ASIATISCHE FORSCHUNGEN

MONOGRAPHIENREIHE
ZUR GESCHICHTE, KULTUR UND SPRACHE
DER VÖLKER OST- UND ZENTRALASIENS

Herausgegeben von
Walther Heissig und Thomas O. Höllmann
unter Mitwirkung von Herbert Franke und Charles R. Bawden

Band 137

2000

Harrassowitz Verlag · Wiesbaden

Elisabetta Chiodo

The Mongolian Manuscripts on Birch Bark from Xarbuxyn Balgas in the Collection of the Mongolian Academy of Sciences

Part 1

2000

Harrassowitz Verlag · Wiesbaden

The signet illustrates birch trees in Mongol style.

Die Deutsche Bibliothek - CIP-Einheitsaufnahme
Ein Titeldatensatz für diese Publikation ist bei der Deutschen Bibliothek
erhältlich

Die Deutsche Bibliothek - CIP Cataloguing-in-Publication-Data
A catalogue record for this publication is available from Die Deutsche
Bibliothek

e-mail: cip@dbf.ddb.de

Printing and binding by MZ-Verlagsdruckerei GmbH, Memmingen
Printed in Germany

ISSN 0571-320X
ISBN 3-447-04246-X

To the people of Dašinčilen Sum

Contents

Foreword

In 1970 the Mongolian archaeologist X. Perlee and the Soviet archaeologist E.V. Šav-kunov discovered a collection of Mongolian and Tibetan manuscripts written on birch bark in a half-destroyed stūpa near the ruins of the ancient town Xarbuxyn Balgas, located 240 km west of Ulanbaatar to the south of Bulgan Ajmag. The texts were written around 1600, and the majority of them had only survived in fragmentary form. Soviet specialists were able to restore a small number of the 1,000 manuscript items. The majority, however, remained untouched. In 1992 the Institute of History of the Mongolian Academy of Sciences, to which the manuscripts belong, and the Mongolian State Library, where the collection was kept, asked the Institute of Central Asian Studies of the University of Bonn to cooperate in the restoration and editing of the complete collection. The completion of the project was possible thanks to the generosity of the Mongolian authorities and the considerable financial support from the German Foreign Office. The present volume is the first result of this work.

Dr. Elisabetta Chiodo, the author of the volume, has edited 240 manuscript items in Latin transcription and facsimile. The texts represent 42 different works which Dr. Chiodo was able to identify. The transcriptions are accompanied by detailed commentaries dealing with the linguistic peculiarities and the contents of the text, which were analysed in a wide frame of reference. No translations were made, because the time taken for such a work would have unduly delayed the process of editing the remaining texts. For the circumstances of the manuscript find, the contents of the text, their importance for the cultural history of the Mongols and the difficulties connected with arranging the disparate items according to the texts to which they belong, the reading and the identification of the manuscripts, which are mostly fragmentary and sometimes even partly charred, I refer to Dr. Chiodo's detailed introduction.

Later volumes will contain the edited version of the remaining Mongolian manuscripts and of the Tibetan texts, which are less numerous than the Mongolian items. A separate volume will be devoted to a revised edition of the birch bark manuscript of the Qalqa Penal Law. Professor Perlee edited this work as early as in 1976, supplying an exhaustive commentary. It turned out, however, that some folios of the original manuscript were omitted in this edition and that some minor corrections had to be made. A detailed description of the technical aspects connected with the restoration of the manuscripts will be added to the last volume.

The completion of an edited version of these unique documents was possible thanks to the cooperation of institutions and individual persons. The Institute of History of the Mongolian Academy of Sciences and the Mongolian State Library sent the manuscripts to Germany. The director of the Institute, Prof. Dr. A. Ochir, agreed to leave the manuscripts in Bonn for the time necessary for restoration and editing. The former director of the State Library, Dr. P. Otgon, and Dr. Ts. Ishdorj, Senior Academic Worker in the Institute of History, brought the manuscripts to Bonn. Dr. Ishdorj joined the technical work in Bonn for a protracted period. The German Foreign Office provided the project funds for more than five years. In addition, it granted substantial financial help for the publication of the present first volume of the text edition. The embassies of Mongolia in Bonn and of the Federal Republic of Germany in Ulaanbaatar have supported our efforts with great sympathy. Particular thanks must be given to Mr. Bayarsaikhan, at present Mongolian ambassador in Germany, and Dr. Dominique Dumas, who was in charge of cultural affairs during the initial time of the project in the German Embassy. The Manuscript Division of the Central Library (Universitäts- und Landesbibliothek) of the University of Bonn gave its consent to keep the precious collection in rare books room. We are especially indebted to the head of the department, Dr. Doris Pinkwart, and to the librarians Mrs. Christine Weidlich and Mrs. Monica Klaus. They library very kindly co-operated in preparing a first exhibition of the manuscripts in July 1994 and in a second exhibition on September 7, 1998, which was arranged for Prof. Dr. Roman Herzog, at that time President of the Federal Republic of Germany, as a part of the preparations for his state visit to Mongolia from September 17 to 22.

Mr. Ivan Bentchev restored the majority of the manuscripts which, removing dirt and grease and joining the broken pieces together. The same was done by Mrs. Katharina Nebel, Cologne University of Applied Sciences, Department of Restoration and Conservation of Archival Material, Books and Graphic Art. The physicist Dr. Ralf Tepest, working in the same department, made partly charred manuscripts visible with the help of infrared reflectography. The director of the department, Prof. Dr. Robert Fuchs, was always ready to give his advice and to offer the help of his institution. Colleagues in Mongolia, particularly the chief librarian of the Gandan Monastery in Ulaanbaatar, Byamba Lama, willingly answered questions arising in connection with the study of the manuscripts. In January 2000 Dr. Otgonbaatar, Senior Academic Worker in the Institute of Language and Literature of the Mongolian Academy of Sciences, joined our work in Bonn. The continuation of the project after November 1998 was possible by the financial support of the German Research Association (Deutsche Forschungsgemeinschaft, DFG). Geshe Pema Tsering, Bonn, provided unstinting support with his knowledge of Tibetan Buddhist practice and birchwood technology. Prof. Dr. Walther Heissig, University of Bonn, accepted this volume for publication in the series "Asiatische Forschungen". The Harrassowitz Verlag in Wiesbaden and Mr. Claudius Naumann, Berlin, produced the book with great care. I wish to thank all these persons and institutions for their substantial help, which enabled us to complete the first part of our project.

I am particularly grateful to Dr. Elisabetta Chiodo for her competent work and for her untiring efforts to complete the first volume of this edition of the manuscripts on birch bark from Xarbuxyn Balgas within the planned period of five years, a time which is rather short considering the difficult path which had to be gone from uncleaned scattered pieces preserved in a great number of envelopes and even in cigarette boxes and soup packets to an edition of transcribed and identified texts.

Klaus Sagaster
German coordinator of the Mongolian-German Manuscript Project

Introduction

The Mongolian collection of manuscripts written on birch bark from Xarbuxyn Balgas consists of about 1,000 items of which 240 are dealt with in this publication. The majority of the texts date from the first part of the 17th century. Most of them survived only in fragmentary form. The manuscripts are designated by their initials XBM (= Xarbuxyn Balgas Mongolian) to indicate the place where they were found and to distinguish them from the Tibetan manuscripts which also form part of the collection (= XBT). The Xarbuxyn Balgas collection is the result of an archaeological find. In 1970, during a joint Mongol-Soviet expedition, the archaeologists X. Perlee and E.V. Šavkunov, while investigating the ruins of the ancient town of Xarbuxyn Balgas, found an astonishing number of Mongolian and Tibetan manuscripts written on birch bark inside a half-destroyed stūpa. The Mongolian manuscripts, however, are far greater in number than the Tibetan ones. Xarbuxyn Balgas is located 240 km west of Ulaanbaatar and 17 km from Dašinčilen Sum in Bulgan Ajmag.

The Mongolian manuscripts from Xarbuxyn Balgas constitute the largest collection discovered during an archaeological expedition. It is also the third important collection of Mongolian documents after those which were found in Turfan and Olon Süme.[1] The Turfan collection consists of fragments of printed books and some manuscripts, mainly dating from the 14th century. The Turfan texts were previously investigated by various scholars in separate studies. In 1993, the Mongol scholar D. Cerensodnom and the German scholar Manfred Taube published the Turfan texts in a single volume.[2]

Moreover, fragments of Mongolian manuscripts were found inside a stūpa in Olon Süme, southern Mongolia, by the Japanese archaeologist Namio Egami in 1937. 211 fragments of the Olon Süme collection, which date from the 16th–17th centuries, were extensively studied by Prof. Walther Heissig, who published them in 1976.[3]

Needless to say, a find such as the Xarbuxyn Balgas manuscripts sheds new light on the history of the transmission of texts in northern Mongolia in the first part of the 17th century.

Above all, we now have the opportunity to examine the Xarbuxyn Balgas manuscripts and compare them with those from Olon Süme. A comparative analysis as such allows us to gain a broader picture of the circulation of texts in northern and southern

---

1 Seventeen Mongolian documents were found by Kozlov among the ruins of the abandoned city of Khara-khoto. See Munkuyev, "Two Mongolian Printed Fragments", pp. 341–57.

2 Cerensodnom and Taube, *Turfansammlung*. For the Turfan texts find and the scholars who investigated them, I refer the reader to the above-mentioned book; see also the Turfan texts in Ligeti, *Monuments préclassiques,* I, pp. 115–237.

3 *Die mongolischen Handschriften-Reste aus Olon süme.*

Mongolia during the 16th–17th centuries—a flourishing period in the intellectual history of the Mongols.[4]

At present, Xarbuxyn Balgas consists of the remnants of a town wall made with black stones which date back to the 10th–11th centuries. Inside the wall there are the ruins of buildings which were constructed with stones in the early 17th century. The settlement site also includes the ruins of a large Buddhist temple in the Tibetan architectural style.[5] A half-destroyed stūpa approximately 8–9 metres high is located near the south-western corner of the town wall. It is inside this stūpa that the archaeologists found the Mongolian and Tibetan manuscripts on birch bark.[6]

While the archaeologists were cleaning the southern wall of the stūpa, they discovered that there were manuscripts in the foundations of the stūpa. The manuscripts were covered with building material and clay mixed with earth and animal dung. The archaeologists also noticed that the stūpa has been ransacked in the course of time.[7]

Several times I was able to travel to Xarbuxyn Balgas and visit the stūpa which had preserved the manuscripts on birch bark until 1970. On those occasions, I noticed that the stūpa is still an object of veneration by people, who place their offerings inside it.

The manuscripts on birch bark consist of used books and fragments. Yet they were placed inside the stūpa at rite of consecration instead of new books. According to a religious custom, used books are placed in a *bungqan* (*'bum-khaṅ*) or *cha-cha-yin ger* (*tsha-khaṅ*), which is a building in which *tsha-tsha* figures and used books are "buried". Used books, however, are also "offered to the fire", i.e. burnt or placed inside a stūpa at the rite of consecration.[8]

As for the religious significance of texts written on birch bark, according to the words of Geshe Pema Tsering, the eastern Tibetans regard birch bark as pure material. Due to the element of purity which is characteristic of birch bark, people use it to make containers for milk and yoghurt. Geshe Pema Tsering also added that the eastern Tibetans believe that the Buddha himself praised birch bark as the best material for writing, and that the *mantra* of the *gDugs-dkar (Sitātapatrā)* on birch bark is the best protective amulet.[9] In the opinion of Mongol scholars and other people whom I consulted in Mongolia, texts written on birch bark do have greater religious significance than those written on paper.[10] The belief that texts written on birch bark have a special religious significance is

---

4 See Heissig, "Zur geistigen Leistung", pp. 101–6, and *Geschichtsschreibung*, I, pp. 15–17 by the same author; see also Žamcarano, *The Mongol Chronicles*, p. 6.

5 Pėrlėė, *Mongol ard ulsyn ėrt dundad üeijn xot suuriny tovčoon*, p. 124.

6 Pėrlėė, "Üjsėnd bičsėn xojor züjl", p. 131; see the photographic reproduction of the Xarbuxyn Balgas stūpa in Majdar, *Arxitektur*, No. 190.

7 I should like to thank Prof. G.S. Kljaštornyj, St. Petersburg, who took part in the expedition to the ruins of Xarbuxyn Balgas in 1970, for this information.

8 I am most grateful to Enxbold Lama, former librarian in the Gandan monastery in Ulaanbaatar, for this information.

9 Pema Tsering, "The Technique of Traditional Ink Production in Tibet". Paper read at the 7th International Congress of Mongolists. Ulaanbaatar, 12–17 August 1997. I am most grateful to Geshe Pema Tsering, Bonn, for allowing me to use his unpublished paper. When the Mongol herdsmen travel long distance, they tie to the saddle a small container made of birch bark with dried milk. See Sampilnorbu, *Mongyol ündüsüten-ü idegen umdayan*, p. 183.

of course interesting, but it should be added that the birch bark is also a suitable and durable writing material, more convenient than paper since birch trees are abundant in the mountain areas of northern Mongolia. The astonishing number of manuscripts from Xarbuxyn Balgas bears witness to the widespread use of birch bark as writing material in the first half of the 17th century.

The Mongols, however, have used birch bark as writing material since the 13th century, evidence of this being the well-known texts found on the left bank of the River Volga in 1930 on land which once belonged to the Golden Horde.[11] We also have further evidence of the use of birch bark as writing material in the first part of the 17th century. Fragments of the well known text *Naiman gegen* were discovered in Almalyk near Tašhkent in 1970.[12] The Tantric text *Sitātapatrā-dhāraṇī (Čaɣan sikürtei)* on birch bark, which was used as an amulet, is preserved in the Royal Library in Copenhagen. The provenance of this text is unknown.[13]

Moreover, four Mongolian texts written on birch bark were found by librarians in the Tibetan section of the Ulaanbaatar Central State Library. One text is complete and bears the title *Erlig-ün čilma-u* (sic!) *sudur orosiba*. The others consist of an invocation to Dayan Degereke; an incomplete text of divination *(tölge)*; one fragment of a text of divination, which also contains Tibetan words.[14] Finally, Perlee mentions a Mongol text of geomancy written on birch bark, which is kept in the Research Institute of Tariat in Arxangaj Ajmag.[15]

The discovery of the Mongolian manuscripts from Xarbuxyn Balgas became known to scholars in 1974, when the work by Perlee "*Xalxyn šinė oldson caaz ėrxėmžijn dursgalt bičig*", was published. It concerns one of the most important documents of the Xarbuxyn Balgas collection, i.e. the book which contains 18 articles of the Qalqa Penal Law *(čaɣaǰa)*. Perlee briefly describes the other Mongolian manuscripts from Xarbuxyn Balgas in the introduction to his work, in which, however, there is no mention of the Tibetan manuscripts which were also found in Xarbuxyn Balgas.[16]

As is well known, Perlee published the articles of the Qalqa Penal Law in Mongol script and Latin transcription, together with a valuable historical commentary, but without a facsimile reproduction of the manuscript.[17] When I had the opportunity to see the original manuscript, I discovered that Perlee had omitted 4 folios (14v–17r) in his publication. This is regrettable, since the folios which Perlee left out contain the earliest

---

10 The question of whether texts written on birch bark have greater religious power than those written on paper was also discussed during the lecture on the Xarbuxyn Balgas manuscripts find. This lecture was held by Prof. Klaus Sagaster and myself at the State University in Ulaanbaatar on 21st September 1994.

11 Poppe, "Zolotoordynskaja rukopis' na bereste", vol. 2, pp. 81–136; see also Ligeti, *Monuments préclassiques*, pp. 279–83; Ceringsodnam, *Mongɣol uran ǰokiyal*, pp. 349–53.

12 Taube, "Mongolische Birkenrinden-Fragmente", pp. 152–5. I am most grateful to Prof. Manfred Taube, Leipzig, for communicating the title of the text.

13 Heissig and Bawden, *Catalogue*, Mong. 158, p. 210.

14 See Chiodo and Sagaster, "The Mongolian and Tibetan Manuscripts", p. 29.

15 "Xalxyn šinė oldson caaz-ėrxėmžijn dursgalt bičig", p. 6.

16 p. 6.

17 From pages 14 to 139.

written evidence hitherto known of the so-called *Yeke tügel,* "The Great Distribution", which is a basic text of the cult of Činggis qaɣan.[18] In the book of the Penal Law, the text bears the title *Ĵirɣuɣan tümen-i yeke tügel,* "The Great Distribution of the Six Tümen" (14v).[19]

The *Yeke tügel* from Xarbuxyn Balgas is a short text which celebrates the deeds of the Yisün Örlög, "The Nine Paladins" of Činggis, while the *Yeke tügel* which was previously available is a lengthy text which also celebrates the deeds of a number of persons who gave their strength to Činggis and his descendants.[20]

The provenance of the *Yeke tügel* from Xarbuxyn Balgas makes this text especially valuable since the texts of the *Yeke tügel* hitherto known were collected in the Ordos region, southern Mongolia. The *Yeke tügel* from Xarbuxyn Balgas gives evidence of the cult of Činggis qaɣan in northern Mongolia in the early 17th century. Moreover, it demonstrates that the hymn in praise of the Yisün Örlög was circulating as an independent text.

Perlee also published two texts of the Xarbuxyn Balgas collection in Mongol script and Latin transcription. They are an incense offering of the Yellow Jambhala and an incense offering of Geser, which are included in a single booklet (XBM 66).[21]

Moreover, Heissig translated this into German and commented on the incense offering of Geser which Perlee had previously published.[22] It is also interesting to note that Heissig has access to one of the two fragments of the Xarbuxyn Balgas hymn to Qongsim Bodisung: *Qutuɣ-tu qongsim bodisung-un aldarsin dügürügsen neretü sudur nom nigen ĵüil-iyer qutuɣ-tu yeke kölge nom sudur,* "One chapter of the holy mahāyāna-sūtra called Perfect Praise of the Holy Qongsim Bodisung" (XBM 48, fols. 2–3). The text also bears different titles. Heissig transcribed the text on folio 2 side by side with the two fragments of the same text which were found in Olon Süme in his work *Die mongolischen Handschriften-Resten aus Olon süme.*[23]

Prof. Klaus Sagaster and myself wrote an article which presents the preliminary results of our research work on the Mongolian and Tibetan manuscripts from Xarbuxyn Balgas. The article was published in 1995.[24] It was translated into Mongolian and Japanese.[25]

In the course of my study of the Mongolian manuscripts from Xarbuxyn Balgas, I translated into English the hymn to Qongsim Bodisung (*Qutuɣ-tu qongsim bodisung-*

---

18 See Chiodo, "History and Legend", pp. 175–95.
19 On the Six Tümen, see *Altan kürdün mingɣan kegesütü,* p. 147; *Ĵangɣ-a-yin urusqal,* p. 171 and note 1.
20 See Yang, *Altan bičig,* pp. 93–8, 186–200; see also Rintchen, *Matériaux,* pp. 76–83; Sayinĵirɣal and Šaraldai, *Altan ordon-u tayilɣ-a,* pp. 78–102.
21 See Perlee, "Üĵsėn bičsėn xojor züjl", pp. 127–51.
22 "Geser Khan-Rauchopfer als Datierungshilfen des mongolischen Geser Khan-Epos", pp. 89–135.
23 Heissig identified the Olon Süme fragments as a section of *Altan quyaɣ-tu kemekü neretü yeke kölgen sudur,* which is one of the titles of the text. See *Handschriften-Reste,* pp. 326–34. The Xarbuxyn Balgas fragment is transcribed on page 329.
24 "The Mongolian and Tibetan Manuscripts", pp. 28–41.
25 Saran and Nima, "Qar-a buq-a-yin balgasu-ača oldaɣsan mongɣol töbed üisün bičig-ün tuqai", pp. 44–9; Osamu Inoue, "Harubohin Barugasu shutsudo no mongoru go. Chibetto-go juhi shahon-joron", pp. 105–22.

un aldarsin dügüregsen neretü sudur nom nigen ǰüil-iyer qutuγ-tu yeke kölge sudur), and the fragmentary hymn to Yamāntaka, without a title (XBM 47; XBM 65).[26]

In 1993, the Xarbuxyn Balgas manuscripts were brought to the Central Asian Institute of Bonn University by Dr. Ts. Ishdorj, Institute of History of the Mongolian Academy of Sciences, and Dr. P. Otgon, the former director of the Central State Library in Ulaanbaatar, to be restored and investigated.

When the Xarbuxyn Balgas collection was brought to Bonn it consisted of manuscripts which were almost entirely in their original state of preservation. A small number of manuscripts had been restored by Russians experts in Ulaanbaatar during the eighties. In the summer of 1993, professional restorers such as Mr. Ivan Bentchev, Bonn, and Mrs. Eva-Katharina Nebel, Cologne, began to restore the rest of the collection. The work was completed about two and a half years later.

At the very outset, the general state of preservation of the Xarbuxyn Balgas collection looked extremely poor. We were mainly dealing with severely damaged, stained and half-burnt items covered with earth, animal dung and fat. There were also folios stuck together which had to be separated by the restorers. Fortunately, the collection also includes fairly well preserved and legible items and even 15 complete texts.

Moreover, the fragments were scattered at random throughout hundreds of envelopes mixed with other items, to which Perlee gave provisional numbers. As a result, my preliminary task consisted of arranging the fragments according to the texts to which they belong. A task like this turned out to be very demanding, but also rewarding. For example, 27 fragments of 21 copies of *Itegel yabuγulqu* (XBM 1–21) were found dispersed throughout the envelopes. A similar problem involved the restoration of the "Four prayers of the *ǰayuradu*" (XBM 110), which has the form of a booklet. Previously, the top corners of the folios of the booklet broke, and were found mixed with other items in different locations.

A substantial contribution to the study of an unexplored collection of manuscripts is the identification of the texts. This task was fulfilled in most of the cases. However, some texts, both fragmentary and complete, are identified according to their contents, while theirs titles remain unknown. For instance, the complete text XBM 73 is clearly a prayer to Geser, but it does not have a title.

In this publication I dealt with 110 texts, which represent 42 different texts. The manuscripts are in different states of preservation: some are fairly well preserved and legible, others are severely damaged and barely legible. We also have half-burnt manuscripts, but the texts are still legible thanks to infra-red reflectography. A characteristic of the Xarbuxyn Balgas collection is that it includes a large number of copies of certain texts. An example is the 27 items of 21 different copies of *Itegel yabuγulqu* (XBM 1 to XBM 21). This turned out to be valuable since, in many instances, the Xarbuxyn Balgas texts were restored on the basis of the other copies. I also considered it worth analysing the Xarbuxyn Balgas texts in relation to other available versions of the same texts. In my own view, a comparative study as such helps to shed light on the history of the

---

26 Chiodo, "A Mongolian Hymn to Qongsim Bodisung on Birch Bark", pp. 224–49; "Yamāntaka and the *Sülde* of Činggis" (in press).

transmission of the texts. In this study, attention was paid to the palaeographic, ortho-graphic, grammatical and lexical features of the texts. The diverse features of the texts were discussed in the notes to the transcription and in the commentaries.

The Xarbuxyn Balgas texts are marked by the frequent use of spellings and grammatical forms which reflect the spoken language. For instance, *qoyor* (for *qoyar*), *qoyoloi* (for *qoyolai*), *urul* (for *uruγul*),[27] etc.; *öberin* (for *öberün*), *noytoi-gi* (for *noyto-yi*), etc.[28] Ancient spellings and terms are also attested in the texts, e.g.: *qumaqi*, *qayaraqai*, *bolad*, *tasuraqai*, etc.;[29] *tenggeri* (XBM 35, 7v), *eng urida*, *nökör següder* (XBM 46, 1v, 2r), *güjügün* (XBM 47, 4r), *uni*, *sülder* (XBM 65, 2r, 2v), *irgen oryon* (XBM 107, 4v), etc. Extremely rare terms are also found. XBM 46 (2r), for example, has *bodančay* (for *bodančar*), *borqan* (plural of *borqai*), *ötög qutuy* (1v), while the term *ilqayan* appears in XBM 47, 3v, 4r.[30]

The Xarbuxyn Balgas collection shows great similarity with that from Olon Süme. Both consist of used book which were preserved inside a stūpa. Moreover, six texts, both complete and fragmentary of the Xarbuxyn Balgas collection, which are presented in this publication, were also found in Olon Süme in fragmentary forms. They are the well known Buddhist prayer *Itegel yabuyulqu*, "To go for refuge";[31] the prayer of penitence *Qutuy-tu yurban čoyča neretü yeke kölgen*, "The holy mahāyāna-[sūtra] called The Three Heaps", which is also known by different titles;[32] a rare text such as *Tabun jayun burqan-u sudur*, "The sūtra of the 500 Buddhas";[33] the hymn to Qongsim Bodisung *Qutuy-tu qongsim bodisung-un aldarsin dügürügsen neretü sudur nom nigen jüil-iyer yeke kölge nom sudur*, "One chapter of the holy mahāyāna-sūtra called Perfect Praise of the Holy Qongsim Bodisung". The text, however, is known by different titles.[34] In addition there is *Ündüsün-i sang*, "Burnt offering of origin"[35] and the "Four prayers of the *jayuradu*" (*bar-do*).[36] However, the poorly preserved fragments of three texts from Olon Süme such as *Itegel yabuyulqu*, *Qutuy-tu yurban čoyča neretü yeke kölgen* and the "Four prayers of the *jayuradu*", which were left unidentified, were identified by myself in the light of the texts from Xarbuxyn Balgas. There is no doubt that the identification

---

27 XBM 59r; XBM 60, 3r; XBM 96, 4r respectively. For other examples, see "Linguistic Features of the Manuscripts".

28 XBM 41, 5r; XBM 73, 4r.

29 Instead of the modern literary forms *qumaki*, *qayarqai*, *tasurqai*, *bolod*. See XBM 29, 2v; XBM 82, *2v; XBM 73, 2r respectively.

30 These terms are discussed in the notes to the texts in which they appear and in the commentaries following the transcription of the texts.

31 From XBM 1 to XBM 21; on the Olon Süme text, see Heissig, *Handschriften-Reste*, OS IV/111–12.

32 From XBM 22 to XBM 27; Heissig, *Handschriften-Reste*, pp. 479–86.

33 XBM 28; Heissig, *Handschriften-Reste*, pp. 334–6, and *Steininschrift und Manuskriptefragmente*, pp. 40–9 by the same author.

34 XBM 47 is complete, while XBM 48, XBM 49 and XBM 50 consist of fragment; on the Olon Süme text which Heissig identified as a section of *Altan quyay-tu kemekü neretü yeke kölgen sudur*, see *Handschriften-Reste*, pp. 326–34.

35 XBM 80, XBM 81; Heissig, *Handschriften-Reste*, pp. 380–408.

36 XBM 110; Heissig, *Handschriften-Reste*, pp. 446–9.

of the fragments of the three above-quoted texts from Olon Süme throws additional light on the history of these texts.

The Xarbuxyn Balgas manuscripts are numerous and deal with a variety of subjects. We have Buddhist prayers, hymns and prayers to Buddhist deities, protective deities, and teachers of the religion, folk religious texts, *dhāraṇī*, calendars, a dream book, manuals of astrology and divinations and the "Four prayers of the *ǰayuradu*".

Contrary to the Olon Süme collection, which includes fragments of the *Bodhicaryā-vatāra*, *Bilig baramid yool ǰirüken* etc.,[37] the Xarbuxyn Balgas collection does not contain Buddhist philosophical *sūtra*. The only text of the Xarbuxyn Balgas collection which is contained in the *Ganǰur* is the short *dhāraṇī Qutuy-tu lingqu-a-yin nidün kemegdekü neretü tarni*, "The holy *dhāraṇī* called Lotus-Eyed" (XBM 41),[38] while *Qutuy-tu yurban čoyča neretü yelke kölgen*,[39] is found in the *Zungdui* with the title *Čoytu čindan* at the beginning of the text and *Qutuy-tu yurban čoyča kemegdekü yeke kölgen sudur* at the end.[40] Various independent copies of this texts are also known.[41]

The Xarbuxyn Balgas collection entirely consists of ritual texts. Texts like this were not necessarily meant for the use of an isolated Buddhist monastic community only. On the contrary, judging from the nature of these texts, we may suppose that they also served the purpose of spreading the basic teachings of the Buddhist religion and the worship of deities of the Buddhist pantheon among the northern Mongol laymen in the first part of the 17th century. What is also striking is the size of the Xarbuxyn Balgas manuscripts, which were written on small pieces of birch bark, obviously with the purpose of making the texts convenient for a person to carry.

It should be stressed that the collection from Xarbuxyn Balgas provides the hitherto earliest available evidence of a number of texts, and what is even more interesting is that it contains texts which were previously unknown. It is thus at this point worth presenting some texts which sufficiently show the contribution of this new collection of manuscripts to our knowledge of the literary and spiritual culture of the Mongols.[42]

Beginning with the "Summary of the *Altan gerel*", we can conclude that this text must have been very popular if we have two complete texts and fragments of 10 different copies.[43] The "Summary" is written in simple language, but it contains profound ideas. The "Summary", which emphasises the Buddhist idea of the miraculous power of the recitation of the prayer, must have served the end of making accessible to people the teachings of the *Altan gerel*,[44] a fundamental *sūtra* in Mahāyāna Buddhism,[45] using ancient Mongol

---

37 Heissig, *Handschriften-Reste*, pp. 13–66, 271–5.

38 Vol. 14, pp. 286–7; vol. 23, pp. 237–8.

39 From XBM 22 to XBM 27.

40 pp. 434v–437r.

41 The texts are quoted in the section of the book Prayer of Penitence (XBM 22 to XBM 27).

42 The texts mentioned below are discussed in separate sections of the book, to which the reader is referred.

43 From XBM 29 to XBM 40.

44 Full title: *Qutuy-tu altan gerel-tü erketü sudur-nuyud qayan yeke kölgen sudur (Ārya-Suvarṇa-prabhāsottama-sūtrendrarāja nāma mahāyāna-sūtra)*.

45 On the worship of the *Altan gerel* in Mongolia see Bira "The Worship", pp. 3–14.

religious ideas. As a matter of fact, this text shows passages which are strongly reminiscent of popular religious texts invoking the spirit-masters of the locality. It is also interesting to note that the "Summary" mentions a golden bridge and a silver bridge over a
river of blood located in hell (*čisutu mören degereki altan mönggön kögergen*, XBM 29,
2 r–3 v). A description like this is rare in the Mongolian sources, though it is found in the
Chinese accounts of journeys to the underworld and in Chinese iconography. However,
an idea of hell such as that indicated above must have been familiar to the Mongols of the
early 17th century if it appears in a popular text like the "Summary".

The Xarbuxyn Balgas collection bears witness to the important role attributed to
Avalokiteśvara, the Buddhist god of compassion, by including nine different texts devoted to this god, who is called by different names and represented in different forms.[46]
The large number of texts to Avalokiteśvara which were found in Xarbuxyn Balgas
points to the existence of a body of texts dedicated to this deity. They also shed light on
the history of the worship of Avalokiteśvara in northern Mongolia. As is well known,
Avalokiteśvara is highly revered by the Buddhist Mongols to this day.[47] The majority of
these texts are fragmentary, but one is complete. It is *Qutuγ-tu qongsim bodisung-un
aldarsin dügürügsen neretü sudur nom nigen ǰüil-iyer qutuγ-tu yeke kölge nom sudur.* As
has been mentioned above, two fragments of the text were found in Olon Süme. The
background of the text, which is a hymn in praise of the extraordinary saving powers of
Avalokiteśvara, was traced back in chapter 24 of the *Saddharma-puṇḍarīka-sūtra*
(Mong. *Čaγan lingqu-a neretü degedü nom yeke kölgen sudur*, "The supreme mahāyāna-
sūtra called The White Lotus"), which is entirely devoted to this deity.[48]

Continuing with the cult of Avalokiteśvara, we have fragments of seven copies of a
text which describes the marvellous Sukhāvatī paradise, the realm of Buddha Amitābha,
expressing the wish for rebirth on Mount Potala, which is the abode of Avalokiteśvara.[49]
This must have been very popular with the Mongols, as the seven copies from Xarbuxyn
Balgas show. It it still popular with the Tibetan laymen, who recite it during the fasting
days on the occasion of Buddhist festivals.[50] The Xarbuxyn Balgas text, which describes
Sukhāvatī, was clearly circulating independently, but it is also found included, with textual variants, in Tibetan works such as the *Maṇi bka'-'bum* (Mong. *Mani gambu*),
rGyal-rabs gsal-ba'i me-loṅ[51] (Mong. *Gegen toli*),[52] *Pad-ma bka'-yi thaṅ-yig*[53] (Mong.

---

46   One text devoted to this god is included in the Book of Prayers (XBM 41). For the other texts,
     see the section of the book entitled "The Worship of Avalokiteśvara" (XBM 47 to XBM 64).
47   See Mėnd-Oojoo, *Bilgijn mėlmij nėėgč,* The book describes in great detail how Mongol peo-
     ple participated in the construction of the huge statue of Avalokiteśvara, which was housed in
     a temple located in the Gandan monastery, Ulaanbaatar, in 1996.
48   The *sūtra* is included in the *Ganǰur,* vol. 66, p. 2–466. The description of the infallible saving
     powers of Guanyin, or Avalokiteśvara, in the *Saddharma-puṇḍarīka-sūtra* contributed to the
     spread of the worship of this deity among Chinese. The work is the most popular *sūtra* of Chi-
     nese Buddhist literature. See Strickman, *Mantras et mandarins,* p. 136.
49   From XBM 51 to XBM 57. Avalokiteśvara is an emanational body of Amitābha.
50   I am most grateful to Geshe Pema Tsering for this interesting information.
51   See Sørensen, *The Mirror,* pp. 98–9.
52   Heissig, *Geschichtsschreibung,* pp. 34–40.
53   See Bischoff, "The First Chapter of the Legend of Padmasambhava", pp. 39, 42.

Badma yatang sudur).[54] It is interesting to note that the description of Sukhāvatī, which is located at the very beginning of the Mongolian *Mani gambu*, [55]coincides almost exactly with that in the Xarbuxyn Balgas text.

On the texts which address dieties, the hymn in alliterative verses to the ferocious Tantric god Yamāntaka (XBM 65) merits special attention. Unfortunately, only three damaged fragments of the hymn have survived. The hymn to Yamāntaka was previously unknown, but a complete text of an incense offering of Yamāntaka, without a title, which is basically similar to that from Xarbuxyn Balgas, forms part of the German collection of Mongol books preserved in Berlin State Library.[56] The hymn to Yamāntaka provides evidence of the worship of this fierce god in northern Mongolia in the first part of the 17th century, though the most significant aspect of this text is that it includes passages which show striking similarity to the texts of the incense offering of the white standard *(čaγan sülde)* and black standard *(qara sülde)* of Činggis qaγan. As a result, the hymn to Yamāntaka from Xarbuxyn Balgas reveals a new aspect of the cult of Činggis, such as the association of Činggis's *sülde* with the wrathful Yamāntaka.

The Xarbuxyn Balgas collection provides evidence of the worship of Geser as a protective deity. The prayer to Geser XBM 73, which was hitherto unknown, is especially valuable. This text describes Geser by terms and expressions which are reminiscent of the description of Geser in the epics, offering evidence of the diffusion of the Geser epics among the Mongols before the first part of the 17th century. The oral tradition of the text is emphasised by means of the frequent occurrence of grammatical forms used in the spoken language.[57]

The fragment, unfortunately severely damaged, of a previously unknown text which invokes Altan Sečen qaγan (XBM 79) should interest the historians. The Xarbuxyn Balgas fragment testifies to the existence of the worship of an Altan Sečen qaγan, but the few lines of the text which are left do not cast light on the question of whether the text actually invokes the famous Altan qaγan of the Tümed or another person.On the other hand, the fact that Altan qaγan of the Tümed was worshipped cannot be surprising if we consider the great reputation of this person, which was not confined to southern Mongolia. There is no doubt that the entire question of the worship of Altan qaγan of the Tümed merits further research. However, in this study I have untertaken a preliminary investigation of this subject using those sources, especially the biography of Altan qaγan known as *Erdeni tunumal neretü sudur,* which suggest that Altan qaγan became an object of veneration after he died.[58]

---

54 See Heissig, *Geschichtsschreibung*, p. 40, and note 5, pp. 40–3, *Blockdrucke*, No. 24, p. 31, and *Mongolische Handschriften*, No. 489, p. 264 by the same author.

55 Heissig and Sagaster, *Mongolische Handschriften*, No. 334, p. 192; see also Heissig, *Blockdrucke*, No. 24, p. 30.

56 Heissig and Sagaster, *Mongolische Handschriften*, No. 466, pp. 253–4.

57 The description of Geser in the incense offering (XBM 66) is also reminiscent of the Geser in the epics. This text, however, is already known, since it was translated into German and commented on by Heissig, who used the text which was previously published by Perlee. See Heissig, "Geser Khan-Rauchopfer", pp. 89–135; Pèrlèè, "*Üjsènd bičsèn xojor züjl*", pp. 127–51.

58 The fragment XBM 79 is discussed in the commentary.

Two texts of the collection especially illustrate the penetration of Buddhist gods and principles into ancient Mongol practices. They are *Ündüsün-i sang* (XBM 80; XBM 81) and the fire-*dalalya*, the ritual of beckoning good fortune, which is usually performed after the sacrifice to the hearth-fire.The diverse aspects of the fragments of *Ündüsün-i sang* which were found in Olon Süme were discussed by Heissig.[59] As far as the fire-*dalalya* is concerned, the Xarbuxyn Balgas collection includes fragments of four copies of the fire-*dalalya*, which constitute the earliest evidence of this text which has been so far available.[60] Apart from some orthographic variants, the various texts of the fire-*dalalya* previously known are the same as those from Xarbuxyn Balgas.[61] However, the Xarbuxyn Balgas texts can be used as early evidence of the interpretation of the fire-*dalalya* in the light of the Vajrayāna. XBM 82 and XBM 84 show the following ending formulas: *včir-du küy-e tegüsbe*, "The thunderbolt *küy-e* has ended", *včir-tu kölgen dayu dayusba*, "The Vajrayāna-(sūtra) has ended".

We also have wedding calendars which were used to select the auspicious date to give a girl in marriage (XBM 97, XBM 98; XBM 99). XBM 99, which displays a fragmentary wedding diagram, is noteworthy. As is well known, the first example of a Mongolian wedding diagram is that from Turfan.[62]

Moreover, there are texts of astrology and divination showing the vast range of protective and therapeutic rituals which, as the texts indicate, were performed by Buddhists practitioners.[63] It is worth observing that three texts of astrology and divination from Xarbuxyn Balgas are substantially similar to those which are contained in the handbook Mong. 301 which is preserved in Copenhagen Royal Library. It was brought from the Tümed, southern Mongolia.[64] One of the Xarbuxyn Balgas texts bears a fragmentary title which was restored on the basis of the Copenhagen text. It is *Kümün-tü mangyus-un birid kölčin qoor kiküi üjekü bičig*, "The book for investigating the harm of the hungry ghosts *(preta)* and the *kölčin*-demons of the *mangyus* upon a person".[65] The similarity of these texts of different provenance points to a common body of Mongol traditions. Moreover, the manual of astrology and divination XBM 107, which takes the form of a booklet, contains three texts. One of these texts is especially valuable, since it provides rare evidence of the method of divination with the twelve *nidāna*,

---

59   *Handschriften-Reste*, pp. 380–408.
60   XBM 82 to XBM 85.
61   See Chabros, *Beckoning Fortune*, pp. 85–110, 216–40; on the other fire-*dalalya*, which are usually included in the fire-*sūtra*, see XBM 82 to XBM 85 below in this volume.
62   See Cerensodnom and Taube, *Turfansammlung*, p. 157; see also Franke, *Mittelmongolische Kalenderfragmente*, pp. 36–40.
63   From XBM 104 to XBM 106; XBM 107; XBM 108; XBM 109; XBM 107 mentions a *joliy* ritual apparently performed by a Buddhist specialist; on the integration of a *joliy* ritual in the body of Buddhist ceremonies, see Lessing, "Calling the Soul", pp. 32–33. As is well known, this ceremony was also performed by a shaman. For this see Heissig, "Schamanen und Geisterbeschwörer", pp. 15–16. Moreover, the idea of a *joliy*, "substitute for another person's life" has a long tradition among the Mongols. As a matter of fact, the term *jol'ia* appears in § 272 of the *Secret History*.
64   Heissig and Bawden, *Catalogue*, pp. 161–3.
65   XBM 104 to XBM 106.

pratīyasamutpāda, "the twelve-link chain of dependent causation". Divination by means of the twelve *nidāna* has a long history in Asian cultures.[66] A Tibetan text dealing with this method of divination was found in Dunhuang.[67] To judge from the later text *Ĵayun ekitü-yin sudur-a*,[68] which includes a section on divination by means of the twelve *nidāna*, one may conclude that the Mongols used this divinatory practice until recently.

Finally, I would like to draw attention to the beautifully written manuscript of the "Four prayers of the *ĵayuradu*" (XBM 110), which are recited to guide the dead in the intermediate state (between death and rebirth). The prayers are usually located at the end of the *Bar-do thos-grol*, a work which is well known to Tibetologists.[69] The prayers were also circulating independently, as the Xarbuxyn Balgas manuscript clearly shows. The Tibetan text was translated into Mongolian with the title *Sonosuyad yekede tonilyayči neretü yeke kölgen sudur*, "The mahāyāna-sūtra called The Great Liberation by Hearing".[70] As was mentioned above, fragments of the four prayers of the *ĵayuradu* were found in Olon Süme. Moreover, a southern Mongolian copy dating from the first part of the 17th century is located in the National Museum of Ethnography in Stockholm. The text is complete and well preserved.[71] The Xarbuxyn Balgas text has a colophon showing the erroneous interpretation of the name of the *gter-ston* Karma Gliṅ-pa, "the man of Karma Gliṅ", who, according to the Tibetan tradition, brought to light the *Bar-do thos-grol*. The name Karma Gliṅ-pa obviously confused the Mongol translator, who took the Tibetan *gliṅ* as a separate word, not as a part of the name of this person (XBM 110, 3v). As I will show below, the same misinterpretation of the name Karma-Gliṅ-pa occurs in both the Stockholm text and in the fragment from Olon Süme, which has preserved a section of the colophon.[72]

The process whereby the manuscripts on birch bark became a collection is not known. As has been mentioned, the settlement site of Xarbuxyn Balgas was a religious centre which included a large Buddhist temple inside the ancient town wall. It is difficult to say whether all the manuscripts on birch bark were written down in Xarbuxyn Balgas, but there is no doubt that they were eventually collected in this place and used to consecrate the stūpa.

It is interesting to note that the incense offering of the Yellow Jambhala, which is published in this book (XBM 66), mentions Altatu monastery. Perlee explains that this monastery existed in the 17th century, and it was situated north of the River Altaad in contemporary Bulgan Ajmag. In Perlee's view, the incense offering was written down in

---

66 Chavannes, "Le cycle turc", pp. 86–7.

67 Mcdonald, "Une lecture", pp. 284–5.

68 The original manuscript belongs to Mr. Süxbat's private collection, Ulaanbaatar, who most kindly allowed me to photocopy it in the summer of 1997.

69 In this work I have used *Bar-do'i thos-grol bźugs-so* (Kalsang ed.); on the English translation of the prayers see Evans-Wentz, *The Tibetan Book of the Dead*, pp. 197–208.

70 See Heissig, *Blockdrucke*, pp. 33–4; Krueger edited *Sonosuyad yekede tonilyayči* in 1965.

71 Aalto, "Catalogue", H. 5827, p. 69. I am most grateful to Mr. H. Wahlquist, the keeper of the Sven Hedin Foundation at the National Museum of Ethnography, Stockholm, for sending the photocopy of the manuscript.

72 H. 5827, 4v:7–5r:2; *Handschriften-Reste*, OS/IV 109–10v, p. 449.

Altatu monastery.[73] It is thus possible that the text was written down in this monastery. It is worth noting that Xarbuxyn Balgas is also located in contemporary Bulgan Ajmag.

Moreover, the ruins of the well-known settlement site such as Cagaan Bajšin (Čaɣan Bayising) are situated 70 km north-east of Xarbuxyn Balgas. Cagaan Bajšin attracted the attention of scholars because of the Tibetan and Mongolian inscriptions engraved on a stele which was erected near the ruins of the palace of Čoɣtu tayiǰi,[74] and the poem engraved on rock dating to 1624, which is a beautiful example of Mongol poetry in alliterative verses.[75] Unfortunately, by now the Tibetan and Mongolian inscriptions are barely legible.[76] Cagaan Bajšin was a centre of the Red School of Tibetan Buddhism at the beginning of the 17th century.[77] According to the Mongolian inscription, Čoɣtu tayiǰi and his mother Buyantu Čing tayiqu had six temples constructed in Cagaan Bajšin in 1601. The construction was concluded in 1617.[78] From the Tibetan inscription we learn that a large number of canonic books and the 84,000 items of the doctrine (dharmaskandha, chos-kyi phuṅ-po) weṙe housed in the temples.[79]

Mongolian sources attribute to Abadai Tüsiyetü qan the diffusion of Buddhism among the Qalqa.[80] Abadai, who had been converted to Buddhism, banned the old worship of the ongyod.[81] Abadai also established close relation with Altan qaɣan of the Tümed, and invited lamas from the Tümed to the Qalqa.[82]

---

73 Pėrlėė, "Üjsėnd bičsėn xojor züjl", p. 143, and note 3, and "Xalxyn šinė oldson", p. 136 by the same author.
74 On the political and religious activities of Čoɣtu tayiǰi, see Ɣongɣor, Qalq-a tobčiyan, I, pp. 390–409; see also the Bolor toli, pp. 484–6.
75 See Huth, Die Inschriften, p. 2, and especially Vladimircov, Nadpisi, pp. 1253–9; see also Damdisürüng, Mongɣol-un uran ǰokiyal, I, pp. 58–75; see the photographic reproduction of the ruins of Cagaan Bajšin in Majdar, Arxitektur, Nos. 144–6.
76 I had the opportunity to see the inscriptions of Cagaan Bajšin in the summer of 1999.
77 Vladimircov, Nadpisi, pp. 1265–1269, 1275–1280; Ɣongɣor, Qalq-a tobčiyan, I, pp. 400–3.
78 Huth, Die Inschriften, p. 44.
79 Huth, Die Inschriften, p. 22. One of the six temples was called bSam-yas after the famous temple in Tibet (Huth, p. 26, note 20). On bSam-yas which the Tibetan king Khri-sroṅ lde-btsan had constructed, see Tucci, "Il tempio di Bsam Yas", pp. 118–23.
80 Qalq-a-yin mongɣol-un yaǰar-a burqan-u šasin delgeregsen, 1v (Ms. belonging to the author); the Third Dalai Lama bestowed on Abadai the title Včirai batu tüsiyetü sayin qan in 1586 (Erdeni-yin erike, p. 88); see also the Erdeni tunumal neretü sudur, pp. 156–7; Asarayči neretü-yin teüke, p. 111; Altan kürdün mingɣan kegesütü, pp. 230–1; Tümengke, Abadai's son, actively contributed to the spread of the Yellow School in the Qalqa. For this see Ɣongɣor, Qalq-a tobčiyan, I, pp. 364–6.
81 The regulations of the Arban buyan-u čaɣaǰa penal law prohibited the worship of the ongyod and ordered people to burn them. If someone did not comply, this person's tent would be destroyed. In place of the ongyod the images of the six-armed Mahākāla were substituted (Altan erike, pp. 118–20); on the cult of the ongyod, objects which designate the support of a protective ancestral spirirt, usually in the form of effiges, see Even Chants de chamanes, pp. 286–392; see also Banzarov, "The Black Faith", pp. 77–9. On an archaeological find which casts light on the worship of the ongyod among the Khidans, see Pėrlėė, "Kidančuud modon ongodyn tuxaj", pp. 154–5.
82 Qalq-a-yin mongɣol-un yaǰar-a burqan-u šasin delgeregsen, 3v; Ɣongɣor, Qalq-a tobčiyan, I, pp. 354–7.

The Mongol historian Galdan writes in his *Erdeni-yin erike* that Abadai had the monastery of Erdeni Ĵoo constructed in 1586, and that he sent envoys to the Ligdan qaɣan of the Čaqar to bring back religious books which had been written in Mongolian by the Sa-skya Paṇḍita.[83] From this one can guess that Buddhist works which were translated into Mongolian by the Sa-skya-pa lamas during the Yuan dynasty were still preserved and the memory of these works was still alive among the aristocrats of northern Mongolia.

There is no doubt that Buddhism declined after the fall of the Yuan dynasty, but the theory of the "two systems" *(qoyar yoson)* which shaped the idea of sovereignty of the Mongol rulers did not end when the Mongols were expelled from China.[84] Moreover, the memory of the "two systems" was still alive among the Mongol nobility of the 16th century, and it played a prominent role in the religious and political alliance between Altan qaɣan of the Tümed and the Third Dalai Lama, the leader of the dGe-lugs-pa in Tibet.[85]

It is a well-known fact that Tibetan Buddhism had great influence upon the Mongol nobility at the Yuan court,[86] though the shamans also played an important part in the performance of rituals.[87] The teachings of Buddhism must have reached a broader circle of Mongols during the 14th century, evidence of this being the hymn to the fierce Tantric goddess Mahākālī by Chos-kyi 'od-zer, which is in fact characterised by motifs from traditional Mongol heroic poetry.[88] However, Buddhism intensively spread among the Mongol steppe dwellers in the second part of the 16th century.[89]

---

83 *Erdeni-yin erike*, p. 89. According to the chronicle *Erdeni ĵoo-yin ba öndör gegen-ü namtar*, envoys from the Čaqar brought Mongol books to the Qalqa (pp. 36–7).

84 Evidence of this is found in the letter written in 1402 by Tsoṅ-kha-pa as an eulogy for Elbeg Nigülesküi qaɣan. See Kaschewsky, *Das Leben des lamaistischen Heiligen Tsongkhapa*, pp. 140–1; see also Grupper, review of the *Weiße Geschichte* by Klaus Sagaster, pp. 130–3.

85 On the historical development of the theory of the "two systems", see the discussion by Sagaster, *Weiße Geschichte*, pp. 9–49; on Cakravartin Altan qaɣan, the recollection of the *qoyar yoso* at the meeting with the Third Dalai Lama in Kökenaɣur in 1578, see the *Erdeni tunumal neretü sudur*, pp. 90–128; see also the *Erdeni-yin tobči* (Urga text), 74r; the discussion of the theory of the "two systems" in the *Bolor erike* by Rasipunsuɣ (II, pp. 176–8). Finally, see Bira, "The Worship", pp. 11–12.

86 On the religious and political relations between the Mongol rulers and the Sa-skya-pa lamas, see the following sources: *Payba lama-yin tuɣuĵi*, pp. 80–95; *Erdeni-yin tobči* (Urga text), 43 r; *Altan kürdün mingɣan kegesütü*, pp. 110–122; *Altan erike*, pp. 97–109; *Bolor toli*, pp. 425–39; *Čaɣan lingqu-a erikes*, pp. 61–8. See also Petech, "Tibet", p. 330. On Buddhism in Qaraqorum, see Cleaves, "The Sino-Mongolian Inscription of 1346", pp. 1–123.

87 The *Yuan shi* gives a great deal of information on Mongol rituals performed by shamans at the Yuan court. See Ratchnevsky, "Über den mongolischen Kult", pp. 421, 425, 429, 433–4.

88 See Cerensodnom and Taube, *Turfansammlung*, pp. 19–20, 115; see also Čeringsodnam, *Mongɣol uran ĵokiyal*, pp. 389–94. It is interesting to note that Buddhist writers of the 19th century used folk poetry and songs to introduce the teachings of this religion to the Mongol herdsmen (Cėrėnsodnom, *Mongolyn burxany šašny uran zoxiol*, pp. 353–80).

89 Serruys remarked that whatever Lamaism existed in Mongolia in the 15th and 16th centuries, it lived side by side with shamanism, and most of the people probably practised a mixture of both. See "Early Lamaism", p. 182; on the social position of the shaman in the 17th century, see Heissig, "Lamaist Suppression", pp. 109–10.

The Mongolian sources available do not provide information on Buddhism in Mongolia during the 15th century, but the Chinese records of the Ming dynasty, regarding tribute missions from the Oyirad and the eastern Mongols, give direct indication of the presence of Tibetan lamas and traces of Buddhism in Mongolia until the middle of the 15th century.[90] Information on the activities of lamas in Mongolia and Mongol-Tibetan contacts appear again in the Chinese records as soon as tribute and diplomatic relations were established between Altan qaɣan of the Tümed and the Ming court in 1570.[91] The lack of information on Buddhism from the middle of the 15th century until 1570 in the Chinese records is not proof of the absence of this religion in Mongolia during that period.[92] Perhaps a careful investigation of the Tibetan sources will eventually throw light on this question.[93] At present, it should be remembered that the memory of the great influence of Tibetan Buddhism on the Yuan court was still alive among the Mongol nobility of the 16th century, who, no doubt, also had some knowledge of the teachings of this religion,[94] and also that the Chinese records testify to the religious activities of Tibetan lamas in Mongolia until the middle of the 15th century and again at the time of Altan qaɣan. In view of this, there are reasons to assume that Buddhism never entirely disappeared from Mongolia.[95] In the second part of the 16th century, historical events supported the revival and the intense diffusion of Buddhism in Mongolia.[96]

---

90 Serruys, "Early Lamaism", pp. 187–201; the 21 hymn to Tārā and the hymn to the five "Dhyāni-Buddhas" in Chinese, Sanskrit, Tibetan and Mongolian were printed in Peking in 1431. See Heissig, "Zwei mutmaßlich mongolische Yüan-Übersetzungen", pp. 8–115; 21 hymns to Tārā in Sanskrit, Tibetan and Mongolian were found among the inscriptions of Arǰai Aɣui, Otoɣ Banner (Ordos). They were dated to the end of the 15th century, providing evidence of the continuity of Buddhism in southern Mongolia. The inscriptions of Arǰai Aɣui, however, necessitate further study. See Qaserdeni et al., *Arǰai aɣui-yin uyiɣurǰin mongɣol bičigesü*, pp. 129–230.

91 Serruys, "Early Lamaism", pp. 201–2; see also *Pei-lou Fong-sou* (translated and commented on by Serruys), pp. 162–3, and note 86, p. 162.

92 In fact, Serruys explains that from 1450 on, tribute missions from the Oyirad and the eastern Mongols gradually became rarer, and disappeared from the Chinese records altogether. See "Early Lamaism", p. 201.

93 In 1434, Śā-kya ye-śes, Tsoṅ-kha-pa's disciple, visited the Ming court in Peking. After this, he propagated the teachings of the Yellow School of Buddhism in southern Mongolia and other regions. For this see Ya Hanzhang, *Dalai lama-yin namtar*, p. 32. According to the *Altan erike*, Śā-kya ye-śes visited the Ming court three times (in 1414, 1416, 1434). This source also sheds light on the close relation between Śā-kya ye-śes and the Chinese emperor Yongle (see pp. 144–51, and notes 37r–41v, pp. 217–22); on Śā-kya ye-śes, see also the *Čaɣan lingqu-a erikes*, pp. 183–5; on Tibetan lamas who visited Mongol areas during the 15th century, see Roerich, *Blue Annals*, p. 551.

94 See the words of Sečen qong tayiǰi addressed to his great-uncle Altan qaɣan, which are quoted in the *Erdeni-yin tobči*, 74r. As Larry Moses remarks, Altan qaɣan's convertion was not an isolated event, nor was it a miraculous one. Buddhism was there, but it lacked support among the nobility or the general populace. See *The Political Role of Mongol Buddhism*, p. 90. In his article "Early Lamaism" (pp. 181–213), Serruys exhaustively demonstrated that Lamaism did not begin with the arrival of the Third Dalai lama in Mongolia.

At the end of the 16th century, the Chinese official Xiao Daheng observed how Buddhism deeply influenced the lives of the ordinary believers of southern Mongolia. He also noted the important role reserved for the lamas in that area.[97] Moreover, the biography of Neyiči Toyin provides a great deal of information on the missionary methods used by this person to propagate Buddhism in eastern Mongolia, but from this source we also learn how Neyiči Toyin made the ordinary people of northern Mongolia recite the Yamāntaka spells and other Buddhist prayers in the first part of the 17th century.[98]

The Xarbuxyn Balgas collection of manuscripts can be examined from diverse viewpoints, but if we place it in the context of the religious climate of a period when Buddhism was intensively spreading in Mongolia, we may suppose that the texts of "popular Buddhism", which belong to the collection, served the purpose of the Buddhists to spread the fundamental teachings of this religion and the worship of gods of the Buddhist pantheon among the people in the first part of the 17th century. Moreover, the wedding calendars, dhāraṇī,[99] manuals of astrology and divination and the "prayers of the ǰayuradu" indicate that lamas were required whenever religious intervention was necessary[100]: to assign the date for a wedding,[101] recite spells which avert obstacles and misfortune, indicate the suitable or unsuitable day for performing any kinds of actions,[102] drive away the evil spirits which provoked disease,[103] and guide the dead during the bar-do,

---

95   In his article "Early Lamaism" (p. 213), Serruys concludes that all the facts point to an uninterrupted Lamaism tradition in southern Mongolia, going all the way back to Mongol Lamaism of early Ming dynasty and ultimately to the end of the Yuan dynasty. See also Jagchid, "Buddhism in Mongolia", pp. 48–60; Čoyiǰi, "Tutaɣar dalai blam-a-luɣ-a aɣulǰaqu-yin uridaki", pp. 10–26; Vladimirtsov, Régime social, pp. 236–7.

96   On the diffusion of Buddhism in the Qalqa, and the methods used by the nobility and lamas to convert people to this religion, see Ɣongɣor, Qalq-a tobčiyan, I, pp. 383–90; on the Qalqa Mongols in the 17th century see Veit, Die Vier Qane von Qalqa, I, pp. 3–15.

97   Serruys, Pei-lou Fong-sou, pp. 137–9, 147–8, 153. Xiao Daheng also noticed the large number of teachers (baysi) among the southern Mongols (pp. 140–1). It is worthy of note here Xiao Daheng's account of the discovery of the Fourth Dalai Lama, the son of Sümer dayičing (p. 139). The Mongol historian Nata narrates this episode in his Altan erike, pp. 141–4.

98   See Heissig, "Lamaist Suppression", p. 126; see also Ɣongɣor, Qalq-a tobčiyan, I, note 1, p. 385; the Altan kürdün mingɣan kegesütü (p. 225) also mentions the missionary activities of Neyiči Toyin in northern Mongolia.

99   See XBM 86 to XBM 90; XBM 91 to XBM 92.

100   The same, of course, happened in Tibet. See Stein, Tibetan Civilization, p. 174; on Mongɣolǰin families who invite lamas to perform rituals such as čalm-a oytolqu, "to cut off the lasso", sor qayaqu, "to throw a sor into a bonfire" etc., and read books, see Altanɣarudi et al., Mongɣolǰin-u šasin surtaqun, pp. 320–9.

101   The Russian scholar Pozdneyev relates that a lama is indispensable for performing a wedding ceremony. See Religion and Rituals, p. 564. Pozdneyev's account refers to late 19th century Mongolia.

102   The Chinese official Xiao Daheng describes how the Mongols strictly observed the rules imposed by lamas, and did not dare to transgress them. People turned to lamas for any action they had to undertake. For this see Serruys, Pei-lou Fong-sou, pp. 147–8. See also Naranbatu et al., Mongɣol buddha-yin soyol, pp. 177–8.

103   For this see Naranbatu et al., Mongɣol buddha-yin soyol, p. 186. On the library of a Čaqar lama, who was apparently a practitioner of magic ceremonies, see Heissig, "The Mongol

"the intermediate period between death and rebirth".[104] Finally, texts such as *Ündüsün-i sang* and the fire-*dalalya* testify to the penetration of Buddhist beliefs and deities in the sphere of popular Mongol religious practices. As is well know, syncretist rituals were already performed during the Yuan period,[105] but the earliest evidence to date of texts which show the penetration of Buddhism in Mongol cult practices is fragments of ritual texts from Olon Süme dating from the 16th–17th centuries.[106]

Needless to say, a collection of manuscripts which covers a vast range of topics such as that from Xarbuxyn Balgas merits further investigation. In this book, however, the task was to give Mongolists access to previously unknown texts which had been restored, identified and analysed. In view of this, the present publication should constitute a basis for future research.

The manuscripts from Xarbuxyn Bagas could never have been restored and investigated without the generous support of the Cultural Section of the Ministry of Foreign Affairs in Bonn. On the occasion of the publication of this work, I should like to express my sincere gratitude to this institution.

I feel deeply indebted to Prof. Klaus Sagaster for various reasons: for encouraging my work, for finding time to discuss and for helping with Tibetan sources.

I am most grateful to Prof. Walther Heissig for showing interest in my research work, and, above all, for his pioneer study *Die mongolischen Handschriften-Reste aus Olon süme,* which paved the way for my present work on the manuscripts from Xarbuxyn Balgas.

I should like to express my gratitude to Geshe Pema Tsering, Bonn, for enlightening me on Buddhist rituals and explaining the significance of Tibetan terms which are found in the Xarbuxyn Balgas texts.

Manuscripts and Xylographs", pp. 161–89. For the discussion of these texts, see Bawden, "The Supernatural Element", II, pp. 101–3.

104   Xiao Daheng relates that when a person dies, lamas are invited to recite prayers for 49 days or seven days, according to the means of the family. The best horse, robes and other objects which belonged to the dead are then offered to lamas. See Serruys, *Pei-lou Fong-sou,* p. 137; in Pozdneyev's words when a sick person is close to death, the presence of a lama in his or her home is absolutely necessary, according to Mongolian custom. On that occasion, lamas read the *Jayuradu-yin sudur.* See Pozdneyev, *Religion and Rituals,* p. 594; see also Naranbatu et al., *Mongyol buddha-yin soyol,* p. 185.

105   On syncretist rituals which were performed at the Yuan court, see Ratchnevsky, "Über den mongolischen Kult", p. 425, and notes 45–7; see also Heissig's remarks on *Ündüsün-i sang* from Olon Süme in *Handschriften-Reste,* p. 574.

106   See the Olon Süme *Rauchopfergebet, Ündüsün-i sang* and *Substitutsopfergebet* = Heissig, *Handschriften-Reste,* pp. 371–423. On the introduction of Buddhist concepts in a popular cult such as that of Dajan Deerx, see Even, *Chants de chamanes,* pp. 398–407. The works composed by Mergen Gegen of the Urad (1717–1766) provide ample evidence of the Buddhist interpretation of Mongol beliefs and ritual practices. See the book *Mergen gegen,* edited by Ȟalluu and Ȟarantai. It should be pointed out that the above-mentioned book also includes ritual texts which Mergen Gegen did not compose. These texts were circulating among the Urad and the Ordos Mongols, and Mergen Gegen wrote them down (p. 22). On the works by Mergen Gegen, see Bawden, "Two Mongol Texts", p. 1–19.

I extend my sincere thanks to Dr. Ts. Ishdorj, Institute of History of the Mongolian Academy of Sciences, for bringing the Xarbuxyn Balgas collection from Ulaanbaatar to Bonn, and, during my stay in Mongolia in 1994 and 1995, providing access to Mongolian and Oyirad manuscripts, which are preserved in Ulaanbaatar Central State Library and in the Institute of Language and Literature of the Academy of Sciences.

I am also grateful to Mr. P. Süxbat, Ulaanbaatar, who most kindly put at my disposal his private collection of Mongolian manuscripts and xylographs during my visit to Mongolia in the summer of 1997, a period when access to Mongolian books preserved in libraries turned out to be especially arduous.

A debt of gratitude is also owed to Mrs. Eva-Katharina Nebel, Cologne, and particularly to Mr. Ivan Bentchev, Bonn, who have restored the manuscripts from Xarbuxyn Balgas. Without the skilful work of the restorers I would never have been able to read most of the texts.

I should like to thank Mr. Frede Møller-Kristensen, Copenhagen Royal Library, for the kind welcome accorded to me during my visit to the Library, and for sending microfilms and photocopies of Mongolian manuscripts. I am also grateful to the librarians of Louvain University Library for allowing me to photocopy a number of Mongolian texts.

Other people placed at my disposal Mongolian materials or helped on different occasions; individual acknowledgements appear in the notes.

Fig. 1: Birch tree in the vicinity of Xarbuxyn Balgas. Photo by Elisabetta Chiodo, August 1999

Fig. 2: The ruins of Xarbuxyn Balgas. Photo by Elisabetta Chiodo, August 1999

Fig. 3: The stūpa of Xarbuxyn Balgas. Photo by Elisabetta Chiodo,
August 1999

Fig. 4: Offering placed inside the stūpa. Photo by Elisabetta Chiodo, August 1999

Linguistic Features of the Manuscripts

Palaeography

The manuscripts from Xarbuxyn Balgas analysed in this volume is the work of more than 100 scribes, who wrote them with a *calamus* in different styles of calligraphy. The manuscripts show either the form of a book with loose folios (Indian *pothī*) or of a booklet *(debter)*, i.e. the left sides or the middle of the folios are stitched together. The palaeographic features of the manuscripts are diverse and necessitate a separate study.[1] Some examples are given below.

In some texts, the letters *q* and *γ* at the beginning of a word are barely distinguishable from an initial *a*, e.g.: *qoγar, γal* (XBM 47, 1 v, 2 v); *qoγoloi* (XBM 60, 3r); *qaγan, γaǰar* (XBM 73, 1 v); *qamqaγ, qamuγ* (XBM 81, *2 v, 3 v); *qaγan, γaγčabar,* (XBM 110, 2 v, 7 v).

Usually, no distinction is made between *č* and *ǰ* in the middle of a word, e.g.: *tegünčilen* (XBM 25, *1v); *küčütü* (XBM 65, 1v); *eǰed* (XBM 81, 8r).[2]

The letters *γ* and *ǰ* are not differentiated at the beginning of various words. For example: *ǰaγun, yeke* (XBM 47, 2v).[3] In some instances, *i, γ, yi, ǰ* and *v* are not distinguished: *dvib, čambudvib,*[4] *yeke, yirtenčü, ǰayaγan* (XBM 110, 3 v, 2 r).

In some words the final *g* is written with two "teeth": *bodisung* (XBM 41, 8v); *bilig,* (XBM 47, 2v; XBM 60, 3 v); *erlig* (XBM 110, 2r), etc., while in others have only one "tooth" (*silüg*, XBM 47, 1 v).[5] There are words with the final *m* written with two "teeth": *oom* (XBM 49, 2v), *qomsim* (XBM 60, 3r) etc., while others have one "tooth": *darm-a* (XBM 48, 2r).[6]

For instance, in the text of the fire-*dalalγa* (see XBM 82, *4 r) the letters *g* and *m* at the end of the words *kesig* and *γuyinam* are in some cases written with one "tooth", in others with two "teeth". Moreover, the letter *n* at the end of the word *buyan* is usually written in the shape of a slightly curved stroke to the left, but in one case it is written with a vertical stroke like the earlier handwriting (XBM 82, *2 r).

---

1 A study was made by Kara. See *Knigi mongol'skix kočevnikov.*
2 See Cerensodnom and Taube, *Turfansammlung,* p. 10; see also the remarks by Žamcarano in *The Mongol Chronicles,* p. 8.
3 See *ǰarliγ, γabuqui* in *Molon Toyin's Journey* (= Lőrincz, vol. 2, chap. 1, 11 a–11b).
4 See *čambudvib* in *Molon Toyin's Journey,* vol. 2, chap. 1, 10 b.
5 See *bölög, qung* in *Molon Toyin's Journey,* vol. 2, chap. 1, 14 a.
6 On these palaeographic features, see Kara, *Knigi mongol'skix kočevnikov,* p. 65; see *oom* in the Olon Süme text OS IV/60 v = Heissig, *Handschriften-Reste,* p. 278.

The final *r* is written with a rounded stroke to the right in some texts (*dotor-a*, XBM 110, 2 r, *sür,* XBM 82, *4 r), while in others it shows a straight stroke to the right, e.g.: *činar* (XBM 8, 2 r); *qoyar, deger-e* (XBM 48, 2 r, 2 v); *temür* (XBM 48, 2 r).[7]

The final *s* is often written like an Uighur *z*: *tus* (XBM 60, 3 r); *simnus* (XBM 56, 1 v); (*erdenis, sonos,* XBM 110, 4 r).[8]

Orthography

We can observe the inaccurate use of the punctuation signs in numerous texts. Diacritical points representing the sounds *n, γ* and *š* are absent in various texts, but some texts use them in the following manner.

The letter *n* is written with the single dot at the beginning of some words: *nemekü, menekei* (XBM 47, 2 r, 3 r). Moreover, *ünesün* (XBM 73, 3 v).

The diacritical points are found before the letter *γ* in intervocalic position e.g.: *doloγan* (XBM 30, 3 r); *čaγan, dutaγaǰu* (XBM 47, 2 r, 3 v), before a consonant and at the end of a word (*quγaγtan, saγsabad, ǰasaγ,* XBM 47, 1 v, 2 v, 3 v).[9]

The letter *š* with two points to the right is found at the beginning of some words: *šagi-a-muni* (XBM 23, 1 v), *šagi-muni* (XBM 41, 2 v), *šigemüni, šatu* (XBM 57, 9 r, 8 v), and at the end of the word *üilš* (for *üileš, üiles,* XBM 28, 9 v).

Moreover, the diacritical points are found before the initial *q,* e.g.: *qan* (XBM 47, 3 v); *qonoγ* (XBM 30, 3 r), and before the initial and medial *q,* as in the word *qamtudqaǰu* (XBM 47, 2 v).

Some texts show traces of the pre-classical orthography. So we find the syllables *qi, γi* (instead of *ki, gi*) in the following words.[10]

- *qumaqi* (XBM 29, 2 v, XBM 34, 2 v; XBM 37 r)
- *saqin* (XBM 47, 1 v)
- *oγiu* (XBM 81, 2 r)
- *qiri* (XBM 110, 3 v)
- *avaloγide* (XBM 51, 1 v)
- *iγindo* (XBM 83, 1 v)[11]

---

7 The same is found in the Olon Süme manuscripts. See, for istance, the letter *r* at the end of *ker ber* in OS IV/96 v (Heissig, *Handschriften-Reste,* p. 305); see also the examples which Kara gives in *Knigi mongol'skix kočevnikov,* p. 67.

8 See von Gabain, *Grammatik,* p. 26; see also Kara, *Knigi mongol'skix kočevnikov,* p. 66.

9 On the irregular use of the diacritical points in the texts of the 17th century, see Žamcarano, *The Mongol Chronicles,* p. 8.

10 Ligeti remarked that the spelling *qi, γi* was employed in the 15th and 16th centuries, and some examples dating from the early 17th century are attested in the Qalqa. See "A propos de quelques textes", p. 265.

11 This word was not identified.

The use of the letters *d*, *t* is inconsistent in the majority of the Xarbuxyn Balgas texts, e.g.:

- *ǰil-d̲ü* (XBM 97, 2 v)
- *burqan-t̲ur* (XBM 11 r)
- *nom-t̲ur* (XBM 11 r)
- *dalai-t̲ur* (XBM 34, 3 r)
- *bügüde-t̲ür* (XBM 22, 5 v)
- *γurban-d̲a* (XBM 57, 10 r)
- *erketü-t̲e* (XBM 28, 7 r)
- *ǰabsar-d̲aki* (XBM 92, 2 r)
- *egüden-t̲eki* (XBM 82, *4 v)
- *eǰen-t̲üriyen* (XBM 47, 4 v)

Moreover, there are *qutuγ-d̲an* (XBM 1, 1 r); *nidü-d̲en* (XBM 1, 2 r); *üjesküleng-d̲ei* (XBM 41, 7 v).

The medial *t* in the words *boltuγai* (XBM 88, 2 r,) and *metü* (XBM 110, 8 v) are written like *d* before a consonant *(bold̲uγai, med̲ü)* while the letter *d* in the word *üyiledküi* (XBM 41, 7 v, etc.) is written like *d* before a vowel *(üyiled̲küi)*.[12]

Occasionally, instead of the initial *t* we find *d* (*degüs* for *tegüs*, XBM 110, 6 r).

The letter *d* is often doubled in intervocalic position, e.g.: *čidderleǰü* (XBM 49, 6 v); *nereyiddügsen* (XBM 56, 1 v); *dongγodduγči* (XBM 66, 8 r); *duradduγsan* (XBM 62, 1 r); *beleddümüi*[13] (XBM 81, *2 v). There is also the spelling *itegem=müi* (XBM 5, 1 v), i.e. a part of the word is written at the end of the line and the rest at the beginning of the next line. In this case, the letter *m* is again written in the next line.

The letter *γ* is often found with front vowels, and the letter *g* with back vowels, e.g.: *üyiledkegülüysen* (XBM 57, 9 r); *kičiyeγsen* (XBM 57, 9 r); *bayasulčagsan* (XBM 22, 3 v); *bolugsan* (XBM 22, 4 r); *uduridugči* (XBM 41, 4 r).[14]

In some instances, *ö* and *ü* in second position are spelt with a superfluous *yod*, e.g.: *bülüge, tölöge, kümün* (XBM 42, *2 r; XBM 83, 3 v; XBM 97, 6 v); the suffix *-lüge* (XBM 110, 8 v)[15] is also spelt with a superfluous *yod*.

Numerous words are written separately in the Xarbuxyn Balgas texts. Words spelt separately such as *es-e* (XBM 16 r), *tus-a* and *bas-a* (XBM 110, 3 v) are also attested in the pre-classical texts. They reflect Uighur orthographic features.[16]

Words, however, are also split in unusual ways: *čoγ-čas* (XBM 2, 1 v); *süm-bür* (XBM 29, 5 r); *maqa-bud* (XBM 56, 3 r); *un-i* (XBM 56, 2 v); *bold̲u-γai* (for *boltu-γai*,

---

12 This orthographic feature is also observed in the earlier texts. See Cerensodnom and Taube, *Turfansammlung*, p. 11.
13 See Róna-Tas, *"Thar-pa čhen-po"*, p. 474.
14 See some examples in Žamcarano, *The Mongol Chronicles*, p. 8.
15 For this see Sárközi, *"Vajracchedikā"*, p. 92.
16 See Cerensodnom and Taube, *Turfansammlung*, p. 11; see also *Sayin ügetü erdeni-yin sang* (J̌aγunasutu et al., p. 384); Ligeti, "A propos de quelque textes", p. 274.

XBM 88, 2v), etc. An orthographic feature like this, however, is observed in both the earlier and later Mongol texts.[17]

A number of words are written separately for reasons of space, i.e. part of a word is written at the end of a line and the rest in the next line, e.g.: *ǰayay=an* (XBM 41, 6v); *nigüles=ügči* (XBM 47, 3v).

Finally, words are written separately in the Xarbuxyn Balgas texts because the scribes used pieces of birch bark with splits in their surface. This obviously prevented the scribes from joining the words. So we have *ungsibas-u; daldari-qu* (XBM 47, 3v), etc. In some cases, we can notice a blank space between the words. The reason is that the surface of the birch bark is uneven at a certain point, and therefore unsuitable to write on it. (e.g.: XBM 43, *2v).

In numerous words the vowels *o* and *u* are written as *ö* and *ü* and vice versa. This orthographic peculiarity is not infrequent in the Mongolian texts.[18] For instance, the words *ǰöb* and *ǰüg* are written *ǰob, ǰug* in the Turfan texts.[19] The Xarbuxyn Balgas texts show the following forms.

- *böluysan* for *boluysan* (XBM 22, 4r)
- *bölbas-un* for *bolbas-un (bolbasun)* (XBM 22, 4v)
- *ǰökiyayči* for *ǰokiyayči* (XBM 22, 3r)
- *tüyuluysan* for *tuyuluysan* (XBM 22, 3r)
- *dütayu* for *dutayu* (XBM 22, 3v)
- *tüsa* for *tusa* (XBM 22, 2r)
- *moron* for *mörön, mören* (XBM 29, 2v)
- *tomür* for *tömür, temür* (XBM 47, 3v)
- *dorben* for *dörben* (XBM 70r)
- *ǰob* for *ǰöb* (XBM 79, 6r)
- *tobed* for *töbed* (XBM 82, *5r)
- *ǰug* for *ǰüg* (XBM 41, 2v)
- *tuyuskegsen* for *tegüskegsen* (XBM 58, 2v)
- *bulčakü* for *bilčaqu* (XBM 41, 8v)

There is also evidence of alternation of consonants:

- *m ~ b*: *kömčin ~ köbčin* (XBM 34, 2v); *namči ~ nabči* (XBM 34, 3r)[20]
- *b ~ m*: *yabbar ~ yambar* (XBM 49, 4r)

---

17 See the remarks by Cerensodnom and Taube in *Turfansammlung,* p. 11; see also de Rachewiltz, "The Preclassical Mongolian Version of the Hsiao-ching", p. 20; Sárközi, *"Vajracchedikā",* p. 93; numerous words are written separately in *Molon Toyin's Journey into Hell* (see Lőrincz, p. 21 et passim).

18 For this see the remarks by de Rachewiltz in "The Preclassical Mongolian Version of the Hsiao-ching", p. 20; the spelling *mörila-* for *morila-* is found in *Les lettres* (Mostaert and Cleaves, p. 17); *mor* for *mör,* etc. also occurs in the *Erdeni-yin tobči.* See Žamcarano, *The Mongol Chronicles,* p. 8.

19 Cerensodnom and Taube, *Turfansammlung,* No. 3r6, p. 56, No. 4r7, p. 58. Moreover, the spelling *ǰug* occurs in *Les lettres* (Mostaert and Cleaves, p. 17); see also *Erdeni dara-yin qorin nigen mayta[yal]* of 1431 = Heissig, "Zwei mutmaßlich mongolische Yüan-Übersetzungen", 6a, p. 26.

20 *namči* (obsolete form of *nabči*) is found in Lessing, p. 1207.

– *m ~ l: menekei ~ melekei* (XBM 47, 3r)
– *n ~ l: minaya*[21] *~ milaya* (XBM 73, 2v)
– *l ~ r: tüyidkel ~ tüyidker* (XBM 41, 1v)
– *r ~ l: keregür*[22] *~ keregül* (XBM 107, *3v)

There is frequent use of suffixes which are joined to the word they modify. This orthographic characteristic is also attested in the earlier Mongol works and throughout the Olon Süme texts.[23]

– *ayulayin* (XBM 28, 3r)
– *yarquyin* (XBM 41, 4v)
– *čayun* (XBM 3, *1r)
– *küjisün* (XBM 54, 2r)
– *möri* (XBM 22, 3v)
– *qarangyusi* (XBM 41, 3v)
– *orodi* (XBM 90, 4v)
– *dayisundu* (XBM 103, 4r)
– *tamudača* (XBM 46, 5r)
– *köldegen* (XBM 57, 10v)
– *köliyer* (XBM 47, 4r)

The plural suffix in *-s* is directly added to the genitive suffix and the accusative suffix:

– *ündü-sün* (XBM 5, 1r)
– *erdeni-sün* (XBM 47, 1v; XBM 52, 1v)
– *lingqu-a-sun* (XBM 81, 3r)
– *üile-si* (XBM 66, 9r)

It is interesting to note that the word *erdeni-sün* is also written in this way in the Olon Süme text OS I/10r.[24]

The Xarbuxyn Balgas texts also show old spellings. Several examples follow:

– *ayay-qa tegimlig* (XBM 1, 2r), MLM *ayay-a tegimlig*[25]
– *kögeregen* (XBM 30, 3v), MLM *kögerge*[26]

---

21 See *minaya* in Lessing, p. 1207.
22 See *keregür* in the Turfan text No. 34v4 (Cerensodnom and Taube, Turfansammlung, p. 126).
23 See de Rachewiltz, "The Preclassical Mongolian Version of the Hsiao-ching", p. 20; Heissig, *Handschriften-Reste,* p. 564.
24 Heissig, *Handschriften-Reste,* p. 564.
25 On *ayay-qa tegimlig,* see Weiers, *Untersuchungen,* pp. 201–202; see also the remarks by Ligeti in "A propos de quelques textes", p. 274; in the Turfan texts we find both *ayay-qa tegimlig* and *ayay-a tegimlig* (Cerensodnom and Taube, *Turfansammlung,* No. 14r8, No. 32r4, pp. 84, 120). See Lessing *(ayay-a tegimlig),* p. 23.
26 On epenthetic vowels within a word, see the discussion by Ligeti, "A propos de quelques textes", note 4, pp. 274–275; the form *kögöröge* is found in the *Čayan teüke* (Sagaster, *Weiße Geschichte,* p. 148).

- *oordo* (XBM 30v; XBM 35, 8r) instead of *ordo*[27]
- *yesün* (XBM 32, 2v), MLM *yisün*[28]
- *tenggeri* (XBM 35, 7v); the forms *tngri, tengri* alternate in the texts (e.g.: XBM 38r; XBM 29, 2v).[29] Occasionally, we find the spelling *tengeri* (XBM 34, 2r).
- *vaiduri, vayiduri* (XBM 41, 3v; XBM 42 *1v) < AT *vayiduri*, <Skr. *vaiḍūrya*, MLM *vayidury-a, bayidury-a*[30]
- *borqan* (XBM 46, 2r), pl. of *borqai*[31]
- *sülder* (XBM 56, 2r), MLM *sülde*[32]
- *qayaraqai* (XBM 57, 4r), MLM *qayarqai*[33]
- *körisütü* (XBM 57, 8r)[34]

---

27 The spelling *oordo* for *ordo* remains a matter of controversy. As far as I known, it is not attested elsewhere, but *oon* instead of *on* is found in the *Bodhicaryāvatāra* (Cleaves, "Bodistw-a Čari-a Avatar-un tayilbur", p. 55, and the remarks by the author in note 352, p. 129); see the discussion of the spelling *oon* by Cerensodnom and Taube in *Turfansammlung*, No. 21 v10, p. 95. Finally, see *noom* instead of *nom* in Kara, "L'inscription mongole d'Aruγ" p. 165, note 74.

28 The Turfan text No. 82r11 has *yesün* (Cerensodnom and Taube, *Turfansammlung*); the Olon Süme fragment OS III/29 Av also has *yesün* (Heissig, *Handschriften-Reste*, p. 428); *yisün* is found in the "Vocabulaire d'Istanboul" (Ligeti, p. 74); *yisün*, however, is also found in both the Olon Süme and Xarbuxyn Balgas texts.

29 *tenggeri* often occurs in the *Secret History*. See, for example, § 1; *tenggeri* is found in the manual *Sanhe Yulu* (Ligeti, "Deux tablettes", p. 208); see *tngri* in the Turfan texts (*Turfansammlung*, 3v3, etc.), and in *Erdeni dara-yin qorin nigen mayta[ya]l* of 1431 = Heissig, "Zwei mutmaßlich mongolische Yüan-Unersetzungen", 7b, p. 46, etc.; *tengri* is listed in the "Vocabulaire d'Istanboul" (Ligeti, p. 68); *tngri* is the prevailing form in the *Altan tobči* (15v et passim). The *Erdeni-yin tobči* (Urga text, 2r et passim) has *tengri*. On the occurrance of *tngri, tengri* in the Mongolian literature of the 13th–17th centuries, see Weiers, *Untersuchungen*, p. 199. Note that *oordo* and *tenggeri* appear in the same text (XBM 35).

30 See von Gabain, *Grammatik*, p. 350; see also *vaiduri* in the *Bodhicaryāvatāra*, *Turfansammlung*, No. 11 r13, p. 79; Ligeti, "A propos de quelques textes", p. 274; see *bayidury-a*, Skr. *vaiḍūrya* in Ishihama and Fukuda eds., *Mahāvyutpatti*, No. 6222; Lessing has *baiduri, baiduriy-a* (p. 74), *viidüriy-e* (p. 894).

31 See *borqai* in § 180 of the *Secret History*.

32 *sülder* appears for the first time in the *Secret History* (§ 63); *sülder* is also attested in the *Altan tobči*, 16v, 111v; the form *sülder* survived in ritual texts of the cult of Činggis qaγan (see XBM 65 below in this volume).

33 *qayaraqai* is found in the *Hsiao-ching* (see de Rachewiltz, "The Preclassical Mongolian Version", 32a, p. 38). It also occurs in the hymn to Mahākālī (*Turfansammlung*, No. 29r 2, p. 116). The *Bodhicaryāvatāra* also shows the spelling *qayarqai* (*Turfansammlung*, No. 20v9, p. 93); see also *qayarqai* in the *Bodhicaryāvatāra* from Olon Süme (*Handschriften-Reste*, OS IV/35–6, p. 253); on this word see the discussion of Jayunasutu et al. in *Sayin ügetü erdeni-yin sang*, p. 616. Finally, see *qayarqai* in Lessing, p. 907.

34 See *körisütei* in § 254 of the *Secret History*; *körisütü* also occurs in the Olon Süme text OS III/29 Av (Heissig, *Handschriften-Reste*, p. 428); see *körüsütü* in Lessing, p. 492, and *körösö* in *Mongyol kitad toli*, p. 712.

- *ile-de* (XBM 110, 3 v); *ilete* (XBM 66, 2 v, XBM 78, 2 r), MLM *iledte* [35]
- *degü* (XBM 73, 1 v), MLM *degüü* [36]
- *bolad* (XBM 73, 2 r), MLM *bolod* [37]
- *öter* (XBM 75, 9 r), MLM *ödter* [38]
- *kir* (XBM 78, 1 v), MLM *kkir* [39]
- *tasuraqai, tamturaqai* (XBM 82, *2 v), MLM *tasurqai, tamturqai* [40]
- *ebečin* (XBM 100, 4 v) MLM *ebedčin* [41]
- *qubčan* (XBM 107, 4 r), MLM *qubčasun* [42]
- *qudal-tu* (XBM 107, 2 r), MLM *qudalduya(n)* [43]
- *degel* (XBM 110, 6 r), MLM *debel* [44]

We find prothetic vowels in the transcription of Tibetan words such as *ibsan, imdo,* (XBM 83, 1 v); *oydarm-a* (XBM 107, 6 v); *isgangga, isganga* (XBM 109, 3 v, 7 r). They

---

35 The Xarbuxyn Balgas texts, however, also have *iledte*. See *ilete* in the *Bodhicaryāvatāra* (de Rachewiltz, "The Third Chapter of Chos-kyi 'od-zers's Translation", 33a, p. 1185); *Sayin ügetü erdeni-yin sang* (Jaγunasutu et al., p. 269); *ilete* is also attested in the *Erdeni-yin tobči* (Urga text, 10 v et passim).

36 See *degü* in the Turfan text No. 35 r2 (*Turfansammlung*, p. 128); *degü* is also attested in the *Erdeni-yin tobči* (Urga text, 18 r et passim); see the plural form *degüs* in the *Altan tobči*, 160 v.

37 *bolad* appears in the *Alexander Saga* (see *Turfansammlung*, No. 3 v5, p. 57); on this term see Cleaves, "Daruγa and Gerege", p. 46.

38 For the spelling *öter*, see Ligeti, "A propos de quelques textes", p. 274, note 3; see *öter* in *Sayin ügetü erdeni-yin sang* (Jaγunasutu et al., p. 259), and *Molon Toyin's Journey into Hell* (= Lőrincz, p. 22).

39 XBM 29, 4 r has *kiir*, but XBM 22, 2 r reads *kkir;* the spelling *kir* appears in the Olon Süme texts, e.g.: OS IV/41 (Heissig, *Handschriften-Reste*, p. 271); *kkir* occurs in the hymn to the five "Dhyāni-Buddhas" of 1431. See Heissig, "Zwei mutmaßlich mongolische Yüan Ubersetzungen", p. 71; *kikir* is found in the inscription of Arjai Aγui which praises one of the 35 Buddhas of penitence. See Qaserdeni et al., *Arjai aγui-yin uyiγurjin mongγol bičigesü,* pp. 58–9.

40 Lessing, pp. 785, 775 respectively.

41 *ebečin* occurs in § 227 of the *Secret History*. It is also found in the *Bodhicaryāvatāra* from Turfan and from Olon Süme (Cerensodnom and Taube, *Turfansammlung*, No. 19 r3, p. 90; Heissig, *Handschriften-Reste*, OS IV/26–8, p. 58); *ebečin, ebedčin*, however, alternate in both the Olon Süme and Xarbuxyn Balgas texts. The *Erdeni-yin tobči* (Urga text, e.g.: 16 r) has *ebečin;* see *ebečin, ebedčin* in the *Altan tobči* (73 v, 158 r).

42 See *qubčan* in § 136 of the *Secret History*, and in the Turfan text No. 14 r9 (Cerensodnom and Taube, *Turfansammlung*, p. 84).

43 The word *qudaldu* is written separately. For this reason, it is spelled *qudal-tu* in the text. See the form *qudaltu* in the Turfan text No. 52 r3 (Cerensodnom and Taube, *Turfansammlung*), and in "L'inscription mongole d'Aruγ" (Kara, p. 162); on *qudaldu*, see the remarks by Jaγunasutu et al. in *Sayin ügetü erdeni-yin sang*, p. 653; the "Vocabulaire d' Istanboul" has *qudalduči* (Ligeti, p. 46); *qudaldu* appears in the *Erdeni-yin tobči* (Urga text, 78 v).

44 *degel* is found in the Olon Süme texts. See OS IV/53 r (Heissig, *Handschriften-Reste*, p. 280). The *Erdeni-yin tobči* has both *degel* and *debel* (Urga text, 22 v, 82 r); *degel* is the prevailing form in the *Altan tobči* (see, for example, 7 v).

transcribe the Tibetan *bzaṅ-po*,[45] *mdo*,[46] *gtor-ma*,[47] *skaṅ-ba*,[48] following an old tradition which goes back to the Uighur translators.[49] We can also observe the use of the *galiγ* alphabet for the transcription of Sanskrit words in some texts (e.g.: XBM 78, 3r–4r); the *birγa* is often found at the beginning of a text, folio or section of a text.[50]

The texts are also marked by the frequent use of spellings which reflect the influence of the colloquial language, e.g.[51]:

- *ǰayaǰu* for *ǰiyaǰu* (XBM 30, 2r)
- *ǰayasu* for *ǰiyasu* (XBM 47, 3r)
- *čadqulang* for *čidqulang* (XBM 49, 4v)
- *aǰarγa* for *aǰirγa* (XBM 82, *4r)
- *čamduqui* for *čimadqui* (XBM 75, 5r)
- *boltola* for *boltala* (XBM 30, 2r)
- *dotoroki* for *dotoraki* (XBM 46, 3v)
- *qotolo* for *qotola* (XBM 46, 4v)
- *qoγor* for *qoγar* (XBM 59r)
- *qoγoloi* for *qoγolai* (XBM 60, 3r)
- *solongγon* for *solonγa(n)* (XBM 110, 7r)
- *toγo* for *toγa* (XBM 30, 2v)
- *toγola* for *toγala* (XBM 98, *4)
- *toγolotuγai* for *toγolatuγai* (XBM 98, *4)
- *omorqoqui* for *omorqaqui* (XBM 110, 5v)
- *γoro-a* for *iru-a* (XBM 107, *3r)
- *bold* for *bolod* (XBM 57, 10r)
- *qalγa* for *qaγalγa* (XBM 110, 5r)
- *ulan* for *aγulan* (XBM 47, 3r)
- *alan* for *alaγan* (XBM 46, 3v)
- *bulγa* for *buγulγa* ("yoke") (XBM 85, 4r)
- *burulasi* for *buruγulasi* (XBM 84, 4r)
- *urul* for *uruγul* (XBM 96, 4v)
- *kerülten* for *keregülten*, XBM 66, 10v

---

45   It means "good". See Das, *Tibetan-English Dictionary*, p. 1109. According to the text in which *ibsan* appears (fire-*dalalγa*), this is a Sanskrit word (*enedkeg-ün keleber: ibsan…*). However, this word is not recognisable as Sanskrit.

46   *sūtra* (Das, p. 675).

47   "Sacrificial objects" (Das, 527).

48   "A kind of expiatory sacrifice to make amends for a duty not performed" (Das, p. 82).

49   See Kara, "Une version mongole du *Maṇi bka'-'bum*", p. 34 and note 29; see *oγdarma* in the fragment of the *Sitātapatrā-dhāraṇī* from Olon Süme (OS IV, 38–9 = Heissig, *Handschriften-Reste*, p. 290, and p. 569).

50   The *birγa* is also found in the Olon Süme manuscripts. See OS IV/37r, OS IV/39–39r, etc., (Heissig, *Handschriften-Reste*, pp. 287, 290); on the use of the *birγa*, see Kara, *Knigi mongol'skix kočevnikov*, p. 51.

51   For the influence of the colloquial language on the orthography of the literary language, see the discussion by Poppe in "The Groups *uγa* and *üge*", pp. 4–5.

- *ebösün* for *ebesün* (XBM 29, 3r)
- *ödür* for *edür,* (XBM 54, 2r)
- *kötegö* (*sibayun*) for *kötege,* (XBM 102r)
- *tireng* for *teyireng* (XBM 109, 7v)
- *sirbiigsen* for *sirbeyigsen* (XBM 65, 1v)

Moreover, the suffix *-san/-sen* instead of *-ysan/-gsen*[52]:

- *arilusan* (XBM 41, 7v)
- *bolusan* (XBM 58, 2v)
- *qamtudasan* (XBM 58, 3r)
- *törögülüsen* (XBM 46, 2v)
- *tügesen* (XBM 46, 4r)
- *idesen* (XBM 109, 3r)
- *bei* instead of *bui* (XBM 41, 8r)
- *bile* instead of *bülüge* (XBM 79, 6r)

Morphological Features

Declension

Genitive suffixes:

- *-yin: ečige-yin* (XBM 82, *1v)
- *-u/-ü: nasun-u* (XBM 88, 2v); *etügen-ü* (XBM 81, *7v)
- *-un/-ün: yal-un* (XBM 81, 3r); *ger-ün* (XBM 84, 4r)

The genitive suffixes of the colloquial language occur frequently in the texts.[53]

- *-yin: čay-yin* for *čay-un* (XBM 57, 9v); *-nugüd-yin* for *-nügüd-ün* (XBM 12v)[54]
- *-i-yin: könjilei-yin* for *könjile-yin* (XBM 82, *3v)
- *-yi-yin: könög-yi-yin* for *könög-ün* (XBM 82, *3v)
- *-in: qumaqiin* for *qumaqiyin* (XBM 37r); *öberin* for *öberün* (XBM 41, 5r)[55]
- *-gi-yin: sang-gi-yin* for *sang-un* (XBM 57, 9v)[56]

---

52 On this suffix see Poppe, *Khalkha-mongolische Grammatik,* pp. 81–2, and by the same author see "Alexandersage", p. 122, note 77; on the occurrence of *-san/-sen* in the Mongolian literature of the 15th–17th centuries, see Weiers, *Untersuchungen,* pp. 168–70.

53 These genitive suffixes also appear in the language of the Geser epic which Poppe investigated. See "Geserica", pp. 14–18, and by the same author see the following two works: *Khalkha-mongolische Grammatik,* pp. 59–60; *Introduction,* pp. 189–90; see also Weiers, *Untersuchungen,* pp. 66–70.

54 See *yajar-yin* in Poppe, *Grammar,* § 284, p. 74.

55 See *öberin* and other examples in Ligeti, "Deux tablettes", pp. 207–8; see also Poppe, "Geserica", p. 16.

56 Poppe quotes *jiryalang-gi-yin* ("Geserica", p. 17).

-i is often used instead of -u after a word ending in n, e.g.[57]:

- amitan-i (XBM 15 r; XBM 28, 2 r; XBM 47, 3 r)
- sinayan-i, mösön-i, qančuni, onini (XBM 81, 8 r)
- könjilen-i (XBM 84, 4 r)
- ökin-i (XBM 97, 2 v)

Accusative suffixes:

- -i: sedkil-i (XBM 9, 5 r)
- -yi: tusa-yi (XBM 6, 4 r)

The accusative suffixes of the colloquial language are also extensively used in the texts. A number of these suffixes occur in the Prayer to Geser (XBM 73), demonstrating the oral tradition of the prayer.[58] The Xarbuxyn Balgas texts show these suffixes:

- -i: duyulyai for duyulyayi (XBM 73, 2 v)
- -i-i: mesei-i for mese-yi (XBM 73, 3 v)
- -i-yi: töröi-yi for törö-yi; bügüdei-yi (XBM 47, 3 v, 4 r)[59]
- -i-gi: noytoi-gi for noyto-yi; üilei-gi (XBM 73, 3 r, 4 r)[60]
- -yigi: meseyigi for meseyi (XBM 73, 2 v)
- -gi ni: bey-e-gini for bey-e-yi inu, "his body" (XBM 107, *6 r)[61]

The use of the dative-locative suffixes -dur/-dür, -tur/-tür is the most inconsistent in the texts[62]:

- burqan-tur (XBM 11 r)
- bey-e-tür (XBM 41, 7 r)
- jambala-tur (XBM 57, 2 v)
- ayulan-tur (XBM 60, 3 r)
- nasun-tur (XBM 90, *3 r)
- dayisun-tur (XBM 100, 2 v)

Occasionally, we find the dative-locative -dur/-dür, -tur/-tür with i (inu), e.g.: delekei-tür-i (XBM 53, *1 v); untaqui-türi (XBM 110, 4 r).[63]

---

57 See Poppe, "Geserica" (p. 17), Grammar, § 284, p. 74; see also Weiers, Untersuchungen, p. 67, and "Bemerkungen", p. 368.

58 On accusative suffixes in the colloquial language, see the following three works by Poppe, "Geserica", pp. 20–2; Khalkha-mongolische Grammatik, pp. 61–2; Introduction, pp. 191–4; see also the following two works by Weiers, Untersuchungen, pp. 93–8; "Bemerkungen", p. 368.

59 For this suffix, see Poppe, "Geserica", p. 21; see also adai-yi in Heissig, Handschriften-Reste, p. 565.

60 See töröi-gi and other examples in Poppe, "Geserica", p. 22; see also Weiers, Untersuchungen, p. 97.

61 See toya-gini in Poppe, "Geserica", p. 21.

62 The inconsistent use of d/t is observed throughout Molon Toyin's Journey into Hell. See Lőrincz ; see also Sárközi, "Vajracchedikā", p. 92.

63 For the use of the dative-locative suffix in conjunction with i, see Weiers, Untersuchungen, pp. 80, 84–5, and note 1, p. 84; see also Poppe, Introduction, § 155, p. 214; Cleaves, "The Sino-

In one instance the double suffix of the dative- locative is employed: *qaγan-a-ṭur* (XBM 22, 3 r).

The suffix *-a/-e* appears frequentely in the texts, e.g.:

– *daruγsan-a* (XBM 22, 1 v)
– *yaǰar-a* (XBM 74, 1v)
– *simnus-a* (XBM 81, 8 v)
– *usun-a* (XBM 81, 8 r)
– *kümün-e* (XBM 97, 2 r)
– *degüner-e* (XBM 97, 3 v)

The suffixes *-du/-dü, -tu/-tü*[64] are mainly found in the texts XBM 93, XBM 94, XBM 95, ("The seats of the soul"), while *-da/-de, -ta/-te* are widely used, e.g.:

– *yarγayči-da* (XBM 22, 1 v)
– *aqada* (XBM 73, 1 v)
– *tngri-de* (XBM 22, 2r)
– *ekede, erede* (XBM 97, *4 r)
– *gereltü-de* (XBM 41, 3 v)
– *törögsed-te* (XBM 22, 4 v)
– *gerte* (XBM 108 r)

The dative-locative *-dur/-dür, -tur/-tür* with the reflexive-possessive suffix *-iyan/-iyen*: *čimadur-iyan* (XBM 78, 2r); *eǰen-ṭüriyen* (XBM 47, 4v).

The dative-locative *-dayan/-degen, -tayan/-tegen*: *mörön-ṭegen* (XBM 73, 2 r); *gertegen* (XBM 29, 2r).

Moreover, the combined dative-locative *-da/-de, -ta/-te* with the ablative suffix *-ča/-če*: *tamudača* (XBM 46, 5 r); *lingquu-ṭača* (XBM 46, 5 r); *lingqu-ṭača* (XBM 56, 5 r).[65]

The possessive suffix joined to the dative locative *-da/-de* is also found e.g.: *čoγ-tuda; kkir kkir ügei-tüde* (XBM 22, 2 r, 2 v).[66]

The frequent occurrence of the plural suffixes *-n, -s, -d, -ud/-üd, -nar/-ner, -nuγud/-nügüd*[67]:

– *borqan* (pl. of *borqai*, XBM 46, 2r)
– *qulaγan* (XBM 47, 3 r)

Mongolian Inscription of 1362", note 260, p. 131; de Rachewiltz, "The Third Chapter of Chos-kyi 'od-zer's Translation", p. 1200, note 138; *töröγsen-dür-i* appears in the *Erdeni-yin tobči* (Urga text, 76 r). The dative-locative suffix with *i* is widely used in *Molon Toyin's Journey into Hell* (see Lőrincz, pp. 24–5 et passim).

64   On the use of these suffixes in the non-literary language, see Ligeti, "Deux tablettes", pp. 208–9; see also Weiers, *Untersuchungen*, pp. 76–8; Poppe, *Grammar*, § 286, p. 75.

65   See Weiers, *Untersuchungen*, pp. 103–6; Poppe, *Grammar*, § 300, p. 78.

66   See some examples in Heissig, *Handschriften-Reste*, p. 564.

67   For the ample use of the plural forms in the ancient language, see the remarks by J̌ayunasutu et al. in *Sayin ügetü erdeni-yin sang*, pp. 123–9; see also Heissig, *Handschriften-Reste*, p. 566; Sárközi, "*Vajracchedikā*", p. 94. Finally, see plural forms such as *ǰidas, üyes, sibaγud, beyes, sükes* etc. in *Molon Toyin's Journey* (Lőrincz, pp. 54–55).

– *qayačaqun* (XBM 9, 6v)
– *sayuqun* (XBM 110, 3v)
– *čoyčas* (XBM 4r)
– *oros* (XBM 41, 3v); *orod* (XBM 22, 3r)
– *elčis* (XBM 81, *7v)
– *erdenis* (XBM 110, 4r)
– *yaǰad* (XBM 56, 3r)
– *todqad* (XBM 73, 3v)
– *čidküd* (XBM 35, 7v)
– *quvaray-ud* (XBM 5, 1r)
– *nom-ud* (XBM 47, 2r)
– *blam-a-nar* (XBM 5, 1v)
– *todqar-nuyud* (XBM 41, 3r)
– *ündüsün-nuyud* (XBM 22, 4v)

Furthermore, the word *qan* with the plural suffixes -*d-ud*: *qad-ud*, i.e. the final *n* of the stem is dropped and the suffix -*d* is added to it (XBM 57, *2r).[68]

Conjugation

The imperative of the second person, which coincides with the stem of the verb, e.g.:

– *yabu* (XBM 104, *2v)
– *ög* (XBM 107, 2r)
– *ungsi* (XBM 109, 3v)
– *sonos* (XBM 110, 4r)
– *udurid* (XBM 110, 5v)

The imperative of the second person of the plural, or the so-called benedictive: -*ytun/ -gtün* (*nisülesügtün*, XBM 110, 1v).

The imperative of the third person -*tuyai/-tügei* is also often found, e.g.: *boltuyai* (XBM 1, 2v) etc.; *sakituyai* (XBM 22, 62); *ungsituyai* (XBM 46, 1v).

The voluntative in -*su/-sü*, which often occurs in the pre-classical language[69]: *bolsu* (XBM 29, 2r); *ögsü* (XBM 29, 2r); the suffix of the modern literary language -*suyai/ -sügei*, e.g.: *bolsuyai* (XBM 47, 3r); *egüskesügei* (XBM 16v).

Moreover, the suffix of the colloquial language -*sai/-sei*: *üǰegdesei* (XBM 29, 1v);[70] we also find *üǰeydesii* (XBM 32, 2r), and *üǰeydesi* (XBM 35, 2r) instead of *üǰegdesei*.

The Present forms in -*mu/-mü*, -*mui/-müi*, -*m*, expressing an action which is present or future, e.g.: *mörgömü* (XBM 24, 3r); *itegemüi* (XBM 12r); *beledüm* (XBM 79, 6r).

The suffix -*yu/-yü* also expressses an action which is present or future: *boluyu*, *ügüleyü* (XBM 28, 9r; XBM 47, 2r).[71]

---

68   See *xādūd* in Poppe, *Khalkha-mongolische Grammatik*, p. 55.
69   See Weiers, *Untersuchungen*, pp. 117–19; see also Poppe, *Grammar*, § 338, p. 90.
70   Weiers quotes *abusai* in "Bemerkungen", p. 369.

The *praeteritum perfecti -ba/-be, -bai/-bei* is sometimes employed as a future tense,[72] e.g.:

– *sonosba* (XBM 29, 2r)
– *bolba* (XBM 47, 2r).
– *kürbei* (XBM 47, 2r)

The *praeteritum imperfecti* of the colloquial language in *-ǰi* is also used: *dayariǰi, bolǰi* (XBM 107, *6v, *8v).[73]

The *nomen futuri -qu/-kü, -qui/-küi* of the passive voice expressing the idea of necessity to act,[74] e.g:

– *tataydaqu; takiydaqu* (XBM 60, 4r)
– *bisilydaqui; tebčigdeküi* (XBM 110, 4r)

The pre-classical plural form of the *nomen futuri -qun/-kün*[75] is attested in two texts: *qayačaqun* (XBM 9, 6v); *sayuqun* (XBM 110, 3v).

In one instance we find the *nomen imperfecti -ya/-ge* with *inaru: boluy-a inaru* (XBM 110, 3v), and *-ge* with *üdügüi* (*irege üdügüi*, XBM 28, 4r).[76]

The plural form of the *nomen perfecti -ysad/-gsed: buliysad* (XBM 22, 3v); *üiledügsed, törögsed* (XBM 22, 3v, 4v).

The *converbum conditionale -basu/-besü* is often used, e.g.: *ungsibasu* (XBM 29, 3v); *olbasu, kürbesü, sedkibesü* (XBM 47, 2v, 3v). Occasionally, the suffix *-basu/-besü* is found with *ber* (see *genübesü ber* in XBM 66, 7r). The suffix *-yasu/-gesü* occurs in the word *besiregesü* (for *bisiregesü*, XBM 41, 8v).[77]

The *converbum imperfecti* in *-ǰi* is used showing colloquial influence: *kiǰi* (XBM 107, *6v, *7r, *7v).[78]

The *converbum modale* in *-n*, e.g.: *kičiyen* (XBM 28, 9v); *oytalun, quyuran* (XBM 100, 3r, 3v); the *converbum modale* with *bui*, expressing continuous actions: *saqin bui* (XBM 47, 1v).[79]

The *converbum perfecti* of the verb *ki-*, i.e. *kiged* with the instrumental suffix: *kiged-iyer* (XBM 66, 8r), and the genitive suffix: *kiged-ün* (XBM 69, 2r; XBM 70r).[80]

---

71   On these suffixes see Weiers, *Untersuchungen*, pp. 131–7, 139–46, and "Bemerkungen", p. 369; see also Poppe, *Grammar*, §§ 344–6, pp. 91–2, §585, 164, § 349, p. 92, § 586, p. 164.
72   See Poppe, *Introduction*, pp. 266–7.
73   See Poppe, *Khalkha-mongolische Grammatik*, p. 80.
74   Poppe quotes the *nomen futuri* of the passive voice in *-qui/-küi*, pointing out that the *nomen futuri* of the passive voice in *-qu/-kü* never occurs. See *Grammar*, § 607, p. 169. However, in the Xarbuxyn Balgas texts we have the *nomina futuri* of the passive voice both in *-qui/-küi* and *-qu/-kü*. On the occurrence of these two forms in the *Hsiao-ching*, see de Rachewiltz, "The Preclassical Mongolian Version", note 37, p. 58.
75   See Poppe, *Grammar*, § 361, p. 94.
76   See Weiers, *Untersuchungen*, pp. 170–7.
77   See Weiers, *Untersuchungen*, pp. 194–7.
78   See Poppe, *Grammar*, § 372, p. 96.
79   Poppe, *Grammar*, § 575, p. 161.
80   See Poppe, *Grammar*, § 432, p. 122.

The occasional occurrence of the *converbum terminale -tala/-tele: boltola* (for *boltala,* XBM 30, 2 r)*; butaratal-a, butaratala* (XBM 56, 2 v; XBM 66, 10 r).

The *converbum praeparativum: -r-un/-r-ün, -run/-rün* recurs in the texts,[81] e.g.: *yabuju bür-ün* (XBM 6, 4 v); *egüskejü bürün* (XBM 6, 4 r); *nomlar-un* (XBM 28, 9 v); *ügülerün, nomlarun* (XBM 29, 1 v, 2 r).

Two texts show the suffix *-ya* as an element of other suffixes, which, as Poppe stated, is a peculiarity of the Qalqa dialect.[82] We have these forms:

– *-γaysan: yabaγaysan* (XBM 107, *3 v); *qariγaysan* (XBM 108 r)
– *-γaju: yabaγaju* (XBM 107, *4 r)
– *-γaqu: yabaγaqu* (XBM 107, *4 r)

The duplication of a word is often attested in the texts. It conveys the idea of completeness. For instance, *burqan burqan bolqu boltuγai,* "May I completely become a Buddha" (XBM 13, 6 r). Furthermore, *[de]gedü degedü* (XBM 16 v); *büri büri* (XBM 30, 3 r); *[e]rdeni erdeni* (XBM 41, 4 r); *jöb jöb* (XBM 66, 3 v; XBM 68, 2 r); *üy-e üy-e* (XBM 66, 9 r); *joriγtu joriγtu* (XBM 66, 10 v); *alin alin* (XBM 110, 8 v).[83]

It is also worth noting that the Xarbuxyn Balgas texts show an unusual duplication of words such as *bu burqan* (XBM 15 r) instead of *burqan burqan; boda bodalang* (XBM 53, *2 v) instead of *bodalang bodalang; ke kes-ig* (XBM 82, *3 r) instead of *kesig kesig; bu buyan* (XBM 82, *5 r) instead of *buyan buyan; daγu daγusba* (XBM 84, 4 v) instead of *daγusba daγusba.*[84]

Finally, the widespread use of the ending formula *sadu edgü* (Skr. *sadhu,* "good"; AT *ädgü,* "good"), which is found in the Uighur Buddhist texts,[85] associates the Xarbuxyn Balgas texts with those from Olon Süme, which are also marked by the frequent occurrence of the formula *sadu edgü.*[86]

In the transcription of the texts, the reader should note that the blank space within square brackets *[ ]* indicates letters, words and lines which are missing in the original, viz. a section of the folio is missing or ink has entirely faded.

Points within square brackets *[…]* denote illegible letters, words and lines.

Superfluous letters and words are given between angle brackets (e.g.: *čayun <un>; a<r>murliγulugči*); words and lines which are misplaced are also given between angle

81 For the diverse uses of the *converbum praeparativum* in the Mongolian literature of the 13th–17th centuries, see Weiers, *Untersuchungen,* pp. 184–9.
82 Poppe only mentions the form *jawāsan.* See *Introduction,* p. 273.
83 See *jük jük* in § 273 of the *Secret History; jüg jüg* appears in the *Hua yi yi yu* (Manduqu, p. 59); on the duplication of a word and the various meanings, see Poppe, *Grammar,* §§ 40–403, pp. 111–12; see also some examples in Sárközi, "*Vajracchedikā*", p. 94.
84 Poppe quotes modal adverbs with the meaning "completely", derived by reduplication of the first syllable of the word with the inserted consonant *-b* (*qab qar-a, qab qarangγui,* etc.). See *Grammar,* § 218, pp. 59–60. However, the forms which are attested in the Xarbuxyn Balgas are different since they consist of the duplication of a part of a word regularly ending in vowel. In my own view, the fact that these forms are attested in different texts should allow us to exclude that we are dealing with words which were left incomplete by the scribe.
85 See Zieme, *Altan yaruq sudur,* p. 112.
86 Heissig, *Handschriften-Reste,* pp. 569–70; see also Kara, "Une version mongole", p. 21.

brackets. Finally, angle brackets are used to indicate words and lines which were deleted by the scribe.

Letters and words written between lines are inserted in the text and printed in bold. Letters and words which were restored are given within square brackets.

The letters *d* and *t* are inconsistent in most of the texts. These letters are underlined in the transcription; spellings which differ from the orthographic rules of the literary language such as *ǰug* (for *ǰüg*), *böluγsan* (for *boluγsan*), *boluγsan* (for *boluγsan*), *čidderleǰü* (for *čiderleǰü*) etc., have been retained in their original forms.

For the sake of convenience, the initial *γ* written without the diacritical points is transcribed *γ* (e.g.: *γaǰar*), while the initial *q* marked with the diacritical points is transcribed *q* (e.g.: *qan*). However, the orthographic peculiarities of certain words are pointed out in the notes to the transcription of the texts. Moreover, the photographic reproduction of the manuscripts will enable the reader to verify the diverse features of the texts.

For punctuation the following signs are used:

.	single *čeg*
:	*dabqur čeg*
::	*dörbeǰin čeg*
+, x	repetitions signs
O	*birγa*

Word division:

The hyphen (-) is used to separate suffixes and word endings. It is also employed to join words which are split in the texts.

A double stroke (=) is used to join words written separately for reasons of space, i.e. a part of the word is at the end of one line and the rest at the beginning of the next line.

Abbreviations:

Skr.	Sanskrit
AT	Ancient Turkic
Tib.	Tibetan
Chin.	Chinese
MLM	Modern Literary Mongolian

Buddhist Prayers

To Go for Refuge (XBM 1 to XBM 21)

The Xarbuxyn Balgas collection provides us with 27 items of 21 copies of a text which was identified as *Itegel yabuyulqu (skyabs-'gro)*, "To go for refuge". The large number of copies of *Itegel yabuyulqu* from Xarbuxyn Balgas shed light on the widespread circulation of this text in northern Mongolia in the first part of the 17ᵗʰ century. It is also interesting to note that the inscription of Cagaan Bajšin (Čaɣan Bayising) of 1601 ends with the section of *Itegel yabuyulqu* called the "four immeasurables" *(dörben čaylasi ügei)*.[1]

Itegel yabuyulqu is a prayer serving as a preliminary contemplative stage for entry to the sacred world of a ritual.[2] The Russian scholar Pozdneyev relates that the Mongol lamas usually start the religious service with *Itegel yabuyulqu*, and that copies of this prayer can be found not only on every lama, but also in the home of almost every layman.[3]

We also have evidence of the circulation of *Itegel yabuyulqu* in southern Mongolia in the 16ᵗʰ–17ᵗʰ centuries. A fragment of the prayer was found in Olon Süme, but Heissig did not identify it.[4]

A large number of copies of *Itegel yabuyulqu* are known to us. The prayer is found either as a single text or included in collections of prayers and other religious texts. The title of the text may also vary.[5]

---

1 Huth, *Die Inschriften*, p. 35; for *dörben čaylasi ügei;* Tib. *tshad-med-pa bźi*, see Ishihama and Fukuda eds., *Mahāvyutpatti*, No. 1506.

2 On the significance of the recitation of this prayer at the beginning of a ritual in Buddhist monasteries in Tibet, see Beyer, *The Cult of Tārā*, pp. 177–9. Numerous examples of the recitation of "To go for refuge" at the beginning of a ritual are found in the book by Savvas and Lodro Tulku, *Transformation*.

3 *Religion and Ritual*, pp. 407–10; *Itegel yabuyulqu* is the only prayer which the lamas of the Gandan monastery in Ulaanbaatar recite in Mongolian.

4 Heissig, *Handschriften-Reste*, OS/IV 111–12, p. 540. The Olon Süme text is discussed in the commentary.

5 See Rintchen, "Manuscrits mongols" *(Itegel)*, No. 26, p. 109; Aalto, "A Catalogue" *(Itegel sudur)*, H-5803, p. 94; Farquhar, "A Description", No. 27, p. 194. Sazykin, *Katalog: Itegel neretü orosiba*, No. 1410, p. 255; *Itegel*, Nos. 1383, 1393, 1435, pp. 251, 253, 257; *Itegel yabuyulqu-yin yoson orosibai*, Nos. 1409, 1422, pp. 254, 256). Numerous copies of the texts are preserved in the Central State Library in Ulaanbaatar. For example, *Itegel yabuyulqu neretü orosiba*, No. 294-2 N-923, and *Itegel yabuyulqu-yin surtayal-un tobči quriyangyui*, No. 294-2 U-913. The latter summarises the teachings of *Itegel yabuyulqu*. The Oyirad version *Itegel orošiboi* (No. 352) is preserved in the Institute of Languages and Literature of the Mongolian Academy of Sciences in Ulaanbaatar.

I was able to see *Itegel yabuyulqu neretü orosiba*,[6] which is a single text. Moreover, I had access to *Itegel yabuyulqu maytayal* included in the collection of Lamaist prayers known as *dBus-yin nom-un ayimay yeke baya-nuyud-tur nomlaysan-u nom-un yabudal-un ǰerge sayin qubitan-u-qoyolai-yin čimeg kemegdeküi*.[7] Finally, I saw *Itegel yabuyulqu-iyan yosun kemegdekü* forming part of *Qutuy-tu degedü yekede tonilyayči neretü sudur*.[8]

XBM 1

2 items of a *pothī* (2 folios, 4 written sides) measuring 15 × 4.5 cm, and comprising 19–17 lines (r/v); the Mongolian page numbers are *nigen, qoyar* (1, 2); 1 v shows 8 lines belonging to a different text and letters of the alphabet written in a different hand. These lines are poorly written. *Itegel yabuyulqu* continues on 2 r, but a section of the text is missing.[9]

1 r

1	O *ba bür-ün*[10] *oy[taryui]*	7	*erdem üiles : nigen-tür*
2	*-yin kiǰayar-a-luy[-a] [sača]*[11]	8	*quriyayad mön činar*
3	*qamuy amitan arban ǰü[g]*	9	*bolǰu :: naiman tümen dörben*
4	*-ün yurban čay-un*	10	*mingyan nom-un čoyč[as]*[13]
5	*qamuy tegünčilen iregsed*	11	*yarqui-yin oron*[14] *boluysan*
6	*-ün bey-e ǰarliy ǰirüken*[12]	12	*qutuy-dan ayay-qa tegil =*

---

6 Heissig and Sagaster, *Mongolische Handschriften*, Libr. Mong. 134, No. 441, p. 245. See also Heissig, *Blockdrucke*, No. 66, p. 57.

7 Heissig and Bawden, *Catalogue*, Mong. 392, pp. 229–30.

8 Heissig and Bawden, *Catalogue*, Mong. 449, pp. 220–1.

9 Restored by Mr. Bentchev; old number 21/9.

10 This copy of text has *ba bür-ün*, "as for we"; the other Xarbuxyn Balgas texts have *ači-tu ečige eke; ačitu ečige eke terigüten; ečige eke terigüten*. Libr. Mong. 134 (1v:1) has *bi kiged*. The Tibetan original has *bdag daṅ*, "I and ..." in the opening passage of *sGrol-dkar yid-bźin 'khor-lo'i sgrub-thabs bźugs-so*. It reads: *bdag daṅ 'gro-ba nam-mkha'i mtha' daṅ mñam-pa'i sems-can mtha'-dag* (1r:2). See Savvas and Lodro Tulku, *Transformation*, p. 44. See *bi bürün*, "as for I", in § 201 of the *Secret History* (de Rachewiltz, *Index*, p. 113). On the *converbum praeparativum -r-un, -run/-r-ün, -rün* meaning "as ...", "because of", "when ..." etc., see Poppe, *Introduction*, § 237, p. 279, and by the same author see "Antworten", p. 46.

11 The words *oytaryui* and *sača* were restored on the basis of the other copies of the text. See XBM 2, 1v:2–3, etc.

12 Mong. 392 (1v), Mong. 449 (1v), Libr. Mong. 134 (1 v:8), and the other copies have *sedkil*.

13 See *čoyčas* in XBM 2, 1 v:10 (*čoy-čas*) and in the other copies of the text. The 84,000 *dharmaskandha*. However, *naiman tümen dörben mingyan* is incorrect. XBM 2, 1v:9 reads *nayan dörben mingyan*. See *nayan tümen dörben mingyan* (which is also incorrect) in Poppe, *Diamond Sutra*, 49b, note 3, p. 158.

14 *yarqu-yin oron*, Skr. *ākara*; Tib. *'byuṅ-gnas*. See Ishihama and Fukuda eds., *Mahāvyutpatti*, No. 7267.

13   *mig*[15] *-nuyud-un auγ-a*
14   *-yin eǰen ačitu ündüsün*
15   *kiged : ündüsülüysen*[16]
16   *selte ber degedü tegüs*

17   *[č]oγ-tu lam-a-nuyud-**tur***
18   *itegemüi ::*[17] *idam*
19   *mandal-un tengri-yin*[18]

1v

1   *o̤m o̤m o̤m*
2   *o̤m o̤m o̤m*
3   *o̤m o̤m o̤m*
4   *namo̤*[19] *gürü*

5   *lovigisuvari*[20] (?)
6   *eǰe[…]*[21] *nigülesküi **ber***
7   *üǰen soyorq[a]*
8   *irügeǰü ene*

2r

1   *tegünčilen iregsen-t̤ür*[22]
2   *itegemüi [::] [ila]ǰu tegü[s]*
3   *nögčigsen burqan-nuyud*
4   *-tur itegemüi [::] degedü*
5   *nom-nuyud-tur itegemüi [::]*
6   *qutuγ-d̤an ayaγ-qa*
7   *tegimlig-[nu]yud*
8   *-tur itegemüi :: [ba]yatur*
9   *daginis-un darm-a balai* (?)

10   *-yin čiγulγan .*[23] *belge*
11   *bilig-ün tegüs nidü-den*[24]
12   *-nuyud-tur itegemüi ::*[25]
13   *burqan nom kiged degedü*
14   *čiγulγan-nuyud-tur*
15   *bodi qutu[γ]-tur*
16   *kürte[le] [i]tegemüi :: bi*
17   *minu [ögli]ge*[26] *terigüten*

2v

1   *üiledügsen buyan-iyar*
2   *amitan-u tusa-yin*

3   *tulada burqan bolqu*
4   *boltuγai [::]*[27] *qamuγ amitan*

---

15   A metathesis of *tegimlig;* the form *ayaγ-qa tegimlig* < AT *ayaγ-qa tägimlig*, appears in the ear-
      lier texts. See, for example, Cerensodnom and Taube, *Turfansammlung,* 13r1, p. 82; see also
      Aalto, "Ayaγ-qa tegimlig", pp. 17–22; Weiers, *Untersuchungen,* pp. 201–2.
16   Instead of *ündüsülügsen.*
17   Mong. 392, 2 r: *qamuγ qutuγ-tan quvaraγ-ud eǰen. ačitu iǰayur kiged ündüsün selte tegüs čoγ-
      tu degedü blam-a-nuyud-tur itegemüi.*
18   XBM 5, 1v:5–7: *idam mandal-un burqan-nuyud-un čiγulγan-t̤ur itegemüi bi*; Libr. Mong.
      134, 2v:7–3r:1: *idam mandal-un burqan-u nököd selte bügüde-dür itegemüi.*
19   The letter *m* is misplaced in this word.
20   This word is incorrectly written.
21   I am unable to read this word.
22   *tegünčilen iregsen* is barely legible in the original.
23   Libr. Mong. 134 (10v:7–8) has *bayatur dagini dharma balsa-dur* in a different passage.
24   *-den* is legible in the original.
25   Mong. 449, 1v: *yidam mandal-un burqan-u čiγulγan nökör selte-nuyud-tur itegemüi. čoγtu
      itegel degedü nom-i tedkügči sakiyulsun belge bilig-ün nidün tegüsügsen-nuyud-tur itegemüi.*
      Libr. Mong. 134, 3r:2.5: *degedü nom-i tedkügči sakiyulsun belge bilig-ün nidün-luγ-a
      tegüsügsen-nuyud-tur itegemüi.*
26   Libr. Mong. 134, 3v:4: *minu öglige;* XBM 11v:3–4: *ö[ber]-ün öglige.*

5   *amuγulang kiged :*
6   *amuγulang-un silta =*
7   *γan-ṯur tegülder boltu =*
8   *γai ::²⁸ ǰobalang kiged*
9   *ǰobalang-un siltaγan-ača*
10 *qayačaqu boltuγai*
11 *ǰobalang ügei degedü*

12 *ǰirγalang-ača ülü*
13 *qayačaqu boltuγai ::*
14 *inaγsi činaγsi urin*
15 *tačiyangγui qoγar-ača*
16 *anggiǰiraqu tegsi*
17 *orosiqu boltuγai [::]²⁹*

XBM 2

1 item of a *pothī* (1 folio, 1 written side), measuring 9.5 × 4.5 cm, with 11 lines; the Mongolian page number is *nigen* (1). The folio is stained, and has splits in its surface. The text is framed with lines.³⁰

1 v

1   *ači-tu ečige eke kiged*
2   *oγtarγui kiǰaγar-luγ-a³¹*
3   *sača qamuγ amitan*
4   *arban ǰüg-ün γurban*
5   *[čaγ]-un qam[u]γ tegünčilen*
6   *iregsed³² bey-e ǰarliγ*

7   *sedkil erdem üiles bügü[de]*
8   *-yin mön činar boluγsan*
9   *nayan dörben mingγan nom*
10 *[-un] čoγ-čas γarqu-yin*
11 *oron boluγsan*

XBM 3

1 item of a *pothī* (1 folio, 2 written sides), measuring 8 × 4 cm, with 8 lines; the page number is illegible, but it is the beginning of the text. Only four lines, which are barely legible, are left on verso.³³

*1 r

1   ○ *ačitu [eči]ge*
2   *eke kiged*

3   *oγtarγui kiǰa =*
4   *γar-luγ-a sača*

---

27 Mong. 449, 1 v has *γurbanta ügüle* at this point.
28 Mong. 449 (2r) and Libr. Mong 134 (5r:7–5v:1) have: *qamuγ amitan ǰirγalang kiged ǰirγalang-un siltaγan-luγ-a tegülder boltuγai.*
29 Mong. 449, 2r: *qamuγ amitan oγira qola tačiγaqui urilaqui qoγar-ača tegsi-dür aqu boltuγai;* Libr. Mong. 134, 5v:9–6r:6: *qamuγ amitan čiqula kiged čiqula busud-ḏa tačiγaqui urilaqui qoγar-ača qayačaγsan tegsi sedkil-ṯur aqu boltuγai.*
30 Restored by Mr. Bentchev; old number 12/2.
31 *kiǰaγar-luγ-a* is legible in the original.
32 It omits the genitive suffix after *iregsed*. See XBM 1, 1r:5–6 and the other copies.
33 Restored by the Russians experts in Ulaanbaatar; old number 8/3.

5   *qamuy amitan*   7   *yurban čayun <un>*[34]
6   *arban jüg-ün*   8   *qamuy [te]günčilen*

*1v

1   *[i]regsed*   3   *[ ]n bügüde*
2   *[ ]i ba sa[...]*   4   *bütükü boltuyai :*

XBM 4

2 items of a *pothī* (2 folios, 3 written sides), measuring 10 × 4 cm, with 11 lines; the page number is missing on the first folio transcribed below, which is also severely damaged, especially on verso; the other folio has the Mongolian page number *jiryuyan* (6).[35]

recto

1   *nayan dörben*   7   *[-tu]*[37] *[ü]ndüsün*
2   *mingyan nom-un*   8   *[de]gedü čoy-tu*
3   *čoycas yarqui-yin*   9   *tegülder blam-a*
4   *oron boluysan:*   10   *-nar-tur itegemüi :*
5   *qutuy-tan quvaray*   11   *burqan-tur*
6   *[-ud   ]*[36] *-un ejen äči*

verso

1   *[...] [ite]gemüi :*   7   *i[te]gemüi itegel :*
2   *[burs]ang quvaray*   8   *nom-un s[a]ki[yu]l =*
3   *[-ud] -tur itegemüi :*   9   *sun eke belge bilig*
4   *[ ]*   10   *-ün nidün*
5   *burqan [ ]*   11   *tegüsügsen*
6   *či[yu]lyan [ ]*

6r

1   *boltuyai: qamuy*   5   *boltuyai qamuy*
2   *amitan jobalan[g]*   6   *amitan ta[či]yangyui*
3   *ügei jiryalang*   7   *urin kilin[g]-eče*
4   *-ača ü [l]ü qaya[č]aqu*   8   *qayačay [sa]n [t]egsi*

---

34   The other versions have *čay-un; ča* is written like *či*. The word *čayun* has the genitive suffix joined to the word. The suffix *-un* which follows is superfluous.
35   Restored by Mrs. Nebel; old number 12.
36   See XBM 5, 1r:10–11.
37   XBM 5, 1r:11.

9 *sedkil [...]*[38]
10 *aqu boltuɣai :*

11 *maṇ gha lam :*

XBM 5

1 item of a *pothī* (1 nearly entire folio, 2 written sides), measuring 14 × 6.5 cm, with 12 lines; the Mongolian page number is *nige[n]* (1). The folio has one edge torn.[39]

1 r

1 O *ačitu eči[ge] [eke kiged]*[40]
2 *oytarɣui-yin [ki]ǰaɣar < >*[41]
3 *-luɣ-a sača qamuɣ amitan : arban*
4 *ǰüg-ün ɣurban čaɣ-un*
5 *qa[m]uɣ tegünčilen iregsed*
6 *-ün bey-e ǰar[l]iɣ sedkil erdem*
7 *üiles bügüde-yin mön <>*

8 *činar boluɣsan : nayan dörben*
9 *mingɣan nom-un čoɣčas ɣarqui-**yin** oron*
10 *boluɣsan qutuɣ-tan quvar =*
11 *aɣ -ud-un eǰen ači-tu ünd =*
12 *<d>-ü-sün*[42] *degedü čoɣ*

1 v

1 *[-tu] blam-a-nar*
2 *-tur i[tegemü]i : burqan-tur*
3 *itegemüi: nom-tur itegemüi*
4 *: bursang quvaraɣ-ud-tur*
5 *itegemüi : iddam*[43] *mandal-un*
6 *burqan-nuɣud-un čiɣulɣan*

7 *-tur itegemüi bi : degedü*
8 *čoɣ-tu itegel nom-un sakiɣu =*
9 *lsun eke belge bilig*
10 *-ün nidün tegüsügsen*
11 *-nuɣud <> -tur itegem =*
12 *<m>ü*[44] *:: ɣurban ta :*

XBM 6

2 items of a *pothī* (2 folios, 3 written sides), measuring ca. 9 × 3cm, with 13 lines; the Mongolian page numbers are *nigen, dörben* (1, 4). The folios are fairly well preserved.[45]

---

38 XBM 8, 5r:4 has *sedkil-tür.*
39 Restored by Mr. Bentchev; old number 22/16.
40 The words *eke kiged* are restored according to the other versions of the texts. See XBM 2, 1 v:1 etc.
41 The word was deleted by the scribe of the text.
42 The letter *d* is written again in the next line. See *itegem =müi* below in the text.
43 Instead of *idam.*
44 The letter *m* is repeated in the next line.
45 Restored by Mr. Bentchev; old number 31/6.

1 v

1	○ *ačitu*	8	*qamuγ tegünčilen*
2	*ečige eke kiged*	9	*iregsed-ün bey-e*
3	*oγtarγui-yin*	10	*ǰarliγ sedkil*
4	*kiǰaγar-luγ-a*	11	*erdem üiles*
5	*sača qamuγ ami =*	12	*bügüde-yin*
6	*tan : arban ǰüg*	13	*mön činar*[46]
7	*-ün γurban čaγ-un*		

4 r

1	*nuγud-tur*	8	*tula : bodi*
2	*bodičid-tur*	9	*sedkili egüskesüge =*
3	*kürtel-e itegemü[i]*	10	*i degedü bodi*
4	*bi : kemen öber*	11	*sedkil-i egüskeǰü*
5	*-ün busud-un*	12	*bürün :*[47] *qamuγ*
6	*tusa-yi saγitur*	13	*amitan-i erkele[n]*
7	*bütügeküi-yin*		

4 v

1	*ǰočilasuγai*	8	*-yin tula burqan*
2	*bi : sedkil*	9	*bol[u]n bütükü*
3	*-tür ǰokis-tu*	10	*boltuγai :*
4	*dege[dü] [bo]di*	11	*qamuγ amitan*
5	*yabudal-iγar*	12	*ǰirγalang kiged*
6	*yabuǰu bür-ün :*[48]	13	*ǰirγalang-un*
7	*amitan-u tusa*		

XBM 7

1 item of a *pothī* (1 nearly entire folio, 1 written side), measuring 15 × 6 cm, with 15 lines, without page number; the lower section of the the folio is missing.[49]

The text of *Itegel yabuγulqu* runs from lines 1–7, while the rest of the folio shows letters of the alphabet. It is interesting to observe how a folio containing an incomplete text was used for other purposes.

---

46 *mön činar* is legible in the original.
47 Mong. 449, 1 v reads: *bodi sedkil-i egüskemüi. degedü bodi sedkil-i egüskeǰü*; Libr. Mong. 134, 4 v:6–8: *bodi sedkil-i egüskemüi. degedü bodi sedkil-i egüskeged.*
48 Mong. 449, 2 r: *degedü bodi yabudal-i sedkil-dür ǰokistai yabusuγai*; Libr. Mong. 134, 5 r:1–3: *degedü bodi yabudal-i taγalan üiledsügei.* See *bodi yabudal-iγar yabuγad* in the *Bodhicaryāvatāra* = Cerensodnom and Taube, *Turfansammlung*, No. 10, p. 77.
49 Restored by Mr. Bentchev; old number 22/19.

1 O *ačitu ečige eke terigü =*
2 *[ten] oγtarγui-yin kiǰaγar*
3 *-luγ-a sača qamuγ amitan*
4 *arban ǰüg-ün γu[rban]*

5 *čaγ-un qamuγ tegünči[len]*
6 *ireg[s]ed-ün bey-e [   ]*
7 *sedkil erdem üile[s]*

XBM 8

2 items of a *pothī* (3 written sides). The first item is a nearly entire folio measuring
ca. 12 × 5 cm, with 9 lines; the Mongolian page number is *qoyar* (2). The second item is a
folio measuring ca. 12 × 7 cm, with 11 lines; the Mongolian page number is *tabun* (5). The
folios are half-burnt, but the text is legible thanks to infra-red reflectography. The text is
written with a thicker and a thinner *calamus*.[50]

2 r

1 *[am]itan-u tusayin*
2 *[tul]a ta [arba]n*
3 *ǰüg-ün γurban*
4 *čaγ-un qamuγ*
5 *tegünčilen iregsed*

6 *-ün beyen kelen sedkil*
7 *ǰirüken erdem üiles*
8 *bügüde mön činar*
9 *[   ] ::[51] nayan dörben*

2 v

1 *mingγan nom[-un]*
2 *[č]oγčas [γarqui-yin][52]*
3 *oron bo[l]uγsa[n]*
4 *qamuγ qutuγ-t[an]*
5 *quvaraγ-ud namai*

6 *eǰelen ündüsün*
7 *barilduγulun*
8 *iregsen-luγ-a*
9 *čoγ-tu tegülder*

5 r

1 *boltuγai qamuγ*
2 *amitan tačiyangγui*
3 *urin kiling[53] qaγačaγ =*
4 *san tegsi sedkil-tür*

5 *aqu boltuγai kemen*
6 *dörben čaγlasi ügei :*
7 *bisilγaydaqui[54] oom*
8 *suba[u]-a siddo sarva*

---

50 Restored by Mrs. Nebel; old number 14.
51 This word should be either *bolǰu* or *boluγsan*. XBM 1, 1r:9 has *bolǰu*; XBM 5, 1r:8 reads
    boluγsan.
52 These words are illegible, but the other copies have *γarqui-yin oron* at this point.
53 The ablative suffix *-eče* is omitted.
54 The passive of the nomen futuri in *-qui, -küi* expressing the idea of necessity to act. See Poppe,
    Grammar, § 607, p. 169.

9　*darm-a subau-a*　　　　　　　　11　*ödgü*[55]
10　*siddo qang [sad]u*

XBM 9

3 items of a *pothī* (3 folios, 5 written sides), measuring 8 × 2.5 cm, with 10–13 lines; the Mongolian page numbers are *nigen, tabun, ǰirγuγan* (1, 5, 6); various words are illegible on 5 v.[56]

1 v

1	O *oγtarγui*	6	*tusa-yin tula*
2	*-yin kiǰaγar*	7	*arban ǰüg-ün*
3	*-luγ-a sača ečige*	8	*γurban čaγ-un*
4	*eke terigüten :*	9	*qamuγ tegünčilen*
5	*qamuγ amitan*	10	*iregsed-ün*

5 r

1	*bodičid [　]*[57]	6	*bodičid sedkil*
2	*itege[müi] öber*	7	*-i egüskebei*
3	*-ün bus[ud]-un*	8	*degedü bodi*
4	*tusa masida*	9	*[sed]kil egüs =*
5	*bütügeküi*[58] *tulada*	10	*keǰü buru[n]*[59]

5 v

1	*[　] amitan-a*	6	*qamuγ amitan-u*
2	*[...]*	7	*tusayin tula*
3	*[...] [ǰo]ki =*	8	*bu[r]q[an] bolun*
4	*[st]u [sedk]il-iyer*	9	*[butü]kü boltuγai*
5	*ya[buǰ]u bür-ün*[60]	10	*γurban t[a] [...]*

55　*ödgü* instead of *edgü*. The formula *sadu edgü* (Skr. *sadhu*, "good", AT *ädgü*, "good") often occurs at the end of the Xarbuxyn Balgas texts. See *satu ädgü* in *Altun yaruq sudur* = Zieme, p. 112. On *sadü edgü* in the Olon Süme texts, see Heissig, *Handschriften-Reste*, pp. 569–70.
56　Restored by Mr. Bentchev; old numbers 33 (fols. 1,5), 30/4.
57　The text is damaged; XBM 6, 4r:2–3 reads *bodičid-tur kürtel-e*.
58　The genitive suffix *-yin* is missing.
59　It reads *buru*, which is a mistake for *burun, bürün*. XBM 6, 4r:11–12 has *egüskeǰü bürün*.
60　XBM 6, 4r:12–4v:6 reads: *qamuγ amitan-i erkele[n] ǰočilasuγai bi. sedkil-tur ǰokis-tu [bo]di yabudal-iyar yabuǰu bür-ün.*

6 r

1	*qamuɣ amitan*	6	*t[u]ɣai :: qamuɣ*
2	*ǰirɣalang kiged*	7	*amitan ǰirɣalang*
3	*ǰirɣalang-un sil =*	8	*ki[ged] [ǰi]rɣalang*
4	*taɣan-ṯur*	9	*-un s[iltaɣa]n-ača*
5	*delbetei (?)[61] bol =*	10	*qayačaqu*

6 v

1	*boltuɣai [::] qamuɣ*	8	*a (?) tačiyangɣui*
2	*amitan ǰobalang*	9	*urin qoyar-ačⁱ[63]*
3	*ügei ǰirɣaɣsan*	10	*qa[ɣa]ča[qu] tegsi*
4	*ǰirɣalang-ača*	11	*sedkil-ṯür*
5	*ülü qayačaqun[62]*	12	*aqu boltuɣai ::*
6	*boltuɣai [::] qamuɣ*	13	*sadu e[d]gü*
7	*amitan olba (?) ǰir[ ]*		

XBM 10

1 item (1 small fragment of a folio, 2 written sides), measuring ca. 5.5 × 3 cm, and consisting of 5–6 lines.[64]

recto

1	*[na]yan dörben mingɣ[an]*	4	*[ ] namai eǰel[en][67]*
2	*[nom-un][65] [čo]ɣ-čas ɣarqui-yi[n]*	5	*[ ] [ir]egsen-lu[ɣa]*
3	*[oron][66] qamuɣ qutu[ɣ]*		

verso

1	*[ ]:: bo[ltuɣai]*	4	*[ ]u boltuɣai ::*
2	*[ ] [qa]muɣ amitan*	5	*[ ] ǰobalang ki[ged]*
3	*[ ]un silta[ɣan]*	6	*[ǰobalan]g-un siltaɣa[n]*

---

61 XBM 13, 6v:5 has *tegülder*.
62 Note the plural of the nomen futuri. For this see Poppe, *Grammar*, § 361, p. 94; see also Weiers, *Untersuchungen*, pp. 180–1; Ligeti "A propos", pp. 255, 275.
63 Mong. 449, 2 r reads: *qamuɣ amitan oyira qola tačiyaqui urilɣaqui qoyar-ača.*
64 Restored by Mr. Bentchev; old number No. 31/6.
65 See *nom-un* in the other copies of the text.
66 *oron* is found in the other copies of the text.
67 *namai eǰelen* is found in XBM 8, 2 v:5–6.

XBM 11

1 item of a *pothī* (1 nearly entire folio, 2 written sides), written by two hands. It measures 14×4 cm, and has 14–16 lines, without page number. A small portion of one side of the folio is missing.[68]

recto

1 *degedü čoɣ-tu te[güs]*
2 *blam-a-nar-tur i[tegemüi :]*
3 *burqan-tur itege[müi:]*
4 *nom-tur itegemüi :*
5 *bursang quvaraɣ [-ud]*
6 *-tur itegemüi : id[am]*
7 *mandal-un burqan-nuɣu[d]*

8 *-un čiɣulɣan-tur ite[ge =]*
9 *müi : degedü čoɣ-tu*
10 *itegel nom-un sakiɣul[sun]*
11 *eke belge bilig ni[dün]*
12 *tegüsügsen-nuɣud-t[ur]*
13 *itegemüi : ɣurban da [ ]*
14 *burqan nom kiged*

verso

1 *degedü čiɣulɣan-nuɣu[d]*
2 *-dur bodičid-tur*
3 *kürtele itegemüi : ö[ber]*
4 *-ün öglige terigüten [üile=]*
5 *dügsen[69] buyan-nuɣud*
6 *amitan-u tusa-yin tul[a]*
7 *burqan bolun bütükü*
8 *boltuɣai :: ɣurban*

9 *erdeni-dür itegemüi :*
10 *qamuɣ kilinčesi öber[e]*
11 *öbere namančilamui : am[itan-i][70]*
12 *buyan-nuɣud-dur daɣa[n]*
13 *bayasulčamui : burqa[n-u]*
14 *bodi qutuɣ-yi [ ]*
15 *tegen barisuɣai[71]*
16 *nom[72] kiged dege[dü][73]*

XBM 12

1 item of a *pothī*, (1 fragment of a folio, 2 written sides), measuring ca. 14×4 cm, with 10 lines. The text is framed with lines; the section of the text surviving is well preserved.[74]

recto

1 *[ ]*
2 *nigen [ ]*

3 *mön [ ]*
4 *nayan d[örbe]n mingɣ[an]*

---

68 Restored by Mr. Bentchev; old number 22/20.
69 See *üiledügsen* in XBM 16r:10.
70 See XBM 16r: 15.
71 XBM 16v:1–2 has: *burqan-u bodi sedkil-iyer barisu[ɣai]*; Libr. Mong. 134, 4 r:7–8 reads: *bodi qutuɣ-i sedkil-iyer barimui.*
72 *nom* is legible in the original.
73 XBM 16 v: 2–3: *burqan nom kiged degedü…*
74 Restored by Mrs. Nebel; old number 32/4.

5 *nom-un čoγ-ča o[ron]*[75]   8 *tegüsügsen-e i[tegemüi :]*
6 *sakiγulsun bel[ge]*   9 *burqan nom kiged*
7 *bilig-ün nid [ün]*   10 *či<l>γulγan*[76] [ ]

verso

1 [   ]r   6 *[bolu]n bütükü boltu =*
2 [   ]u   7 *[γai] γurban erdeni*
3 [   ]n [   ]ila   8 [ ][77] *itegemüi : qamuγ*
4 [   ]an qa[muγ] [am]itan-u   9 [ ] *-nügüd-yin*[78]
5 *[tus]a-yin tula burqan*   10 *[öbe]r-e öber-e*

XBM 13

2 items of a *pothī* (4 written sides). The first item is a folio measuring ca. 7 × 4.5 cm, and comprising 8–7 lines (r/v); the Mongolian page numbers is *jirγuγan* (6). The second item is a nearly entire folio, measuring ca. 7 × 4.5 cm, with 7–6 lines (r/v); the Mongolian page number is *dolo[γan]* (7); a portion of folio 7 is missing, but the text is fairly well preserved.[79]

6r

1 ○ *qamuγ amitan ene*   5 *-iγar yabuju amitan*
2 *čaγ-ača ekilen jočila =*   6 *tus[a]-yin tula burqan*
3 *suγai bi sedkil-dü*   7 *burqan*[80] *bolqu boltuγai :*
4 *jokistu bodi yabudal*   8 *küsek[ü] oroqu*

6v

1 *sedkil egüske :*   5 *-tur tegülder*
2 *qamuγ amitan*   6 *boltuγai : qamuγ*
3 *[jir]γalang kiged*   7 *amitan jobalang*
4 *jirγalang-un siltaγan*

---

75 The other copies have *γarqui-yin oron*.
76 There is a superfluous *l* in the word *čiγulγan*.
77 Either *-dür* or *-tür*. The dative-locative suffix is inconsistent in the texts. XBM 11v:9 has *erdeni-dür*, while XBM 18, 4r:1 reads *erdeni-tür*.
78 Instead of *-nügüd-ün*.
79 Old numbers 5/4, 26/27; 5/4 was previously restored by the Russians experts in Ulaanbaatar and then by Mr. Bentchev; 26/27 was restored by Mr. Bentchev.
80 The word *burqan* is repeated twice.

7r

1 *kiged [ǰ]obalang*   5 **lang** *ügei ǰiryalaqui*
2 *-un [s]ilt[aya]n-ača*   6 *-ača ülü qayačaqu*
3 *qayačaqu boltuyai [:]*   7 *boltuyai ::*
4 *qamuy amitan ǰoba =*[81]

7v

1 *qamuy [am]itan*   4 *alayčilaqui*
2 *tačiya[q]ui*   5 *-ača qayačaysan*
3 *urilaqui*   6 *tegsi*

XBM 14

1 item of a *pothī* (1 folio, 2 written sides), measuring 10×4 cm, with 10–11 lines, the page number is illegible. The folio is stained, especially on verso.[82]

recto

1 O *ǰočilas-uyai*[83] *bi ::*   6 *yabuǰu bürün :*
2 *sekil-tür*   7 *amitan-u*
3 *ǰokis-tu*   8 *tusa-yin tula*
4 *degedü bodi*   9 *burqan bo[l]un*
5 *yabudal-iyar*   10 *bolqu boltuyai :*

verso

1 *qa[muy] [amitan]*[84]   7 *qamuy amitan*
2 *ǰir[yalan]g kiged*[85]   8 *ǰobalang kiged*
3 *ǰiryalang-un*   9 *ǰobalang-un*
4 *siltayan-tur*   10 *siltayan-ača*
5 *tegülder*   11 *qayačaqu*
6 *boltuyai :*

---

81 There is a stroke on the right side of the *ba* of *ǰoba =lang*. Perhaps it is a superfluous *l*.
82 Restored by Mr. Bentchev; old number 9/1.
83 This word is written separately because there is a split in the folio, which obviously existed when the text was written.
84 *qamuy amitan* is found in XBM 4, 6r:1.
85 *kiged* is still legible in the original.

XBM 15

1 item of a *pothī* (1 folio, 2 written sides), measuring 9 × 6 cm, consisting of 11–10 lines (r/v). The folio is stained on recto and the page number is barely legible *[yu]rban* (3) (?).[86]

recto

1 *[…] kiged : quvaraɣ*
2 *[…] [bo]di jirüken-tür*
3 *kür[tele] […] nasun ürgül=*
4 *jide [   ] [bel]ge bilig*
5 *[   ] nigen*
6 *bi [   ] qamuɣ amitan-i*[87]

7 *tusa-yin tul-a*[88] *bu burqan-u*[89]
8 *emüne bi aju bür-ün [tuɣu =]*
9 *luɣsan* (?) *burqan büged boltu[yai ::]*
10 *bodi se[d]kil egüs-kebei :*[90]
11 *[   ] [a]mitan jirɣalan[g]*

verso

1 *kiged jirɣalang-un silta[ɣan]*
2 *-tur **tegülder boltuɣai** :: qamuɣ*
   amitan jobala[ng]
3 *kiged : jobalang-un*[91]
4 *qayačaqu boltuɣai :: qamuɣ*
5 *amitan jobalang <> ügei*

6 *jirɣalang-ača ülü qayačaqu*
7 *boltuɣai :: […] urin kiling*
8 *-eče [qaya]čaɣsan tegsi*
9 *[se]dkil-tür a[q]u boltuɣai ::*
10 *[   ] [d]örben čaɣ[lasi]*

XBM 16

1 item of a *pothī* (1 folio, 2 written sides), measuring 13 × 5.5 cm, with 15–16 lines, the page number is illegible. The folio is stained on both sides, and the ink has faded, making numerous words difficult to read.[92]

recto

1 *erdem […] burqan-nuɣud-un*
2 *burqan-tur itege[m]üi [bi] :: […]u*

3 *sayitur tegül[der] saki[ɣu]l[sun]*[93]
4 *belge bilig-ün nidün [te]güsügsen-e*

---

86 Restored by Mr. Bentchev; old number 12.
87 Instead of *amitan-u*. For the genitive suffix *-i* after a word ending in *n* see Poppe, "Geserica", pp. 16–18.
88 The word *tula* is written separately.
89 Note *bu burqan* instead of *burqan burqan* in XBM 13, 6r:6–7.
90 This word is written separately because there is a split in the folio.
91 Instead of *jobalang-ača*.
92 Restored by Mrs. Nebel; old number 33.
93 XBM 11 r:9–10 reads: *degedü čoɣ-tu itegel nom-un sakiɣul[sun]*.

5 itege[müi bi ::]⁹⁴ qorin nigen ba e[s-]e⁹⁵
6 bügesü yambar čidaqui ber ügei
7 burqan nom kiged degedü čiyul[ya]n
8 -nuyud-tur bodi qutuy-tur
9 kürtele itegemüi b[i] :: öber-ün
10 ög[l]ige terigüten üiledüg[s]en tedeger

11 a[m]itan-u tusa-yin⁹⁶ tula burqan
12 [   ] bütükü boltuyai : yurban
13 [er]d[en]i-tür⁹⁷ [i]tegemüi :: qamuy⁹⁸
14 [kilinč]esi [...] öber-[e] öber-e
      naman =
15 čilasuyai .⁹⁹ a[m]itan-i buyan-tur

verso

1 [   ] burqan-u bodi¹⁰⁰
2 [se]dkil-iyer barisuyai burqan nom¹⁰¹
3 kiged degedü čiyulyan-tur bodičid
4 -tur kürtele itegemüi : öber busud
5 -un qoyar tusa-yi sayitur bütüge[kü]i
6 -yin tula : bodi sedkil-i egüskesügei
7 b[i] [de]gedü degedü¹⁰² bodi sedkil-i
8 egüskejü bürün : qamuy amitan-i
9 erkelen jočilasuyai sedkil-tür

10 jokistu degedü bodi yabudal-iyar
11 yabuju qamuy amitan-u tusa-yin
12 tula : burqan bolun bütükü boltuyai :
13 qamuy amitan jiryalang kiged jirya=
14 [la]ng[-u]n siltayan-tur tegülder
      boltu[yai:]
15 qamuy amitan jobalang kiged :
16 jobalang-un¹⁰³ silta[yan-ača]¹⁰⁴

XBM 17

1 item of a *pothī* (1 fragment of a folio, 2 written sides), measuring ca. 6×5.5 cm, comprising 5–2 lines. The text is framed with lines, and is incomplete on verso.¹⁰⁵

recto

1 siltayan-t[ur] [   ]
2 boltuyai :: qamuy
3 amitan jobalang kiged

4 [j]obalang-un siltayan
5 -ača qayačaqu

verso

1 [   ] [te]gsi sedkil

2 -tur aqu

---

94 A part of the word is still legible in the original.
95 The word *ese* is written separately. On this orthographic feauture in the early texts, see Cerensodnom and Taube, *Turfansammlung*, p. 11.
96 The word *tusa* is barely legible.
97 XBM 11v:9 has *erdeni-dür*; XBM 18, 4r:1 reads *erdeni-tür*.
98 This line is damaged, but still legible in the original.
99 *namančilasuyai* is legible in the original.
100 *burqan-u bodi* are barely legible in the original.
101 *burqan nom* are legible in the original.
102 *degedü* is repeated twice.
103 *jobalang* is not very clear in the original.
104 *-ača* is barely legible in the original.
105 Restored by Mr. Bentchev; old number 25/4.

XBM 18

1 item of a *pothī* (1 fragment of a folio, 2 written sides), written by two hands. It measures 15×6 cm, and comprises 19–16 line (r/v); the Mongolian page number is *dörben* (4); the text is damaged on recto, and some words are barely legible.[106]

4r

1 *γurban erdeni-tür*	11 [ ] *de* (?) *buu* <>
2 *itegemüi qamuγ*	12 [ ]*sügei kemen*
3 *nigül [...] -iyen* (?)	13 [ ]*γdaqui*
4 *öber-e öber-e*	14 [ ] *buyan* <>
5 [ ]*la* [ ] *namančilamui*	15 [ ]*gčid-ün qaγan*
6 [ ]*küi* [ ] *čaγ* (?) *[...]*	16 [ ]*qu bodi*
7 *[a]rban [qa]ra nigül*	17 [ ] *[e]güskesügei*
8 [ ] [*ǰa]bsar ügei*	18 [ ]*i [se]dkil*
9 [ ] *[üile]dügsen qamuγ*	19 [ ] *kiged*(?) *amitan*
10 [ ] *namančilamui*[107]	**tusayin**

4v

1 *tula burqan bolun bütü =*	9 *singgeged öber [-iyen]*
2 *kü boltuγai :: kemen sedkigde =*	10 **öber-iyen** *boluγsan qamuγ am[itan]*
3 *küi : qamuγ amit[a]n ǰirγalang*	11 *kiged ǰobala[n]g-un s[iltaγan]*
4 *kiged ǰirγalang-u[n] silta[γan]*	12 *-ača qayačaqu boltuγ[ai :]*
5 *-tur tegü[l]der bol[t]uγai :*	13 *čaγ-tur öber-ün* [ ]
6 *kemeküi čaγ-t[ur]*	14 *kiǰaγar dorona ger[*]
7 *tere* <> *-eče* [ ]	15 *qamuγ amitan tus[a]* [ ]
8 *ača* (?) *γaruγad* [ ]	16 *amuγulang-tu bolγa[*]

XBM 19

1 item of a *pothī* (1 folio, 1 written side), measuring ca. 12×7 cm, consisting of 10 lines, without page number. The folio is stained and has splits in its surface. The text is framed with lines.[108]

1 *qayačaqu boltuγai : qamuγ*	3 *[-ač]a [ü]lü qayačaqu boltuγai ::*
2 *[ami]tan ǰobalang ügei ǰirγalang*	4 *qamuγ amitan tačiyangγui-yin*

---

106 Restored by Mr. Bentchev; old number 28/8.
107 *Qutuγ-tu γurban čoγča neretü* (XBM 22, 5v:9–12), which is shown below, has a passage which reads: *arban qar-a nigül kiged tabun ǰabsar ügei ba se[dk]il nisvanisun erke-ber üiledügsen. qamuγ kilinčesi namančilamui.*
108 Restored by Mr. Bentchev; old number 28/6.

5 *[...]*[109] *qayača-ɣsan*   8 *bisilɣaɣdaqui : maṅ gha*
6 *tegsi [sedki]l-ṯür aqu boltuɣa[i]* ::   9 *lam bavantu*[110]
7 *kemen dörben čaɣalasi [üge]i*   10 *bavantu*

XBM 20

1 item (1 small fragment of a folio, 2 written sides), measuring 7.5 × 2.5 cm, with 8–7 lines (r/v).[111]

recto

1 *tur bodičid [   ] [kürtel =]*   5 *da (?): amitan [   ]*
2 *e itegemüi b[i] [   ]*   6 *tula burq[an] [   ]*
3 *da (?) öglige [   ]*   7 *bütükü b[oltuɣai   ]*
4 *üiledügs[en]*   8 *ɣurban e[rdeni] [   ]*

verso

1 *[ite]gem[ü]i*   5 *[   ] qamuɣ amitan*
2 *[keme]n bodi sedkil*   6 *[   ][ǰo]čilasuɣai*[114]
3 *[egüskes]ügei*[112] *degedü*   7 *[sedki]l-ṯür*[115]
4 *[sedki]l-e*[113] *egüske[   ]*

XBM 21

1 item of a *pothī* (1 folio, 1 written side), measuring ca. 10 × 4 cm, with 7 lines; the Mongolian page number is *tabun* (5). The folio is dark and stained, and the ink has faded.[116]

5 r

1 *tačiyangɣui*   3 *-eče qayača[ɣsan]*
2 *urin [ki]ling*   4 *tegsi [...]*[117]

---

109 XBM 8, 5r:2–3 has *tačiyangɣui urin kiling*.
110 The ending formula *manggalam bavantu* occurs in the inscription of Cagaan Bajšin. See Huth, *Die Inschriften*, p. 35.
111 Restored by Mrs. Nebel; old number 25/2.
112 XBM 16v:6 has: *bodi sedkil-i egüskesügei*.
113 Instead of *sedkil-i*.
114 XBM 16v:7–9 reads: *[de]gedü degedü bodi sedkil-i egüskeǰü bürün. qamuɣ amitan-i erkelen ǰočilasuɣai*.
115 XBM 16v:9 also reads *sedkil-ṯür*.
116 Restored by Mrs. Nebel; old number 12.
117 The text is illegible; XBM 9:6r:11 has *sedkil-ṯür*. The inscription of Cagaan Bajšin reads *tegsi sedkil-tü-ṯür* (Huth, p. 35).

5 [...]   7 maṅ ga laṃ
6 boltuyai

The fragments of 21 copies of *Itegel yabuyulqu* are written by 23 scribes (XBM 11 and XBM 18 are written in two hands). This is especially interesting from the palaeographic point of view. The copies of the text dealt with above show the inconsistent use of the dative-locative suffix *-dur/-dür*, *-tur/-tür* (*siltayan-tur*; *erdeni-tür*, *nuyud-dur*, XBM 1, 2v:6–7; XBM 18, 4r:1; XBM 11v:2, etc.). Moreover, we have numerous words written separately in the texts, e.g.: *čoy-čas*, *čoy-ča*, *tul-a*, *es-e* (XBM 2, 1v:10; XBM 12r:5; XBM 15r:7; XBM 16r:5), and the repetition of words: *burqan burqan*, *degedü degedü* (XBM 13, 6r:6–7; XBM 16v:7). We also find an unusual form such as *bu burqan* in XBM 15r:7, and the use of the final formula *sadu edgü* (XBM 9, 6v:13); XBM 8 has *sadu ödgü* at the end of the text. Finally, XBM 9 is the only text in which the ancient plural form of the *nomen futuri* is found (*qayačaqun*, 6v:5).

As has been mentioned, I was able to identify a fragment of *Itegel yabuyulqu* from Olon Süme (OS IV/11–12), which Heissig did not transcribe.[118] The fragment consists of 12 lines. The first section of the text is damaged, while the rest is fairly well preserved and legible. OS IV/11–12 is transcribed as follows.

> 1) *eng urida beyen-ü čiyulyan- i* 2) [   ] *blam-a* [...] *idam* 3) *mandal-un burqan* [...]*qui* 4) [...] *[ki]ged. qamuy amitan-u* 5) *tusayin tula arban jüg-ün* 6) *yu[rba]n čay-un qamuy tegünčilen* 7) *iregsen-ü bey-e kele jirüken* 8) *[er]dem üiles bügüde mön činar -un* 9) *nayan dörben mingyan nom-u čoyča* 10) *yarquyin oron boluysan* 11) *qamuy qutuy-dan quvarayud* 12) *namai-yi ejelen ündüsün-ü.*

The opening section of the Olon Süme fragment does not correspond to the Xarbuxyn Balgas fragments, which also show a number of textual variants in each. OS IV/11–12 has the formula *eng urida*, "in the very beginning", which often occurs in the earlier texts.[119] It is also attested in one of the Xarbuxyn Balgas texts discussed below (XBM 46).

The rest of the Olon Süme text is the same as some of the copies from Xarbuxyn Balgas. The spellings *tusayin*, *qutuy-dan* in OS IV/11–12 are also found in XBM 8 (2r:1) and XBM 1 (1r:12) respectively.

We can, however, observe the following variants: OS IV/11–12 has *čoyča* instead of the plural form *čoyčas*[120] in the majority of the Xarbuxyn Balgas fragments; *quvarayud* is spelt *quvaray-ud* in XBM 4 (r:5–6) and XBM 8 (2v:5), but XBM 1 (1r:12–13) has *ayay-qa tegimlig* instead; *namai-yi* in the Olon Süme fragment is *namai* in both XBM 8 (2v:5) and XBM 10 (r: 4).

* * *

---

118 Heissig, *Handschriften-Reste*, OS IV/11–12, p. 540.
119 See *eng urida* in the *Bodhicaryāvatāra* = Cerensodnom and Taube, *Turfansammlung*, No. 42, p. 137. For other examples, see XBM 46 below in this volume.
120 XBM 2, 1v has *čoy-čas*.

Prayer of Penitence (XBM 22 to XBM 27)

The Xarbuxyn Balgas collection includes one complete text and five fragments of five copies of the same text whose title is found in both XBM 22 and XBM 25. They are *Qutuy-tu yurban čoyča neretü yeke kölgen* (Tib. *'Phags-pa Phuṅ-po gsum-pa źes-bya-ba theg-pa chen-po'i mdo*),[121] "The holy mahāyāna-[sūtra] called The Three Heaps", and *Bodisug-nar-un aldal namančilaqui neretü*, "[The sūtra] called Confession of Sins of the Bodhisattvas". The text is also known by other titles.

The three heaps (*yurban čoyča*, Tib. *phuṅ-po gsum-pa*), which are mentioned in the title of the text quoted above (XBM 22), indicate the practice of confessing non-virtues, the practice of rejoicing and the practice of dedication.[122]

The text is a prayer of confession of sins which is recited in front of the 35 Buddhas of penitence, who are invoked as Tegünčilen Iregsen (Skr. Tathāgata), "Thus Came", with their epithets and physical qualities.[123] Lamas recite the prayer during the religious service.[124]

The text was also circulating in southern Mongolia between the end of the 16th century and the beginning of the 17th centuries, as six fragments which belong to the Olon Süme collection demonstrate. Heissig did not identify the Olon Süme fragments, which are, however, severely damaged. The Olon Süme fragments are discussed below.[125]

Copies of the text which are concerned with are numerous. I had access to the following. The text with the title *Čoytu čindan* at the beginning of the text, and *Qutuy-tu yurban čoyča kemegdekü yeke kölgen sudur*. It is included in the *Zungdui*;[126] the Buriat xylograph *Čoytu candan-u yučin tabun burqad-un emün-e gem unal namančilaqu yoson orošiba*, "Rules to confess sins in front of the 35 Buddhas of the Blessed Sandalwood".[127] Moreover, *Čoytu čandan sudur orosiba*, "The [sūtra] called The Glorious Sandwood", which has *Qutuy-tu yurban čoyčas kemekü sudur* at the end of the text,[128] and *Čoy-tu čindan-a orosiba*.[129] Finally, the Oyirad version *Bodhi sadva-yin unal namančilaxui orošibai*.[130]

---

121 *gZuṅs-'dus* (272v:5–274v:7). The title is located at the end of the text.
122 For this see Rigzin, *Tibetan-English Dictionary*, p. 172; see also *Bod-rgya tshig-mdzod chen-mo, Zang han da cidian*, p. 1716.
123 See Olschak et al., *Mystik und Kult Alttibets*, pp. 136–45.
124 See Pozdneyev, *Religion and Ritual*, p. 406.
125 *Handschriften-Reste*, pp. 479–86.
126 434v–437r.
127 See Heissig and Sagaster, *Mongolische Handschriften*, No. 410, Libr. Mong. 18, p. 235.
128 Heissig, *Blockdrucke*, No. 6, pp. 11–12 (Libr. Mong. 125).
129 Heissig and Sagaster, *Mongolische Handschriften*, No. 409, Ms. Asch 125, pp. 234–5.
130 Heissig and Sagaster, *Mongolische Handschriften*, No. 415, Ms. or. fol. 594-3, pp. 236–7. The text is preserved in various collections of Mongolian books. See Rintchen, "Manuscrits mongols", p. 108; Heissig and Bawden, *Catalogue*, Mong. 392, pp. 229–30; Farquhar, "A Description", p. 191. Fragmentary hymns to the 35 Buddhas of penitence form part of the inscriptions of Arǰai Ayui in Otoy Banner, one of the seven Banners of the Ordos in southern Mongolia. See the hymns in Qaserdeni et al., *Arǰai ayui-yin uyiyurǰin mongyol bičigesü-yin sudulul*, chap. 1, pp. 12–110.

A *sūtra* with the title *Qutuγ-tu γurban čoγča neretü yeke kölgen sudur (Ārya-Tri-skandhaka nāma mahāyāna-sūtra)* is found in the *Ganǰur,*[131] but, apart from the same title and topic, it is different from the text under discussion.

XBM 22

1 complete *pothī*, composed of 6 folios (10 written sides), measuring ca. 14 × 6 cm, consisting of different numbers of lines. The Mongolian page numbers are *nigen, qoyar, [γurban], dörben, tabun, ǰirγuγan* (1–6); folio 2r has the Tibetan number *gñis* (2). The title is found on folio 5 v. The text is fairly well preserved.[132]

1 v

1 O *bi kiged qamuγ amitan*
2 *nasu ürgülǰi blam-a-tur : itegemüi :*
3 *burqan-tur itegemüi : nom-tur itegemüi :*
4 *bu[r]sang quvaraγ-ud-tur itegemüi :*
5 *ilaǰu tegüs nögčigsen tegünčilen iregsen*[133]
6 *dayini daruγsan ünen tegüs tuγuluγsan*
7 *ilaγuγsan čoγ-tu šagi-a-müni*[134] *burqan*[135]
8 *-tur mörgömüi : tegünčilen iregsen vačir*
9 *ǰirüken sayitur daruγsan-a*[136] *mörgömüi :*
10 *tegünčilen iregsen erdeni-ün*[137] *gerel γarγaγči-da*[138]
11 *mörgömüi :: tegünčilen iregsen luus-un erke-tü*
12 *qaγan-a*[139] *mörgömüi : tegünčilen iregsen bayat[u]d-un*
13 *ayimaγ-a*[140] *mörgömüi : tegünčilen iregsen*

---

131 Vol. 84, pp. 134–78.
132 Restored by the Russians experts in Ulaanbaatar; old number 9.
133 The Oyirad Ms. or. fol. 594-L. UB, has *tögünčilen boluqsan*.
134 XBM 23,1v:6 has *šagi-a-muni*. On the various spellings of Sākyamuni, see Mostaert and de Rachewiltz, *Houa i i iu*, II, p. 32.
135 *ilaǰu tegüs nögčigsen tegünčilen iregsen dayini daruγsan tegüs tuγuluγsan ilaγuγsan čoγ-tu šagiamuni burqan*. See in the gZuṅs-'dus (Abbr. ZD): *De-bźin gśegs-pa dgra-bcom pa yaṅ-dag-par rdzogs-pa'i saṅs-rgyas dpal śākya thub-pa*.
136 *Zungdui,* 434v:9–10: *včir ǰirüken-iyer sayitur ebdegčide mörgömü,* Libr. Mong. 18, 2r:18–29 and Ms. Asch 125, 1v:10–13 read *tegünčilen iregsen vačir-un ǰirüken-iyer sayitur ebdegčide mörgömü;* Libr. Mong. 125, 2v:3–7: *tegünčilen iregsen dayini daruγsan ünen tegüs tuγuluγsan sayin ilaγuγsan včir ǰirüken-e mörgömü;* ZD: *De-bźin gśegs-pa rDo-rje sïṅ-pos rab-tu 'joms-pa*.
137 See *erdeni-yin* in XBM 23, 1 v:9.
138 Ms. Asch 125, 1 v:14: *erdeni-yin gerel γarγaγčida;* Libr. Mong. 18, 2r: 21–2: *erdeni-yin gerel sačuraγuluγčida;* Libr. Mong. 125, 3r: 2–3: *erdeni-yin gerel γarγaγči-da;* Ms. or. fol. 594-L., 2r: 12–14: *tegünčilen boluqsan gerel γarxui erdeni-dü;* ZD: *De-bźin gśegs-pa Rin-cen 'od-'phro*.
139 ZD: *De-bźin gśegs-pa Klu-dbaṅ-gi rgyal-po*.
140 ZD: *De-bźin gśegs-pa dPa'-bo'i sde*.

2r

1 *bayasqulang čoɣ-tu<r>-da*¹⁴¹ *mörgömüi :: tegünčilen*
2 *iregsen ɣal erdeni-tü-de mörgömüi ::*¹⁴² *tegünčilen*
3 *iregsen sara-yin gerel erdeni-tüde*¹⁴³ *mörgömüi:*
4 *tegünčilen iregsen üǰegseger tüsa-tüda*¹⁴⁴
5 *mörgömüi : tegünčilen iregsen saran erdeni*
6 *-tüde*¹⁴⁵ *mörgömüi : tegünčilen iregsen kkir ügei*
7 *-tüde*¹⁴⁶ *mörgömüi : tegünčilen iregsen čoɣ-i*
8 *öggügči-de*¹⁴⁷ *mörgömüi:* **tegünčilen [iregsen] ariɣun-a**¹⁴⁸ **mörgömüi:** *tegünčilen iregsen*
9 *ariɣun-i öggügčide*¹⁴⁹ *mörgömüi : tegünčilen*
10 *iregsen usun tngri-t̲ür*¹⁵⁰ *mörgömüi[:] tegünčilen*
11 *iregs[e]n usun tngri-yin tngri-de*¹⁵¹
12 *mörgömüi : tegünčilen iregsen sayin čoɣ*
13 *-tuda*¹⁵² *mörgömüi : tegünčilen iregsen*
14 *čoɣ-tu čindan-a*¹⁵³ *mörgömüi : tegünčilen*
15 *iregsen kiǰayalal ügei kündü ǰibqulang-a*¹⁵⁴
16 *mörgömüi : tegünčilen iregsen čoɣtu gerel*

141 For *čoɣ-tu-da.* Zungdui, 435r:4–5: *čoɣtu bayasuɣčida*: Ms. Asch 125, 2r:4 reads *čoɣ-tu bayasqulang-a*; Libr. Mong. 125, 3v:8–9 has *bayasqulang-tu bayatur-a*; ZD: *De-žin gśegs-pa dPal-dgyes.*

142 Ms. or. fol. 594-L. UB, 2v:12: *ɣal erdeni-dü*; Libr. Mong. 18, 2r:29–2b:1: *erdeni-yin ɣal-dur*; ZD: *De-bžin gśegs-pa Rin-cen me.*

143 The possessive and dative-locative suffixes written together often appear in the text. See also XBM 23 below; Libr. Mong. 18, 2v:2–3: *erdeni saran gerel-dür*; Ms. or. fol. 594-L. UB, 2v:15–3 r1: *sarayin gerel erdeni-dü*; ZD: *De-bžin gśegs-pa Rin-cen zla-'od.*

144 For *tusa-tuda*; Mr. or. fol. 594-L. UB, 3r:3–4: *tusatu-du*; ZD: *De-bžin gśegs-pa mThoṅ-ba don-yod.*

145 ZD: *De-bžin gśegs-pa Rin-cen zla-pa.*

146 Libr. Mong. 18, 2r:7–8: *erdeni saran-dur… kkir ügei-dür*; Libr. Mong. 125, 4v:10: *kkir ügegü-tüde*; ZD: *De-bžin gśegs-pa Dri-ma med-pa.*

147 ZD: *De-bžin gśegs-pa dPal-sbyin.*

148 ZD: *De-bžin gśegs-pa Tshaṅs-pa.*

149 ZD: *De-bžin gśegs-pa Tshaṅs-pas sbyin.*

150 ZD: *De-bžin gśegs-pa Chu-lha.*

151 ZD: *De-bžin gśegs-pa Chu-lha'i lha.*

152 ZD: *De-bžin gśegs-pa dPal-bzaṅ.*

153 Ms. or. fol. 594-L. UB, 4v:1–2: *čoq čečeq-dü*; ZD: *De-bžin gśegs-pa Tsan-dan dpal.*

154 Libr. Mong. 18, 2v:22–3: *kiǰayalaši ügei sür ǰibqulang-tuda*; Zungdui, 435r: 24 omits *kündü*; Ms. Asch 125, 2v:5–6: *ki[ǰa]yalasi ügei čoɣ ǰali-tuda*; ZD: *De-bžin gśegs-pa gZi-brjid mtha'-yas.*

2v

1   -tüde[155] mörgömüi : tegünčilen iregsen
2   yasalang ügei čoy-tuda[156] mörgömüi :
3   tegünčilen iregsen qu[ri]čaqui ügei[157]
4   köbegün-e[158] mörgömüi : tegünčilen [ireg]sen
5   čečeg-ün čoy-tüda[159] mörgömüi : tegünčilen
6   iregsen ariyun gerel-iyer čenggen ile
7   medegči-de[160] mörgömüi : tegünčilen iregsen
8   l[in]qu-a-yin gerel čenggen ile medegči-de[161]
9   mörgömüi : tegünčilen iregsen ed-ün čo[y]
10 -tuda[162] mörgömüi : tegünčilen iregsen durad[qui]
11 čoy-tüda[163] mörgömüi: tegünčilen iregsen
12 čoy-tu belge-tü masi oyoyata[164]
13 aldarsiysan-a[165] mörgömüi [:] tegünčilen iregsen
14 degedü [o]ki ilayuysan čimeg-tü qayan-a[166]
15 mö[r]gömüi : tegünčilen iregsen masi teyin
16 bü[ge]d daruyči čoy-tuda[167] mörgö[müi :]
17 tegünčilen iregsen qad[q]ulduyan-i teyin

---

155 ZD: De-bźin gśegs-pa 'Od-dpal.
156 ZD: De-bźin gśegs-pa Mya-ṅan med-pa'i dpal.
157 ri of quričaqui is barely legible in the text. Zungdui, 435:r28: quričaqui ügei; Libr. Mong. 18,
     2v :28: quričal ügei; Ms. Asch 125, 2v: 10: bay-a ügei.
158 ZD: De-bźin gśegs-pa Sred-med-kyi bu.
159 For čoy -tuda. ZD: De-bźin gśegs-pa Me-tog dpal.
160 Zungdui, 345r:31–3: ariyun gerel teyin büged čenggegsen-iyer ile medegčide; Libr. Mong.18,
     3r1–3: ariyun gerel teyin čenggeküi ber ilerkei ayiladuyčida; Ms. Asch 125, 2v 13–15: teyin
     činggemel ariyun gerel il[e]gey-e ayiladugčida; Ms. or. fol. 594-L. UB, 4v:4–8: teyin čenggeküi
     aruun gerel ilerkei ayiladuqči-du; ZD: De-bźin gśegs-pa Tshaṅs-pa'i 'od-zer rnam-par
     rol-pas mṅon-par mkhyen-pa.
161 Zungdui, 435r:33–4: lingqu-a-yin gerel teyin büged čenggegsen-iyer; Ms. Asch 125,
     2v16–3a1: teyin činggemel badm-a-yin gerel ilerkei ayiladuyčida; Ms. or. fol. 594-L UB,
     4v9–12: teyin čenggeküi badmayin gerel ilerkei ayilayuqči-du; ZD: De-bźin gśegs-pa
     Padma'i 'od-zer rnam-par rol-pas mṅon-par mkhyen-pa.
162 ZD: De-bźin gśegs-pa Nor-dpal.
163 The same as above. Zungdui, 435v:2–3: duradqu-yin čoytu-da; Libr. Mong. 18, 3 r:9: duradqu-
     yin čoy-a; Ms. Asch 125, 3 r:4: sanal-un čoy-a; Libri Mong. 125, 9v:2–3: duradqui-tu čoytu-da;
     Ms. or. fol. 594-L. UB, 5 r:4–5: sanal čoqtu; ZD: De-bźin gśegs-pa Dran-pa'i dpal.
164 masi oyoyata are legible in the original.
165 Zungdui, 345v:3–4: belgen čoy masi sayitur dayurisqaysan-a; Libr. Mong. 125, 9v:7–8: masi
     ariyun-a oyoyata aldarsiysan-a; ZD: De-bźin gśegs-pa mTshan-dpal śin-tu yoṅs-grags.
166 Zungdui, 435v: 6: erketü oki dhuvaza-yin qayan-a; Libr. Mong. 18, 3r: 13–15 erketü-yin oki
     dhuvaza-yin qayan-a; Ms. Asch 125, 3 r :9–1: oki ilayuyan belge-yin erketü qayan-a; Libr.
     Mong. 125, 10r: 3–6: ilayaqu belgetü oroi-yin čimeg-ün qayan-a; ZD: De-bźin gśegs-pa
     dBaṅ-po'i tog-gi rgyal-mtshan-gyi rgyal-po.
167 Libr. Mong. 18, 3r:16: maši-da dayin daruyči čoy-a; Libr. Mong. 125, 10 v:1–2: masi
     darumtatuda; ZD: De-bźin gśegs-pa Śin-tu rnam-par gnon-pa'i dpal.

3 r

1 *büge[d] ilayuysan-a*[168] *mörgömüi :*
   tegünčilen
2 *iregsen teyin büged daruyči*[169]
   tegünčilen
3 *iregsen mörgömüi : tegünčilen iregsen*
   bügüde
4 *-yi geyigül-ün jökiyayči čoy-tüda*[170]
5 *mörgömüi : tegünčilen iregsen*
   linqu-a-yin
6 *erdeni masi darumta-tuda*[171]
   mörgömüi :
7 *tegünčilen iregsen dayin-i daru[y]san*
8 *üneger tuyuluysan burqan erdeni*
9 *-tü linqu-a-tur sayitur sayuysan*

10 *qutuy-tu ayulus*[172] *-un erketü qayan-a*
11 *-tur*[173] *mörgömüi :: namo tedeger*
    terigü =
12 *ten arban jüg-ün yertenčü-yin qamuy*
13 *orod-tur*[174] *tegünčilen iregsen dayini*
14 *daruysan üneger tüyuluysan*[175] *burqan*
15 *ilaju tegüs nögčigsen ali yambar*
16 *büküi sayuysan ilaju tegüs nögčigsen*
17 *burqan-nuyud tedeger-dür düraddun*
18 *soyorq-a :*[176] *minu ene töröl kiged :*
    terigülesi ügei töröl ba *ečüs-tür*
19 *orčilang-tur orčiqui qamuy töröl*
20 *-nuyud-tur-i kilinčesün üyilesi*[177]

---

168 *Zungdui,* 435v:9: *bayilduyan-i masi teyin büged ilayuysan-a;* Libr. Mong. 18, 3r: 18–19:
     bayilduyan-ača maši-da teyin ilayuysan-a; Ms. Asch 125, 3a:14–15: *bayilduyan-i teyin masi-da*
     ilayuysan-a; Libr. Mong. 125, 10v:7–8: *bulyalduqui masi ilayuysan-a;* Mr. or. fol. 594-L. UB,
     5v:1–3: *bayildāyani teyin maši ilayuqsan-du;* ZD: *De-bźin gśegs-pa g'Yul-las śin-tu rnam-par*
     rgyal-ba. See *qatquldu'an* and *bulqalduqui* in §§ 91, 249 of the *Secret History.*
169 *Zungdui,* 435v:10–12: *teyin büged daruysan-iyar oduyči čoytu-da;* Libr. Mong. 18, 3r:20–21:
     teyin darun ajirayči čoy-a; ZD: *De-bźin gśegs-pa rNam-par gnon-pas gśegs-pa'i dpal.*
170 For *jökiyayči čoy-tuda;* Ms. Asch 125, 3v:4–5: *büküi-eče gilgen jökiyayči čoy-tu-da;* Libr.
     Mong. 125, 11r:3–5: *qamuy-a üjügül-ün jökiyaysan čoytu-da;* ZD: *De-bźin gśegs-pa Kun-nas*
     snaṅ-ba bkod-pa'i dpal.
171 *Zungdui,* 435v:15–16: *erdeni lingqun-iyar teyin büged daruyčida;* Libr. Mong. 18, 3r:24–6:
     erdeni lingqu-a-bar teyin daruyči-da; Ms. Asch 125, 3v:6–8: *erdeni-yin badm-a-bar dayini*
     daručida; Libr. Mong. 125, 11r:9–11v1: *linqu-a-yin erdinis-i daruysan-a;* Ms. or. fol. 594-L.
     UB, 5v:9–12: *erdeni padma-bar teyin daruqči-du;* ZD: *De-bźin gśegs-pa Rin-cen padma'i*
     rnam-par gnon-pa. Note *erdinis* in Libr. Mong. 125, 11v; *erdini* appears in 12r. The form
     erdini is attested in the earlier texts. See, for example, *the Bodhicaryāvatāra* = Cerensodnom
     and Taube, *Turfansammlung,* No. 11, p. 79.
172 For *ayulas.*
173 Note the double suffix of the dative-locative *-a-tur.* Libri Mong. 18, 3r:29–31: *lingqu-a-yin*
     tabčang-tur; Ms. Asch 125, 3r:11: *badm-a-tur;* Libri Mong. 125,12r:2–5: *erdini-tü linqu-a-yin*
     sayurin-tur sayitur sayuysan qutuy-tu ayulasun qayan-a; Ms. or. fol. 594-L. UB, 6r2–5:
     padma-du sayitur suuqsan uulayin erketü xān burxan-du; ZD: *De-bźin gśegs-pa dGra-bcom-*
     pa yaṅ-dag-par rdzogs-pa'i saṅs-rgyas rin-po-che daṅ padma-la rab-tu bźugs ri-dbaṅ-gi
     rgyal-po.
174 Libr. Mong. 125, 12v:1–3: *arban jüg-ün qamuy yirtinčü ulus-tur.*
175 For *tuyuluysan.*
176 For *duraddun, duradun; Zungdui,* 435v:24–26: *ali kedüi bükü sayun amiduraysan ilaju tegüs*
     nögčigsen tedeger qamuy burqan-nuyud namayi durad-un soyorq-a; Libr. Mong. 18,
     3v:13–18: *ali kedüi činegen sayuju amiduran aysan ilaju tegüs nögčigsen burqad tedeger*
     bükün namai-yi ayiladun soyorq-a; Ms. Asch 125, 4r:4–9: *al[i]ba kedüi sayuyču dayalyaqui*
     qamuy ilaju tegüs nögčigsen burqad tedeger namai ayiladun soyorq-a.

3v

1 *üyiledüysen ba :*[178]
    üyiledkegülüysen[179]
2 *ba: üyiledügsed-tür dayan bayasul =*
3 *čagsan*[180] *ba : suburyan-u ed ba :*
4 *bursang quvar[a]y-ud-un ed ba :*
5 *arban jüg-ün bursang quvaray*
6 *-ud ed-i buliysan ba : buliyulug =*
7 *san*[181] *ba : buliysad-ta dayan*
8 *bayasulčaysan ba : tabun jabsar*
9 *ügei-yi üyiledügsen ba : üyiled =*
10 *kegülügsen ba : üyiledügsed-tür*
11 *dayan bayasulčaysan ba : arban*

12 *qar-a nigül-tü möri*[182] *üneger abču*
13 *oroysan ba : oroyuluysan :*
14 *ba : oroysan-ta dayan bayasulčag =*
15 *san ba : alimad üyilesün tüidker-e*[183]
16 *tüyidtejü bür-ün : bi [ami]tan-u*
17 *tamu-tur törökü ba :*[184] **adayusun-u**
    töröl oron-tur törökü ba *:[bi]rid-ün*
18 *yajar-a törökü ba : kijayar yajar-a*
19 *törökü ba : <> buruyu törö =*
20 *kü ba : urtu [n]asutu tengri-tür*
21 *törökü ba :*[185] *erketen dütayu*[186] *bolqu*

4r

1 *ba : buruyu üjel-i bariqu ba :*[187]
2 *iregsen burqan-i bayasqan ülü*

3 *üyiledkü ba : alimad üyile<ü>s-ün*
4 *tüidker tedeger-nuyud-yin ilaju*

177　The genitive suffix -*ün* is joined to the word *kilinčes* (plural of *kilinče*); the accusative suffix -*i* is joined to the word *üyiles* (plural of *üyile*).

178　Instead of *üiledügsen*; *Zungdui*, 435v:27–31: *biber ene töröl kiged. terigülesi ügei ečüs ügei töröl-eče. orčilang-dur orčiysan qamuy töröl-nuyud-tur nigül kilinče-tü üiles-i üileddügsen ba*; Libr. Mong. 18, 3v:19–26: *bi ene töröl kiged. terigün ečüs ügei töröl-eče orčilang-a orčiqui qamuy töröl oron-dur. nigül kilinče-yin üiles-i üiledügsen ba. üiledküi-dür dayan bayasulčaysan buyu. uy töröl-nuyud-tur nigül kilinče-tü üiles-i üileddügsen ba*; Ms. Asch 125, 4r:8–16: *bi ene töröl kiged. terigün ečüs ügei töröl-eče ene orčilang-a orčiqu busu qamuy torol (töröl) orod-tur kilinčetü üile üledügsen (üiledügsen) ba. üledügülüysen (üiledügülüysen, üiledügülügsen) kiged. üledüysüd (for üiledügsed)-te. dayan bayasulčays[a]d-ta. dayan bayasulčaysad buyu.*

179　The verb *üyiled-* (*üiled-*) with the double causative suffix -*ke*/-*gül.*

180　The literary form is *bayasulčaysan.*

181　The literary form is *buliyuluysan.*

182　*Zungdui*, 436r:6–7: *arban jüil nigül kilinče-tü üiles-ün mör-i.*

183　This word is barely legible in the original.

184　*Zungdui*, 436r 9–11: *ali üile-yin tüidker-iyer tüidtejü. bi amitan tamu-dur unaqu ba*; Libr. Mong. 18, 4r13–15: *üileyin tüidker alin-iyar tüidčü bi amitan tamu-dur odqu buyu*; Ms. Asch 125, 5r3–6: *jayayan-u tüidker alin-i tüidüsen-iyer bi tamu-yin amitan-tur törökü ba*; Libr. Mong. 125, 14v3–6: *ali üile-yin tüidker-e tüidtejü bi amidu tamu-tur unaqu ba.*

185　*Zungdui*, 436r:13–15: *tere buruyu törö ügegün-dür törökü ba*; Libr. Mong. 18, 4r:18–22: *jiq-a kijayar oron-a törökü buyu. ters-üd bolun törökü buyu. urtu nasutu tngri-ner-e törökü buyu*; Ms. Asch 125, 5r:9–14: *kijayar-a küseküi oron-a törökü ba. taduru buruyu-tan t[ö]rököi kiged.*

186　For *dutayu.*

187　*Zungdui*, 436r:16–17 and Libr. Mong. 12515r:7–8 read *buruyu üjel-tü bolqu ba.*

5 *tegüs nögčigsen burqan belge bileng*[188]
6 *böluysan*[189] *nidün böluysan erke*
   bolug =
7 *san : üliger böluysan :*[190] *medegči*
8 *üjegči : tedeger-ün nidün-ü ide aril =*
9 *yan namočilamui :*[191] *ülü bučan : ülü*
10 *niyun :*[192] *jiči tasulsuyai*
   jan[ggi]dsuyai[193]

11 *ilaju tegüs nögčigsen burqan-nuyud*
12 *tedeger namai dürad-un*[194] *soyorq-a :*
13 *minu ene töröl kiged : terigülesi ügei*
14 *töröl ba : ečüs-tür orčilang-tur*
15 *orčiqui busu töröl-nuyud-tur*
16 *öglige-yin ečüs aduyusun-u töröl*

4v

1 *oron-tur törögsed-te*[195] *nigen emkü*
   idegen
2 *öggügsen-ü buyan-u ündüsün-nuyud*
3 *ba :*[196] *saysabad*[197] *sakigsan-u*[198]
   buyan-[u]
4 *ündüsün-nuyud ba : minu ariyun*
5 *yabuysan-u ündüsün-nuyud ba :*[199]
6 *minu amitan oyoyata bölbas-un*[200]

7 *boluysan-u buyan-u ündüsün-nuyud*
8 *ba : minu bodi qutuy-tu<r> sedkil*[201]
9 *egüskegsen-ü buyan-u*
   ündüsün-nuyud
10 *ba : minu tengsel ügei*[202] *belge bilig*
11 *-ün buyan-u ündüsün-nuyud tedeger*
   bügü =
12 *de-yi nigen-e quriyaju qamtudqaju :*

---

188 Instead of *bilig*.
189 For *boluysan*; *Zungdui*, 436r:17–20: *ali bükü tede bügüde üiles-ün tüidker-i ilaju tegüs nögčigsen burqan belge bilig-tü boluysan*; Ms. Asch 125, 5v:2–5: *jayayan-u tüidker yambar bügesü tedeger bügüde-yi ilaju tegüs nögčigsen burqan belge bilig boluysan*; Libr. Mong. 125, 15v:1–7: *ali jüil üile-yin tüidker minu. boluysan bügesü tedeger bügüde-yi ilaju tegüs nögčigsen burqan-u belge bilig-ün nidüber ger-e boluysan*.
190 *Zungdui*, 436r:21–2: *nidütü boluysan. ger-e boluysan. üliger boluysan*; Libr. Mong.18, 4v:3–5: *gereči boluysan. šilyaday boluysan*; Ms. Asch 125, 5v:7–8: *nidün boluysan. gerenči boluysan. keb boluysan*; Libr. Mong. 125, 15v78: *üliger boluysan*; Ms. or. fol. 594-L. UB, 8v2–4: *belge biliq boluqsan nidün boluqsan gereči boluqsan. keb boluqsan*.
191 For *namančilamui*; *Zungdui*, 436r:23–4: *tedeger-ün nidün-ü iledte arilyan namančilamui*; Libr. Mong. 18, 4v:5–7: *ayiladun üjegči tedeger-ün gegen-ü emün-e namančilamui*.
192 The negative *ülü* with the *converbum modale*.
193 *Zungdui*, 436r: 24–6: *buu bučasuyai. buu niyusuyai. qoyinaysida ber tasulju janggidsuyai*.
194 For *duradun*.
195 *Zungdui*, 436r:32–3: *öglige kedüi yadabasu aduyusun-u töröl-dür törögsed-e;* Libr. Mong. 18, 4v:23–6: *öglige-yin aday adayusun-u töröl oron-a törögsed-tür nigen emküi tedüi idegen-i öggügsen*; Ms. Asch 125, 7r: 4–7: *torol (töröl)-nuyud-tur öglige yadabaču adayusun-u töröl-dür dürsün*.
196 *Zungdui*, 436r:34–436b1:*nigen emkü-yin tedüi idegen-i idegülügsen ali tere buyan-u ündüsün ba*.
197 The regular spelling is *šayšabad*.
198 The literary form is *sakiysan*.
199 *Zungdui*, 436v:3–4: *ariyun-iyar yabuysan-u minu ali buyan-u ündüsün ba*.
200 For *bolbasun*.
201 *Zungdui*, 436v: 6–7 and Libr. Mong. 125, 17v:3 read *degedü bodičid sedkil*.
202 *tengsel ügei*, Skr. *anuttara;* Tib. *bla-na med-pa, Mahāvyutpatti*, No. 2521.

13 *ǰanggidču tengsel ügei : deger-e ügei*
14 *degedü-yin degedü blam-a-yin*
   blam-a-ṯur

15 *oyoyata irüger bolyan tengsel ügei ene*
16 *üneger tuyuluysan bodi qutuy-tur*
   <tuyuysan tuyuluysan>[203]

5r

1 *oyoyata iregemüi :*[204] *yambar*
   [n]ögčigsen
2 *čay-un ilaǰu tegüs nögčigsen*
3 *burqan-nuyud irügeküi bölug =*
4 *san*[205] *ba : yambar edüge sayuysan ilaǰu*
5 *tegüs nögčigen burqan-nuyud oyoyata*
6 *irüger ǰokiyaysan ba : [te]günčilen ba:*
7 *[...] oyoyata ǰo[r]in irügemüi : qamuy*
8 *kilinčesi öber-e öber-e*
   namančilamui :[206]

9 *buyan-nuyud-tur dayan*
   bayasulčamui :
10 *burqan-nuyud-tur durad-un ǰalbarin*
11 *öčimüi :: bi ber tengsel ügei bel =*
12 *ge bilig-ün degedü olqu boltuyai ::*
13 *kümün-ü degedü ilayuysan ali edüge*
14 *sayuysan*[207] *kiged : alimad nögčigsen*
   ba :
15 *tegünčilen ali irege edüi erdem-üd-i*
16 *maytaysan : kiǰayalal ügei dalai-ṯur*

5v

1 O *adali bügüde-ṯür alayaban qamtudqan*
2 *čiqula ǰalbarisuyai ::*[208] *qutuy-tu<r> yurban*
3 *čoy-ča neretü yeke köl-gen te[gü]sbe ::*[209]

---

203 These words are misplaced.
204 Instead of *irügemüi; Zungdui,* 436r:11–17: *tengsel ügei. degere ügei. degedü-yin degedü.*
   dabsiydaqu-yin ber dabsiydaqu bolyan sayitur ǰorin irügeküi-ber. degere ügei üneger
   tuyuluysan bodhi qutuy-tur sayitur ǰorin irügesügei; Libr. Mong. 125, 18r:5–8: *tengsel ügei*
   ünen tegüs tuyuluysan bodi qutuy-tur oyoyata irügemüi.
205 For *boluysan.*
206 *Zungdui,* 436v:17–29: *ker ali nögčigsen čay-un ilaǰu tegüs nögčigsen burqan-nuyud ber sayitur*
   ǰorin irügegsen ba. ker ali irege edügüi čay-un ilaǰu tegüs nögčigsen burqan-nuyud ber sayitur
   ǰorin irügeküi bolqu ba. ker ali edüged-tür sayuysan ilaǰu tegüs nögčigsen bügesü tegünčilen kü.
   bi ber sayitur ǰorin irügesügei. qamuy nigül kilinče-i öber-e öber-e arilyan namančilamu;
   Ms. Asch 125, 6v14–7r12: *bi yambar nögčigsen čay-un ilaǰu tegüs nögčigsen burqan-nuyud*
   yambarčilan oyoyata irügsen kiged. iregedüi ilaǰu tegüs nögčigsen burqan-nuyud yambar
   bügesü oyoyata irügeküi kiged. yambar edüged-dür sayuysan ilaǰu tegüs nögčigsen burqan-
   nuyud oyoyata yambar irügen üiledüysen tere metü bi oyoyata irügen üiledümü qamuy
   kilinčes-yin (-ün) öber-e öber-e arilyan namančilamui. The text from Xarbuxyn Balgas has
   edüge while the *Zungdui* and Ms. Asch 125 have *edüged-tür, edüge-dür* respectively. For
   edö'e-tür, edüge-dür see Mostaert and de Rachewiltz, *Hua i i iu,* II, pp. 40–41.
207 Libr. Mong. 125 20r2–3: *ali edüged-ḏür sayuysan.*
208 *Zungdui,* 437r:1–7: *alimad nögčigsen kiged. tegünčilen irege edügün-ü maytaydaqui erdem-*
   üd kiǰayalal ügei dalai-dur adali bügüde-de. alayaban qamtudqaǰu itegen mön deger-e
   odsuyai; Libr. Mong. 125, 20r:4–20v6: *tegünčilen irege edügüi maytaydaqui erdem-üd-i*
   kiǰayalal-un dalai-dur adali bügüde-de alayaban qamtudqaǰu ürgülǰi-de itege[m]üi.
209 There is a split which damaged this word. The passage which follows is omitted in both Libr.
   Mong. 125 and in Ms. or. fol. 594-L. UB.

4 *sayin buyan boltuyai :: bey-e-yin*
5 *yurban ǰüil-i kiged : kelen-ü dör =*
6 *ben ǰüil ba : ali basa sedkil-ün*
7 *yurban ǰüil :²¹⁰ arban <> qara nigül-i*
8 *öber-e öber-e namančilamui :: terigüle =*
9 *si ügei-eče [e]düged-tür arban qar-a nigül²¹¹*
10 *kiged tabun ǰabsar ügei ba sed[ki]l*
11 *nisvsnisun²¹² erke-ber üyiledügsen :²¹³ qamuy*
12 *kilinčesi namančilamui : tačiyangyui urin*
13 *mungqay-un erke-ber bey-e kelen kiged*
14 *tegünčilen sedkigsen kilinčisi²¹⁴ bi yambar*
15 *üyiledügsen tedeger bügüde-yi öber-e*
16 *öber-e namančilamui bi mörgöged takiyad*

6r

1 O *namančilamui ba: dayan bayasun*
2 *durad-un ǰalbariysan*
3 *üčüken quriyaysan²¹⁵ buyan-i qamuy*
4 *tüyuluysan²¹⁶ yeke bodičid-tur*
5 *itegemüi :: : ::²¹⁷ maṅ gha lam*
6 *oṃ maṇi bad me hūṃ ::*

7 *oṃ maṇi bad me hūṃ ::*
8 *oṃ maṇi bad me hūṃ ::*
9 *sadu sakituyai::*
10 *[tegü]-sbe (?)²¹⁸ :: : ::*
11 *tüyuluysan burqan*
12 *bolun bütükü boltuyai ::*

210 *Zungdui*, 437 r:8–10: *beyen-ü yurban ǰüil üile. kelen-ü dörben ǰüil üile. ali ber sedkil-ün yurban ǰüil üile.* Note *ali basa* in the Xarbuxyn Balgas text and *ali ber* in the *Zungdui* text; the first meaning of *ber* is "too".
211 *Zungdui*, 437 r:12–13: *terigülesi ügei-eče edüged-tür kürtele;* Libr. Mong. 18, 6r:79 *terigüleši ügei nasun-ača edüge kürtele quriyaysan. testeši ügei arban nigül.*
212 For *nisvanisun* (the genitive suffix -*un* is joined to the word *nisvanis*); *nisvanis*, "attachment" is a borrowing from Uighur *nïzvanï* < Sogdian *nyzβān*, corresponding in meaning to Skr. *kleśa*. See the remarks by Poppe in *The Twelve Deeds*, note 26, p. 74; see also Cerensodnom and Taube, *Turfansammlung*, 33r11, pp. 121–2.
213 *Zungdui*, 437 r:15–16: *sedkil nisvanis-un erke-dür oroysan-dur-i.*
214 For *kilinčesi*.
215 This word is difficult to read in the original.
216 For *tuyuluysan*.
217 *Zungdui*, 437 r:18–25: *bey-e kelen tegünčilen sedkil-iyer. biber-yin ber nigül kilinče-yi. öber-e öber-e namančilamui. mörgöged takiyad namančilayad. dayan duraduysan-iyar minu üčügüken. aliber üiledügsen buyan-nuyud-i qamuy-i tuyuluysan bodhi qutuy-tur ǰorin irügemüi.*
218 The word is not entirely legible. It was probably deleted. The folio also shows words which are written in a different hand.

XBM 23

1 item of a *pothī* (1 folio, 1 written side), measuring 11×5 cm, comprising 13 lines; the Mongolian page number is *nigen* (1). The folio is fairly well preserved.[219]

1v

1 ○ *bi : kiged qamuy amitan nasu ürgülǰi*
2 *blam-a-tur itegemüi : burqan-tur itegemüi :*
3 *nom-tur itegemüi : bursang quvaray-ud-tur*
4 *itegemüi : ilaǰu tegüs nögčigsen tegünčilen*
5 *iregsen dayin-i daruysan ünen tegüs tuyuluy =*
6 *san ilayuysan čoy-tu šagi-a-muni burqan*
7 *-tur mörgömüi : tegünčilen iregsen včir ǰirüken*
8 *sayitur daruysan-a mörgömüi : tegünčilen*
9 *iregsen erdeni-yin gerel yaryay[či]-da mörgömüi :*
10 *tegünčilen iregsen luus-un erketü [qa]yan-a mörgömüi :*
11 *tegünčilen iregsen bayatud-un ayimay-a mörgömüi :*
12 *tegünčilen iregsen bayasqulang čoy-tuda mörgömüi :*
13 *tegünčilen iregsen yal erdeni-tüde mörgömüi :*

XBM 24

1 item of a *pothī* (1 folio, 2 written sides), measuring 11.5×2.5 cm, consisting of 14 lines on recto, while only 4 lines are left on verso; the Mongolian page number is *yurban* (3).[220]

3r

1	*mörgömü : tegünčilen*	8	*tengri-yin ten[gri]*
2	*iregsen ariyun-i*	9	*burqan-a mörgömü :*
3	*öggügči-de mörgömü :*	10	*tegünčilen iregs[en]*
4	*tegünčilen iregsen*	11	*sayin čoy-tu*
5	*usun tengri burqa[n-a]*	12	*mörgömü : tegünčilen*
6	*mörgömü : tegü[nčilen]*	13	*iregsen čoy-du*
7	*iregsen usun*	14	*čindan-a mörgö[mü :]*

3v

1	*[tegün]nčilen [iregsen]*	3	*kündü ǰibqulang-a*
2	*ki[...][221] ügei*	4	*[mö]rgömü [...]*

---

219 Restored by Mrs. Nebel; old number 25/4.
220 Restored by the Russians experts in Ulaanbaatar; old number 6/4.
221 XBM 22, 2r:15 has *kijayalal;* the other versions read *kijayalaši, kijayalasi.*

XBM 25

1 item of a *pothī* (1 folio, 1 written side), measuring ca. 14 × 5.5 cm, with 16 lines; the page number is illegible. It is the beginning of the text. One side and edge of the folio are torn. The text is framed with lines.[222]

*1v

1   O *bodisug-nar-un aldal*
2   *namančilaqui neretü : öber*
3   *-ün nereben nereyidčü bür =*
4   *ün :: burqan-tur itegemüi :*
5   *nom-tur itegemüi :*
6   *bursang quvaray-ud-tur*
7   *itegemüi :*[223] *ila[ǰu] tegüs*
8   *[n]ögčigsen tegünčilen iregsen*

9   *[dayin]-i daruysan üneger*
10 *[tegüs] [tuy]uluysan*[224] *sigiy-a-muni*
11 *burqan-tur mörgömü :*
12 *[te]günčilen iregsen sayitur ebdeg =*
13 *či vačir*[225] *ǰirüken-e*[226]
14 *mörgömü : tegünčilen iregsen*
15 *erdeni-yin gerel yaryayči*
16 *[-da] mörgömü : tegünčilen*

XBM 26

1 item of a *pothī*, (1 small fragment of a folio, 2 written sides), measuring ca. 6 × 3 cm, with 6 lines; the Mongolian page number is *[a]rban nigen* (11).[227]

11r

1   [   ]*yin blam-a*
2   [ˊ] *[oy]o[y]ata irüger*
3   *[boly]an tengsel*[228] *ügei*

4   *[ün]eger [tuyu]lu =*
5   *ysa[n] bod[i] qutuy*[229]
6   [   ]*i bi*

11v

1   *burqan-nuyud*
2   *oyoyata yam[   ]*
3   *irügegsen ba [   ]*[230]

4   **yambar** *edü[g]e say[uy =]*
5   *saṅ*[231] *ilaǰu tegüs*
6   *nögčigse[n]*

---

222   Restored by Mr. Bentchev; old number 26.
223   The letter *i* is written like *y* at the beginning of the word *itegemüi*.
224   See XBM 22, 1v:6.
225   *vačir* or *včir*. There is a split in the folio at this point.
226   XBM 22, 1v: 8–9 has *tegünčilen iregsen vačir ǰirüken sayitur daruysan-a*. On the other textual variant see the note to this passage.
227   Restored by Mr. Bentchev; old number 26.
228   This word is damaged but legible.
229   XBM 22, 4v: 14–16 has *degedü-yin degedü blam-a-yin blam-a-tur oyoyata irüger bolyan tengsel ügei ene üneger tuyuluysan bodi qutuy …*
230   Ms. Asch 125, 6v–7r has *burqan-nuyud yambarčilan oyoyata irügesen kiged.*
231   See *yambar edüge sayuysan* in XBM 22, 5r:4.

XBM 27

1 item of a *pothī* (1 fragment of a folio, 2 written sides), measuring ca. 10.5 × 3 cm, with 13 lines; the Mongolian page number is *yesün* (9).[232]

9 r

1	*üliger bol[uysan]*	
2	*medegči ü[jegči]*	
3	*tedeger [ ]*	
4	*ide arilya[n] [ ]*	
5	*bi ülü [ ]*	
6	*niyun[233] jiči[234] [ ]*	
7	*yai oytal[ ]*	

8	*sayitur [ ]*
9	*suyai[235]*
10	*ilaju t[egüs] [nögči =]*
11	*gsen qa[ ]*
12	*oyo[ ]*
13	*durad[ ][236]*

9 v

1	*[ ] [e]ne töröl*
2	*[ ] [ter]igülesi*
3	*[ ] [t]öröl-eče*
4	*[ ] [o]rčilang*
5	*[ ] [or]čiju <>*
6	*[ ] [tö]röl oron*
7	*[ ]gün : ögli =*

8	*[ge] [ ] [e]čüs*
9	*[aduyus]-un tö =*
10	*[röl] [ ] tur*
11	*[ ]de*
12	*[ ] [i]degen*
13	*[ ]n[237]*

The Olon Süme collection includes 6 fragments of folios of the text discussed so far. Unfortunately, only a few lines are left.[238] The Olon Süme fragments analysed here are OS IV/75 r to OS IV/72 r. They contain the following words: *[ ] eteged-t[ ] [ ]uysan tegünčilen [ ] irege üdügün-u may[ ] [ ]üd inu qajayalal üge[ ] [ ] adali bügüdeger [ ] [ ]amtudqan ürgülji [ ]gei qutuy-tu yurban [ ]ča [ ] [ ]udur.*

The parallel passage in XBM 22 (5 r:13–5 v:3) reads: *ali edüge sayuysan kiged. alimad nögčigsen ba. tegünčilen ali irege edüi erdem-üd-i maytaysan. kijayalal ügei dalai-tur adali bügüde-tür alayaban qamtudqan čiqula jalbarisuyai. qutuy-tu yurban čoy-ča neretü yeke köl-gen te[gü]sbe.*

---

232   Restored by Mr. Bentchev; old number 26/21.

233   *niyun* is clear in the original.

234   Part of the final *i* is still visible.

235   XBM 22, 4 r:7–9 reads *medegči üjegči. tedeger-ün nidün-ü ide arilyan namančilamui: ülü bučan: ülü niyun: jiči tasulsuyai jan[ggi]dsuyai.*

236   XBM 22, 4 r:11–12: *ilaju tegüs nögčigsen burqan-nuyud tedeger namai dürad-un soyorq-a.*

237   XBM 22, 4 r:11–4 v:2 has *ilaju tegüs nögčigsen burqan-nuyud tedeger namai dürad-un soyorq-a : minu ene töröl kiged : terigülesi ügei töröl ba : ečüs-tür orčilang-tur orčiqui busu : töröl-nuyud-tur öglige-yin ečüs aduyusun-u töröl oron-tur törögsed-te nigen emkü idegen öggügsen.*

238   Heissig, *Handschriften-Reste*, pp. 482–3.

We can observe that XBM 22 has *edüge* instead of *eteged-t[ür]* in the Olon Süme text. *Čoɣ-tu čindan-a* (7r) and the *Zungdui* text (436v) read *edüged-d̲ür*, *edüged-tür* respectively.

XBM 22 has *irege edüi*, while the Olon Süme text has *irege üdügün*. The form *üdügün* is the ancient plural of *üdügüi*, *edügüi*.[239] It is preserved in the *Zungdui* text (*irege edügün*, 437r).

XBM 22 has the spelling *kiǰaɣalal*, while the Olon Süme text shows the pre-classical form *qiǰaɣalal*.

The Olon Süme text contains the word *ürgülǰi*, which is not found in XBM 22, but it occurs in *Čoɣtu čandan sudur* (20v): *alaɣaban qamtudqaǰu ürgülǰi-de itege[m]üi*.

The words after *[   ]gei* in the Olon Süme fragment OS IV/72r are obviously the title of the text. It can be restored as *Qutuɣ-tu ɣurban [čoɣ]ča [neretü (?)][240] [s]udur*.

On the basis of the spellings *irege üdügün* and *qiǰaɣalal*, the Olon Süme text can be regarded as the earliest Mongolian translation of the Tibetan '*Phags-pa phuṅ-po gsum-pa źes-bya-ba theg-pa chen-po'i mdo*.

* * *

The Sūtra of the 500 Buddhas (XBM 28)

The fragmentary text XBM 28 was identified as *Tabun ǰaɣun burqan-u sudur*, "The sūtra of the 500 Buddhas", on the basis of the Olon Süme the text, which Heissig investigated. The Olon Süme text consists of fragments of four different copies.[241]

Tabun ǰaɣun burqan-u sudur is an invocation to the Buddha with his epithets. The last part of the text invokes Bodhisattvas. Some of the epithets of the Buddha are also found in the five-language work *Sayin galab-un mingɣan burqan-u ner-e* (Tib. *bsKal-bzaṅ rnam-'dren stoṅ-gi mtshan*).[242] *Tabun ǰaɣun burqan-u sudur* forms part of the Buddhist works translated into Mongolian at an early time which were collected by lČaṅ-skya Qutuɣtu Rol-pa'i rdo-rje on the order of the emperor Qianlong in 1742. A Mongolian version of the text is preserved in the library of the Palace Museum in Peking.[243] Unfortunately, the original from which the text was translated is as yet unknown.

---

239 See Poppe, *Introduction*, § 114, p. 176.

240 XBM 22 has *neretü*, while Libr. Mong. 125 and the *Zungdui* text have *kemekü* and *kemegdekü* respectively.

241 Heissig, *Steininschrift und Manuskriptfragmente*, pp. 40–9, and *Handschriften-Reste*, pp. 334–46 by the same author.

242 See Heissig and Sagaster, *Mongolische Handschriften*, No. 486, p. 262; see also *Sayin ɣalaba-yin mingɣan burqan-u aldar*, which is included in the recently published *Oyun-u dotoraɣuluɣči erdeni toli* (Rasisereng ed., pp. 558–632).

243 Heissig, "Übersetzungsgeschichte", pp. 43, 48; a passage from the Peking text is quoted by Heissig in *Steininschrift und Manuskriptfragmente* (p. 49, note 1).

Copies of *Tabun ǰayun burqan-u sudur* are scanty,[244] but the versions from Olon Süme and Xarbuxyn Balgas demonstrate that this text was known both in southern and northern Mongolia in the 16th–17th centuries. The two texts were transmitted in the same form, though the last sections do not coincide. The following orthographic variants can be observed. The Olon süme text (OS IV/80r–80v) writes *bikiged, amitani, bürün, iridi, irege edüi, očirtu*,[245] while the Xarbuxyn Balgas text has *bi kiged, amitan-i, bür-ün, ridi, irege üdügüi, včir-tu*. Finally OS IV/55–56 reads *oytaryui-daqi*,[246] which is *oytaryui-tur* in the Xarbuxyn Balgas text.

XBM 28

6 items of a *pothī* (12 written sides). The first item is a folio which measures 11 × 5 cm, and comprises 10 lines; the Mongolian page number is *qoyar* (2). The folio is stained, but the text is legible.

The second item is a folio which measures ca. 10 × 5 cm, and comprises 10 lines; the Mongolian page number is *yurban* (3); the text is written in a different hand. The folio is badly damaged, and one side is missing.

The third item is a folio which had broken into three pieces. It measures 10 × 5 cm, and comprises 10 lines; the Mongolian page number is *dörben* (4).

The forth item is a fragment of a folio. It measures 6 × 5 cm, and comprises 5 lines; the Mongolian page number is *tabun* (5). The remaining text is barely legible on 5v.

The fifth item is a folio measuring 10.5 × 5 cm, comprising 10 lines; the Mongolian page number is *doloyan* (7). The text is badly damaged on 7v.

The sixth item is a folio measuring 10.5 × 5 cm, comprising 10 lines; the Mongolian page number is *yisün* (9) There are splits in the folios, and some words are illegible.[247]

2r

1 O *ürgülǰi bi kiged :*
2 *qamuy amitan-i*[248] *tusayin*
3 *tula ünen mayad*[249]
4 *kemen medeǰü bür-ün*
5 *bilig-üd činadu*
6 *kiǰayar-a kürügsen-ü*

---

244 The iconographical set of 500 Buddhist gods, which is usually called *Five Hundred Gods of Narthang*, is not related with *Tabun ǰayun burqan-u sudur* under discussion. See Tachikawa et al., *Five Hundred Buddhist Deities*.

245 pp. 335–7; the fragments OS IV/81–82, OS II/3A have *bi kiged, amitan-u*.

246 pp. 338–9.

247 Restored by Mr. Bentchev; old numbers 28/2; 28/3; 26/5; 26; 23. Previously folio 4 had broken into three pieces, which were found scattered in different locations with different numbers. They are: 26/29; 26/6; 26/21.

248 Instead of *amitan-u;* on the genitive suffix *-i* after a word ending in *n*, see Poppe, "Geserica", pp. 16–17.

249 The word is written with diacritical points before *y*.

7 *yeke uqayan-u*   9   *yeke ge[ge]gen tarni*
8 *tarni :*[250] *deger-e oki*   10 *sača bu[s]u-luɣ-[a]*

2v

1 *sačayu tarni :*[251] *qamuɣ*   6   *niɣuča burqan-a mörgö =*
2 *ǰobalang-ud-i*   7   *mü :: nom-un sang*[253] *burqan-a*
3 *usadqan amurliɣuluɣči*   8   *mörgömü :: arslan daɣubar*[254]
4 *tarni : namo mörgömü ::*   9   *ridi qubilyan-u*
5 *ariɣun gegen gerel-tü*[252]   10 *köldür*[255] *mörgömü ::*

3r

1 *burqan-u [...]ɣsan*[256]   6   *sakiɣči burqan[-a]*
2 *[s]ümbür aɣulayin*   7   *mörgömü :: arslan*[260]
3 *giskigürleǰü ɣaruɣsan*   8   *dürüber*[261] *alt[an]*
4 *burqan-a mörgömü :*[257]   9   *včir-tu saran metü*
5 *sasin no[m]*[258] *-i eǰelen*[259]   10 *yabuɣči burqan-a*

3v

1 *mörgömü : qutuɣ*   4   *gerel-tü yeke otač[i]*[262]
2 *[...] erdeni-tü*   5   *burqan-a mörgömü :*
3 *burqan-a mörgömü :*   6   *tügemel*[263] *neretü aɣulayin*

---

250 *uqayan-u tarni*, Skr. *vidyā;* Tib. *rig-sṅags.* See Ishihama and Fukuda eds., *Mahāvyutpatti,*
     No. 4223.
251 *sača busu-luɣ-a sačayu*, Skr. *asamasama;* Tib. *mi mīyam-pa daṅ mīyam-pa, Mahāvyutpatti,*
     No. 2537.
252 See *ariɣun gerel-tü* in *Mingɣan burqan-u ner-e*, chap. 1, f. 77.
253 *nom-un sang*, is found in *Mingɣan burqan-u ner-e*, chap. I, f. 11.
254 The word *daɣubar* has the diacritical points before *ɣ;* see *arslan daɣun-u küčütü*, Skr.
     siṃhasvaravegā; Tib. *seṅ-ge'i sgra'i śugs*, in *Mahāvyutpatti*, No. 475.
255 See *dörben ridi köl-ün ner-e;* Tib. *rdzu-'phrul-gyi rkang-pa źi'i ming*, in *Mahāvyutpatti,*
     Nos. 968–77; see also *dörben ridi qubilyan köl-ün ner-e* in *Mahāvyutpatti* (Sárközi ed.),
     No. 966.
256 OS/IV 80r:17 has *nomlaɣsan* (*Handschriften-Reste*, pp. 335, 337).
257 The initial *m* is barely legible, and the split in the folio damaged part of the letter *m* in second
     position.
258 The final *m* is blurred in the word *nom.*
259 *nom-un eǰen*, Skr. *dharmasvāmī;* Tib. *chos-kyi rje, Mahāvyutpatti*, No. 18.
260 OS IV/80r:19 (p. 335) has *arsalanu.*
261 *dürü* for *düri.* OS IV/80r:20 (p. 335) has *dürüber; düri ber* is found in *Steininschrift und
     Manuskriptfragmente* (p. 49, note 1).
262 Part of the letter *i* is missing; see *yeke otači* in *Mingɣan burqan-u ner-e*, chap. I, f. 9.
263 The ink is faded, but the word *tügemel* is legible; *tügemel* is found in the Peking text (*Stein-
     inschrift und Manuskriptfragmente*, p. 49, note 1); *tügemel eǰen*, Skr. *vibhu;* Tib. *khyab-
     bdag, Mahāvyutpatti*, No. 31.

7 ejen²⁶⁴ burqan-a mörgömü :   9 mörgömü [:] nögčigsen
8 s[u]baradisdi²⁶⁵ burqan-[a]   10 doloyan burqan-a

4r

1 O mörgömü :: irege   6 čečeg burqan-a mörgö[mü ::]
2 üdügüi²⁶⁶ mingyan burqan-a   7 jayun galab-ud-un²⁶⁷
3 mörgömü :: mingyan tabun   8 včir-tu²⁶⁸ sang burq[an-a]
4 jayun burqan-a mörgö =   9 mörgömü :: amurliy[san]²⁶⁹
5 mü :: tabun jayun   10 burqan-a mörgömü [::]

4v

1 jiryuyan jüg-ün   6 mörgömü :: sara-yin
2 jiryuyan burqan-a   7 [ ]rsi-tu²⁷² burqan-a
3 ereš-iyer²⁷⁰ mörgömü ::   8 [mö]rgömü :: barayun
4 jegün jüg-ün yeke   9 [jü]g-ün küčün
5 erdeni gerel-tü²⁷¹ burqan-a   10 [ ]a²⁷³ yeke-tü

5r

1 O burqan-a mörgömü ::   4 -tü burqan-a mörgömü ::²⁷⁴
2 umar-a-tu jüg   5 deged[ü] [ ]²⁷⁵
3 -ün ariyun gerel

264 There is a hole in the folio, but the word *ejen* is legible.
265 OS IV/80v:4 (p. 336) reads *suburyadisdi;* the Peking text has *suburya disdi* (*Steininschrift und Manuskriptfragmente*, p. 49, note 1).
266 OS IV/80v:5 (p. 336) has *irege edüi;* the Peking text reads *irege edügüi* (*Steininschrift und Manuskriptfragmente*, p. 49, note 1).
267 OS IV/80v:8 (p. 336) has *galabisun.*
268 OS IV/80v:9 (p. 336) has *očirtu.* Heissig transcibes this word *uridu* (p. 337).
269 See OS IV/80v:9 (p. 366).
270 OS IV/80v:11 (p. 366) has *arasiyar.* Heissig reads *nagsiar* (p. 337); *arasiyar* is found in the Peking text, which Heissig transcribed (*Steininschrift und Manuskriptfragmente,* p. 49, note 1); *eres-iyer*, "resolutely, decidedly, etc.", Lessing, p. 323.
271 See *erdeni gereltü* in *Mingyan burqan-u ner-e*, chap. I, f. 100.
272 OS IV/80v:12 (p. 336) has *nangsitu.*
273 As one would expect it, this word is *auya.* See OS IV/80v:14 (p. 336) has *auya; auy-a küčütü* is found in *Mingyan burqan-u ner-e*, chap. I, f. 7.
274 The ink has faded at this point, but the word *mörgömü* is still legible.
275 OS IV/80v:15 (p. 366) has *jüg-ün.*

5v

1 *yeke erd[enitü]*   4 *mör[gömü ::] [   ]*
2 *burqan-a mö[rgöm]ü [::]*   5 *[   ]²⁷⁶*
3 *sigem[üni] [   ]*

7r

1 O *dayu[s]taqu²⁷⁷ [...]gči :*   6 *bodhi saduva-tur*
2 *e[r]ketü-te [mö]rgömü ::*   7 *mörgömü :: tügemel*
3 *oytaryui-tur bükü*   8 *gerel-tü tegünčilen*
4 *bodhi saduva-tur*   9 *iregsen-e mö[r]gömü [::]*
5 *mörgömü ::²⁷⁸ visivari*   10 *tarni i[...]en buy[u]²⁷⁹*

7v

1 *[...] [   ] [s]ubau-a*   6 *arban jüg-ün*
2 *gi[...] [suba]u-a*   7 *bodhi saduva inu*
3 *[   ]i [...]*   8 *qamuy amitan*
4 *mayidari balasdi (?)*   9 *abura-qui-yin tula :*
5 *[...] ::*   10 *[...] arilaju ken mayu (?)²⁸⁰*

9r

1 O *-iyar (?)²⁸¹ törökü boltuyai :*   6 *ene nom inu oytar =*
2 *ükükü üiles [u]čira =*   7 *yui <>²⁸² busu (?)²⁸³*
3 *basu : ene nom-i*   8 *bui : qamuy burqan*
4 *ungsiysan-iyar*   9 *-nuyud ber qud[a]l*
5 *[...]qu boluyu :*   10 *ülü ügüleyü :*

9v

1 *burqan nomlar-un*   3 *qongsim bodi<i> sa[du]va*
2 *degedü nom-un²⁸⁴ qan*   4 *ene burqan nomlay[s]an*

---

276 The text is badly damaged on this side of the folio. See OS IV 80v:19–21 (p. 366), which
     reads: *yeke erdenitü burqan-a mörgömü. sigemüni burqan-a mörgömü. maidari burqan-a
     mörgömü. a bun (?) burqan-a [mör]gömü.*
277 The *s* of *dayustaqu* is not visible because there is a split in the folio at this point; see *erketü* in
     the next line.
278 OS IV/55–56 (p. 339) reads: *oytaryui-daqi bodisug maqasug namo mörgömü.*
279 OS IV/55–56:16–17 (p. 339): *bey-e-yi ibegen sakiyči tarni inu ene buyu.*
280 The text on this side of the folio is different from that from Olon Süme. However, lines 11–12
     in OS IV/55–56 (p. 339) read:*nigül tüidker arilyayči.*
281 Either *-iyar* or *-iyer* : folio 8 is missing.
282 A word was deleted by the scribe.
283 This word is not clear in the text.
284 *degedü nom*, Skr. *dharmottara;* Tib. *chos-mchog, Mahāvyutpatti*, No. 3500.

5   *egenegte ǰobalang-i*
6   *abu[r]ayči*[285] *ečüs-tür*
7   *qamuγ berke üilš*[286]

8   *-eče tonilaqu boluyu :*
9   *ese*[287] *naiman bodi<i>*
10 *saduva-nar*[288] kičiyen

* * *

Summary of the *Altan gerel* (XBM 29 to XBM 40)

The two complete texts and the 14 fragments of 10 copies of the text dealt with below have no title. I was, however, able to see five Oyirad versions of this text which bear the following titles. *Yeke külgüni altan gerel neretü nomiyin xurangγui,*[289] "Summary of the book called the Golden Light of the Mahayāna", and four texts with the title *Altan gereliyin xurangγui,* "Summary of the Golden Light". The four texts belong to the collection of Oyirad manuscripts preserved in the Institute of Languages and Literature of the Mongolian Academy of Sciences in Ulaanbaatar.[290]

I also had access to the Oyirad *Altan gereliyin xurangγui* and the Mongol *Altan gerel-tü quriyangγui.* These texts, however, are different from those quoted above.[291]

XBM 29

1 complete booklet *(debter),* composed of 5 folios (8 written sides). Two folios are stitched together, while the others are loose. They measure 13.5x7 cm., and have 11–12 lines, without page numbers. The top corner of the last folio is missing, otherwise the booklet is fairly well preserved. The last section of the text, which invokes deities is not found in the other copies from Xarbuxyn Balgas.[292]

---

285   There is a split in the folio at this point; see *maγui ǰayayad-i aburayči* in *Molon Toyin's Journey into Hell* (Lőrincz, p. 120).

286   Instead of *üileš, üiles;* the final *s* has the two points to the right. See *üileš* in the *Bodhicaryāvatāra* from Olon Süme (Heissig, *Handschriften-Reste,* OS I/4, OS I/5 verso, p. 30); for *berke-yi üiledkü, berke üiledküi* (Skr. *duíkarakāraka;* Tib. *dka'-ba byed-pa*), see the *Mahāvyutpatti,* No. 6652.

287   The verb is omitted after the negative *ese.* Perhaps the original text had *ese bügesü,* "if not, otherwise".

288   For the Eight Bodhisattva, see Das, *Tibetan-English Dictionary,* p. 485; the Eight Bodhisattva are also mentioned in *Molon Toyin's Journey into Hell* (Lőrincz, p. 120).

289   Heissig and Sagaster, *Mongolische Handschriften,* No. 446, Ms. or. quart. 770-2, pp. 246–7. See also No. 447.

290   Nos. 143, 144, 145, 535.

291   *Altan gereliyin xurangγui* is preserved in the Ulaangom Museum, while *Altan gerel-tü quriyangγui* in the Ulaanbaatar Central State Library (No. 254-2 A-521); on two texts extracted from the *Altan gerel,* see Ligeti, "La collection", pp. 152–3.

292   Restored by Mr. Bentchev; old number 12.

1v

1   O *namo budday-a* :: : ::
2   O *namo darmay-a* :: : ::
3   O *namo sanggy-a* :: : ::
4   *burqan-u nomlaysan-i nigen ongγočan*
5   *-ţu naiman tümen ayaγa namo tegebe*[293]
6   *ünen burqan nidündü minu üǰegdesei* :[294]
7   *namoni*[295] *nigen oom mani bad mi qung*
8   *geǰü: tere kümün ügülerün ünen burqan* :
9   *minu nidündü [üǰe]gdesei burqan* :
10 *ireǰü öroi*[296] *degere su[γuna]γ*[297]
11 *tataba*[298] *[en]e*[299] *kümün bisirel bisirebe* :
12 *bar[a]γun ebüdüg-iyer sögödčü ala* =

2r

1   *γaban qamtudqaǰu oroi deger[   ]*[300]
2   *mörgöǰü aman aldaba : burqan burqan*[301]
3   *bi : čini ǰarliγ-iyar bolsu*[302] *bi* :
4   *kümün či namoni nigen ungsiǰu*
5   *ülü güičem burqan nomlarun bi* ::

6   *čimadu ǰiγaǰu ögsü bi* :: *ene kümün*
7   *gertegen qariba arban ǰil boltala*
8   *güičem burqan tengri sonosba* :
9   *ene erdeni burqan nom lam-a-ţur*
10 *mörgömü bi* :: *γurban ǰirγuγan*
11 *tümen burqan-ţur mörgömü bi* ::

2v

1   *qorin qoγar tümen yesün mingγan*
2   *toγa ügei burqan-ţur mörgö* =
3   *mü bi* :: *tabun ǰaγun tümen*
4   *molor bey-e-tü gegegen gereltü*

5   *burqan-ţur mörgömü bi* ::[303] *köbčin γaǰar*
6   *degereki burqan-ţur mörgömü bi* ::
7   *doloγan qonoγ narin qura oroǰu to* =

---

293   Ms. or. quart. 770-2, 1v:2 has *naiman tümen ayaxa tagilmaq*.
294   We have the voluntative suffix *-sei;* Ms. or. quart. 770–2, 1v:3 reads *üǰüqdesei*. On this suffix see Poppe, *Introduction*, § 199, p. 25; see also Weiers, "Bemerkungen", p. 369.
295   It should stand for *namova (namo); namoni* also appears in XBM 30, 1v:6, XBM 31, 1v:6, XBM 35, 2r:3.
296   For *oroi*.
297   This word is not clear in the original, but XBM 32, 2r:3 and XBM 35, 2v:2 have *suγunaγ;* Ms. or. quart. 770-2, 1v:7 has *suunaq*.
298   The suffix *-ba/-be* is used as future tense in the text. See Poppe, *Introduction*, p. 266.
299   *ene* is barely legible in the original; See *ene* in XBM 30, 2r:2 and XBM 32, 2r:4.
300   XBM 30, 2r:4 has *degereben*.
301   *burqan* is repeated twice.
302   For the use of *-su/-sü*, see Weiers, *Untersuchungen*, pp. 127–31.
303   The passage from 2r-1 to 2v:5 is not found in Ms. or. quart. 770-2 (2r:1–4), which reads: *keltü sanātu burxan-dü mürgümüi. bi mini amār ungšiqsan burxan-du mürgümüi. bi tenggeriyin nigen burxan-du mürgümüi. bi*.

8 *squ büri burqan-tur mörgömü bi ::*
9 *köbčin qamuy moron-u*[304] *usun-i*
   qoyar

10 *jaqayin ur[u]sugsan*[305] *qumaqiyin*[306]
   eke
11 *burqan-tur mörgömü bi :: tengri*

3 r

1 *yajar qamuy modon-i*[307] *nabči büri*
2 *burqan-tur mörgömü bi :: ebösün*[308]
3 *usun degereki büri burqan-tur*
4 *mörgömü bi :: qamuy burqan diyan*
5 *sayuysan ayulayin ejen burqan*
6 *-tur mörgömü bi :: doloyan üy-e*

7 *önggeregsen ebüge ečige eke*[309] *burqan*
8 *-tur mörgömü bi :: köbčin burqan-a*
9 *mörgömü bi :: ene nom ungsibasu*
10 *erlig qayan-u emüne jobalang-tu*
11 *dalai-tur čisutu mören degereki*

3 v

1 *altan mönggön kögergen degere medeg =*
2 *demü : ene nom-i dörben te ungsi =*
3 *basu tüg tümen nom-i ungsiysan*
4 *-tur adali boluyu ::*[310] *qamuy čidkedün*[311]
5 *eliy-e bügüde yarba : arban naiman tamu*
6 *qoyoson bolba : erliy qayan-u burqan*
7 *bolba :*[312] *tengri yajar naran saran modon*
8 *dalayin dotoraki luu-yin oordo*[313] *usun*
9 *-i ede bügüde amurliba*[314] *ene nom-i ungsi =*
10 *basu arban tümen naiman mingyan*
11 *burqan ireǰü sonosumu*[315] *jayun tümen*

---

304 It should be read *mörön-ü, mören-ü*.
305 Instead of *urusuysan*.
306 Note the ancient spelling *qumaqi* instead of MLM *qumaki*.
307 Instead of *modon-u*; the genitive in *-i* after a word ending in *n* often occurs in the Xarbuxyn Balgas manuscripts. It reflects the spoken language. Poppe provides various examples of this suffix in his work "Geserica"(pp. 14–18).
308 Instead of the literary form *ebesün*; the spelling *ebösün* also occurs in the other copies of the text.
309 *eke* is omitted in the Oyirad version (Ms. or. quart. 770-2, 2v).
310 Ms. or. quart. 770-2, 3r:1–3:*ene nomi dörbön te ungšibasu tuq tümen nom ungšiči sanaqsandu adali buluyu*.
311 For *čidköd*; the genitive suffix is joined to the word.
312 Ms. or. quart. 770-2, 3r:3–6: *xamuq čidkür ali bügüde yurban mou jayātan naiman tamu xōsun bolxu*.
313 *oordo* instead of *ordo*. The spelling *oordo* is pointed out in the section of the book Linguistic Features of the Manuscripts.
314 Ms. or. quart. 770-2, 3r:6–9: *tenggeri yajar dalai dotoroki kluyin oroni usuni ejen ede bügüdedü xor kürgeqči amaraba*.
315 For the suffix *-mu/-mü* used both as present and future see Poppe, *Grammar*, § 346, p. 91.

4 r

1   *bodisug ireǰü sonosumu yesün tümen*
2   *doloyan mingyan lam-a ireǰü*
      ungsilčamui
3   *ungsiysan minu burqan-ṯur adali*
4   *bolumui ene nom-i ungsibasu nigen*
      tüg
5   *tümen altan nom-i ungsiysan metü*

6   *boluyu bodi sini*[316] *tegüsbe oom a*
7   *qung baǰar guru badm sidi qung*
8   *bad :: : :: ○ adqay ügei yeke*
9   *sang\<γ\>un eǰen ariy-a avalogi =*
10   *de isvari kiir*[317] *ügei bügüdei*
11   *-yi medegči erketü manǰusiri času*
12   *-tu yaǰar-t[ur] mergen oroi[-yin]*

4 v

1   *čimeg ǰongga-ba čoytu tegülder*
2   *lam-a-yin köldür ǰalbarin itegemüi ::*
3   *kkir ügei köke : ayurun*
4   *dum-da bayu-ysan : gigi . li dagini*
5   *sir (?) ǰar küriye-legsen kirče =*
6   *gei*[318] *mayu silmusi daruysan*

7   *kkir-eče qayačaysan badm sambau =*
8   *a baysi-ṯur maytan mörgömü ::*
9   *ünen yurban erdeni-tür: üneger*
10   *tusa kürgegsen ürgülǰi sedkil*
11   *-tü ünen ünen bisirel-tü burqan baysi*

5 r

1   *[-ṯur] [ma]ytan mörgömü :: sečen yur =*
2   *[ban] [er]deni-ṯür semeger tusa*
3   *[   ] semügen (?) sečen burqan*
4   *[-ṯur] maytan mörgömü :: balamud*
5   *[   ] iyan tonilyaysan baysi*
6   *[   ] uriyaysan bal si**k**ir metü*
7   *[   ]örösen burqan baysi*

8   *[-ṯur] [may]tan mörgömü :: süm-bür*
      ayu =
9   *[lan]i bey-e-tü sün dalai metü*
10   *[   ]ytu :: **či** sido törögsen*
11   *[burqan] [ba]ysi-ṯur maytan*
      mörgömü ::
12   *bi ::*

XBM 30

1 complete, but damaged booklet *(debter)*. It is composed of 5 folios (8 written sides), measuring ca. 8.5 × 7 cm, consisting of 8–10 lines, without page numbers. The first folio is torn; the second folio has a hole in its surface and some words are missing; 3 v and 4 r are also severely damaged, and a section of the text is missing in both.[319]

---

316   The text reads *bodi sini*, which probably stands for *bodičid*. The forms *bodhi sin-i, bodi čin-yi* are found in the other copies from Xarbuxyn Balgas; Ms. or. quart. 770-2 has *bodhi* in the following passage: *ene nomi nigente ungšibasu tuq tümen altan gerel ungšiqsan metü bolxu bodhi olxu tögüsbei* (3 v:5–7); Ms. No. 114 has: *bodi sadu: tuq tümen gereltü nom ungšiqsan metü bolxu bodi sadu tögüsbei* (3 v–4 r); Ms. No. 145 reads: *ene nomi unšibasu nigen tümen tabun mingyan altan gerel nomi ungšiqsan metü bolxu bodhi satv tögüsbei* (4 r).
317   The spelling *kiir* occurs once in the text; *kkir* appears below (4 v).
318   *kirčigei* for *kerčigei, kerčegei* (Lessing, p. 455).
319   Restored by Mr. Bentchev; old number 32/7.

1 v

1 *[namo] buday-a :: namo d[armay-a ::]*
2 *[namo] sanggay-a :: bu[rqan]*
3 *[nomlays]an nigen ongyoča*
4 *[   ] tümen ayay-a namo tege[be]*
5 *ünen burqan nidü-tü minu*

6 *[üjey]desei*[320] *namoni*[321] *nigen oom*
   mani ba[d]
7 *[mi] [qu]ng gejü tere kümün ügülerün*
8 *burqan nidüdü üjeydesei či*

2 r

1 *[bu]rqan irejü oroi degere suyu[nay]*
2 *[   ]*[322] *ene kümün bisirel bisirebe :*
3 *[barayu]n*[323] *ebüdüg-iyer sögedčü*[324] *alayaba[n]*
4 *[qamtud]qaju oroi degereben mörgöjü*
5 *[   ]ba*[325] *burqan burqan bi činu jarliyar (?)*[326]
6 *[bol]su bi : kümün či namoni nigen ungsi[ju]*
7 *[   ] burqan nomlarun bi čimadur jaya =*
8 *[ju ögsü]*[327] *bi : ene kümün gertegen qariba*
9 *[arba]n jil boltola*[328] *güijü güijü güijü (?)*
10 *[burqa]n tengri sonos-ba*

2 v

1 *[   ]*[329] *bur[qan] nom lam-a-tur mörgö[mü]*
2 *[bi ::]*[330] *[   ] [jiryuy]an*[331] *tümen burqan-tur mö[rgömü]*
3 *[bi ::] [   ] [qoy]ar*[332] *[tü]men yesün mingyan toyo*[333] *ügei*
4 *burqan-tur mörgömü bi :: tabun jayun*
5 *tüg tümen [mol]or*[334] *bey-e-tü gegegen ge[re]l*

---

320 Line 8 reads *üjeydesei* instead of *üjegdesei*.
321 *namoni* is also found in XBM 29, 1v:7 and XBM 31, 1v:6.
322 XBM 29, 1v:11 has *tataba*.
323 XBM 29, 1v:12.
324 MLM *sögödčü*.
325 *aman aldaba* in XBM 29, 2r:2.
326 The letter *r* at the end of the word is not clear in the original, but see *amayar* below in the text
     (2v:8); *jarliy-iyar* appears in XBM 29, 2r:3.
327 *jaya-* for *jiya-*; see *jiyaju ögsü* in XBM 29, 2r:6.
328 Instead of *boltala*, reflecting the spoken language.
329 XBM 29, 2r:9 reads *erdeni burqan*.
330 *mörgömü bi* recurs in the next lines.
331 *yurban jiryuyan* in XBM 29, 2r:10.
332 XBM 29, 2v:1 has *qorin qoyar*.
333 *toyo* instead of the literary form *toya*; both *mingyan* and *toyo* are written with the diacritical
     points before *y*; see the spelling *toyo* in a manuscript from eastern Turkestan which
     Murayama published ("Zwei mongolische Manuskripte", p. 283).
334 *molor* in XBM 29, 2v:4.

6　*-tü [　] [mö]rgömü bi :: naiman ǰayun*
7　*[　]n-tu burqan-tur mör[gömü]*
8　*b[i ::] [mi]ni amayar³³⁵ ungsiysan burqan*
9　*-tur mörgömü bi ::³³⁶ tengri-yin nutuy*
10　*[n]igen burqan-tur mörgömü bi ::³³⁷*

3r

1　*köbčin yaǰar degere ki burqan*
2 - *tur mörgömü bi :: doloyan qonoy³³⁸*
3　*na[rin] qura oroǰu tosqu³³⁹ büri burqan*
4　*-t[ur] [mör]gömü bi :: köbčin qamuy mör[en-ü]³⁴⁰*
5　*[...]³⁴¹ qoyar ǰaqayin urusuysan qumak[i]*
6　*eke burqan-tur mörgömü bi :: eke burqan*
7　*-tur mörgömü bi :: tengri yaǰar qamuy*
8　*modon-i³⁴² nabči büri büri³⁴³ burqan-tur*
9　*mörgömü bi :: ebesün usun*
10　*degere ki³⁴⁴ burqan-tur*

3v

1　*mörgömü bi :: qamuy diyan sayu =*
2　*[ysan] ayulayin eǰen burqan-tur*
　　mörgömü
3　*[bi] :: dolo[yan] üy-e önggöröy =*
4　*se[n]³⁴⁵ [e]büge ečige eke burqan-tur*

5　*[mörgömü] bi :: [　] burqan-tur*
6　*[mörgömü bi ::] [　] [un]gsibas[u]*
7　*[　]*
8　*tu [da]l[a]i-tu čisutu mören-ü*
9　*altan mönggön kögeregen³⁴⁶ degere*

4r

1　*medegdemü : ene nom-i dörben te<n>*
2　*ungsiba[s]u tüg tüme[n] nom-i*

3　*un[　] qamu[y]*
4　*[　] arban*

335　*amayar, ama-bar;* Ms.or. quart. 770–2, 2r:2 has *amār;* see *amayar* in Heissig, *Handschriften-Reste,* OS IV/95r; see also Poppe, "Geserica", p. 23.
336　Ms. or. quart. 770-2, 2r:2–3 reads *bi amār ungšiqsan burqan-du mürgümü.* This line is not found in XBM 29.
337　Ms. or. quart. 770-2, 2r:3–4 has *tenggeriyin nidün nigen burxan-du mürgümüi bi.*
338　The word *qonoy* is written with the diacritical points before *q.*
339　*tosqu* has the diacritical points before *q.*
340　*mören-ü* occurs in XBM 34, 2v:10; Ms. or. quart. 770-2, 2r: 8 reads *möreni.*
341　This word is illegible; XBM 29, 2v:9 has *usun-i.*
342　*modon-i* instead of *modon-u* as in XBM 29.
343　*büri* is repeated twice.
344　*degere ki* is barely legible in the original.
345　Instead of the regular form *önggeregsen.*
346　MLM *kögerge(y), kökörge(n).* The latter is found in *Mongyol kitad toli,* p. 699; see the form *kögöröge* in the *Čayan teüke* = Sagaster, *Weiße Geschichte,* p. 148, note 9.

5 *naiman tamu qoyo[son] [bol]ba*
   erli<n>g
6 *qa[γan-u]³⁴⁷ burqan burqan³⁴⁸ bolba*
   tengri

7 *[ ] naran s[aran] modon dalai*
8 *[-yin] [do]tora luu-yin ordo usun-i*

4v

1 *[e]de bügüde amurliba nom-i³⁴⁹*
2 *ungsibasu arban tümen naiman*
3 *mingγan burqan ireǰü sonosumui :*
4 *yesün tümen bodisug ireǰü*

5 *sonosumui : yesün tümen doloγ[an]*
6 *mingγan lam-a-nar ireǰü ungsilčamui :*
7 *ungsiγsan minu burqan-tur adali*
8 *bolumui :: ene nom ungsibasu*

5r

1 *nigen tüg tümen altan nom-i*
2 *ungsiγsan metü boluyu ::*

3 *bodhi sin-i tegüsbe ::*
4 *sadu edgü :: : ::*

XBM 31

1 item of a *pothī* (1 fragment of a folio, 1 written side), measuring ca. 12×3.5 cm, comprising 10 lines. It represents the first folio of the manuscript.³⁵⁰

*1v

1 *[ ] [na]mo*
2 *[ ]a :: ::*
3 *[ ] [nige]n ongγoča³⁵¹*
4 *[ ] tu*
5 *[ ] [üne]n³⁵² burqan nidün*

6 *[ ] [na]moni nigen*
7 *[ ] [h]ūm :: geǰü*
8 *[ ] [ügeler]ün :³⁵³ ünen*
9 *[ ] [ü]ǰegdesei či*
10 *[ ] [dege]re³⁵⁴ suγunaγ*

XBM 32

1 item of a *pothī* (1 fragment of a folio, 2 written sides), measuring ca. 9.5×5 cm, consisting of 9 lines; the Mongolian page number is *qoγar* (2). The fragment is stained.³⁵⁵

---

347 *qaγan-u* is found in XBM 29, 3v:6.
348 *burqan* is repeated twice.
349 *ene* before *nom-i* is omitted. See XBM 29, 3v:9.
350 Restored by Mr. Bentchev; old number 32/2.
351 XBM 29, 1v:4 reads *nigen ongγočan*.
352 See *ünen* in XBM 29, 1v:6.
353 See *ügülerün* in XBM 29, 1v:8.
354 See *degere* in XBM 29, 1v:10.
355 Restored by Mr. Bentchev; old number 31/3.

2r

1 [   ] minu [   ]
2 üǰey[d]esii³⁵⁶ bü[ri] burq[an] [   ]
3 oroi dege-e suyunay [   ]
4 ene kümün bisire bisir[ebe] [   ]
5 [ebü]düg-iyer sögödč[ü] [   ]

6 qamtudqad oroi deger[e]
7 mörgöǰü aman aldaba bu[rqan]
8 burqan bi : činu ǰarliy-iya[r]
9 bolsu bi :: kümün či [na]mon[i]

2v

1 [   ] ülü gü[ičem] [   ]
2 [   ] bi : čimadu [ǰi]yaǰu
3 [   ] [en]e kümün gertegen
4 [   ] [arba]n ǰil boltala güičem
5 [   ] sonosba : ene erdeni

6 [   ] lam-a-ṯur mörgömü
7 [bi] [yurba]n ǰiryuyan tümen
8 [burqan-ṯ]ur³⁵⁷ mörgömü bi [:] qorin
9 tümen yesün mingyan toy-a

XBM 33

1 item of a *pothī* (1 fragment of a folio, 2 written sides), written in a similar hand as that of XBM 32. It measures ca. 9.5 × 5 cm, with 9 lines; the Mongolian page number is *naiman* (8). The fragment is damaged and some words are illegible.³⁵⁸

8r

1 eke burqan-ṯur mörgömü bi ::
2 tengri yaǰar qamuy modon-i nabči
3 [b]üri burqan-ṯur mörgömü bi ::
       ebös[ün]
4 usun degereki büri burqan-ṯur m[ör =]

5 gömü bi :: burqan diyan say[uysan]³⁵⁹
6 ayulayin eǰen burqan-ṯur mör[gömü]
7 [bi ::] [d]ol-oyan³⁶⁰ üy-e [   ]
8 [   ] ebü[ge]³⁶¹ ečige ek[e] [   ]
9 [   ] köbčin [   ]

8v

1 mörgömü bi :: ene nom ungsibasu
2 erlig qayan-u emün-e ǰobalang-tu
3 [dal]ai-ṯur čisu-tu mören degere

4 [a]ltan mönggön kögörgen deger-e
       me[degde =]
5 müi .³⁶² ene nom-a³⁶³ dörben te
       ungsibasu

---

356   For *üǰegdesei*, reflecting the colloquial language.
357   Line 6 has *lam-a-ṯur*.
358   Restored by Mr. Bentchev; old number 23.
359   See XBM 29, 3r:4–5.
360   There is a small hole in the text which obviously prevented the copyist of the manuscript
        from joining the word *doloyan*. This word is hardly legible in the original.
361   See *ebüge* in XBM 29, 3r:7.
362   See *medegdemüi* in XBM 29, 3v:1–2.
363   Instead of *nom-i*.

6 *[tü]g tümen nom [ung]siγsan-tu[r]*   8 *[   ]*
7 *[adal]i*[364] *boluyu [   ]*   9 *[   ] [ta]mu qoγoson bolba*

XBM 34

3 items of a *pothī* (3 folios, 5 written sides), measuring ca. 11 × 6–11.5 × 7–12 × 6.5 cm, comprising 11 lines (4r has 10 lines); the Mongolian page numbers are *qoyar, γurban, dörben* (2, 3, 4). The folios have numerous splits, and a section of one side of folios 2 and 4 are missing, but the text is legible.[365] The text shows various incomplete words which were deleted and written again by the scribe of the text. There are also spelling errors in the text.

2r

1 *tataba barayun ebüdüg-iyer*
2 *sögödčü : alayaban qamtudγad*
3 *oroi degere mörgöjü aman*
4 *aldaba burqan <>*[366] *burqan bi :: či[ni]*
5 *jarliγ-iyar bolsu bi : kümün*
6 *či namoni nigen ungsiju ülü*

7 *güičem burqan tengeri*[367] *sonosba ene*
8 *erdeni burqan nom lam-a-tur*
    mörgöm[ü]
9 *bi :*[368] *γurban jirγuyan tümen*
10 *burqan-tur mörgömü bi : <>*
11 *γučin*[369] *qoyar*[370] *yesün mingγ[an]*

2v

1 *<> toγo ügei*[371] *burqan*
2 *[-t]ur mörgömü bi : tegün*[372] *jayun*
3 *[tü]g tümen molor beye-tü*
4 *[ ]n*[373] *gerel-tü <> burqan-tur*
5 *[mö]rgömü <> bi : kömčin*[374] *yaǰar*
6 *[de]gereki burqan-tur mörgömü*

7 *[b]i : doloγan qonoγ narin qura*
8 *[o]roju tosqu büri burqan-tur*
9 *mörgömü bi : kömčin qamuγ*
10 *mören-ü*[375] *urusuγsan*
11 *[q]o[γ]ar ǰaqayin qumaqi-yin*[376]

---

364 *adali* is found in XBM 29, 4r:3.
365 Restored by Mr. Bentchev; old numbers 26/6; 26/10; 31/8.
366 The scribe of the text deleted a part of the word *burqan*, then he wrote it again.
367 This version of the text shows the spelling *tengeri* instead of *tenggeri* in XBM 35.
368 This copy omits the passage which is found in XBM 29, 2r:5 8.
369 XBM 29, 2v:1 has *qorin*.
370 The letter *y* is written like *v* in the word *qoyar* . See also *qoyar* on the left side of the folio.
371 See *toγo ügei* (for *toγa ügei*) in XBM 30,3r:3.
372 The text reads *tegün*, which is obviously an error for *tabun*: the scribe of the text wrote *gü* instead of *bu*.
373 XBM 29, 2v:4 has *gegegen*.
374 Instead of *köbčin*. Note the alternation *b ~ m*. This kind of alternation is not unusual in the Mongolian language, e.g.: *qabar ~ qamar; narbai ~ narmai* (*narbai* appears in *Erdeni tunumal neretü sudur*, p. 143). On the alternation *b ~ m*, see Poppe, *Introduction*, p. 100.
375 *usun-i* is omitted; see XBM 29, 2v:9.
376 The genitive suffix is barely legible.

3r

1	eke burqan-ṯur mörgömü bi :	7	burqan-ṯur mörgömü bi : ene nom
2	<> tengeri yajara³⁷⁷ modon-u namči³⁷⁸	8	-i ungsibasu erlig qayan-u emüne
3	buri³⁷⁹ burqan-ṯur mörgömü bi :	9	jobalang-tu dalai-ṯur čisutu
4	ebösün usun degere ki buri	10	moren³⁸¹ degere ki altan mönggön
5	burqan-ṯur mörgömü bi : qamuy	11	kögergen degere medegdemüi
6	burqan diyan sayuysan ayula-yin ejen³⁸⁰		

3v

1	ene <> nom-i dörben ḏe	7	yajar naran saran modon
2	un<s>gsibasu³⁸² tüg tümen nom-i	8	dalai dotor-a ki luu-yin ordo
3	u[n]ysiysan³⁸³ -ṯur adali boloyu ::	9	usun-yi³⁸⁶ ende³⁸⁷ bügüde <>
4	qamuy čidköd <>³⁸⁴ eliy-e	10	amurliba ene nom³⁸⁸ <>
5	bügüde yarba arban [na]iman	11	ungsibasu arban tümen
6	tamu qoyoson bolba tengeri³⁸⁵		

4r

1	<> naiman mingyan³⁸⁹	6	[ča]mui ungsiysan minu burqan-ṯur
2	[bu]rqan irejü : sonosumui jayun	7	[ad]ali boluyu ene nom-yi³⁹⁰ ungsibasu
2	[t]ümen bodisung irejü : sonosumui	8	[nige]n tüg tümen altan nom-yi
4	[ja]yun tümen doloyan	9	[u]ngsiysan <> metü boluyu ::
5	[min]gyan lam-a irejü : ungsil=	10	[ ]ï³⁹¹ čin-yi tegüsbe :: : ::

377 The text has *tengeri yajara,* which likewise appear in XBM 37r:2; XBM 29 and XBM 30 have *tengri yajar* (2v:11–3r:1; 3r:7 respectively).
378 *namä ~ nabči.* Same alternation of consonants as above *(kömčin).*
379 For *büri.*
380 *ejen* is legible in the original.
381 *moren* for *mören* is written in a different hand.
382 The letter *s* of *ungsibasu* is misplaced.
383 It is a spelling error for *ungsiysan.*
384 XBM 35, 7v:2–3 reads *čidküd-ün.*
385 The previous passage also has *tengeri.*
386 Instead of *usun-i.*
387 The other copies of the text have *ede* (XBM 29, 3v:9 etc.).
388 The accusative suffix is omitted.
389 The split in the folio which runs from lines 1–3 existed before the text was written, since the words are entirely preserved.
390 Instead of *nom-i,* which appears in the preceding passage (3v).
391 XBM 29, 4r:6 has *bodi;* XBM 30, 5r:3 reads *boḏhi.*

XBM 35

4 items of a *pothī* (4 small folios, 6 written sides), measuring 5.5 × 5 cm, consisting of 8–9 lines; the Mongolian page numbers are *qoyar, yurban, doloyan, naiman* (2, 3, 7, 8). From lines 5 to 8 only a few words are left on 3r, while the ink has entirely faded on 3v and 8v.[392]

2r

1 *burqan nidündü*
2 *minu üǰeydesi*[393]
3 *namoni nigen oom*
4 *mani bad mi qung*

5 *geǰü : ter-e kümün*
6 *ügü[ler]-ün ünen*
7 *bu[rqa]n : minu nidündü*
8 *üǰeydesi či*

2v

1 *burqan ireǰü*
2 *oroi deger-e suɣ =*
3 *unaɣ tataba ene*
4 *kümün bisirel bisire =*

5 *be : barayun ebüdü =*
6 *g-iyer sögödčü*
7 *alaɣaban qamtudqa =*
8 *ǰu oroi degereben*

3r

1 *mörgöǰü aman alda =*
2 *ba : burqan burqan*
3 *bi : čini ǰarliɣ*
4 *-iyar bolsu bi :*

5 *kümün či [   ]*
6 *ni[ge]n [   ]*
7 *ülü [   ]*
8 *[   ] bi*

7r

1 *tu dalai-tur čisu*
2 *-tu mören degereki*
3 *altan mönggön*
4 *kögörge degere*

5 *medegdemüi : ene nom*
6 *-i dörben de ung =*
7 *sibasu tüg tümen*
8 *nom-i ungsiɣsan*

7v

1 *-tur adali boluyu*
2 *:: qamuɣ čidköd*
3 *-ün eliy-e bügüde*
4 *yarba : arban*
5 *naiman tamu qoɣo =*

6 *son bolba erl<l>iɣ*[394]
7 *qayan-u burqan*
8 *bolba : tenggeri*[395]
9 *yaǰar naran saran*

---

392 Restored by Mr. Bentchev; old number 31/3.
393 Instead of *üǰegdesei*.
394 Here we have the aberrant form *erlliɣ* for *erlig*.
395 This version of the text has the ancient form *tenggeri; tenggeri* often appears in the *Secret History* (see, for example, § 1).

8r

1 *modon dalayin*	6 *ungsibasu arban*
2 *dotoraki luu-yin*	7 *tümen naiman*
3 *oordo*[396] *usun*	8 *mingyan burqan*
4 *ede bügüde amur =*	9 *irejü sonosum[ui]*[397]
5 *liba : ene nom-i*	

XBM 36

1 item of a *pothī* (1 fragment of a folio, 2 written sides), measuring ca. 10×3 cm, with 9 lines; the Mongolian page number is *[d]oloyan* (7). The last section of the fragment is stained.[398]

7r

1 *[ ] [t]egen*[399] *qariba arban*	5 *[tü]men*[401] *burqan-tur mörgömü [bi:]*
2 *[ ] güičem burqan tengri*	6 *[qo]rin qoyar tümen jayun*
3 *[ ] [b]i : ene erdeni burqan nom*	7 *[mi]ngyan*[402] *toya ügei bur-q[an]*
4 *[-tur]*[400] *mörgömü bi : yurban*	8 *[-tur] mörgömü bi : [...]*
jiry[yuyan]	9 *[...]*

7v

1 *[gege]gen*[403] *gerel-tü burq[an]*	6 *[bür]i*[406] *burqan-tur mörgöm[ü]*
2 *[-tur] mörgömü bi : köbčin*	7 *[bi] : köbčin qa[m]uy möre[n-ü]*[407]
3 *[ ] degere-yi*[404] *burqan [-tur]*	8 *[us]un-i*[408] *qoyar [ ]*
4 *mörgömü doloyan qo[noy]*	9 *[u]ru[suysan]*[409] *[ ]*
5 *[nari]n*[405] *qura oroju tosqu*	

---

396   The spelling *oordo (ordo)* also occurs in this text. See *oordo* in XBM 29, 3v:8.

397   Some versions have *sonosomu*, while others read *sonosumui*. Note that 7r above has *medegdemüi*; the suffixes *-mu/-mü*, *-mui/-müi* are not used consequently in these texts.

398   Restored by Mr. Bentchev; old number 26/14.

399   XBM 29, 2r:7 and XBM 30, 2r:8 have *gertegen*.

400   See *burqan-tur* in the next line.

401   *yurban jiryuyan tümen* is found in XBM 29, 2r:10–11.

402   XBM 29, 2v:1 reads *qorin qoyar tümen yesün mingyan*.

403   *gegegen* occurs in XBM 29, 2v:4.

404   XBM 29, 2v:6 reads *degereki*.

405   *qonoy* and *narin* appear in XBM 29, 2v:7.

406   See *büri* in XBM 29, 2v:8.

407   XBM 34, 2v:10 has *mören-ü*.

408   XBM 29, 2v:9.

409   See *urusuysan* in XBM 30, 3r:5; XBM 29, 2v:10 has *ur[u]sugsan*.

XBM 37

1 item a *pothī* (1 nearly entire folio, 2 written sides), measuring ca. 10 × 6 cm, comprising 13–12 lines (r/v); the page number is missing. This item is half-burnt, but the text is legible thanks to infra-red reflectography.[410]

recto

1	*[quma]qiin*[411] *eke burqan*	8	*burqan diyan sayuysa[n]*
2	*-ţur mörgömü bi :: tengeri*[412]	9	*ayula-yin eǰen <> burqa[n]*
3	*yaǰar-a qamuy modon-i nabči*	10	*-ţur mörgömü bi :: doloyan*
4	*büri burqan-ţur mörgömü*	11	*üy-e öngereysen*[414] *ebüge*
5	*bi :: ebösün usun-a*[413]	12	*ečike eke burqan-ţur*
6	*degereki büri burqan*	13	*mörgömü bi :: köbčin*
7	*-ţur mörgömü bi :: qamuy*		

verso

1	*bu[rqan] [ ]*	7	*[de]ger-e medegdemüi : ene*
2	*ene n[o]m [-i] [u]ngsi[basu] erl[ig]*	8	*nom-i dörben ḏe*
3	*qayan-u emün-e ǰobalang*	9	*ungsibasu tüg*
4	*-tu dalai-ţur čisu-tu*	10	*tümen nom-i*[415] *ungsi =*
5	*mören degereki altan*	11	*ysan-ţur adali bolu =*
6	*[m]önggön kögörge*	12	*yu qamuy čidköd-ün*

XBM 38

1 item of a *pothī* (1 fragment of a folio, 2 written sides*)*, measuring ca. 10 × 3 cm, with 9 lines. Only a few words are left on recto.[416]

recto

1	*[ ] tngri [ ]*	3	*[ ]*
2	*[bur]qan-ţur [ ]*	4	*[ ] ene nom-i*

---

410 Restored by Mrs. Nebel; old number 14.
411 *qumaqiin* instead of *qumaqiyin* in XBM 29, 2v:10. For the genitive suffix *-in* in the pre-classical language, see Weiers, *Untersuchungen*, p. 58; on the genitive *-in*, which occurs in the Geser epic, see Poppe, "Geserica", pp. 15–16; see also Ligeti, "Deux tablettes", pp. 207–8.
412 As shown, the form *tengeri* appears in XBM 34.
413 The other copies of the text omit the dative-locative suffix *-a* after *usun* (*ebösün usun*, XBM 29, 3r:1–2, etc.).
414 For *önggeregsen*.
415 XBM 29, 4r:5 and XBM 30, 5r:1 have *altan nom*.
416 Restored by Mr. Bentchev; old number 13/3.

5　[　] erl[　]　　　　　　　　　　7　[　] mören [　]
6　[　]　　　　　　　　　　　　　8　mönggön

verso

1　[　]n⁴¹⁷ deger-e [　]　　　　　6　naiman tamu qo[γoson] [　]
2　[　] dörbe[n]⁴¹⁸ [　]　　　　　7　erliγ⁴²¹ [qa]yan-u [　]
3　[　]n nom [　]　　　　　　　　8　tengri yaǰar [　]
4　[adal]i⁴¹⁹ boluyu : qa[muγ]⁴²⁰ [　]　9　dal[a]i-yin dotor[a]
5　[　] [e]liy-e bügüde [　]

XBM 39

1 item of a *pothī*(1 folio, 2 written sides), measuring 10×5 cm, consisting of 8–9 lines; the Mongolian page number is *naiman* (8).The text is incomplete, it ends in the middle of 8v:6, otherwise it is well preserved.⁴²²

8r

1　O eke burqan-ṯur mörgömü bi ::　　5　mörgömü bi :: ene nom <>
2　tengri yaǰar qamuγ modon-i　　　6　ungsibasu erliγ⁴²⁴ qayan-u
3　nabči büri burqan-ṯur　　　　　7　emüne ǰobalang-tu dalai
4　mörgömü bi :: köbčin burqan-a⁴²³　8　-ṯur čisu-tu mören degere-yi⁴²⁵

8v

1　altan möngeön⁴²⁶ kögergen dege =　4　tümen⁴²⁷ nom-i ungsiysan-ṯur
2　re medegdemüi : ene nom　　　　5　adali boluyu : qamuγ čid =
3　dörben te ungsibasu tüg　　　　　6　köd-ün eliy-e

417　This word is *kögergen* according to XBM 29, 3v:1, but we find different spellings in the copies from Xarbuxyn Balgas.
418　*dörben* in XBM 29, 3v:2.
419　XBM 29, 3v:4.
420　XBM 29, 3v:4.
421　*erliγ* for *erlig*.
422　Restored by Mr. Bentchev; old number 26.
423　Line 1 reads *burqan-ṯur*, here we have the dative-locative *-a* instead of the usual *-ṯur*.
424　The word *erlig* is misspelt in most of the copies of the text.
425　Instead of *degereki* in the others versions of the text (XBM 29, 3r:11, etc.); *degere-yi* is also found in XBM 36, 7v:3.
426　We have the spelling *möngeön* for *mönggön*.
427　This copy also omits *altan* before *nom*.

XBM 40

1 item of a *pothī* (1 folio, 2 written sides). It measures 9.5 × 5 cm., with 9–7 lines (r/v); the Mongolian page number is *yesün* (9). The text is well preserved and legible.[428]

9r

1 *erlig qayan-u burqan bolba tengri*
2 *yaǰar . naran . saran modon-u dalai*
3 *-yin dotoraki luu-yin ordo*
4 *usun-i ede bügüde amurliba :*
5 *ene nom-a*[429] *ungsibasu arban*

6 *tümen naiman mingyan burqan ireǰü*
7 *sonosumu: ǰayun tümen bodisug*
8 *-nar ireǰü sonosumu : yesün*
9 *tümen doloyan mingyan lam-a-nar*

9v

1 *ireǰü ungsilčamu ungsigsan*
2 *minu burqan-tur adali bolu =*
3 *mui :: ene nom-a ungsibasu*
4 *nigen tümen altan nom-a*

5 *ungsiysan metü boluyu ::*
6 *boddi*[430] *sin-i tayulba :: : ::*
7 *sadu edgü ::*

The 12 copies of the Xarbuxyn Balgas text do not mention the *Altan gerel*, but a passage in XBM 29 (4r:4–6) reads: *ene nom-i ungsibasu nigen tüg tümen altan nom-i ungsiysan metü boluyu*, "If someone reads this book, it will be the same as if someone has read the Golden Book countless times". The Oyirad version *Yeke kölgöni altan gerel neretü nomiyin xurangyui* mentions the *Altan gerel* both in the title and in the following passage (3v:4–6): *ene nomi nigentei ungšibasu tüq tümen altan gerel ungšiqsan metü bolxu*, "If someone reads this book once, it will be the same as if someone has read the *Altan gerel* countless times". It is thus possible that the "golden book" in the Xarbuxyn Balgas text indicates the *Altan gerel*.

The *Ārya-Suvarṇa-prabhāsottama-sūtrendra-rāja nāma mahāyāna-sūtra, Qutuy-tu altan gerel-tü erketü sudur-nuyud qayan neretü yeke kölgen sudur* (Abbr. *Altan gerel*), "The holy mahāyāna-sūtra called the Supreme Golden Light, the Powerful King of the Sūtras", is one of the basic and highly revered *sūtra* of Mahāyāna Buddhism. Altan qayan had the *Altan gerel* engraved on tablets in 1577, and from this period the *sūtra* extensively spread among the Mongols.[431] The *Altan gerel* is included in the *Ganǰur*.[432]

As for the question of the relation between the short "Summary of the *Altan Gerel*" and the voluminous *Altan gerel*, the two texts share the same idea of the power of the recitation of a religious book emphasising the benefits that a person will obtain as a result.

---

428 Restored by Mr. Bentchev; old number 21/7.
429 For *nom-i*. See also line 4. Perhaps *nom-a* is the result of a careless orthography.
430 Instead of *bodi*, or *bodhi*.
431 Mong. 395, chap. 17, 22r = Heissig and Bawden, *Catalogue*, pp. 204–6.
432 Vol. 13, No. 177, pp. 393–692; see also vol. 14, Nos. 176, 178. On the description of the three texts, see Ligeti, *Catalogue*, pp. 55–6; see also Heissig, *Blockdrucke*, pp. 9, 52. On the worship of the *Altan gerel*, see Bira, "The Worship", pp. 3–14.

One of the benefits is described in these words in the *Altan gerel: erlig-ün yirtinčü-deki qamuy ǰobalang-ud-i qoyoson bolyayči,* "It makes all sufferings in the realm of Erlig become emptiness",[433] while the "Summary" (XBM 29, 3v:5–6) reads: *arban naiman tamu qoyoson bolba,* "The Eighteen Hells will become emptiness". Moreover, the *Altan gerel* contains passages which invoke the Buddhas, but they are different from the invocations to the Burqans in the "Summary".[434] One may conclude that when using the "Summary" to disseminate the teachings of the *Altan gerel,* the Buddhists attributed to this text the religious power of the *Altan gerel.*

The "Summary" is a many facetted text, which is composed of a variety of themes. What is note-worthy is the following passage which is reminiscent of folk religious texts invoking the spirit-masters of the locality: *doloyan qonoy narin qura oroǰu tosqu büri burqan-ṯur mörgömü bi,* "I bow to each Burqan of the light rain which falls for seven days and nights"; *tengri yaǰar qamuy modon-i nabči büri burqan-ṯur mörgömü bi,* "I bow to each Burqan of Heaven and Earth and the leaves of all trees" (XBM 29, 2v:6–8).[435]

The "Summary" also has a passage which shows the ancient idea of the association of female deities with earth and water. It reads: *köbčin qamuy moron (mörön)-ü usun-i qoyar ǰaqayin ur[us]uysan qumaqiyin eke burqan-ṯur mörgömü bi* (XBM 29, 2v:9–11), "I bow to Mother Burqan of the fine sand, and the water of all rivers running within two banks".[436]

Finally, the text invokes the paternal and maternal ancestors of seven generations in this passage: *doloyan üy-e önggeregsen ebüge ečige eke burqan-ṯur mörgömü bi* (XBM 29, 3r:6–8), "I bow to father and mother Burqan, the ancestors of seven past generations".[437]

It is interesting to note that the "Summary" mentions a bridge of gold and a bridge of silver over a river of blood (*čisutu mören degereki altan mönggön kegergen,* XBM 29, 3r:12–3v:1), which are located in the realm of Erlig qayan. A description of hell like this is rare in the Mongol written sources, but the fact that it appears in a text of popular Buddhism such as the "Summary" indicates that it was familiar to the Mongol people.[438]

---

433 *Ganǰur,* p. 543.

434 *Ganǰur,* pp. 521–5; Mong. 395, chap. 7, pp. 2–3.

435 The text called *Iaǰar usun-i sang,* "Incense offering of the locality" has a passage which reads: *mörön usu bulay čögem nayur ayula qada čilayuu oboy-a oi modon ebesü... qur-a usu čaytayan oroyad ebesün tariyan eldeb yarayad* (1r–2r). Copy of the Ms. belonging to the author (Mr. Süxbat's private collection). On an invocation to the spirit-masters of the locality, see Even, *Chants de chamane mongols,* pp. 309–11.

436 See Even, *Chants de chamane mongols,* pp. 311–312. The Mongols also associate females with rocks, caves, tree and fire. See Altangarudi et al. *Mongyolǰin-u šasin surtaqul,* pp. 7–22; Nima, *Böge mörgöl-ün tuqai,* pp. 275, 286; See also the prayer to the fire in Rintchen, *Matériaux,* p. 32, and the expression *eke selengge* in the same work, p. 74; *Qad Ėėž* (Mother-Rock) is worshipped by the contemporary Mongols in Sergelen Sum, Töv Ajmag.

437 On the Mongol custom of counting on the basis of seven generations, see Čeringsodnam, *Mongyol-un niyuča tobčiyan,* note 337, p. 398; on the term *ebüge,* "ancestor", and its plural form *ebüges,* see the discussion by Mostaert and Cleaves in *Les lettres,* pp. 65–6; see also *ebüges ečiges,* "ancestors and fathers" in § 133 of the *Secret History.*

The idea of a "bridge thin as hair" located in the underworld has been observed among the Mongol-Turkic speaking people of Siberia.[439] As far as the Mongol texts are concerned, an early version of *Naran-u gerel dagini tuyuǰi,* which shows the influence of the Chinese narrative tradition, describes a river of blood into which impure women are condemned, but it does not mention a bridge.[440] Four bridges, however, appear in the description of hell which is found in the so-called "Story of Güsü Lama". The four bridges are made of gold, yellow copper, red copper and iron, and lead to the land of the Buddhas, the realms of Amitābha, the Tngri and Erlig respectively.[441] In conclusion, I have not yet found another Mongol written source where a river of blood and a bridge appear side by side.

Turning to the Chinese accounts of journeys to the underworld we find that the *Xiyang ji,* "Records of the Western Ocean", does mention a river of blood and a bridge over the River Nai.[442] Moreover, according to the *Yüli,* "Precious Records", which is an account of a journey to the nether regions dating back to the Song dynasty, six bridges are located in the Tenth Hall of Judgment of the Taoist hell. The six bridges are made of gold, silver, jade, stone, wood and planks. According to this work, souls from different hells are liberated into one of the four continents by the appropriate bridge.[443] It is thus in the *Yüli* that one finds a bridge of gold and a bridge of silver corresponding to the bridges of gold *(altan)* and silver *(mönggön)* of the "Summary".

It is worth adding that the representation of a bridge over a river in hell is also old in Chinese iconography. The *Foshuo Shiwangjing,* "The sūtra of the Ten Kings", dating back to the 10th century, depicts a virtuous woman crossing a bridge over a river in which the wicked, who are being tormented by demons are floating.[444]

* * *

---

438   See the description of the Eighteen Hells in the *Čiqula kereglegči,* 20r–24v (facsimile in Heissig, *Geschichtsschreibung,* I). One of the hells of the *Institutes of Vishnu* is called Dīpanadī. It is a river of flame which has a stinking odour and is full of blood (Goodrich, *Chinese Hells,* p. 16). A Tibetan thangka representing Mañjuśrī-Yamāntaka shows a sea of blood as a symbol of the sea of suffering. For this see Essen and Thingo, *Die Götter des Himalaya,* p. 173.

439   Quotation from Potanin *Očerki Severo-zapodnoj Mongolii,* in Sazykin "Erzählung über Güsü-Lama", p. 121.

440   Damdisürüng, *Jayun bilig,* vol. 2, p. 793; Sazykin noticed that a river of blood is not found in the later versions of this work ("Mongol and Oirat Versions", pp. 283–7); see also the discussion by Heissig in *Geschichte der mongolischen Literatur,* vol. I, pp. 109–19; *Molon toyin u eke aǰi qariyuluysan sudur,* the well-known work which narrates Molon Toyin's journey into hell, tells us that women who committed impure actions are condemned into a pool of blood *(čisun balčiy)*. See *Jayun bilig,* vol. 2, p. 885. According to the Chinese description of hell, a pool of blood is located in the Cold Hell, and is a special place for impure women. See Goodrich, *Chinese Hells,* pp. 55–6.

441   I had access to the Mongol and Oyirad version of this text which Sazykin published. See "Erzählung über Güsü-Lama", pp. 126, 133; "The Story of Güsü-Lama", pp. 33, 36.

442   Duyvendak, "A Chinese Divina Commedia", pp. 272–3.

443   See Clarke, "The Yü-Li or Precious Records", pp. 235, 389; see also Goodrich, *Chinese Hells,* pp. 80–6.

444   *Sérinde,* pp. 333–4.

Book of Prayers (XBM 41)

XBM 41 is a booklet which includes four texts. The first text, without a title, is an invocation to Lamas, Bodhisattvas and Buddhas.[445]

The second text is *Itegel yabuyulqu*, of which the Xarbuxyn Balgas collection includes 27 items of 21 copies. They were dealt with above in this volume.[446]

The third text bears the title in Sanskrit, Tibetan and Mongolian. They are *Ary-a badma ločan-a; Jabčin bagsba badm-a-yi sbčan sis bunu-a; Qutuy-tu lingqu-a-yin nidün kemegdekü neretü tarni*, "The holy dhāraṇī called Lotus-Eyed". The *dhāraṇī* is included in the *Ganjur* only with the Mongolian title *Qutuy-tu lingqu-a-yin nidün neretü tarni*.[447] It is found in the *bKa'-'gyur* with the title *'Phags-pa Padma'i spyan žes-bya-ba'i gzuńs*.[448]

The fourth text bears no title. It praises the saving powers of Qongsim[449] Bodisug[450] (Avalokiteśvara), the Buddhist god of compassion, who, according to this text, revived a person from death.[451] Moreover, the text tells us that the god descends to earth on the 13th day of the 5th month, and as a result the crops of the year grow abundantly. The description of Avalokiteśvara, who saves human beings from the sufferings of hunger, is found in the *Mani gambu*.[452] It is worth at this point mentioning that the Xarbuxyn Balgas collection bears witness of the widespread circulation of texts of the worship of Avalokiteśvara. As a matter of fact, it includes nine different texts, mainly fragmentary, devoted to this deity. The texts are described below in this volume (XBM 47 to XBM 64).

XBM 41

1 booklet *(debter)* including 4 complete texts, written by 3 hands. Originally the left sides of the folios were stitched together, but now most of the folios are loose. The booklet is composed of 8 folios (16 written sides), without page numbers. It measures ca. 11 × 8.5 cm; the number of lines varies. The folios are in different states of preservation. Folios 1v and 2r are stained and some words are illegible; the last folio is torn.[453]

---

445   On a text which invokes the teachers of the religion, Bodhisattvas and Buddhas, see Heissig, *Handschriften-Reste*, pp. 449–56.

446   See XBM 1 to XBM 21.

447   Vol. 14, pp. 286–7; vol. 23, pp. 237–8. See also Ligeti, *Catalogue*, Nos. 250, 507, pp. 70–124.

448   Vol. 11, p. 98/4/2–98/4/8.

449   This name is also spelt in other ways. A Turfan text uses Qonš-im (< Chin. Guanshiyin) as in ancient Turkic (Cerensodnom and Taube, *Turfansammlung*, No. 45, p. 144, and note 45 r 6); the Xarbuxyn Balgas text XBM 48 (2 r:8) has Qonsiim.

450   In others texts the spelling is Bodisung.

451   On therapeutic rites among the Chinese associated with Guanyin, see Strickmann, *Mantras et mandarins*, pp. 149–59.

452   Vol. I, 48v = Heissig and Sagaster, *Mongolische Handschriften*, Libr. Mong. 47.

453   Restored by Mr. Bentchev; old number 32/2.

1v

1 viri ǰir[   ]
2 ǰokiyayči lam-a bui : lam-[a]
3 -tur mörgömü : lam-a-yin bey-e-yi
4 včir-un bey-e üjebesü bulilaqui
5 bei (?) ügei sedkisi ügei⁴⁵⁴ tegüld[er]
6 erdem-tü lam-a-tur mörgömü :
7 lam-a-yin ǰirliy⁴⁵⁵ esrun egesig⁴⁵⁶

8   tüyidkel⁴⁵⁷ ügei arsalan-u
9   dayun-tur tegülder buruyu
10 üjelten-i [...] ǰokiyayči
11 lam-a-yin [...]
12 lam-a-yin sedkil oytaryui
13 metü nam[...][   ] [...]

2r

1 činar yosu-tu [...]
2 sayitur tuyulu-ysan la[m]-a-yin
3 sedkil-tür mö[r]gömü : [sedkis]i
4 ügei yeke sang nigülesküi
5 nidüber üjegči :⁴⁵⁸ kir ügei⁴⁵⁹

6   medegči erketü manǰusiri časutan-u
7   merged-ün oroyin čimeg ǰöngga-ba
8   čoy-tu tegülder lam-a va (?) ban (?)
9   -tur mörgömü : [...]
10 degedü buyan -du čim[   ]

2v

1 bey-e-tü sayin üge-tü [...]
2 egesig-iyer dayurisqayči ǰarliy (?)
3 -tu medeküi yoson qočorlig⁴⁶⁰
4 tüyidkel ügei medegči sedkil-tü
5 mergen-ü ǰug-tu⁴⁶¹ dalayin itegel
6 -tür ǰalbarimui :: mergen ary-a⁴⁶² ber

7   [n]igülesküi šagi-muni burqan terigün
8   -türi[ye]n tabun titimtü
9   nigülesküi nidü-ber olan amitan-i
10 üjegči örösiyen nidü
11 -ber üjegčide mörgömü :

---

454 sedkisi ügei, Skr. acintya; Tib. bsam-gyis mi-khyab-pa. Ishihama and Fukuda eds.,
      Mahāvyutpatti, No. 7904.
455 For ǰarliy.
456 esru-a (text: esrun)-ü egesig dayun-iyar dayurisqayči; esru-a-yin egesig dayurisqayči, Skr.
      brahmasvararutāravitā; Tib. tshangs-pa'i sgra-dbyaṅs bsgrags-pa, Mahāvyutpatti, No. 481.
457 tüidkel ~ tüidker. For the alternation of l ~ r, see Poppe, Introduction, p. 158; tüidker, Skr.
      nivaraṇa; Tib. sgrib-pa, Mahāvyutpatti, No. 2156.
458 sedkisi ügei yeke sang nigülesküi nidüber üjegči is found in the hymn to the Panchen Lama
      and Dalai Lama (see XBM 78, 2v:1–2).
459 See the spelling kir in Heissig, Handschriften-Reste, OS IV/41, p. 271; gkir ügei, Skr. nirmala;
      Tib. dri-ma med-pa, Mahāvyutpatti, No. 73.
460 The form qočorliy appears in one of the versions of the Čayan teüke. See Sagaster, Weiße
      Geschichte, p. 84.
461 For ǰüg-tü. On the form ǰug in the early pre-cassical texts, see Poppe, "Ein mongolisches
      Gedicht", p. 267. See also the discussion by Cleaves, "Sino-Mongolian Inscription of 1362",
      p. 101, note 34; the spellings ǰüg, ǰug alternate in the inscriptions of Arǰai Ayui, which date
      back to the end of the 15ᵗʰ century. Unfortunately, the originals are barely legible. See
      Qaserdeni et al., Arǰai ayui-yin uyiyurǰin mongyol bičigesü-yin sudulul, pp. 48–9, 53–4.
462 mergen ary-a-tu, Skr. upāyakauśalya; Tib. thabs-la mkhas-pa, Mahāvyutpatti, No. 1349.

3r

1 *geikübtür arsi-ṭaki degedü tangyari[y]*
2 *-ḏa ayui-ṭur : niyuča tarni*
3 *okis dayisun bügüdeyin ejen anu :*
4 *buruyu tatayči*[463] *todqar-nuyud*
5 *-un čiyulyan-i ebdegči ilaju*

6 *tegüs baǰar-bani*[464] *-ṭur mörgömü :*
7 *nom-un bey-e*[465] *oytaryui metü ilyal*
8 *ügei :*[466] *öngge bey-e solongya meḏü*
9 *öbere öbere geyigülügči : uran*
10 *kiged degedü bilig-tür erke*

3v

1 *oluysan: tabun iǰaǰur emküyul[küi]*[467]
2 **-iyer** *oduysan-a mörgömü :: naran*
   metü
3 *ülü üǰeküi-yin qarangyusi*[468]
4 *geyigülügči : saran metü nisvanisun*
5 *tabun orosi*[469] *arilyayči :*

6 *yurban oroi-yin*[470] *ebedčin-i*
7 *arilyayči otači burqan vaiduri*
8 *erdeni*[471] *gereltü-de mörgömü :: tengsel*
9 *ügei üǰügülegči burqan e[r]deni*
10 *tengsel [ügei]*[472] *<>*[473] *itegel*
   degedü <>

4r

1 *[e]rdeni erdeni*[474] *tengsel ügegü*
   uduridugči[475]
2 *bursang quvaray-ud [er]deni :*

3 *tengsel ügei yurban erdeni*
4 *-ṭür mörgömü :: : ::*[476]
5 O *ačitu ečige eke kiged :*

---

463 See *buruyu uduriduyči, buruyu tatayči,* Skr. *vināyaka;* Tib. *log-'dren, Mahāvyutpatti,*
     No. 3162
464 See the spelling Baǰar bani in Poppe, "On Some Mongolian Manuscripts", p. 83.
465 *nom-un bey-e,* Skr. *dharmakāya;* Tib. *chos-kyi sku, Mahāvyutpatti,* No. 114.
466 *qoličal ügei buyu ilyal ügei; ese qoličaysan ba ilyal ügei.* Skr. *asaṃbheda;* Tib. *ma- 'dres-pa*
     dbyer-med-pa, Mahāvyutpatti, No. 5188.
467 For *emkügül[küi].*
468 *qarangyusi* is the plural of *qarangyu,* with the accusative suffix joined to the word. See
     nisvanis-un qarangyu[d]i činar-i [geyi]gülügči in Heissig, *Handschriften-Reste,* OS IV/123v,
     p. 455.
469 The initial *o* is written like *qo* in the word *orosi.* See also *oroi, uduridugči* and other words
     below; *oros* is the plural of *oro* with the accusative suffix joined to the word. The usual plural
     of *oro* is *orod.* However, words ending in vowels also take the plural suffix in *-s.* See
     Poppe, *Introduction,* pp. 177–9. The five delusive poisons (*nisvanis-un tabun oron,* Skr.
     pañcakleśavisa; Tib. *ñon-moṅs dug-lṅa*) are desire attachement, hatred-anger, ignorance,
     pride and jealousy. For this see Rigzin, *Tibetan-English Dictionary,* p. 98.
470 On the genitive suffix *-i-yin* see Poppe, "Geserica", p. 16.
471 AT *vayiduri;* Skr. *vaiḍūrya.* See *vaiduri erdini* in the *Bodhicaryāvatāra* (Cerensodnom and
     Taube, *Turfansammlung,* No. 11r13, p. 79).
472 4r below has both *ügegü* and *ügei; tengsel ügei,* Skr. *anuttara;* Tib. *bla-na med-pa,*
     Mahāvyutpatti, No. 2521.
473 A word was deleted by the scribe of the text.
474 The word *erdeni* is repeated twice.
475 *uduriduyči,* Skr. *nāyaka;* Tib. *'dren-pa, Mahāvyutpatti,* No. 20.
476 The first text ends here.

6 oγtarγui-yin kiǰayar-luγ-a
7 sača : qamuγ amitan arban ǰüg-ün

8 γurban čaγ-un qamuγ tegünčilen
9 iregsed-ün bey-e ǰarliγ sedkil

4v

1 erdem üiles bügüde-yin mön činar
2 boluγsan : naiman tümen dörben
3 mingγan nom-un čoγčas γarquyin
      oron
4 qamuγ qutuγ-tan quvaraγ-ud-un
5 eǰen ači-tu ündüsün kiged čoγ
6 -tu tegülder lam-a-nar-tur mörgömü ::

7 burqan-tur mörgömü :: nom-tur
      mörgömü ::
8 bursang quvaraγ-ud-tur mörgömü ::
9 idam mandal-un tengri-yin
10 čiγulγan nökör selte-tür itegemüi ::
11 belge bilig nom-un sakiγulsun
12 -tur it[e]gemüi burqan nom kiged :

5r

1 degedü čiγul[γan]-nuγud-tur bodičid-tur
2 kü[r]tele itege[müi] ba :⁴⁷⁷ öberin öngelge⁴⁷⁸
3 terigüten tedeger üiledügsen amitan
4 tusayin tula burqan bütükü boltuγai :
5 γurban erdeni-t[ü]r ite[ge]m[ü]i :
6 qamuγ kili[n]če-yi ö[be]re öber-e
7 nomačilamui :⁴⁷⁹ qamu[γ] [...]n⁴⁸⁰ buyan-nuγud
8 -tur daγan bayasulčamui : burqan
9 bodi-yi sedk[il]-iyer barimui :
10 qamuγ amitan ǰirγalang kiged :
11 ǰirγalang-un siltaγan-tur tegülder
12 boltuγai :: **qamuγ amitan** ǰobalang kige[d] ǰobalang

5v

1 -un siltaγan-ača qaγačaqu boltuγai ::
2 ǰobalang ügei ǰirγalang-ača ülü
3 qaγačaqu boltuγai :: tačiyangγui
4 urin kiling-eče qaγačaqu
5 tegsi sedkil-tür aqu bo[l]tuγai ::
6 sadu edgü maṅ gha lam⁴⁸¹
7 nigen namo buday-a :: namo darmay-a ::
8 namo sangay-a :: ened[ke]g-ün keleber :

---

477 ba, "we".
478 The genitive suffix -in joined to öber reflects the influence of the colloquial language. On the genitive suffix -in, see the discussion by Ligeti in "Deux tablettes", pp. 207–8 and note 36; öngelge is obviously a mistake for öglige. See öber-ün öglige in Itegel yabuγulqu (XBM 11).
479 For namančilamui.
480 XBM 16r: 15 has amitan-i.
481 The second text ends here.

9   *ary-a badm-a locan-a -yin tarni : töbed-ün*
10 *keleber : ǰabčin bagsba badm-a-yi sbčan*
11 *sis byau-a : mongγolun keleber :*
12 *qutuγ-tu lingqu-a-yin nidün kemegdeküi*

6r

1   *neretü tarni :: γurban erdeni-ṯür mörgömü ::*
2   *tegünčilen iregsen dayin-i daruγsan ünen*
3   *mayad tuγuluγsan : lingqu-a-yin [n]idü-tü* [482]
4   *burqan-a mörgömü :: bodisung maqas[u]ng qamuγ*
5   *tüidker teyin büged arilγaγ-či-ṯur* [483]
6   *mörgömü :: dadyata oom dar-a dar-a diri*
7   *diri: duru duru : gala gala gili gili :*
8   *gülü gülü : bar-a bar-a : bari bari : buru*
9   *buru : bay-a bay-a : gürü gürü :*
10 *sarva avarana ǰay-a [...]*
11 *braba sv[...] [...]*

6v

1   *bay-a suvaq-a: gürü bay-a*
2   *[l]i suu ha : sagar sman biro-a suu qa : sarva*
3   *dataaggada distadi suu qa :* [484] *ene tarni*
4   *ǰayun naiman-ta ungsiγulun*
5   *üyiledbesü ele qorin nigen*
6   *qonoγ bolqu učir-tur* [485] *ǰayaγ =*
7   *an-u qamuγ tüidker barayda =*
8   *qu boluyu :* [486] *nidüber* [487] *teyin*
9   *büged arilqu boluyu :*
10 *tegün-ṯür nidün-ü*

---

482   *Ganǰur*, vol. 23, p. 237: *ünen tegüs.*
483   *Ganǰur*, vol. 23, p. 237: *qamuγ tüidker-i teyin ber arilγaγsan-a bodhi saduva ma ha saduva-dur.*
484   The Bkaḥ-ḥgyur text (84v–86v) includes this *mantra: tadyathā / oṃ ta ra ta ra / ti ri ti ri / tu ru ru tu ru / ka la ka la / ku lu ku lu / bha ra bha ra / bhi ri bhi ri / bhu ru bhu ru / bha ya bha ya / ku ru ku ru / sa rba karma a ba ra ṇa dza nu me śa pra bha ya svāhā / dzva la ne ba dhi ni svāhā / ku ru paṃ dza li svāhā / sa ga ra / saṃ pi ro svāhā / sarba ta thā ga tā a dhi ṣṭhi te svāhā.*
485   On *čay učir* meaning "time" see Poppe, *The Diamond Sutra*, p. 83, note 3.
486   *Ganǰur*, vol. 23, p. 237: *ene tarni-yin ǰang üile ene buyu. erte manaγar bosču ǰayun naiman ta uribasu qorin nigen qonoγsan qoyin-a ǰayayan-u tüidker bügüde baraγdaqu bolai.*
487   *Ganǰur*, vol. 23, p. 237: *tabun nidü ber.*

7r

1 *ebečin ügei bolqu boluyu : bey-e-tür*
2 *ebečin ügei bolqu <> boluyu : sedkil*
3 *-tür gem ügei bolqu boluyu :*[488]
4 *tegüle kü*[489] *sed[ki]l teyin*
5 *büged arilusan*[490] *tabun*

6 *sedkil-i ber olqu bolqu*
7 *boluyu : qamuy torol*[491] *tutum*
8 *-tur burqan iregsen-luy-a*
9 *učiraldugsan boluyu :*[492] *bodičid*
10 *-un jirüken-tür ayui*

7v

1 *niyur burqan-i üjeküi kiged*
2 *nom sonosqui ba bursang*
3 *quvaray-ud-tur kündülen*
4 *üyiledküi-luy-a : qamuy*
5 *amitan oyoyata balbara =*
6 *yulun*[493] *üiledküi-luya : ülü*

7 *anggijaraqu boluyu :*[494]
8 *üje[s]küleng-dei bey-e-tü :*
9 *boluyu : tunggalay*[495] *sedkil-tü*
10 *bo[l]uyu :*[496] *qutuy-tu lingqu-a*
11 *[-yi]n nidün kemegdekü ner[e]tü*

8r

1 *[tarn]i tegüsbe :: : ::*[497]
2 *[oo]m mani bad mi hum ::*
3 *[yu]rban delekei-yin ulusun*
4 *noyan kumün*[498] *tusai neretü*
5 *noyan kümün yurban edür*
6 *ükügsen <> kumün*[499] *-i qongsim*[500]

7 *bodasug*[501] *edegebe tabun sara*
8 *-yin arban yurban edür qongsim*
9 *bodasug bayuju ene jil-ün*
10 *tariyan adabasi yarqu bei*[502]
11 *idekü kümün bui : yeke tergegür*

---

488 *Ganjur*, vol. 23, pp. 237–8: *tegün-dür nidün-ü ebedčin ülü bolqu boluyu. bey-e-dür ebedčin ülü bolqu boluyu. sedkil-ün eregüü bolqu ülü boluyu.*
489 The *Ganjur* text has *tegünčilen kü*. See note 48.
490 Instead of *ariluysan*. The form *bitügdesen* occurs in the *Alexander Romance* (Cerensodnom and Taube, *Turfansammlung*, 4v10, p. 58). Poppe regards *-san/-sen* as a suffix of the spoken language. See "Alexandersage", p. 122, note 77.
491 For *töröl*.
492 *Ganjur*, vol. 23, p. 238: *tabun nidün ber teyin büged arilqu boluyu. tegünčilen kü ariyun tabun sedkil-i ber olqu boluyu. qamuy töröl tutum-dur iregsed burqad-luy-a učiralduqu boluyu.*
493 For *balbasurayulun, bolhasurayulun.*
494 *Ganjur*, vol. 23, p. 238: *bodhi jirüken-dür orosiqui-dur kürtele burqan-i üjeküi nom-i sonosqui quvaray-ud-i kündüleküi kiged. qamuy amitan-i oyoyata bolbasurayul-un üiledküi-eče ülü qayačaqu boluyu.*
495 For *tungyalay*. The word has the diacritical points before g and before the final *y*.
496 *Ganjur*, vol. 23, p. 238: *bey-e üjesküleng-tü boluyu. sedkil süsüg-tü boluyu.*
497 The third text ends here.
498 For *kümün*.
499 The text has *kumün* instead of *kümün* as in line 4.
500 This word is entirely legible in the original.
501 For *bodisug;* the same spelling appears in line 9.
502 Instead of *bui,* which is found in the next line.

8v

1   *deger-e yabuqu kümün ed*   6   [   ] *ken kümün ese besiregesü*[503]
2   *ügei bui : [q]ongsim bodisug*   7   [   ] *r ükükü bui: egüni m[...]i*
3   [   ] *ǰayun naiman da ungsiqu*   8   [   ] *ese salyabasu ter-e*
4   [   ] *bey-e-yin tula mingyan*   9   [   ] *čisu ber bulčakü*[504]
5   [   ] *ungsi ker-iyer tonilqu*   10   [   ] *čikin-iyer <>*

9r

1   [...] *arban kümün*   3   [   ] *sayad ügei tonilqu :*
2   [   ] *čiǰu irebesü ter-e*   4   [   ] *:: : ::*

Qutuy-tu lingqu-a-yin nidün kemegdekü neretü tarni, "The holy *dhāraṇī* called Lotus-Eyed", is the only text of the Xarbuxyn Balgas collection dealt with in this volume which is found in the *Ganǰur*.

The *dhāraṇī* addresses the Lotus-Eyed Buddha (Padmanetra), and describes the wordly and spiritual benefits that a person who recites the *dhāraṇī* will obtain.

The Xarbuxyn Balgas text shows the inconsistent use of *d, t (bey-e-tür, tutum-tur)*, and spellings such as *arilusan, torol, tunggalay*, etc.

Comparing passages from the Xarbuxyn Balgas text with those in the *Ganǰur* text, the following textual variants can be observed:

The Xarbuxyn Balgas text has (11:3–8) : *ene tarni ǰayun naiman ta ungsiyulun üiledbesü ele qorin nigen qonoy bolqu učir-tur ǰayayan-u qamuy tüidker baraydaqu boluyu*, "If someone has this *dhāraṇī* recited 108 times, when 21 days have passed, all obstacles of fate *(karma)* will be eliminated".

The *Ganǰur* reads (Vol. 23, p. 237): *ene tarni ǰang üile ene buyu. erte manayar bosču ǰayun naiman ta uribasu qorin nigen qonoysan qoyin-a ǰayayan-u tüidker bügüde baraydaqu bolai.*

The words *ene tarni ǰang üile ene buyu* ("this is the ritual of this *dhāraṇī*"), and *erte manayar bosču* ("rising tomorrow morning"), are not found in the Xarbuxyn Balgas text. Moreover, the latter has *ungsiyulun üiledbesü ele,* which the *Ganǰur* text renders as *uribasu* ("if someone recites"). The *Ganǰur* text also uses the expression *qorin nigen qonoysan qoyin-a* ("after 21 days have passed") instead of *qorin nigen qonoy bolqu učir-tur* in the Xarbuxyn Balgas text.

The passage in the *Ganǰur dhāraṇī* quoted above precisely corresponds to that in the *bKa'-'gyur.* It reads: *gzuṅs -'di-'i cho-ga ni 'di yin-te naṅ-bar laṅs brgya-rtsa brgyad bzlas- brjod byas-na zag ni śu-rtsa gcid lon-pa'i tshe las-kyi sgrib-pa thams-cad zas-par 'gyur-ro.*[505]

---

503   For *bisiregesü;* the form *büsiren* is found in a Buddhist text from Turfan. See Cerensodnom and Taube, *Turfansammlung,* No. 22, and note 22r5, pp. 98–9. See also *büsire-* in § 170 of the *Secret History;* on the suffix *-yasu/-gesü*, see Poppe, *Grammar,* § 369, p. 96.
504   For *bilčaqu*, "to smear all over", Lessing, p. 103.
505   Vol. 11, 98/4/4–5.

It is also worth observing a phrase construction such as *qamuy amitan oyoyata balbarayulun (bolbasurayulun) üiledküi-luya ülü anggiǰiraqu boluyu* in the Xarbuxyn Balgas text. The *Ganǰur* has *qamuy amitan-i oyoyata bolbasurayul-un üiledküi-eče ülü qayačaqu boluyu* ("all living beings in their entirety will be not separated from achieving ripening"). The comitative *-luya* in the Xarbuxyn Balgas text follows the Tibetan, which reads *byed pa daṅ bral bar mi 'gyur ro.*[506]

* * *

Prayer for Rebirth (XBM 42 to XBM 45)

The text presented here is a prayer in the form of a litany expressing the wish to be born in front of the abodes of deities. The title of the text, of which we have 4 fragmentary copies, is as yet unknown. The Xarbuxyn Balgas prayer is especially interesting since it mentions the names of the abodes of deities. A fragmentary text of a prayer asking for rebirth in the realms *(ulus)* of deities was found in Olon Süme.[507] The Olon Süme text, however, does not indicate the names of the realms of these deities. Heissig regarded the Olon Süme text as the composition by a Mongol author.[508]

XBM 42

3 items (3 folios, 4 written sides) of a booklet *(debter)*, measuring ca. 15×5–15×5.5–16.5×5.5 cm, and having different numbers of lines, without page numbers. The text is written in two hands. The edges and sides of the folios are torn, but the text is well preserved.[509]

*1v

1 O *ilaǰu tegüs nögčigse[n]*
2 *tegünčilen iregsen dayini*
3 *daruysan üneger tuyuluysa[n]*
4 *abida burqan-tu mörgön*
5 *takin ǰalbarin itegemüi ::*
6 *abida burqan-tur mörgöm[üi]*

7 *umar-a ǰüg sükavadi-yi[n]*
8 *oron-tur*[510] *abida* **burqan** *say[un]*[511]
9 *bülüge yeke irügel-den-ü*
10 *törögsen yaǰar bui ::*
11 *tegün-ü emüne <> inu*
12 *törökü boltuyai ::*

---

506 Vol. 11, 98/4/7.
507 Heissig, *Handschriften-Reste*, pp. 456–66.
508 *Handschriften-Reste*, p. 465.
509 Folio *1 was restored by Mrs. Nebel; old number 32/5. Folios *2–*3 were restored by Mr. Bentchev; old number 31/6.
510 The text places the Sukhāvatī paradise, which is the realm of Buddha Amitābha, in the north instead of in the west. On the realm of Amitābha see Schwieger, *Ein Tibetisches Wunschgebet*, p. 14.
511 See *sayun* below in the text.

13 *emüne jüg vaiyiduri*[512] *erdeni*   16 *yurban oros*[514] *-i*
14 *oron-tur otočin-u*   17 *tebčin törögsen yajar*[515]
15 *qayan burqan sayun bül[üge]*[513]

*2r

1 *bui: tegün-ü emüne*   9 *töröku boltuyai :: öröne*
2 *inu töröku boltuyai ::*   10 *jüg čoy-tu ayulan-tur :*
3 *gandarigudun*[516] *ayulan-tur*   11 *qutuy-tu nagajuna*[517] *ečige*[518]
4 *ilaju tegüs nögčigsen*   12 *köbegün* **qoyar** *sayun bülüge ::*
5 *sigemuni burqan sayun*   13 *qoyar kijayar arilyan*
6 *bülüge :: qoyar čiyulyan-i*   14 *törögsen yajar bui : tegün-ü*[519]
7 *quriyan törögsen yajar*   15 *emüne inu törökü boltuyai ::*
8 *bui : tegün-ü emüne inu*   16 *kitad utaisang*[520]

*2v

1 *ayulan-tur ilayuysad-un*   5 *yajar bui : tegün-ü emüne*
2 *köbegün qutuy-tu*   6 *inu törökü boltuyai :: ayui*
3 *manjus[ir]i sayun bülüge ::*[521]   7 *yeke bodalang ayulan-tur*[522]
4 *yeke bilig-den-ü törögsen*   8 *idam qongsim*[523] *bodisung*

---

512 The letter *v* at the beginning of the word *vayiduri* (Skr. *vaidūrya*) is written like the letters *j*
     and *y* in the text. The Turfan text No. 46 has *vaiduri*. On this word, see the discussion by
     Cerensodnom and Taube in *Turfansammlung*, note 46r3, pp. 144–5; see *baiduri* the same as
     viidürij-e, "lapis lazuli" in Lessing, pp. 74, 894. The land of Bhaiṣajyaguru is located in the
     east, the colour of the land and god is dark blue (Tucci, *Painted Scroll*, p. 360). The Xarbuxyn
     Balgas text, however, has *emüne jüg* (south). For Bhaiṣajyaguru, "the master of medicine",
     also known as "the king of the blue lapis lazuli light", see Essen and Thingo, *Die Götter des
     Himalaya*, pp. 33–4.
513 The letter *ü* in second position is written with a superflous *yod* in the word *bülüge*. See also
     below in the text.
514 The plural form *oros* instead of the usual form *orod*; *oros* is also found in the Book of Prayers
     (XBM 41, 3v).
515 The word *sayun* and lines 16–17 are written in a different hand.
516 *gandiragud ayula* appears in "The Sino-Mongolian Inscription of 1346" (Cleaves writes
     gantiragud, p. 71). See *qajir sibayun čoylaysan ayula*, Skr. Gṛdhrakūṭaparvata; Tib. *bya-rgod
     phuṅ-po'i ri*, in Ishihama and Fukuda eds., *Mahāvyutpatti*, No. 4101; see also Monier-
     Williams, "vulture peak, name of a mountain near Rājagṛha", p. 361.
517 For *nagarjuna*. Nāgārjuna is the great Buddhist philosopher, who was deified and included
     among the northern Buddhist deities. See Getty, *The Gods of Northern Buddhism*, pp. 174–5.
518 *ečige* is legible in the original.
519 *tegün-ü* is legible in the original.
520 Wutai shan is the abode of Mañjuśrī.
521 The text reads *bülige*. Note that the scribe wrote the letter *ü* on the left of the word.
522 On Mount Potala, the abode of Qongsim Bodisung (Avalokiteśvara), see XBM 51–57 below
     in this volume.
523 There is a small split in the folio, which damaged the word *qongsim*, but the inital *q* is still legible.

9 *sayun bülüge yeke örösi* =[524]
10 *yelten-ü törögsen yaǰar bui :*
11 *tegün-ü emüne inu törökü*
12 *boltuyai :: čom qas dan-u* (?)[525] *degedü*

13 *ayui-tur niyučasun*
14 *eǰen*[526] *včir-a bani sayun bülüge ::*
15 **yeke** *küčü-den-ü törögsen yaǰar*
16 *bui : tegün-ü emüne inu*

*3r

1 *törökü boltuyai :: ulanbur*
2 *qarsi-tur qutuy-tu*
3 *<bodisung>*[527] **boyda** *dar-a eke*
4 *sayun bülüge :*[528] *urin*
5 *tačiyangyui-i*[529] *<>*[530]
6 *tebčin törögsen*
7 *yaǰar bui : tegün-ü emüne*

8 *inu törökü boltuyai ::*
9 *tabun küčün tegüsügsen*
10 *balyasun-tur* **yum-un** *qutuy-tu*
11 *bodisung sayun bülüge ::*
12 *<> berke qatayuǰil-iyar*
13 *törögsen yaǰar bui : tegün-ü*
14 *emüne inu törökü boltuyai :: oyoyata*

XBM 43

2 items of a *pothī* (2 fragments of folios, 3 written sides), measuring ca. 10.5 × 5, 6 × 3.5 cm, consisting of 13, 10–9 (r/v) lines respectively; the page number is missing on the fragment which was numbered *2v, according to the sequence of the text. The other fragment has the Mongolian page number *yurban* (3). This fragment is half-burnt.[531]

*2v

1 [   ] [sa]*yun bülüge : yurban*
2 [   ] *tebčin törögsen yaǰar*
3 [   ] *emüne inu törökü*

4 *[boltuyai] :: gandaragud*[532]
5 *[ayulan-t]ur*[533] *ilaǰu tegüs*
6 *[nögčigsen] sayun bülüge :: qoyar*

---

524 The letter *r* of *örösiyelten* is barely legible.
525 The abode of Vajrapāṇi is called *lcaṅ-lo-can*. See *Zang han da cidian*, p. 765. On the abode of this god, see also the *Čiqula kereglegči*, 28r (facsimile in Heissig, *Geschichtsschreibung*, I).
526 *niyuča-yin eǰen*, "lord of mysteries", is the epithet of Vajrapāṇi. The text has the plural form *niyučas* with the genitive suffix *-un* joined to the word.
527 This word was dotted by the scribe of the text.
528 According to *Noyoyan dar-a eke orosiba* (xylography belonging to the author) the abode of Tārā is a cave in Mount Potala (*bodalang ayula-yin ayui*, 1v), which is also the abode of Avalokiteśvara; *bodalang ayulan*, the abode of Tārā, appears at the very beginning of the 21 hymns to this goddess which form part of the inscriptions of Arǰai Ayui, Otoy Banner. Unfortunately, the original is illegible. See Qaserdeni et al., *Arǰai ayui-yin uyiyurǰin mongyol bičigesü*, pp. 129–30.
529 The accusative suffix *-i* instead of *-yi* after the word *tačiyangyui*.
530 A word was deleted by the scribe of the text.
531 The fragment without a page number was restored by Mrs. Nebel; old number 25/4; the other one was restored by Mr. Bentchev; old number 22/21.
532 For this name see the note to XBM 42, *2r:3.
533 See *ayulan-tur* in line 11.

7 *[čiɣulɣa]n-i*[534] *quriyan törögsen*
8 *[ɣaǰa]ar*[535] *bui :*[536] *tegünü emüne*
9 *[inu] töröküü*
10 *[boltuɣ]ai :: öröne ǰüg*

11 *[čoɣ-]tu*[537] *ayulan-tur*
12 *[qu]tuɣ-tu nagarǰun[a]*
13 *[e]čige*[538] *köbegün*

3r

1 *qoɣar sayun bülü[ge]*
2 *kiǰaɣar-i [ar]ilɣan*[539]
3 *ɣaǰar bui : tegün-ü [emüne inu]*
4 *töröküü boltuɣai :: [   ]*
5 *utai sang ayulan [   ]*

6 *ilaɣugsan-ud köbe[gün] [   ]*
7 *tu manǰusiri [   ]*
8 *yeke bilig [   ]*
9 *ɣaǰar bui : [   ]*
10 *töröküü [boltuɣai ::]*

3v

1 *[   ] aɣui-tur niɣučasun*[540]
2 *[   ] včirabani sayun*
3 *[   ] yeke küčüten-ü*
4 *[törögs]en*[541] *ɣaǰar bui :*
5 *[   ] inu töröküü*

6 *[boltuɣai ::] [ula]bur qarsi*
7 *[   ] boɣda dara*
8 *[   ] urin*
9 *[   ] törögsen*[542]

XBM 44

2 items (2 fragments of folios, 3 written sides); the first item (*1) measures 3 × 6 cm, and
has 2 lines; the second item (*2) measures 2.5 × 6 cm. The latter has 3 lines belonging to
the text on one side, while the other side shows 2 lines, which most probably belong to a
different text.[543]

*1

1 *emüne inu törögsen töröküü*

2 *[boltuɣai ::]*

---

534 See *čiɣulɣan* in XBM 42, *2v:6.
535 See XBM 42, *2v:7.
536 The section of the text (from lines 8 to 13) has a blank space between the words. Note that the
surface of the birch bark is uneven at this point.
537 See XBM 42, *2:10.
538 *qutuɣ-tu* and *ečige* appear in XBM 42, *2:11.
539 XBM 42, *2:13.
540 *niɣučasun* as in XBM 42, *2v:13.
541 XBM 42, *3:15.
542 This text is fragmentary. See the complete passage in XBM 42 (*1v:15–*3r:6).
543 Restored by Mrs. Nebel; old number 25/4.

*2r

1 *[...] mon*[544] *oron itegel*   3 *[...] oron-u bodisung*
2 *mayidari sayun bü[l]üge*

*2v

1 *süsüg-iyer itegen* < >[545]   2 *jalbaribasu alin-u nigülesküi*

XBM 45

1 item (1 small fragment of a folio, 1 written side), measuring 2 × 5 × 6 cm, with 3 lines on
one side, only the word *ǰug-ün (ǰüg-ün)* is left on the other side.[546]

1 *degedü ayui-ṯur törökü bol[tuyai ::]*   3 *sayitur medegči qutu[y]*
2 *kitad-un u[t]ai sang ayulan-ṯur*

* * *

Prayer for Salvation (XBM 46)

XBM 46 is a complete text in alliterative verses without a title. The text is a prayer expressing the wish to be reborn freed from sins and fear of hell, which includes all beings,
starting from the earliest ancestors to the small insects which live on earth. The origin of
the text remains a matter of controversy. However, on the basis of the alliteration of the
verses, the assonance of the words and especially the lexical content, which is discussed
below, one may infer that this text was written by a Mongol author.

XBM 46

1 complete *pothī*, composed of 5 folio (9 written sides), measuring 13 × 4.5 cm, and composed of different numbers of lines; the Mongolian page numbers are *nigen, qoyar,
yurban, dörben, tabun* (1–5). The text is well preserved.[547]

---

544 For *mön*.
545 The text reads *ǰalbasu*, which was correctly written in the next line (*ǰalbaribasu*).
546 Restored by Mr. Bentchev; old number 25/3.
547 Restored by Mr. Bentchev; old number 12.

Buddhist Prayers

1v

1	O *namo buday-a* :: : ::	5	*ǰaddam*[549] **ötög qutuɣ** *ungsiǰu*
2	O *namo darmay-a* :: : ::	6	*ungsituɣai :*
3	O *namo sangɣay- a*[548] :: : ::	7	*eng urida*[550]
4	*oom savasid-ṭi*		

2r

1	*elingčüɣ qulingčuɣ*[551]	6	*qanilan yabuɣsan*
2	*borqan bodančaɣ*[552]	7	*nökör següder*
3	*[e]büge ečige*	8	*qataɣuǰin*
4	*qamtu*[553] *törögsen :*	9	*[a]rɣaɣsan : baɣsi*
5	*ečige eke*		

2v

1	*sibi tebirigsen*[554]	3	*sen*[555] *köbegün*
2	*eme törögülü =*	4	*ači ür-e*[556]

---

548 For *sanggay-a*.

549 Instead of *suvasdi siddam, svasti siddhaṃ*.

550 The formula *eng urida* is often attested in the early texts, though it also occurs in the later sources. See Manduqu, *Hua yi yi yu* (p. 111) *ang urida; ang* is an orthographic feature going back to Uighur; see also *eṇg urida* in the "Summary of the *Bodhicaryāvatāra*" = Ceren-sodnom and Taube, *Turfansammlung* (No. 42, p. 137). The Olon Süme fragment OS IV/ 111–12 also has the formula *eng urida* (Heissig, *Handschriften-Reste*, p. 540), which likewise appears in the *Erdeni-yin tobči* (Urga text, 1r); on *eng türün, eng uridu, eng urida, angqa urida* etc., see the discussion by de Rachewiltz in "The Preclassical Mongolian Version of the Hsiao-ching", note 29, pp. 57–8. For the occurance of *eng urida* in a ritual text, see the passage quoted in note 556 below.

551 Instead of *elinčüg qulinčuɣ, qulunčuɣ*.

552 *borqan* is the plural of *borqai; bodančaɣ* must be an error for *bodančar*. These terms are discussed in the commentary.

553 The ink is faded at this point, but the word *qamtu* is still legible in the original.

554 For *šabi, teberigsen*.

555 For *törögülügsen*. The text shows the irregular use of the suffixes (*-ɣsan, -gsen/-san, -sen*); Poppe regards *-san/-sen* as a suffix of the spoken language ("Alexandersage", p. 122, note 77). It is thus possible that this is a suffix of the colloquial language as Poppe states. The text, however, contains numerous spelling errors.

556 A text of the incense offering of the fox (*ünegen sang*) of the Qadagin Mongols includes a passage which shows similar words to those which appear in the Xarbuxyn Balgas text. It reads: *eng urida ečige eke elünčeg qulunčaɣ-tur burtaɣ boluɣsan bolbasu ünegen-ü miqan čisun-iyar takin arilɣatuɣai. emege eke-yin emege eke-dür burtaɣ boluɣsan bolbasu ünegen-ü üsün yasun-iyar takin arilɣatuɣai. qoyitu köbegün ači-nar-tur burtaɣ boluɣsan bolbasu ünegen-ü tabun erketen-iyer takin arilɣatuɣai.* See Qurčabaɣatur, *Qadagin arban ɣurban ataɣ-a tngri*, p. 146.

5　etügen <>[557]
6　degereki simuɣul

3r

1　ǰirɣuɣan költü
2　ba : dörben
3　költü ba :
4　qoyar költü

3v

1　görögesün ulusun
2　kiling usun
3　dotoroki[558] **amitan-u** kiling
4　[a]man-ṯu ide[g]sen

4r

1　quriɣaɣsan
2　buruɣu kilinče
3　üiledügsen burtaɣ
4　idegen idegsen

4v

1　siditü ba [:][562]
2　sidi ügei
3　ba [:] qoyolai
4　tula alaɣsan

7　sirɣulǰi naiman
8　költü ba :

5　ba : köl ügei
6　ba : deger -e
7　niskü sibaɣun
8　güikü

5　alan-ṯu[559] unuɣ =
6　san köldü
7　dayarigsan
8　nidün-ṯü

5　küčir kelegsen
6　kundü[560] nigül
7　kilinče üiles
8　tügesen[561] deger-e

5　mal qotolober[563]
6　toniltuɣai :
7　törötügei :

557　A word was deleted by the scribe of the text. However, one would expect the word *eke* after *etügen*.
558　The regular form is *dotoraki*; see *qotolober* below. These forms reflect the spoken language.
559　For *alaɣan*, reflecting the spoken language.
560　Instead of *kündü*.
561　For *tügegsen*.
562　The previous passage has the *dabqur čeg* after *ba*.
563　For *qotala*; on the Qalqa *xotol* see Cėvėl, p. 699; the form *qotola* appears both in the *Secret History* (§ 105), and Turfan text No. 31, while *qotol* appears in a Turfan text dating back to a later period (No. 96). See Cerensodnom and Taube, *Turfansammlung*, pp. 119, 197.

5r

1	*qoyitu töröl*	6	*toniltuyai :*[567]
2	*-tür ayud*[564]	7	*törötügei :*[568]
3	*tamudača*[565]	8	*oom man i*
4	*altan öngge-tü*	9	*bad mi*
5	*lingquu-tača*[566]	10	*qung ::*

5v

1	*sadu edgü*	3	*boltuyai*
2	*nasun qutuy*		

The text was transcribed according to the sequence in the original. In so doing, however, the alliteration of the verses is not evident. The text should be arranged as follows. *oom suvasid-ti ǰaddam / ötög qutuy ungsiǰu ungsituyai / eng urida / elingčüy qulingčuy borqan bodančay / ebüge ečige qamtu törögsen | ečige eke | qanilan yabuysan nökör següder / qatayuǰin [a]ryaysan baysi sibi,* etc.

The Xarbuxyn Balgas prayer is an interesting text, which is composed of compound words. It also contains terms which merit scrutiny.

We can observe the rare occurrence of *ötög qutuy* (1v:5). The first term, *ötög,* appears in the *Secret History (ötök)* in the meaning of "drink which is offered".[569] The term is also attested in *Boyda činggis qayan-u takil-un sudur,* "The book of the offerings to the holy

---

564　The text has the plural form of *ayul.* For this plural, see Poppe, *Grammar,* § 267, p. 71. As Kara remarks, the term *ayis, ayus,* which occurs in combination with *tamu,* has been related to the Mongol verb *ayu-* (> and ~ *ayi-*). Kara also adds that this is a popular etymology based on the erroneous interpretation of the Uighur *aviš* in the expression *aviš tamu.* The latter ultimately corresponds to the Indian *avīci* ("L'ancien ouighur dans le lexique mongol", p. 319); see *ayuš tamu* in the Olon Süme fragment OS IV/97r (Heissig, *Handschriften-Reste,* p. 418); *ayis tamu* occurs in *Molon Toyin's Journey into Hell* (Lőrincz, p. 75).

565　In *tamudača* we have the combined pre-classical dative-locative suffix *-da* and the ablative suffix *-ča* joined to the word. For the combined suffix *-dača /-deče, -tača /-teče* see Poppe, *Grammar,* § 300, p. 78; see also Weiers, *Untersuchungen,* pp. 105–7. See the form *tamu-tača* in Cerensodnom and Taube, *Turfansammlung,* No. 36, p. 132, and in Heissig, *Handschriften-Reste,* OS IV/91v, p. 472.

566　*lingquu* instead of the usual spelling *lingqu-a.* The text refers to the two Cold Hells called *badma (padma),* "lotus", and *udbala (utpala),* "blue lotus", in which, because of the great cold, the flesh of the sufferers falls away from the bones like the petals of a lotus. See the *Čiqula kereglegči,* 24r–24v (facsimile in Heissig, *Geschichtsschreibung,* I); see also Waddel, *Buddhism of Tibet,* p. 96. On the Cold Hell called *padma* in a Tibetan prayer, see Poucha, "Das tibetische Totenbuch", pp. 150–1.

567　See the expressions *tamu-tača tonilbasu* in Cerensodnom and Taube, *Turfansammlung,* No. 36, p. 132, and *küiten tamu-ača toniltuyai* in Heissig, *Handschriften-Reste,* OS IV/33, p. 459.

568　See *küiten tamu-ača toniltuyai qonsiim bodisung-un ulus-tur törötügei* in the Olon süme text quoted in the note above.

569　See §§ 154, 272; see also Haenisch *Wörterbuch,* p. 129.

Činggis qaγan", which dates back to the 17th century. It is a ritual text which describes the ceremonies in honour of Činggis. In this text, the term *ötög* refers both to kumiss and milk brandy which are offered during the ceremonies, accompanied by the songs 'in the language of the gods' and the music of the *čargi*.[570] The term *ötög* is listed in dictionaries of the modern Mongolian dialects, but with different meanings.[571]

The Mongol word *ötög* corresponds to the Turkic *ötüg*, which means "prayer, rite of invitation, invitation formula".[572] The term *ötügči* appears in the Uighur *Altun yaruq sudur* in the meaning of "suppliant".[573] Moreover, the Turkic verb *ötün-*, "to say, to pray", corresponds to the Mongolian *öči-*,[574] meaning "to say, to pray, to chant, to inform, to report".[575] The Mongolian noun *öčig* means "prayer, eulogy, ceremonial song, report";[576] the Ordos *ö'ts'ök* has the meaning of "prayer recited in high voice at an offering".[577] The second element *qutuγ*, "happiness" is well-known.[578]

In conclusion, the phrase *ötög qutuγ ungsiǰu ungsituγai* (1v:5–6) can be translated as "let one recite the prayer which brings happiness", (lit. "let one recite, reciting, the happiness-prayer").

The text has *elingčüγ qulingčuγ* (2r:1) (for *elinčüg qulinčuγ, qulunčuγ*). The term *elinčüg* appears in the *Secret History*, and also in other early texts. It means "great- grandfather".[579] Ramstedt lists *elṇtsǝɢ* in the meaning of "Die ahnen in der vierten und fünften generation rückwärts".[580]

---

570   See Chiodo, "The Book of the Offerings", part I, pp. 198, 207, and part II, pp. 86, 89–90, 108–9.

571   *ötög* means "manure" (Lessing, p. 646); "kumiss or liquid which settle to the bottom of a container" (Cévél, p. 448).

572   Pelliot, "Note sur le Turkestan", p. 31 and note 1; see also *ötüg*, "Bitte, Gebet, Eingabe, Frage" in von Gabain, *Grammatik*, p. 352.

573   See Zieme, p. 222.

574   Doerfer, *Türkische und Mongolische Elemente*, vol. 2, No. 574, p. 134.

575   *Mongγol üges-ün iǰayur-un toli*, p. 460; on *öči-* "dire, rapporter, communiquer (inférieur à supérieur)", see the discussion by Mostaert and Cleaves in *Les lettres*, p. 26.

576   Lessing, p. 629; *Mongγol üges-ün iǰayur-un toli*, p. 461; see *öči'üli* in § 103 of the *Secret History*.

577   Mostaert, *Dictionnaire ordos*, p. 543a.

578   See § 200 of the *Secret History*; Kowalewski lists *qutuγ* meaning "bonheur, félicité, bénédiction, sainteté, divinité", p. 918; on the term *qutuγ*, see also the remarks by Mostaert and Cleaves (*Les lettres*, p. 26); the *qut* indicates one of the three souls of a person in Turkic, and it became synonimous of happiness (Kotwicz, "Formules initiales", p. 147); von Gabain lists *qut* in the meaning of "Glück, Segen, Würde, Majestät, Geist" (*Grammatik*, p. 360).

579   § 180; see Haenisch, *Wörterbuch*, p. 43; see also Cleaves, "The Sino-Mongolian Inscription of 1362", p. 63, and the discussion of the term in note 56, pp. 104–5; Mostaert and Cleaves, *Les lettres (alinčeg, elinčeg)*, p. 55; de Rachewiltz, "The Preclassical Mongolian Version", *(elinčüg)*, pp. 33, 45 and note 90, p. 73.

580   *Kalmückisches Wörterbuch*, p. 120; see also Lessing (*elünče, elünčeg*, "great-grandfather", p. 311); the *Mongγol üges-ün iǰayur-un toli* (p. 222) has *elünče, elünčig*; the *Wu-T'i Ch'ing-Wen-Chien* (vol. I, Nos. 4484–5) has *elunče ebüge, elünče emege*.

The term *qulingčuɣ* is usually attested as *qulunča* in the meaning of "great-great-grandfather".[581] Ramstedt registers both *χulṇtsʋɢ*, "Grossvaters Grossvater",[582] and the compound *elṇtsəɢ χulṇtsʋɢ*, "Die Urväter".[583] In the *Wu-T'i Ch'ing-Wen-Chien* we find that the earliest ancestors are called *öndör ebüge* (Chin. *shizu*), while the great-great-grandfather and the great-great-grandmother are called *qulunča ebüge, qulunča emege*.[584] According to Vreeland, the Qalqas refer to all preceding generations as *öndör ebüge*.[585]

It is also interesting to note the unique occurrence of *borqan bodančaɣ* in the Xarbuxyn Balgas text. The first element *borqan* is the ancient plural in *-n* of *borqai*.[586] The term *borqai* appears in §180 of the *Secret History*, and is glossed as *gaozu*, "great-great- grandfather";[587] *borqai, boroqai* is also found in the *Hua yi yi yu*. Haenisch translates this term as "Vorfähren 4. Grades".[588]

The second element *bodančaɣ* must be an error for *bodančar*. It is possible that this error occurred because the original copy of the text had a final *r* written in an early orthography, which the copyist took as a *ɣ*. It is also possible that the form *bodančaɣ* was used to create assonance with the preceding words *ötög qutuɣ, elingčüɣ qulingčuɣ*.[589] As far as I know, the term *bodančar* did not survive in the eastern dialects, but dictionaries of the western dialects list this term. Ramstedt has *bodṇtsᵊr*, "Vorfahr, Ururgrossväter", pointing out that this is a rare term.[590] Moreover, Coloo registers *bodantsar* in the dictionary of the Oyirad dialect which he compiled.[591]

As a result, the prayer from Xarbuxyn Balgas provides us with a list of kinship terms beginning with *elinčüg qulinčuɣ* down to *törögsen ečige eke*, "one's own parents" (2r:4–5). As has been indicated, according to Ramstedt, *elṇtsəɢ χulṇtsʋɢ* are the earliest ancestors.[592]

581   *Mongɣol üges-ün iǰaɣur-un toli*, p. 1128; Lessing, p. 985.
582   p. 196.
583   p. 120.
584   Vol. I, Nos. 4482–3.
585   Vreeland, *Mongol Community and Kinship Structure*, p. 57a.
586   On this plural form see Poppe, *Grammar*, §272, p. 72.
587   See Haenisch, *Wörterbuch*, p. 19.
588   *Sinomongolische Glossare*, vol. I, p. 21; the term *borqai, boroqai* is listed in *Mongɣol üges-ün iǰaɣur-un toli*, p. 775. It is interesting to note that the ancient term *borqai* is found in the section of the book *Mongɣoljin-u šasin surtaqun* (Altanɣarudi et al., p. 21), which deals with ancestor worship.
589   I am most grateful to Prof. Igor de Rachewiltz for his suggestions regarding the form *bodančaɣ*.
590   *Kalmückisches Wörterbuch*, p. 48; see also Muniev, *Kalmycko-russkij slovar'*, p. 104; both *xulanč* and *bodončar* are found in Doerfer, *Türkische und mongolische Elemente*, vol. I, pp. 217–218.
591   *BNMAU dax' mongol xėlnij nutgijn ajalguuny tol' bičig*, II, Ojrd ajalguu, p. 103.
592   A list of kinship terms is also included in *Köke ǰula. Mongɣol ulamǰilaltu amidural-un toli*, (Vangǰil, chap. 2, pp. 10–13); see *manu sayin alinčeg sayin abüge sayin ačige sayin aqa* in the letter of Ölǰeitü (Mostaert and Cleaves, *Les lettres*, p. 55).

The text under discussion also has the expression *nökör següder,* (2r:7), lit. "companion-shadow", which is placed after *törögsen ečige eke,* thus stressing the close relationship of a *nökör següder* with a person. The expression *nökör següder* occurs in §214 of the *Secret History (nökör se'üder)*[593] and in other early works.[594] Haenisch correctly translates *nökör següder* as "unzertrennlicher Gefährte".[595]

As for the question of whether the prayer from Xarbuxyn Balgas is a Mongolian composition or a translation, it has been pointed out that the text shows the alliteration of the verses and the assonance of the terms, which are features of Mongolian poetry. It is, of course, true that there are examples of Mongolian translations of Tibetan poetry in alliterative verses,[596] but the terms and expressions which have been discussed so far, suggest a Mongolian cultural background.

---

593 de Rachewiltz, *Index,* p. 123.
594 See Cleaves, "The Lingǰi of Aruγ", p. 43, and the discussion in note 63, pp. 65–6; see also Ligeti, "*Subhāṣitaratnanidhi* mongol", p. 256; de Rachewiltz, "The Preclassical Mongolian Version of the Hsiao-ching", p. 38 and the discussion in note 290, p. 80; Cerensodnom and Taube, *Turfansammlung,* No. 9, p. 70; *nökör següder* is also found in the *Altan tobči* (6v).
595 *Wörterbuch,* p. 134.
596 See the poems in alliterative verses which form part of the *Vajracchedikā* (Poppe, *Diamond Sutra*); see also the discussion by Cerensodnom and Taube in *Turfansammlung,* pp. 122–3, and in the same work (No. 33, pp. 120–2) the poem on the *Prajñapāramitā,* which is regarded as being the composition by a Mongol author. On the history of the Mongolian verse forms, see the the article by Kara "Old Mongolian Verses", pp. 162–8.

The Worship of Avalokiteśvara

The Xarbuxyn Balgas collection includes numerous copies of eight different texts,[1] mainly fragmentary, devoted to Avalokiteśvara, the Buddhist god of compassion, pointing to the existence of a body of texts dedicated to this deity in northern Mongolia in the first part of the 17th century. Avalokiteśvara is given different names in the texts. This god is also described in different manifestations.

Hymn to Qongsim Bodisung (XBM 47 to XBM 50)

We have a complete text (XBM 47)[2] and fragments of three copies of a hymn to Qongsim Bodisung. The title of the text is found at the end of XBM 47 and XBM 49. XBM 47 has *Qutuγ-tu qongsim bodisung-un aldarsin dügürügsen neretü sudur nom nigen ǰüil-iyer qutuγtu yeke kölge nom sudur*, "One chapter of the holy mahāyāna-sūtra called Perfect Praise of the Holy Qongsim Bodisung",[3] while XBM 49 reads *Qongsim bodi sadu aldarsin dügürgegsen neretü su[dur] nom-a [ni]gen ǰüil-yi-iyer*. The original from which the text was translated is as yet unknown.

The text describes Qongsim Bodisung with eight hands and eleven heads (Ekādaśamukha-Avalokiteśvara)[4], and emphasises the power of the recitation of the six-syllable formula *oṃ maṇi padme hūm*.

The same hymn to Qongsim Bodisung as that from Xarbuxyn Balgas was circulating in southern Mongolia at the turn of the 16th century, as two fragments from Olon Süme show. Heissig identified the fragments as a section of *Altan quyaγ-tu kemekü neretü yeke kölgen sudur*, "The mahāyāna-sūtra called The Golden Armour", which is one of the titles of the text.[5] The Olon Süme fragments are regarded as the earliest stage of transmission of the text hitherto known. We can, however, observe the occurance of early

---

1 One text dedicated to this deity is included in XBM 41.
2 The complete text XBM 47 was translated into English and discussed by Chiodo in the article "A Hymn to Qongsim Bodisung on birch bark from Xarbuxyn Balgas (Bulgan Ajmag)", pp. 223–49.
3 On the meanings of *ǰüil*, see Lessing, p. 1193; see also *dharma-paryāya*, "discourse on dharma" in Conze, *Vajracchedikā Prajñāpāramitā*, pp. 37, 74.
4 See Toyka-Fuong, *Ikonographie und Symbolik* (B), between pp. 78–9; Essen and Thingo, *Die Götter des Himalaya*, p. 77; on the various iconographies of Avalokiteśvara see Tachikawa et al., *Hundred Buddhist Deities*, pp. 295–300.
5 See Heissig, *Handschriften-Reste*, pp. 326–34.

spellings such as *sanggay-a* and *saqin* in both the Olon Süme fragment OS/IV 101–4 r[6] and XBM 47.

Copies of the hymn to Qongsim Bodisung are included in catalogues of Mongolian books.[7] I had access to the following: *Qongsim bodisung-un aldarsiysan dügüregsen neretü sudur*, "The sūtra called Perfect Praise of Qongsim Bodisung". The text was found in Khiakta by Jaehrig in 1795.[8]

Altan quyay-tu kemekü neretü yeke kölgen sudur, "The mahāyāna-sūtra called The Golden Armour". The latter is found on the title page, while *Qomsim bodisung aldarsin dügüregsen neretü nom nigen bačag nigen ǰüil-iyer* is found at the end of the text. The text was found in Inner Mongolia and is preserved in Louvain University Library.[9]

Moreover, there is a fragmentary text without the title page. This text was incorrectly identified as being the *Ganǰur dhāraṇī Mahākāruṇika-nāma-āryāvalokiteśvara*, and listed under this title in the catalogue *Mongolische Handschriften*.[10] The Mongolian *Ganǰur* does contain a *dhāraṇī* called *Mahākāruṇika-nāma-āryāvalokiteśvara-dhāraṇī-anuśaṃsā-sahitā sūtrāt saṃgṛhitā, Qutuy-tu yeke nigülesügči qomsim bodisung bodhisaduva-yin tarni ači tusa tobčilan quriyaysan neretü*, "The *dhāraṇī* of the great holy compassionate Qomsim Bodisung called Collection of Benefits".[11] However, despite the textual similarities with the text with which we are concerned it is a different text.

Finally, there is a copy of the text which I acquired in Ulaanbaatar in 1996. The title page bears *Altan quyay-tu-yin sudur*, "The sūtra of the Golden Armour", while *Qutuy-tu qongsim bodisung aldarsin dügüregsen neretü sudur nigen ǰüil-iyer* is found at the end of the text. On the basis of palaeographic and orthographic features this manuscript can be dated back to the end of the 17th century.[12]

XBM 47

1 complete booklet *(debter)*, measuring ca. 16×9.5 cm, and composed of 4 folios (7 written sides), without page numbers; it has 15–17 lines. Previously the left sides of the folios were stitched together, but now the folios are loose. Apart from holes and splits in the folios, the text is fairly well preserved and legible.[13]

It should be noted that various words are written separately in this text. For example, *nigülesüg-čiyin* (2v:15) etc. However, in a number of cases words are written separately because the copyist used pieces of birch bark with holes and splits in their surface. This

---

6 *Handschriften-Reste*, p. 328.
7 On *Altan quyay-tan orosiba*, which is preserved in the Library of the Hungarian Academy of Sciences, see Heissig, *Handschriften-Reste*, p. 326, note 2.
8 Heissig and Sagaster, *Mongolische Handschriften*, Ms. Asch 130, No. 453, p. 249.
9 Heissig, "The Mongol Manuscripts and Xylographs", No. 27, p. 174.
10 Heissig and Sagaster, Ms. or. oct. 422-6, No. 202, p. 125.
11 *Ganǰur*, vol. 17, No. 385, pp. 91–9.
12 Further evidence of the circulation of the text under discussion in northern Mongolia is *Qongsim bodi sadu-yin aldarsigsan degüregsen neretü sudur*. The manuscript belongs to Mr. Süxbat's private collection. I was able to see this text in the summer of 1997.
13 Restored by Mr. Bentchev; old number 31.

obviously prevented the copyist from joining the words, e.g.: *ungsi-gči* (3 r:2), *ungsibas-u* (3 v:12) etc.

1 v

1 O *namo buday-a :: kemejü ene nigen silüg ungsi* =
2 *basu ači inu arban qoyar altan quyaytan*
3 *doloyan erdeni-ber* [14] *čimegsen duyulyatu* O *namo darmay* =
4 *a :: kemejü ene nigen silüg ungsibasu ači inu*
5 **arban** *qoyar mönggön quyaytan* [15] *altan duyulyatu*
6 O *namo sanggay-a ::* [16] *kemejü ene nigen silüg*
7 *ungsibasu ači inu arban qoyar temür*
8 *quyaytan mönggön duyulyatu yerü yučin jiryu* =
9 *[yan] <ulsun>* **sakiyulsun** [17] *saqin bui ::* [18] *ene yurban*
10 *silü[g]* [19] *kemebesü yurban erdeni=sün* [20] *sitügen inu*
11 *[...]n* [21] *buyu :: küseküi sedkil-iyer egüskebei* [22] *teri* =
12 *gülesi ügei olan amitan-i qongsim* [23] *bodisung-un*
13 *qutuyolqu boltuyai ::* O *oom qung subauu-a sido*
14 *qang* [24] *kemen qoyoson* [25] *kü boltuyai :: qoyoson kü ayar*
15 *-tur bam üsüg badm-a lingqu-a sečeg-ün* [26] *üjüg*

---

14 For *doloyan erdeni* "the seven kinds of gems" see Sárközi ed., *Mahāvyutpatti*, p. 260.

15 The Olon Süme version has *quyay-tan*. See Heissig, *Handschriften-Reste*, OS IV/101–4r, p. 328.

16 As has been mentioned, *sanggay-a* occurs in OS IV/101–4r. This form also occurs in Tantric Uighur texts. See, for example, Kara and Zieme, *Fragmente*, p. 40; Ms. Asch 130, (1v:9), Louvain No. 27 (1r:8) and the Ms. belonging to the author have *sangghay-a*.

17 The top section of the folio is torn at this point so that only a part of the word *sakiyulsun* remains; it was written again between the lines.

18 The pre-classical form *saqin* follows the modern form *sakiyulsun*; *sakiyulsun*, side by side with *saqin*, also occurs in OS IV/101/104r (*Handschriften-Reste*, p. 328). Ligeti states that the spelling *qi, yi* was employed in the 15th and 16th centuries, and some examples dating from the early 17th century are attested in the Qalqa. See "A propos de quelques texts", p. 265. The converbum modale *saqin* with *bui* expresses continuous actions. See Poppe, *Grammar*, § 575, p. 161.

19 XBM 48, 2r:4 has *silüg-üd-i;* XBM 49, 2r:5 has *silüg-yi* (see below); Ms. Asch 130, 2r:2 has *silüg-üd*.

20 The spelling *erdeni-sün* occurs in another Olon Süme text. See Heissig, *Handschriften-Reste*, OS I/10r, p. 411.

21 Ms. or. oct. 422-6, 2r:7 has *sitün;* Ms. Asch 130 (2r:3), Louvain No. 27 (1v:13–14) and XBM 48, 2r:5–6 (see below) have *sitügen inu bui*.

22 XBM 48, 2r:6–7 reads *küseküi sedkil egüskeküi;* Ms. Asch 130, 2r:4: *küseküi sedkil egüskejü;* Louvain No. 27, 1v:14–15: *küseküi sedkil egüskebesü*.

23 OS IV/101–4r has *qonsiim*. The same spelling is found in XBM 48, 2r:8; Ms. or. oct. 422-6, 2v:10 has *qomsim*. In a Turfan fragment we find *qonši-im* (< Chin. *guanshiyin*) as in ancient Turkic. See Cerensodnom and Taube, *Turfansammlung*, No. 45, p. 144, and note 45r6.

24 OS IV/101–4r, also reads *qang;* Louvain No. 27, (1r:17) reads *ham*. The *mantra* for the dissolution of oneself into emptiness is oṃ svabhāva-śuddhāḥ sarva-dharmāḥ svabhāva-śuddho haṃ. See Beyer, *The Cult of Tārā*, p. 144.

25 See the spelling *qoyoson* in the *Mongyol kitad toli*, p. 653.

2r

1　*edeni nigen de ungsibasu minu bey-e qubilǰu beki*
2　*<> bolba :*[27] *ariɣun sedkil-iyer minu ǰirüken degereki*
3　*bam üǰüg qubilǰu lingqu-a čečeg bolba :*
4　*tere degere*[28] *üǰüg saran mandal degere qung*
5　*üǰüg-eče čayan önggetü gerel talbibai : olan*
6　*amitan-i geyigülüged qongsim bodisung bolbai :*
7　*mön gerel ɣarɣayulǰu siri*[29] *üǰüg-tür kürbei*
8　*siri üǰüg qubilǰu qongsim : bodisung bol[bai :]*
9　*čayan önggetü arban nigen niɣur-tu naiman ɣar*
10　*-tu gürü sarva namo oom mani bad mi qung ::*
11　*ene ǰirɣuyan üǰüg-tü kemeǰü ene tarni-yi üngsi =*
12　*basu*[30] *mön bey-e qubilǰu mingɣan ɣar-tu mingɣan*
13　*nidü-tü qongsim bodisung-un bey-e bütükü : boltuɣai*[31]
14　*:: qamuɣ nom-ud-i medekü boluɣu:: ene tarni-yi üng =*
15　*sibasu nidün*[32] *gegegen nemekü bolqu boluɣu :: qamuɣ*
16　*amitan-i tonilɣaqu*[33] *boluɣu :: uran arɣa*

2v

1　*bilig-yi olqu boluɣu :: sečen mergen bilig-yi*
2　*olqu boluɣu ::*[34] *mayui ǰobalang-ača tonilqu*
3　*boluɣu :: saysabad-un tergegüri olqu boluɣu::*
4　*qutuɣ möri olqu boluɣu ::*[35] *ene tarni-yi ungsibasu*

26　*sečeg, čečeg.*
27　Ms. Asch 130, 2r:9–14: *qoyoson-u ayar-dur bam süsüg-eče badm-a lingqu-a üǰüg-eče saran mandal-un deger-e ede-i kemeǰü. nigen-te ungsibasu. minu bey-e qubilǰu beki bolba;* Ms. or. oct. 422-6, *qoyoson-u ayar-tur bam üǰüg qubilǰu badm-a lingqu-a edeni. kemen nigen-te ungsibasu minu bey-e beki bolba.*
28　A word is missing at this point. XBM 48, 2v:3 has *a üsüg;* XBM 49, 2v:6: *e e üǰüg.* Louvain No. 27, 2r:11: *e üsüg.*
29　Ms. Asch 130, 2v:10: *qari üǰüg;* Louvain No. 27, 2v:16: *hari üsüg.*
30　Instead of *ungsibasu.* See the spelling *üngsibasu* in lines 14–15; XBM 48, 3r:8–9: *ene ǰirɣuyan tarni-yi ǰayun naiman da ungsibasu;* Ms Asch 130, 3r:4–5: *ene ǰirɣuyan üǰüg-tü tarni-yi kemeǰü ungsibasu;* Louvain No. 27, 2v:5–6: *ene ǰirɣuyan üsüg-tü tarni kemeǰü ǰayun naiman ta ungsibasu;* the Ms. belonging to the author, 2v:11–12: *ene ǰirɣuyan üsüg tarni-yi ünen čing sedkil-iyer ungsibasu.*
31　Ms Asch 130 3r:6–8: *mön bey-e qubilǰu mingɣan ɣar-tu qongsim bodisug bolba. minu bey-e bütükü boltuɣai.* This text omits *mingɣan nidü-tü.*
32　Louvain No. 27, 2v:8: *nidün-dür;* Ms. or. oct. 422-6, *nidü-tür.*
33　Ms. or. oct. 422-6, 4r:3: *qamuɣ amitan-i ǰobalang-ača tonilɣaqu.*
34　XBM 49 and Ms. Asch 130 omit *sečen mergen bilig-yi olqu boluɣu.*
35　XBM 48, 3v:10–11, Louvain No. 27, 3r:2–3, Ms. or. oct. 422-6, 4v:1–2, and Ms. Asch 130, 3v:5–6 add *nom-un bey-e-luɣ-a teng bolqu boluɣu.*

5 *yambar ba ǰebendü*³⁶ *ülü dayariydaqu boluyu :: qala =*
6 *yun usun yal ber sirgireǰü*³⁷ *sönekü boluyu :*³⁸ *asu =*
7 *ri-nar-tur kürbesü sedkil-iyer inu nomoqan boluyu ::*
8 *aduyusun-u töröl-eče-(tür ?) tonilqu boluyu ::*³⁹ *[ni]gen*⁴⁰
9 *sedkil-iyer qongsim bodisung namai sedkibesü*
10 *ǰayun mingyan yalabad-un kilinče bügüde aldara =*
11 *qu boluyu : ene bey-e tebčiküi čay-tur qamuy erketü*
12 *burqan bodisung-nar oyta-ryui-tur*⁴¹ *ireǰü alayan*
13 *-ban qamtudqaǰu oroi degere talbiǰu sükavadi*⁴²
14 *neretü*⁴³ *yirtinčü-tür uduridču odqu boluyu : ene*
15 *yeke nigülesüg-čiyin ene tarni-yi ken ungsiqui*

3r

1 *bolbasu*⁴⁴ *ǰiryuy[a]n mayui töröl*⁴⁵ *ülü abqu*
2 *boluyu :*⁴⁶ *ked ber ungsi-gči*⁴⁷ *kümün tamu-tur*
3 *odbasu bi büged burqan buu bolsuyai :*

---

36 Louvain No. 27, 3r:5: *ir ǰebe ülü dayariqu boluyu;* the Ms. belonging to the author, 3r:13 has *ǰebe-tü.* The *dhāraṇī* A *ary-a avalogide šuvari-yin arban nigen niyur-tu kemegdekü,* which is included in the *Zungdui,* reads: *eregün-i tarqayči. mese-i tebčiküi. qoor-a-yi tarqan üiledküi kiged. ked ber nigen nigen qarsilan üiledküi tere boluyu* (206r).
37 Louvain No. 27, 3v:6–8: *qalayun usun ba. yal ber sirgeǰü sönökü boluyu. birid-tür kürbesü čadqulang boluyu.* The latter sentence is omitted in The Xarbuxyn Balgas text. The *Zungdui* has: *usun-iyer ükükü ülü bolumui. yal-iyar ükükü ülü bolumui* (207r).
38 See a similar passage in the *Gegen toli* (8r–8v): *yal usun quura irtü mese degere dooraki qoor tan büged. alan ülü čidayu. Gegen toli* = Ligeti, "La collection", p. 173.
39 *Ganǰur,* No. 385, p. 93: *bi büged asuri-nar -un oron-dur odbasu. mayui sedkil öber-iyen bügüde nomoyadqu boluyu. bi büged aduyusun-u oron-dur odbasu. öber-iyen bilig-i olqu boltuyai.* The *Gegen toli* (8v) has *ma üǰüg asuri-yin bayilduyan-ača tonilyayu … bad üǰüg aduyusun-u ǰobalang-ača tonilyayu. mi üǰüg birid-ün ǰobalang-ača tonilyayu.* On this passage see Sørensen, *The Mirror,* p. 106.
40 A part of this word is legible in the original.
41 The word *oytaryui* is written separately because there is a hole in the folio.
42 Skr. *Sukhāvatī.*
43 Ms. Asch 130, 4r:12–13 and XBM 49, 5r:6 add *ǰiryalang-tu;* Ms. or. oct. 422-6, 5r:11 writes *ǰiryalang-du.*
44 Ms. Asch 130 4v:3: *ungsibasu;* Ms. or. oct. 422-6, 5v:4: *ungsigči bolbasu.*
45 *ǰiryuyan mayui töröl* are the six *gati,* "the six evil rebirths" (i.e. hell, hungry ghosts, animal, man, demi-gods and gods). On Avalokiteśvara, who goes to these places to preach the teachings of the six-syllable formula, see Sørensen, *The Mirror,* pp. 111–12.
46 Ms. or. oct. 422-6, 5v:6: *ülü töröku boluyu;* Ms. Asch 130 (4v:3–5), Louvain No. 27 (3v:6–7) and the Ms. belonging to the author (4r:3–4) have *ülü odqu boluyu.*
47 This word is written separately because there is a split in the folio.

4 *qutuy ese olbasu*[48] *ene tarni-yi üngsigči*[49]
5 *kümün čing ǰoriy sedkil ügei bügesü*
6 *ülü bütükü*[50] *[e]ne yeke nigülesügči-yin ene tarni*
7 *ungsigči kü[mü]n ber ger-tür ungsibasu*
8 *uribasu ger dotora yabuyči*[51] *amitan-u kilinče*
9 *bügüde aldaraqu boluyu : usun-tur nomlabasu*
10 *tere usun uyuysan ba dayariysan ba amitan-i*[52]
11 *kilinče bügüde aldaraqu boluyu : ulan*[53] *-tur*
12 *yabubasu qoor-tan luusun qad qab ǰayasu*[54]
13 *ariyatan menekei*[55] *ülü qaluyu :*[56] *ker ber dayisun*
14 *bulya*[57] *östen qulayan*[58] *buliy-a*[59] *tede teyimüi*[60]
15 *üiles učirabasu tedenü sedkil-i ǰögöleregülǰü*[61]

---

48 The copyist skipped a passage at this point. XBM 49, 5r:3–8 reads: *qamuy amitan qutuy ol[su]yai ene tarni-yi ungsiyči küm[ün] yayun sedkibesü sedkil-iyer inu boluyu. kedber ese bolbasu bi burqan buu bolsuyai;* Louvain No. 27, 3v:10–14: *qutuy olsuyai. ene tarni-yi ungsiyči kümün yayun sedkibesü sedkil-iyer inu boluyu. kerber ese bolbasu bi burqan buu bolsuyai.*
49 Instead of *ungsigči.*
50 XBM 49, 5v:11–6r:5 adds: *qatuytai [kümü]n ungsiysan-tur noyaytai kümün. töröl ese olbasu bi burqan buu bolsuyai. kedber seǰig abubasu yayun sedkibesü ülü bütükü.* The same passage is found in Louvain No. 27, 4r:1–5: *qatuytai kümün ungsiysan-dur noyaytai kümün-ü töröl ese olbasu bi burqan buu bolsuyai. ker ber seǰig abubasu yayun sedkibesü ülü bütükü;* Ms. Asch 130, 4v:12–5r:5 adds the same passage with some variants.
51 XBM 49, 6r:5–10 reads: *ene yeke nigülesügči-yin tarni-yi ungsiyči kümün-ü ger-tür ungsibasu ger tergen-ü dotor-a yabuyči bükü amitan-u kilinče aldaraqu boluyu;* Ms Asch 130: 5r:5–10: *ene yeke nigülesügči-yin ene tarni-yi ungsigči kümün kerbe ungsiju yabubasu. ger dotor-a ki yabuyči amitan-u kilinče bügüde aldaraqu boluyu.*
52 Instead of *amitan-u.* On the genitive *-i* after a word which ends in *n,* see Poppe, "Geserica", pp. 15–17.
53 For *ayulan,* reflecting the colloquial language. XBM 49, 6v:2–3 has *ayulan-tur.*
54 For *ǰiyasu,* reflecting the colloquial language.
55 *menekei, melekei.* For the alternation *n ~ l* see Poppe, *Introduction,* p. 159.
56 Ms. Asch 130, 5v:5 has *qaldayu.* On the verb *qal-* see Haenisch, *Wörterbuch,* p. 58; see also Cleaves, "The Mongolian Documents in the Musée de Téhéran", p. 31; Cerensodnom and Taube, *Turfansammlung,* 34v5, p. 126.
57 Ms. Asch 130, 5v:6: *dayisun buliyan.* See *bulqa* in §150 of the *Secret History;* on this term see Cleaves, "Sino-Mongolian Inscription of 1362", p. 64, and note 89, p. 111; see also the discussion by Sagaster in the *Weiße Geschichte,* p. 119, note 8, and the remarks by Manduqu in the *Hua yi yi yu,* pp. 89–90.
58 Plural of *qulayai.* See Poppe, *Grammar,* § 272, p. 72.
59 The Ms. belonging to the author, 4v:8–9: *östen buliyan qulayai.* See *buliy-a qulayai,* "bandit, voleur", in Kowalevski, p. 1186.
60 The accusative suffix *-i* is joined to *teyimü;* the other versions have *teyimü.*
61 Instead of *ǰögelere-;* see *ǰö'ölen* in § 189 of the *Secret History* (de Rachewiltz, *Index,* p. 98); *ǰögölen* is found in *Sayin ügetü erdeni-yin sang* (J̌ayunasutu et al., p. 261).

3v

1　*qariɣuluyu:*[62] *< ked ilqayan-u*[63] *ǰasaɣ töröi-yi<n>*[64] *köndeǰü*
2　*bayulilaǰu ginǰi*[65] *tomür*[66] *čider -iyer čiderleǰü*[67] *alaqui*
3　*-ṯur orobasu čing sedkil-iyer ene tarni-yi ung =*
4　*sibasu qan*[68] *nigülesügčiyin sedkil egüskeǰü talbiqu*
5　*boluyu : mayui sedkil-ten irgen qoor ba kibesü*
6　*čing sedkil -iyer ǰögöleregülǰü qariɣuluyu : >*[69] *ked*
7　*ilqayan-u ǰasaɣ töröi-yi köndeǰü bayulilaǰu ginǰi =*
8　*leǰü temür čider-iyer čiderleǰü alaqui-ṯur orobasu*
9　*čing sedkil-[i]yer ene tarni-yi ungsibasu ene yeke nigüles =*
10　*ügčiyin sedkil egüskeǰü talbiqu boluyu :*[70] *mayui*
11　*sedkilten*[71] *irgen qoor ba kibesü čing sedkil-iyer*
12　*ene tarni-yi ungsibas-u*[72] *qoor-a aldaraǰu rasiyan*
13　*boluyu :: qatuytai kümün ǰirmüsün bolbasu ked ber*
14　*töröküi čay-tür: qamuɣ qoor ada*[73] *kiküi-ṯür ene tarni*

62　Ms. Asch 130, 5 v:9: *qariqui.*
63　The word *ilqayan* is written with the diacritical points before *q* and *y* as in Ms. Asch 130, 5 v:10; the Ms. belonging to the author (4 v:12) has *ilqayan* without diacritical points; Louvain No. 27, 4 v:3 and Ms. or. oct. 422-6, 7 r10 have *il qayan* . This term is discussed in the commentary.
64　The accusative suffix *-i* is joined to the word *törö;* the genitive suffix *-yin* is erroneous. Line 7 has *töröi-yi.*
65　XBM 49, 6 v:11 and Ms. or. oct. 422-6, 7 r:11 have *bayulaǰu ginǰi;* Louvain No. 27, 4 v:4–5: *ginǰi bayulyaǰu.* See *ginǰi bayu bayulaǰu* in the *Altan tobči,* ed. Bawden, p. 42, and *Quriyangyui altan tobči,* Liu ed., p. 24 and note 152. The *Altan tobči* reads *ginǰi bayu-bar-iyan …,* p. 19 r. See also *buqa'u,* in § 81 of the *Secret History.* In the *Erdeni-yin tobči* (Urga text) we read: *temür ginǰi temür tusiy-a emüsken,* p. 27 v. The term *tusiy-a* has the same meaning as *čider,* "hobbles for horses, shackles for the feet" (Lessing, pp. 178, 845). The *Ganǰur* text No. 374, has *temür tusiyan.*
66　For *tömür, temür.*
67　The spelling *čider, čiderle-* is also found in the *Erdeni-yin tobči* (Urga, 100 r).
68　The word is written with diacritical points before *q;* Ms. or. oct. 422-6, 7 v:5 also reads *qan;* Ms. Asch 130, 6 r:2 has *qayan;* Louvain No. 27, 4 v:8 has *ene.* See *ene* in line 9.
69　The words from *mayui* to *qariɣuluyu* are misplaced (see lines 10–13), and the passage which follows is a repetition of that given between angle brakets. However, the two passages show some variants. See the next note.
70　The two passages show variants as follows: line 1 has *töröi-yin,* line 7 has *töröi-yi;* line 2 has *bayulilaǰu ginǰi tomür,* lines 7–8 have *bayulilaǰu ginǰileǰü temür;* line 4 has *qan,* line 9 has *ene.* The occurrence of *ene* instead of *qan* in the second passage shows that the copyist had another copy of the text at his disposal; *ene* is found in Louvain No. 27 (4 v:8).
71　The scribe of the text used too much ink to write the letter *d* in the word *sedkilten,* he wrote it again between the lines.
72　The word *ungsibasu* is written separately because there is a split in the folio. See also the words *ungsibasu* and *daldariqu* in the next lines.

15 -yi nigen sedkil-iyer ung-sibasu ada todqar⁷⁴ inu

16 urgün⁷⁵ dutayaǰu daldari-qu boluyu : mayui ebedčin-tür

17 odbasu ülü qalda[yu] : luusun qad yaǰar-un eǰen-i

4r

1 köndeǰü bey-e qabu[d]ču⁷⁶ güǰügün⁷⁷ uryuǰu ögö[s]ün⁷⁸

2 čisun čiburiqui čay-tur : ene tarni-yi ungsibasu

---

73 On the expression *qoor ada*, "harm and misfortune" = "harm", see de Rachewiltz's remarks in "The Preclassical Mongolian Version", note 111, p. 65; on *qor ada* in the *Hua yi yi yu* see the discussion by Manduqu, pp. 73–4; for *ada-tu*, "dangerous", see Cleaves, "The Sino-Mongolian Inscription of 1362", note 78, p. 110. The text says that people inflict harm on the woman at the moment of birth of the child. The Chinese worship Guanyin as bestower of children and wealth. The goddess is the protector of mothers and helps at delivery. For this see Cheng Manchao, *The Origin of the Chinese Deities*, pp. 8–9. A thanka from Mongolia describing the female manifestation of Avalokiteśvara as goddess of fecundity, gives rare evidence of the worship of Avalokiteśvara as goddess of fecundity in Mongolia, see Sárközi, "A Thanka from Mongolia", pp. 393–401. See also Chiodo, "A Hymn to Qongsim Bodisung", p. 236, note 120.

74 Both *ada* and *todqar* mean "demon, evil spirit". Texts of popular religion often mention these evil spirits, though not necessarily together. See Bawden, "The Supernatural Element", I, pp. 72, 74. See *ada todqod* in the Hymn to Mahākālī = Cerensodnom and Taube, *Turfan-sammlung*, No. 30, p. 118.

75 For *ürgün*, *ürgen*. Ms. Asch 130, 6v:1: *ürgen*.

76 Ms. Asch 130, 6v:5 and Louvain No. 27, 5r:5 have *qabudču*. There is a small split in the folio at this point which damaged the word. The folio also shows a long split which runs from lines 1 to 7. As in the case indicated above, the split existed on the bark before the copyist wrote the text on it.

77 The term *güǰügün* is not listed in dictionaries of the modern language. The forms *güǰigün*, *geǰi'ün* < *geǰigün* are often attested in the pre-classical texts in the meaning "ulcer, abcess, sore". See Bosson, *A Treasury (mayui güǰigüten)*, p. 150, and note 112, p. 323; on *güǰigün* see the discussion by J̌ayunnasutu (et al.) in *Sayin ügetü erdeni-yin sang*, pp. 690–1. See also Mostaert and de Rachewiltz, *Houa i i iu (geǰi'ün)*, p. 87; Poppe, *Twelve Deeds (güǰigün)*, p. 65, and note 9, p. 108; *Mukkadimat al-adab*, pp. 189, 226, 389. The term often occurs in the later texts, for example in two *dhāraṇī* which are included in the collection of *dhāraṇī* preserved in Copenhagen (= Heissig and Bawden, *Catalogue*, Mong. 468, pp. 230–1). They are Čoytu qara yeke ökin tngri činggegči usniša neretü tarni (12v, 15r, 16r), and Čayan sikürtei (Qutuy-tu tegünčilen iregsen oroi-ača yaruysan čayan sikür-dei budud-da ülü ilaydaqu yeke-de qariyuluyči degedü bütügsen nertü tarni, 20r); on another occurrence of this term, see Sárközi, *Political Prophecies*, p. 24 (5a), and the discussion of the term in note 65, p. 140. According to a Tibetan Mongol belief, the masters of earth and water, if offended, provoke ulcers, abcesses, sores etc. Sayang Sečen, for example, calls *luus un qayan-u ebečin*, "the disease of the kings of the *luus*", the disease which afflicted Göden qayan (*Erdeni-yin tobči*, 42v; see also the *Altan tobči*, 131v). This disease is what the Tibetans call *klu-nad*, "leprosy" (Hoffmann, *Quellen*, p. 158). For the term *güǰügün* in association with Tibetan and Mongol popular beliefs, see the discussion by Chiodo, "A Hymn to Qongsim Bodisung", pp. 244–5. On this popular belief, which is observed among the contemporary Mongols, see Sampilnorbu, *Mongyol-un ǰang ayali*, p. 383.

78 Louvain No. 27, 5r:7 reads *ögesün*.

3 *darui-tur anaqu boluyu : ked ber ene yeke nigüles =*
4 *ügčiyin ene tarni-yi ungsibasu*[79] *baribasu ilqayan*
5 *-u yirtinčü-yin*[80] *aduyu-sun-u nasu ülü abqu boluyu :*
6 *qamuy mayui ǰayayan-tur odqui-tur ayul ügei*
7 *boluyu : ked ber ene yeke nigülesügči-yin tarni-yi*
8 *ungsibasu masi ǰiryalang-tu yirtinčü-yin abida*
9 *burqan-u ulus-tur törökü boluyu : ked ber **ene** yeke nigü =*
10 *lesügči-yin ene tarni-yi kičiyebesü sakibasu .*[81] *yurban*
11 *erdeni-tür itegeǰü tabun čoyčas-iyar bököyiǰü mörgö =*
12 *besü : qoyar köliyer ergin toyoribasu: qamuy tegün =*
13 *čilen iregsen burqan-u ulus-tur töröku boluyu :*
14 *yučin yurban tengri-ner-ün sudaram sal*[82] *ne[r]etü*
15 *balyasun-tur törökü boluyu : busu yabudal ber*
16 *yayun üiles bügüdei-yi čidaqu boluyu :*

4v

1 *qutuy-tu qongsim bodisung-un aldarsin*
2 *dügürügsen neretü sudur nom nigen ǰü[il]*
3 *-iyer qutuy-tu yeke kölge nom sudur*
4 *dayusba :: : ::*[83]
5 *sadu edgü*[84] *eǰen-türiyen*[85] *ölǰei-tü*
6 *qutuytu-tu*[86] *boltuyai ::*

XBM 48

2 items of a *pothī* (2 folios, 4 written sides) written in a beautiful hand, each measuring 13 × 6–13 × 5 × 6 cm, consisting of 12–13; the Mongolian page numbers are *qoyar, yurban* (2–3); the text on folio 2 is bordered with lines, folio 3 ends in the middle of the sentence. The text is well preserved.[87] The text on folio 2r–2v was previously transcribed by Heissig side by side with the Olon Süme fragments.[88]

---

79 Ms. Asch 130, 6v:11 and Louvain No. 27, 5r:11: *uribasu baribasu.*
80 Louvain No. 27, 5r:11–12: *il qayan-u yirtinčü-tür.*
81 Ms. Asch 130, 7r:12–13 and Louvain No. 27, 5b:6–7 add *bačay baribasu šayšabad sakibasu.* Louvain No. 27 writes *saysabad.*
82 *sudaram sal* may be an error for *sudarasun (sudarśana).* On *sudarasun,* the abode of the 33 Tngri, see the *Čiqula kereglegči,* 27v (facsimile in Heissig, *Geschichtsschreibung,* I). Ms. Asch 130, 7v:8 and Louvain No. 27, 5v:13 have *sudaram.*
83 On *dayus-, tegüs-,* see Weiers, *Untersuchungen,* p. 201.
84 The ending formula *sadu edgü* is not found in the other versions of the text used in this work.
85 The dative-locative suffix *-tür* and the reflexive-possessive suffix *-iyen* are written together.
86 See *ölǰeitü qutuytu* in § 200 of the *Secret History.*
87 Restored by Mr. Bentchev; old number 24/4.
88 *Handschriften-Reste,* p. 329.

2r

1 *qoyar temür quyay-dan :*[89] *möng =*	7 *keküi : terigülesi ügei olan*
2 *gön duyulyatu :: yerü yučin*	8 *amitan qonsiim*[92] *bodisung-un*
3 *jiryuyan sakiyulsun inu sakin*[90]	9 *qutuy olqu boltuyai :: oom*
4 *bui : ene yurban silüg-üd-i*	10 *qung subau-a siddo qang sarva*
5 *kemebesü : yurban erdenis-ün*[91]	11 *darm-a : subau-a siddo qang*
sitügen	12 *kemen qoyoson kü boltuyai ::*
6 *inu bui : küseküi sedkil egüs =*	

2v

1 *qoyoson kü ayar-tur: bam*	7 *ariyun sedkil-iyer minu*
2 *üsüg qubilju badm-a lingqu =*	8 *jirüken degere bam üsüg qu =*
3 *a čečeg bolbai : a üsüg*	9 *bilju lingqu-a čečeg bolba :*
4 *saran mandal-un degere edeni*	10 *tere deger-e a üsüg saran*
5 *jayun nigen ungsibasu minu*	11 *mandal-un deger-e qung üsüg*
6 *bey-e qubilju beki bolba :*	12 *-eče čayan öngge-dü gerel*

3r

1 *talbibai : olan amitan-i geyigülüged*	8 *badmi qung :: ene jiryuyan :*
2 *qonsiim bodisung bolba: mön gerel*	9 *tarni-yi jayun naiman da kemejü*
3 *yaryayulju siri üsüg-tür kür =*	10 *ungsibasu mön bey-e qubilju*
4 *bei : siri üsüg qubilju qonsi =*	11 *mingyan yartu minyan nidü*
5 *m*[93] *bodisung bolba : čayan öngge-tü*	12 *-dü qonsim bodisung-un bey-e*
6 *arban nigen niyur-du naiman yar*	13 *bütüküi boluyu :: qamuy nom-ud-i*
7 *-du gürü sarva namo oom mani*	

3v

1 *medeküi boluyu :: ene tarni-yi*	8 *< > saysabad-un tergegüri*
2 *ungsibasu nidün gegen nemekü*	9 *olqu boluyu :: qutuy möri*
3 *bolqu boluyu :: qamuy amitan-i*	10 *olqu boluyu :: nom-un bey-e-luy-a*
4 *tonilyaqu boluyu :: uran ary-a*	11 *teng olqu boluyu :: ene tarni*
5 *bilig-yi olqu boluyu :: sečen*	12 *-yi ungsibasu yambar ba jeben*
6 *mergen bilig olqu boluyu ::*	13 *-tür ülü*
7 *mayui jobalang-ača tonilqu boluyu ::*	

---

89 See the spellings *öngge-dü*, *niyur-du* etc. below.
90 XBM 47, 1v:9 has *saqin*.
91 XBM 47, 1v:10 writes *erdeni-sün*.
92 XBM 47, 1v:12: *qongsim*.
93 Instead of *qonsiim* in the lines above.

XBM 49

6 items of a *pothī* (5 entire folios and 1 nearly entire folio, 11 written sides).

The first item measures 12 × 6 cm, and has 9–11 lines; the Mongolian page number is *qoyar* (2). The text is fairly well preserved.[94]

The second item measures 12 × 6 cm, and has 9–11 lines; the Mongolian page number is *dörben* (4). Some words are damaged, otherwise the text is legible.[95]

The third item measures 12.5 × 6 cm, and has 11 lines; the Mongolian page number is *tabun* (5). The folio is stained on verso.[96]

The forth item measures 11 × 7 cm, and has 11 lines; the Mongolian page number is *ǰiryuyan* (6). It is well preserved.[97]

The fifth item measures ca. 12.5 × 6 cm, and has 6–9 lines; the Mongolian page number is *naiman* (8). The folio is stained, but legible.[98]

The sixth item is a nearly entire folio which measures 12.5 × 6.5 cm, and has 12 lines; the Mongolian page number is *yesün* (9). The folio is damaged, the sides and edges are torn and there is a long split in its surface.[99]

2r

1	ene nigen silüg-yi ungsibasu	6	[γ]urban erdenis-ün sitügen inu
2	ači inu arban qoyar [te]mür quyaγ =	7	küseküi sedkil-i egüskebei
3	tan mönggün duyulyantu γ =	8	:: [terigü]lesi ügei olan amitan
4	učin ǰiryuyan sakiyulsun	9	[qong]sim bodisung-un qutuγ
5	sakin bui :: ene silüg-yi kemebesü :		

2v

1	olqu boltuyai : oom suvabau-a	7	ede-e[100] nigen de ungsibasu minu
2	sido sarva dharma suvabau-a		bey-e
3	sudo qan qoyoson kü boltuyai:	8	qubilǰu : beki bolba : sedkil-i
4	qoyoson kü ayar-tur badm-a	9	-iyer minu ǰirüken degere bam
5	üǰüg qubilǰu lingqu-a čečeg	10	üǰüg qubilǰu : lingqu-a čečeg
6	bolba: e e üǰüg saran mandal	11	bolba :

4r

1	bolqu bolu[yu] :: qamuγ amitan-i	3	bilig olqu b[o]luyu :: mayui
2	[t]onilqu boluyu :: uran arγ-a	4	ǰobalang-ača tonilqu boluyu ::

---

94 Restored by the Russians experts in Ulaanbaatar; old number 7/3.
95 Restored by Mr. Bentchev; this folio was preserved in the Ulaanbaatar Central State Library, but no number was assigned to it.
96 Restored by Mr. Bentchev; old number 32/8.
97 Restored by Mrs. Nebel; old number 32/5.
98 Restored by Mrs. Nebel; old number 21/2.
99 Restored by Mr. Bentchev; old number 12/2.
100 For *ede-i*.

5 saysabad tergegür [...]¹⁰¹ boluyu
6 :: qutuy möri [o]lqu boluyu ::
7 nom-un [bey]-e [lu]y-a [...]¹⁰²

8 o[l]qu boluyu [::] [e]ne ta[r]ni-yi
9 ungsibasu yabbar¹⁰³ ba

4v

1 ǰeben-dü ülü dayaydaqu
2 boluyu :: qalayun usun yal
3 <> ber sirgireǰü sönökü boluyu ::
4 birid-tür kürbesü čadqulang¹⁰⁴
5 boluyu :: asuru-nar-tur¹⁰⁵ kürbe =
6 sü sedkil-i-iyer nomoqan bolu =

7 yu :: adayusun-u töröl-eče
8 tonilqu boluyu :: nigen sedkil-i-iyer
9 qongsim bodisung namai sedkibe =
10 <be>sü¹⁰⁶ ǰayun mingyan yalab
11 -ud

5r

1 kilinče bügüde aldaraqu boluyu ::
2 ene bey-e-yi tebčiküi čay-tur
3 qamuy erketü burqan bodisung <un>
4 -nar : oytaryui-tur ireǰü
5 alayaban oroi degere talbiǰu
6 sükavadi neretü ǰiryalang-tu yirt[in =]

7 čüi-tür uduridču odqu bolu =
8 yu :: ene yeke nigülesügči-yin tarni
9 -yi ken ungsiyči bügesü ǰiryuyan
10 mayui töröl-tür ülü
11 odqu boluyu ::

5v

1 kedber ungsayči¹⁰⁷ kümün ta[mu]
2 -tur odbasu bi büged burqan
3 buu bolsuyai : qamuy amitan
4 qutuy ol[su]yai ene [t]arni-yi
5 ungsiyči küm[ün] yayun sedkibe =
6 sü sedkil-i-iyer inu boluyu ::

7 kedber ese bolbasu bi burqan
8 buu bolsuyai :: ene ta[rni]-yi ungsiy =
9 [či] [kümün] [či]ng ǰoriy sedkil ügei
10 bügesü ü[l]ü bütükü
11 qatuytai [kümü]n¹⁰⁸ ungsiysan

6r

1 -tur noyaytai küm[ü]n : töröl
2 ese olbasu bi burqan buu
3 bolsuyai :: kedber seǰig abu =

4 basu yayun sedkibesü ülü
5 bütükü : ene yeke nigülesügči-yin
6 tarni-yi ungsiyči kümün-ü ger

---

101 XBM 47, 2v:3 has olqu.
102 The other versions have teng at this point of the text (XBM 48, 3v:10–11, etc.).
103 Instead of yambar. On the alternation b~m see Poppe, Introduction, p. 100.
104 For čidqulang, reflecting the spoken language. See ǰayasu for ǰiyasu in XBM 47, 3r:12.
105 For asuri. Skr. asura.
106 be of -besü is repeated in the next line.
107 Instead of ungsiyči.
108 qatuytai kümün is not found in the complete text XBM 47. As has been indicated, it occurs in Ms. Asch 130, 4v and in Louvain No. 27, 4r.

7 -tür ungsibasu ger tergen-ü[109]
8 do[t]or-a yabuyči bükü amitan-u
9 kilinče aldaraqu bolu =

6v

1 dayariysan amitan-u kilinče
2 bügüde aldaraqu boluyu : ayulan
3 -tur yabubasu qoor dan luu =
4 sun qad yekes ariyatan minekei[110]
5 ülü qaluyu :: kerbe dayisun
6 bulya östen qulayai[111] buliy-a

8r

1 kerber ene yeke nigülesügči-yin
2 ene tarni ungsibasu masi
3 jiryalang-tu yirtenčü abida
4 ber burqan-u ulus-tur
5 törökü boluyu :: mayui jayayan

8v

1 basu <yurban>[114] saysaba =
2 d <> -yi sakibasu
3 yurban erdeni-tür itegejü

9r

1 toyoriyulbasu qa[muy]
2 tegünčilen iregsen burqan ene
3 ulus-tur törökü boluyu ::
4 yučin yu[r]ban qad tengri-ner
5 suda[…]an[115] neretü balyasun-tur
6 törökü bo[l]uyu :: busu yabudal ber

10 yu : usun-tur nomlabasu
11 tere usun uyuysan ba

7 tede-e teyimü üiles učira =
8 basu tede-ü sedkil-i jögele =
9 rügüljü qariyuluyu: kerbe
10 ilqayan [-u] jasay töröi köndejü
11 bayulaju ginji temür čidderi
12 -iyer čidder-lejü[112] alaqui

6 -u möri-iyer ülü odqu
7 boluyu :: ked ber ene yeke
8 nigülesügči-yin tarni-yi
9 kičiyebesü bančy[113] bari =

4 tabun čoyčas-i-iyar
5 bököyijü mörgöbesü
6 qoyar köl-iyer ergin

7 yayun ba üiles bügüdei-yi
8 čidaqu boluyu ::[116] qutuy-tu
9 qongsim bodi sadu aldarsin
10 dügürgegsen neretü su[dur] [no]m-a
11 [ni]gen jüil-i-iyer tegüsbe sad[u]
12 [edgü] :: : ::

---

109 XBM 47, 3r:7 has ger-tür. See ger tergen "tent cart" in § 121 of the Secret History; see also
     Cleaves, "An Early Mongolian Loan Contract", note 26, p. 37.
110 For menekei.
111 XBM 47, 3r:14 has the plural form qulayan.
112 čidder for čider; čidderle- for čiderle-. On this orthographic feature see Cleaves, "Sino-
     Mongolian Inscription of 1362", p. 64; see also Róna-Tas, "Thar-pa čhen-po", p. 474.
113 It is a metathesis of bačay.
114 The word yurban is misplaced. It was placed before erdeni-tür.
115 On sudarasun see the note to XBM 47, 4r.
116 The l of boluyu is barely legible.

XBM 50

1 item of a *pothī* (1 fragment of a folio, 2 written sides), measuring ca. 12.5×6 cm, with 14–13 lines; the Mongolian page number is *doloyan* (7). It is severely damaged and half-burnt; various words are illegible on 7r.[117]

7r

1	*qal-daqu [ ]*	8	*[ ]*
2	*qa[ ]*	9	*[ ]*
3	*köndeǰü [ ]*	10	*[ ] yeke [ ]*
4	*qabudču güǰügün*	11	*[ ]*
5	*uryuǰu ked ber*	12	*[ ]*
6	*čisun [ ]*	13	*[ungsi]basu bari[basu]*[118]
7	*[ ]*	14	*[ ]*

7v

1	*[ ] ǰayayan*	8	*[yirti]nčü -yin abida*
2	*[ ] tur*	9	*[burq]an-u ulus-tur*
3	*[ ] boluyu*	10	*[tör]ökü boluyu*
4	*ked ber ene yeke*	11	*[may]ui ǰayayan möri*
5	*nigülesügči-yin ene*	12	*[ül]ü abqu boluyu*
6	*tarni-yi ungsibasu*	13	*[ ] yeke nigüle*[119]
7	*[ ] [ǰi]ryalang-tu*		

The hymn in praise of the saviour Qongsim Bodisung emphasises the power of the recitation of the six-syllable formula *oṃ maṇi padme hūm* of the deity which counteracts danger and ensures rebirth in the paradise Sukhāvatī.

The idea of a saviour Avalokiteśvara is very old in the history of Buddhism, and it can be traced in two important works such as *Ārya-kāraṇḍa-vyūha nāma mahāyāna-sūtra*, *Qutuy-tu quyurčay-un ǰokiyal kemegdekü yeke kölgen sudur*, "The holy mahāyāna-sūtra called The Array of Baskets", and the *Saddharma-puṇḍarīka-nāma mahāyāna-sūtra*, *Čayan lingqu-a neretü degedü nom yeke kölgen sudur*, "The supreme mahāyāna-sūtra called The White Lotus". The two works are included in the *Ganǰur*.[120] Various versions of the *Saddharma-puṇḍarīka* are listed in catalogues of Mongolian books.[121]

---

117   Restored by Mr. Bentchev; old number 12/4.
118   *ungsibasu baribasu* is found in XBM 47, 4r:4.
119   See the complete passage in XBM 47, 4r.
120   Vol. 66, No. 871, pp. 512–633; vol. 66, No. 868, pp. 2–466 respectively.
121   On five Mongolian versions of the work I refer the reader to Higuchi's article "Mongolian Versions", pp. 21–35; see also Farquhar, "A Description", Nos. 6–7, pp. 167–8.

The *Kāraṇḍa-vyūha* was translated into Tibetan in the 9th century,[122] and played an important role in the introduction of the cult of Avalokiteśvara to Tibet.[123] The *Kāraṇḍa-vyūha* is the first *sūtra* in which the six-syllable formula is attested.[124]

As is well-known, the *Mani gambu* (*Maṇi bka'-'bum*), a work devoted to the myth and cult of Avalokiteśvara, extensively describes the benefits of the six-syllable formula. It is, however, with the *Saddharma-puṇḍarīka* (*Čayan lingqu-a*) that the hymn to Qongsim Bodisung shows a close link. The *Saddharma-puṇḍarīka* is one of the most popular works of Mahāyāna Buddhism. It was translated into Chinese in the 3rd century and into Tibetan in the 9th century.[125]

Two fragments found in Turfan give early evidence of the translation into Mongolian of the *Saddharma-puṇḍarīka*, or at least of the chapter dealing with Avalokiteśvara, which was probably circulating as an independent text.[126]

According to chapter 24 of the *Saddharma-puṇḍarīka*, solely by uttering Avalokiteśvara's name living beings are saved from fire, water, spirits, demons, knives, prison and thieves.[127] The close link between the hymn to Qongsim Bodisung from Xarbuxyn Balgas and chapter 24 of the *Saddharma-puṇḍarīka* can be observed by comparing some passages from the two sources as follows.

XBM 47, 2v:4–5: *ene tarni ungsibasu yambar ba ǰebendü ülü dayariydaqu boluyu.*
Čayan lingqu-a, p. 428: *ker ber alan toyoribasu ele. nidü-ber üǰegči erketü-yin dayudabasu ele. tedeger alayčin-u tede mesen keseg keseg quyuran kemkerekü boluyu.*

XBM 47, 2v:6: *qalayun usun yal ber sirgireǰü sönekü boluyu.*
Čayan lingqu-a, pp. 427–8: *ked ber yal-un čoyča-dur unabasu ber. tedeger bügüde bodhi saduva ma ha saduva nidü-ber üǰegči erketü-yin čoy ǰibqulang-iyar masida sitaysan yal-un tere čoyča-ača tonilqu boluyu ... usun sačuysan metü yal sönökü boluyu.*

XBM 47, 3v:6–7: *ked ilyaqan-u ǰasay töröi-yi köndeǰü bayulilaǰu ginǰileǰü temür čider-iyer čiderleǰü ...*
Čayan lingqu-a, pp. 428–9: *ǰarim amitan temür čider kiged. modun čider-iyer čiderleküi-dür. gem-tü ba daki gem ügei bügesü. bodhi saduva ma ha saduva ary-a*

---

122   Imaeda, "Note préliminaire", pp. 71–2; see also Regamey, "Motifs vichouites", p. 419.

123   Sørensen, *The Mirror*, p. 494.

124   Imaeda, "Note préliminaire", p. 71; see also the *Ganǰur* text, No. 871, pp. 585–8; Regamey, "Motifs vichouites", p. 417.

125   On the Chinese translation, see Gockel, *Kuan-shi-yin*, p. 24; *Sérinde*, p. 351. On the Tibetan translation, see Schulemann, *Die Botschaft des Buddha*, p. 67.

126   See Cerensodnom and Taube, *Turfansammlung*, Nos. 27–8, pp. 108–13. It should be observed that the Chinese Buddhists made independent copies of chapter 25 of the *Saddharma-puṇḍarīka*. It was given the title *Guanyinjing* "The sūtra of Guanyin". Evidence of the circulation of chapter 25 of the *Saddharma-puṇḍarīka* as an independent text is the scroll from Dunghuang called *Guanyinjin yijuan*, "The sūtra of Guanyin in one scroll" (*Sérinde*, pp. 357–61).

127   *Ganǰur*, No. 868, p. 428. On the same powers attributed to Tārā see Beyer, *The Cult of Tārā*, p. 229.

avologide šuvari-yin ner-e-yi nereyiddügsen-iyer temür čider kiged modon čider-iyer
čiderlegsed. öber-iyen aldaraqu boluyu …[128]

XBM 47, 3r:11–14: *ulan-ṯur yabubasu qoor-tan luusun qad qab ariyatan menekei ülü*
qalayu. ked ber dayisun bulya östen qulayan buliy-a…
Čayan lingqu-a, pp. 429, 436: *kerbe yurba mingya yeke mingya yirtinčüs-ün ene orod-tur*
ary-a-tan kiged. buliyan qulayai. dayisun-u yar-tu mese bariysan ber. dügürčü ele.
tende yayča sardavaki ber olangki ǰiyulčid arad-luy-a erdeni-tü bey-e sardavaki-luy-a
oduysan-dur-i. tedeger oduysan ber ary-a-tan buliyan qulayai. dayisun yar-tu mese
bariysan teden-i üǰeǰü ele. üǰeged ayuǰu emiyeǰü. bida bükün ber itegel aburan öggün
kemegsen-dür. tere sardavaki ber olan ǰiyulčid-tur ber eyin kemen buu ayuytun.
iǰayurtan-u köbegün e buu ayuytun. ayul ügei öggügči bodhi saduva ma ha saduva
ary-a avologide šuvari-yin nigen dayun-iyar dayutaytun. tegüber ta buliyan
qulayan-u ayul kiged. ene dayisun ariyatan küriyelebesü ber. ary-a avologide
šuvari-yi duradbasu. ödter türgen bükün-dür buruyudču odqu boluyu.[129]

There is no doubt that the *Saddharma-puṇḍarīka* forms the background of the hymn to
Qongsim Bodisung.[130] The same applies to a number of *dhāraṇī* in praise of the saving
powers of Avalokiteśvara. The Mongolian *Ganǰur* contains various *dhāraṇī* like these.
Some examples are quoted in the notes to the transcription.[131]

The lexical content of the hymn to Qongsim Bodisung is interesting. We can observe
the occurrence of the term *ilqayan* in the phrase *ked ilqayan-u ǰasay töröi-yi köndeǰü*[132]
… *alaqui-ṯur orobasu*,[133] "If anyone transgresses the code of law and rules of conduct of
the ilqayan … they will incur the capital sentence". The term *ilqayan*, of course, does not
refer to the title of the imperial Mongol princes of Persia, which is, however, *il qan*.

---

128 See the following passage in the *Ganǰur* text No. 385, p. 97: *alimad qayan-u ǰasay-tur*
      toruysan-dur. ginǰi döngge gindan qoriyan-dur oroyulqui čay-tur. nigen üǰügür-tü sedkil-iyer
      nigülesügči-yin tarni-yi uribasu. qayan örösiyeküi sedkil-iyer talbiqu boluyu.

129 The passage refers to the danger that a caravan leader (*sārthavāha*) meets with when travel-
      ling on the roads of Central Asia. This episode and also the others in the preceding passages
      are depicted in the sūtra of Guanyin from Donghuang (*Sérinde*, p. 359); See the following
      passage in the *Ganǰur*, No. 374, p. 700: *ked be ayula kiged aylay čöle oduysan-a. bars kiged*
      čino-a doysin ariyatan kirülegsen moyai kiged eliy e ragša ayulǰabasu ber. ene tarni-yi
      ungsiqu-yi sonosbasu qoor kürgen yadamui …

130 On the association of prayers for rebirth in the Sukhāvatī paradise with the *Ārya-*
      amitābha-vyūha-nāma-mahāyāna-sūtra, see Schwieger, *Ein tibetisches Wunschgebet*, p. 90.

131 See also vol. 16, Nos. 370–4; vol. 17, Nos. 375, 379; vol. 23, Nos. 539–40, 544. For the descrip-
      tion of the texts, see Ligeti, *Catalogue*.

132 See *ǰasaq könde-* in § 277 of the *Secret History*; see also *ǰasay kömde- (könde-)* in the *Hsiao-*
      ching (= de Rachewiltz, "The Preclassical Mongolian Version", note 140, p. 68), and *Sayin*
      ügetü erdeni-yin sang (J̌ayunasutu et al., p. 257).

133 See *yisün aldal-tur ere'ü-tür bu orotuyai* in § 277 of the *Secret History* (de Rachewiltz, *Index*,
      p. 126); see also *aldal-dur oroyu* in the *Hsiao-ching* = de Rachewiltz, "The Preclassical Mon-
      golian Version", pp. 25, 27, and note 241, p. 77.

Mostaert and Cleaves translate *il qan* as "khan soumis", adding that *il, el* means "paix", being the opposite of *bulya* "révolté".[134]

It is interesting to note that the term *il qan* appears in an Uighur text of divination from Turfan. In this text we find *iltïn qantïn acïy bolur mu*, which Bang and von Gabain translate as follows: "wird dann von Il-Qan Zorn (Kummer sein?")".[135] In a note to the translation the two scholars remark that *il qan* means "König" in a general sense.[136]

In the Xarbuxyn Balgas we find the term *qan* referring to *ilqayan* in the preceding passage, while two other versions of the text have *ilqayan* and *qayan* respectively. As a result, *ilqayan* has the same meaning as *qan, qayan* in the text, and it should be understood as "lord, ruler, etc." in a general sense.[137]

The term *ilqayan*, however, is not entirely unknown in the Mongolian texts. In fact, it appears in *Qutuy-tu qamuy tegünčilen iregsed-ün oroi-ača yaruysan Čayan sikür-dei busud-da ülü ilaydaqu yeke-de qariyuluyči degedü bütügsen nertü tarni*,[138] and in *Mañjusiri-jñān-a saduva-yin ünemleküi ner-e-yi üneger ügülegči*, which is included in the *Zungdui*.[139]

* * *

Prayer Asking for Rebirth on Mount Potala (XBM 51 to XBM 57)

The fragmentary text, of which we have 7 copies bears no title, nor does it mention the name of Avalokiteśvara. However, the text is a prayer which describes the Sukhāvatī paradise, containing the refrain "May I be reborn on Mount Potala" *(bodalang ayulan-tur töröküi boltuyai)*. As is well-known, the western paradise Sukhāvatī is the realm of Buddha Amitābha,[140] and Avalokiteśvara is an emanational body of this Buddha.[141]

---

134 *Les lettres*, p. 27. For these terms see also Pelliot, *Les Mongols et la Papauté*, pp. 126–7, and note 1 on p. 127; see *il bulya* in the seal of Güyüg (Dobo and Bayan-a, *Uyiyurjin mongyol üsüg*, p. 15).

135 *Turfan-Texte*, I, p. 252.

136 Note 170, p. 265.

137 On this term see the discussion by Chiodo in "A Mongolian Hymn to Qongsim Bodisung", pp. 241–3.

138 Mong. 468, 18v = Heissig and Bawden, *Catalogue*.

139 20r.

140 See Schwieger, *Ein tibetisches Wunschgebet*, pp. 7, 14; on prayers for rebirth in the Sukhāvatī paradise, see Heissig and Sagaster, *Mongolische Handschriften*, Nos. 480–2, pp. 258–9; on two prayers describing Sukhāvatī composed by Tsoṅ-kha-pa, see Heissig, *Blockdrucke*, No. 124, p. 111, and notes 9–10; I was able to acquire the manuscript *Sukavadi-yin oron-u namtar orosiba* by Čaqar gebsi blam-a Lobsang Čulkrims in Ulaanbaatar in 1997; on prayers asking for rebirth on the pure land of Amitābha, which form part of the colophons of various Uighur *sūtra*, see Zieme, *Religion und Gesellschaft*, pp. 86–8.

141 *Mani gambu*, vol. 1, chap. 1, 3r = Heissig and Sagaster, *Mongolische Handschriften*, No. 334, p. 192; on the *Mani gambu*, see also Heissig, *Blockdrucke*, No. 24, p. 30, and by the same author see "Eine kleine Klosterbibliothek", pp. 557–90.

Moreover, Mount Potala is the mythical abode of Avalokiteśvara. In view of this, the identification of the fragmentary text from Xarbuxyn Balgas was not a difficult task. I soon discovered that, apart from the refrain and some minor variants, the text from Xarbuxyn Balgas is in fact the same as the hymn describing the Sukhāvatī paradise, which is found at the very beginning of the Mongolian *Mani gambu (Maṇi bka'-'bum)*.[142] This work includes another hymn in praise of Sukhāvatī paradise, which has the refrain "May I be reborn on Mount Potala", but it coincides only in part with that found in the opening section.[143] The beautiful hymn which praises Sukhāvatī was very popular with the Tibetans;[144] it is included not only in the *Maṇi bka'-'bum*, but also in *rGyal-rabs gsal-ba'i me-loṅ*[145] and *Padma bka'-yi thaṅ-yig*.[146] The two Tibetan works were translated into Mongolian with the titles *Gegen toli*[147] and *Badma yatang sudur*[148] respectively.

The fragments of seven copies of the prayer from Xarbuxyn Balgas provide evidence of the popularity of this text among the Mongols, which was obviously circulating independently. The same applies to another Mongol text which, despite a number of textual variants, is basically the same as that from Xarbuxyn Balgas. It is preserved in Louvain University Library with the title *Jiryuyan jayuradu*, "The six intermediate states (between death and rebirth)". The Louvain prayer invokes Amitābha, asking this Buddha to lead the dead to Sukhāvatī, while the following section, which describes Sukhāvatī expresses the wish to be reborn on Mount Potala.[149]

Finally, Prof. Kara transcribed and translated into French the first lines of the hymn describing the Sukhāvatī paradise, which is included in the copy of the Mongolian *Maṇi bka'-'bum* preserved in St. Petersburg.[150]

XBM 51

1 item (1 small fragment of a folio, 1 written side), measuring ca. 5 × 6.5 cm, with 5 lines. The Mongolian page number is *nigen* (1). The fragment is half-burnt, but the text is

---

142 Vol. 1, chap. 1, 2 r–3 v.

143 Vol. 1, chap. 4, 47 v–48 v.

144 According to Geshe Pema Tsering, Bonn, the hymn in praise of Sukhāvatī is very popular with the Tibetan laymen, who recite it during the days of fasting at Buddhist festivals.

145 See Sørensen, *The Mirror*, pp. 98–9.

146 See Bischoff, "The First Chapter of the Legend of Padmasambhava", pp. 39–42. This text is a *gter-ma* rediscovered by the *gter-ston* O-rgyan Gliṅ-pa. See Sørensen, *The Mirror*, p. 644.

147 See Heissig, *Geschichtsschreibung*, pp. 34–40.

148 Heissig, *Geschichtsschreibung*, p. 40 and note 5, pp. 40–3. See *Blockdrucke*, No. 25, p. 31 by the same author; see also Heissig and Sagaster, *Mongolische Handschriften*, No. 489, p. 264.

149 See Heissig, "The Mongol Manuscripts and Xylographs", No. 39, p. 179. On prayers expressing the wish to meet Amitābha at the moment of death see Schwieger, *Ein tibetisches Wunschgebet*, p. 50; a painted scroll from Khara Khoto depicts Guanyin being invoked to lead the dead to the land of Amitābha (Pjotrowskij ed., *Die Schwarze Stadt*, pp. 206–7).

150 See "Une version mongole du *Maṇi bka'-'bum*", pp. 19–23.

legible thanks to infra-red reflectography. There are Tibetan words on the left side of the fragment.[151]

Judging from the style of calligraphy, XBM 51 is the earliest copy of the hymn, probably dating back to the 16th century. Unfortunately, only a few lines survived.

1v

1 O *nigülesküi-yin eje[n] ariy[-a]*
2 O *avaloyide*[152] *suvar -a-tur*
   mörgöm[ü]i :

3 O *öröne jüg-ün badm-a kemekü*[153]
4 *[süka]vadi-yin*[154] *ayui anu erdenisün*
5 *[   ] [del]ekei-tür*[155] *[   ]*

XBM 52

1 item of a *pothī* (1 fragment of a folio, 1 written side), measuring ca. 12.5 × 5 cm, with 11 lines. The Mongolian page number is *nigen* (1).[156]

1v

1 O *nigülesküi-yin ejen*
2 *ary-a avalogi-de*
3 *süvr-a-tur mör =*
4 *gömüi + : öröne*
5 *jüg-ün badma kemekü*
6 *sü[kavad]i-yin*[157] *ayui*

7 *a[   ]*[158] *[er]deni-sün*
8 *alt[an] [de]lekei-tür*[159]
9 *eld[deb] [   ] jayalmai*
10 *čo[yolburi]-ača*[160] *öber =*
11 *e busu*

XBM 53

2 items of a *pothī* (2 fragments of folios, 3 written sides), without page numbers. The first item measures 12 × 5 cm, and has 9 lines. The second item measures 11 × 5 cm, and has 9–13 lines (r/v); the text on verso is barely legible.[161]

---

151 Restored by Mr. Bentchev; old number 12/3.
152 The word is written with *y* before *i*.
153 Louvain No. 39, 3 v:1–5 begins as follows: *asuru jiryalang-tu sükavadi-yin degedü ayui-daki. abida burqan-a vivanggirid ögtegsen. asarayči qomsim bodisaduva-dur mörgömü.*
154 XBM 53, *1v:5 has *[s]ükavadi.*
155 XBM 53, *1v:7 reads *altan delekei-tur-i.*
156 Restored by Mr. Bentchev; old number 10/4.
157 XBM 53, *1v:5 has *[s]ükavadi.*
158 XBM 51, 1v:4 has *anu;* XBM 54, 1v:5 reads *aqu.*
159 XBM 53, *1v:6–7: *erdenis-ün altan delekei-tür-i.*
160 XBM 53, *1v: 8–9: *eldeb [j]üil jalyamai čoyolburi-ača...*
161 Restored by the Russians experts in Ulaanbaatar; old numbers 5/4, 7/3.

*1 v

1 [nigül]esküi-[y]in e[j]en
2 [a]ry-a avalo-gidv
3 [   ]¹⁶² -tur mörgömü :
4 [örön]e jüg-ün badm-a
5 [kemekü]¹⁶³ [s]ügavadi-yin

6 [ayu]i¹⁶⁴ erdenis-ün
7 altan delekei-tür-i¹⁶⁵
8 eldeb [j]üil jayalmai
9 čoyolburi-ača öber-e

*2 r

1 busu [s]iroi [kig]ed
2 gürüi-yin¹⁶⁶ nereber
3 ügei¹⁶⁷ boda bodalang¹⁶⁸
4 [ayu]la[n] [   ]ur¹⁶⁹ törökü
5 [boltuy]ai om + ::

6 [   ]r čimeg-sen bodi
7 [mo]don-ača öber-e
8 [bu]su busu : oi
9 [   ]un modon-u nereber¹⁷⁰

*2 v

1 [üge]i [   ]
2 [törö]kü boltu[yai]

3 [naim]an [   ] diyan-u
4 [usu]un [   ] ača

---

162 A part of the name of Avalokiteśvara is missing. The copies of this text show different forms of this name (süvra, šuvara). For this reason, it is not possible to restore the word.

163 kemekü is found in XBM 51, 1v:3 and XBM 54, 1v:4.

164 See ayui in XBM 52, 1v:6 and XBM 54, 1v:5.

165 On the various uses of -dur-i/-dür-i, -tur-i/-tür-i, see Weiers, Untersuchungen, pp. 80–7.

166 On the genitive suffix -i-yin, see Poppe, "Geserica", pp. 16–17.

167 The Mani gambu (vol. I, chap.I, 1r–1v) reads: singgekü jüg-ün badm-a-tu sükavadi-yin tariyalang-un oron kemekü eldeb erdeni altan yajar delekei-de olan nidü-tü-yin jiruqai-da jiruqayilaysan-ača busu siroi kiged. čilayun ner-e čü ügei; Kara ("Une version mongole", p. 22): öröne jüg-ün Badma kemekü Sukhāvati-yin ayui inu.erdenis-ün altan delekei-tür eldeb jüil jalyamai čoyolburi-ača anggida busu siroi kiged kürü-yin nere ber ügei. The passage which Kara transcribed is similar to that from Xarbuxyn Balgas. The latter has öber-e busu, while the other has anggida busu, but the meaning is the same: "apart from". The Mani gambu has singgekü jüg, which is öröne jüg in the other two versions. Moreover, there is tariyalang-un oron instead of ayui; tariyalang-un oron, "field" translates žiṅ-khams of the Tibetan Mani bka'- 'bum (1v:1). The Mani gambu also shows the expression olan nidü-tü-yin jiruqai jiruqayilaysan, corresponding to the Tibetan mig-maṅ ris-su bris-pa (1v:2). These words also appear in the Oyirad version of the Mani bka'-'bum, which Kara quotes in his article ("Une version mongole", p. 23, note 8). Finally, the Mani gambu uses the expression ner-e čü ügei, "not even the name" instead of nere ber ügei in the other two versions. However, both čü and ber mean "even".

168 boda bodalang instead of bodalang bodalang.

169 -dur or -tur. This suffix is inconsistent in the text. See, for example, delekei-tür (*1v:7).

170 The passage from lines 6 to 9 is not found in XBM 54; Mani gambu (vol. 1, chap. 1, 2r) has: bodi modon-iyar čimegsen-ečč busu: jimis-tü modon kiged oi siyui-yin ner-e čü ügei. See also Kara, p. 22.

5 [   ] olan
6 [   ] usun nereber[171]
7 [   ] bilig-ün
8 [   ]
9 yal-ača öber - e

10 busu [yi]rtinčü-yin
11 tüleküi [   ][172] un ne[re]
12 ber ügei + .::
13 [o]yoyat[a]

XBM 54

2 items of a *pothī* (3 written sides). The first item is a fragment of a folio measuring 11 × 4.5 cm, and has 10 lines; the Mongolian page number is *nigen* (1). The second item is a nearly entire folio with the edges and sides torn, which measures 18 × 6.5 cm, and has 18 lines; the Mongolian page number is *qoy[ar]* (2). The remaining is legible.[173]

1v

1 O nigülesküi ejen [   ]
2 avalogide šuvar-a [   ]
3 mörgömüi öröne [   ][174]
4 badm-a kemekü süka[vadi]
5 ayui aqu : erdenis [-ün]

6 altan delekei-tür el[deb][175]
7 jüil jayalmai čoyol-bu[ri-ača]
8 öber- e busu : sir[oi] [kiged][176]
9 gürü-yin nerebe[r] [ügei]
10 bodalang [   ]

2r

1 [be]lge bilig-ün čoy-tu
2 [ba]darangyui yal-ača öber-[e]
3 [bu]su : yirtinčü-yin tülekü[i]
4 yal-un nereber ügei +
5 oyoyata tonilaqui küjisü[n][177]

6 ünüd anggilaqui-ača öbere
7 busu : kei salkin-u nereber ügei + :
8 nom-un činar-un tegsi delekei yajad
9 -ača öbere busu : siroi kiged
10 maqabud-un nereber ügei + :[178]

---

171 The passage from lines 1 to 6 is not found in XBM 54; *Mani gambu* (chap. 1, 2r):*naiman üy-e-tü diyan-u usun bayatur-ača busu eldeb usun-u ner-e čü ügei; Maṇi kha'-'bum* (Kara, p. 22) reads: *naiman erdem-tü diyan-u usun urusquy-ača. anggida busu olan jüil usun-u nere ber ügei.*
172 XBM 54, 2r:4 has *yal-un.*
173 Restored by Mr. Bentchev; old numbers 26/6, 10/4.
174 *jüg-ün* is found in XBM 51, 1v:3 and XBM 52, 1v:5.
175 XBM 53, *1v:8 has *eldeb.*
176 XBM 53, *2r:1 has *[kig]ed* at this point. See *siroi kiged maqabud* below in this text.
177 The genitive suffix *-ün* is joined to the word *küjis,* the plural of *küji.*
178 *Mani gambu* (vol. I, chap. I, 2r): *nom-un činar-un delekei toytaysan-ača busu. maqabud-un yajar-un ner-e čü ügei.* The Xarbuxyn Balgas text has *tegsi delekei yajad,* while the *Mani gambu* reads *delekei toytaysan.* The element earth is *siroi* in Xarbuxyn Balgas text, but is *yajar* in the *Mani gambu.* The Tibetan text has this line (1v:4): *chos-kyi dbyiṅs-kyi sa-gźi brdal-ba-las 'byuṅ-sa'i miṅ yaṅ med;* Louvain No. 39, 5v:7–8 reads: *adqay-tu tabun maqabud-un nereber ügei. aldarsiysan bodalang +.* The expression *siroi maqabud,* referring to the five elements occurs in *Ariyun oron-du getülküi sudur* (4v). This text is located in Ulaanbaatar Central State Library (No. 294.2 A-816).

11 *belge bilig-ün gerel-tü sikür*
12 *-iyer geyigülküi-eče öber-e busu :*
13 *naran saran-u nereber ügei + :*
14 *qutuy-dan-u [ge]gen gerel-tü bili[g]*
15 *-üd-eče öber-e busu : ödür*[179]

16 *kiged*[180] *söniyin nereber ügei:*[181]
      bodala[ng + :]
17 *nom-un qad köbegüd ö[besüben]*[182]
18 *[tö]rögsen-eče öbere [busu :]*

2v

1 *[qa]yan kiged*[183] *tüsimed*
2 *[nere]ber ügei + :*[184] *bi minügei*
3 *[   ] barimtalaqui-ača öber[-e]*
      [busu :][185]
4 *[   ] keregül ayidangyui*
5 *[nere]ber ügei + :*[186] *samadi diyan*
6 *i[de]gen idegeküi-eče öbere*
7 *bus[u] : ye[rü] ide[gen]-ü*
8 *nereber ügei*[187] *bodalang + : duran-i*[188]
9 *qangyayči rasiyan-u usun-i uyuqui-ača*

10 *öber -e busu :*[189] *busu umdayan-u*[190]
11 *nereber ügei + :*[191] *ariyun saysabad*
12 *-un qubčad-i emüsküi-eče öbere*
13 *busu : yirtinčü-yin qubčad-un*
14 *nereber ügei + :*[192] *linqua-tača*[193]
15 *qubilyan-iyar törökü-eče*
16 *[ö]ber-e busu :*[194] *[d]örben jüil*
17 *[tör]öl-ün nereber ügei*[195] *bodalang*
18 *[ayulan] -tur törökü boltuyai :*

---

179 Instead of *edür*. The spelling *ödür* also appears in the other copies of the text.
180 *kiged* is barely legible.
181 Louvain No. 39, 5v:2–3: *edür söni-yin nereber ügei. ülemji tere bodalang +.*
182 XBM 56, 3v:7 and XBM 57, *2v:6 have *öbesüben*.
183 *kiged* is legible in the original.
184 Louvain No. 39, 6v:10–12: *kerčigei yertenčü-yin qayan tüsimel-ün nereber ügei. kelberil ügei tere bodalang +.*
185 See *ülü barimtalaqui-ača* in XBM 57, *2r:11–12; *Mani gambu* (chap. 1, 2r) reads *bi kiged minügei ber ülü bariqui-ača busu.*
186 *Mani gambu* (chap. 1, 2r): *temčel bayilduyan-u ner-e čü ügei.*
187 *Mani gambu* (chap. 1, 2r): *diyan-u idegen-iyer amiduran aqui-ača busu. idegen kemeküi ner-e čü ügei.*
188 This word is legible in the original.
189 Louvain No. 39, 5v:15–6r:2: *imayta ükül ügei rasiyan-u idegen-i ideküi-eče öber-e. ilangyuy-a čoyča orod-un idegen-ü nereber ügei. altan tere bodalang +; Mani gambu* (chap. 1, 2v): *eril qan[g]yaqui rasiyan-u usu joyoylaqui-ača busu.*
190 The words *busu umdayan-u* are legible in the original.
191 Louvain No. 39, 6r: 3–4: *eldeb kedüi bükü umdayan-u ilyal inu; Mani gambu* (chap. 1, 2v): *umdayan kemeküi ner-e čü ügei.*
192 Louvain No. 39, 6r:8–13: *sayin qubčad-un kedüi bükü ilyal inu. sača tegsi ilyal ügei qubčad-i emüsküi-eče öbere. samayu yirtenčü-yin qubčad-un nereber ügei. sayaral ügei tere bodalang +.*
193 The combined pre-classical dative-locative suffix *-ta* and the ablative suffix *-ča*. For this suffix see Weiers, *Untersuchungen*, pp. 105–7.
194 *Mani gambu* (chap. 1, 2v): *lingqu-a deger-e qubil-un töröküi-eče busu; Sukavadi-yin oron-u namtar* (chap. 5): *imayta badm-a lingqu-a čečeg-eče qubilaju busu.*
195 XBM 56, 5r:5 and *Mani gambu* (chap. 1, 2v) have *töröl-ün;* Louvain No. 39, 5v:10–13 reads: *ülemji lingqu-a-yin degere qubilju töröküi-eče öbere. ürgüljide dörben jüil törölün nereber ügei.*

XBM 55

1 item (1 small fragment of a folio, 1 written side), measuring 10 × 2.5 cm, and consisting of 11 lines. Lines 9–11 are illegible.[196]

1	*[bo]dala[ng]* [ ]	7	*oluɣsan* [ ]
2	*törökü* [ ]	8	*busu ötel[küi]*[197]
3	*busu* [ ]	9	[ ]
4	*töröl-ün* [ ]	10	[ ]
5	*ügei +* :: [ ]	11	[ ]
6	*ügei nasun* [ ]		

XBM 56

2 items of a *pothī* (2 folios, 4 written sides), measuring 11 × 4–11.5 × 4 cm respectively, and comprising 13–12 lines (r/v); the Mongolian page numbers are *ɣurban, tabun* (3, 5); folio 3 is well preserved, while folio 5 is stained.[198]

3r

1	O *nom-un činar-un tegsi*	8	*sikür-iyer geyigülküi*
2	*delekei yaǰad-ača öber =*	9	*-eče öber-e busu : naran*
3	*e busu : siroi kiged*	10	*saran-u nereber ügei*
4	*maqa-bud-un nereber*	11	*bodalang aɣulan-ţur törökü*
5	*ügei bodalang aɣulan*	12	*boltuɣai +* :: *qutuɣtan*
6	*-tur törökü boltuɣai +* ::	13	*-u gegen gerel-tü*
7	*belge bilig-ün gerel-tü*		

3v

1	*bilig-üd-eče öber =*	7	*köbegün öbesüben*
2	*e busu : ödür*[199] *söni*	8	*törögsen-eče öber =*
3	*-yin nereber ügei*	9	*e busu: qaɣan kiged*
4	*bodalang aɣulan-ţur*	10	*tüsimed-ün nereber*
5	*törökü boltuɣai +* ::	11	*ügei bodalang aɣulan*
6	*nom-un qad-un*	12	*-ţur törökü boltuɣai +* ::

---

196 Restored by Mr. Bentchev; old number 24.

197 XBM 56, 5r:12 has *ötelküi*; *Mani gambu* (chap. 1, 2v) reads: *gegen iǰaɣur-un nasun-a erkesil oluɣsan-ača busu ötelküi baɣuraqu-yin ner-e ču ügei.*

198 Folio 3 was restored by Mr. Bentchev; old number 32/3. Folio 5 was restored by the Russians experts in Ulaanbaatar; old number 7/3.

199 The spelling *ödür* is also found in the other copies of the text.

5 r

1	O törökü boltuγai + ::	8	boltuγai + :: yegüd =
2	lingqu-_t_ača qubilγan	9	kel ügei alin-u[200]
3	-iγar töröküi-eče	10	erkei-yi oluγsan
4	öbe[r]-e busu : dörben	11	-ača öber-e busu :[201]
5	ǰüil töröl-ün [ne]r-e	12	ötelküi üküküi
6	ber [üge]i bodalang	13	-yin nereber ügei
7	aγulan-_t_ur tö[rö]kü		

5 v

1	bodalang aγulan-_t_ur	7	-yin nereber ügei[203]
2	törökü boltuγai + ::	8	bodalang aγulan-_t_ur
3	töröküi[202] üküküi ügei	9	törökü boltuγai + ::
4	möri bisilγaγsan	10	tere oron-_t_ur
5	-ača öber-e busu :	11	[...]γči qotalaγar
6	töröküi üküküi	12	bodi yabudal-iγar[204]

XBM 57

2 items (2 folios, 4 written sides) of a booklet *(debter)*. They measure ca. 11.5 × 5 cm, and have different numbers of lines, without page numbers. The first folio is severely damaged and only a few words are legible.[205]

*1 r

1	öber-e busu	7	[ ]
2	törökü üküküi	8	[ ] nereber
3	[ ]	9	ügei [boda]lang aγulan
4	[ ]	10	-_t_ur [törö]kü boltuγai
5	[ ] boltuγai	11	+ ::
6	[ ] yabuqui-ača		

---

200 The letter *l* is still legible in the word *alin*.
201 *Mani gambu* (chap. 1, 2v): *gegen iǰaγur-un nasun a erkesil oluγsan-ača busu.*
202 *töröküi* is legible in the original.
203 *Mani gambu* (chap. 1, 2v): *törökü ükükü ügei mör bisilγaγsan-u tula töröku üküku bui-yin ner-e ču ügei; Sukavadi-yin oron-u namtar* (chap. 6) reads: *enelül ǰobaqu terigüten tamu ba. ölösün umtasqu terigüten birid ba.teneg mungqay büged ačiγlal onoγdaqu ügei.*
204 *Mani gambu* (chap. 1, 2v): *burqan-u tariyalang-un oron tende. qamuγ bodičid edleküi-eče busu ǰobalang qoor-un ner-e ču ügei.*
205 Restored by Mr. Bentchev; old number 12/22.

*1v

1 O küjis-ün ünüd[206]
2 angilaqui-ača[207] öber-e busu
3 kei salkin-u nereber
4 ügei + :: nom-un činar-un
5 tegsi delekei yajad
6 -ača öber-e busu siroi

7 kiged maqabud[-un] ner-e ber
8 ügei + :: belge bilig gerel
9 -dü sikür-iyer geigülküi
10 -eče öber-e busu naran
11 saran-u nereber
12 ügei + :: qutuy-tan-u

*2r

1 gegen gereltü bilig-üd
2 -eče öber-e busu
3 ödür kiged söni-yin
4 nereber ügei + :: nom-un
5 qad-ud köbegün
6 öbesüben törögsen-eče
7 öber-e busu :[208] qayan

8 kiged tüsimed-ün
9 nereber ügei + ::
10 bi <>[209] minügei
11 kemen ülü barimtalaqui
12 -ača öber-e busu :
13 keregül

*2v

1 ayidangyui-yin ner-e ber
2 ügei [...][210] diyan-u
3 idegen ideküi-eče öber-e
4 busu yerü idegen-ü
5 nereber ügei + :: [du]rani
6 qangyayči rasiyan-u usun
7 uyuqui-ača öber-e

8 busu busu umdayan-u
9 nereber ügei + ::
10 ariyun [says]abad-un
11 qubčad emüsküi
12 [-eč]e öber-e busu :
13 yirtinčü-yin qubčad-un
14 [ne]r-e ber ügei[211] + ::

* * *

206 The plural forms of the words küji and ünür.
207 For anggilaqui.
208 The Mani gambu (chap. 1, 2r) has: nom-un qayan oron öber-iyen uryuysan-ača busu. This copy from Xarbuxyn Balgas has the word qan with two plural suffixes (qad-ud). XBM 54, 2r:17 reads nom-un qad köbegüd, while XBM 56, 3v:6–7 has nom-un qad-un köbegün. It is possible that qad-ud is a mistake for qad-un, but Poppe quotes xādūd in his Khalkha-mongolische Grammatik (p. 55).
209 The copyist of the text left the word minügei incomplete at this point, subsequently writing it again; Mani gambu (chap. 1, 2r) has bi kiged minügei ber ülü bariqui-ača busu.
210 This word is illegible. XBM 54, 2v:5 has samadi diyan; the word samadi is not found in the Mani gambu (chap. 1, 2v).
211 The word ügei is legible in the original.

Hymn to Ariyabalo (XBM 58; XBM 59)

The fragmentary text XBM 58; XBM 59 bears no title. It is a hymn which praises Ariyabalo (Skr. Āryabala), "He of the noble powers", in the form of one head and four arms (Ṣadakṣarī).[212] I was unable to find a text similar to that from Xarbuxyn Balgas,[213] but at least the description of the deity, is similar to that found in the *Gegen toli,* "Bright Mirror".[214]

XBM 58

3 items of a *pothī* (5 written sides). The first item is a nearly entire folio which measures 11.5 × 5.5 cm, and has 13 lines, without page number. The edges of the folio are torn. The second item is a folio which measures 12.5 × 5.5 cm, and has 16 lines; the Mongolian page number is *qoyar* (2). The folio shows various vertical splits, and is stained on recto. The third item is a folio which measures 12.5 × 5.5 cm, and has 14 lines; the Mongolian page number is *yurban* (3). It is damaged on verso.[215] The text is careless in its orthography.

*1v

1 [ ] su[va]sdi sidam
2 [ ] blam-a idam
3 kiged: yurban erdeni
4 -tür mörgömü :: om + ::
5 bodalan ayulani[216] orgil
6 agi (?) oron-tur bütügsen
7 ülisi ügei[217] nom-un

8 činar-un qarsi (?)[218] -tur
9 burqan [na]ran saran
10 sayurin [...]n sayuysan-u
11 boyda [a]riy-a bal[o] adi[s]ti =
12 d[219] öggün soyorqa
13 :: x :: oo[m]

---

212 See Essen and Thingo, *Die Götter des Himalaya*, pp. 74, 76.
213 The hymn called *Ariy-a balo-yin maytayal,* which I saw in the Central State Library in Ulaanbaatar (No. 294.2 A-819), is different from the Xarbuxyn Balgas text; a payer for salvation and blessing addressed to Ariyabalo is included in Mong. 149 (Heissig and Bawden, *Catalogue*, p. 241).
214 Ligeti, "La collection", p. 173; on this source, see Heissig, *Geschichtsschreibung*, I, pp. 34–40.
215 Restored by Mr. Bentchev; old numbers 22/15, 26.
216 Instead of *ayulanu*.
217 *ülisi ügei,* Skr. *anupama;* Tib. *dpe-med-pa.* See Ishihama and Fukuda eds., *Mahāvyutpatti,* No. 68.
218 This word is not clear in the original, but a similar phrase is found in the text which describes Sukhāvatī composed by Blo-bzan tshul-krims. It reads (11 v, 13 r): *ülisi ügei sayin qarsi ger ... ülisi ügei sayin ordo qarsi* = Heissig and Sagaster, *Handschriften,* Libr. Mong. 93, No. 494, p. 266.
219 *adistid,* Skr. *adhiṣṭhāna;* Tib. *byin-rlabs, Mahāvyutpatti,* No. 4250.

2r

1	*qotala amitan-u*	9	*asru²²⁰ gerel ɣarɣači*
2	*itegel bodičid sedkil*	10	*čaɣan öngge beyetü :*
3	*-tü qoyoson kiged*	11	*[…]un²²¹ kkir ügegü²²²*
4	*[ni]gülesküi ilɣal ügei*	12	*[…]²²³*
5	*sedkil-tü qutuɣ-tu yeke*	13	*selteyin ariluysan bey-e*
6	*nigülesküi-de mörgön*	14	*-tür [mö]rgön maɣtamu x ::*
7	*maɣtamu x :: asida (?) yeke*	15	*[…] […]küi*
8	*nigülesküi ariy-a balo anu*	16	*čira[i] niɣur-tu*

2v

1	*unduyuliy nidü-tü*	9	*ɣar-tu bolusan²²⁸ ta[…]da (?)*
2	*[…]tur qa<a>bar (?)²²⁴-tu ulaɣan*	10	*alačilaqu²²⁹ ügei amitan-u*
3	*nidü-ü iǰayur inu*	11	*tusalaqui belgetü tuyuskesen²³⁰*
4	*qotala-yi üǰegči : uduridu =*	12	*itegel-tür-iyer (?)²³¹ mörgön*
5	*či²²⁵ ariy-a balo-tur mörgön*	13	*maɣtamu x :: baraɣun ɣartaɣan*
6	*ma[ɣ]tamu x :: dörben<e>²²⁶ ǰüil*	14	*subud erike bariɣsan²³²*
7	*čalasi²²⁷ ügei gerel tegüsügsen*	15	*barasi²³³ ügei yeke*
8	*-iyer tunumal dörben<e> ǰüil*	16	*nigülesküi [ ]*

3r

1	*balamad amitan-i uduridqu*	6	*bariɣsan²³⁵ tegsi ǰirɣuɣan*
2	*bel<i>ge²³⁴ -tü baɣatur yeke*	7	*ǰüil amitan-i tusalabai*
3	*nigülesügči-tü-de mörgön*	8	*taduru orčilang-un²³⁶ gem*
4	*maɣtamu : x :: degedü ǰegün*	9	*-üd-eče ese qaldaɣsan*
5	*ɣartaɣan čaɣan badm-a*	10	*belgetü :: degere ügei burqan*

---

220 For *asuru*.
221 There is a split in the folio. Probably this word is *ariɣun*.
222 *gkir ügegü, gkir ügei*, Skr. *vimala*; Tib. *dri-ma med- pa*, *Mahāvyutpatti*, No. 449.
223 This line is illegible.
224 The passage below reads *ɣaar* for *ɣar*.
225 *uduridduɣči, uduriduɣči*, Skr. *nāyaka*; Tib. *'dren- pa*, *Mahāvyutpatti*, No. 20.
226 This is an orthographic mistake for *dörben*.
227 Instead of *čaɣlasi*.
228 Instead of *boluɣsan*.
229 For *alaɣčilaqu*.
230 For *tegüskegsen*.
231 Probably erroneous for *-tür-iyen*.
232 *baraɣun ded ɣar-daɣan čaɣan erike* is found in the *Gegen toli* (7 r).
233 For *baraɣdasi; baraɣdasi ügei, baraɣdaqu ügei*, Skr. *avyayībhāva*; Tib. *zad-par mi-'gyur-ba*, *Mahāvyutpatti*, No. 4717.
234 Instead of *belge*.
235 *ǰegün ded ɣar-daɣan čaɣan čečeg barigsan* (*Gegen toli*, 7 v).
236 The letter *u* of the suffix *-un* is written like *v*.

11   -a mörgön maytamu :: x::
12   qoyar ya<a>r-iyar ǰirüken<e>[237]

13   tus alayaban qamtudasan[238]
14   <san> qoyoson kiged

3v

1   nigülesküi [   ]lal
2   [   ]
3   qot[   ]
4   taqu[...] [...]ysan belgetü (?)
5   : qo[y]ar ügei ya<a>r
6   -tuda mörgön maytamu
7   : x :: kelen-tür ǰiryuyan

8   [   ] badm-a [   ]san
9   -iyar (?) si[...]kei ǰiryuyan
10   üjüg-i aldarsiyuluči
11   ǰarliy-tu gegegen ǰiryuyan
12   üjüg-iyer tüidkeri
13   ari[lyay]či [...]u :
14   geyigülün [   ]či-tur

XBM 59

1 item of a *pothī* (1 fragment of a folio, 2 written sides), measuring ca. 8.5 × 4.5 cm, and consisting of 10–11 lines; the page number is missing.[239]

The text is written in two hands, one of which is similar to that of XBM 58. The text shows the same orthographic features as XBM 58. Thus, this fragment could be either a part of XBM 58 or of another copy of the text. The orthography of the text is extremely careless. There is hardly a single word which is correctly written. As a result, the transcription of the text is uncertain.

recto

1   mörgön maytamu
2   om x :: om ma ni
3   [bad] ma hum günbeli
4   [   ]n niluyun (?) [...]sim[240] -de

5   [   ]r čimeg<en>sen[241] girben alčilqu[242]
6   [üge]i tabun ǰüil gerel yarqu (?)
7   küsilitü ǰirlayang-un[243] oronsa[244]
8   qaraysan (?) küsili[245] qangyači-da

---

237   The text has *yaar* for *yar*, *ǰirükene* for *ǰirüken*.
238   For *qamtuduysan*; the *Gegen toli* (7r) has *degedü qoyar yar-tu ǰirüken tus alayaban qamtudqaǰu*.
239   Restored by Mr. Bentchev; old number 26.
240   I am unable to read this word.
241   For *čimegsen*.
242   Probably for *gilben alayčilaqu*.
243   For *küseltü ǰiryalang*.
244   This word is probably an error for *oronasa*, which would make sense in the present context. On the ablative suffix *-asa/-ese* see Poppe, *Grammar*, § 292, p. 75, and by the same author see "Geserica", pp. 22–23.
245   For *küseli*.

9 *mörgön maytamu [x ::] [om] m a [ni]*   10 *quy (?)²⁴⁶ tanyi qoyor köl̲dyin²⁴⁷*
   bad [ma]   11 *ǰbilan²⁴⁸ [sa]yuysan čiqu[ ]*

verso

1 *[   ] [be]lge bilig<e>²⁴⁹*   6 *maytamu om :: tabun<a>²⁵⁰*
2 *[...] bolyan kergesen (?)*   7 *iǰayur-tu [   ] yi*
3 *belge bilig<e>-ün belge [   ]*   8 *oroi-t̲ur [   ] tegüsügsen*
4 *ünen gegegen s[   ]*   9 *tabun belge bilig<e>-ün*
5 *medegči-de mörgön*   10 *[m]ön čina<a>r-tu*

* * *

Sādhana of Qomsim Bodisu(n)g (XBM 60)

Continuing with the texts devoted to Avalokiteśvara, XBM 60 is a *sādhana* of Qomsim Bodisu(n)g in the form of one head and four arms (Ṣaḍakṣarī-Lokeśvara). The title of the text is unknown to me. Although I was unable to find a text similar to this one, I observed that the Xarbuxyn Balgas text describes the god using phrases which are similar to those found in works of the cult of Avalokiteśvara, such as the *rGyal-rabs gsal-ba'i me-loṅ²⁵¹ (Gegen toli),²⁵²* and the *Maṇi bka'-bum (Mani gambu).²⁵³*

XBM 60

2 items of a *pothī* (2 folios, 4 written sides), written in a beautiful hand, measuring ca. 12 × 6 cm, and comprising 11–13 lines; the Mongolian page numbers are *yurban, dörben* (3–4). Folio 3 has the sides and edges torn, otherwise the text is well preserved.²⁵⁴

3 r

1 O *yar-tur čayan lingqu-a :*   3 *ayulan -t̲ur naran-u gerel*
2 *čikin tus bariǰu : času-tu*   4 *aysan metü öber-iyen čoy-tu*

---

246 It should be *qung*.
247 For *tan-u qoyar köldüiyen*.
248 For *ǰabilan*, "to sit cross-legged" (Lessing, p. 1019).
249 *bilige* is clearly an error for *bilig*.
250 For *tabun*.
251 The work was translated into English by Sørensen. See *The Mirror*.
252 The *Gegen toli* was mentioned above. It should be pointed out that the version of the *Gegen toli* to which I had access (= Ligeti, "La collection" p. 173), does not coincide completely with the *rGyal-rabs gsal-ba'i me-loṅ*.
253 Heissig and Sagaster, *Mongolische Handschriften*, No. 334, pp. 192–3.
254 Restored by the Russians experts in Ulaanbaatar; old number 7/3.

5 *gerel-tü qomsim bodisug*
6 *bolba bi :*[255] *kemen sedkigdeküi*[256]
7 *oroi-tur čaɣan öngge-dü :*
8 *oom üjüg : qoyoloi-tu*[257]

9 *ulaɣan öngge -tü e üjüg*
10 *: jirüken-tür köke öngge*
11 *-tü qung üjüg : ede ɣurban*
12 *üjüg-üd-eče gege[n] [na]ran*

3v

1 *ɣaruɣsan-iɣar egenisda*[258] *beyen*
2 *tengri-yin oroi-taki viročana*
3 *bu[r]qan-u jirüken-tür kürčü*
4 *bilig-ün kei öber-ün bey-e*
5 *-tür iregsen-iyer öber-ün*
6 *tergen oɣtarɣui-tur*
7 *qomgsim bodisug-nar*[259]

8 **kiged** *egülen metü dügürčü bayiju :*
9 *oom mani bad mi qung ::*
10 *kemekü tarni ber nomlamui : bi ber*
11 *nomlaldusuɣai kemen mutur janggid =*
12 *ču : sayuju: oom ma ni bad*
13 *mi qung :: kemekü tarni ber*

4r

1 ○ *küčün čidaɣsan ber erke*
2 *tataɣdaqu*[260] *burqan burqan-iɣan*[261]
3 *uriju iregülügsen včir-tu<r>*
4 *sedkil-ün tabun naiman takil-iɣar*

5 *takiɣdaqu tabun-a naiman ede buyu ::*
6 *oom arvam a qung : oom badim*
7 *a qung : oom busbim a qung :*
8 *oom dubam a qung : oom*

---

255 The *Gegen toli* describes Avalokiteśvara in the form of one head and four arms as follows: *nigen niɣur-tu dörben ɣar-tu. degedü qoyar ɣar-tu jirüken tus alaɣaban qamtudqaju. baraɣun ded ɣar-daɣan čaɣan erike bariju. jegün ded ɣar-daɣan čaɣan čečeg barigsan ... öngge inu času-tu aɣulan-dur naran ɣarugsan metü* (7r–7v), "He has one head and four arms. The first two have the palms of the hands joined together in front of his heart. The lower right hand holds a white rosary. The lower left hand holds a white flower (lotus). His body complexion resembles the colour of the sun rising upon the glacier mountains". In the *rGyal-rabs gsal-ba'i me-lon*, we find a passage which reads (Sørensen's translation) "(in the form of) one head and four arms of which the first two are joining together the palms of the hands in front of the breast, the lower right hand holding a rosary of white crystal, the lower left hand (holds) a white lotus blossoming in the direction of the ear ... a body complexion resembling the rising sun shining upon a Massif of glacier-mountains". *The Mirror*, pp. 100–1. See also the *Mani gambu*, chap. 2, 24v–25r. For a similar description of Qonšim Bodistv in Uighur, see Kara and Zieme, *Fragmente tantrischer Werke*, pp. 67–8.

256 The future noun in *-qui/-küi* of the passive verb expresses the idea of necessity to act. See Poppe, Grammar, § 607, p. 169. However, the future noun in *-qu/-kü* can also express the same idea. See *tataɣdaqu* in 4r:2 below in this text; on the future noun of the passive verb see the remarks by de Rachewiltz in "The Preclassical Mongolian Version", note 37, p. 58.

257 For *qoɣolai*, reflecting the spoken language.

258 For *aganista* (Akaniṣṭha).

259 *qomsim bodisug* with the plural suffix *-nar*.

260 The *nomen futuri* in *-qu /-kü* of the passive verb expressing the idea of necessity to act. See *takiɣdaqu* in line 5.

261 *burqan* is repeated *twice*.

9   *alogi a qung : oom g̱andi*   11   *oom sabda a qung :*[262]
10   *a qung : oom nabede a qung :*

4v

1   *bradi ǰa qung :*   7   *-tür-iy[e]n tabun titim-tü*
2   *suvaq-a : ede takil-nuyud*   8   *nigülesküi nidü-ber olan amitan-i*
3   *-iyar takiyad : basa ber*   9   *örösiyegči : üǰegči erketü*
4   *maytayal ede buyu : <> :*   10   *yeke nigülesügči-de mörgömü :*[263]
5   *gem-eče ese qaldaysan čayan öngge*   11   *manayar erte*[264] *ür čayiqui čay*
6   *-tü tuyuluysan burqan terigün*

* * *

Prayer to Lokeśvara (XBM 61)

XBM 61 is a fragment which bears witness to a prayer which invokes Lokeśvara,[265] although it is difficult to establish whether we are dealing with a text which is entirely devoted to this deity.

XBM 61

1 item of a *pothī* (1 nearly entire folio, 1 written side), measuring ca. 14 × 5 cm, comprising 16 lines; the Mongolian page number is *ǰiryuyan* (6). The text is framed with lines. The folio has a hole in its surface and the lower part of the text is missing. The folio is also framed with lines on verso, but the text was not written on this side.[266]

6r

1   *O yeke nigülesügči-de*   5   *siǰimi tasu[l]umui*[267] *om + ::*
2   *mörgömü yerüde itegen*   6   *giri u[ ] üǰüg*
3   *takimui yertenčüi-yin ǰobalang*   7   *-tür ǰalba[ri]mui [ ]tu*
4   *-ača tonilumui yesün*   8   *sedkil-i talbimui nom[...]*

---

262   The 8 offerings are the following: *argha, pādya, gandha, puṣpa, dhūpa, āloka, naivedya, śabda*. See Waddel, *The Buddhism of Tibet*, p. 426; see also Savvas and Lodro Tulku, *Transformation*, p. 75, et passim; on offering materials and their meanings see Wayman, *The Buddhist Tantras*, pp. 71–81.
263   In the *rGyal-rabs gsal-ba'i me-lon* we find the following description of the deity (Sørensen's translation): "his hair was endued with five knots ... and decorated with precious jewels", *The Mirror*, p. 101.
264   See *manaqar erte* in § 90 of the *Secret History*.
265   On the iconography of Lokeśvara see Clark, *Two Lamaistic Pantheons*, p. 219.
266   Restored by Mr. Bentchev; old number 32/1.

9	*jiryalang-tur türidkem[üi]*	13	*jalbarimui mayu[ ]*
10	*orodu (?) logisvari-ṭur*	14	*bilig-tür sid[ ]*
11	*mörgömü om + :: [ ]*	15	*manduyulugči [ ]*
12	*ma üjüg-tür [ ]*	16	*[…] takimui manju[ ]*

* * *

Prayer to Mahākāruṇika Ārya-Avalokiteśvara (XBM 62)

The beginning of the text in the fragment XBM 62 transcribed below invokes the great compassionate Avalokiteśvara (the text has *ma-ha-a garuni-ga; mahākāruṇika*).

XBM 62

1 item of a *pothī* (1 folio, 2 written sides), measuring 11.5 × 5 cm, consisting of 12 lines; the Mongolian page number is *nigen* (1). The text is framed with lines. Some sections of the folio are stained, making some words difficult to read.[268]

1r

1	O *yeke nigülesügči ar-y-a*	7	*nuyuluyad tonilqui-yin möri*
2	*duradduysan-iyar burqan bolqu*	8	*üjügül-ün bodi qutuy-un giskigüri*[269]
	keme =	9	*bayiyuluyad : tuyuluysan*
3	*besü bodi saduva ma ha a saduva*	10	*burqan-u taniyultuyai*
4	*ma ha a garuni ga : ary-a avalovgi =*	11	*nigülesügči ber : adistidlan soyorq =*
5	*de suvar -a-ṭur mörgömü :*	12	*a :: nidü-ber üjegči [ ]*
6	*itegemüi bi : mayui jayayan-u egüden*		

1v

1	*soyorq-a :: yirtinčü-yin […]u [ad]is =*	7	*-yi buyan-iyar nögčigül-ün soyorq-a ::*
2	*tidlan soyorq-a [::] amitan-u itegel*	8	*minu kelen-i buyan-iyar nögčigül-ün*
3	*adistidlan soyorq-a :: čindamani*	9	*soyorq-a :: minu sedkil-i buyan*
4	*erdeni adistidlan soyorq-a ::*[270]	10	*-iyar nögčigül-ün soyorq-a : edür*
5	*ilayuysad-un degedü köbegün*	11	*söni ügei örösiyen soyorq-a :*
6	*adistidlan soyorq-a :: minu bey-e*	12	*yabuqui sayuqui-ṭur s[a]kin*

* * *

---

267 See *sijim tasuraysan, nasuda tasuraqui*; Skr. *prabandhoparama*; Tib. *rgyun-chad-pa*, in Ishima and Fukuka eds., *Mahāvyutpatti*, No. 2023.

268 Restored by Mrs. Nebel; old number 32/5.

269 *giskigür, giškigür*.

270 On Ārya Avalokita Cintāmaṇi, see Sørensen, *The Mirror*, p. 192 and note 801, p. 267.

Hymn to Yeke Nigülesügči (XBM 63)

The small fragment XBM 63 is what we have left of a text devoted to Avalokiteśvara, who is called *yeke nigülesügči (mahākāruṇika)*, "great compassionate". The text was not identified; however, it contains terms which suggest that we are dealing with a hymn to Avalokiteśvara in his fierce manifestation. The text has *[ye]ke [ni]gülesügči-de maytan mörgömü*, "Praising, I bow to the great compassionate". Moreover, terms like *ǰalayu bey-e, ada todqar, butaratala* occur in other Mongol hymns in praise of fierce Tantric deities such as Mahākālī[271] and Yamāntaka (see XBM 65 below). Finally, the description of Avalokiteśvara as a fierce deity, who defeats enemies and evil forces, is found in the *Mani gambu*.[272]

XBM 63

1 item of a *pothī* (1 fragment of a folio, 2 written sides), measuring ca. 7 × 4.5 cm, with 9–8 lines (r/v). The fragment is badly damaged, and the sequence of the text is tentative.[273]

recto

1 [ ]mi
2 [ ]i
3 [ye]ke [ni]gülesügči
4 [-d]ür maytan mörgö[m]ü ::
5 oṃ (?) ma ni bad

6 mi hūm + ǰalayu
7 bey-e-ben [...]ysan
8 be[l]ge bi[l]ig-ün[274]
9 [   ]n nidüber

verso

1 ba[ ]
2 qam[ ]
3 butaratala [ ]gči[275]
4 kedtür doysid-i

5 qamuy ada todqar[276]
6 -i eǰelegči(?) [...]ge [...]m
7 č[...] qamuy-a [...]
8 [...] ki (?) erke[t]ü

* * *

271 See the hymn to Mahākālī = Cerensodnom and Taube, *Turfansammlung*, No. 30, pp. 117–19.
272 Vol. 1, chap. 2, 39v–40r.
273 Restored by Mr. Bentchev; old number 25/3.
274 *belge bilig* are legible in the original, but the letter *l* is missing in both.
275 It is possible that this word is *kiduyči* (spelled *kidugči*); the hymn to Yamāntaka (see XBM 65 below) has *butaratala kiduysan*.
276 *ada todqod* is found in the hymn to Mahākālī = Cerensodnom and Taube, *Turfansammlung*, No. 30, p. 118; *ada todqod* also appears in the passage of the *Mani gambu* describing Avalokiteśvara in his fierce manifestation (vol. 1, chap. 2, 40r).

Prayer to Nidüber Üjegči Erketü (XBM 64)

The last text of the worship of Avalokiteśvara (Mong. *nidüber üjegči erketü*) only consists of one damaged fragment.[277]

XBM 64

1 item of a *pothī* (1 folio, 1 written side), measuring 10×3.5 cm. The ink has entirely faded in the first section of the text, and only 8 lines are left.[278]

1 [ ]*ysan burqan*
2 [ ] *küjigüben*
3 *čimegsen nigülesküi*
4 *nidüber amitan-i*

5 *üjegči nidüber*
6 *üjegči erketü*
7 *-de*
8 *mörgömü*

277 A text with the title *Nidüber üjegči-yin maytayal tarni* is included in Mong. 163 (Heissig and Bawden, *Catalogue*, p. 231).
278 Restored by Mr. Bentchev; old number 25/3.

Hymn to Yamāntaka

XBM 65 is a fragmentary hymn in alliterative verses in praise of the fierce god Yamāntaka, "The Ender of Yama".[1] I was able to find, in a collection of ritual texts, a complete copy of an incense offering of Yamāntaka, without a title, which basically coincides with the text from Xarbuxyn Balgas.[2]

The hymn to Yamāntaka is one of the most interesting texts of the Xarbuxyn Balgas collection. The text provides evidence of the worship of Yamāntaka in northern Mongolia in the first half of the 17th century. Moreover, it sheds light on an important aspect of the cult of Činggis qaγan, such as the worship of the white standard and black standard (*čaγan sülde, qara sülde*)[3] As a matter of fact, the hymn to Yamāntaka includes passages which show striking similarity to those which are found in the texts of the incense offering of the white standard and black standard of Činggis qaγan.

Various printed texts of the incense offering of the standards of Činggis were used in this work.[4] I also used the photographic reproduction of a manuscript which bears the title *Činggis eǰen boyda-yin sakiγulsun čaγan sülde-yin sang takily-a kiged sarqud čai sayalin-u ǰüil-üd yoson tegüs orosiba*, "Incense offering to the protective white standard of the holy lord Činggis, and the perfect ritual to offer various kinds of ceremonial milk

---

1 On the various iconographies of this god see Getty, *The Gods of Northern Buddhism*, p. 153; Essen and Thingo, *Die Götter des Himalaya*, pp. 168–71; Tsultem, *Mongyol ǰiruγ*, No. 72. On texts of the cult of Yamāntaka, see Heissig and Sagaster, *Mongolische Handschriften*, No. 366 (*Ya ma ndaga-yin dbang sudur orosiba*), No. 374 (*Yamandaga sudur orosiba*), pp. 208, 210–11; see also Heissig, *Blockdrucke*, pp. 47–9.

2 Heissig and Sagaster, *Mongolische Handschriften*, No. 466, Ms. or. quart. 771-5, pp. 253–4.

3 The term *sülde* conveys various concepts; *sülde* expresses the idea of sacred, charismatic power, vital force and vigour. On this important term see Bawden, "Vitality and Death", pp. 10–14; Skrynnikova, "Sülde", pp. 51–9; Even, *Chants chamanes mongols*, pp. 437–9; *sülde* means "object of veneration, majesty of a person" (Šaγ ǰa, *Mongyol ügen-ü tayilburi toli*, p. 888). In the cult of the standard (*sülde, tuγ sülde*) of Činggis, *sülde* refers both to the protective ancestral spirit of Činggis and to the standard which embodied it. See Sayinǰirγal and Šaraldai, *Altan ordon-u tayily-a*, p. 321; Mostaert, "Sur le culte", p. 548 and note 37. As Altangarudi et al. state, *sülde* is Činggis qaγan himself. For this see *Mongyolǰin-u šasin surtaqun*, p. 325.

4 Rintchen, *Matériaux*, pp. 60–1; *Eǰen sülde-yin sang* in Sayinǰirγal and Šaraldai, *Altan ordon-u tayily-a*, pp. 324–9; *Eǰen sülde-yin sang* in *Ordos-un tayily-a takily-a irügel maytaγal*, pp. 9–15; *Eǰen sülde-yin sang* in Γaluu and J̌irandai eds., *Mergen gegen*, pp. 488–500; the Ordos text *Boγda eǰin-ü sülde-yin sang orošibai* was translated into English and commented on by Serruys. See "A Mongol Prayer to the Spirit of Činggis-Qan's Flag", pp. 527–35.

brandy, tea and milk products".[5] Moreover, the facsimile reproduction of *Altan sülde-yin sang*, which is included in the *Altan bičig*.[6]

XBM 65

3 items (3 folios of a *pothī*, 5 written sides), measuring ca. 11 × 6–11 × 6.5 cm, comprising 9–10 lines; the Mongolian page numbers are *nigen, qoyar, γ[ur]ban* (1, 2, 3). The folios are severely damaged; folios 1 and 2 are half-burnt, but the text is legible using infra-red reflectography; folio 3 is stained, and some words are illegible.[7]

1v

1 O *yamandaga kemen nereyiddügsen*[8]   5 *mörgömü ::*[10] *ǰalaman včir ǰida barin*[11]
   -iyer :   6 *ǰalayu čirayiban baruyiysan*[12]
2 *yambir ba*[9] *berke simnus-un dayisun-i* 7 *ǰayidugsan üsün-iyen sirbüügsen*[13]
3 *daruys-an yayaramtayai dayun-iyar*   8 *ǰalayu boyda yamandaga burqan-ṯur*
4 *dayudaysan yamandaga : burqan-ṯur*   9 *mörgömü :*[14] *niyur turquran (?)*[15]

---

5 The original manuscript is preserved at the home of the Tuγči, the person in charge of the cult of the white standard, in a place called Alabur in Üüsin Banner, one of the seven banners of the Ordos in southern Mongolia. Prof. Sagaster and myself visited Alabur in April of 1990, and on that occasion the Tuγči allowed us to photograph the text.

6 Yang Haiying, *An Introduction to Altan bičig,* pp. 150–4.

7 Restored by Mrs. Nebel; old numbers 14 (fols. 1–2), 25/4 (fol. 3).

8 For *nereyidügsen.*

9 For *yambar ba.* Ms. or. quart. 771-5, 12r:8, *Altan sülde-yin sang* (p. 150), Rintchen (*Matériaux,* p. 60) and Serruys ("A Mongol Prayer", p. 528) have *yambar ba; Eǰen sülde-yin sang* has *yamarba* (*Ordos-un tayilγ-a takilγ-a,* p. 9).

10 The text should be arranged as follows. *yamandaga kiged nereyiddügsen-iyer / yambir ba simnus dayisun-i daruys-an / yayaramtayai dayun-iyar dayudaysan / yamandaga burqan-ṯur mörgömü* etc.

11 Ms. or. quart. 771-5, 12r:6 has *barin kilingleysen.*

12 Ms. or. quart. 771-5, 12r:7: *ǰalayu čirai niyur-tu.*

13 For *sirbeyigsen (sirbeigsen),* reflecting the spoken language; Ms. or. quart. 771-5, 12r: 6–7 reads *üsün-iyen degegsi sirbeyigsen.*

14 *Čaγan sülde-yin sang* (1v:13–2r:9) reads: *altan sülde kemen nereyidügsen yambhar ba berke simnus-un dayisun ni daruysan qariy-a yeketü čaγan sülde yayaramtayai dayun dayudaysan altan sülde čimadur takin mörgömüi. ǰalaman včar-ḏu ǰida-iyan barin kilinglegsen ǰalayuu čirai niyur-ḏur jayiduysan üsün-iyen serbeilgegsen ǰalayuu boyda sülde čimadur takin mörgömü.*

15 This word is not clear. The correct form must be *niyur-turiyan. Čaγan sülde-yin sang* (2v:9) reads *niyur-ḏur-iyan.* Serruys, "A Mongol Prayer" (p. 528) has *niyur-tur-iyan.* The latter is also found in Sayinǰirγal and Šaraldai (*Altan ordon-u tayilγ-a,* p. 325), Rintchen (*Matériaux,* p. 60), *Eǰen sülde-yin sang* (*Mergen gegen,* p. 490) and *Eǰen sülde-yin sang* (*Ordos-un tayilγ-a takilγ-a,* p. 10); *Altan sülde-yin sang* (p. 150) has *niyur-tayan.*

2r

1 O *mingyan nidün-i niγ[uča]*[16] *-yin*
   e[j]en
2 *manjusi[r]i :*[17] *minu [ ]*[18] *üilesi*
3 *ü[l]ü medegči niγur toγorin či[m]eg*
4 *-tü boyda yamandaga :: sülder-tü*[19]
5 *küčütü-yin tulada : sümbür*

6 *-ün orgil deger-e : südara[s]un-u*[20]
7 *ejen qormusta tngri-yi :*
8 *sogödke[gü]l-ün*[21] *bayiγsan boyda*
9 *yamandaga :*[22] *sayaral ügei sedkil*
10 *-dü- yin tulada : sangsar-tu*

2v

1 O *yabuqu amitani: samaγu maγu*
2 *simnus-us*[23] *ejen-i [ ] [...]*[24]

3 *boyda yamandaga : irekü simnus-un*
4 *adasi*[25] *qariγulqui-yin tulada :*

---

16 Ms. or. quart. 771-5, 12r:9–10 has *mingyan nidü-tei niγuča ...*
17 See Vajrabhairava (Yamāntaka or Yamāri), the fierce manifestation of Mañjuśrī, in Essen and Thingo, *Die Götter des Himalaya*, pp. 168–9. The text invokes Mañjuśrī as *niγuča-yin ejen*, "lord of mysteries", which is an epithet of Vajrapāṇi (Lessing, p. 1177). See *niγučasun ejen včir-a bani* in XBM 42, *2v:13–14.
18 There is a hole in the folio. Ms. or. quart. 771-5, 12r:19: *nigeken ber.*
19 Apart from *Ejen sülde-yin sang* (*Mergen gegen*, p. 491), in which the form *sülde* occurs, the other versions of the incense offering to the *sülde* of Činggis have *sülder. Altan sülde-yin sang* (p. 151); Rintchen (*Matériaux*, p. 60); Serruys ("A Mongol Prayer", p. 529); *Ejen sülde-yin sang* (*Altan ordon-u tayily-a*, p. 325); *Ejen sülde-yin sang* (*Ordos-un tayily-a takily-a*, p. 10).
20 For *sudarasun*. On Sudarasun, the abode of Qormusta Tngri, see the *Čiqula kereglegči*, 16v (facsimile in Heissig, *Geschichtsschreibung*, vol. I).
21 The text has *sogödkel-ün* instead of *sögödkegülün*. Ms. or. quart. 771-5, 13r:4 has *sögedkegülün*.
22 *Čaγan sülde-yin sang* (2r:9–2v:5): *niγur-dur-iyan mingyan nidütei niγuča-yin üiles-i nigeken ber ülü medegči niγur-dur -iyan toγorin čimegtü boyda čaγan sülde čimadur takin mörgömüi. sülder yeke küčütü (küčütü)-yin tulada sümber aγula-yin orgil deger-e sudarsun ejen qaγan qormusta tngri emün-e-ben sögödkegülün bayiγsan boyda čaγan sülde ...;* See *niγuča-yin üiles* in Serruys ("A Mongol Prayer", p. 528); Sayinjirγal and Šaraldai (*Altan ordon-u tayily-a*, p. 325); *Ejen sülde-yin sang* (*Mergen gegen*, p. 491) has *niγučas-un üiles*. Rinchen (*Matériaux*, p. 60) writes *niγuča ulus-i*, which Rintchen corrects as *niγuča-yin üiles* on the basis of a ritual text to Geser; *Altan sülde-yin sang* (p. 150) reads *niγuča ulus-i.*
23 *simnus* < AT *šimnu ~ šamnu, šumnu; simnus* is a plural form in *s*, but is also used as a singular in the early texts. For this, see Cerensdom and Taube, *Turfansammlung*, No. 10, p. 77, and note 10r14, pp. 76–7. The term *simnus* means, "demon, evil spirit, Māra (in Buddhism)". See Lessing, p. 710.
24 These two words are illegible. Ms. or. quart. 771-5, 13r:5–7 reads *sangsar-tu yabuqu amitan-i samaγu yeke tulada. sakisuγai kemegsen; Čaγan sülde-yin sang* (2v:6–9) reads: *sangsar-dur yabuγči amitan samaγu maγu yeke tulada sakisuγai kemen.*
25 The plural form *adas* with the accusative suffix *-i* joined to the word. See *čisutan dayisun adas-i* in the hymn to Mahākālī = Cerensodnom and Taube, *Turfansammlung*, No. 31, p. 119.

5 *u[l]ayan*[26] *bey-e-ben qubilǰu : ilegü*
6 *[du]tayu*[27] *simnus-un čerig-üd-i*
7 *un-i*[28] *butaratal-a kiduysan*

8 *boyda yamandaga :*[29] *mital ügei sedkil*
9 *-tü-yin tulada : min[gy]an yal qar-a*

3 r

1 *nidün -iyen qar[...]*[30] *mun [ü]gei*[31]
    [   ]
2 *[si]mnus-un adasi m[...]*[32]

3 *[boyda] yamandaga*[33] *[...]*
4 *[amit]an-i örösiyeküi-yin sedkil*
5 *[-tü]-yin tu[l]ada :*[34] *[ü]nen degedü*

---

26 The letter *l* in the word *ulayan* is not legible. Ms. or. quart. 771-5, 13r:8 has *ulayan*.

27 Ms. or. quart. 771-5, 13r:9 has *ülegü dutayu ügei*.

28 The word *uni* is written separately *(un-i)*. This word is attested in various sources; *hüni* is found in §§ 177, 242 of the *Secret History* meaning "smoke"; § 242 has *hüni butara'ulčaǰu*. See de Rachewiltz, *Index*, p. 139; see also Haenisch, *Wörterbuch*, p. 79 (*huni*, "Rauch"); *ünin* appears in a Turfan text. See the discussion by Cerensodnom and Taube, *Turfansammlung*, note 69r10, p. 172; see also *unin* in *Yeke včir ayuyuluyči tantr-a* (Siklós, *The Vajrabhairava Tantras*, p. 164); see *unin butaraǰu* in Ishihama and Fukuda eds., *Mahāvyutpatti*, No. 5240; the term *uni*, "smoke", is listed in *Mongyol üges-ün iǰayur-un toli*, p. 388.

29 *Čayan sülde-yin sang* (2v:10–16): *öber öber-ün šimnus dayisun olan-u tulada. olan ridi qubilyan ni qubilyaǰu ilegüü dutayuu simnus-un čerig-üd-i unayan sayitur kiduyči boyda sülde...; Eǰen sülde-yin sang* (*Mergen gegen*, pp. 492–3) reads: *öber öber-ün silmus-un dayisun olan tulada. ünen degedü ridi qubilyan-i qubilyaǰu. ilegüü dutayu silmus-un čerig-üd-i. ünen sayitur butaratal-a kiduyči.*

30 This word is not entirely legible. Ms. or. quart. 771-5, 13r:12 has *yaryaǰu; Čayan sülde-yin sang* (3r:3); *Altan sülde-yin sang* (p. 151); Rintchen (*Matériaux*, p. 61); Serruys ("A Mongol Prayer", p. 529) and the other version have *qaraǰu*.

31 Ms. or. quart. 771-5, 13r:12 has *müng ügei; Altan sülde-yin sang* (p. 151) has *mün ügei;* Sayinǰiryal and Šaraldai (*Altan ordon-u tayily-a*, p. 326), *Eǰen sülde-yin sang* (*Mergen gegen*, p. 493), *Eǰen sülde-yin sang* (*Ordos-un tayily-a takily-a*, p. 11) have *mung ügei;* Rintchen (*Matériaux*, p. 61) has *mön ügei;* Serruys ("A Mongol Prayer", p. 529) transcribes *mö[n]g ügei*, and translates this expression as "dispirited" (p. 533), referring to the armies of evil spirits. In my own view, however, this expression refers to the *sülde* of Činggis in the text which Serruys translates, and to Yamāntaka in the text from Xarbuxyn Balgas. Moreover, in a note Serruys writes that Mostaert suggested the spelling *möng* meaning, "inconsistent, disheartened, discouraged" (note 25, p. 533). I propose the term *mung, müng*, which is rare, but not unknown; the spelling *mung* occurs in § 90 of the *Secret History* meaning "difficulty" (Haenisch, *Wörterbuch*, p. 112), while *müng* is found in the *Erdeni-yin tobči* (Urga text, 28v). See Chiodo, *Erdeni-yin tobči. A Manuscript from Kentei Ayimay*, p. 13.

32 These words are illegible; Ms. or. quart. 771-5, 13r:13 has *olan simnus-un adas-i. mölkegülün geskiysen (giskigsen)*.

33 *Čayan sülde-yin sang* (3r:1–7): *matal (mital) ügei ǰoriy-du-yin tulada mingyan qar-a nidün-iyen kelinglen (kilinglen) qariyaǰu mong ügei olan šimnus-un čerig-üd-i köl door-a-ban mölkögülün geskegsen (giskigsen) boyda čayan sülde ...*

34 Ms. or. quart. 771-5, 14r:1–2 has *olan ǰobulang-tan amitan-i örösiyen sedkil-tü-yin tulada.*

6 *[manjusi]ri*[35] *bodis[un]g qubilju :*[36]
7 *[örö]siyen*[37] *bayiɣsan boyda*

8 *[yamandaga :]*[38] *[doɣ]sin*[39] *sedkil-tü-yin*
9 *[tulada :]*[40] *[tongɣo]raɣ*[41] *gabalad*

3v

1 ○ *bariju tüg tümen adasun*
2 *[čer]ig-üd-i terigün-i oɣtalju*
3 *m[on]čaɣ*[42] *jegügsen boyda*
   yamandaga [:][43]
4 *[boɣ]da-yin [j]arliɣ-iyar ülü yabu[ɣči]*[44]

5 *büküi nom-tur [ü]lü kičiyegči*[45]
6 *bu[r]uɣu maɣu yabudal-dan-i ü[ ]*
7 *badanči (?) boyda yamandaga :*[46] *[ ]*
8 *amitan-i tonilɣaqu[i] [   ]*[47]
9 *qamuɣ-iyar tonil[   ]*[48]

---

35 Ms. or. quart. 771-5, 14r:3.

36 Serruys, "A Mongol Prayer" (p. 529) reads: *orošin sakiqu-yin tulada ünen degedü olan ridi qubilyan-i qubilyaju; Ejen sülde-yin sang* (*Mergen gegen*, p. 494) has *örösiyen qaraju. sakiqu-yin tulada. ünen degedü ridi. qubilyan-i qubilyaju.*

37 Ms. or. quart. 771-5, 14r:4.

38 *Čaɣan sülde-yin sang*, 3r:13–15 reads *olan jobalang-tan amitan-i öröšiyen sakiqu-yin tulada. olan ridi qubilyan-i ɣarɣaju öröšiyen sakiyči …*

39 Ms. or. quart. 771-5, 13r:4.

40 See *sedkil-tü -yin tulada* above (2r:9–10). Serruys, "A Mongol Prayer" (p. 529) reads *doɣšin sedkil-tü-yin tulada.*

41 Ms. or. quart. 771-5, 13r:15, Serruys ("A Mongol Prayer", p. 529) and *Ejen sülde-yin sang* (*Mergen gegen*, p. 494) have *tongɣoraɣ; Altan sülde-yin sang* (p. 151) has *tongɣoriɣ.*

42 *mončaɣ* is found in Ms. or. quart. 771-5, 14r:1.

43 *Čaɣan sülde-yin sang* (3r:7–12): *doɣšin yeke küčütü-yin tulada tongɣoriɣ jida-iyan barin kilinglejü tüg tümen čerig-üd-ün terigün-i oɣtalun mončoɣlan jegügsen boyda čaɣan sülde …; Ejen sülde-yin sang* (*Mergen gegen*, p. 494) reads: *tüg tümen silmus-un. toloɣai-yi oɣtolun mongčoɣlan morin-dur-iyan čimeglen jegügsen;* Rintchen, (*Matériaux*, p. 61): *doɣsin sedkiltei-yin tulada. tongɣoraɣ jida-ban bariju. tüg tümen čerig-ün dayisun-i terigün-i oɣtalun molčuylan. erike bolɣan jegügsen; Altan sülde-yin sang* (pp. 151–2): *doɣsin sedkil-tei-yin tulada. tongɣoriɣ jida-iyan bariju. tüg tümen čerig-üd-ün dayisun-u terigün-i oɣtalun molčoɣlan erike bolɣan jegügsen.*

44 See *ülü kičiyegči* in the next line; *Altan sülde-yin sang* (p. 152) reads: *boyda-yin jarliɣ-iyar ülü yabuɣči;* Serruys, "A Mongol Prayer" (p. 529) has *boyda sülde-yin jarliɣ-iyar ülü yabuɣči; Ejen sülde-yin sang* (*Mergen gegen*, p. 495): *boyda sülde-yin üiles-iyer ülü yabuɣči.*

45 *ülü kičiyegči* is found in *Altan sülde-yin sang* (p. 152), Rintchen (*Matériaux*, p. 61), Sayinjirɣal and Šaraldai, *Altan ordon-u tayily-a,* (p. 327), and *Ejen sülde-yin sang* (*Mergen gegen*, p. 495).

46 Ms. or. quart. 771-5, 14r:6–9 has the following passage: *buruɣu maɣu yabudal-tan-i daruɣči. boyda +. erkin burqan nom-i olba. eteged maɣu-i üiledügsen maɣu olan bolba. erdem-ten sayid maɣu čögidbe (čögedbe). engke amurliɣuluɣsan boyda +; Čaɣan sülde-yin sang* (3v:6–11): *boyda sülde-yin jarliɣ-iyar ülü yabuɣči büküi nom-dur ülü oroɣči buruɣu maɣu omoɣ-tan-i doroyitaɣulun daruɣči boyda čaɣan sülde …; Altan sülde-yin sang* (p. 152): *boyda-yin jarliɣ-iyar ülü yabuɣči. büküi nom-dur ülü kičiyegči buruɣu yabudaltan-i doroyitaɣulun daruɣči…;* Rintchen (*Matériaux*, p. 61): *jarliɣ bolun yabuɣad. jaliqai buruɣu omoɣtu yabudaltan-i doruyitaɣulun daruɣči;* Sayinjirɣal and Šaraldai (*Altan ordon-u tayily-a,* p. 327): *buruɣu maɣu yabudaltan-i doroyitaɣulun daruɣči; Ejen sülde-yin sang* (*Mergen gegen*, p. 496): *buruɣu maɣu nomtan-i doroyitaɣulun daruɣči.*

47 Ms. or. quart. 771-5, 14r:10 has *qamuɣ amitan-i tonilqu-yin tulada.*

The worship of Yamāntaka among the Mongols goes back to the Yuan dynasty. 'Phags-pa Lama, the spiritual teacher of Qubilai, composed prayers to Yamāntaka.[49] The Tantra of Yamāntaka (Vajrabhaivara), the fierce manifestation of the Bodhisattva Mañjuśrī, played an important role in all Tibetan Schools, especially the Sa-skya-pa and dGe-lugs-pa.[50] Yamāntaka was the Yidam of Tsoṅ-kha-pa.[51]

Information on the cult of Yamāntaka in northern Mongolia during the first part of the 17th century is as yet rather scanty.[52] Contrast this with the worship of Yamāntaka in eastern Mongolia and Buddhist circles in Peking where the worship of this fierce Tantric deity spread during the first part of the 17th century.[53]

The hymn to Yamāntaka should be linked with the literary tradition of poems composed in praise of fierce deities, of which the hymn to Mahākālī by Chos-kyi 'od-zer is the earliest example in Mongolian religious literature.[54]

It is also important to stress that the hymn to Yamāntaka shows surprising similarity to the texts of the incense offering of the white standard and black standard (čaɣan sülde, qara sülde) of Činggis. The majority of these texts were collected in the Ordos, where the worship of the two standards continues in Üüsin Banner and Eǰen Qoroɣa respectively.[55]

---

48 Ms. or. quart. 771-5, 14r:11–12 reads: *qaranɣui sansar-ača ɣarɣaǰu. qamuɣ nom-ud-iyar tonilɣaɣsan;* Serruys ("A Mongol Prayer" p. 530): *qamuɣ amitan-i qaranɣui sansar-ača ɣarɣaqu tulada qamuɣ nom-ud-iyar tonilɣaɣči;* Sayinǰirɣal and Šaraldai (*Altan ordon-u tayilγ-a,* pp. 328–9): *qamuɣ amitani qaranɣui sansar-ača ɣarɣaqu-yin tulada qamuɣ nom-ud-iyar qariyulun tonilɣaɣči.* The same passage is found in both *Altan sülde-yin sang* (p. 153) and *Čaɣan sülde-yin sang* (4v:4–7). The latter has *daruɣči* instead of *tonilɣaɣči; Eǰen sülde-yin sang* (*Mergen gegen,* p. 499) has *qamuɣ nom-iyar qariyulun. tonilɣaɣči siditü.*

49 *Pagba lama-yin tuɣuǰi,* pp. 82, 183.

50 Essen and Thingo, *Die Götter des Himalaya,* p. 168.

51 Lessing, *Yung-ho-kung,* pp. 75–6. On the diverse aspects and traditions of the cult of Yamāntaka, see the book by Siklós, *The Vajrabhairava Tantras.*

52 Heissig, "A Mongolian Source to Lamaist Suppression", p. 126; the history of the monastery of Erdeni J̌oo tells us that the fierce Tantric deities have been worshipped in this monastery since its foundation in 1586, but there is no mention of the cult of Yamāntaka in this source (*Erdeni ǰoo-yin ba öndör gegen-ü namtar,* pp. 34–5). The manuscript is preserved in Ulaanbaatar Central State Library, No. 517-3 E-734; on the worship of Yamāntaka and other fierce deities in Mongolia, see Pozdneyev, *Religion and Ritual,* pp. 380, 417–43.

53 Heissig, "A Mongolian Source to the Lamaist Suppression", pp. 124–9; see *Blockdrucke,* pp. 47–9 by the same author. The *Altan erike* tells us that Altan qaɣan of the Tümed had a temple devoted to Yamāntaka constructed in Čabčiyal (p. 123, and note 22r–22v, p. 210); on the worship of Yamāntaka in Peking, see Lessing, "The Topographical Identification of Peking with Yamāntaka", pp. 89–90.

54 See Cerensodnom and Taube, *Turfansammlung,* Nos. 29–32, pp. 114–22; see also the poem to Mahākāla Darqan Güjir Tengri in Poppe, "Opisanie", pp. 155–8.

55 On the history of the worship of the white standard in Üüsin Banner, see Erkesečen, *"Yisün költü čaɣan tuɣ",* pp. 43–53; see also Chiodo, "The Worship of the White Standard (*čaɣan tuɣ sülde*) in Üüsin Banner", pp. 618–26. Unfortunately, this article contains numerous printing mistakes. On the worship of the black standard in Eǰen Qoroɣa, see Sayinǰirɣal and Šaraldai, *Altan ordon-u tayilγ-a,* pp. 280–329.

We also have a great deal of information about the worship of both the white standard and black standard in northern Mongolia.[56]

The cult of Činggis qaγan is an ancestor-cult. The cult of Činggis, however, developed in different forms, and Činggis's *sülde* was also interpreted in the light of Buddhist beliefs, as the texts of the incense offering show. The Buddhist interpretations of Činggis qaγan as Cakravartin, an incarnation of Vajrapāṇi, and as a fierce deity *(doysin)* were discussed elsewhere.[57]

Finally, it is worth quoting passages from the hymn to Yamāntaka and the incense offering of the *sülde* of Činggis respectively, which are good demonstrations of the association of the *sülde* of Činggis with Yamāntaka.

The hymn to Yamāntaka describes the god in these words: *doysin sedkil-tü-yin [tulada] [tongyo]ray gabalad*[58] *bariǰu tüg tümen adasun [čer]ig-üd-i terigün-i oytalǰu m[on]čay ǰegügsen boyda yamandaga* (3r:8–3v:3), "Holy Yamāntaka, because you have a fierce mind, you hold a chopper and a skull bowl. You cut off the heads of countless armies of demons, and wear them as a garland (around the neck)."

Similar words describe the *sülde* of Činggis in *Čayan sülde-yin sang: doyšin yeke küčütü-yin tulada tongyoriy ǰida-iyan barin kilingleǰü tüg tümen čerig-üd-ün terigün-i oytalun mončoylan ǰegügsen boyda čayan sülde čimadur takin mörgömü* (3r:7–12), "Making an offering I bow to you, holy White Standard. Because you are fierce and powerful, angrily you hold a chopper and spear. You cut off the heads of countless armies and wear them as a garland (around the neck)."

The two passages show minor textual variants, but the representation of Yamāntaka and the *sülde* of Činggis coincide.[59]

---

56   Arjasüren and Njambuu, *Mongol jos zanšlyn ix tajlbar tol'*, Vol. I, pp. 160–2. On two temples dedicated to Činggis qaγan in northern Mongolia, in which the standards were housed, see Rintschen, "Zum Kult", p. 9; see also Sagaster, "Ein Dokument", pp. 201–2. Information on the white standard in Baruun Xüree is found in Navaan, *Övgön Dèndèv*, p. 30; for the revival of the worship of the black standard in Baruun Xüree, see Chiodo, "The Worship of the Black Standard *(qara sülde)* of Činggis qaγan in Baruun Xüree", pp. 250–4.

57   On Cakravartin Činggis qaγan, and Činggis qaγan as an incarnation of Vajrapāṇi, see the following works: Sagaster, *Weiße Geschichte*, pp. 35–7, 315; Qurča, "*Yekes lamanar*", p. 32; Rintchen, *Matériaux*, p. 62. On the interpretation of Činggis as a *doysin*, see Sagaster, "Ein Dokument", pp. 206–9; Qurča, "*Yekes lamanar*", p. 33. On the association of the worship of the black standard with that of Mahākāla in a Qalqa text see Heissig, *Volkreligiöse Texte*, pp. 159–63, especially p. 159. The section of the text which invokes Mahākāla is different from that devoted to the *sülde* of Činggis. Finally, on the association of the white standard with Sülde Tngri, see Rintchen, *Matériaux*, p. 83.

58   The word *gabala* is in the plural form in the text. The *Yamandaga sudur* (2v:11–12) has *tongyoriy kiged gabala bariysan. Yamandaga ber öber egüskeǰü inu* by Mergen Gegen has *tongyoruy ba yabala-yi bariysan*. See *Mergen gegen*, p. 867.

59   Yamāntaka is depicted with a bull's head and a crown of skulls. The god has a vajra crowned chopper in his right hand and a skull bowl in his left hand. Yamāntaka also wears a garland of human heads around his neck. See Tsultem, *Mongyol ǰiruy*, No. 72.

It is also interesting to note that both Yamāntaka and Činggis are described as possessing *sülder*.[60] The term *sülder* is found in the *Secret History* with the meaning "sign of good fortune and majesty".[61] This term is associated with the person of Činggis and his clan in this source.[62] The expression *süldertü beye*, indicating Činggis's power to frighten enemies, appears in §249 of the *Secret History*. The expression *sülder-tü bey-e*, referring to Činggis is attested in the *Altan tobči*.[63]

---

60 See *sülder-tü* in 2 r:4. On the various concepts of *sülde*, see note 3 above. It is interesting to note that the ancient form *sülder* occurs in all the texts of the incense offering to the *sülde* of Činggis quoted so far. However, in *Eǰen sülde-yin sang*, which is included in Mergen Gegen's collection of ritual texts, we find *sülde* (*Mergen gegen*, p. 491). It is worth pointing out that *Eǰen sülde-yin sang* is one of the numerous texts which Mergen Gegen did not compose. These texts were circulating among the Urad and the Ordos, and Mergen Gegen wrote them down (*Mergen gegen*, p. 22).
61 Haenisch, *Wörterbuch*, p. 137.
62 See §§ 63, 201, 249 of the *Secret History*.
63 111 v.

Incense Offerings

Incense Offerings of the Yellow Jambhala and Geser (XBM 66)

The booklet numbered XBM 66 contains two texts of an incense offering devoted to both the Yellow Jambhala (Skr. Pīta Jambhala) and Geser respectively. The two texts were previously published by Perlee in Mongol script and Latin transcription, and given the titles *Sir-a ǰambala-yin sang* and *Geser boyda-yin sang* respectively.[1] However, the two texts are without titles in the original. Moreover, the text of the incense of Geser, which Perlee published, was translated into German and analysed by Heissig.[2]

Beginning with the texts of the incense offering of the Yellow Jambhala, I had access to the text *Ene šara ǰimbhala-yin takil ene bui*, "This is the offering of the Yellow Jambhala", which is included in the handbook of divination *Tngri-yin qara noqai-yin sudur*, "Sūtra of the black dog of Tngri".[3] Furthermore, during my stay in Bulgan Ajmag in the summer of 1998, Mr. Damdinsüren, a herdsman who lives in Dašinčilen Sum, allowed me to photograph the manuscript which bears the title *Sira ǰambala-yin ubsang*. It belongs to Mr. Damdinsüren's private collection of Mongolian manuscripts and xylographs. Dašinčilen Sum is located in the vicinity of Xarbuxyn Balgas.[4]

Jambhala (Vaiśravaṇa-Kubera) is the Buddhist god of wealth, and the protector of the northern quarter of the world.[5] The Mongols usually call this god Namsarai,[6] and invoke him as "lord of treasury" *(sang-un eǰen)* in prayers. The Yellow Jambhala, and Jambhala of other colours, is also highly venerated in the popular religion of the Mongols. It is also interesting to note that the Ordos regard Qutuɣtai Sečen as an incarnation of the Yellow Jambhala.[7]

---

1 "*Üisènd bičsèn xojor žüjl*", pp. 127–51.
2 "Geser Khan-Rauchopfer", pp. 89–135.
3 Heissig and Sagaster, *Mongolische Handschriften*, Ms. Asch 128-A, No. 89, p. 65.
4 I am most grateful to Mr. Damdinsüren for allowing me to photograph the manuscript.
5 On Vaiśravaṇa, god of wealth and protector of the north, see Essen and Thingo, *Die Götter des Himalaya*, pp. 229, 231, 234–5, and Pīta Jambhala on p. 239; see also Toyka-Fuong, *Ikonographie und Symbolik*, (B), pp. 90–1; Tachikawa, *Five Hundred Buddhist Deities*, pp. 356–7; on Vaiśravana, Kubera and Jambhala, see the description by Nebesky-Wojkowitz in *Oracles and Demons*, pp. 68–81.
6 See *Buddyn šašin, sojolyn tajlbar tol'*, (compiled by Čojmaa et al.), vol. 1, p. 368.
7 Mostaert, "Sur le culte", pp. 555, 558. Mostaert discusses the various aspects of the Yellow Jambhala in the Ordos folklore in note 95, pp. 560–1; see also *Ordos-un tayily-a takily-a*, pp. 502–8. On a shamanist invocation which also addresses the Yellow Jambhala, see Heissig, "Invocation of a Female Shaman", pp. 55, 59. For the significance of Kubera in the Hindu folklore, see Zimmer, *Miti e simboli*, p. 70.

Texts of the incense offering of Geser are numerous. I was able to see *Geser-yin ubsang neretü sudur,* "The sūtra called Incense Offering of Geser",[8] and two texts called *Geser-ün bsang*, which are located at the end of the Geser epic known as *Cay-a-yin geser.*[9] Moreover, I used an incomplete manuscript consisting of a collection of ritual texts devoted to Geser. I purchased this manuscript during my stay in Ulaanbaatar in the summer of 1998.

The Mongols worship Geser as a protective deity of war, domestic animals, especially horses, and game.[10] Ritual texts also describe Geser as an incarnation of the ferocious deity Jamsaran (lCam sring).[11]

XBM 66

1 booklet *(debter)* including two complete texts, without titles, written in two hands, and composed of 12 folios (22 written sides), of which 10 are stitched together and 2 are loose; it measures ca. 10–11×9 cm, and has different numbers of lines; without page numbers. The folios are in a different state of preservation; 12r is severely damaged, and the text difficult to read.[12]

1v

1 *om a qung :: : :*	5 *qana qana qung bad om subau-a*
2 *om a qung :: : :*	6 *sudda sarva darm-a sabau-a soddu*
3 *om a qung :: : :*	7 *[ ]g qoyoson kü*
4 *om bajar amirda gündali*[13]	8 *boltuy[ai]*

2r

1 *qoyoson kü ayar-tur ene sir-a*[14]	2 *čambala*[15] *-yin takil bsang-yi delgeregüljü*

---

8   Heissig and Sagaster, *Mongolische Handschriften,* Libr. Mong. 130, No. 75, p. 54; see also Nos. 71–4. On other texts of the incense offering of Geser, see Heissig and Bawden, *Catalogue,* Mong. 166–70.

9   pp. 549–56.

10 On the the diverse aspects of the worship of Geser among the Mongols, see Heissig, *Religionen,* pp. 401–20; for a detailed study of the the worship of Geser in northern Mongolia, see Rintchen, "En marge", pp. 3–50; the worship of Geser among the Qorčin Mongols is dealt with by Kürelbayatur and Urančimeg in *Qorčin-u jang ayali,* pp. 262–3

11 Rintchen, "En marge", p. 29; on lCam sring see Nebesky-Wojkowitz, *Oracles and Demons,* pp. 88–93. According to Nebesky-Wojkowitz (p. 88), lCam sring or Beg tse was originally a pre-Buddhist deity of the Mongols, who began to be venerated by the Tibetans after bSod nams rgya mtsho turned this deity into a protector of Buddhism.

12 Restored by Mr Bentchev; old number 34.

13 *amṛtakuṇḍalī.*

14 The initial *s* is barely legible in the word *sir-a.*

15 Skr. Jambhala is written *čambala* in the text, but in 3v:2 we find the spelling *zambala.* The incense offering of Geser has *jambala.*

3　*ariyun belge bilig-yi dügürejü el-e*
4　*alimad küsegsen erdem-üd-i ilete ünen*
5　*aldarsiysan sir-a čambala-ṯur*

6　*ariyun takil takimui ::*
7　*qamuy nom-ud-un sang-yi dügürgejü*
8　*bodi sedkil-iyer [...]ǰi*[16]　*urbal ügei*

2v

1　*a[sa]rayči sir-a čambala-dur*
2　*ariyun takil takimui :: mayui*
　　alyasangyui-yi
3　*arilyayči mayad belge bilig-ün ǰula-yi*
4　*ilete dayurisqayči sir-a čambala-ṯur*

5　*ariyun + :: masi sayitur dörben*
6　*qosiyun mal kesig-i öggün soyorq-a ::*[17]
7　*altatu keyid*[18]　*kiged :: arban ǰüg-ün*
8　*burqan-nuyud-un qutuy-yi nadur*

3r

1　*sayitur bütügejü öggün soyorq-a ::*
2　*sasin-u erdem-üd-i ilete ündüsülen*
3　*nigülesügči samayu mayu sedkil-i*
4　*tungy[a]n sayitur ǰasayči sir-a + ::*

5　*sanduraysan bügüdeyi sayitur nuta*
　　ǰasayči
6　*samayuraysan bügüdeyi idqan sayitur*
7　*undurayayči sir-a čambala-ṯur + ::*

3v

1　*[ ]muni-yin*[19]　*erdem-ün sang boluysan*
2　*sir-a zambala*[20]　*-ṯur ariyun takil takimui ::*
3　*simsiredügsen bügüdeyi sergegen nigülesügči*
4　*sirgegsen bügüdeyi unduryan öggügči sir-a + ::*
5　*ünen ǰöb ǰöb-iyer s[a]yitur küsegsen üiles*
6　*bügüdeyi öber-e öber-e qangyayči sir-a[+ ::]*
7　*ügegü dutayu bügüde-yi engkeǰigül-ün*
8　*bayaǰiyuluyči : sir-a + :: ölösügse[d]*

4r

1　*undaya***sug***ad bügüde-yi qangyan čidqayči sir-a [+ ::]*
2　*erigsen sanaysan bügüde-yi öber-e öber-e*
3　*olyayuluyči sir-a + :: ebečiten taqul-ḏan-i*
4　*qurdun-a anayayči sir[-a] + :: qamuy ters*
5　*buruyu sedkil-ḏen-i esergüčel ügei*
6　*daruyči sir[-a] + :: qar-a ǰirüke-tü qoor*
7　*-tu sedkil-ḏen-i ečin-e büged sögö[d]keǰü :*

16　This word is missing in *Sira ǰambala-yin ubsang*. It reads *bodi sedkil-iyer urbal ügei...* (1v–2r).
17　*Ene šara ǰimbhala-yin takil ene bui* = Ms. Asch 128-A, 7v:14–17: *masi sayitur dörben qosiyun mal kiged kesig-yi öggün soyorqayči*; *Sira ǰambala-yin ubsang* (2r) *masi sayitur dörben qosiyu mal kiged-ün kisig-i öggün soyor-ha a*.
18　*altatu keyid* (Altatu monastery) is also mentioned in *Sira ǰambala-yin ubsang* (*alta-tu keyid*, 2r).
19　*[ ]müni* (?); Asch 128-A, 8r:3 and *Sira ǰambala-yin ubsang* (2v) have *sigemüni*.
20　The text reads *zambala* at this point.

8 *ilete sögedkegülüyči sir-a + :: qaya =*
9 *raqai²¹ sabatan-u saba-yi nögkön²² öggügči*

4v

1 *qayačaysan bügüde-yi qamtudqan*
     jiryayu =
2 *luyči sir-a + :: [q]otala-yin erkin*
3 *burqan-u qutuy orosiyuluysan*
4 *sir-a + :: qoličal ügei degedü nom-un*

5 *qutuy-yi quriyaysan sir-a + ::*
6 *qoladaysan bügüd[e]-yi oyiratayulun*
7 *öggügči qočoruysan bügüde-yi teg =*
8 *silen güičegülügči sir-a + :: qutuy*
9 *-tai quvaray-ud-un irüger-i čiqula*

5r

1 *irügegči sir-a + :: qutuy-dan-u belge*
2 *bilig-üd-i oyoyata orosiyulun ayči*
3 *sir-a + :: quriyaysan-i minu arbidqayči*
4 *qumiysan-i minu delgeregülügči*
     sir-a + ::

5 *kimuraqui temečeldüküi bügüde-yi*
6 *a<r>murliyulugči kinal-dan-u jasay*
7 *jam-ača anggijirayuluyči :²³ sir-a + ::*
8 *kilinče-tü üiles-eče jayilayuluyči ::*

5v

1 *kinal-dan-u ö[si]yeten d[a]yisud²⁴ -i²⁵*
     kölberi =
2 *gülün uytuy-ul[uyči]²⁶ [sir-a] + ::*
3 *oṃ quu [   ]ng hiri : hūṃ a a*
4 *hiri hūṃ oṃ čambala jalend[ra]yi*

5 *suvva ha-a oṃ čambala idam bilig*
6 *da ba ba a yi hi ga a hi idam*
7 *čambala sabari var-a argam: badim*
8 *busbin dubam : aulogi gandi naibedi :*

6r

1 *sabda²⁷ baradi jay-a suvva ha-a ::*
2 *ene sir-a čambala-yin takil bsang*
3 *tasural ügei takiysan-iyar :: sedkil anu*

---

21 *qayaraqai* is the ancient spelling of *qayarqai*. *Sira jambala-yin ubsang* (3v) also reads *qayaraqai*. On the occurrence of *qayaraqai* in the early texts, see de Rachewiltz, "The Preclassical Mongolian Version of the Hsiao-ching", p. 38; on this term, see the remarks by Jayunasutu et al. in *Sayin ügetü erdeni-yin sang*, p. 616.
22 For *nökön*.
23 A similar passage is found in the incense offering of the *sülde* of Činggis. It reads: *kimuraqu temečeldükü-yi amurjiyuluyči kinal-tu dayisun jakirtala* (*Ejen sülde-yin sang = Ordos-un tayily-a takily-a*, p. 14); *Sira jambala-yin ubsang* has *kimuraqui temečeküi* (3v).
24 The ink has faded at this point, and the word *dayisud* is barely legible.
25 *Sira jambala-yin ubsang* (5v) has *ösiyeten-ü dayisun*.
26 *Sira jambala-yin ubsang* (5v) has *kölberegülün oytoluyči*; Asch 128-A, 8v:12–13: *kölberilün üiledügülügči*; XBM 68, 2v:14: *untayuluyči*.
27 The eight offerings to the Yellow Jambhala are the following: *argha, pādya, puṣpa, dhūpa, āloka, gandha, naivedya, śabda*. See "The practice of the single Yellow Jambhala" in Savvas and Lodro Tulku, *Transformation*, pp. 121–4.

4   *tüdel ügei qanqu*[28] *boltuyai :: yayun*
5   *sanaysan sedkigen üiles minu bügüde čindamani*
6   *erdeni metü ündüsülen bütükü boltuyai ::*
7   *bey-e kelen sedkil minu blam-a burqan nom-un*

6v

1   O *činar bolun bütükü [boltuyai ::]*
2   *om a a hūm čay[an] ö[ng]ge-tü om*
3   *üsüg oroi-tur minu orositu =*
4   *yai adistid-un ündüsün degedü*
      qamuy[29]

5   *blam-a -nar nigülesküi tunumal čayan*
6   *gerel-iyer oroi-tur minu adislan*
7   *getülgen soyor-ha a ::*[30] *ulayan öngge*
8   *-tü e e üsüg qoyolai-tur minu*
9   *bol[tuyai]*

7r

1   *ǰol-un tengri kümün-eče buu qayačaqu*
2   *boltuyai ǰayasun-luy-a usun nököčegsen*
3   *metü : ǰol-un tengri kümün-eče buu qayačaqu bol=*
4   *tuyai sitügen mör üile yurban qamuy bügüde*
5   *-tür bida baysi sabi nökör selte qamiy-a*
6   *genübesü ber: ǰol-un tengri iǰayur-ača nökö =*
7   *[…]n sitügen bolun soyor-ha a : aman abun qoyi[si =]*
8   *da minu ömilen nököčen soyor-ha a :*[31] *om a a*
9   *hūm yurban da* **ügüle**: *gigis subasu: deger-e tengri-ner-ün*
10   *boyda : gerčüyin qubilyan*[32] *čerig-ün terigün bolu =*
11   *gsan boyda minu : dayisun-u omoy süri sinta =*

7v

1   *rayuluyad qariyuluyci boyda minu : nar[a]n saran*
2   *kiged odod-un quyay-i morin-iyan del deger-e*
3   *delgere[n]ggüi ayulul-un bariysan boyda minu : činadusun*
4   *čerig-ün terigün-i omoy süri daruyad : kei*
5   *möndör metü altan toyona -bar gilbelün qarbuyči*
6   *boyda minu [:] kei salkin-u činar-i qamurun qamtudqa =*

---

28   For *qanuqu*.
29   Perlee reads *kümün* (*Sir-a ǰambala-yin sang*, p. 135), which is incorrect; the word *qamuy* is also found in *Sira-ǰambala-yin ubsang* (5v).
30   The letter *h* instead of *q* in the word *soyorqa*. The same spelling appears in *Sira ǰambala-yin ubsang*.
31   The text of the incense offering of the Yellow Jambhala ends here. The last section in *Sira ǰambala-yin ubsang* is different from that in the Xarbuxyn Balgas text (folio 7r, lines 1–8).
32   Libr. Mong. 130, 1r:6: *garudi-yin qubilyan*; *Geser-ün bsang* (*Cay-a-yin geser*, p. 552): *degere tngri-ner-ün boyda yirtinčü-deki qubilyan*; the Ms. belonging to the author (3v): *degere tngri-ner-ün qubilyan geser boyda minu*.

7 gči :[33] morin ǰayan unuysan-u düri-ber
8 yabuyad :[34] bosun güin yabuyči boyda minu :[35]
9 dayisun-u köbegün-i güičen bariyad :[36] köke

8r

1 [lu]u[37] ber kürkire[gü]l-ün[38] dongyodduyči[39] boyda
2 [m]inu : adal mal amin bey-e-tü ergičegči : day =
3 [i]sun-i dalai kiged-iyer[40] d[a]ldalayad[41] qoyar
4 garudi ber derbegül-ün ni[s]ügči boyda minu : ali-ba
5 ǰüg yabubasu emüne-eče minu qoyar luu ber kür =
6 kiregülügč[i] qoyar garudi ber niskegülüged :
7 činadus-un süri doroyitayuluyči boyda minu [:]
8 köke oytaryui körisütü etügen eke-yi ergin
9 toy[o]riyad[42] qamuy dayisun-i qamur-un alayči
10 boyda minu : qayar[q]ai[43] aman-ṭur künesün

8v

1 öggügči boyda minu [:] qalturiqu köl-ṭür m[inu]
2 tüsiy-e öggügči boyda minu : qara [   ][44]
3 gegen ǰula bolyan[45] öggügči qabčal ǰam-i ayu[46] bolyan

---

33 Libr. Mong. 130, 3v:3–7: yar-tayan altan toyon-a gilbel-ün qarbubasu. qamuy dayisun-i
    qočorli ügei alan daruyči; the same passage is found in Geser-ün bsang (Cay-a-yin geser,
    p. 551); on toyona, meaning "arrow", see Pèrlèè, " Üjsènd bičsèn xojor züjl," note 9, p. 124, and
    especially Heissig, "Geser Khan-Rauchopfer", p. 110, and note 42, p. 124.
34 Libr. Mong. 130, 2v:3–5: türgen gilbel-gen-ü morin ǰayan unuysan.
35 Libr. Mong. 130, 6r: 5–7: ginggis geküle bosun güigči-de ariyun takil takimui.
36 Libr. Mong. 130, 2v:6–7: dayisun-u köbegün-ü morin güičen bariysan.
37 Following Geser-ün bsang (Cay-a-yin geser, p. 553).
38 Geser-ün bsang (Cay-a geser, p. 553) has kürkir[e]gülün.
39 dongyodduyči instead of dongyoduyči.
40 kiged with the suffix of the instrumental.
41 Geser-ün bsang (Cay-a-yin geser, p. 554) has damdoluyad, damdaluyad; damda-, "to cover,
    enclose, close", is similar in meaning to daldala-, "to hide, conceal, to cover etc.", Lessing,
    pp. 228, 226. Heissig suggests the reading tamtuluyad. See "Geser Khan-Rauchopfer",
    note 15, p. 100; tamtu- means "to break to pieces, crush, ruin, etc.", Lessing, p. 775.
42 Libr. Mong. 130 (3r:3–7) and the Ms. belonging to the author (3v) have namayi aliba ǰüg-dür
    odaqui-dur minu deger-e köke oytaryui-dur kürkiren ködölümüi. doora etügen eke ergin toyori-
    mui. See körisütei etügen körbeǰü in § 254 of the Secret History = de Rachewiltz, Index, p. 150.
43 Part of this word is illegible. Perlee transcribes it qayarqai (Geser boyda-yin sang, p. 137).
    Judging from the space between the letters r and a (qayar[q]ai), it is also possible that this
    word is qayaraqai, as in the incense offering of the Yellow Jambhala (4r: 8–9).
44 Geser-ün ubsang (Cay-a-yin geser, p. 554): söni-yi.
45 Libr. Mong. 130 5r:1–2: qarangyui söni gegen ǰula boluysan-a; the Ms. belonging to the author
    (4v) reads qarangyui söni ǰula boluysan.
46 ayu, ayuu.

4   öggügči boyda minu : qas qada-yi šatu bolyan
5   öggügči boyda minu : aru-yi atayatu dayisun
6   -i altan toyona-bar alan qarbuyči boyda minu :
7   öber-ün ösiy-e-den-i bars ötege ber dob =
8   tolyan alayči tengri-ner-ün geser boyda
9   minu : čerig-i minu : terigülen uduridun

9r

1   soyorq-a boyda minu : e e boyda minu : gi
2   gis sabasu kei-yin dergede qutuy-tu blam-a
3   -yin batuda yeke ǰabilalčan ǰayaysan : badm-a
4   li[n]gqusi köl dooraača uryuluysan baral ügei sasin
5   -u sang-tu boluysan : eke-tü :⁴⁷ alalduyan qadqul =
6   duyan-i daruysan aginista-yin eǰen šigemüni-yin
7   sasin-i sakiysan : eserun qormusta ečige-tü
8   üy-e üy-e kögǰemel⁴⁸ bayasqulang-tu : ütegerümte =
9   gei⁴⁹ mayu dayisun-i silmusi sakin kiduyči ökin
10 tengri egeči-tü :⁵⁰ uralaqui üile-si⁵¹ kičiyeysen :

9v

1   uqayan-u bodi sedkil-ün siddi güičegsen ünen
2   kü yeke sang-**gi-yin**⁵² eǰen ǰambala aqa-tu :⁵³ yurban čay
3   -yin⁵⁴ burqan-i činar-i abuysan čindan <>

---

47   Rintchen, "En marge", p. 22: *kei-yin deger-e qutuy-tu yeke blam-a-yin batuda arsalan-u
     sayurin deger-e ǰabilan sayugsen. badm-a lingqusi köl dour-a-ača uryuyulugsen. barasi ügei
     saǰin-u sang-tu bolugsen eke-tü eke daginis-un sidi olugsen geser qayan-a mörgümü.*
     Rintchen's transcription was not modified.
48   For *kögǰimel*.
49   The verb *ütegerü-*, *ütegere-* with the suffix *-mtegei*. On the suffixes *-mdayu/-mdegü*, and
     -mtayai/-mtegei, see Cleaves's remarks in "The Sino-Mongolian Inscription of 1335",
     note 176, p. 122.
50   Rintchen, "En marge", p. 22: *edüge sayugsen sigemüni burqan-u saǰin-i barigsen. samayu
     dayisun simnusi as-kin kidügči ökin tengri ečige-tü.*
51   The plural suffix *-s* is joined to the accusative suffix *-i*.
52   Note *sang-gi-yin*. For this suffix see Poppe, "Geserica", p. 17; *Geser-ün bsang (Cay-a-yin
     geser,* p. 554) has *sang-un eǰen,* "lord of the treasury"; see *sang-un eǰin,* in the *ǰulay* text from
     Üüsin = Serruys, *Kumiss Ceremonies,* p. 61.
53   Rintchen, "En marge", p. 22: *ilaǰu tegüs nögčigsen dibinggar-a burqan-u uqayan bodi sedkil-
     ün sidi güičegsen. ünen kü yeke sang-un eǰen ǰambala aq-a-tu.* In another passage of the same
     text the Yellow Jambhala is described as follows: *qalay kölčin-i qamur-un daruyči. qamuy ed
     mal-du arbin bolugči šir-a ǰambala,* p. 22.
54   The word *čay* with the suffix of the genitive *-yin* instead of the usual *-un*. See also below. Perlee
     transcribes *čay-un* (*Geser boyda-yin sang,* p. 149). On the use of the genitive in the non-
     classical language, especially in the language influenced by dialects, see Poppe, *Grammar,*
     § 284, p. 74.

4 *yongqorun-iyar ibegen beyeben čimegsen :*[55] *čirai öngge*
5 *-ben ese aldaysan čayaryu mayu dayisun-i* **simnus-i** *ǰarkira =*
6 *tala kiduyči yurban čay-yin geser boyda minu :*
7 *ütele busu üile-yi ese üileddügsen ünen kü*
8 *yurban erdeni-yin küčün-iyer qamuy dayisun*
9 *-i*[56] *kiduyči geser boyda minu : egüden neng-tü*

10r

1 *qar-a bold*[57] *-iyan ürün qurčadqayči sasin-i domči =*
2 *layči :*[58] *ütegerümtügei mayu sedkilten-i ünesün*
3 *butaratala kiduyči geser boyda minu : qatayu*
4 *qurča bold-iyan qabtayalan yabuǰu : qamuy dayisun-i*
5 *qamurun kiduyči : geser boyda minu : amin sünesün-iyen*
6 *[saki]qui*[59] *-yin tula : aldartu sigemüni-yin sasin-i*
7 *[delge]regülküi*[60] *-yin tula : adal mal em-e köbegün-iyen üreǰi =*
8 *gülküi-yin tula : e geser boyda-tur takin maytan mö[r]gö =*
9 *mü bi :: e e hūm yurban da basu basu la gi gi*
10 *sa ǰalyi : qubilyan minu: küisün čigeǰin*[61] *-eče arban*
11 *ǰüg-ün burqan-u bey-e : köl ebüdüg kürte[l]e*

10v

1 *dörben*[62] *luusun qad-un bey-e tegüsügsen : kösi =*
2 *gün aburitan-i köldegen*[63] *sögödkegsen : qubilyan*
3 *burqan-u bey-e-tü külüg boyda-yuyan takin mörgömü*
4 *[   ] ters irutan-i terigün-i oytaluysan :*[64]
5 *derü (?)*[65] *buruyu-dan-i erke-tür-iyen oroyuluy =*
6 *san : tengri-[yin] [te]ngri burqan-u qubilyan boyd[a]*
7 *eǰen-tür-iyen terigüd-ber-iyen mörgön*
8 *maytan + :: gegen gerel-tü naran metü bey-e-tü*

---

55 *Geser-ün bsang* (*Cay-a-yin geser*, p. 554): *yongqor door-a-bar bey-e-ben čimegsen.*
56 *Geser-ün bsang* (*Cay-a-yin geser*, p. 555): *qarsilayči dayisun-i.*
57 For *bolod.*
58 *Geser-ün bsang* (*Cay-a-yin geser*, p. 554), *doromǰilayči; domčila-* is the denominal verb from *dom*, "sorcery or ceremony for ridding diseases or calamities, magic formula or cure", Lessing, p. 260.
59 *Geser-ün bsang* (*Cay-a-yin geser*, p. 555): *sakiqu-yin tula.*
60 *Geser-ün bsang* (*Cay-a-yin geser*, p. 555): *delgeregülkü-yin tula.*
61 For *čegeǰin.*
62 *dörben* is still legible in the original.
63 The suffix of the dative-locative *-degen* is joined to the word *köl.*
64 *oytal-, oytol-.*
65 Perlee suggests the forms *derü, terü, daru, taru* (*Geser boyda-yin sang*, p. 150).

9   *getemsiküi* (?) *ǰoriytan-i doroyitayuluyči*
10 *sedkil-tü kerülten*[66] *amitan-i qayiralayči*

11r

1   *geser boyda qayan-ṯur-iyan + :: sintaral*
2   *üǰel ügei ǰoriytu ǰoriytu serigün*[67]
3   *sedkil-ḏen-i sintarayuluyči sirayiyo[l]-un*
4   *qayan-i alaǰu*[68] *silege yaryaysan*
5   *siddi-tü törögsen geser-[tü]r-iyen + ::*
6   **mayui** *dayisu[n]-i [i]laysan mongyol ul[u]si*[69] *eǰelegsen*
7   *moqosi ügei ǰoriy-tu molor erdeni*

11v

1   *metü bey-e-tü :*[70] *geser qayan-ṯur-i[yan]*
2   *+:: ayalan odqui [-ṯur]*[71] *qoor-ḏ an dayisun-i*
3   *doroyitayulu-yči : abalan odqui*
4   *-ṯur a[…] [an]g görögesün-i učarayu =*
5   *lu[yči] : sayuqui-ṯur adal*
6   *mal*[72] *küsel qangyayči :*[73] *arban*
7   *ǰüg-ün eǰen geser qayan-ṯur-iyan*
8   *gegegen sayiqan qatun-tu : keger qalǰan morin kölge-tü :*
9   *ken-i ber ayayulun čidayči küčütü : kelkü*[74] *ulusun*
10 *kereg tusa-i bütü**geg**či : geser qayan-ṯur-iyan + ::*
11 *busud-un toroi-yi*[75] *buliyči : buruyu sedkil-ḏe[n] [   ]*

---

66 *kerülten* for *keregülten*, reflecting the spoken language.
67 For *sirügün, siregün.*
68 The hole in the folio existed when the text was written. This is clear from the sequence of the text.
69 The text reads *ulansi*, which is meaningless. It seems that the ink has faded at this point, damaging the letter *u* in the word *ulusi*. The term *ulus* makes sense in the present context.
70 See in the *Erdeni-yin tobči* (Urga text)*: molor erdini metü ene kü bede ulus minu,* 29r.
71 See *odqui-ṯur* in lines 3–4.
72 Perlee transcribes *asayuqui-ṯur adal metü* …, which is incorrect. However, the original is difficult to read at this point. See *Geser boyda-yin sang*, p. 141.
73 *Geser-ün bsang* (*Cay-a-yin geser*, pp. 555–6): *qudalduy-a keger-e odqui-dur. asiy tusa boluysan geser qayan-dur ariyun takil-iyar takimui. sayuqu ger tergen-dür tüsiy-e boluysan*; Libr. Mong. 130, 4v:3–7: *qudal-du kiy-e odqui-dur minu asiy tusa boluysan-a minu ariyun takil takimui. sayuqu ger te[r]gen-tü tusiyen (tüsiyen) boluysan-a*; Rintchen, "En marge" p. 33: *ayalan yabubasu ǰam-un tngri bolun qarayalǰamui. ger-tü sayubasu beyen-ü següder metü sakimui.*
74 *kelkü, kelekü.* On *kelekü* meaning "tout" in *kelekü bügüde*, "tout" see Mostaert, "Introduction" to the *Erdeni-yin tobči*, I, p. 74; see also the form *kelkü* in Sárközi, *Political Prophecies*, p. 26.
75 For *töröi-yi* with the accusative suffix *-i-yi (-i* is joined to the word); Perlee transcribes *durui-yi* and also suggests the reading *dur-a-yi* (*Geser boyda-yin sang*, p. 151); see also Heissig, "Geser Khan-Rauchopfer", note 75, p. 102. However, the word *törö* makes sense in this context.

12r

1   *arban jüg-ün* **ges**er *qayan-i qamuy amitan*
2   *-ṯu tusatu ubsang negüküi-yin usu[n]-u*
3   *qutuy-i ö<n>ggügsen-e minu bayuqui*
4   *nutuy-un qutuy-i egü[gsen]-e*[76] *minu + ::*
5   *keger*[77] *tala-yin kesig-i [ög]gügsen-e*
6   *minu + :: keseg t[o]l[oy]ai bayuri*
7   *jayay[   ] [   ] öggügsen-e*[78] *minu + :: uyuqu*
8   *[   ]*[79] *kesig[-i] [ö]ggügsen-e minu*
9   *+ :: tonilqui čay-i öggügči dibanggarayin*[80]
10 *erdem-ün sa[n]g-i öggügsen-e sigemüni-yin mandal*
11 *-ṯur sayin yabudal-i öggügsen-e minu + :: üküküi-***yin**
12 *čay-i m[…]gči*[81] *mayidari-yin kög dayun dorm[-a]*
13 *-yin*[82] *mandal-ṯur sayin yabudal-i öggügsen-e minu [+ ::]*
14 *öber-ṯür kereg-ṯü […]*[83] *öggügsen-e*
15 *minu + ::*

The inclusion of two texts of an incense offering of the Yellow Jambhala and Geser in a single booklet points to the close relationship between the two deities;[84] it also demonstrates the joint worship of these deities. This type of worship was observed among the eastern Tibetans, who used to perform an incense offering to both the Yellow Jambhala and Geser before starting out on a journey.[85] We have evidence that the Mongols also asked for the protection of Geser before setting out on a journey.[86] Finally, the incense offering to Geser describes the Yellow Jambhala as the elder brother of Geser (9v:2).

An interesting aspect of the incense offering of the Yellow Jambhala is that it mentions Altatu monastery *(Altatu keyid)*, which does not appear in the other Xarbuxyn Balgas copies of the incense offering of the Yellow Jambhala dealt with below (XBM 67–71). Yet *Sira jambala-yin ubsang,* the text which I was able to photograph in Dašinčilen Sum, does mention Altatu monastery. The Xarbuxyn Balgas text refers to Altatu monastery in this passage: *altatu keyid kiged. arban jüg-ün burqan-nuyud-un qutuy-i nadur sayitur*

---

76 For *öggügsen-e.*
77 For *keger-e;* the Ms. belonging to the author (5r) has *kkir ügei.*
78 The Ms. belonging to the author (5r–5v) reads *kkir ügei tala-yin kesig-i öggügsen. keseg toloyai-yin bayuri tübsin-e jayan* (for *jayayan ?*) *öggügsen.*
79 The Ms. belonging to the author (6v): *dalai-yin.*
80 Dibanggara (Dīpaṅkara). See Lessing, p. 254.
81 The Ms. belonging to the author (6v) has *manayači,* so this word should be *managči.*
82 The Ms. belonging to the author (6v): *dormayin.*
83 The Ms. belonging to the author (6v): *öber kereg-ṯü erdem-ün sang.*
84 The association of the Tibetan Gesar with Kuvera, Vaiśravaṇa is shown by Stein in his work *Recherches,* p. 272.
85 I am most grateful to Geshe Pema Tsering, Bonn, for this information.
86 Rintchen, "En marge", p. 25.

bütügejü öggün soyorq-a (3:7–4:1), "Deign to give us, fulfilling it perfectly, the blessing of Altatu monastery and of the Buddhas of the ten directions".

Perlee, tells us that Altatu monastery existed in the 17th century, and it was situated north of the Altaadyn Gol (River Altaad) in what is now Bulgan Ajmag.[87] In Perlee's view, the fact that the text mentions Altatu monastery may indicate that the incense offering was written down in this monastery.

Perlee's view is, of course, interesting. However, the Mongol scholar associates Altatu monastery with *dörben qosiyun*, which appears in the passage located in the preceding lines (2v:5–6). It reads: *masi sayitur dörben qosiyun mal kesig-i öggün soyorq-a*, "Deign to give us perfectly the fortune of the four species of animals". *Sira jambala-yin ubsang* from Dašinčilen Sum has these words: *masi sayitur dörben qosiyu mal kiged-ün kisig-i öggün soyor h-a a.*

Perlee interprets *dörben qosiyun* as "the four banners", i.e. of Tüsiyetü qan, Sečen qan, and the two of Jasaɣtu qan. According to the Mongol scholar, the members of the "four banners" had the two texts of the incense offering written down in Altatu monastery when, in 1614, they gathered to enact one article of the Qalqa Penal Law on the bank of the River Altaad.[88]

In my own view, however, Perlee's interpretation is incorrect, since the text refers to *dörben qosiyun mal*, meaning "the four species of animals".[89] Furthermore, the same words are found not only in the other copies of the incense offering to the Yellow Jambhala from Xarbuxyn Balgas (XBM 69, 2r:4–6; XBM 70r:7), but also in *Ene šara jimbhala-yin takil* (Ms. Asch 128-A, 7v:14–17). As a matter of fact, these texts do not mention Altatu monastery.

XBM 66 also includes an incense offering of Geser. The text constitutes the earliest known written evidence of the worship of Geser in northern Mongolia. Moreover, the text includes expressions which are stongly reminiscent of the Geser epic, offering evidence of the spread of the Mongolian version of the Geser epic before the first half of 17th century.[90] The incense offering addresses Geser as *arban jüg-ün ejen geser qayan*, "Geser qayan, lord of the ten directions" as in the epic.[91] Geser is also adressed as *külüg boyda* in this text (10v:3), i.e. like Činggis qayan in the famous lament of Kilügedei Bayatur.[92]

Moreover, a passage in the incense offering describes Geser, who annihilated the Sirayiɣol. It reads: *sirayiyo[l]-un qayan alaju silege yaryaysan* (11r:3–4), "(Geser) killing

---

87   Pėrlėė, "Üjsėnd bičsėn xojor züjl", p. 143, note 3, and "Xalxyn šinė oldson", p. 136 by the same author. Perlee writes Altadu in the first work and Altatu in the other.

88   Pėrlėė, "Üjsėnd bičsėn xojor züjl", p. 128, and note 2, p. 143.

89   To request the fortune of the four species of animals is a motif of the folk religious texts. See Chabros, *Beckoning Fortune*, pp. 222, 226; see also the fire-*dalalɣa* dealt with in this volume (XBM 82 to XBM 85).

90   This important aspect of the incense offering of Geser is discussed by Heissig in his article "Geser Khan-Rauchopfer".

91   On *Arban jüg-ün ejen geser qayan-u tuyuji*, which was printed in Peking in 1716, see Heissig, *Blockdrucke*, No. 35, pp. 35–6. This text was published in two volumes in Kökeqota in 1955–1956.

92   See, for example, the *Altan tobči*, 126v.

the qaγan of the Sirayiγol eliminated the contagious disease". The Geser epics often refer to the three qans of the Sirayiγol *(sirayiγol-yin γurban qan)*.[93] The expression *silege γarγa-* also occurs in other folk religious texts. It is found both in the so-called *Baγa öčig*, "Small Prayer", which celebrates Činggis's campaigns,[94] and in the incense offering of the *sülde* of Činggis.[95] The term *silege* survived in the Ordos dialect. The *Dictionnaire ordos* lists *šilē* in the meaning of "maladie contagieuse".[96]

Another interesting feature is the expression *köke oγtarγui körisütü etügen eke-yi ergin toγoriγad* (8r:8–9), "The Blue Heaven and Mother Earth with layers revolved", which is reminiscent of the phrase occurring in § 254 of the *Secret History (hodutai tenggeri horčiǰu büle'e ... körisütü etügen körbeǰü büle'e*,[97] "the Heaven with stars was turning round about ... the Earth with layers was turning backward and forward").

* * *

Incense Offering of the Yellow Jambhala (XBM 67 to XBM 71)

The Xarbuxyn Balgas collection also includes fragments of five copies of the incense offering of the Yellow Jambhala.

XBM 67

1 item of a *pothī* (1 folio, 1 written side), measuring ca. 16.5 × 7.5 cm, and consisting of 17 lines; the Mongolian page number is *nigen* (1). The first section of the text is damaged.[98]

1v

1 O o[om] baǰar <emirada>[99] gündali
2 qana qana [q]ung [ba]d oom
3 sübau-a sodu sarava drm-a
4 sübau-a sido qung [qoγ]oson kü
5 [bo]ltuγai qoγoson kü
6 aγar-tur ene sara[100]
7 [ǰa]mbala-yin takil ene bui[101]

8 ariγun buyan bili<n>g-i maγad
9 dügürgeǰü ele alimad qamuγ erdem
10 -üd-ün ilete üne[...]-iyer[102]
11 aldarsiγsan sara ǰambala-tur
12 ariγun takil-**iyar** takimui qamuγ
    ed-ün
13 sang dügürgeǰü bodi sedkil-iyer

---

93 *Arban ǰüg-ün eǰen geser qaγan-u tuγuǰi*, vol. I, p. 153; vol. II, p. 289.
94 See Sayinǰirγal and Šaraldai, *Altan ordon-u tayilγ-a*, p. 50.
95 See Serruys, "A Mongol Prayer", p. 530.
96 Mostaert, p. 616a; see also Serruys's remarks in "A Mongol Prayer", note 44, p. 534.
97 de Rachewiltz, *Index*, p. 150.
98 Restored by Mr. Bentchev; old number 26/27.
99 This word is dotted in the text; *emirada* for *amirada (amrita)*.
100 Instead of *sira*.
101 *bui* is legible in the original.
102 XBM 66, 2r:4 has *ünen*.

14   *urbal ügei asarayči sara*   16   *takimui mayui [a]lyasangyui qarangyui*
15   *ǰambala-ṯur ariyun takil-iyar*   17   *-yi arilyayči may[a]d*

XBM 68

1 item of a *pothī* (1 folio, 2 written sides), measuring 11.5 × 4.5 cm, with 16 lines; the Mongolian page number is *qoyar* (2). The folio has numerous splits, and the text is difficult to read on verso.[103]

2r

1   *ṯur ariyun takil*[104] *taki* =   9   *esergüčel ügei daru[yči]*[107]
2   *[mui] s[ ]muni-yin*[105] *erdem*   10   *sir-a ǰambala-ṯur a[ri]* =
3   *-üd-ün sang boluysan*   11   *yun takil takimui : qota* =
4   *ünen ber ǰöb ǰöb-iyer*[106]   12   *la-yin erkin burqan-u*
5   *sayitur qamuy küsegsen*   13   *qutuy orosiyuluysan*
6   *-i öber-e öber-e*   14   *qoličal ügei degedü*
7   *qangyayči qamuy <> ters*   15   *nom-un-yi qutuy-i quri* =
8   *buruyu sedkil-ḏen-i*   16   *yaysan qutuy-ḏan-u*

2v

1   *quvaray [-ud-un]*[108]   9   *ǰasay ǰam-ača <>*
2   *ir[ü]ger-i či[qula]*[109]   10   *[an]ggiǰirayuluyči kilinče*
3   *irüge[gč]i [oyoya]ta*[110]   11   *[ ]*[114] *üiles-eče <>*
4   *orosin [...]*[111] *sir-a*   12   *ǰayilayuluyči ösiye*
5   *ǰambala-ṯur ariyun*   13   *-den dayisun-i kölberin*
6   *takil takimui :: kimuraqui*   14   *untayuluyči sir-a*
7   *t[emče]ldüküi*[112] *a-murili* =   15   *ǰambala-ṯur ariyun*
8   *[yulu]gči*[113] *kinal-tu*   16   *takil takimui :: sir-a*

---

103   Restored by Mr. Bentchev; old number 31.
104   Part of the *l* of *takil* is still legible.
105   This word is not entirely legible in XBM 66, 3v:1; Ms. Asch 128-A, 8r:3 and *Sira ǰambala-yin ubsang* (2v) read *sigemüni*.
106   *ǰöb* is repeated twice; see *ǰöb ǰöb* in XBM 66, 3v:5.
107   *daruyči* is found in XBM 66, 4r:6.
108   See *quvaray-ud-un* in XBM 66, 4v:9.
109   *irüger-i čiqula* occurs in XBM 66, 4v:9.
110   XBM 66, 5r:2 has *qutuy-ḏan-u belge bilig-üd-i oyoyata;* however, these lines are the same as those in XBM 69, 2v:5–6: [ ] *irügegči čiqula irügeyči [o]yoyata orosin ayči.*
111   This word is illegible, but XBM 69, 2v:6 has *ayči* at this point.
112   XBM 66, 5r:5 has *kimuraqui temečeldüküi.*
113   Part of the word is legible in the original; this word is written separately because there is a split in the folio.
114   XBM 66, 5r:8 has *kilinče-tü;* Ms. Asch 128, 8v:9: *kilinčeten-i.*

XBM 69

1 item of a *pothī* (1 fragment of a folio, 2 written sides), measuring ca. 7.5×6.5 cm, with 8–9 lines, the Mongolian page number is *qoyar* (2).[115]

2r

1 *belge bilig-ün ǰula-yi [   ]*[116]
2 *dayurisqayči sira ǰambala-ṯur*
3 *ariyun takil-iyar takimui masi*
4 *sayitur dörben qosiyu ma[l]*

5 *kiged-ün*[117] *kisig-yi*[118] *ögkü*
6 *soyorqa[q]ui*[119] *[s]ira ǰambala-ṯ[ur]*
7 *ariyun takil-iyar ta[kimui]*
8 *[   ]*

2v

1 *[o]rosiyuluysan qoličal <> ügei*
2 *[de]gedü nom-un qutuy-yi*
3 *quriyaysan qutuy-tan*
4 *[q]uvaray-ud-un <>*
5 *[   ] irügeči čiqula irügeyči*

6 *[o]yoyata orosin ayči sira*
7 *[ǰambal]a-ṯur ari[y]un takil-iyar*
8 *[takimui] [ki]mura-qui*[120]
    temeče[l]düküi
9 *[   ]*

XBM 70

1 item of a *pothī* (1 folio, 2 written sides), measuring 7.5×4 cm, and consisting of 9 lines, with the page number missing; the folio is severely damaged on verso, and only some words are legible.[121]

recto

1 *belge bilig-ü[n]*
2 *ǰu[la]-i*[122] *ile*[123]
3 *dayurisqayči [sir-a]*
4 *ǰambala-ṯur*
5 *ariyun takil taki =*

6 *mui :: masi sayitur*
7 *dorben*[124] *qusiyun mal*
8 *<yun>*[125] *kiged-ün*
9 *kiseg*[126] *-ün öggün*

---

115 Restored by Mr. Bentchev; old number 22/16.
116 XBM 66, 2v:4: *ilete*.
117 *kiged* with the suffix of the genitive.
118 Instead of *kesig-i*.
119 Ms. Asch 128- A, 7v:17: *öggün soyorqayči*.
120 This word is written separately because there is a split in the folio.
121 Restored by Mr. Bentchev; old number 26.
122 XBM 66, 2v:3 has *ǰula-yi*.
123 This word is barely legible in the original; XBM 66, 2v:4 reads *ilete*.
124 Instead of *dörben*.
125 *yun* is part of the word *qusiyun*, but it is written after the word *mal* in the next line.
126 Instead of *kesig*.

verso

1 *[s]oyor-qayči sir-a*
2 *ǰambala-ṯur*

3 *ariγun takil ta[ki]* =
4 *mu[i]*[127]

XBM 71

1 item of a *pothī* (1 nearly entire folio, 1 written side), measuring 11.5 × 5 cm, with 9 lines; the Mongolian page number is *dörben* (4).[128]

4r

1 *ene sir-a ǰambala*
2 *-yin takil-i takibasu*
3 *aliba sanaγsan üiles*
4 *bütükü boluyu :*
5 *ene si[r]-a ǰambala-yin*

6 *neng tegüskü boltuyai :*
7 *[na]sun torqaru ölǰei*
8 *[q]utuγ orosiqu*
9 *[bol]tuyai :: manganam a ::*

---

127 The rest of the text is illegible.
128 Restored by Mr. Bentchev; old number 21/9.

The Worship of Geser

Incense Offering of Geser (XBM 72)

The Xarbuxn Balgas collection bears witness to another text of an incense offering of Geser. Unfortunately, only a small fragment has survived.

XBM 72

1 item of a *pothī* (1 fragment of a folio, 2 written sides), measuring ca. 10×3 cm, with 11 lines.[1]

recto

1	*al[ ]*	7	*qočorlig ü[gei]*
2	*minu [ ]*	8	*eǰen-ṯür takin [ ]*
3	*ködel [ ]*	9	*ǰarliɣ-iyar ya[ ]*
4	*toɣo[ ]*	10	*aysan yaǰar [ ]*
5	*čakil[ ]*	11	*tümen dörben [ ]*
6	*gilbelgen ya[ ]*		

verso

1	*[ ] tul[a]*	5	*[ ] minu tusa*
2	*[ ] m[i]nu*	6	*[ ] [a]rasu-tu bey-e*
3	*[ ] qarangɣui*	7	*[ ] [bo]luɣsan-u tula x::*
4	*[ ] tula*	8	*[doro]yitaɣuluyči eriküi*

---

1 Restored by Mrs. Nebel; old number 25/4.

9 [   ]u qangyayuluyči-da   11 [   ]n [yes]ün³ küsel minu⁴
10 [   ]n-i inu² dürbel ügei

* * *

Prayer to Geser (XBM 73)

Continuing with the worship of Geser, we have a prayer, which was hitherto unpublished. It is interesting to note that the prayer to Geser from Xarbuxyn Balgas is substantially the same as that which is included in the incomplete manuscript, which I was able
to find in Ulaanbaatar. It was described above (XBM 66). The prayer also contains expressions which are similar to those which occur in other ritual texts dedicated to Geser.

XBM 73

1 booklet *(debter)*, which includes a complete text, without a title, and *mantra* at the end of
the text. It is written in two hands, and composed of 5 folios (8 written sides) stitched together. It measures ca. 11 × 5.5 cm, with different numbers of lines; the folios are not numbered. Some words are damaged in the first section of the text, but the remaining text is
well preserved and legible. The last two folio, which include *mantra*, are damaged.⁵

1v

1 ○ dönürüb⁶ [...]   3 ○ kirčün luus [   ] ača
2 ○ e dö[nürüb] : mürei mürei   4 yaruysan suu čerig-ün geser⁷

---

2 *inu* is legible in the original.
3 Either *yesün* or *yisün;* the former is the prevailing spelling in the Xarbuxyn Balgas texts.
4 *minu* is legible in the original. The complete passage in *Geser-ün bsang* (= *Cay-a-yin geser,*
   pp. 501–2) reads: *namayi aliba jüg-dür oduqui-dur minu köke oytaryui kürkiren ködölmüi.
   door-a etügen eke ergin toyorimui. aman-ača minu yal gilbel-ün čakilabasu yartayan altan
   toyona gilbelgen qarbubasu qamuy dayisun anu qočorli ügei alan daruyči. boyda ejen-dür-iyen
   ariyun takil-iyar takimui. boyda-yin jarliy-iyar yabuyči arban jüg-dür aysan sayuysan yajar
   usun-u ejen naiman tümen dörben mingyan jarudasun nököd-tür ariyun ... qarangyui söni
   gegen jula boluysan-a ariyun ... ayuqu amin-dur minu tusa boluysan-a ariyun ... arasutu
   beyen-dür minu quyay boluysan-a ariyun ... ergigüü-tü dayisun-i doroyitayuluyči eriküi yisün
   küsel-i minu qangyayuluyči-dur ariyun ...;* Libr. Mong. 130, 5r:7–6r:4: *arasutu bey-e-dür minu
   quyay boluysan-a minu ariyun takil takimui. ene takil-nuyud-i minu dörbel ügei amsayad
   erigsen yisün küsel-i minu öggün soyorqayči-da ariyun ... eriküdü dayisun-i minu
   doroyitayuluyči-da ariyun ... erigsen yisün küsel minu qangyuluyči-da (qangyaluyči) ariyun ...;*
   Rintchen, "En marge" (p. 21) includes this line: *geser qan arasutu beyen-dü biden-i quyay
   boluyči.*
5 Restored by Mrs. Nebel; old number 34.
6 Tib. Don-grub.
7 The word *geser* is still legible in the original.

5 *qayan-a takimui : čayan luus [...]*[8]   9 *sira ulabir gerel-tü ǰarudasu =*
6 *itegel aqada*[9] *takimui : luus luu*   10 *na takimui :*[12] ○ *dayisun-i yaǰar*
7 *čayan gerel-tü degüde*[10] *takimui :*   11 *-tur čerig čoqorlaqu čayan :*
8 *čayan darai-yi egeči[d]e*[11] *takimui :*

2r

1 *naran-u gerel-tü duyulyan*[13] *[t]erigün*   6 *qurča bolad*[17] *ildün-iyen mörön*
2 *-tegen emüsčü*[14] *sara[n-u] neretü*   7 *-tegen deleyin :*[18] *qoor-tu dayisun*
   bambai   8 *-i esergüben ülü <>*
3 *mö[rö]n-tegen [qalqabč]ilaǰu*[15] *tümen*   9 *qanduyulun : [   ] [...]lyayči*[19]
4 *odon neretü quyay-i bey-e*   10 *gray od[on] neretü*[20] *[q]oor-tu*
5 *-tegen emüsčü :*[16] *belge bilig neretü*   11 *sumun-iyan degegside*[21] *qarbun*[22]

---

8   The Ms. belonging to the author (2r) has *luusun*.
9   This word is written with the diacritical points before *q*, and has the dative-locative suffix
    joined to the word.
10 In *degüde* (*degü* is the ancient form of *degüü*) we find the dative-locative suffix joined to the
    word. The same spelling *(degüde)* is found in the Ms. belonging to the author (2v).
11 See *ökin tengri egeči-tü* in the incense offering of Geser (XBM 66, 9r:9–10); the Ms. belonging
    to the author (2v) reads *čayan gereltei dara*.
12 Libr. Mong. 130, 4r:5–8: *nayan tümen dörben mingyan ǰarudasun-dur ariyun takil takimui* (=
    Mongolische Handschriften, No. 75, p. 54).
13 The Ms. belonging to the author (2v): *naran-u gerel neretü duyuly-a*.
14 The epic *Cay-a geser* (p. 240) reads: *erdeni sigedkegsen qubilyan-u duulyaban erdenitü
    terigün-degen emüsbe*.
15 The Ms. belonging to the author (2v): *saran neretü bambai-yi mörön-degen qalqabčilaǰu*;
    Geser-ün sang (Cay-a-yin geser, p. 555): *naran-u bambai-yi mörön-degen ayuluysan*.
16 The Ms. belonging to the author (2v) has *tümen odod neretü quyay-i beyen-degen emüsčü*.
17 *bolad* instead of *bolod*. On the occurrence of the form *bolad* in the early pre-classical texts see,
    for example, Cerensodnom and Taube, *Turfansammlung*, No. 3, p. 57, and note 3v5.
18 The Ms. belonging to the author (3r): *belge bilig neretü qurča bolod ildüben mörön-degen
    deleyisen* (for *deleyigsen*); Libr. Mong. 130, 2r:19–2v:1: *naran-u altan duyuly-a. oroi-tayan
    talbiysan saran-u bambai mörön-degen emüsügsen. odod-un quyay-i bey-e-dür emüsügsen.
    qurča urtu belge bilig-ün ildü mutur-tayan ǰayiduysan*; *Geser-ün bsang (Cay-a-yin geser*,
    p. 551): *qurča neretü belge bilig-ün ildü-i mutur-tur-iyan ǰayiduysan*; Rintchen, "En marge",
    (p. 27): *naran metü duyulya-i terigün-degen asuysan saran metü bambai-i mörün-tegin
    ayuyuluysan odud metü quyay-i beyen-degin emüsegsen qurča iretü beleg bilig-ün ildü-i
    mutur-tayan dalayiysan*.
19 The Ms. belonging to the author (3r): *ečüs bolyayči*.
20 *neretü* is still legible in the original.
21 *degegside* is still legible in the original.
22 The Ms. belonging to the author (3v): *gray odon neretü. qurdun sumun-iyar degegside
    qarbun*; Libr. Mong. 130, 2v:1–2: *odod-un raqu-da sumun tataysan*; *Geser-ün bsang (Cay-a-
    yin geser*, p. 550): *garay odon-u kiling-ün sumun-iyar qarbuyči*.

2v

1 *türgen čakilyan neretü qurdun*	7 *kümün-i sakiyad morin-i saki :*[29]
2 *morin-iyan unuǰu*[23] *könggen singgen*[24]	8 *nasun-i sakiyad amin-i saki :*[30]
3 *gilbelgen minaya*[25] *-bar nisin ayuli*	9 *qubčasun-i sakiyad meseyigi*[31]
4 *ayul dayisun-u ulus-tur ayul*[26]	10 *saki : quyay-i sakiyad duyul =*
5 *dayisun-i tebčiged dayisun-u*	11 *yai*[32] *saki :*[33] *numun-i sakiyad sumun*
6 *adal-i*[27] *barayan-i ab :*[28] *öber-ün*	

3r

1 *-i saki : emegeli sakiyad qaǰayari*[34]	4 *urulduqu bügesü minu morin*
2 *saki : noytoi-gi*[35] *sakiyad čidöri*	5 *-i uduridqa*[38] *dayisun-u kučün*[39] *-i*
3 *saki :*[36] *kümün-i*[37] *morin minu morin*	6 *doroyidtayul :*[40] *busud-un <>*

---

23 The Ms. belonging to the author (3r): *türgen čakilyan neretü qurdun morin-i unuǰu*; Libr. Mong. 130, 2v:3–5: *türgen gilbel-gen-ü morin ǰayan unuysan*.

24 The Ms. belonging to the author (3r): *könggen singgen ayuluyči. arban ǰüg-ün eǰen geser qayan-i ene edür takiyad ǰalbarimui.*

25 *minaya ~ milaya*, "whip".

26 The word *ayul* is written with diacritical points before *y*.

27 *adal* often appears in combination with *mal*. See *adal mal* in XBM 66, 8r,10r; *adal*, "cows and horses", is listed in *Mongyol üges-ün iǰayur-un toli*, p. 133.

28 The Ms. belonging to the author (3v):*adal mal-dur minu ölǰei boluyči*; Libr. Mong. 130, 8v:7–9: *dayisun kümün-i ed aduyusun-i nadur olan olǰayul-un soyorq-a*; *Geser-ün bsang* (*Cay-a-yin geser*, p. 550): *kümün-ü ed-yi nadur öggüged.*

29 The Ms. belonging to the author (6v): *namai-yi ba öber-ün kümün-yi sakiyad morini saki*; *Geser-ün bsang* (*Cay-a-yin geser*, p. 550): *minu kümün-dür sakiyad. morin-dur minu ibege.*

30 The Ms. belonging to the author (6v): *nasun-i sakiyad amigi saki*; Libr. Mong. 130, 9r:9–9v:1–2: *nasuda sakiyad amin-dur minu ibegen soyorq-a*; *Geser-ün bsang* (*Cay-a-yin geser*, p. 550): *nasun-dur sakiyad. amin-dur ibege.*

31 The word *mese* with the accusative *-yi -gi*, reflecting the spoken language. On examples of this form in the Mongolian dialects, see Poppe "Geserica", p. 22; the Ms. belonging to the author (6v) has *mesegi*.

32 The accusative suffix *-i* is joined to the word *duyulya*; the Ms. belonging to the author (6v) has *duyulyan-i*.

33 Libr. Mong. 130, 9r:7–9: *quyay minu sakiyad asiy-da ibegen soyorq-a*; *Geser-ün bsang* (*Cay-a-yin geser*, p. 550): *quyay-dur minu sakiyad. mese-dür ibege.*

34 The same as above: the accusative suffix is joined to the word *qaǰayar.*

35 *noyto* with the accusative *-i -gi;* for *noyto, noyta* see Sagaster, *Weiße Geschichte*, p. 136.

36 The Ms. belonging to the author (6v): *noytai-i sakiyad čider-i saki.*

37 Instead of *kümün-ü.*

38 The Ms. belonging to the author (6v): *kümün-i mori minu morin-luy-a urulduqu bügesü minu morin uduridq-a*; Rintchen, "En marge" (p. 28): *nayadum-un čay-tu kimori-i delgeregül.*

39 *kü* is written without the *yod* at the beginning of the word *küčün*. See also *kümün* (line 7).

40 The Ms. belonging to the author (6v): *dayisun-i kümün-i morin doroyitayul.*

7 kümün minu kumün-luya üge
8 bulyalduqu[41] bügesü **minu** kümün-i

9 oyun-i oyutu bolya :[42] dayisun
10 kümün-i oyun-i uqayan-i

3v

1 jüdegül[43] kümün-ü mese minu
     mese-i[44]
2 <> qatan bolad bulyaldubasu : minu
3 mese qatan[45] bolad bolyau :[46] dayisun
4 -u mesei-i[47] uyadqa[48] dayisun-i

5 tebčijü kesegejü ög :[49] minu
6 sedkigsen sedkil-i bütege : <>
7 dayisun todqad-i ünesün[50]
8 tobaray bolya.[51]

4r

1 üileddügsen üilei-gi minu minu
2 bütügen soyorq-a :: tögörög
3 yeke tögörög : tngri
4 doroyidtayulbai ::[52] murai murai

5 < m[...] [tng]ri>[53] tngri darubai ::[54]
6 sadu edgü
7 <> aqidqaqui (?)

4v

1 om bajar saduva
2 samay-a manu balay-a
3 bajar saduva dvenuva ba
4 dista [dr]dhuva me bha va
5 suduva șayuva me bha va

6 anu rayduva me bha va
7 subuva șayuva me bha va
8 sarva sidhi me barica sarva
9 gar ma succa me cadam siri

5r

1 yam gürü hum ha ha

2 [ha ha] [hu]va [bha] ga van[55]

---

41 See bulqalduqu in § 185 of the Secret History, buly-a bulyalduqui is found in the Altan tobči, 111v.
42 The Ms. belonging to the author (6v): busud-un kümün-lüge üge bulyalduqu bügesü minu oyun-i sayin oyutu boly-a.
43 The Ms. belonging to the author (6v): busud-un kümün-i uqan (uqayan) oyun-i jüdegül.
44 Instead of mese-yi.
45 The word qatan is written with the diacritical points before the letter q.
46 The Ms. belonging to the author (3v): quyay mesen-dür minu qatan bolod boluyči.
47 Instead of mese-yi.
48 The Ms. belonging to the author (7r): busud-un mese-yi uyadq-a.
49 The same words are found in the Ms. belonging to the author (7r).
50 The word ünesün is written with a dot before the letter n in middle position.
51 The Ms. belonging to the author (7r): dayisun todqar-i ünesün tobray bolya soyorq-a.
52 The Ms. belonging to the author (7v): tögöreg tögöreg tögöreg yeke tögöreg esurun qormusta tngri todqar-nuyud-i doroyitayulbai.
53 It seems that these two words were deleted.
54 The Ms. belonging to the author (7v): mürei mürei mürei yeke mürei esurun qan qormusta tngri darubai.
55 ha ha ha ha huva bha ga van appears in XBM 78, 4r:1–2.

3   *sarva dha ta-a gada baǰar*
4   *ma me munca bacar pa*
5   *va ma ha a samay-a*
6   *saduva a maṅ ga laṃ : ::*

7   *oṃ [...] saduva*
8   *[...] [ ]*
9   *[...] [ ] bacar*
10 *guru badm-a [sid]i huṃ*[56]

The prayer to Geser from Xarbuxyn Balgas provides further evidence of both the diverse aspects of the worship of Geser as a protective deity and the spread of the Geser epics in Mongolia in the first part of the 17th century. This text, in fact, is also marked by phrases which are reminiscent of the Geser epics, in particular when describing Geser's armour and weapons. It is also worth pointing out that Geser is invoked by his Tibetan name Döngürüb (Don-grub) in the prayer. This name seldom appears in the Mongolian epics,[57] though Geser Sarbo Dörüb is found in *Arban ǰüg-ün eǰen geser qayan-u tuγuǰi*.[58]

The Xarbuxyn Balgas text tells us that Geser's armour is called "ten thousand stars" *tümen odon neretü quyaγ* (2r:3–4). The same description of Geser's armour is found in the epic *Arban ǰüg-ün eǰen geser qayan-u tuγuǰi (tümen odon neretü quyaγ)*.[59]

Moreover, according to the text under discussion, Geser wears on his head "a white helmet with the light of the sun" (*čayan naran-u gerel-tü duyulyan-u terigün-tegen emüsčü*, 1v:11–2r:2), while the epic *Arban ǰüg-ün eǰen geser qayan* has *čayan duyuly-a-ban terigün-tegen emüsbe*,[60] "(Geser) wore on his head a white helmet".

Geser's sword is "a sharp sword of steel called wisdom" (*belge bilig neretü qurča bolad ildü*, 2r:5–6) in the prayer from Xarbuxyn Balgas. It is interesting to note that the epic *Cay-a-yin geser* uses similar words to describe Geser's sword (*tabun belge bilig-ün tegüsügsen erdenitü bolod*).[61]

According to the Xarbuxyn Balgas text, Geser's whip is "light, thin and shining" (*könggen singgen gibelgen minaya*, 2v:2–3). Geser's whip, at least to my knowledge, is not mentioned in other ritual texts of Geser, but *Arban ǰüg-ün eǰen geser qayan-u tuγuǰi* describes Geser's whip as a "wisdom whip" (*bilig-ün tasiyur*).[62]

Geser is the protective deity of war, thus people invoke him to protect armour and helmet (*quyaγ-i sakiyad duyulyai saki*, 2v:10–11). Moreover, bow and arrow (*numun-i sakiyad sumun-i saki*, 2v:11–3r:1).

As a protective deity of horses, Geser is requested to protect saddle and bridle, halter and hobbles (*emegeli sakiyad qaǰayari saki. noytoi-gi sakiyad čidöri saki*, 3r:1–3), and asked for victory in a horse race. The Xarbuxyn Balgas text reads: "If my horse and another person's horse compete, make my horse lead the race" (*kümün-i morin-u urulduqu bügesü minu morin-i uduridqa*, 3r:3–5).

---

56 See the *mantra oom a qung banǰar gürü badma sidi qung* in XBM 78, 2v:7–8.
57 For this see the remarks by Ölǰei, *Mongγol töbed 'geser'-ün qaričaγ-a*, p. 152.
58 See vol. I, p. 8; the epic *Paǰai geser-ün tuγuǰi* has Geser Γarbo, vol. I, p. 25.
59 Vol. I, p. 120.
60 Vol. I, p. 127.
61 p. 240.
62 See vol. I, p. 142; on the significance of the magic whip of Geser, see Heissig, *Geser-Studien*, p. 324.

Prayers to Lamas

Prayer to Tsoṅ-kha-pa (XBM 74 to XBM 77)

We have fragments of four copies of a prayer to Tsoṅ-kha-pa (1357–1419), the founder of the dGe-lugs-pa School of Tibetan Buddhism, who is invoked as an incarnation of Mañjuśrī.[1] I was unable to find a similar text to that from Xarbuxyn Balgas.[2]

XBM 74

1 item of a *pothī* (1 folio, 1 written side), measuring, 10 × 4.5 cm, and comprising 18 lines; the Mongolian page number is *nigen* (1). The folio is well preserved. The text is bordered with lines.[3]

1v

1 *h̲e̲n̲d̲k̲e̲g-ün*[4] *kele-be[r]*
2 *qarsi-t̲ur manǰusiri*
3 *girdi metü : ene času*
4 *-tu yaǰar-a čoy-tu*
5 *sumadi girdi edüge qami =*
6 *γ-a abasu ber tengsen*
7 *sačalalduqui ügei*
8 *boluyad : ende ber anu*
9 *oroi-yin čimeg boluysan*

10 *ǰongkaba öčin ǰalbari =*
11 *mui ge[t]ü[l]gečĭ*[5] *boyda*
12 *ǰongkaba örösiyeǰü*
13 *adistidlan*[6] *soyorq-a :*
14 *manǰusiri-yin*
15 *qubilyan bey-e-tü*[7] *e e :*
16 *öber busud-i*
17 *bolbasun tonilqui*
18 *ber*

---

1 On Tsoṅ-kha-pa see the work by Kaschewsky, *Das Leben des lamaistischen Heiligen Tsongkhapa*, especially pp. 106–20; see also Essen and Thingo, *Die Götter des Himalaya*, pp. 146–9.
2 See the *dhāraṇī* of Tsoṅ-ka-pa in Mong. 163 (Heissig and Bawden, *Catalogue*, p. 230); see also the prayer composed by Mergen Gegen (*Mergen gegen*, pp. 141–3).
3 Restored by Mr. Bentchev; old number 24/10.
4 On *enedkeg*, *hendkeg* see Weiers, *Untersuchungen*, p. 202; see also Heissig, *Manuskript-fragmente*, p. 47
5 *getülgegčĭ*, Skr. *tāraka*; Tib. *sgrol-ba-po*. See Ishihama and Fukuda eds., *Mahāvyutpatti*, No. 414.
6 *adistid*, Skr. *adhiṣṭhāna*; Tib. *byin-rlabs*, *Mahāvyutpatti*, No. 4250.
7 *qubilyan bey-e*, Skr. *nirmāṇakāya*; Tib. *sprul-pa'i-sku*, *Mahāvyutpatti*, No. 116.

XBM 75

5 items of a *pothī* (5 folios, 8 written sides), measuring 14×4.5 cm, and consisting of 12 lines; the Mongolian page numbers are *nigen, tabun, ǰiryuyan, doloyan, yesün* (1, 5, 6, 7, 9); folio 5 is torn. Apart from folio 9, the other folios have the text bordered with lines.[8]

1v

1	*namo guru urida*	7	*ünen čoy-tu*
2	*orčilang nirvan-u*	8	*qotala arilqu*
3	*nom erdem-üd üǰen*	9	*mön činar-ud-i :*[9]
4	*ulam ǰabsar-tur*	10	*ülemǰi teyimü-yi*
5	*abqu gegeküi-yin*	11	*ilyal ügei medemü*
6	*čenggel-eče nögčiged*	12	*aburan manu blam-a*

5r

1	*esergülegči qalayun*	7	*-tur : čing nigen*
2	*küiten ǰobalang*	8	*üǰügür-tü gegen sed =*
3	*-ud-i küličeged*	9	*kil-iyer aysan ǰovangka =*
4	*čamdqui*[10] *ürikü*[11]	10	*[b]a öčin ǰalbarimui*
5	*ǰoriy-tu öberün*	11	*[ ] boyda*
6	*sedkil-i nomoyadqu*	12	*[ ] ba :*

5v

1	*örösiyeǰü adis =*	7	*tonilqui ber adis =*
2	*tidlan soyorq-a :*	8	*tidlan soyorq-a :*
3	*manǰusiri-yin*	9	*ügüleküi bütügeküi*
4	*qubilyan bey-e-tü*	10	*sasin delgere[gül] =*
5	*e e öber busu =*	11	*ün soyor[q-a :]*
6	*d-i bolbasun*	12	*sayin [ ]*

6r

1	*oyoyata bariy =*	7	*-tur tögörigsen ba*
2	*daqui oroi čimeg*	8	*bürin-i tonilyaqui*
3	*olduysan tedüi*	9	*-tur ülemǰi yayiqamsiy*
4	*ken-yin sayin idegen*	10	*tonilqu möri*
5	*-tür adali idegelegči*	11	*üǰügülügči ǰovangkaba*
6	*orčilang-un dalai*	12	*öčin ǰalbarimui*

---

8   Restored by Mr. Bentchev; old numbers: 12/4 (fols. 1, 6–7), 32 (fols. 5–9).
9   *mön činar*, Skr. *tattva;* Tib. *de-kho-na-ñid, Mahāvyutpatti*, No. 1714.
10   Instead of *čimadqui.*
11   For *ürekü.*

6v

1 *getülgegči boyda*
2 *ǰovangkaba örösiyeǰü*
3 *adistidlan soyorq-a :*
4 *manǰusiri-yin*
5 *qubilyan bey-e-tü*
6 *e e öber busud*

7 *-i bolbasun tonilqu*
8 *ber adistidlan*
9 *soyorq-a : ügüleküi*
10 *bütügeküi sasin-i*
11 *delgeregül-ün soyorq =*
12 *a : erdem- tü kin (?)*

7r

1 *kelemürči metü egüskeküi*
2 *ǰerge-yin ečüs-tür*
3 *kürügsen siravang*[12]
4 *lavaba (?) metü tegüs =*
5 *keküi ǰerge-yi*
6 *i[l]edte*[13]

7 *bolyaysan sari*
8 *budari*[14] *metü*
9 *ünen-i üǰegsen*
10 *sa[ča]lal ügegüi*[15]
11 *delekei deger-e ülegsen*
12 *ǰovangkaba*

7v

1 *öčin ǰalbarimui*
2 *getülgegči boyda*
3 *ǰovangkaba örösiyeǰü*
4 *adistidlan soyorq-a :*
5 *manǰusiri-yin qubilyan*
6 *bey-e-tü e e öber*

7 *busud-i bolbasun*
8 *tonilqui ber adis =*
9 *tidlan soyorq-a :*
10 *ügüleküi bütügeküi*
11 *sasin-i delgeregül-ün*
12 *soyorq-a ::*

9r

1 O *öter*[16] *olqu boltuyai*
2 *oṃ ma ṇi bad*
3 *me hūṃ ḥri*

4 *mangghalam nasun qutuy*
5 *nemekü boltuyai*
   oṃ ma ṇi pad me hūṃ ḥri[17]

XBM 76

1 item of a *pothī* (1 nearly entire folio, 2 written side), measuring 13 × 4.5 cm, and containing 11 lines; the Mongolian page number is *qoya[r]* (2). The text is bordered with lines.[18]

---

12 Skr. Śrāvaka.
13 *iledte, ilete,* Skr. *pratyakṣa;* Tib. *mṅon-sum, Mahāvyutpatti,* No. 4405.
14 Śāriputra. See Kaschewsky, *Das Leben des lamaistichen Heiligen Tsonkhapa,* p. 182.
15 *sačalal ügei,* Skr. *asama;* Tib. *mñyam-pa med-pa, Mahāvyutpatti,* No. 2536.
16 MLM *ödter;* on the form *öter* see Ligeti, "A propos de quelques textes", p. 274, note 3.
17 The *mantra* is written in Tibetan.
18 Restored by Mr. Bentchev; old number 25/4.

2r

1 adistidl[an] [soyor =]
2 q-a¹⁹ ügüleküi [bütügeküi]²⁰
3 sasin-i delgere[gülün]
4 soyorq-a ǰaliqai
5 -yi tebčiǰü sayin
6 ǰarliγ dayun-i

7 [d]ayurisqaqui [...]
8 üjesküleng-tü
9 yurban γray debel
10 emüsüged : [...]
11 terigüten küsegdekün

2v

1 [ ] ali ba ol-daysan
2 [ ]tegelegči : čaylasi
3 [ügei] [ ]lduba metü
4 boluysan (?) ǰovangkaba
5 öčin ǰalbari[m]ui
6 getülgegči boyda

7 ǰovanggaba örösiyen
8 adistidlan
9 soyorq-a manǰusiri
10 -yin qubilyan bey-e-tü
11 e e : öber busud-i

XBM 77

1 item of a *pothī* (1 folio, 2 written sides), measuring ca. 14×4.5 cm, with 12–13 lines; without page number. The text is damaged and some words are illegible.²¹

recto

1 a[s]uru qarigči sedkil
2 -iyer [...]
3 dör[ben] [...] ǰüg-yi
4 nomla[...] tüidkel ügei-yi
5 uqayan [...]gči [ǰo]vangkaba
6 [ö]čin ǰalba[r]imui

7 [qu]tuy-tu boyda
8 [...] örösiyeǰü
9 adistidlan soyor[q-a]
10 manǰusiri-yin qubilya[n]
11 bey-e-tü e e öber
12 busud-i bo[l]ba[sun]

verso

1 [ ]
2 [ ] ügüleküi
3 bütü[ge]küi [sasin-i]²²
4 delgere[gülün] [ ]
5 [...] töröl [...]

6 [ ]
7 [ ]
8 [...] nom [ ] [...]
9 ber [a]tala [...]
10 [...] [ ]

---

19 *soyorq-a* is written with diacritical points before *q*.
20 See XBM 75, 7v:10.
21 Restored by Mr. Bentchev; old number 26/15.
22 See XBM 75, 7v:11.

11 *sayitur [   ]*   13 *[   ][...]*
12 *[ya]yiqamsiy t[onilqu]*[23]

Hymn to the Panchen Lama and Dalai Lama (XBM 78)

The text from Xarbuxyn Balgas, which invokes both the Panchen Lama and Dalai Lama, can be regarded as the earliest evidence yet known of a Mongol text devoted to the two highest religious personalities of Tibet. If text dates back to the first part of the 17th century, the Panchen Lama whom the text invokes, must be Blo-bzaṅ chos-kyi rgyal-mtshan (1570–1662), while the Dalai Lama could be either the Fourth or the Fifth. The Fourth Dalai Lama was Yon-tan rgya-mtsho (1589–1617), the great-grandson of Altan qaγan of the Tümed. The Fifth Dalai Lama was Ṅag-dbaṅ blo-bzaṅ rgya-mtsho (1617–1682).[24] The Fourth Dalai Lama and the Fifth Dalai Lama became disciples of the Panchen Lama Blo-bzaṅ chos-kyi rgyal-mtshan in 1613 and 1625 respectively.[25]

XBM 78

1 booklet *(debter)*, including a complete text, written in two hands. It is composed of 4 folios (6 written sides) stitched together. The folios measure 10×8cm, and has a varying number of lines, without page numbers. A vertical line marks the beginning of the *mantra*. The text is fairly well preserved.[26]

1v

1 *tegüs sayin buyan-u erd[e]m-üd*[27]   7 *lam-a bančen-u köl-ṯür*
2 *qočorliy*[28] *ügei yarq[u]i-yin oron*   8 *jalbarimui*
3 *temdegtei-e kir*[29] *ügei jonggaba*   9 O *bodalang-un ayula-ača*
4 *-yin sasi[n]-u ker-ün deger-e*   10 *bayuju iregsen burqan-u*
5 *tenggel ügei*[30] *nom-un tuy-i bariyči* 11 *qutuy-ača yarču iregsen*
6 *ülemji erdem-tü tegüs čoy-tu*

---

23 See XBM 75, 6r:10.
24 Petech, "Tibet", pp. 334–6.
25 See Ya Hanzang, *Bančin erdeni-yin namtar,* pp. 57, 65.
26 Restored by Mr. Bentchev; old number 31/1.
27 There is a split in the folio which damaged the word *erdem.*
28 *qočorliy* appears in the *Čayan teüke.* See Sagaster, *Weiße Geschichte*, p. 84; *qočorlig* is found in XBM 41, 2v:3.
29 The spelling *kir* occurs in the Olon Süme text OS /IV 41 (Heissig, *Handschriften-Reste*, p. 272).
30 *tenggel ügei* "incomparable" appears in *The Twelve Deeds* (see Poppe, p. 43). Poppe explains that *tenggel ügei* is synonimous with *tengsel ügei*: the primary stem is *teng*, "half, equal, equivalent, etc." Poppe also remarks that the verb *tengge-* is found in Qalqa (note 4 to f. 33r, p. 94); *tengsel ügei*, Skr. *anuttara*; Tib. *bla-na-med-pa* (Ishihama and Fukuda eds., *Mahāvyutpatti*, No. 2521).

2r

1 *bügüde olan amitan-i*
2 *tusalan törögsen bodi*
3 *sedkili ilete tuyuluysan*

4 *qutuy-tu dalai lam-a čimadur-iyan*
5 *maytan mörgömü bi*

2v

1 *sedkisi ügei yeke sang nigüleskü*i
2 *[n]idüber üjegči kir ügei medegči*
3 *erketen-ü [man]jusir[i] [ča]sutan-u*
4 *merged-ü[n] oroi-yin čimeg*
   jŏnggabai [31]

5 *čoy-tu tegülder lamayin köl-tür*
6 *maytan mörgömü* ::
7 O *oom a qung ba<n>jar gürü*
8 *badma sidi qung* :: : ::
9 *oom mari gam suu qa* :: : ::

3r

1 *oom namo bagavadi baranja*
2 *bramiday-e oom nadda dida*
3 *ilisi ilisi binayay-e binayay-e*
4 *namo bagavadi bradaaryam*

5 *bradi iriy-a iriy-a*
6 *suridi suridi usur-i*
7 *usur-i buyu y-e buyu y-e*
8 *suuya* [32]

3v

1 O *oṃ bacar saduva*
2 *samay-a. manu palay-a*
3 *bacar saduva d[v]enuva*
4 *ba dista [dṛ]dhuva*
5 *me bhava suduva ṣayuva me*

6 *ba va anu rayduva me bha va*
7 *subuva ṣayuva me bha va* :
8 *sarva sidhi me barica sarva*
9 *gar ma succa me cddam siri*

4r

1 *yam gürü hūṃ ha ha ha ha*
2 *huva bha ga van s[a]rvada*
3 *ta ga da bacar ma me munca*

4 *bacar bha va ma ha a*
5 *samay-a saduva a*

---

31 See *[sedkis]i ügei yeke sang nigüleskü*i *nidüber üjegči. kir ügei medegči erketü manjusiri*
časutan-u merged-ün oroyin čimeg jŏngga-ba in XBM 41, 2r:3–7.

32 This *mantra* (lines 1–8) is found at the end of the *Vajracchedikā*. The Xarbuxyn Balgas text,
however, omits some words. See Poppe, *Diamond Sutra*, p. 49b, p. 32; see also Conze,
Vajracchedikā Prajñāpāramitā, p. 63, note 3.

Invocation to Altan Sečen Qaγan

XBM 79 is a fragment of a previously unknown text which invokes Altan Sečen qaγan. This fragment is badly damaged, but particularly interesting and worth of scrutiny. It is discussed below.

XBM 79

1 item of a *pothī* (1 folio, 2 written sides), measuring ca. 14 × 8 cm, and consisting of 12–14 lines (r/v); the Mongolian page number is *ǰirγuγan* (6). The folio has various splits in its surface, and the text is severely damaged, especially on 6v. As a result, the transcription of numerous words on 6v is tentative.[1]

6r

1 *[alta]n sečen qaγan minu sa[…] sü[ ]*
2 *[ ] süm-e barigsan qoyitu-yin*
3 *deledügsen ai altan sečen*
4 *[qaγan] minu buyui-yin ülü yabuqu*
5 *buyura temegen-iyer ayalan bile :*
6 *[ ]u du ǰobtu albitu[2] bile :[3]*
7 *altan sečen qaγan minu tanyi-yin (?)*

8 *[ül]ü yabuqu yaǰar temegen-iyer*
    ayala[n]
9 *[bil]e : tende ki ende ki tegsi albit[u]*
10 *[bil]e : ai altan sečen qaγan minu*
11 *oi-yin ayula-du söb beledüm*
12 *[bil]e : ai altan sečen qaγan*

6v

1 *tala yaǰar tariγ-a tariγsan ami[ ]*
2 *[ ] yin buyan bariγsan [ai] [alt]an*
3 *sečen qaγan minu tala-gi […]*
4 *dayi[s]ud (?)[4] tümen-i olǰa bolγan*
    [bile :][5]
5 *[ai] [a]ltan sečen qaγan minu [ ]*

6 *[ ]un bile : […]ruda (?) tü[…]*
7 *bolγan bile : ai altan sečen [qaγan]*
8 *[m]in[u] yar a[ ]ri[6] [ ]*
9 *[…]liqu bolγan ǰang (?) […]busi kim*
    bi[le :]
10 *a[i] altan [se]čen qaγan minu*

---

1 Restored by Mr. Bentchev; old number 26/27.
2 For *ǰöbtü albatu*.
3 The colloquial form of *bülüge*.
4 There are two splits in the folio at this point.
5 The word *bile* recurs in the text.
6 There is a split in the folio which damaged this word.

11 [   ]čiγad [...] [...]uda (?) ba[...]m   13   ai [altan] [se]čen qaγan m[inu] [...]
    [bile :]   14   [...]i gegen [...]m bile : delekei
12 [...] [   ] ǰ[...]r[...]

The text under discussion is marked by the refrain *ai altan sečen qaγan minu*, "Ah my Altan Sečen qaγan". It also mentions a monastery which was constructed *(süm-e bariγsan)* and cultivated fields *(tariy-a tariγsan)*. It is well-known that Altan qaγan of the Tümed had monasteries constructed,[7] and that as early as the middle of the 16th century there were Chinese farmers in the territory of the Tümed.[8] Unfortunately, the few lines of the damaged fragment which are left do not provide enough information to allow us to state that the invocation is actually addressed to Altan qaγan of the Tümed (1507–1581). On the other hand, the fact that Altan qaγan of the Tümed was worshipped cannot be surprising if we consider the immense reputation of this person. Altan qaγan was both a great warrior and an eminent political leader. Moreover, we should remember the prominent role that Altan qaγan played in the spread of Buddhism in Mongolia before and after the famous meeting with the Third Dalai Lama in 1578.[9]

The worship of Altan qaγan was until recently unknown, but if we pay careful attention to the biography of Altan Qaγan, which is known as *Erdeni tunumal neretü sudur* (Abbr. *Erdeni tunumal*), we find that this source does suggest that Altan qaγan was venerated by the Mongols. Beginning with the appellation, Altan qaγan is called Altan Sečen qaγan both in *Erdeni tunumal*[10] and in the Xarbuxyn Balgas text. Altan qaγan, however, is also given other epithets in *Erdeni tunumal*.

It is interesting to note that the account of the military achievements of Altan qaγan in *Erdeni tunumal* is clearly a eulogy on a person who became legendary. For example, when relating Altan qaγan's victory over the Chinese, *Erdeni tunumal* says that "a ray of light of five colours irradiated from the body of the blissful Altan qaγan" *(bayasqulang-tu altan qaγan-u bey-e-deče tabun öngge-tü gerel γarbai)*.[11]

It is also worth noting that the section in *Erdeni tunumal* which narrates Altan qaγan's exploits is reminiscent of the prayer to Činggis qaγan *Boγda činggis-un öčig*, which is found in the *Altan bičig*.[12] It is a hymn in praise of the victorious campaigns of Činggis. We can also find passages in *Erdeni tunumal* which are similar to those in *Boγda činggis-un öčig*. A passage in *Erdeni tunumal* describes Altan qaγan using these words: *qan tngri-yin ǰayaγ-a-bar törögsen qari dayisun -i toyin-ṯur-iyan oroγuluγsan. qan čola*

---

7   See Altan-orgil, *Köke-qota-yin süm-e keyid*, p. 75.
8   *Erdeni tunumal neretü sudur* (Ĵürongγ-a ed.), p.61, and note 1; see also Serruys, *Pei-lou Fong-sou*, pp. 141–2.
9   Altan qaγan had the *Altan gerel* printed in 1577. See Heissig and Bawden, *Catalogue*, Mong. 395, pp. 204–6. See the description of Altan qaγan in the colophon of the *Altan gerel*, which is transcribed and translated on pp. 205–6; see also the study by Čoyiǰi, "*Tutuγar dalai blam-a-luγ-a ayulǰaqui-yin uridaki*", pp. 10–26.
10 15v (the page number refers to the facsimile reproduction of the manuscript which is included in the volume).
11 11r.
12 Yang Haiyin, *Altan bičig*, pp. 114–16, 212–17.

ner-e-yi bey-e-tür-iyen orosiγuluγsan. γayiqamsiγ-tu boγda altan qayan,[13] "The marvellous holy Altan qaγan, who was born by the destiny of Lord Heaven, who subdued the enemies, and incorporated the title qan."[14]

Passages in the *öčig* celebrate Činggis as follows: *deger-e tngri-yin ǰayaγabar törögsen tenggerlig yeke ner-e beyendür-iyen orosiγuluγsan… toγmoγ dayisun-i toyin-dur-iyan oroγulǰu,*[15] "(Činggis qaγan) was born by the destiny of Heaven above, and incorporated the great name heavenly… (Činggis qaγan) subdued the enemies Toγmoγ."

Another passage in *Erdeni tunumal* referring to Altan qaγan says: *deger-e tngri-yin ǰayaγ-a-bar törögsen delekei takin-u eǰen boγda altan sečen qaγan,*[16] "The holy Altan Sečen qaγan, the lord of the whole world, who was born by the destiny of Heaven above."

Moreover, the *Čaγan teüke* uses similar words to describe Činggis. It reads: *deger-e tngri-yin ǰayaγabar egüdčü delekei dakin-i eǰelen törögsen tngrlig suutu boγda činggis qaγan …,*[17] "The heavenly, fortunate holy Činggis qaγan, who was born to rule the whole world, originated by the destiny of Heaven above."

The expression *de'ere tenggeri-ece ǰaya'atu töreksen*[18] refers to Börte čino-a in the *Secret History*, while *tenggeri-ece jaya'atu*[19] is attributed to Činggis in the same source. The term *tenggerlig (tngrilig)* does not occur in the *Secret History*. It is found associated with Činggis in the later Mongol sources. Yet *Erdeni tunumal* calls Altan qaγan *tngrilig*.[20]

The fact that Altan qaγan was a person who possessed sacred power is stressed in the section of *Erdeni tunumal* enumerating the prodigious signs which people saw when the ashes of Altan qaγan were placed inside a stūpa. This episode is also narrated in detail in the *Čaγan lingqu-a erikes*, a source which suggests that Altan qaγan became an object of veneration after he died.[21] It is, however, *Erdeni tunumal* which includes words which are especially interesting to our investigation. This source tells us that "all the people of five colours took (the ashes of Altan qaγan) as an object of veneration" *(tabun öngge ulus tus tus büri mörgöl-ün oron bolγan abubai).*[22]

The expression "people of five colours" is not found in the *Secret History*, but it refers to the people of the countries conquered by Činggis qaγan in the later Mongolian sources.[23] The *Yeke öčig*, "The Great Prayer" describes the "people of five colours" as

---

13 10v–11r.

14 On the expression *toyin-dur-iyan oroγul-* (= to subdue), see the discussion by Chiodo in *Erdeni-yin tobči. A Manuscript from Kentei Ayimaγ*, pp. 22–3.

15 Yang, Haiyin, *Altan bičig*, pp. 114–15, 212–15.

16 17r.

17 See Sagaster, *Weiße Geschichte*, p. 82.

18 de Rachewiltz, *Index*, § 1, p. 13.

19 de Rachewiltz, *Index*, § 201, p. 113.

20 54r.

21 pp. 193–7.

22 45r.

23 On *tabun öngge dörben qari*, see Sagaster, *Weiße Geschichte*, pp. 304–17; see also the *Altan tobči*, 169v, 172r; *Erdeni-yin tobči* (Urga text), 76v; on *tabun öngge ulus*, see the *Altan kürdün mingγan kegesütü*, pp. 4, 77, 83, 212, 240.

those who gave their strength to Činggis.[24] Hence when the *Erdeni tunumal* associates "the people of the five colours" with Altan qaγan, it stresses the military might of Altan qaγan, which was no less than that of Činggis.[25] This source also emphasises the idea of an universal worship of Altan qaγan as that of Činggis.

Moreover, the expression *mörgöl-ün oron* indicates both the object of veneration and the place of veneration;[26] *mörgöl-ün oron lam-a öglige-yin eǰen*, referring to Sa skya Paṇḍita and Göden qaγan is found in the *Erdeni-yin tobči*,[27] while *öglige-yin eǰen takil-un oron*, indicating Altan qaγan and the Third Dalai Lama, appears in the *Erdeni tunumal*.[28]

Returning to the Xarbuxyn Balgas fragment of the invocation to Altan Sečen qaγan, the fact that this fragment was found in northern Mongolia is not proof that the invocation cannot address Altan qaγan of the Tümed, whose reputation, as is well known, was not confined to southern Mongolia.[29] We should also remember the close relationship between Altan qaγan and Abadai of the Qalqa,[30] and the presence of Tümed lamas in northern Mongolia.[31] There is also the fact that the monastery of Erdeni J̌oo, which Abadai had constructed in 1586, was modelled on the Yeke J̌oo monastery in Kökeqota. The latter was founded by Altan qaγan, and is also known as "the monastery of Altan qaγan" *(altan qaγan-u süm-e)*.[32]

Finally, I would like to draw attention to the wall paintings of Daxiong temple which is located inside Maidari monastery *(Meidai zhao)* in the western Tümed Banner, southern Mongolia. In view of the fact that Maidari monastery plays a significant role in the

---

24   Sayinǰirγal and Šaraldai, *Altan ordon-u tayily-a*, pp. 192–4.
25   This is also evident from a passage in the *Altan tobči*, see 169v.
26   See *mörgöl-ün oron, burqan-u oron* in Naranbatu et al., *Mongγol buddha-yin soyol*, p. 174.
27   43r.
28   29v.
29   As far as Šoloi of the Qalqa (1577–1652) is concerned, as is well known, this person bore the title Sečen qan, but, at least to my knowledge, there is no evidence of Šoloi being called Altan Sečen qaγan in the Mongolian sources. The *Bolor toli* (p. 493) has Sečen qaγan Šoloi as in Γongγor, *Qalq-a tobčiyan* (I, 380); the *Sir-a tuγuǰi* (p. 145) has Siloi dalai ǰinong, while Solo sečin dalai ǰinong maha samadi appears in the *Altan kürdün mingγan kegesütü*, p. 237. This person is called Maha samadi sečen qaγan in the *Qayučin manǰu dangsa*. See Čimeddorǰi, "*Ligdan qaγan nögčigsen-ü daraγaki*", pp. 19–20. Moreover, a document from Kentei Ayimaγ dated to 1694 does provide evidence of the worship of Šoloi by his ninth son Dalai ǰinong Ananda, but in this source Šoloi is referred to as Maqasamidi gegen dalai sečen qan Šoloi. For this see Veit, "Das Testament des Sečen qan Šoloi", pp. 408, 410. It is worth adding that the paleographic features of the Xarbuxyn Balgas fragment point to early 17th century. Thus, I would exclude that Šoloi is the person whom the Xarbuxyn Balgas text invokes. Finally, the Qalqa prince Šoloi ubasi qong tayiǰi (1540–1586) was also called Altan qan/qaγan. This person, however, is not called Altan Sečen qaγan in the sources. See *Mongγol-un ubasi qong tayiǰi* in Damdinsürüng, *Mongγol uran ǰokiyal*, pp. 638–47; see also Badai et al., *Oyirad teüke surbulǰi bičig*; Γongγor, *Qalq-a tobčiyan*, I, pp. 368–76.
30   *Erdeni-yin erike*, p. 89.
31   *Qalq-a-yin mongγol-un γaǰar-a burqan-u sasin*, 13v (manuscript belonging to the author); *Asaraγči neretü-yin teüke*, pp. 126–127; Γongγor, *Qalq-a tobčiyan*, I, pp. 356–7.
32   Altan-orgil, *Köke-qota süm-e keyid*, pp. 75, 79.

history of the diffusion of Buddhism among the Mongols, this monastery should interest the specialists in this religion and the historians as well. The wall paintings of Daxiong temple describe the meeting of Altan qaγan with the Third Dalai Lama, and depict Altan qaγan with a rosary in his right hand and a wish-granting jewel in his left hand. Another section of the wall represents Altan qaγan holding the banner of victory.[33] There is no doubt that the wall paintings of Maidari monastery in association with the worship of Altan qaγan of the Tümed merit investigation.

---

33 Zhang Weiban, *Meidai zhao*, pp. 12–13. I acquired the booklet *Meidai zhao* when I visited Maidari monastery in August of 1998.

Burnt Offering of Origin

The importance of a text such as *Ündüsün-i sang*, "Burnt offering of origin", of which we have fragments of two copies, was pointed out by Heissig, who investigated the fragments of *Ündüsün-i sang* from Olon Süme within a broad frame of reference.[1] It is therefore interesting to note that this text was circulating in both southern and northern Mongolia in the 16th–17th centuries.[2] The Xarbuxyn Balgas text XBM 81 shows an archaic style of calligraphy. For example, the letter *q* at the beginning of a word is written like an initial *a*. Moreover, we find the ancient spelling *oyiu* (instead of *ogiu*) in the text. Unfortunately, the Xarbuxyn Balgas fragments and those from Olon Süme have only a small portion of the text in common. The other fragments belong to different parts of the text.[3]

In the course of his investigation of *Ündüsün-i sang* from Olon Süme, Heissig associated this work with the texts of popular religion, especially those which are recited on the occasion of the summer ceremonies, when libations of mare's milk are offered to the gods, mountains and rivers, and places of religious significance.[4] Heissig also regarded *Ündüsün-i sang* as one of the earliest examples of a syncretic text which blends Buddhist gods and beliefs with ancient Mongol religious practices.[5]

Ündüsün-i sang differ from the entirely Buddhist texts of the incense offering such as *Ündüsün bsang* and *Ariyun ubsang*,[6] but it can be associated, to some extent, with the Louvain text (Ms. No. 24a), which bears the title *Ariyun sang orosiba*.[7]

A complete text of *Ündüsün-i sang* is available. This copy was found by Jaehrig in Khiachta in 1794, and, apart from some minor textual variants, it is the same as the texts from Olon Süme and Xarbuxyn Balgas, providing evidence of the continuity of the transmission of *Ündüsün-i sang*.[8]

---

1 See Heissig, *Handschriften-Reste*, pp. 380–408.
2 *Handschriften-Reste*, p. 380.
3 Part of folio 3v (XBM 81) corresponds to OS/IV 48, folio 6 (XBM 81) to OS IV/52v.
4 *Handschriften-Reste*, pp. 380–408, and Heissig, *Manuskriptfragmente*, pp. 48–55; on texts which are recited on the occasion of the summer ceremonies see Serruys, *Kumiss Ceremonies* (*julay* text), pp. 23–56; see also Damdinsürüng, *Gegün-ü sün-ü sačuli* (*Jayun bilig*), vol. I, pp. 323–336.
5 *Handschriften-Reste*, p. 574.
6 *Ündüsün bsang* was translated into English and commented on by Serruys. See "A Mongol Lamaist Prayer", pp. 321–418; on *Ariyun bsang*, see Heissig and Sagaster, *Mongolische Handschriften*, No. 420, pp. 238–9.
7 Heissig, "The Mongol Manuscripts and Xylographs", pp. 173–4.
8 Heissig and Sagaster, *Mongolische Handschriften*, Ms. Asch 122, No. 421, p. 239.

XBM 80

2 items of a *pothī* (2 fragments of folios, 2 written sides). The first item measures ca. 16 × 5 cm, with 13 lines; the second item measures ca. 16 × 9 cm, with 15 lines. The folios are severely damaged and the text is barely legible.⁹

*1v

1 [   ] [qun]g :: [...] qung::
2 [   ] [qun]g :: baǰar amirda kündeli
    qa[   ]
3 [   ] bun : oom sibau-a sod[   ]
4 [   ]dadu qang qoyoson kü [   ]
5 [aya]r¹⁰ bsang-un idegen öngge sa[   ]
6 [   ] tatu-nuyud küsel-ün

7 [   ] ölǰei qu[tuy]
8 [   ]i bura bu[   ]
9 [   ] abara[   ]
10 [   ] oom a qung
11 [   ] ariyun t[   ]
12 [   ] ündüs[   ]
13 [   ]

*2r

1 qung :: : ::
2 [   ] egüskemüi takil [   ]
3 [   ] ečige oytary[ui] [   ] un dayun
    kürkireged
4 [   ] [d]alai-ača yal gilbeleged : tere
    qoyar-un
5 [   ]r-ača dalayin [   ] čayan [   ]en
    tuyuluyad:
6 [   ]ülen-ü ǰirüken-eče rasiyan-u qura
    o[r]oyad:

7 [   ] ǰirü[ken] [   ] modon [...]
8 [   ]g- ün idegen quriyayad ::
9 [   ] bui [   ]
10 [   ] bui :: doron[a] [   ] takil-un
11 [   ]an-ača labai-yin ča[yan] [...]
12 [   ] [...] [   ]
13 [   ] [...] modon [...] [   ]
14 [   ] ača suqai [...] [   ]
15 [...] arča-yin modo[n] [   ]¹¹

---

9   Restored by Mr. Bentchev; old number 9.
10 Ms. Asch 122,1v:8 reads *qoyoson ayar-tur*. This expression appears frequently in the Buddhist texts (see *qoyoson ayar-tur* in XBM 47, 1v).
11 See the complete passage in Ms. Asch 122, 1v:8–3r:14: *qoyoson kü boltuyai. qoyosun-u ayar-tur ubsang-un idegen öngge sayitu dayun dayalaqui amtatu-nuyud küselün ǰögelen čimeg. ireküi küsel bügüdeyin ölǰei qutuy-iyar büridkü boltuyai. oṃ sarvan bindidi bura bura sura sura ayaraday-a ayaraday-a bačir isbaran-a qanag. oṃ a a huu. oṃ a a hūṃ. oṃ a a hūṃ. ariyun takil-un ündüsün qamiy-a-ača egüsemüi. takil-un ündüsün oytaryui-ača egüsemüi. ečige oytaryui-ača luusus-un dayun-i kürekireged. eke dalai-ača yal gilbeleged. tere qoyar ǰabsar-ača dalai-yin ǰirüken čayan egülen-i bayiyulan tulugsan-iyar. tere egülen-ü ǰirüken-eče rasiyan-u qur-a oroyad. yaǰar-un ǰirüken-eče ubsang-un modon oroyuyad. tere ubsang-un modon-u ǰirüken-eče ubsang-un ǰirüken-i quriyayad. ubsang-un ečige inu oytaryui bui. eke inu delekei bui. köbegün inu arban yurban takil-un modon bui. dorona ǰüg-ün čayan labayin čayan modon-i abču. emün-e ǰüg-ün noyoyan kökemdüge öngge-tü ongydayin(?) ayula-ača kökemdüge modon-i abču. umar-a ǰüg-ün ulayan ǰes ayulan-ača ulayan čandan modon-i abču. oron-a ǰüg-ün qar-a temürün ayulan-ača qar-a suqai modon-i abču. kökemdüge nabčin möčirtei arča modon kiged.*

XBM 81

5 items of a *pothī* (10 written sides), written in a beautiful hand.

The first item is a nearly entire folio which measures ca. 12.5 × 5 cm, and has 14–15 lines. It was numbered *2r- *2v, according to the sequence of the text. The top section of the folio is missing, and the edges are torn.

The second item is a fragment of a folio. It measures ca. 12 × 6 cm, and has 14–15 lines; the Mongolian page number is *ɣur[ban]* (3). The folio is stained, especially on recto and numerous words are illegible.

The third item is a small fragment of a folio. It measures ca. 4 × 4 cm, and has 4–3 lines; the Mongolian page number is *ǰirɣuɣan* (6).

The forth item consists of two pieces of the same folio, which measure 3.5 × 3–10 × 3 cm respectively. It was numbered *7r-*7v, according to the sequence of the text.

The fifth item is a nearly entire folio. It measures 12 × 7 cm, and has 14–15 lines; the Mongolian page number is *naiman* (8); sections of the folio are missing. The text is severely damaged.[12]

*2r

1 *[oom a] qung :: oom a qung*
2 *[ ] un ündüsün qam[i]ɣ-a-ača egüsü =*
3 *[ ]*[13] *[e]čige oɣtarɣui-ača luus-un*
4 *[ ] [kürki]reged :*[14] *eke delekei-eče ɣal gilbelüged :*
5 *[ ]*[15] *un ǰabsar-ača dalai-yin ǰirüken-eče*
6 *[ ]en*[16] *bayiɣuluɣad : tere egülen-ü*
7 *[ ]e*[17] *rasiyan-u qura oroɣad : yaɣar-un*
8 *[ ]e*[18] *ebösün modon-u ǰirüken-eče ub =*
9 *[sang-un]*[19] *[i]degen quriyaɣad :*[20] *ubsang-un ečige*
10 *[oɣta]rɣui*[21] *bui: eke inu delekei bui :*

---

12 Old numbers 22/20; 12/4; 25/4; 22/34; 32/4; 32/4; 25/4 and 32/4 were restored by Mrs. Nebel, the others by Mr. Bentchev.
13 Ms. Asch 122, 2r: 10: *egüsemüi.*
14 Ms. Asch 122, 2r:12–13: *luusun-un dayun-i kürkireged.*
15 Ms. Asch 122, 2r:14–15: *tere qoyar-un.*
16 Ms. Asch 122, 2r:15: *čaɣan egülen-i*
17 Ms. Asch 122, 2v:2–3: *ǰirüken-eče.*
18 Ms. Asch 122, 2v:4–5: *ǰirüken-eče.*
19 Ms. Asch 122, 2v:9.
20 A similar passage is found in *Ündüsün bsang.* It reads: *onča dalai-yin ǰirüken-ü čaɣan egülen bayin toɣtaǰu. egüles-ün ǰirüken-ü narin qur-a-yin oroɣulǰu el-e. üjesküleng-tü čambu-dvib-un yaɣar delekei-eče yaɣar-un ǰirüken mod öbesün sayitur delgereǰü.* See Serruys, "A Mongolian Lamaist Prayer", p. 364.
21 Ms. Asch 122, 2v:10.

11 [   ] [i]nu²² arban γurban takil-un modon bui :
12 [   ]²³ [jü]g-ün čayan labai-yin ayulan
13 [-ača] [   ]a-yin²⁴ čayan modon abču : emüne
14 [jüg-ü]n noγoγan kö[kemdüge]²⁵ oγiui²⁶ -yin

*2v

1   ayulan-ača kökemdüge modon [abču:] [   ]²⁷
2   jüg-ün ulaγ[a]n ǰisün²⁸ ayulan-ača [   ]²⁹
3   čindan-i modon abču : umara jüg [-ün] [   ]³⁰
4   temür-ün ayulan-ača qara suqai mod[on] [abču :]
5   kökemdüge nabčis möčir-dü arčai-yi[n] [modon]
6   kiged : ungγaril-du čayan qamqaγ lam[   ]³¹
7   möčir-dei ba : qarabtur qamqaγ sira al[tan]³²
8   möčir-dei ba: sodu (?)³³ modon kiged: s[   ]
9   -yin modon ba : qamqaγ kiged ǰür[   ]
10 ebösün ba :³⁴ čayan čulu qulusun ki[ged]
11 köndei qulusun ba: baltu modon kiged : [   ]³⁵
12 modon ba : čandan kiged : ayuru b[a]
13 edeger takil-un arban γurban modon-i [qoγo =]
14 sun sedkil-ün čina[r]-[tu]r büridken bayt[ayaǰu]³⁶
15 takil beleddümü[i] [ede]ger takil-un köke [   ]

3r

1   [   ] degegsid[e] [   ] oγtarγui
2   [luγ-]a sača [bolu]γad :³⁷ oγtarγui ber dügüren
3   [qa]muγ burqan-nuγud-tur + ::³⁸ ulaγan γal-un

---

22 Ms. Asch 122, 2v:12: köbegün inu.
23 Ms. Asch 122, 2v:14: dorona.
24 Ms. Asch 122, 2v:15 has labayin.
25 See Ms. Asch 122, 3r:2; see also this word in *2v:5.
26 This word is written with γ before i; Ms. Asch 122, 3r:3 has ongγdayin ayula-ača.
27 Ms. Asch 122, 3r:5: umar-a.
28 Ms. Asch 122, 3r:6: ǰes.
29 Ms. Asch 122, 3r:7: ulaγan.
30 Ms. Asch 122, 3r:8: qar-a; Ms. Asch 122 has örön-e ǰüg instead of umara jüg in the Xarbuxyn Balgas text.
31 Ms. Asch 122, 3r:16 has labai; this may be a case of alternation m ~ l in this word.
32 Ms. Asch 122, 3r:18: altan.
33 The Qorin nigetü tayilburi toli (p. 579) lists sonduu, "similar to the jujube tree".
34 Ms. Asch 122, 3v:1–4: sodu (?) modon ba. qamqaγ kiged ǰirüken-ü sün. ebesün-ü sidi-nuγud ba.
35 Ms. Asch 122, 3v:8: üǰümte-ün modon ba.
36 Ms. Asch 122, 3v:13: baytaγaǰu.
37 Ms. Asch 122, 3v:14–4r:1: edeger takil-un köke yeke utaγa inu degegside γaraγsan-iγar köke oγtarγui-luγ-a sača boluγad.
38 Ms. Asch 122, 4r:4–5: ariγun takil takimui.

 4 [   ]³⁹ inu yaruγsan-iyar ǰabsar-luγ-a sač[a]
 5 [   ]⁴⁰ ǰabsar-iyar dügüren qamuγ nom-un
 6 [   ]ud-tur + ::⁴¹ qara negüresün inu
 7 [   ] [...]⁴² delekei
 8 [   ] [...]⁴³ [de]lekei ber dü[gü]ren
 9 [   ]⁴⁴ bur[sang] quvarad-ud[tur] +:: [   ]
10 [oom a qung ::] oom a qung ::
11 oom a qung :: gürü norbu badm-a
12 [sam]bau-a baysi-tur + :: [   ]⁴⁵ γayi[qam =]
13 siγ-i ilete maydamui : γirtenčü-yin
14 itegel lingqu-a-sun⁴⁶ qaγan inu [i]ndi bod[i]⁴⁷

3v

 1 qaγan-u kö[   ] [qaγa]γčaγad⁴⁸
 2 qamuγ-i nomoγadqan se[ri]gün [   ] tur⁴⁹ iled[   ]⁵⁰
 3 [q]oγar gegen-iyer bütümǰi časutu yaǰar-a sas[in]
 4 [   ]⁵¹ delgeregülbei ○ : edüge öröne uma[ra]
 5 qoγar-un ǰabsar-tur aburasun aman-i [   ]
 6 γulun⁵² sayuγči yasalang-**ača** ülü nögčin [   ]⁵³
 7 amitan-i γayča kü itegel yeke-yin yeke dege[dü]
 8 tngri-ner-ün qan: qamuγ burqan bodisun[g]
 9 -nar-un qubilγan badm-a sambau-a nigülesküi
10 adisdid-un eǰen-i⁵⁴ edüge duradumui ǰalbarimui ::⁵⁵
11 [a]disdid-i öggün soyorq-a :: qoyoson kü
12 [ayar]⁵⁶ -tur ene adisdid-un takil oytarγui-yin
13 [kiǰaγ]ar-luγa sača boltuγai ::⁵⁷ oom a qung ::

39 Ms. Asch 122, 4r:6: *ilči*.
40 Ms. Asch 122, 4r:8: *boluγad*.
41 Ms. Asch 122, 4r:10–11: *čoγčas-nuγud-tur ariγun takil takimui*.
42 Ms. Asch 122. 4r:13: *yaǰar-a bayugsan-iyar*.
43 Ms. Asch 122, 4r:14–15: *delekei-luγ-a sača boluγad*.
44 Ms. Asch 122, 4r:16: *qamuγ*.
45 Ms. Asch 122, 4v:6–7: *terigüten-tür*.
46 The plural suffix in *-s* is joined to the genitive suffix.
47 Lines 7–14 are severely damaged, but the words transcribed above are still legible in the original.
48 Ms. Asch 122, 4v:13–14: *köbegün inu gem-eče qaγaγčagsan*.
49 Ms. Asch 122, 4v:15–16: *serigün ayur-tur*.
50 Either *iled[te]* or *ilet[e]*; Ms. Asch 122, (4v:16) has *ilete*.
51 Ms. Asch 122, 5a: 2–3: *časutu yaǰar-a šača* (for *šasin?*) *nom-i delgeregülbei*.
52 Ms. Asch 122, 5r:7: *daruγulan*.
53 Ms. Asch 122, 5r:9: *qamuγ*.
54 There is a split in the folio, but the word *eǰen* is legible.
55 *duradumui ǰalbarimui* are legible in the original.
56 Ms. Asch 122, 5v:3 and OS IV/48v (Heissig, *Handschriften-Reste*) read *aγar*, as expected.
57 OS IV/48v: *qiǰaγar-luγ-a sača boltuγai*.

14 *[oom] a qung :: oom a qung :: ene ariyun*
15 *[aldars]iysan*[58] *takil-iyar včir-a dara terigüten*

6r

1 *yayiqamsiy čoy dai-a [   ]*[59]   3 *ayulas doyaloqan*[61] *rasiyan [   ]*
2 *qan sümbür tay- tur + [   ]*[60]   4 *erdem-dü*[62]

6v

1 *[   ] :: siričig-ün*   3 *[   ] [teri]güten: naran saran gangga*
2 *[   ] möngke yajar usun-a*   4 *[   ]a + ::*[63]

*7r

1 *[   ]güd-tür + ::*   8   *[   ] ene yirtenčü-tü[r]*
2 *[   ] yajar-un ejed*[64] *teri[güten]*   9   *[   ]la qoyitu*
3 *[   ]*   10 *[   ] [bu]rqan-u čiyulyan*
                                              11 *[   ] [...]a terigü[ten]*
     — — —   12 *[   ] dayun*[65] *metü*
4 *[   ] [oy]tary[ui] [   ]*   13 *[   ]*
5 *[   ] [te]rigüre[n] [   ]*   14 *[   ]*[66]
6 *[   ]a [   ]*
7 *[   ] [...]*

*7v

1 *[   ] un qubilyan bey[-e] [   ]*   4 *[   ] eki[   ]*
2 *[   ] tü -tür + :: qang[   ]*   — — —
3 *[   ] : qamuy qan yaja[r] [usun-a +]*[67]   5 *[   ]*

---

58 Ms. Asch 122, 5v:10 has *aldarsigsan*.
59 Ms. Asch 122, 9v:15: *bayigsan*.
60 Ms. Asch 122, 10r:1: *doloyan altan ayula*.
61 For *doloyaqan*?
62 Ms. Asch 122, 10r: 2–4:*doloyan rasiyan-u nayur naiman yeke erdem-tü mörön.*
63 M. Asch 122, 10v:14–11r:2: *siričigün-ün terigüten. dumdatu möngke yajar usun-tur +. gandis toregüten (terigüten). naran saran ganga mörön kiged. qamuy qan yajar usun-tur +.*
64 The word *ejed* is still legible in the original.
65 *dayun* is legible in the original.
66 The text is fragmentary. The complete passage in Ms. Asch 122, 11v:4- 12r:13 reads: *köbegün kiged-tür +. dorkiran quraqui yajar-un ejen terigüten čorkiran čiyulqui usun-u ejed terigüten. čayan dabasun kiged-tür +. oytaryui -yin nayur köke nayur qar-a nayur terigüten. qamuy nayur-tur +. tayising sačun terigüten qutuy-tu naiman bodisug-nar-un čiyulyan qamuy qan yajar usun-tur +. ene yirtinčü-tür qutuy ügei-yin tula čambala qoyitu boldoy neretü jimis-ün sang-un burqan-u čiyulyan ba qamuy qan yajar usun-tur +. arbus alay terigüten. barayun eteged-tür čau ke[n]gge-yin dayun metü dungginegči (dünggginegči). jegün eteged-tür čau čanggi-yin dayun metü čingginayči čayayibir čayan öngge-dü.*
67 See *yajar usun-a* in line 8.

6 [   ]   10 ḏu keibüng kürtü [   ]
7 [   ]   11 qamuy qan yaǰar u[sun-a +]⁶⁸ [   ]
8 yaǰar usun-a + :: tem[   ]   12 elči qondan⁶⁹ etügen-ü [   ]
9 terigüten: qamuy qan [yaǰar usun-a +]   13 [...] yeke elčis⁷⁰ [   ]
   [   ]   14 [   ]⁷¹

8r

1 [   ] ün neretü [   ] :
2 [qa]muy yeke sayuri[   ]⁷² + :: da[lan] dol[oyan]⁷³
3 etügen eke-yin [   ]i⁷⁴ činegen čila[yun] [   ]⁷⁵
4 eǰed : sinayan-i [čine]gen mösön-i eǰ[e]d :
5 qančuni činegen yool-un eǰed :⁷⁶ tüigüre (?)⁷⁷
6 činegen toloyai-yin eǰed : toliyin
7 činegen nayur-un eǰed : onin-i činegen⁷⁸
8 kötel-ün eǰed : kilyasun-u činegen ǰamun⁷⁹

---

68 These words are legible in the original.
69 Ms. Asch 122, 13r:3 has qudas. The term qondan means "crimson", see Mongγol üges-ün
    iǰayur-un toli, p. 1076.
70 elčis is still legible in the original.
71 Ms. Asch 12r:13- 13r:8 reads: čakravadun qubilyan bey-e-ḏü čayasu-ḏu čöle gerel-ḏü-ṯür +.
    yangyayin qatayana terigüten qamuy qan yaǰar usun-ṯur +. altayin qan erketü arban qoyar
    mörön čidqulang-ḏu. alyas sübele belčir-ḏü qatun eke terigüten qamuy qan yaǰar usun-ṯur +.
    anggir vayiqaya terigüten. qamuy qan yaǰar usun-ṯur +. temür ulqu dörben terigüten. qamuy
    qan yaǰar usun-ṯur +. keibüng kürtü balyasun terigüten qamuy qan yaǰar usun-ṯur +. ariyun +.
    tngri elči qudas ötügen-ü elči dayisun terigüten qamuy yeke elči sibim raydan sibe sisung
    singgün neretü tüsimel.
72 Ms. Asch 122, 13r:9: sayuris-tur ariyun +.
73 Ms. Asch 122, 13r:10.
74 Ms. Asch 122, 13r:11: siyayin.
75 Ms. Asch 122, 13r:12 has čilayun-u. The Xarbuxyn Balgas text has sinayan-i, mösön-i, qančuni
    instead of sinayan-u, mösön-ü, qančunu. On the genitive suffix -i after a word ending in n, see
    Poppe, "Geserica", pp. 14–16.
76 Ms. Asch 122, 13r:14–15 has qulu eǰed. The Xarbuxyn Balgas text has yool-un eǰed.
77 Ms. Asch 122, 13r:15 has tüinggi. Heissig transcribes this word tüngge and translates it
    "Schlaufe", following Poppe's suggestion. See Handschriften-Reste, pp. 397, 400 and
    note 112. The term tüngge is listed in Mongγol üges-ün iǰayur-un toli, (p. 1989), meaning "loop
    for fastening leather strings". This dictionary also registers tünggerče, "small leather bag", and
    quotes the expression tünggerčeg-ün činegen (p. 1989).
78 Ms. Asch 122, 13v:3: onun-i činegen; oni(n), onu(n), "notch on an arrow", Lessing, p. 614.
79 Heissig transcribes yamun eǰed, "Amtsherren", Handschriften-Reste, pp. 397, 400 and
    note 113. In my own view, ǰamun (ǰam-un) eǰed, "road spirit-masters", is more suitable in this
    context. See above yool-un eǰed, "river spirit-masters"; toloyai-yin eǰed, "hill spirit-masters";
    nayur-un eǰed, "lake spirit-masters"; kötel-ün eǰed, "mountain pass spirit-masters";
    tergegürün eǰen, "highway spirit-masters", is found in Mong. 301, 19v (= Heissig and
    Bawden, Catalogue, pp. 161–3).

9 *ejed : terigüten qamuy qan [yaja]r usun*
10 *-a + :: buta*[80] *büri burqan qada*[81] *büri*
11 *[qa]n*[82] *boluysad-tur + :: qamuy amitan-i*
12 *[ne]gükü nu[t]uy*[83] *bayuqu [qu]duy*[84] *terigüten*
13 *[qamuy] [q]an yajar usun-a + :: qamiy-a*[85]
14 *sayuysan yajar usun-a kiged: qamiy-[a]*[86]

8v

1 *[sayu]ysan ya[jar] [usun-a] + :: ene takil*
2 *[   ] buyan [   ]ur oytaryui*
3 *[   ] burqan [   ] bodisug*
4 *[   ] qutuy [oros]iqu boltuyai ::*[87]
5 *dum[da]*[88] *ber dügüren qa[muy]*[89] *nom-nuyud*
6 *-un qutuy or[o]siqu boltuyai :: delekei*
7 *ber dügüren [qamuy] burs[a]ng quvaray-ud-un*
8 *qutuy orosiqu boltuyai :: qayan qatun*
9 *terigüt[en] erdeni-dü ečige eke kiged :*
10 *qamuy amitan engke [a]muyulang-iyar jiryaqu*
11 *boltuyai :: ečüs-tür bur-qan-u*[90] *qutuy-i*
12 *türidkel ügei olqu boltuyai ::*
13 *[esergülü]gči*[91] *dayisun simnus-a öber-iyen*
14 *[   ]*[92] *ügei bolqu boltuyai :: kei*
15 *[qura] [ke]reg*[93] *čay-tur bolqu*[94]

---

80 The word *buta* is legible in the original.
81 *qada* is legible in the original.
82 Ms. Asch 122, 13v:8 has *qan; Gegün-ü sün-ü sačuli* (p. 331) reads *buta büri burqan qada büri qan.*
83 The *t* of *nutuy* is barely legible; Ms. Asch 122, 13v:10–11: *negükü nituy* (for *nutuy*).
84 *Gegün-ü sün-ü sačuli,* (pp. 331–2): *negüküi nutuy bayuqui quduy.*
85 *qamiy-a* is still legible in the original.
86 This line is still legible in the original.
87 Ms. Asch 122, 14r 2–6: *ene takil takigsan buyan-u küčün-iyer oytaryui her dügüren qamuy burqan-nuyud-un qutuy orosiqu boltuyai.*
88 Ms. Asch 122, 14r:7: *dumda-du.*
89 Ms. Asch 122, 14r:8.
90 The word *burqan* is written separatedly because there is a split in the folio, which already existed when the text was written.
91 Following Ms. Asch 122, 14v:6, which reads *esergülügči.*
92 Ms. Asch 122, 14v:8: *sunuju* (?) *ügei; Gegün-ü sün-ü sačuli* (p. 336): *qotala bügüde dayisun ügei boltuyai.*
93 Ms. Asch 122, 14v:9–10 has *kei qur-a kereg.* The expression *kei qura* often occurs in the Mongol texts. See, for example, the *Bodhicaryāvatāra* (Cerensodnom and Taube, No. 21r6, p. 94).
94 *Gegün-ü sün-ü sačuli* (p. 335): *tngri luus-un bilig-ün qur-a bayuju.*

The opening section of *Ündüsün-i sang* relates the origin of the burnt offering *(ubsang)*,[95] which has heaven as father, earth as mother, and thirteen kinds of woods as sons: *ubsang-un ečige [oyta]ryui bui. eke inu delekei bui. [köbegün] [i]nu arban yurban takil-un modon bui* (XBM 81, *2r:9–11). Thirteen woods are the requisites of the burnt offering. Thirteen is a symbolic number of cosmic and religious meaning for both the Tibetans and the Mongols;[96] it also plays an important role in divinatory practices.[97] The cosmic significance of the burnt offering is emphasised by the provenance and colours of the thirteen woods, which are taken from mountains located in the four cardinal directions. e.g.: *umara jüg[-ün] [qara] temür-ün ayulan-ača qara suqai mo[don] [abču]*, "Take black tamarisk wood from the black iron mountain in the north" (XBM 81, *2v:3–4).

In rituals the account of their origin is essential. The prayers recited at the sacrifice to the hearth-fire also relates the origin of fire: *qatan temür ečige-tü qayir čilayun eke-tü*,[98] "(Fire) has hardened iron as father, pebbles as mother".

It is also notable how *Undüsün-i sang* describes the spirit-masters located in the land: *sinayan-i [čine]gen mösön-i ej[e]d. qančuni činegen yool-un ejed*, "Ice spirit-masters the size of a ladle. River spirit-masters the size of a sleeve" (XBM 81, 8r:4–5).

The same figure of speech is used in other contexts. The fire-*dalalya*, for example, describes navel and womb in these words: *könög-yi-yin činegen küi. könjilei-yin činegen umai*, "A navel the size of a bucket. A womb the size of a bedcover".[99]

Finally, the Geser epic has this variant: *emüne jüg-eče qoni činegen čayan egülen. qoyitu jüg-eče üker-ün činegen qar-a egülen*, "White clouds the size of a sheep from the south. Black clouds the size of an ox from the north".[100]

---

95 For the account of origins of the *bsang* and other rituals among the Tibetans, see Stein, *Tibetan Civilization*, pp. 198–9.

96 Ekvall, "Significance of Thirteen", pp. 188–192; on the occurrence of thirteen and the various meanings of this number in the Mongol epics, see Sagaster, "Bemerkungen zur Dreizehn im mongolischen Epos", pp. 141–55; on the association of the number thirteen with the worship of the *oboy-a* and other ritual pratices, see Altangarudi et al., *Mongyoljin-u šasin surtaqul*, pp. 51–82.

97 Divinations are made by means of thirteen stones, as we learn from *Arban yurban čilayun-yin sudur*, "The sūtra of the thirteen stones". This book of divination also mentions "thirteen birds of long life" *(urtu nasun-u arban yurban sibayun)*, 10v. I am most grateful to Prof. Heissig for putting at my disposal a copy of the manuscript.

98 Rintchen, *Matériaux*, p. 17; for the account of the origin of the fire, see the remarks by Mostaert, "Prière", pp. 201–2.

99 See the fire-*dalalya* dealt with below in this volume (XBM 82).

100 *Arban jüg-ün ejen geser qayan-u tuyuji*, I, p. 255.

The *dalalγa* for the Sacrifice to the Hearth-fire

XBM 82 to XBM 85

The *dalalγa*, "the rite to beckon good fortune" is one of the most profound expressions of the ritual culture of the Mongols. It is therefore interesting that the Xarbuxyn Balgas collection includes an almost complete text and fragments of three copies of the *dalalγa* for the sacrifice to the hearth-fire.[1]

The fire-*dalalγa* is usually found included in the fire-*sūtra (γal-un sudur)*, of which a large number of texts are known,[2] but sometimes it also consists of an independent text.[3]

XBM 82

1 booklet *(debter)*, which includes a nearly complete text, written in two hands. It is composed of 6 folios (9 written sides) measuring ca. 13 × 4 cm, without page numbers, and having different numbers of lines. Previously the folios were stiched together in the middle, and their ends folded. The folios have the lower sides torn, but the text is well preserved and legible. The first section of the text is missing.[4]

*1 v

1   *[   ]bad-un[5] qaγan*

---

1   On the fire-*dalalγa* see Chabros, *Beckoning Fortune*, pp. 85–110, 216–40. On the *dalalγa* ritual which is performed on other occasions, I refer the reader to the book quoted above; the fire-*dalalγa* is also discussed by Poppe in "Zum Feuerkultus", pp. 140–5.

2   The following fire-sūtra, which include the *dalalγa*, were used in this work. They are: *Qutuγ-tu burqan baγsi-yin ǰokiγaγsan γal-un burqan-yi takiqu sudur-nuγus orošiba* = Mong. 401 (Heissig and Bawden, *Catalogue*, pp. 123–4); *γal-un eke kölgen sudur, γal-un takilγ-a sudur* (Mss. belonging to the author. They were acquired in Ulaanbaatar); Rintchen, *Matériaux*, pp. 18–24; *γal-un sudur orosibai, γal-un takilγ-a* = Bulaγ ed., *Mongγolčud-un γal takilγ-a*, pp. 192–204, 406–21; *γal takilγ-a-yin öčig = Ordos-un tayilγ-a takilγ-a*, pp. 116–37.

3   See, for example, Rintchen, *Matériaux*, pp. 30–32.

4   Restored by Mr. Bentchev; old number 23.

5   The *dalalγa* included in *γal-un eke kölgen sudur* (Ms. belonging to the author) has *čagarabad*, while *čagrabad* is found in *γal-un sudur* (Bulaγ, ed., p. 199); *čagiravarun < čagiravard* appears in *Sayin ügetü erdeni-yin sang* (J̌aγunasutu et al., p. 183); *cakravar-un* is found in the *Čaγan teüke*. See Sagaster, *Weiße Geschichte*, p. 81; see also *čakiravarun* in *The Twelve Deeds* (Poppe, f. 17b, note 5, p. 155).

2   -u nom-un bu buyan kesig[6]
3   činu ɣuyinam[7]
4   qurui + ::[8]
5   včira dara[9]
6   terigüten
7   arban ǰüg
8   -ün burqan bodisug-nar

9   -un nom-un
10   buyan kesi[g]
11   činu ɣuyi[nam]
12   qurui +
13   erdeni-yi[n]
14   qan bism[an]
15   tengri[10] buy[an]

*2r

1   kesig čin[u]
2   ɣuyin[am]
3   qurui +::
4   möngke teng[ri]
5   ečige-yin bu[yan]
6   kesig činu
7   ɣuyinam
8   qurui +::

9   dalan dolo=
10   ɣan[11] etügen
11   eke-yin ɣaǰar
12   -un buyan[12]
13   kesig činu
14   ɣuyinam
15   qurui +::
16   naran saran gerel-d̲ü

*2v

1   köbegün-ü buyan
2   kesig činu ɣuyi=

3   nam[13] qurui + :: dolo=
4   ɣan ebüged teri=

---

6   Forms such as *bu buyan, ke kes-ig* (*2v:4), *daɣu daɣusba* (XBM 84, 4v:4) are pointed out in the section of the book Linguistic Features of the Manuscripts. As far as *buyan kesig* is concerned, according to Šaɣǰa (*Mongɣol ügen-ü tayilburi toli*, p. 278), the compound *buyan kesig* means "portion which let good come", and the term *kesig* means "portion" (p. 366). On the term *kesig* in the *Secret History*, see the discussion by Mostaert in *Passages*, pp. 374–9; see also Ligeti, "Le sacrifice", pp. 150–1; *kesig* means "favour, blessing, good fortune" (Lessing, p. 460); On the Uighur expression *qut buyan* see Bang and von Gabain, *Türkische Turfan-Texte*, p. 254, note 2.

7   *ɣuyinam* is also found in the other *dalalɣa* texts from Xarbuxyn Balgas (see below). It likewise occurs in the *dalalɣa* included in *Ɣal-un eke kölgen sudur*; see *ɣuyi-* instead of *ɣuyu-* in Cerensodnom and Taube, *Turfansammlung*, No. 5, p. 59.

8   The cry *qurui*, accompanied by a circular gesture, is characteristic of the *dalalɣa*; *qurui* also appears in other ritual texts which are recited to promote good fortune. See, for example, Sárközi, "A Mongolian Hunting Ritual", pp. 200–1; the cry *qurui* is also found in the litanies for calling back the soul. See Bawden, "Calling the Soul", pp. 218–19; Chiodo, "A J̌arud Mongol Ritual", pp. 155–6. Chabros discusses the word *qurui* in *Beckoning Fortune*, pp. 142–50. According to the *Mongɣol kitad toli* (p. 684) *qurui* means "cry to call, to invite somebody"; the verb *quruyila-* (Mong.) means "faire tourner en l'air un object long et flexibile en le tenant par un de ses bouts, faire le moulinet avec le bras ou avec quelque chose qu'on tient en main par de ses bouts" (Mostaert, *Dictionnaire ordos*, p. 373a).

9   Mong. 401, 4r has *vačir-a dhar-a blam-a*.

10   Mong. 401, 4r has *erdeni-yin qaɣan bisman tngri*.

11   Mong. 401, 4v adds *dabqur*.

12   The final *n* in the word *buyan* shows a straight stroke.

5 güten tüg tümen
6 költi ododun[14] buyan
7 kesig činu yuyinam
8 qurui +:: gangg[a]
9 mören-ü dal[ai]

10 metü[15] sirgisi [ügei]
11 buyan kes[ig]
12 činu yuyinam
13 qurui +::

*3r

1 sümbür ayul[a][16]
2 metü baraydas[i]
3 ügei bu-yan ke
4 kes-ig[17] činu yu[yinam]
5 qurui +:: qa[s][18]
6 qadan metü ebdere=
7 si ügei buyan

8 kesig činu yuyinam
9 qurui +:: tasu=
10 raqai-yi[19] minu
11 jalγayči[20] tamtu=
12 raqai-yi minu
13 nököji[21] ögügči

*3v

1 buyan kesig
2 činu yuyinam
3 qurui +::
4 ügeyiregsen
5 minu bayaji=
6 γuluγči:

7 ükügsen-i[22]
8 minu tölöjü
9 ögügči
10 buyan kesig
11 činu yuyinam
12 qurui +::

*4r

1 dumdai minu
2 dügürejü dülimi[23]
3 minu güičejü

4 öggügči[24] buyan kesig
5 činu yuyinam
6 qurui +:: könög

---

13 Mong. 401, 4v: naran saran odon metü gereltei köbegün-u buyan kesig činu.
14 Mong. 401, 4v: ḳolti odon-u.
15 Mong. 401, 4v: gangga dalai metü; Rintchen, Matériaux (p. 22) has gangga mören dalai metü.
16 Mong. 401, 4v: qaγan sümbür ayula.
17 Note ke kesig instead of kesig kesig.
18 Mong. 401 (4v) writes the word qas with diacritical points before q.
19 tasuraqai (MLM tasurqai). See tamturaqai (MLM tamturqai) in the next line. On this ortho-
    graphic feature see Cerensodnom and Taube, Turfansammlung, p. 12; Mong. 401 (4v) has
    tasarqai; Γal-un eke sudur (Ms. belonging to the author, 4r) reads tasuraγsan-i.
20 Mong. 401(4v): jalγaju öggügči.
21 Instead of nököjü.
22 Rintchen, Matériaux (p. 31) has öggügsen; Γal takily-a-yin öčig (Ordos tayily-a takily-a,
    p. 132) reads ükügsen-i mini amijiraγulju.
23 Mong. 401 (4v) reads dulum-a; Γal-un eke kölgen sudur (4r) has dulim-i; Rintchen, Matériaux
    (p. 23) has dulim. See duli, dulim in Mongγol üges-ün ijaγur-un toli, p. 2136; see also düli,
    "mediocre, average, halfway", etc. in Lessing, p. 280; düli appears in Γal-un sudur (Bulaγ, p. 156).
24 Mong. 401 (4v) has dumdaγur-yi minu güičegejü dulum-a-yi minu dügürgejü.

7   -*yi-yin*[25] *činegen küi*[26]
8   *könǰilei-yin*[27] *činegen*
9   *umai ködegedü*
10 *bayiqu dörben*
11 *qosiɣun-tu aduɣusun*

*4v

1   *buq-a: del yeketü*
2   *aǰarɣa*[28] *deleng yeketü*
3   *gegüü-yi*[29] *sür sünesün*
4   *činu ɣuyinam qurui* +::
5   *baydar sayari-tu*[30]
6   *ayta barim kökötü*
7   *ünegen-i*[31] *sür sünesün*
8   *ölǰei qutuɣ-yi*[32] *činu*

12 -*u sür sünesün*
13 *buyan kesig činu*
14 *ɣuyinam qurui* +::
15 *ǰoydor yeketü buyura*
16 *buyulɣan yeketü*

9   *ɣuyinam qurui* +::
10 *daldariɣsan daɣa b[   ]*
11 *riɣsan*[33] *buruyu*[34] *t[ögeri=]*
12 *gsen tölöge eld[eri =]*
13 *gsen*[35] *esige-yi minu*
14 *sür sünesün-i*
15 *činu ɣuyinam qurui* [+::]

---

25 On the genitive suffix -*yi-yin*, see Poppe, "Geserica", pp. 16–18.
26 Mong. 401(5r): *ködege-yin činegen küi*.
27 On the genitive suffix -*i-yin*, see Poppe, "Geserica", pp. 16–18.
28 Instead of *aǰirɣa*.
29 Instead of *gegüü-yin;* Mong. 401(5r): *ǰoydor yeketü buyur-a. dayun yeketü buq-a. del yeketü aǰiry-a. deleng yeketü gegüü üniy-e.* The expression *dou yeketü buxu* is found in the Oyirad *Čaɣan dalalɣa* (copy of the manuscript belonging to the author, 2v), while *dayu yeketü buq-a* occurs in *Arban ɣurban sang,* 5v (this manuscript belongs to the author; it was acquired in Ulaanbaatar).
30 Rintchen, *Matériaux* (p. 23) reads *baydaɣar sayaritu;* Mostaert, "Prière" has *baydar sayaritu* (p. 196). See also the discussion by Mostaert on p. 210 of the same article; see *boydoɣor* meaning "plump" in *Mongɣol kitad toli*, p. 472; *sayari* with the meaning of "buttock" is found in § 140 of the *Secret History*. For this see "Prière", p. 211, and *Dictionnaire ordos*, p. 563a.
31 Instead of *ünigen~üniyen; Γal-un eke kölgen sudur* (4r) has *ünegen;* Rintchen, *Matériaux* (pp. 23, 32) reads *üniyen* and *ünigen* respectively; on *barim, barim-a* see Lessing, "width of fist", p. 87, and *Mongɣol kitad toli*, p. 440.
32 The accusative suffix -*yi* after the word *qutuɣ*. For this see Poppe, "Geserica", p. 20; Rintchen, *Matériaux* (p. 23) omits *ölǰei qutuɣ*, "fortune and happiness". See *ölǰeitü qutuɣtu* in § 211 of the *Secret History*. On the terms *sür, sünesü* and *qutuɣ*, see Kotwicz, "Formules initiales", pp. 131–57.
33 XBM 83, 3v: 4 has *bultariɣsan*.
34 For *birayu*. This word is mispelt in various sources. On *idam bariqu*, which appears in the *Erdeni-yin tobči* from Kentei Ayimaɣ, see Chiodo, *A Manuscript from Kentei Ayimaɣ* (32r), and the discussion on pp. 18–21; see *idam birayu* in the *Altan tobči*, 95v.
35 XBM 84, 4r:10 has *elderigsen*, while XBM 85, 4v:2 reads *elderiɣsen;* Rintchen, *Matériaux* (p. 32) has *eyilügsen, eyil-*, "to run away, to flee", Lessing, p. 303. See *eyilbesü (ǰayilabasu)* in the *Altan tobči* (39b), *ǰayila-*, "to go away from" (Lessing, p. 1026). Mong. 401 has *elderegsen; eldere-~aldara-*, "to come loose, to disappear, to vanish", Lessing, p. 30.

*5r

1	*buruγulasi ügei*	8	*noqai egüden*
2	*bu buyan kesig-i*	9	*-teki ara*[38] *büle*[39]
3	*ölǰei qutuγ-y[i]*	10	*kitad-un kegüked*
4	*γuyinam qurui +*	11	*-i*[40] *činu minu*
5	*kegür-ün*[36] *tedüi*	12	*sür sünesün*
6	*bosaγ-a-taki*[37]	13	*-i činu γuyinam*
7	*aran boyol*	14	*qurui +.:*

*5v

1	*qagi üy-e üy-e*	6	*-ün keleber: igindo*
2	*qurui qurui: küy-e*	7	*imdos:*[41] *mongγol-un*
3	*küy-e: müy-e müy-e:*	8	*keleber: qurui qurui:*
4	*balboi-yin keleber:*	9	*včir-du küy-e*[42] *tegüs=*
5	*müy-e müy-e: enedkeg*	10	*be s[a]du edgü:*

XBM 83

3 items of a *pothī* (5 written sides). The first item is a fragment of a folio measuring ca. 9×6 cm, with 7 lines; the Mongolian page number is *nigen* (1). The second item is a folio measuring 12×5.5 cm, with 12 lines; the Mongolian page number is *qoyar* (2). This folio has a hole in its surface, and the text is badly damaged on verso. The third item is a folio measuring 10.5×6.5cm, with 12 lines; the Mongolian page number is *γur[ban]* (3); 3r is badly damaged, and various words are illegible.[43]

---

36 XBM 85, 4v:4 reads *kegürün* (see below); *Γal-un eke kölgen sudur* (4v), and *Γal-un sudur* (Bulaγ, p. 158) have *ger-ün tedüi*.

37 Instead of the usual form *bosoγ-a*.

38 See *hara* in § 246 of the *Secret History*; Heissig, *Volkreligiöse und folkloristische Texte*, (p. 87) has *egüde aru boyol*.

39 Mong. 401 has *ger-ün bosiγ-a-daki boyol noqai egüden-deki arad boyol*; Mostaert, "Prière" (p. 197): *egüden-deki boyol sayin daγutu noqai*. See the following passage in § 180 of the *Secret History*: *borqai-yin minu bosoq-a-yin bo'ol elinčüg-ün minu e'üden-ü emčü bo'ol* (de Rache-wiltz, *Index*, p. 91); on *büle*, *büli*, "family, strenght" see Lessing, p. 145; see also *büle*, "strength" in *Mongγol kitad toli*, p. 518; Šaγ ǰa lists *büli* in the meaning of "people's labour" (*Mongγol ügen-ü tayilburi toli*, p. 304).

40 Mong. 401 (5r): *gerün bosiγ-a-daki boyol noqai egüden-deki arad boyol*; Rintchen, *Matériaux* (p. 23): *egüden-deki ere boyul kitad keüked-ün...*

41 One would expect *imdo* (Tib. *mdo*) as in XBM 83 below; *imdos* should transcribe the Tibetan *mdos*, but this word means "thread-cross" (Das, pp. 676, 677).

42 *Γal-un eke kölgen sudur* (4v) has *mongγol-un keleber. včir küy-e*; *Γal-un takilγ-a sudur* (5r) reads: *vačir küy-e*; see the interjections *xüüe, xööe*, expressing calling, attracting attention in Kullman and Tserenpil, *Mongolian Grammar*, p. 353.

43 Restored by Mr. Bentchev; old numbers 24; 21/3; 12/4 respectively.

1v

1   O *enedkeg-ün keleber: ibsan*[44] *küy-e*
2   *küy-e tobed-ün*[45] *keleber : iyindo*[46]
3   *imdo*[47] *mongyolun keleber: qurui*
     qurui:[48]
4   *yurban da dalal: nom-un qayan*
     sigemüni

5   *bu[rq]an [   ] un buyan ki[sig]*[49] *ölǰei*
6   *q[utuy] yuyinam qurui qurui:*
7   *[   ] tngri*

2r

1   *[bo]disung-narun nom-un buyan*
2   *[kisig] [či]nu yuyinam qurui qurui:*
3   *[   ] qan bisman tn<r>gri buyan*
4   *[kisig] [či]nu yuyi[nam] qurui qurui:*
5   *tngri ečige-y[in] [buya]n kisig činu*
6   *[yuyinam] qurui qurui : dalan doloyan*

7   *[etüge]n*[50] *eke-yin yaǰarun buyan kisig*
8   *[činu] [y]uyinam qurui qurui : naran*
9   *[sara]n*[51] *odon gereltü köbegün-ü*
10   *[buyan] kisi[g] [činu] [qur]ui qurui :*
11   *[dolo]yan ebüged terigüten tüg*
12   *[tüme]n költi odod-un buyan kisig*

2v

1   *činu yuyi[nam] qurui qur[ui :]*
2   *gangga [   ] dalai [...] [   ]*[52]
3   *ügei buyan kisig [činu] yu[yinam]*
4   *qurui qurui [   ]*[53]
5   *ayulan [me]tü [barayd]asi [ügei]*[54]
6   *buyan ki[sig] [činu yuyinam] qur[ui]*
7   *qurui : [   ]*

8   *buyan ki[sig] činu [yuyinam qurui*
     qurui :]
9   *[ta]suraqai-yi [...] [   ]*
10   *yi minu güiče[ǰ]ü [öggüg]sen] [buyan]*
11   *kisig činu [yuyinam qurui qurui]*
12   *[üg]eyireyse[n] [minu] [   ]*

3r

1   *ükügsen [minu] tölöǰü öggügči*[55]
     [buya]n
2   *ki[s]ig [č]in[u] yuyinam qur[ui]*
     [qurui :]

3   *[...] [m]inu dü[...] [...]*
4   *[...]*
5   *[...]*
6   *[...] umai ködege [...]*

---

44   Tib. *bzaṅ-po*, "good" (Das, p. 1109).
45   For *töbed*.
46   XBM 82, *5v:5 has the spelling *igindo*. This word was not identified.
47   Tib. *mdo*, "sūtra" (Das, p. 675).
48   Rintchen, *Matériaux* (p. 22): *enedkeg-ün keleber sang küy-e küy-e küy-e. töbed-ün keleber*
     yanduling yanduling yanduling. mongyol-un keleber qurui qurui quri-a.
49   Instead of *kesig*. See *kisig* in the next lines.
50   See XBM 82, *2r:10.
51   XBM 82, *2r:16.
52   XBM 82, *2v:8–10 has *gangg[a] mören-ü dal[ai] metü sirgisi ügei.*
53   XBM 82, *3r:1 has *sümbür.*
54   See XBM 82, *3r:2.
55   *tölöǰü öggügči* are legible in the original.

7   *[ ]*

8   *buyan kisig [ci]nu γuyina[m] qurui*

     quri :

9   *joydor ye[ke]-tü buγ[ura]*[56] *[buγu]lγan*

3v

1   *baydar sayaritu ayta barim kökötü*

2   **ügen**[58] *gegüni minu sür s[ü]nesü öljei*

     qutuγ-i

3   *činu γuyinam qurui qurui : daldariγsan*

4   *dayayan bultariγsan biruγu*

     togeriγsen[59]

5   *tolöge*[60] *elderiγsen isige-yi minu sür*

6   *sünesün-i činu buyan kisig γuyinam*

     qurui

10   *yeke-tü [bu]qa [ ] [yeke]-tü*

     [ajï]rγan[57]

11   *delen yeke-tü gegü[-γ]i [...] [sü]r*

12   *sünesü činu γuyinam qurui qurui :*

7   *qurui : buruγulasi ügei buyan kisig*

8   *öljei qutuγ-i γuyinam qurui qurui :*

9   *tegegürün tedüi bosaγan-ṯaki aran*

10   *boγol noqai egüden-ṯeki ara bule*[61]

11   *kitad kegüküd-i činu minu sür*

12   *sunesün*[62] *-i činu γuyinam qurui qurui*

XBM 84

1 item of a *pothī* (1 folio, 2 written sides), measuring ca. 14.5 × 6.5 cm, with 21–4 lines (r/v); the Mongolian page number is *dörben* (4). The folio has a long split, and the top section is torn.[63]

4r

1   *[köde]gen-i činegen küi: könjilen-i*

2   *[činege]n*[64] *umai ködegen-ṯü bayiqu:*

3   *[dör]ben*[65] *qosiγun aduγusun-i*

4   *[mi]nu: sür sünesün buyan kesig*

5   *:: baydar sayari-tu ayta :*

6   *[ba]rim köke-tü*[66] *gegün unaγan-u sür*

7   *sünesün-i öggügči +:: daldariγsan*

8   *dayayan unaγan-i kesig bultariqu*

9   *biraγu tögörigsen tölöge*

10   *elderigsen esige-yi minu sür*

11   *sünesün-i ög[gü]gči +:: burulasi*[67]

12   *ügei buyan kesig öljei*

13   *kelberisi ügei ger-ün dotora*

14   *-yi boγol egüden-ṯü yabuqu*

---

56 See *buγura* in XBM 82, *4r:15.

57 See *buγulγan yeketü buqa. del yeketeü ajarγa* (for *ajïrγa*) in XBM 82, *4r:16-*4v:2.

58 This must be an error for *ünegen*.

59 For *tögerigsen*.

60 Instead of *tölöge*. Note that the vowel *ö* in second position is written with a superfluous *yod*.

61 For *büle ~ büli*.

62 Instead of *sünesün*.

63 Restored by Mr. Bentchev; old number 21/8.

64 Note again the genitive suffix *-i* instead of *-u* after a word ending in *n [köde]gen-i činegen, könjilen-i [činege]n*.

65 See *dörben* in XBM 82, *4r:10.

66 Instead of *kökö; XBM 82, *4v:6 has *kökötü*.

67 For *buruγulasi*.

15 *ügei (?) ara büle kedün nököd-ün*[68]   19 *he[n]dkeg-ün keleber +:: ghu yę*
16 *minu sür sünesün öggügči +::*   20 *ghu yę + töbed-ün*
17 *[ ]ge-yi qurui +:: muy-a muy-a*   21 *[kel]eber :*
18 *balboyin keleber +:: muni muni*

4v

1 *ngayvang-tu*[69]   3 *včir-tu kölgen*
2 *mongγolčilabasu*   4 *dayu dayusba*[70] *:: : ::*

XBM 85

3 items of a *pothī* (5 written sides). The first item is a small fragment of a folio which measures ca. 6×2 cm, and has 1 line. It shows the Tibetan letter *ta* on the left side. The second item is a fragment of a folio measuring 9×7 cm, and having 7 lines, without page number. It was numbered *3r–*3v, according to the sequence of the text. The third item consists of three scattered pieces of a folio. They measure ca. 6×2–5×2–5×2.5 cm respectively; the Mongolian page number is *dörben* (4).[71]

1 *enedkeg-ün keleber*

*3r

1 *[bis]man tengri-yin buyan kesig činu*   5 *yaǰar-un buyan (?) činu γuyinam [x::]*
2 *γuyinam x:: möngke tengri-yin*   6 *[kolti] [o]don-u gerel-tü*
3 *[buyan] kesig činu γuyinam [x::]*   *kö[begün-ü]*[72]
4 *[ ] etügen eke-yin*   7 *buyan kesig činu γuyinam x::*

*3v

1 *aγula metü baraγ[d]asi [ü]gei [buya]n*   5 *ǰalγagči tamturaqai mi[n]u [ö]ggügči*
2 *kesig činu γuyinam x:: qas*   6 *[buyan] [kesi]g činu γuyinam x::*
3 *qada metü ebderesi [ügei buyan]*   7 *[üge]yireysen-i minu*
4 *kesig činu γuyinam x:: [tas]uraqai*   *bayaǰ[iγu]l[uyči]*[73]

---

68 Lines 13–15 differ from the other texts of the *dalalγa*.
69 Tib. *ṅag-dbaṅ*, following Prof. Sagaster's suggestion.
70 *dayu dayusba* instead of *dayusba dayusba*.
71 The first item was restored by the Russians experts in Ulaanbaatar; old number 25/2. The second item had previously broken into two pieces: the first piece was restored by the Russian experts, the other by Mr. Bentchev; old numbers 4, 25/3. The third item was restored by Mr. Bentchev; old numbers 25/4, 31.
72 See *köbegün-ü* in XBM 82, *2v:1.
73 See *ügeiyiregsen minu bayaǰiγuluyči* in XBM 82, *3v:4–6.

4r

1 *[ü]kügsen-i minu tölöji*

— — —

2 *[könji]le-yin*[74] *činegen umai*
3 *köde[ge]dü bayiqu [dö]rben*

— — —

4 *yuyinam x:: joydor yeke-tü*
5 *buyur-a bulya*[75] *yeke [-tü]*

4v

1 *buqa: del yeke-tü ajarya dele[ng]*[76]

— — —

2 *[tölö]ge elderiysen esige inu*

— — —

3 *ölǰei qutuy-i*
4 *[yuyina]m x:: kegürün*

The Xarbuxyn Balgas fragments provide the earliest evidence of a *dalalya* for the sacrifice to the hearth-fire which is at present known.[77] As has been mentioned above, previously the booklet XBM 82 had the ends of the folios folded, suggesting that this text of the fire-*dalalya* was used as an amulet, and the folios were folded to reduce their size in order to fit the booklet into a box or a small pocket to be worn on the body.[78] The Xarbuxyn Balgas collection also includes a *dhāraṇī* which was found with the folios folded to form a square. It is possible that this *dhāraṇī* was used as an amulet.[79]

The opening section of the fire-*dalalya* requests good fortune *(buyan kesig)* from the deities who preside over the ritual. As in other folk religious texts, in the fire-*dalalya* too the dieties involved in the ritual are both those of the Buddhist pantheon (Vajradhara, "the thunderbolt holder", Bisman Tngri, the god of wealth, etc.), and those of the

---

74 XBM 82, *4r: 8 reads *könjilei-yin činegen*.
75 This is a spelling mistake for *buyulya*.
76 See *ajarya* (for *ajirya*) *deleng* in XBM 82, *4v:2.
77 The first printed edition of a text of a fire worship dates back to 1641. See Heissig, *Block-drucke*, p. 1.
78 The Mongols use a text such as *Sitātapatrā-dhāraṇī (Čayan sikürtei)* as an amulet. See Heissig and Bawden, *Catalogue*, Mong. 158, p. 210; on the use of amulets see Heissig, "Ein mongolisches Handbuch", pp. 70–83; see also Bawden, "The Supernatural Element", II, p. 93; Waddel, "The *Dhāraṇī*", p. 156, and the book by Douglas, *Tibetan Tantric Charms and Amulets*.
79 The *dhāraṇī* is not published in this volume, but is mentioned by Chiodo in the article, "The Mongolian and Tibetan Manuscripts", p. 36.

Mongolian folk religion such as Eternal Heaven *(möngke tngri)*, Mother Earth *(etügen eke)*, the constellation of the Seven Old Men *(doloγan ebügen)* etc.[80]

The fact that the fire-*dalalγa* is an old ritual in the history of the Mongols is also demonstrated by the occurrence of terms such as *ara*, "simple people", *boγol*, *kitad kegüked*, "household slaves", *nököd*, "companions, military vassals of a chief of a clan".[81] These terms point to an early nomadic society where the sacrifice to fire was performed by the chief of a clan with the participation of those who belonged to the clan.[82]

It is also interesting to note that the fire-*dalalγa* XBM 82 shows the formula *balbo-yin keleber... enedkeg-ün keleber... mongγol-un keleber...*, which is *töbed-ün keleber* instead of *balboyin keleber* in XBM 83. These formulas are found in the Mongol Buddhist works which were translated from Sankrit and Tibetan, but, as we may assume, they were included in the fire-*dalalγa* in order to ascribe an origin to this Mongol ritual.[83]

Moreover, the final formulas in the fire-*dalalγa* show that this ritual was integrated into the sphere of the Vajrayāna. XBM 82 has these words: *včir-du küy-e tegüsbe*, "The thunderbolt *küy-e* has ended", while XBM 84 reads: *mongγolčilabasu včir-tu kölgen dayu dayusba*, "In Mongolian. The Vajrayāna (sūtra) has ended".

---

80 It is worth mentioning that the text known as *Γal-un takiqu ǰang üile bayasqulang-un γarqui-yin oron kemekü orosiba* has a colophon which reads: *egüni sumadi šiila neretü ber nom-un yoson kiged uridus-un qayučin ǰirum qoyaγula-luγ-a ülü qaršilaqu-yin yoson bolγaǰu nayiraγulbai* (13r), "Sumadi Šiila compiled this book, making it a custom which does not disagree with the practice of the religion and the ancient practice of the elders" (copy of the manuscript belonging to the author. The original manuscript forms part of Mr. Süxbat's private collection). The text quoted above is also found in *Mongγolčud-un γal takily-a-yin sudur*, (Bulaγ, pp. 10–28), however, the colophon in the text at my disposal is more complete than in the one which Bulaγ edited.

81 On these terms, see Vladimirtsov, *Régime*, pp. 114, 154, 213–14.

82 On the *dalalγa* for the sacrifice to the hearth performed in the tent of the qan on behalf of the whole *ulus*, see Pallas *Sammlungen*, I, pp. 327–9; on the same subject see Bergmann, *Nomadische Streifereien*, III, pp. 179–81; on the participation of the slaves in the sacrifice to the hearth, see Dumas, *Aspekte und Wandlungen*, pp. 306–7.

83 These formulas are also found in other fire-*dalalγa*. See Rintchen, *Matériaux*, p. 22.

Dhāraṇī against Misfortune

XBM 86 to XBM 90

The fragments of five copies of a *dhāraṇī* which counteracts misfortune *(γai qarsi)* for each year in a person's life testify to the popularity of a text like this in northern Mongolia in the first part of the 17th century. The title of the *dhāraṇī* is incomplete in both XBM 86 and XBM 87; XBM 86 (1 v) reads: *enedkeg-ün keleber: arban qoyar ǰil-ün qarsi qariqu boltuγai: töbed-ün keleber : ǰiran nigen nasun-u dayalta albin čidkür amur[l]in qari[q]u bo[l]tuγai*, "In Sanskrit. May the obstacles of the twelve-year cycle turn back. In Tibetan. May the retinue of demons of 61 years be pacified and turn back". As it is evident, the title of the *dhāraṇī* is only given in Mongolian, but at least an effort was made to link this text with Indian and Tibetan religious cultures.

XBM 87 reads: *mongγol-un keleber [ar]ban qoyar [ǰil-ün] ǰiran nigen temür qadaγasutu doγsi[n] ada todqar-i qariγuluγči tarni*, "In Mongolian. The *dhāraṇī* possessing 61 iron daggers, which counteracts the fierce demons of the twelve-year cycle". The title was restored on the basis of an Oyirad version of the *dhāraṇī* to which I had access. It bears the following title: *Arban xoyor ǰiliyin ǰiran nigen tömür γadasu-tu doqšin ada todxor arilγaγči tarni.* The text belongs to the collection of Oyirad manuscripts preserved in the Institute of Language and Literature of the Mongolian Academy of Sciences in Ulaanbaatar.[1]

XBM 86

1 item of a *pothī* (1 fragment of a folio, 1 written side), measuring 7 × 6cm, and consisting of 6 lines.[2]

*1 v

1 *enedkeg-ün keleber : arban qoyar ǰil*
2 *-ün qarsi qariqu boltuγai: töbed*
3 *-ün keleber : ǰiran nigen nasun-u*
    dayalta
4 *albin čidkör amur[l]in qari[q]u*
    bo[l]tuγ =
5 *ai :: mongγol-un keleber : arban qoyar*
6 *ǰil-ün ǰiran nigen temür qadaγasutu*

---

1 No. 171. I am most grateful to Prof. Tsolmon, Institute of History of the Mongolian Academy of Sciences, Ulaanbaatar, for putting at my disposal the photocopy of the text.
2 Restored by Mr. Bentchev; old number 18/2.

XBM 87

1 item of a *pothī* (1 folio, 1 written side), measuring ca. 13.5 × 5 cm, with 21 lines; the Mongolian page number is *nigen* (1). The folio has a long split in its surface, and the text is badly damaged.[3] The text is legible by using infra-red reflectography.

1 v

1   O *namo buday-a :: namo*
2   *darmay-a :: namo sanggay-a ::*
3   *enedkeg-ün keleber*
4   *arban ǰiryuyan ǰilün qar =*
5   *[si][4] [qa]riqu boltuyai ::*
6   *töbed-ün keleber*
7   *ǰiran nigen nasun[-u] dayal-da*
8   *albin [čidkör][5] a[m]urlin qari =*
9   *[q]u [boltu]yai mongyol-un*
10 *keleber a[r]ban qoyar [ǰil-ün][6] ǰiran*
11 *nigen temür qadayasu-tu*

12 *doysin ada todqar-i*
13 *qariyu[l]uyči tarni qamuy*
14 *bur[qa]n bodisung maqasung*
15 *[-tu] m[ör]gömü : nigen*
16 *nasun-u [y]ai qarsi ba*
17 *qorin nasun-tu kürtele*
18 *činaysi qariqu boltuyai*
19 *qorin nasun-u yai*
20 *qarsi yučin nasun-tu*
21 *kürtele činaysi qariqu*

XBM 88

1 item of a *pothī* (1 folio, 2 written sides), measuring ca. 18 × 8 cm, and consisting of 14–13 lines (r/v); the Mongolian page number is *qoyar* (2).[7]

2 r

1   *saduva-dur mörgömü: eyin*
2   *kemen [m]in-u sonosuysan*
3   *nigen čay-tur qamuy burqan*
4   *bodhi saduva sit[ü]ged[8]*
5   *nomlabai :: nigen nasun-u yai*
6   **qarsi** *čayasi qariqu bolduyai :[9] qoyar*
7   *nasun-u yai qarsi čayasi*

8   *qariqu bolduyai :[10] yurban nasun*
9   *ba: dörben nasun ba : tabun*
10 *nasun ba : ǰiryuyan <> nasun*
11 *b[a] : doloyan nasun ba :*
12 *naiman nasun ba : yesün nasun*
13 *nasun-u dayalta albin čidkör*
14 *čayasi qariqu boltuyai[11] :: : ::*

3   Restored by Mr. Bentchev; old number 22/15.
4   See *qarsi* in XBM 86, 1 v:2; the Oyirad version has *xarši* (1 v).
5   XBM 86 above has *čidkör* at this point.
6   See *ǰil-ün* in XBM 86, 1 v:6; The Oyirad version reads *ǰiliyin* (2 r).
7   Restored by Mr. Bentchev; old number 28/9.
8   The Oyirad version has *sütēd* (2 r).
9   The letter *t* is written like *d* before a consonant in the word *boltuyai*.
10 The same spelling as above.
11 *boltuyai* is spelt, according to the usual orthography in this line.

2v

1   arban nasun-u γai qarsi
2   ba [:][12] qorin nasun-ṯur kürtele
3   čaγasi qariqu boldu-γai :[13]
4   qorin nasun-u γai qarsi
5   ba [:] γučin nasun-ṯur kürtele
6   čaγasi qariqu boldu-γai :
7   γučin nasun-u γai qarsi ba [:]

8   döčin nasun-tur kürtele [čaγa]si
9   qariqu boltu-γai : döčin nasun
10   -u γai qarsi ba [:] tabin
11   nasun-ṯur kürtele čaγasi
12   qariqu boldu-γai : tabin nasun
13   ba: ǰiran nasun ba [:] dalan nasun

XBM 89

1 item of a *pothī* (1 folio, 2 written sides), measuring 9 × 6.5 cm, and comprising 15–12 lines (r/v); the Mongolian page number is *γurban* (3); various words are illegible on 3v.[14]

3r

1   amurl-in[15] qariqu boltu =
2   γai : arban [na]sun-u
3   γai qarsi ba qorin
4   nasun-ṯu kürtele
5   činaγsi qariqu boltu =
6   γai : qorin nasun-u
7   γai qarsi ba γučin
8   nasun-u činaγsi qari =

9   qu boltuγai : γučin
10   qarsi döčin nasun
11   -ṯu kürtele [č]inaγs[i]
12   qariqu boltuγai :
13   döčin nasun-u γai
14   qarsi ba tabin nasun
15   [-ṯ]u kürtele činaγsi

3v

1   [qar]iqu boltuγa-i :
2   tabin nasu[n] ba ǰiran
3   nasun ba dalan nasun
4   ba nayan nasun ba yeren
5   nasun ba maγui daγal =
6   ta [alb]in[16] čid[kör] [...]

7   [...] [qariqu] boltu =
8   γai[17] ǰaγun nasun kige[d] (?)
9   [ ]n-u[18] maγui aγul
10   -ača tonilači ariγun
11   tngri-yin γaǰar-a[19]
12   tör[ö]kü boluγu[20]

---

12   The *dabqur čeg* is omitted after *ba*.
13   The word *boltuγai* is written separately, and the letter *t* is written like *d* before a consonant.
14   Restored by Mr. Bentchev; old number 18/2.
15   This word is written separately because there is a split in the folio.
16   XBM 86, 1v:4 and the Oyirad version have *albin* (2v).
17   This section of the text is damaged; the Oyirad version reads: *yerēn nasuni aliba čidker mou daγaltas xarši xarixu boltuγai* (3r).
18   The Oyirad version has *ǰayāni* (3v).
19   *γaǰar-a* is legible in the original; XBM 90, *4v:6 reads *ariγun tengri-yin or[ ]*.
20   The Oyirad version: *dēdü tenggeriyin oroni medekü boluγu* (3v).

XBM 90

1 booklet *(debter)*, of which 5 folios (8 written sides) are left. The folios have different sizes and numbers of lines. The booklet is burnt, but the text is legible in part thanks to infra-red reflectography.[21]

*1v

1 [ ]
2 *bad oom [...]*
3 *qung bad [...]*
4 *qung bad ǰoo* (?)
5 *bad oom aa* (?) *q[ ]*
6 *qung bad qana* (?)

*2r

1 *mongɣolun keleber*
2 *arban qoyar ǰilün*
3 *nigen temür [qadaɣasu]*[22]
4 *-tu doɣsin ada [...]*
5 *ariluɣayči ta[rni]*
6 *burqan bodisung*
7 *maqasung*

*2v

1 *nom-labai [ ]*
2 *si qariqu [ ]*
3 *[q]oyar nasun-u [ ]*
4 *si qariqu [ ]*
5 *ɣurban nasun-u* **qarsi**
6 *čaɣag-si*[23] *qariqu [boltu =]*
7 *ɣai ɣurban nasun*
8 *dörben nasun-u*

*3r

1 *nasun ba ǰirɣuɣ[an]*
2 *nasun ba doloɣa[n]*
3 *[nasun] ba naiman nas[un] [ba yesün]*[24]
4 **nasun** *ba [m]aɣui*
5 *[albi]n čidkör*
6 *amurlin [qariqu]*[25]
7 *boltuɣai*

*3v

1 *nasun-u ɣai*
2 *q[ars]i nasun [...]*
3 *[ča]ɣag-si [qariqu]*
4 *boltuɣai :: [ ]*
5 *nasun-u ɣai qars[i]*
6 *ɣučin nasun-t̲ur*

*4r

1 *kürtele čaɣag-si [qariqu]*
2 *boltuɣai :: [ ]*

---

21 Restored by Mrs. Nebel; old number 12/1.
22 See XBM 87, 1v:11.
23 For *čaɣasi*.
24 It is *yesün* (or *yisün*) at this point.
25 The Oyirad version: *mou daɣaltas albin čidkür cāši xarixu boltuɣai* (2v).

3 *yai qarsi ba*
4 *čayag-si qariqu bol[tuɣai ::]*
5 *ɣučin nasun-u ɣai qa[rsi]*

6 *ba döčin nasun [-ṭur]*
7 *kürtele čayag-[si]*

*4v

1 *nasun ba ǰiran*
2 *dalan nasun ba [   ]*
3 *nasun ba ɣa[i] [qarsi]*
4 *ba ǰaɣun **nasun** qa[rs]i*

5 *maɣui aɣul (?)*[26]
6 *ariɣun tngri-yin or[   ]*[27]
7 *medekü boluyu bursan[g]*

*5r

1 *[...]*[28] *sayur- <r>in qutu[ɣ]*
2 *olqu boluyu :: buya[ntu]*[29]
3 *orodi*[30] *tegüskekü b[oluyu ::]*[31] *a[rban]*

4 *qoyar nasun-u ǰil [   ]*
5 *tarni inu ene bu[i]*[32]

The *qadaɣasu* or *ɣadasu*, of which the *dhāraṇī* holds 61, is the *p'ur-bu (kīla)*, the magic dagger used in Tantric rituals to slay demons.[33] We have accounts of the use of the dagger performed by eastern Mongol shamans in rituals to expel evil forces.[34]

From the *dhāraṇī Čoɣtu qara ökin tngri čenggegči usniša neretü*, we learn how magic formulas and dagger annihilate the demons which provoked disease.[35] This *dhāraṇī* has the formula *ɣadasu-iyar qadamui*, "I stab (the demons) with the dagger". A formula like this also recurs in other *dhāraṇī*.[36]

The *dhāraṇī Arban qoyar ǰil-ün ǰiran nigen temür doysin ada todqar-i qariɣuluɣči* is composed in the form of a litany, and shows the use of the refrain *ɣai qarsi činaɣsi qariqu boltuɣai*. A similar repetition formula occurs in a *dhāraṇī* from Olon Süme (*ɣai qarsi-yi činaɣsi qariɣul*).[37]

---

26 XBM 89, 3v:9–10 has *ayul-ača*.
27 The Oyirad version has *oro ni* (3v).
28 The Oyirad version: *xamuq burxadiyin* (3v).
29 The Oyirad version has *buyantu* (3v).
30 The plural form of *oro* with the accusative suffix *-i* joined to the word.
31 The Oyirad version reads *boluyu* (3v).
32 The Oyirad version: *arban xoyor nasun ǰiliyin ǰürekini tarni bui* (4r).
33 The daggers are usually made of *khadira* wood or iron, but also of human bones. See Siklós, *The Vajrabhairava Tantras*, pp. 31–32, and note 33; on the use of the dagger in destructive magic, see Nebesky-Wojkowitz, *Oracles and Demons*, p. 486.
34 Heissig, "Schamanen und Geisterbeschwörer", p. 12.
35 Mong. 468 = Heissig and Bawden, *Catalogue*, pp. 230–1. A passage in the *dhāraṇī* reads: *čegeǰi inu daruydaqu metü bolbasu qara ragsas-un ada buyu. včar-bani-yin arvis tarni-bar oytalamui. čisun uyuɣči včar-un ɣadasu-iyar qadamui*, 12r.
36 See *Čoɣtu vačir kimusutai neretü tarni* = Mong. 468, 3r.
37 See Heissig, *Handschriften-Reste*, OS/III, 29Av, pp. 428–9. On terms and formulas which occur in *dhāraṇī*, see pp. 424–5 of the same book.

Dhāraṇī against Obstacles

XBM 91 to XBM 92

XBM 91 and XBM 92 are most probably sections of two copies of the same *dhāraṇī*. They both have the same *mantra* and the repetition formula *ulu bolqu qarsi*, "there will not be obstacles". The title of the Xarbuxyn Balgas *dhāraṇī*, which averts all types of obstacles, was not identified. However, it can be associated with *Qutuγ-tu mariči nertü tarni*, which has the formula *ulu bolqu*,[1] and *Činayči qariγuluγči maγui tarnis-un kürdün*, in which we find a passage showing similar words to those in the Xarbuxyn Balgas text, i.e. *ĵil-ün qarsi ba. sarayin qarsi ba. odod-un qarsi ba qonoγ qarsi ba. todqad-un qarsi ba ebčin[-ü] qarsi ba. ükül-ün qarsi ba.*[2]

XBM 91

1 item of a *pothī* (1 fragment of a folio, 2 written sides), measuring 10×5.5 cm, with 11 lines; the Mongolian page number is *γurban* (3).[3]

3 r

1 [ ] *gara gara süva*	7 *car-a car-a süva h-a*
2 [*h-a*] [*gu*]*ru guru süva h* =	8 *cu*[*ru*] [*cu*]*ru süva h-a*
3 *a bar-a bar-a süva h-a*	9 [ ] *gesigün-i*
4 *buru buru süva h-a*	10 [ ] *on-u ül*[*ü*]
5 *dar-a dar-a süva h-a*	11 [ ] *sarayin* [*ülü*]
6 [*d*]*uru duru süva h-a*	

3 v

1 *bolqu qarsi ba* : [ ]	5 *ulu*[5] *bolqu qarsi ba* :
2 *un*[4] *ülü bolqu qar*[*si*] [*ba*:]	6 *odod-un* [*ülü*] *bolqu*
3 *idegen-ü ülü bolq*[*u*]	7 *qarsi ba edür* [*-ün*] *ulu*[6] <>
4 *qarsi ba* : *graγ odon-u*	8 *bolqu qars*[*i*] *ba* : [*sö*]*ni*[7]

---

1   Mong. 468, 8 v.
2   Mong. 468, 30 v.
3   Restored by Mr. Bentchev; old number 26.
4   Either *un* or *ün*.
5   For *ülü*.

9   -yin ülü bol[q]u [qarsi]   11   [   ] ülü [bolqu]
10 [ba :] [e]dür söni [   ]

XBM 92

1 item of a *pothī* (1 fragment of a folio, 2 written sides), measuring ca. 12.5 × 8 cm, and consisting of 11–12 lines; the Mongolian page number is *qoyar* (2); written with a thicker and thinner *calamus*. The text which remained is well preserved.[8]

2r

1   *ǰabsar-ḏaki tengri-de mörgömü : γurban*
2   *sansa[r]-un erke-tü aburan soyorq-a :*
3   *γurban oron-u sansar-i erkeber orči =*
4   *γuluyči bügüde-de[9] mörgöged dayan takimui*
5   *minu tabun bey-e-yin čoyčas ba nigülesküi*
6   *ber adaslan[10] soyorq-a: tegün-i ǰirüken*
7   *eyin kemen nomlabai :: om gara gara süva*
8   *h-a : giri giri süva h-a : gürü [gürü]*
9   *süva h-a : bara bara süva h-a: [biri]*
10 *biri süva h-a : buru buru [süva h-a :]*
11 *dhrm dhrm süva [h-a :] [   ]*
12 *duru duru [   ]*

2v

1   *qarsi ba: graγ-un ülü* **bolqu** *qarsi ba : edür*
2   *-ün ülü bolqu qarsi ba : ǰabsar-un ülü*
3   *bolqu qarsi ba : söni-yin ülü bolqu qarsi*
4   *ba : üdesi manaγar-un ülü bolqu qarsi ba :*
5   *ǰüg-ün ülü bolqu qarsi ba : ǰobkis-un*
6   *ülü bolqu qarsi ba : minu tabun čidkör kiged*
7   *ada oytaluγči simnus ba : tede bügüde-eče*
8   *aburan s-oyorq-a[11] : tegün-i ǰirüken-i eyin kemen*
9   *nomlaba-i :: om brmicha brmicha*
10 *[…] avalogidi biriy-a bau-a radadi*
11 *[   ]dasdi ary-a čala nama manǰu ay-a*
12 *[   ] bey-e-yin čoyčas ba :*

---

6   The same spelling as in line 5.
7   See *söni* in XBM 92, 2v:3.
8   Restored by Mr. Bentchev; old number 22/15.
9   The dative locative suffix *-de* is written like *ün*.
10 For *adislan*.
11 There is a long split in the folio.

Calendars

The Seats of the Soul (XBM 93 to XBM 96)

Calendars concerned with the seats of the soul *(sünesü)*[1] must have been popular in northern Mongolia if the Xarbuxyn Balgas collection includes four fragments of four copies of these kinds of calendars.

Both XBM 93 and XBM 94 enumerate the locations of the soul of a man on each day of the month, while XBM 95 lists the locations of the soul of a man on each month of the twelve-animal cycle. XBM 96 is especially interesting since it indicates the seats of the soul according to the cycle of the twelve animals, which is repeated every 13 years.

To know the locations of the soul is also important in the practice of cauterisation. In fact, the book of Mongol medicine called *Erten-ü mongyol tögen-e-yin bičig,* "The book of cauterisation of the ancient Mongols" contains a section which is devoted to the seats of the soul of a man on each month and day.[2]

Texts dealing with the residence of the soul usually form part of manuals of astrology and divination,[3] but they are also known as independent texts.[4] I had access to *Ĵayun ekitü-yin sudur-a,*[5] "The 100-section sūtra", a section of which deals with the seats of the soul.

XBM 93

1 item of a *pothī* (1 fragment of a folio, 2 written sides), measuring ca. 8×4.5cm, and comprising 7 lines. The page number is missing.[6]

---

1 *sünesü,* "soul", is the spiritual part of a living being (Šaўja, *Mongyol ügen-ü tayilburi toli,* p. 882); *sünesü* is the "soul" which leaves the body of a person and wanders about as a result of a fright or because it was stolen by evil spirits. The absence of the "soul" is the cause of malaise such as the physical strength and phychic energy. Moreover, *sünesü* is the "soul" which departs at death. On this term, see Bawden, "Vitality and Death", pp. 17–19, and "Calling the Soul", pp. 216–17; see also Chiodo, "The Ĵarud Mongol Ritual", pp. 158–9.
2 Gombojab ed., pp. 20–3.
3 See the following texts in Heissig and Bawden, *Catalogue:* Mong. 299, p. 165; Mong. 375, p. 173; Mong. 127, p. 170. Mong. 375 includes sections referring to the residences of the soul of a man, the house and ground; Mong. 127 has a section which deals with the locations of the soul of the beast. See also Bawden, "Calling the Soul", p. 206, note 1.
4 Heissig and Sagaster, *Mongolische Handschriften,* No. 105, p. 72, No. 119, p. 77.
5 Photocopy of the manuscript belonging to the author (Mr. Süxbat's private collection).
6 Restored by Mr. Bentchev; old number 18/3.

recto

1 *nigen-tü*[7] *qabar-un üjügürtü :*[8] *[arban qoyar]*
2 *-tu üsün-ü sančig-tu :*[9] *arba[n] [yurban-du]*[10]
3 *sidün-ü sigimiqan-du :*[11] *arban [dörben-dü]*
4 *erigün-tü :*[12] *arban tabun-du bükü [   ]*[13] *[arban]*
5 *jiryuyan-du geji[ge]n-dü :*[14] *arba[n] [doloyan-du]*
6 *küisün-dü :*[15] *arban naiman-du jilb[ang-un]*[16]
7 *dotora : arban yisün-dü köldü :*[17]

verso

1 *[u]čiraqu bui : yučin-tu ükül učiraqu*
2 *[   ] eki-dü s[ü]nesün*[18] *yabuqui üjekü*
3 *[   ] sinede kö[l]ün yeke erekei-tü :*
4 *[   ] yin yadana bui :*[19] *jilbang-un dotora*
5 *tabun sinede ama[n]du :: jiryuyan*
6 *[d]oloyan sinede siyai-yin*[20] *dotora ::*
7 *[   ] un üyestü :*[21] *yisün si[ne]de bögsedü :*

XBM 94

1 item of a *pothī* (1 fragment of a folio, 1 written side), measuring 11 × 7.5 cm, with 12 lines; the Mongolian page number is *yurba* (3). The vertical line on the folio marks the end of a different text.[22]

---

7 The split in the folio damaged the letter *t* which is, however, legible. The split in the folio existed before the text was written.
8 *Jayun ekitü-yin sudur (42r)* has *qabar-tu.*
9 *Jayun ekitü-yin sudur (42r): üsün küjügün jabsar-a.*
10 The use of *-du-dü/-tu-tü* is inconsistent in the text. Note *nigen-tü, tabun-du, yučin-tu.* As a result, it could be either *yurban-du* or *yurban-tu.*
11 *Erten-ü mongyol tögene: sidün-ü sigin-tü (13v); Jayun ekitü-yin sudur (42r): ebčigün-dü.*
12 *eregüü, ereü,* "chin"; *Erten-ü mongyol tögen-e: mörön-tü (13v); Jayun ekitü-yin sudur (42r), jirüken-dü.*
13 *Erten-ü mongyol tögen-e: bükü beyen-tü (13v); Jayun ekitü-yin sudur (42r): bükü bey-e tügemel aru.*
14 *Jayun ekitü-yin sudur (42r): ebčigün-dü.*
15 *Jayun ekitü-yin sudur (42r): belkegesün-dü.*
16 See *jilbang-un dotora* below; *Erten-ü mongyol tögen-e: jilbing-un dotora (13v); Jayun ekitü-yin sudur (42r): yuya dotor-a.*
17 *Jayun ekitü-yin sudur (42r): köl-ün čimüge-dü.*
18 The same as above; the split in the folio damaged some words.
19 *Erten-ü mongyol tögen-e: qoyar sin-e šay-a-yin yadan-a* (p. 21).
20 Same as *šaya,* "anklebone".
21 *Erten-ü mongyol tögen-e:naiman sin-e-dü yar-un üy-e-tü (13v).*
22 Restored by Mrs Nebel; old number 25/4.

3r

1 ○ sang tegüskü boltuyai ::
2 nasun qutuy nemekü boltuyai ::
   — — —
3 arban doloyaqana²³ aman dotang (?)
4 arban naiman-a kü[i]sün-t̠ü
5 arban yesün-e küi[s]ün oyto
6 qorin-a sinai-t̠u²⁴ qorin nigen-e

7 kölün sigeǰei-t̠ü²⁵ qorin dörbe-e²⁶
8 y[ar]un alayan-t̠u²⁷ qorin ǰiryuyan²⁸
9 manglai²⁹ qorin < >³⁰
10 doloyan ebüd-e<n>g-t̠ü³¹ qorin
11 naima[n] [ ]kin-ü quriyudu³²
12 [ ]u yadana

XBM 95

1 item of a *pothī* (1 folio, 2 written sides), measuring 12×5cm, and comprising 13–14 lines; the Mongolian page number is *dörben* (4). The folio has splits, and is stained on recto.³³

4r

1 ○ edür küin (?) beyen-t̠ü³⁴ ba[rs +]
   ebče=
2 gün-t̠ü :³⁵ taulai + qabiryandu :³⁶ luu +
3 geǰigendü : moyai + küǰügündü :
4 morin + ǰirüken-t̠ü :³⁷ [q]onin +
   köldü :³⁸
5 bečin + ekindü : takiy-a+ ü[s]ün-t̠ü :
6 noqai + üyedü [ya]qai + morödü³⁹

7 bui : ○ nigen sinedü kölün erekei-t̠ü :
8 qoyar -tu siyan-u yadan-a : [y]urban-t̠u
9 silbindü : dörben-t̠ü beldü : tabun-t̠u
10 naiman-tu ǰiryuyan-t̠u qoyolai-t̠u :
11 doloyan [-t̠u] naiman-tu üyendü :
   yesün
12 -t̠ü bögsen-t̠ü : arbandu niruyundu :
13 arban nigendü qabirun⁴⁰ üǰügürtü :

---

23 For *doloyana*.
24 *J̌ayun ekitü-yin sudur* (42r): *ayusgin-du*.
25 *J̌ayun ekitü-yin sudur* (42r): *erekei quruyun-du*
26 Instead of *dörben-e;* the text omits *qorin qoyar, qorin yurban* and *qorin tabun*.
27 *J̌ayun ekitü-yin sudur* (42v): *siyai-du*.
28 The suffix of the dative-locative -*a* is omitted after *qorin ǰryuyan*. See also below, *qorin doloyan* etc.
29 The suffix after the word *manglai* is omitted; *J̌ayun ekitü -yin sudur* (42v): *ebüdeg-tü*.
30 The words were deleted by the copyist of the manuscript.
31 For *ebüdüg*. The split in the folio prevented the scribe from joining this word; *J̌ayun ekitü-yin sudur* (42v): *sidün-dü*.
32 For *quruyudu;* note the alternation *u ~ i*.
33 Restored by Mr. Bentchev; old number 21/7.
34 *Erten-ü mongyol tögen-e: üker edür bükü bey-e-t̠ü* (14r).
35 For *ebčigün*.
36 *Erten-ü mongyol tögen-e: qamar-tu* (14r).
37 *Erten-ü mongyol tögen-e: ebčigün-t̠ü* (14r).
38 *Erten-ü mongyol tögen-e: bel-t̠ü* (14r).
39 For *mörödü*.

4v

1 *arban qoyar-tu sančigtu :*[41] *arban*
2 *yurban-tu sidün-ü sim miqan-tu :*[42]
3 *arban dörben-tü uruldu :*[43] *arban*
4 *tabun-tu bükü beyendü : arban*
5 *jiryu[yu]yan-tu čegejindü :*[44] *arban <>*[45]
6 *doloyan-tu küisün-tü : arban naiman-tu*
7 *jilbing-un dotora : arban yesün-tü*

8 *köldü : qorin-tu dotoyadu üyedü :*
9 *qorin nigen-tü yarun sigijei-tü : qorin*
10 *qoyar-tu siyan-tu :*[46] *qorin yurban-tu*
11 *eligedü : qorin dörben-tü yarun alayan-tu :*
12 *qorin tabun-tu kölün bulčin-du :*[47] *qorin*
13 *jiryuyan-tu sigijei-tü : qorin doloyan*
14 *-tu ebüdüg-tü : qorin naiman-tu*

XBM 96

1 item of a *pothī* (1 folio, 1 written side) measuring ca. 13×5.5 cm, and consisting of 12 lines; the Mongolian page number is *nigen* (1). The text is well preserved.[48]

1v

1 O *edüge sunesün*[49] *unusuyin (?) jüil*
2 *bui : nigen nasun arban yurban*
3 *qorin tabun yučin doloyan*
4 *döčin yesün jiran nigen dalan*
5 *yurban nayan tabun yeren doloyan*
6 *ede nasun-tur sunesün*[50]

7 *amandur*[51] *sayumui :: O qoyar nasun*
8 *arban dörben qorin*
9 *jiryuyan yučin naiman tabin*
10 *jiran qoyar dalan dörben nayan*
11 *jiryuyan jaran naiman ede nasun-tur*
12 *sünesün qoyolai-tur*[52] *sayu-mui::*

As has been mentioned, XBM 96 lists the residences of the soul of a person according to the twelve-animal cycle, which recurs every 13 years. The Mongols call the 13th year, the 25th, the 37th etc. of a person's life *jil oroqu.*[53] These years are considered critical, and special rites to avert danger are performed.[54]

---

40 For *qabarun ~ qamarun.*
41 For *sančiy*, "side whiskers", Lessing, p. 671.
42 XBM 93r:3 has *sigimiqan.*
43 For *uruyuldu*, reflecting the spoken language.
44 XBM 93r:5 has *gejigen.*
45 The word *jiryuyan* was deleted by the copyist of the text.
46 *Jayun ekitü-yin sudur* (42r): *ölmei-dü.*
47 For *bulčing.*
48 Restored by Mr Bentchev; old number 9/1.
49 For *sünesün.*
50 The same spelling as above.
51 *Jayun ekitü-yin sudur* (41v) also has *aman-dur.*
52 *qoyolai-dur* is also found in *Jayun ekitü-yin sudur* (41v).
53 For this see Sampilnorbu, *Mongyol-un jang ayali-yin toyimu*, p. 434.
54 On rites performed by a lama see Pozdneyev, *Religion and Ritual*, pp. 562–4.

The Xarbuxyn Balgas fragments show a number of variants in each, nor do they precisely coincide with the corresponding sections in *Erten-ü mongyol tögen-e-yin bičig* and *Jayun ekitü-yin sudur*. This points to diverse traditions and variety of texts on the residence of the soul. A manual of divination, without a title page, which I had the opportunity to see in Ulaanbaatar, includes a chapter called *Edür-ün toy-a-nuyud-un üreyin sayin mayu ilyal inu sayitur nomlaysan eng terigün bölög bolai* (7v),[55] which shows that the seats of the soul of a man and animal are determined by astrologers by means of dice. This text has the term *sülde*, (*kümün-ü sülde, mal-un sülde,* 2v) instead of *sünesü*.

It is worth adding that the use of folk calendars dealing with the residence of the soul has a long history among Asian cultures. A Chinese manuscript from Dunhuang dating from the 10th century provides the earliest evidence of these types of calendars. Moreover, an Uighur text, which precisely coincides with the Chinese text from Dunhuang, was found in Turfan (Ms. No. 20).[56] The Uighur Turfan collection also includes two other fragmentary texts which refer to the residence of the soul (Ms. No. 19, Ms. No. 21). Ms. No. 19 bears the following title: Öz *qonuq kaz-igi ol,* "The sequence of the residences of the soul"; Ms. No. 21 is a calendar used for the practice of cauterisation.[57]

Wedding Calendars (XBM 97 to XBM 99)

Wedding calendars are used by astrologers to select which date is auspicious for giving a girl in marriage, in accordance with the year of birth of the girl. The Xarbuxyn Balgas collection provides early evidence of wedding calendars. We have a nearly complete text (XBM 97), and a small fragment (XBM 98), which, judging from the few words which are left, must be the same text as XBM 97; XBM 99 is a different text.

Beginning with XBM 97, this calendar calculates the suitable or unsuitable months for giving a girl in marriage. Moreover, prognostications are made according to the directions in which a bride turns her face when she is taken to the bridegroom's household. The *Manual of Mongolian Astrology and Divination* which Mostaert published includes a section on these topics.[58]

XBM 97

9 items of a *pothī* (17 written sides); 8 items are folios which measure ca. 8×5.5 cm, and have 9–10 lines; the Mongolian page numbers are *qoyar, yurban, tabun, jiryuyan, naiman, yesün, arban, arban nigen* (2, 3, 5, 6, 8, 9, 10, 11). Moreover, 1 fragment of a folio

---

55 Mr. Süxbat's private collection.
56 See Eberhard's remarks in Rachmati, "Türkische Turfan-Texte VII", p. 382.
57 See Rachmati, "Türkische Turfan-Texte VII", pp. 319–20, and the commentary on the texts by Eberhard on pp. 282–3. The Tibetans believe that the soul resides in various objects. See Tucci, *Le religioni,* p. 237.
58 pp. 45–9; see also *Eldeb kereg-tü qas qayurčay* = Heissig and Bawden, *Catalogue,* Mong. 234, p. 168

measuring 6 × 5.5 cm, and comprising 7 lines. This fragment was numbered *4r–*4v, according to the sequence of the text. The text is fairly well preserved and legible.[59]

2r

1	*ögbesü qadum*	6	*-de mayu dörben sara*
2	*ečige eke kürgen*	7	*arban sara ögbe =*
3	*mayu tabun sara*	8	*sü ǰayučin kümün-e*
4	*arban nigen sara*	9	*mayu üker qonin*
5	*ögbesü mön beye*		

2v

1	*ǰil-ḏü ökin-i tabun*	6	*-yuyan daruqu mayu*
2	*sara arban nigen sara*	7	*ǰiryuyan sara kögeler*
3	*ögbesü ǰokiqu*	8	*sara ögbesü*
4	*qubi sara doloyan*	9	*mön ökin -i*[60] *beyede*
5	*sara ögbesü ere*		

3r

1	*mayu dörben sara*	6	*ögbes[ü] ökin-i*
2	*arban sara ögbe =*	7	*ečige ekede mayu*
3	*sü ǰayučin kümün-e*	8	*quǰir sara naiman*
4	*mayu yurban sara*	9	*sara ögbesü*
5	*yesün sara*		

3v

1	*ökin-ü ečige eke ereyin*	6	*sara yesün sara*
2	*degüner-e*[61] *mayu :*[62] *bars*	7	*ögbesü qadum ečige*
3	*bečin ǰil-ḏü ökin-i*	8	*ekede ereyin degüner-e*
4	*quǰir sara naiman sara*	9	*auyan köbegün-e*
5	*ögbesü ǰokiqu yurban*		

*4r

1	*[ ] sara*	3	*ečige ekede >*[63]
2	*[ög]besü <qadum*	4	*ökin-ü beyetü*

---

59 Old numbers 8/2, 27; No. 8/2 (fols. 2–3, 5,–6, 8) was restored by Russians experts; No. 27 (fols. *4, 9, 10, 11) was restored by Mr. Bentchev.
60 Instead of *ökin-ü*
61 *degü* (MLM *degüü*) with the plural suffix *-ner* joined to the word.
62 Punctuation signs are selsom used in this text.
63 The words marked with dots by the copyist are misplaced.

5   *mayu dörben sara*   7   *ečige ekede mayu*
6   *arban sara ögbesü*

*4v

1   *mön [   ]*   5   *mayu taulai takiy-a*
2   *ečige ekede mayu*   6   *ǰil-dü ökin-i qubi*
3   *ǰiryuyan sara kögeler*   7   *sara doloyan sara*
4   *sara ögbesü erede*

5r

1   *ögbesü ǰokiqu*   6   *sara ögbesü qadum*
2   *quǰir sara naiman*   7   *ečige ekede mayu ǰir =*
3   *sara ögbesü mön*   8   *quluyuna*[64] *sara kögeler*
4   *ökin-ü beyede mayu*   9   *sara ögbesü erede*
5   *tabun sara arban nigen*

5v

1   *mayu :: luu noqai*   6   *sara ǰayučin kümün-e*
2   *ǰil-dü ökin-i dörben*   7   *ökin-ü beyede mayu*
3   *sar-a arban sar-a*   8   *ečige ekede mayu quǰir*
4   *ögbesü ǰokiqu*   9   *sara naiman sara*
5   *qubi sara doloyan*

6r

1   *ögbesü ere[de]*   5   *yaqai ǰil-dü ökin-i*
2   *mayu qubi sara*   6   *yurban sara yesün*
3   *yesün sara ögbesü*   7   *sara ögbesü*
4   *ökin-tü mayu moyai*   8   *ǰokiqu quǰir sara*

6v

1   *naiman sara ögbe =*   5   *sara ögbesü qadum*
2   *sü auyan köbegün-e*   6   *ečige ekede mayu*
3   *ǰayučin kümün*[65] *mayu*   7   *ǰiryuyan sara kögeler*
4   *qubi sara doloyan*   8   *sara ögbesü mön*

8r

1   *moyai mori qonin*   3   *inu emüne qandun*
2   *ǰil-dü ökin-i ni[yur]*   4   *bayubasu sayin*

---

64 An error for *ǰiryuyan*.
65 The *ü* in second position is written with a superfluous *yod*.

5 bečin takiy-a noqai
6 [ǰil]-dü ökin-i niɣur

7 inu dorona qandun
8 bayuba[su] sayin bui

8v

1 q[   ] sara nere
2 qudalabasu aliba
3 adaɣusun qoor
4 ada bolqu quǰir sara
5 nere qudalabasu

6 üčüken köbegün-e
7 ɣai ǰobalang yeke
8 bolqu siltayantu
9 qatun [qo]or ada yeke

9r

1 bolqu ɣurban sara
2 nere quda[l]abasu
3 üyer usun yeke
4 bolqu dörben sara

5 nere qudalabasu
6 yeke bulɣ-a qadqul =
7 duyan bolqu tabun
8 sara nere qudalabasu

9v

1 niskü sibayun
2 güikü görögösün
3 dalai mören-ü
4 ǰayasun ösčü olan
5 bolqu ǰirɣuyan sara

6 nere qudalabasu
7 ebečin **kölčin** bolqu
8 buyantu sayin üile
9 üiledčü seregdekü

10r

1 kereg :: doloɣan
2 sara nere qudalabasu
3 görögesün sibayun
4 olan bolqu qura
5 usun delberekü

6 naiman sara nere
7 qudalabasu mören
8 usun sirgikü
9 boloɣad usun

10v

1 tasuraqu yesün
2 sara nere qudalabasu
3 kei boroɣan ǰud
4 turaqan bolqu
5 arban sara nere

6 qudalabasu
7 yirtenčü degere
8 dayisun bulɣ-a
9 bolqu

11r

1 arban nigen sara nere
2 qudalabasu ebül inu

3 küiten qabur inu
4 eyin öter⁶⁶ irekü

---

66 Instead of the modern literary form *ödter*.

5 *sayin bolqu :: kögeler*   8 *yeke dayisun buly =*
6 *sara nere qudalabasu*   9 *a bolqu medekü*
7 *kei boroyan küiten*   10 *sereg-dekü*

XBM 98

XBM 98 is a small fragment of a folio, which measures 3×6.5 cm, with 5 lines.[67]

1 *[ ] yesün sara*   4 *[ ] mayu dörben [sa]r[a]*
2 *[ ] kürgen mayu:*   5 *ögbes[ü]*
3 *[ ]gen sara ögbesü*

XBM 99

XBM 99 is a fragmentary calendar which calculates which month is suitable or unsuitable for giving a girl in marriage. It also includes sections dealing with both the years when a girl should not be given in marriage and the "rules of dismounting from a horse" *[mori]n-ača bayuqu yoson ene bui*, (2r:6). This calendar is especially interesting since it includes a divinatory diagram which was used to select the auspicious day for a marriage (see the photographic reproduction of XBM 99, *4). The earliest yet known Mongolian wedding diagram is that from Turfan.[68] Wedding diagrams are also found in *Qas erdeni-yin qayurčay kemegdekü toy-a bičig*[69] and the *Manual of Mongolian Astrology and Divination.*[70]

XBM 99 has 4 items of a *pothī* (6 written sides), without page numbers.

The first item is a fragment of a folio which measures ca. 10 × 8 cm, with 8–7 lines (r/v); the second item is a fragment of a folio which measures ca. 11 × 8 cm, with 7 lines; the third item is a fragment of a folio which measures ca. 10 × 5 cm, with 5 lines; the forth item is a fragment of a folio which measures ca. 14 × 8 cm, with 6 lines. The folios are half-burnt, but text is legible by using infra-red reflectography.[71]

*1r

1 *[jil]tü ökin-i [ ]*   5 *[ ] mayu : qubi doloyan*
2 *bui :: yurban yesün sa[ra]*   6 *[sara] [ö]kin [-tü][72] mayu : dörben*
3 *[ ] mayu : jir[y]uyan kögeler sara*   *arban*
4 *[ečig]e [ek]e-de may[u]: tabun arban*

---

67 Restored by Mr. Bentchev; old number 25/2.
68 Cerensodnom and Taube, *Turfansammlung*, p. 157; see also the remarks by Franke in *Mittel-mongolische Kalenderfragmente*, pp. 36–40.
69 66r. See Heissig and Sagaster, *Mongolische Handschriften*, No. 101, Libr. Mong. 101, p. 70.
70 Mostaert, 51v.
71 Restored by Mrs. Nebel; old number 18/1.
72 *ökin-tü* appears in *1v:1.

7 *[sara] [kür]gen-tü mayu : taulai takiy-a*   8 *[ ] ökin-tü qubi doloyan sar[a]*

*1v

1 *bui : qujir naiman sara ökin-tü*
2 *[ ] yurban yesün sara kür-gen-de*[73]
   mayu:
3 *[ ]ban sara qadum ečige eke-de*

4 *[ ] kögeler sara jayuči-tu*
5 *[ ] [yu]rban arba[n] [s]ara ečige eke*
6 *[ ] ○ luu noqai jil-tü ökin-i*
7 *arban sara sayin bui*

*2r

1 *[büü] [ö]g :*[74] *bečin jil-tü [ökin]*
2 *[büü] ög : takiy-a jil-tü üker*
3 *[ ] jile büü ög : noqai jil*
4 *[ ] [ü]ker jile büü ög :: yaqai*

5 *[ ] bars jile büü ög ::*
6 *[ ] [mori]n -ača bayuqu yosun ene*
   bui[75]
7 *[...] üker yaqai jil-tü ökini*

*2v

1 *emüneside qandun bayubasu*
2 *[ ] :: bars taulai luu jil-tü*
3 *[ökini] [ ]da*[76] *qandun bayubasu*
4 *[ ] morin qonin jil-tü ökini*

5 *[ ]g qandun bayubasu sayin bui ::*
6 *[ ] [taki]y-a noqai jil-tü ökini*
7 *[ ] [qa]ndun bayubasu*

*3

1 *[ ] t[u] talbi ::*
2 *[ ]g-tü yal-tu talbi::*
3 *[ ]g-tür mo[n]ggö (?) talbi-ju*

4 *[ ] ali qamuy üiles*
5 *-iyer bütükü masi sayin*

*4

1 *○ yeke sara büg[esü]*
2 *kürgen-eče nere*
3 *job toyola :*[77]

4 *[bay]a sara bügesü ökin-eče nere*
5 *[buruy]u toyolotuyai*[78] *nutuy bayu[ri]*
6 *[y]olom-ta eden-tü (?) [ ]*[79]

---

73 The word *kürgen* is written separately in the text.
74 See *buu ög* below.
75 Mostaert, *Manual* has *beri bayulyaqu*, "faire descendre une brue", p. 39; on *beri bayulyaqu*, and the rituals performed when the bride dismounts and enters the bridegroom's house, see Lobsangčoyidan, *Mongyol-un jang ayali*, pp. 67–73.
76 ...*da* or ...*de*.
77 For *jöb toyala*.
78 For *toyalatuyai*.
79 *Qas erdeni-yin qayurčay kemegdekü toy-a bičig* (66r) has: *yeke sar-a bügesü kürgen-eče jöb toyola. bay-a sara bügesü ökin-eče buruyu toyolamui. qadam ečige qadam eke bui bolbaču bolqu. ügei bolbaču bolqu;* Mostaert, *Manual* (51v) reads: *yeke sara bügesü kürgen-eče jöb toyala. bay-a sara bügesü bayuri-ača buruyu toyola. bayuri nutuy qayaly-a sayin bui.* The passage in the *Manual* has both *toyala* and *toyola*.

Both XBM 97 and XBM 99 use the ancient names for months such as *qubi sara, kögeler sara and qujir sara;*[80] *qubi sara* and *kögeler* sara occur in the Turfan wedding calendar.[81]

The directions in which a bride turns her face when she dismounts from a horse are regarded as auspicious or inauspicious signs in wedding ceremonies. The calendar XBM 97 has: *moyai mori qonin jil-dü ökin-i niyur inu emüne qandun bayubasu sayin,* "If a daughter born in the snake year, horse year or sheep year dismounts from a horse and turns her face towards the south, it is good" (8r:1–4).

The lexical content of XBM 97 is interesting. This text is marked by the use of compound words such as *qoor ada,* "harm and misfortune, (harm)",[82] *yai jobalang,* "calamities", *üyer usun,* "flood", *bulya qadqulduyan,* "battles",[83] *dalai mören,* "ocean",[84] *kei boroyan,* "wind and rain, (storm)",[85] *qura usun,* "rain"[86], *dayisun buly-a,* "revolts",[87] etc.

XBM 99 contains a wedding diagram. The words which remained are *bayuri,* "base on which a tent is erected", *kürgen,* "bridegroom", *qadum,* "in-laws", and *ger,* "tent". The term *bayuri* is not found in the Turfan wedding diagram, but it appears in the Ordos wedding diagram *(ökin-i boytalaqu kürdün),* which is included in the *Manual of Mongolian Astrology and Divination.*[88] The wedding diagram *(gergei abqu kürdün)* in *Qas erdeni-yin qayurčay kemegdekü toy-a bičig* has both *bayuri* and *ger* (66r).

From the text on folio *4 we learn that *nutuy,* "nomad grounds", and *[y]olom-ta,* "hearth" formed part of the diagram. This section of the text explains how to use the diagram, e.g.: *yeke sara büge[sü] kürgen-eče nere job toyola,* "if the month is long (= 30 days), count the name clockwise, starting from bridegroom" (*4:1–3).

80　They correspond to the 1st month, 12th month and 2nd month respectively. See Mostaert, *Dictionnaire ordos,* pp. 375a, 427b, 364a; *Mongyol üges-ün ijayur-un toli,* p. 2950. See also Namjildorji, *Ordos jang üile-yin tobči,* pp. 436–7.

81　Cerensodnom and Taube, *Turfansammlung,* No. 55, pp. 156; *qubi sara* also occurs in the *Čayan teüke*. See Sagaster, *Weiße Geschichte,* p. 133.

82　On *qoor ada,* which occurs in the *Hsiao-ching,* see de Rachewiltz, "The Preclassical Mongolian Version", p. 31, for the discussion of the expression *qoor ada,* "harm and misfortune" = "harm", see note 53, p. 60.

83　The two terms appear in the *Secret History.* See Haenisch, *Wörterbuch,* pp. 21, 63. On *bulya,* see Pelliot, *Les mongols et la papauté,* pp. 126–127. On the term *bulya* see XBM 47, 3r dealt with above.

84　On *dalai müren,* "ocean", see Cerensodnom and Taube, *Turfansammlung,* No. 2, p. 55, and note 2v6.

85　*kei boroyan* is a variant of the expression *kei qura,* which often occurs in the pre-classical texts. See the *Bodhicaryāvatāra* from Turfan = Cerensodnom and Taube, *Turfansammlung,* No. 21, p. 94, and note 21r6; see also Sarközi, "*Vajracchedikā*", p. 75.

86　The expression *usun qur-a* appears in an Oyrad *irügel.* See Sečenmöngke and Gerelčečeg eds., *Oyirad mongyol-un irügel maytayal,* p. 70.

87　*dayisun bulya* appears in XBM 47, 3r (see above in this volume); *dayisun buly-a* in also found in the *dhāraṇī Qutuytu tegünčilen iregsen-ü oroi-ača yaruysan čayan sikür-dei,* 22r = Mong. 468, (Heissig and Bawden, *Catalogue*); on *bulya dayisun,* see Sarközi, "*Vajracchedikā*", p. 75.

88　Mostaert, 51v.

Dream Handbook

XBM 100 to XBM 103

A complete text and the fragments of three copies of a dream handbook provide evidence of the distribution of a text like this in northern Mongolia. The titles of the text are found in both XBM 101 and XBM 103. They are *Niyuča ǰarliγ mayui ǰegüdeni qariγulqu bičig ene bui*, "This is the book with secret words which counteract bad dreams"; *Qamuγ mayui ǰegüdeni qariγ[u]luγči sudu[r]*, "The sūtra which counteracts all bad dreams".

I had access to the text which bears the title *Jegüdün-ü qariγulqu nom ene bui*, "This is the book which counteracts dreams", and *Niyuča ǰarliγ mayui ǰegüden-i qariγulqu bičig ene bui* at the beginning of the text. It is basically similar to that from Xarbuxyn Balgas.[1]

XBM 100

1 complete *pothī*, composed of 5 folios (8 written sides), measuring 13.5 × 6 cm, and consisting of 15 lines; the Mongolian page numbers are *[nigen], qoyar, γurban, dörben, tabun*, (1, 2, 3, 4, 5). The text is severly damaged and the ink has faded; numerous words are illegible on 4v and especially on 5r.[2]

1v

1	*lam-[a]-[t]ur mörgömü bi :*	7	*boltuγai :: irüger-ün qan*
2	*burqan-tur mörgömü bi :*	8	*čagirbad-un qayan-u mayui*
3	*nom-tur mörgömü bi :*	9	*ǰegüdülegsen qara ragsa*
4	*bursang quvaraγ-ud-tur*	10	*čidkör-tür qariqu boltuγai*
5	*mörgömü bi : qamuγ mayui*	11	*öglige-yin eǰen qayan qatun-u*
6	*ǰegüdün ǰedker qariqu*	12	*mayui ǰegüdülegsen beger-e (?)*[3]

---

1 Heissig and Sagaster, *Mongolische Handschriften*, No. 111, Ms. Asch 129, pp. 74–5; see also 3 Oyirad versions of this text, Nos. 112, 113, 114, p. 75; see also the following texts in Sazykin, *Katalog*: *Jegüdü-yi qariγulγan orosibai* (No. 1970, p. 346), *Jegüden-ü sayin ba mayui-yi sinǰileků sudur orosibai* (No. 347, p. 1974), and the Oyirad version (No. 346, p. 1972). The text with the title *Jegüden-i tayilburi neretü sudur* includes a section with the title *Niyuča tarni-yi ǰarliγ mayui ǰegüden-i ariluaqu bičig bui*. This section coincides almost exactly with the text from Xarbuxyn Balgas. It is preserved in Ulaanbaatar Central State Library (No. 294.2 J 995).
2 Restored by Mrs Nebel; old number 21/6.
3 According to the *Mongγol üges-ün iǰayur-un toli* (p. 695), *begere* derives from *bebei*. This term means "fainthearted".

13 *dayisun-tur qariqu boltuyai ::*   15 *[tö]bed⁵-ün čidköd-tür qariqu*
14 *[ban]di⁴ kümün-ü mayui*   16 *[boltuyai] :*
        jegüdülegsen:

2r

1 *[sn]aggsba⁶ kümün-ü mayui*   9 *boro boljomor siba[yun]-tu qariqu*
2 *jegüdülegsen ada todqar-tur*   10 *boltuyai : qakilig¹⁰ sibayun-u mayui*
3 *[qari]qu boltuyai : qajir*   11 *jegüdelegsen uyuli*
4 *sibayun-u mayui jegüdülegsen*   12 *sibayun-tu qariqu boltuyai :*
5 *[   ]⁷ sibayun-tu [qariqu] boltuyai :* 13 *kököge sibayun-u mayui jegüdülegsen*
6 *[...]⁸ sibayun-u mayui jegüdülegsen* 14 *delekei kötege¹¹sibayun-tu qariqu*
7 *ša[ra]⁹ sibayun-tu qariqu boltuyai :* 15 *boltuyai : toyoriyu¹² sibayun-u*
8 *toti siyayun-u mayui jegüdülegsen*

2v

1 *mayui jegüdelegsen: ölöng*   9 *qariqu boltuyai :¹⁵ köke luu oytaryui*
2 *qudqur¹³ sibayun-tu qariqu*   10 *-tur¹⁶ unan jegüdülebesü bombo*
3 *boltuyai : čayan arsalan-u mayui*   *kümün*
4 *jegüdülegsen : sabar arsalan-tur*   11 *ükükü belge bui : tegüni mayui*
5 *qariqu boltuyai : garudi*   12 *dayisun-tur qariqu boltuyai :*
6 *sibayun-u čindamani¹⁴ unan*   13 *angir¹⁷ sibayun dalai-tur unaju*
       jegüdülegsen :   14 *ükün jegüdelebesü bandi kümün*
7 *törö-yin sayin kümün ükükü belge*   15 *[ü]kükü belge bui : tegüni mayui*
8 *bui : tegün-i mayui dayisun-tur*

---

4 Ms. Asch 129, 1v:16.
5 Ms. Asch 129, 2r:1.
6 A part of this word is illegible. Ms. Asch 129, 2r:3 has *šayšabad*. However, this word must be
   snaggsba, which is *sṅags-pa,* "sorcerer", in Tibetan. See Nebesky-Wojkowitz, *Oracles and
   Demons,* p. 470.
7 Ms. Asch 129, 2r:7: *eliy-e.*
8 Ms. Asch 129, 2r:9: *küiküqan* (?). It must be an error for *kökögen,* "cuckoo".
9 Ms. Asch 129, 2r:10: *sira.*
10 Ms. Asch 129, 2r:14: *qakili; qakiliy,* "snipe" (Lessing, p. 915).
11 *kötege,* "turtledove, pigeon" (Lessing, p. 493).
12 Ms. Asch 129, 2r:3: *toyoru.*
13 See *öleng* in § 255 of the *Secret History,* and *ölöng qudqur* in the *Altan tobči,* 79r; see also *ölön
    xutguur* in Cèvèl, p. 435; Lessing (p. 633) gives *öleng qodqur,* "lapwing, peewit, green plover,
    Vanellus cristatus".*
14 Ms. Asch 129, 2v:8: *čindamani-ača.*
15 Ms. Asch 129, 2v:10–12: *tegün-ü mayui iru-a dayisun-tur qariqu +.*
16 Ms. Asch 129, 2v:12–13: *oytaryui-ača.*
17 *angir, anggir.*

3r

1 *[dayisun]-ṯur qariqu boltuγai :*
2 *[ü]kügsen kümün-i dayudan*
   ǰegüdelebe =
3 *sü [...]*[18] *qaγan-u tengsegül irekü*
4 *belge bui : tegüni maγui dayisun*
5 *-ṯur qariqu boltuγai : bars ükül*
6 *[ǰegüdülebesü] qoyar*[19] *er-e kümün*
   ükükü
7 *[belge] bui : tegüni maγui dayisun*

8 *-ṯur qariqu boltuγai : köbegün-ü*
9 *geǰige oγtalun ǰegüdülegsen ečige*
10 *[ükükü] [bel]ge bui : tegüni maγui*
    dayisun
11 *[-ṯur] [qariqu] boltuγai : altan*
12 *[ ]*[20] *ǰegüdülegsen ökin*
13 *[ ] [bel]ge*[21] *bui : tegüni maγui*
14 *dayisun-ṯur qariqu boltuγai :*
15 *duγulγan-u oroγa*[22] *quγuran*

3v

1 *ǰegüdülebesü qan kümün ükükü belge*
2 *bui : tegüni maγui dayisun-ṯur*
3 *qariqu boltuγai : sumun-i onin*
4 *quγuran ǰegüdülebesü er-e dumda*
5 *kümün ükükü belge bui : tegüni maγui*
6 *dayisun-ṯur qariqu boltuγai :*
7 *nidün soqoran ǰegüdülebesü niγun*
8 *köbegün ükükü belge bui : tegüni*

9 *maγui dayisun-ṯur qariqu boltuγai :*
10 *sidün unan ǰegüdülebesü aq-a degü*
11 *nigen uruγ*[23] *ükükü belge bui : tegüni*
12 *maγui dayisun-ṯur qariqu boltuγai :*
13 *γar quγuran [ǰegü]dülebesü sayid*
14 *tüsimed ükükü belge bui : tegüni*
15 *maγui dayisun-ṯur qariqu boltuγai :*

4r

1 *ildü quγuran ǰegüdelebesü*
2 *ǰirüken*[24] *aldaraqu belge bui : tegüni*
3 *maγui dayisun-ṯur qariqu boltuγai :*
4 *ǰidanu*[25] *esi quγuran ǰegüdülebesü*
5 *γool tasuraqu belge bui : tegüni*
6 *maγui dayisun-ṯur qariqu boltuγai :*
7 *odon unan ǰegüdülebesü bayan*
   kümün
8 *ükükü belge bui : tegüni maγui*
   dayisun

9 *-ṯur qariqu boltuγai : čino-a qonin*
10 *alan ǰegüdülebesü qa[ ] [ ]rkü*[26]
    [bel]ge
11 *bui : tegüni maγui dayisun-ṯur*
12 *qariqu boltuγai : ebesün čečeg*
13 *-tür [mö]ndör*[27] *bayun ǰegüdülebesü*
14 *[...] kegüken*[28] *ükükü belge bui :*
    tegüni
15 *maγui dayisun-ṯur qariqu boltuγai :*

---

18 Ms. Asch 129, 3r:3 and XBM 102v:5 have *erlig*.
19 Ms. Asch 129, 3r:7 omits *qoyar*.
20 Ms. Asch 129, 3r:12: *altan süike quγuran*.
21 Ms. Asch 129, 3r:13: *ökin kümün ükükü belge buyu*.
22 Ms. Asch 129, 3r:15: *oroγo-a*. For *oroγoi, orγoi*.
23 Ms. Asch 129, 3v:6: *uruγ eligen*.
24 *ǰi* of *ǰirüken* is written like *ki*. Ms. Asch 129, 3v:11: *ǰirüken*.
25 The same as above: *ǰi* of *ǰidan* is written like *ki*. Ms. Asch 129, 3v:13 reads *ǰida-nu*.
26 Ms. Asch 129, 4r:3–4 has *qariyal kürkü*.
27 Ms. Asch 129, 4r:6 reads *möndör*.
28 Ms. Asch 129, 4r: 6–7 has *em-e köbegün*.

4v

1 *gerte yeke tüimer aldan ǰegüdülebe =*	9 *tngri-yin³² noqai čidkör-ün belge*
2 *sü yeke γamsiγ bolqu bui :*	10 *bui : [te]güni maγui dayisun-ṯur*
3 *tegüni maγui dayi[su]n-ṯur qariqu*	11 *[qariqu] boltuγai : dörben ǰaγun*
4 *boltuγai : to[γos] [sibaγun] otaγan*	12 *ebečin³³ činaysi qariqu boltuγai :*
5 *-ača²⁹ qayačan ǰegüdülebesü*	13 *nayan³⁴ mingγan čidköd³⁵ činaysi*
6 *ger [ba]raγan³⁰ qayačaqu belge bui :*	*qariqu*
7 *tegüni maγui dayisun-ṯur [qariqu]*	14 *boltuγai : sarayin γai³⁶ činaysi*
8 *boltuγai : [ ]basu³¹*	15 *qariqu boltuγai : edür söni-yin³⁷*

5r

1 *γai činaysi qariqu boltuγai :*	9 *[ ] činaysi [qariqu boltuγai]*
2 *ǰil-ün [γai činaysi] qariqu*	10 *[ ] buyan [ ]*
3 *boltuγ[ai :] [ ]*	11 *[ ] boltuγai : [...]*
4 *[ ]*	12 *[...] tabun*
5 *[ ] qariqu [boltuγai:]*	13 *[ ]ǰu [...]*
6 *[ ] [...]*	14 *[ ] [...] kelen*
7 *[ ] qariγulqu*	15 *[ ]³⁸*
8 *[ ]*	

XBM 101

1 item of a *pothī* (1 folio, 1 written side), measuring 16 × 6 cm, with 16 lines, without page number, but it is the beginning of the text. The text is fairly well preserved.[39]

*1v

1 O *[na]mo budday-a :: : ::*	6 *-ṯur mörgömü bi : nom-ṯur mörgö =*
2 O *namo darmay-a :: : ::*	7 *mü bi : burqan-ṯur mörgömü bi :*
3 O *namo sanggay-a :: : ::*	8 *bursang quvaraγud-tur mörgömü*
4 *niγuča ǰarliγ maγui ǰegüdeni*	9 *bi : qamuγ maγui ǰegüden-i jed[ker]*
5 *qariγulqu bičig ene bui :: lam-a*	10 *-i arilγaqu boltuγai ::⁴⁰ irüge[r]*

---

29 *-ača* is legible in the original; Ms. Asch 129, 4r:13: *toγos sibaγun öndegen-eče*.
30 *ger baraγan* are barely legible in the original; Ms. Asch 129, 4r:14: *baraγan-ača*.
31 Ms. Asch 129, 4r:17: *genedte noqai ulir-basu*; XBM 103, 4r:10–4b:1 has *g[ ] noqai ulin qučabasu*.
32 *tngri-yin* is barely legible in the original.
33 *ebečin* is legible in the original; Ms. Asch 129, 4v: 2–3: *dörben ǰaγun nayan naiman ebedčin*.
34 *nayan* is still legible in the original.
35 Ms. Asch 129, 4v:4: *mingγan nayan čidkör*.
36 Ms. Asch 129, 4v:5: *on sarayin γai qarsi*.
37 *söni* is legible in the original.
38 The last section of the text is severely damaged. See the complete passage in XBM 103.
39 Restored by Mr. Bentchev; old number 31/6.
40 XBM 100 has *qariqu boltuγai*.

11 -ün eǰen čigir-badun qaɣan-u maɣui
12 ǰegüden qara ɣaɣsa čidkör-dü
13 qariqu boltuɣai :: öggligeyin⁴¹

14 eǰen noyan qatun⁴² qoyar-un maɣu
15 [ǰegü]delegsen bagiy-a (?)⁴³ dayisun-du
16 [qari]qu boltuɣai :: bandi kümün

XBM 102

1 item (1 fragment of a folio, 2 writen sides), measuring 6 × 4.5 cm, and comprising 5 lines.⁴⁴

recto

1 [...] du [...]
2 [ ] ǰegüdel-egsen uɣul-i
3 [...] kököge sibaɣun-u

4 [ ]den kötegö⁴⁵ sibaɣun-du
5 [ ] [toɣ]oriɣu sibaɣun-u maɣu
    ǰegü[delebsü]⁴⁶

verso

1 anggir [si]ba-ɣun⁴⁷dal[ai] [ ]
2 ükün ǰegüdelebesü⁴⁸ bandi [ ]
3 ükükü belge bui tegüni maɣ[ui] [ ]

4 -du +. ükügsen kümün daɣu[dan]
    [ǰegüdele =]
5 besü erlig qaɣa[n]-u⁴⁹ tengs[egül]⁵⁰

XBM 103

2 items of a *pothī* (2 folios, 3 written sides), measuring 10 × 5 cm, with 10–11 lines; the Mongolian page numbers are *dörben, tabun* (4–5). Folio 4 has a hole in its surface, and a section of folio 5 is missing, but the text is fairly well preserved.⁵¹

4 r

1 bayun ǰegüdelebesü em-e köbegün-i
2 ükükü belge bui : tegüni maɣu
3 dayisundu :: + gerte yeke tüimer

4 aldan ǰegüdelebesü yeke qamsiɣ
5 bolqu belge bui : tegüni maɣu
6 dayisundu :: + toɣos sibaɣun

---

41 The regular form is *öglige*.
42 *noyan qatun* is also found in Ms. Asch 129, 1 v14; XBM 100, 1 v:11 has *qaɣan qatun*.
43 *bagiy-a* (?); XBM 100, 1 v:12 reads *beger-e*.
44 Restored by Mr Bentchev; old number 24/6.
45 For *kötege*. See XBM 100, 2 r:14.
46 See the complete passage in XBM 100, 2 r:11–15.
47 The word *sibaɣun* is written separately. It is also barely legible in the original.
48 *ǰegüdelebesü* is still legible in the original.
49 *erlig qaɣa[ ]* is legible in the original.
50 See the complete passage in XBM 100, 2 v:13–3 r:3; the word *erlig* is illegible in XBM 100, 3 r:3.
51 Restored by Mr Bentchev; old number 26/26.

7   *otayan-ača qayačan ǰegüdelebe =*
8   *sü ger barayan-ača qayačaqu*

9   *belge bui : tegü[ni] mayu*
10   *dayisundu :: + g[   ]⁵² noqai*

4v

1   *ulin qučabasu tengri-yin*
2   *noqai čidkör-ün belge bui :*
3   *tegüni mayui dayisundu :: +*
4   *dörben ǰayun ebedčin činaysi*
5   *:: + mingyan ada todqar*
6   *činaysi :: + on sarayin yai*

7   *qarsi činaysi :: + ǰil*
8   *čayun yai qarsi činaysi :: +*
9   *qoyar ǰi[l]-un yai qarsi*
10   *činays[i] :: + yai ǰobalang*
11   *kiged ni[gü]l kilinče tede*

5r

1   *bügüdeger činaysi qariqu*
2   *boltuyai :: ügei bolqu*
3   *boltuyai :: ö<n>gligeyin eǰen*
4   *noyan qatun kiged : qamuy*
5   *amitan-tur buyan kesig*

6   *nemekü boltuyai :: qamuy*
7   *mayui ǰegüdeni qariyu =*
8   *luyči su-du[r]*
9   *[t]egü[sbe]*

The dream handbook was both used to counteract bad dreams and as a manual of divination. Dream divination is an old practice among the Mongols,[53] which has been observed to this day.[54] The Mongol epics also provide a great deal of evidence of the close link between dream and presage *(ǰöng sobing)*.[55] Moreover, the Mongols attribute great power to dreams since they believe that in a dream the soul of a person leaves the body, wonders about and meets with the spirits of the ancestors.[56]

---

52   *genedte* is found in Ms. Asch 129.

53   See the premonitory dream of Dei Sečen about the great destiny of Temüjin in § 62 of the *Secret History*. To dream that the sun and the moon set together meant for Toyon Temür, the last emperor of the Yuan dynaty, that he would lose his throne. See the *Erdeni-yin tobči* (Urga text, 46v); on the association of dream and divination see the study by Róna-Tas, "Dream, Magic, Power and Divination", pp. 227–36.

54   In the past, the Qorčin Mongols used dreams as divination *(tölge)*, and consulted a diviner *(üǰegči)* to interpret them. If an enemy caused a bad dream, the Qorčin Mongols used to invite a shaman to conjure and perform special magic rites. To counteract bad dreams, the contemporary Qorčin Mongols invite a lama to read a special book and perform an incense offering of the hearth-fire. Nima, *J̌egüdün-ü tuqai tobči temdeglel*. I am most grateful to Mr. Nima, Beijing, for putting at my disposal his unpublished material. On dream divination among the Tibetans see Ekvall, *Religious Observances in Tibet*, pp. 272–3.

55   See Geser's dream, consisting of nine auspicious signs in *Arban ǰüg-ün eǰen geser qayan-u tuyuǰi*, II, p. 466; on studies of dreams in the Mongolian epics, see the two following articles: Erkimbayar, "*Mongyol bayatur-un tuuli-daki ǰegüdü-yi sinǰilekü ni*", pp. 114–18; Sininbayar, "*Mongyol tuuli-daki ǰöng sobing*", pp. 107–12, especially p. 108; see also Heissig, "From Verse Epic to Prosimetrum", pp. 358–9.

56   Erdemtü, "*Mongyol uran ǰokiyal-du tusqaydaysan ǰegüdü ǰöng*", p. 65.

The dream handbook enumerates various species of birds in connection with bad dreams. The idea that birds possess prophetic ability is old and widely diffused.[57] The ancient Mongols also attributed to birds a divinatory power,[58] and Mongol folklore gives evidence of the continuity of this belief.[59]

The text also mentions bad dreams which are signs, omens *(belge)* of death and calamities. For example, it is a bad omen to dream that a dog howls.[60] The handbook has these words: *g[enedte]*[61] *noqai ulin qučabasu tngri-yin noqai čidkör-ün belge bui* (XBM 103, 4r:10–4v:2), "If someone dreams that all of a sudden a dog howls, it is the sign of the dog of tngri and demons".

It is interesting to note that in the *dhāraṇī Čayan sikürtei (Sitātapatrā)* people pray to the deity to avert this bad omen: "Avert the bad omen of the howling of the dog during the night" *(söni düli noqai ulin qučaqu mayu iru-a qariyul)*; "Avert the bad omen of the howling of the wolf, the lord of death" *(ükül-ün ejen čino-a ulin qučaqu mayu iru-a qariyul)*.[62]

The magic formula "May it turn back to the evil enemies" *(tegüni mayu dayisun-tur qariqu boltuyai)* associates the dream book with the *dhāraṇī* which counteract evil. The repetition formula *činadus-tur qariqu boltuyai* "May it turn back to the adeversaries", recurs in *Öljei qutuytu tarni.*[63]

57 On bird divination among the Tibetans, see Laufer "Bird Divination", pp. 1–110; see also Ekvall, *Religious Observances in Tibet,* pp. 271–2.

58 The fate of the future Činggis qayan was announced by a white gerfalcon, which was a highly revered bird in the Middle Ages. See §§ 63, 239 of the *Secret History;* in the *Mukadimat al-Adab,* we find *tölge bariba sibawunla-,* "(He) made divinations by means of birds", (Poppe, p. 353).

59 Lobsangčoyidan, *Mongyol-un jang ayali,* p. 243; on a Mongolian text dealing with bird divination, see Heissig and Sagaster, *Mongolische Handschriften,* No. 88, pp. 63–4; see also Bawden, "Astrologie und Divination", p. 33; on the significance of birds among the Mongol herdsmen, see the *dalalya* of the birds in Chabros, *Beckoning Fortune,* pp. 25–30, 241–53.

60 The Tibetans interpret the howling of a dog as favourable or unfavourable sing, depending on the hour of the day. See Ekvall, *Religious Observances in Tibet,* p. 272.

61 The word *genedte* occurs in Ms. Asch 129.

62 Mong. 468, 7v–8r = Heissig and Bawden, *Catalogue,* pp. 230–1.

63 Mong. 468, 10r.

Astrology and Divination

XBM 104 to XBM 106

We have three fragmentary copies of a text whose title is partly preserved at the beginning of XBM 104. It reads: *Kü[m]ün-t̲ü mangyus [　] kölčin qoor kikü üje[kü] bičig.* A text which is the same as that from Xarbuxyn Balgas is available. It is *Kümün-t̲ü mangyus-un birid kölčin qoor kiküi üjekü bičig*, "The book for investigating the harm of the *preta* and the *kölčin*-demons of the *mangyus* upon a person". This text forms part of Mong. 301, which is a manual of astrology and divination, including various therapeutic rituals, without a title. It is preserved in Copenhagen Royal Library.[1]

XBM 104

3 items of a booklet *(debter)* (3 fragments of folios, 5 written sides), which originally had the left sides of the folios stitched together. The three items measure ca. 5 × 3.5–6.5 × 4.5–7 × 5 cm, with 4, 6, 5 lines respectively, without page numbers. The text which is left is legible.[2]

*1v

1　*hūm̲ manǰusiri : [　]*	3　*kölčin qoor kikü*[3]
2　*kü[m]ün-t̲u mangyus [　]*	4　*üje[kü] bičig [　]*[4]

*2r

1　*yaqai [t]aulai [　]*[5]	3　*erlig qayan-u bi[čig-tü]*[7]
2　*yurban ǰiltü [　]*[6]	4　*bičimüi :: ter-e*

1　See Heissig and Bawden, *Catalogue,* pp. 161–3.
2　Restored by Mrs Nebel; old number 25/4.
3　The text is fragmentary so that it is possible that this word is *kiküi,* which is found in Mong. 301.
4　Mong. 301, 22v:7–10: *om̲ a a hūm̲. manǰusiri-t̲ur mörgömü. basa kümün-t̲ü mangyus-un birid kölčin qoor kiküi üjekü bičig ene bui.*
5　Mong. 301, 23r:4: *yaqai qonin taulai.*
6　Mong. 301, 23r:5: *kümün-i.*
7　Mong. 301, 23r:5: *bičig-tü;* see also XBM 106, 5r:10.

*2v

1 *jiltü kümün ebed[besü]*	4 *kereg kilge dayisun [ ]*[8]
2 *mayui bui : qola bu[u]*	5 *buu qad[qu]ldu : kümü[n]*
3 *yabu : amin-u sakiyul[sun]*	6 *[ ]reldü*[9] *be[ ]*[10]

*3r

1 *[ ]ra [ ]*	4 *jiryuyan-a noqai mo[rin]*[11]
2 *buu ya[bu] :: : :: jun [-u]*	5 *bars jiltü kümün*
3 *dumdadu sara-yin ar[ban]*	

*3v

1 *m[an]gyus-un čeri[g] [ ]*[12]	4 *qonin taulai jil[tü]*
2 *čay*[13] *bui :: ečüs [sara- yin]*[14]	5 *kümün [erli]g qayan-[u]*
3 *qorin qoyar-a [ ]*	6 *[bičig-tü] [bi]čimüi*[15]

XBM 105

1 item of a *pothī* (1 fragment of a folio, 2 written sides), measuring ca. 7×6.5 cm, and comprising 7–8 lines, without page number. The text is damaged.[16]

recto

1 *l[ ]*	5 *[kümü]n-i*[19] *abqu ja[y]aya[t]u*
2 *čege[rle]jü y[a]bu*[17] *[ ]*[18]	6 *kölčin bayuju ter-e edür*
3 *qorin [q]oyar-a takiy-a*	7 *ebed-besü mayu **ter-e** edür*
4 *üker moyai ene y[ur]ban jiltü*	8 *amin-u saki[yulsun] [kereg]*[20]

---

8 Mong. 301, 23r:8: *luy-a.*

9 Mong. 301, 23r:9: *kümün-lüge buu kereldü.*

10 Mong. 301, 23r:10: *beyeben čegerlejü yabu.*

11 Mong. 301, 23r:21: *morin.*

12 Mong. 301, 23v:1: *mordaqu;* XBM 106, 5r:7 has *mordoqu,* reflecting the colloquial language.

13 The word *čay* is damaged.

14 Mong. 301, 23v:3.

15 For the restoration of *[bičig-tü] [bi]čimüi,* see the note to *2r:3–4.

16 Restored by Mrs. Nebel; old number 25/4.

17 Mong. 301, 23r:8–10: *dayisun-luy-a buu qadquldu. kümün-lüge buu kereldü beyeben čegerlejü yabu.*

18 Mong. 301, 23r:11: *ečüs sara-yin.*

19 *kümün-i* is barely legible in the original.

20 XBM 104, *2v:4 has *amin-u sakiyul[sun] kereg kilge;* Mong. 301, 23r:14–15: *amin sakiyulsun kereg kilge.*

verso

1 *kilge :* [   ]
2 *čegerlejü [yabu]*[21]
3 *basa ǰun-u terigün sara-yin*
4 *dörben sinede quluyun-a*

5 *bars luu ene γurban [ǰi]ltü*
6 *[kümün] [d]ayisun-u γaǰar-a*
7 *[qo]čorqu ča[γ]*[22] [   ]
8 *edür* [   ]*[23]

XBM 106

2 items of a *pothī* (4 written sides). The first item is a fragment of a folio which broke into three pieces. It measures ca. 7 × 7.5 cm, and has 8 lines; the Mongolian page number is *dör[ben]* (4). The reader should note that 4r is the last section of a different text of divination.[24]

The second item is a folio which measures ca. 13 × 7 cm, and has 16 lines; the Mongolian page number is *tabun* (5). Some sections of the folio are stained, and various words are illegible.[25]

4r

1 O *sinaγ-a ebde: amaraγ-un tula […]g*
   ebde:
2 *quda anda-yin*[26] *tula qurubči*[27] *ebde :*
3 *yeke naγaču-yin tula γa[   ] [e]bde :*
   [   ]*tad (?)*

4 *boγol-yin tula siremün [ebde]* [*]ǰi*
5 *baγsi-yin*[28] *odumar borogi* [   ]
6 *suvva-h-a :: baγsi-yin […]* [   ]
7 *torγ-a debüsčü ungsi : door[*]
8 *elige-gi čöm oγtaba kemeǰü* [   ]

4v

1 *metü keb keǰiy-e ülü talbiyu: tere mangγus*
2 *-un čalma-yi medebesü ed aman-tu kiǰü*[29]
3 *tegün-i čalma-yi oγtalbasu sayin bui : ese*
4 *bügesü ene yirtinčü-yi orkiǰu aγulan-tu*
5 *diya[n] saγubasu*[30] *blam-a bolbasu γurban on*

21 See line 2 on recto.
22 See *qočorqu čaγ* in XBM 106, 5r:3.
23 Mong. 301, 23r:18–19: *qočorqu čaγ bui. tere edür qola buu yabu.*
24 Restored by Mrs. Nebel; old numbers 12/3, 32/11.
25 Restored by Mr. Bentchev; old number 32/9.
26 The words *quda* and *anda* appear in the *Secret History,* See Haenisch, *Wörterbuch,* pp. 70, 7 respectively.
27 Instead of *quruγubči.*
28 The *baγsi* mentioned in the text must be a practitioner. On the occurrence of the term *baγsi* in the Mongolian texts of divination, see Bawden, "The Supernatural Element", I, p. 77, and especially p. 79; on a *baγši*, "officiant", see Mostaert, *Manual,* p. 27, and "Les Erkut", p. 7 by the same author.
29 Mong. 301, 22v:19 reads *mangγus-un ildü kiǰü.*

6   [   ]³¹ ○ *dumda-ṭu sara-yin ɣurban tabun-a*

7   [   ]³² *[ta]ulai ene ɣurban ǰil-tü kümün-ṭü* ³³

8   [   ]³⁴ *bičig-tü bičimüi : tere edür*

5 r

1   ○ *sara-yin ɣurban sine ṭe quluɣuna luu*

2   *bečin ene ɣurban ǰil-tü kümün dayisun-u*

3   *ɣaǰar-a qočorqu čaɣ bui : tere edür*

4   *olan ɣaǰar-a buu yabu :* ○ *dumda sara*

5   *-yin arban ǰirɣuɣan-a noqai morin*

6   *bars ene ɣurban ǰil-tü kümün-[t]ü*

7   *mangɣus*³⁵ *čerig mordoqu čaɣ bo[lumui] :*³⁶

8   ○ *ečüs sa[r]a [   ]*³⁷

9   *qonin taulai ene [ɣurban ǰil]-tü [kü]mün-ṭü*

10 *erlig-üd[-ün]*³⁸ *bičig-tü [bicimüi] [nam]urun*

11 *terigün sara-yin ɣu[rban] [ ]*³⁹ *kürtele*

12 *takiy-a üke[r] [m]oɣai [ene ɣurban ǰil-tü]*

13 *kümün-i mangɣus maɣu [ ]*⁴⁰

14 ○ *dumda-ṭu sara-yin [ ]*⁴¹

15 *ɣučin kürtele [ ]*⁴²

16 *ene ɣurban ǰil [-tü kümün-ṭü]*

5 v

1   *mangɣus čalma orkimu :* ○ *ečüs sara-yin*

2   *naiman sine kürtele noqai morin bars*

---

30   Mong. 301, 23 r:1–2: *diyan sayuǰu.*

31   Mong. 301, 23 r:2 has *nasulaɣu.*

32   Mong. 301, 23 r:4: *ɣaqai qonin.*

33   5 v:3 has *kümün-i;* Mong. 301, 23 v:4 also reads *kümün-i.*

34   XBM 104, *2:3 has *erlig qaɣan-u.*

35   The genitive suffix *-un* is omitted. Both XBM 104, *3 v:1 and Mong. 301 have *mangɣus-un čerig.*

36   See *čaɣ bolumui* in 5 v:10.

37   Mong. 301, 23 v:2–3: *basa ečüs sara-yin qorin qoyar-tu ɣaqai …*

38   The text omits the genitive suffix after *erlig-üd.* Mong. 301 has *erlig-ün;* XBM 104, *2 r:3 has *erlig qaɣan-u.*

39   Mong. 301, 23 v:6–7: *ɣurban sinede-eče ɣučin-a.*

40   The word *mangɣus* appears without the genitive suffix. See also below *mangɣus calm-a, mangɣus sayali;* Mong. 301, 23 v:7–9: *ene ɣurban ǰiltü kümün-tü mangɣus-un maɣu sedkiküi čaɣ bui.*

41   Mong. 301, 23 v:10 has *arban sinede-eče.*

42   Mong. 301, 23 v:11–12: *quluɣuna luu meči.*

 3   *ene yurban ǰil-tü kümün-i mangyus*
 4   *sayali ǰegümü :*[43] O *öbülün*[44] *terigün*
 5   *sara-yin ǰiryuyan sine-de yaqai*
 6   *qonin taulai ene yurban ǰil-tü kümün*
 7   *-tü yaǰar -un samba*[45] *čerig mordoqu*
 8   *čay bui :* O *dumda-tu [sa]ra-yin qorin*
 9   *yurban-tu takiy-a noqai üker moyai ene*
10   *yurban*[46] *[ǰil-t]ü kümün yasalaqu čay bolumui:*
11   O *[ečü]s sa[r]a-[y]in*[47] *qorin yesün-tü quluyuna*
12   *[l]uu be[či]n* (?) *ene yurban ǰil-tü kümün*[48] *ügürčü*
13   *[ü]lü [d]ayaqu*[49] *ǰobalang bolumu : man gha lam*

The text mentions the register *(bičig)* of Erlig qayan (Yama), in which the fate of a person born in a certain year is written down: *erlig qayan-u bi[čig-tü] bičimüi* (XBM 104, *2r:3–4). Yama (Tib. gSin-rje) is the god of fate and death and the judge of the dead.[50] The representation of Yama with a register is old in the history of Asian cultures. According to a Tibetan manuscript from Dunhuang, Yama reads his register *(dkar-chag)* when the dead are summoned to his presence.[51] The Mongol work *Naran-u gerel dagini-yin tuyuǰi*, which describes Naranu Gerel's journey to the underworld, also mentions the register *(bičig)* of Erlig qayan.[52] The belief that Yama and his messengers bring disease and death to people is observed throughout Asia.[53]

---

43 Mong. 301, 23v:14–16 has *ene yurban ǰiltü kümün-tü mangyus-un sayali ǰegümü.*
44 Instead of *ebülün.*
45 Instead of *sambaya.*
46 The text mentions four years of the animal cycle instead of three. Mong. 301, 23v:21 reads *takiy-a üker moyai.*
47 Mong. 301, 24r:2: *ečüs sara-yin.*
48 Mong. 301, 24r:3 has *kümün-tü.*
49 Mong. 301, 24r:4: *ülü dayaqu.*
50 On the Indian idea of Yama, the god of fate who brings death to people, see Von J. Scheftelowitz, "Die Zeit als Schicksalgottheit", p. 18. On Yama, the judge of the dead who weighs the soul of the dead on scales in the *Bar-do thos-grol*, see Poucha, "Das Tibetisches Totenbuch", pp. 148–9; see also the four prayers of the *ǰayuradu* (XBM 110) below in this volume.
51 Mcdonald, "Une lecture", p. 372.
52 Damdinsürüng, *J̌ayun bilig*, vol. II, p. 792; see also *Molon Toyin's Journey into Hell* (= Lőrincz, p. 46); on the register *(bičig)* of Erlig qayan see the four prayers of the *ǰayuradu* (XBM 110) dealt with below.
53 In the Hindu mythology the dogs of death are the messengers of Yama. See Dandekar, "Yama in the Veda", p. 209; the Tibetans call both Yama and a class of death-bringing demons gSin-rje. For this see the following works. Nebesky-Wojkowitz, *Oracles and Demons*, p. 82; Hoffmann, *Quellen*, p. 162; Stein, "Trente-trois fiches", pp. 315–18. The Altai Tatars and the Telengites believe that the *körmös* are the messengers of *ärlik* and cause disease, death and other calamities. See Harva, *Vorstellungen*, pp. 367–9.

In Mongolian texts of divination the term Erlig also refers to Erlig's harmful messengers.[54]

In *Kümün-tü mangγus-un birid kölčin qoor kiküi üĵekü bičig* the messenger of Erlig is the *mangγus*,[55] who is represented as a demon who throws his death-causing lasso (*čalma*) on a person born in a certain year. To cut off the lasso (*čalma oytalqu*),[56] is the remedy for warding off disease and death.

In order to counteract the evil influence of Erlig qaγan, a protective ritual must be performed. The text recommends: "Have a *kereg* of a protector of life made" (*sakiγulsun kereg kilge*, XBM 104, *2 v:3–4). The protector of life is one of the numerous *dharma-pāla*. Perhaps the *Srog-lha*, the god of life,[57] while *kereg* must refer to a ritual.

According to the *Sumatiratna*, the Tibetan term *mdos*, corresponds to the Mongolian *dongli*, *kereg*; *mdos* means "thread-cross",[58] but it is is also used as a general term for ritual devices of various kinds.[59]

The term *kereg* often occurs in texts dealing with magic therapeutic rituals. A text of the Louvain collection (Ms. No. 35)[60] has the term *kereg* in the following context: *kereg kiĵü emüne γarγ-a sayin bolqu* (2v), "Make a *kereg* and put it out towards the south. It will be good". Although the text does not specify what a *kereg* is, it is evident that we are dealing with some kind of ritual object.

The terms *dongli* and *kereg* appear side by side in another passage of Ms. No. 35. It reads: *qan dongli kiged. ekener-ün kereg emün-e ĵüg γarγ-a* (5v), "Put out a royal thread-cross and a female thread-cross towards the south". The Mongolian *qan dongli* corresponds to the Tibetan *rgyal mdos* "royal thread-cross", while *ekener-ün kereg* must

---

54 Bawden, "The Supernatural Element", I, p. 64 and note 70; this belief is also observed in the *dhāraṇī Činayči qariγuluγči mayui tarnis-un kürdün*, which contains the following line: *qamuγ erlig-ün kürdün ergigülügsen bügüdüger urban qarituγai*, "May all those who turn the wheel of all the *erligs* go back" (Mong. 468, 29r) = Heissig and Bawden, *Catalogue*, pp. 230–1; the expression *erlig qaγan-u elči*, "the messenger of Erlig qaγan", appears in *Arban γurban ataγ-a tngri-yin öčig* (= *Ordos-un tayilγ-a takilγ-a*, p. 181).

55 *mangγus* correspond to the Tibetan *srin-po* (Skr. *rākṣasa*). See Nebesky-Wojkowitz, *Oracles and Demons*, p. 14; the form *mayus* occurs in the *Bodhicaryāvatāra*. See Cerensodnom and Taube, *Turfansammlung*, 12r, pp. 80–1; the *mangγus* often appear in the *dhāraṇī*. See, for example, *Čaγan sikürtei* (6v), and *Činayči qariγuluγči mayui tarnis-un kürdün kemekü*, which mentions various forms of the *mangγus*. The two texts are included in Mong. 468.

56 On this expression see Kowalewski, p. 2100; on a text which lists various demons who bring harm and disease and has the refrain *bi ber činu čalam (čalma)-yi oγtalmui*, "I cut off your lasso", see Heissig and Sagaster, *Mongolische Handschriften*, No. 88, p. 64; see the description of a *čalma oγtalqu* ritual in the article by Sárközi, "Cutting of the Lasso", pp. 39–44; see also the description of the same ritual performed by a lama in *Mongγolĵin-u šasin surtaqun*, (Altanγarudi et al., pp. 328–9).

57 Nebesky-Wojkowitz, *Oracles and Demons*, p. 327; on the *mdos* offered to gods, see Hoffmann, *Quellen*, p. 183.

58 Vol. I, p. 1092; see also Nebesky-Wojkowitz, *Oracles and Demons*, p. 369.

59 For this see Snellgrove, *The Nine Ways of Bon*, p. 300. Bawden was the first who pointed out the wide semantic scope of the term *kereg*, which can refer both to a ritual and various objects employed in the ritual. See "The Supernatural Element", II, pp. 109–10.

60 Heissig, "The Mongol Manuscripts and Xylographs", p. 178.

correspond to *ma mdos*, "female thread-cross"[61] In fact, in the Xarbuxyn Balgas text XBM 109, which is described below, we find *ekener-ün dongli*, "female thread-cross", suggesting that the terms *dongli* and *kereg* are also used synonymously.

XBM 107

XBM 107 is a booklet which includes three fragmentary texts. The first text is a divinatory calendar which sets out the suitable or unsuitable days of the twelve- animal cycle for performing all kinds of actions.

The earliest evidence of a Mongol calendar listing the days of the twelve-animal cycle when it is suitable or unsuitable to perform actions is a fragment from Turfan,[62] which is regarded as being based on Chinese calendars.[63] Various fragments of calendars were found in Olon Süme.[64] In these fragments we can observe the use of the pre-classical forms *joqiqu, ülü joqiqu*[65] ("it is suitable, it is not suitable") as in the Turfan calendar.[66]

The book of astrology and divination, *Eldeb kereg-tü qas qayurčay*, has one section which indicates the days when certain actions are permissible or forbidden, and another which only mentions the suitable days.[67] The *Manual of Mongolian Astrology and Divination*, which Mostaert published, also contains a section on the suitable and un-suitable days.[68]

The second text provides rare evidence of the method of divination with the twelve *nidāna* (Skr. *pratītyasamutpāda*) "the twelve-link chain of dependent causation" *(arban qoyar sitün barilduqu ündüsün-ü bolγaysan üy-e).*[69] The method of divination by means of the twelve *nidāna* has a long history among the Tibetans. A Tibetan text which associates auspicious and inauspicious days with the twelve *nidāna* was found in Dunhuang. According to the later Tibetan sources, texts dealing with a method of divination like this

61 Nebesky-Wojkowitz, *Oracles and Demons*, p. 374; see also Stein, "Trente-trois fiches", pp. 318–19.
62 Cerensodnom and Taube, *Turfansammlung*, No. 51, pp. 150–2. The Turfan collection includes other fragments of calendars, see pp. 146–63.
63 Franke, *Mittelmonglische Kalenderfragmente*, pp. 28–30, 34–6; on an Uighur calendar from Turfan which only lists the unsuitable days, see Rachmati, "Türkische Turfan-Texte VII", pp. 334–84.
64 Heissig, *Handschriften-Reste*, pp. 504–16; the text which is left in OS IV/152 indicates actions which should not be performed (p. 511).
65 OS IV/157, OS IV/147 respectively, pp. 504–6.
66 See No. 51 in *Turfansammlung*, pp. 150–2.
67 See Mong. 234 = Heissig and Bawden, *Catalogue*, pp. 168–9.
68 57r–58v.
69 See Ishihama and Fukuda eds., *Mahāvyutpatti*, Nos. 2251–2262; see also Sárközi ed., *The Mongolian Mahāvyutpatti*, Nos. 2242–53; Lessing, p. 1183. On the Buddhist concept which postulates twelve links in the chain of causation, see Conze, *Buddhist Thought in India*, pp. 156–7; for the meaning of the twelve *nidāna* which fill the outher circle of the 'wheel of life', see Pozdneyev, *Religion and Ritual*, pp. 127–34; see also Waddel, *The Buddhism of Tibet*, pp. 105–122.

were translated from an Indian language at the beginning of the reign of Sroṅ-btsaṅ-sgaṅ-po.[70]

To divine by means of the twelve *nidāna* is a practice which continued in Mongolia. As a matter of fact, a later text such as *J̌ayun ekitü-yin sudur-a* includes a short section which predicts the recovery or death of a sick person using the twelve *nidāna*,[71] but apart from the same method of divination, the section in *J̌ayun ekitü-yin sudur-a* is entirely different from the Xarbuxyn Balgas text.

The third text describes a *ǰoliy* ritual (*ǰoliy yaryaqu*).[72] The fragmentary text from Xarbuxyn Balgas is similar to that included in Mong. 301, which is preserved in the Royal Library in Copenhagen.[73] A *ǰoliy* is a substitute for a sick person in the shape of an effigy representing the patient for whom the ritual is performed. The disease and the evil forces are transferred into the effigy, which is ritually expelled.[74] The Xarbuxyn Balgas text has both the terms *ǰoliy-a* and *ǰoliy*; *ǰol'ia* appears in § 272 of the *Secret History*. It is glossed in Chinese as *tisheng*, "substitute".[75] Evidence of a *ǰoliy* ritual in the 16th–17th centuries southern Mongolia is a fragment from Olon Süme in which we find the spelling *ǰolyi*.[76] The terms *ǰoliya* and *ǰoliy* are often used synonymously in Mongol texts, but in the Xarbuxyn Balgas text *ǰoliya* refers to the ritual, while *ǰoliy* to the effigy.[77] The term *ǰoliy* corresponds to the Tibetan *glud*.[78]

---

70 Mcdonald, "Une lecture", pp. 284–5; see also *Choix des documents tibetains*, p. 120; on a Chinese sūtra dealing with divinations by means of the twelve *nidāna*, see Chavannes, "Le cycle turc", pp. 86–7.

71 13v–14r. Photocopy of the ms. belonging to the author (Mr. Süxbat's private collection).

72 See Mostaert, *Dictionnaire ordos*, p. 209b.

73 Heissig and Bawden, *Catalogue*, p. 161.

74 Accounts of a *ǰoliy* ceremony performed by a shaman or a lama are well known. See the two following works by Heissig, "Schamanen und Geistbeschwöre", pp. 15–16, and "Banishing of Illness", pp. 158–67; see also Sárközi, "A Mongolian Text of Exorcism", pp. 325–39, and by the same author see "Cutting of the Lasso", pp. 39–44; on the various aspects of a *ǰoliy* ceremony, see the discussion by Bawden in "The Supernatural Elements", II, pp. 101–7. On *ǰoliy* ceremonies performed by a lama on different occasions, see Pozdneyev, *Religion and Rituals*, pp. 559–61, 591–4; see also Lessing, *Yung-ho-kung*, pp. 148–49, and "Calling the Soul", pp. 34–6.

75 Haenisch, *Wörterbuch*, p. 92.

76 Heissig, *Handschriften-Reste*, OS IV/77, pp. 520–1.

77 In Mong. 301 (17r) *ǰoliy* indicates the ritual and objects employed. Marie-Dominique Even noted that *ǰoliya* refers to the idea of substitution, while *ǰoliy* refers to the effigy in the text which she investigated (*Chants de chamanes mongols*, p. 300).

78 *Sumatiratna*, vol. I, p. 358; on *glud* rituals among the Tibetans see the following works: Waddel, *The Buddhism of Tibet*, p. 448; Hoffmann, *Quellen*, p. 181; Nebesky-Wojkowitz, *Oracles and Demons*, pp. 507–14; Stein, "Trente-trois fiche", pp. 10–11; on effigies used as substitutes for sick people among the ancient Chinese Buddhists, see Strickmann, *Mantras et mandarins*, pp. 152–3.

XBM 107

1 booklet *(debter)*, without a title, written by two hands, and composed of 8 folios (16 written sides); 6 folios are stitched together and 2 are loose. They measure ca. 13.5 × 6 to 10 × 7 cm, and have a different number of lines, without page numbers. The folios are in different states of preservation: some are fairly well preseved and legible, others are stained and difficult to read (*6r,*6v, *7v); 2 folios are badly damaged, and the text is illegible; 14 written sides are transcribed below.[79]

*1v

1   O *moγai edür-tür ebečidten-i*
2   *emčilebesü önide ǰobaqu : quduγ*[80]
3   *ülü erükü*[81] *beri uγtuqu*[82]
4   *negüdel ülü negükü: daruqui*
5   *üile-tür sayin bui :*
6   *morin edür-tür üile kereg negebesü*
7   *<> bütükü : ger ülü bariqu*
8   *indüldüküi morin nomoγdqui*[83]
9   *ibegel eriküi-tür sayin bui ::*

10   *qonin edür-tür em ülü*
11   *nayiraγulqui : negüdel*
     negü[kü]yidür[84]
12   *maγu : morin qonin oroγulqui*
13   *kiged tngri-ner takiqui*[85] *-tur*
14   *sayin bui :: bečin*[86] *[edür-tür]*
15   *ker qubčasun-yi* (?) *oyabasu*[87]
16   *tegüni el[...] urida ükükü*
17   *maγu :*

*2r

1   O *bars edür-tür tngri-ner-i ülü*
2   *takiqu*[88] *takibasu takiqu*
3   *kümün mese-tür ükükü : čerig*
4   *tataqui-tur sayin*[89] *bui ::*
5   *taulai edür-tür qota balγasun*
6   *ülü bariqu : baribasu*
7   *ger-ün eǰen-tür ölǰei*

8   *ügei : sadaγ-a buu ög :*
9   *qan oro sayuqui-tur*
10   *sayin bui :: luu edür-tür*
11   *qudal-tu*[90] *kiged quraqui čiγulqui*
12   *-tur maγui ülü üiledtekü :*
13   *buyan-tu [...] kiged eliy-e*
14   *nomoγdq-ui-tur sayin bui ::*

---

79   Restored by Mrs. Nebel and Mr. Bentchev; old number 31.
80   *quduγ* or *qudduγ,* "well"; see *quduγ subaγ erübesü* in Cerensodnom and Taube, *Turfansamm-lung,* No. 53, p. 154.
81   Mostaert, *Manual* (57r) has *taulai edür quddug (qudduγ) ülü maltaqu.*
82   See *beri baγulbasu* in Cerensodnom and Taube, *Turfansammlung,* No. 51, p. 151.
83   The regular spelling is *nomoγadqui.*
84   The word *negüküi* is erroneously written in most of the cases. See below in the text.
85   *takiqui* is legible in the original.
86   The word *bečin* is still legible in the original.
87   MLM *oyobasu.*
88   The ink is faded at this point, but the text is still legible in the original. Mostaert, *Manual* (57r) has *bars edür yaγun ber ülü takiγdaqu.*
89   The word *sayin* is still legible in the original.
90   *qudal-tu* for *qudaldu;* see *qudaltu* in Cerensodnom and Taube, *Turfansammlung,* No. 57, p. 159; see also Franke, *Mittelmongolische Kalenderfragmente,* pp. 30–1.

*2v

1 negüdel ülü [n]egükü: beri
2 abqui-tur sayin bui :
3 takiy-a edür-tür qurim ülü
4 qurimlaqu⁹¹ yala bolqu : negüdel
5 ne[gü]küi kiged em nairayulqui
6 -tur sayin bui :: noqai edür-tür
7 beri abubasu qayačaqu ölǰei

8 ügei : ülü negügdekü : üile
9 kereg ülü negekü : qubčasun
10 eskeküi terigüten uralaqui
11 üiles⁹² -tür sayin bui :: yaqai
12 edür-tür darasun uyuqui
13 kiged kegür orosiyulqui-tur
14 mayu : ecüs-tür samsiydaqu

*3r

1 negüdel ülü negükü : buy eliy-e
2 daruqui-tur sayin bui ::
3 quluyan-a edür-tür yoro-a⁹³
4 buu üǰegül :⁹⁴ üǰegülbesü
5 ber ülü onoqu :
6 ebečiten-tür mayu :

7 negüdel ülü negükü :
8 qayaly-a ǰasaqui ularqui⁹⁵
9 terigüten eriküi üiles-tür
10 sayin bui :: üker edür
11 -tür qudal-tu n[e]güdel kiged
12 ügen dayun ülü⁹⁶

*3v

1 ner-e⁹⁷ öngge-tür [ba]rayun-iyar
2 [i]degen olqu : ǰegün-iyer
3 dayisun-u qoor ayul bolqu :⁹⁸
4 ǰiryuyan orod-tur barayun-iyar
5 ayuǰu (?) ǰegün-iyer keregür
6 temečel bolqu :⁹⁹ kürteküi-tür
7 barayun-iyar ayul bolqu :

8 ǰegün-iyer ǰočid irekü :¹⁰⁰ sereküi
9 -tür barayun-iyar yoo-a
10 sayin : ǰegün-iyer yabayaysan¹⁰¹
11 ed tavar¹⁰² oldaqu :
12 quričaqui-tur barayun
13 -iyar [a]maray tayalaqun-i
14 üge¹⁰³ sonostaqu : ǰegün

---

91 Mostaert, *Manual* (58r): *takiy-a edür ülü qurimlaqu.*
92 The word *üiles* is damaged, but legible in the original.
93 The regular form is *iru-a;* the spelling *yoron* appears below in the text (*4r:16); *yoro* occurs in a fragment from Olon Süme (OS IV/146 = Heissig, *Handschriften-Reste*, p. 511); *yoro* is listed in the *Mongyol kitad toli*, p. 1377.
94 Mostaert, *Manual* (57r): *quluyan edür iru-a ülü üǰekü.*
95 *ularqui* should stand for *ulariqui.*
96 This is where the first text ends.
97 *ner-e* is legible in the original.
98 *Jayun ekitü-yin sudur* (13v) has *nere öngge-dü* 32 *qonoy-ača sayin bolqu.* The text has the Mongolian figures.
99 *Jayun ekitü-yin sudur* (13v): *ǰiryuyan erketen-dü* 34 *qonoy-tu ese ükübesü* 10 *qonoy-ača sayin bolqu.* The text has *ǰiryuyan erketen* instead of *ǰiryuyan orod (saḍāyatana).*
100 *Jayun ekitü-yin sudur* (13v): *kürteküi-dü* 3 *qonoy-tu ese ükübesü* 8 *qonoy-tu sayin bolqu.*
101 *yabayaysan:* the suffix *-ya* is an element in the compound suffix *-yaysan* in Qalqa (*jawāsan,* "went"). See Poppe, *Introduction*, p. 273. The text also shows the forms *yabayaǰu, yabayaqu.* See the next lines.
102 The letter *v* is witten like *i* in the word *tavar.*
103 The word *üge* is still legible in the original.

15 -iyer sayin kemen nomlaju[104]
16 amui :[105] abqui-tur

17 ◯ barayun-iyar busud
18 -da **tusalaydaqu** ǰegün-iyer yoo-a

*4r

1   sayin : bolqui-tur
2   sayin üge sonostaǰu :
3   ǰegün-iyer sayin :: töröküi
4   -tür barayun-iyar aliba
5   tayalaysan erdem-üd
6   sonostaqu : ǰegün-iyer
7   yabayaǰu bürelüysen[106]
8   suray yarqu ::
9   ötelküi üküküi edür-tür
10 barayun-iyar čikin ungsibasu
11 ebečin-eče amiduraqu : ǰegün-iyer

12 ungsibasu : üčüken yabayaqu
13 samsiqu üile bolqu :: : ::
14 ◯ qoyolai uruyul tataqui onoqui
15 kemebesü : mungqay [e]dür-tür uruyul
16 qoyolai tatabasu: umar-a-ača yoron
17 -u üile ireküi : üiledeküi-tür[107] erte
18 urudaki üile bolǰu : erken-ü aq-a-tur
19 ölǰei bolqu : medeküi edür-tür sayin :
20 ner-e öngge-tü üge [s]onostaǰu
21 idegen qubčan[108] oldaqu :

*4v

1   [ǰi]ryuyan orod-tur qola-ača ǰalaǰu
2   ireǰü sedkil ǰobaqu : kürteküi-tür
3   amuyulang[109] -un ary-a-tur učiraqu :
4   busud-da keregül temečel bolqu
        kememüi : sereküi
5   -tür ayuyad üǰes**küleng** ber bolqu
        kemeyü :[110]
6   quričaqui-tur gerte [i]rgen oryon[111]
        ireku
7   abqui-tur ükügsen lagsan[112] üge
8   sonostaqu :

9   bolqu-tur ǰiyulčin ireküi qubčasun
10 oldaqu : töröküi-tür bügede-tür
11 ayul bolqu : yalačin kümün ber ireküi
12 kememüi : öteleküi üküküi edür-tür
13 ters ulus-dayan ürgügdekü boluyu ::
14 **qay**[ ][ ]lküi mungqay . üiledküi .
        medeküi
15 [ner-]e orod kürteküi sereküi quriča =
16 <> qui bolqui töröküi üiledküi
17 medeküi ner-e öteleküi töröküi
18 bolqui abqui quričaqui sereküi

---

104 This line is legible in the original.
105 amui is legible in the original.
106 For bürilügsen.
107 edür-tür is sometimes omitted in the text.
108 See qubčan (MLM qubčasun) in § 136 of the Secret History, and in the Turfan text No. 14r9,
     p. 84.
109 The letter l is misplaced in the word amuyulang.
110 kemeyü: usually the form in -yu/-yü expresses an action which may be considered the oppo-
     site of the previous action. See Poppe, Grammar, § 587, p. 164.
111 On the expression irgen orqa, irgen orqo, irge orqa, irge orqo, irgen orqan in the Secret His-
     tory, see Mostaert's discussion in "Passages", pp. 360–1; irgen oryan often occurs in other
     pre-classical texts. See de Rachewiltz, "The Preclassical Mongolian Version of the Hsiao-
     ching", 1 b, p. 28; Cerensodnom and Taube, Turfansammlung, No. 6 r, p. 60; on irgen oryon in
     the Čayan teüke, see Sagaster's discussion in Weiße Geschichte, note 6, p. 122; irgen oryan ap-
     pears in the Erdeni-yin tobči, see the Urga text, 81 v.
112 Instead of layšan.

19 kü[r]teküi orod ner-e medeküi
20 üiledküi mungqay bolqui
21 abqui quričaqui :: : ::
22 ○ bars **quluyana** mungqay üiledküi
       medeküi ner-e

23 orod kürteküi sereküi quričaqui :
24 abqui bolqui töröküi öteleküi :
25 medeküi ner-e orod mungqay öteleküi
26 töröküi bolqui abqui quričaqui
27 sereküi kürteküi orod

*5r

1 edür-t[ür] qubčasun olqu
2 bolqui edür-tür qoor[113] ada
3 bolqu : töröküi edür[-tür] jočid
4 irekü : ötel[e]küi üküküi
5 -tür jegün-iyer emüskü o[l]qu :
6 barayun-iyar elči kiged amaray
7 -ud ba nököd olqu
8 [...]mlaqui (?) :: : ::
9 čikin ungsiqui onoqui

10 kemebesü : mungqay edür-tür
11 čikin ungsibasu : barayun-iyar
12 tayalaydaqun čiyulqu :
13 jegün-iyer idegen umd[a]yan olqu :
14 üiledeküi-tür b[aray]un-iyar
15 sayin : jegün-iyer ed tavar
16 olqu : medeküi-tür
17 sayin bolqu :

*5v

1 kelelčekü kele-besü ečüs-[t]ür
2 mayu : buyan ülü üiledkü :
3 qota balyasun bariqui tariyan kiged
4 -tür sayin bui :: : ::
5 ○ nidün tataqui onoqui kemebesü :
6 mungqay edür-tür nidü tatabasu ečige
7 eke-tür ayul bolqu : üiledküi-tür
8 jegün-iyer üjesküleng-tü bolqu :
9 barayun-iyar üčüken üile bütükü :
10 medeküi-tür jegün-iyer qubčasun
      olqu :
11 barayun-iyar temečel bolqu: ner-e
      öngge-dü

12 ed tavar[114] olqu : jiryuyan orod-tur
13 jegün-iyer sayin : barayun-iyar ed
      idegen
14 sammiqu : (?)[115] kürteküi-tür
      jegün-iyer temečel
15 bolqu : barayun tatabasu ed tavar
16 olqu kememüi : sereküi edür jegün
17 -iyer idegen umdayan oldaqu :
18 quričaqui-tur jegün-iyer sadud
19 nököd (?)[116] su[   ] egüdkü (?) :
      barayun
20 -iyar yaba-ysan jayur-a
21 [ol]daqu : abqui[117]

*6r

1 bügesü usun-tu
2 yabuqu amit[an]-u miq-a-ača yai
      boluy =

3 san buyu :: ese bügesü sir-a
4 toson idegegsen [-eče] [ya]i boluysan
5 buyu :: tegün-tür qabt-yai[118] čilayun

---

113 qoor is still legible in the original.
114 The letter v is written in the usual manner in the word tavar.
115 It is probably an error for samsiqu "to be spent, squandered", or šamsiqu "to appropriate"
       (Lessing, pp. 668, 751).
116 There is a split in the folio.
117 The second text ends here.

6   -iyar negüresün-iyer qaralayu[l]ǰu[119]
7   degere sibayun-i ulayan[120] örbölge
8   naiman [qa]ra[121] [či]layun yoson (?)
9   modon deger-e-i tarni-yin usun-iyar
10 bey-e-gini[122] ugiyaǰu doloyan alqui-yin

11 yarya :: üdei-yin [...][123]
12 qara [ra]qui-yin čay-tur ebedbesü
13 öröne ǰüg belbesün [   ]
14 kümün [   ][124]
15 ügei bügesü[125] soq[or] kümün[126]

*6v

1   [abuy]san-ača yai boluysan buyu
2   ügei bü[ge]sü ulayan öngge-tü
3   ed abuysan-ača yai boluysan [buyu]
4   [...][127] oydarm-a[128] talbi [   ]r
5   usun čečeg terigün kiǰi[129] yu[lir]
6   -iyar kümün [kiǰi] tarni-yin usun-iyar
       [...][130] gi
7   ugiyaǰu barayun ǰüg yary-a :[131]

8   O üdesi toyona (?)[132] raqui-yin čay
9   -tu ebedbesü kümün-ü yasun
10 bari[ysan] [i]regsen-eče yai bolugsan
11 bu[yu] : ese bügesü kümün-i
12 yasun day[a]riǰi [ire]gsen kümün
13 -eče yai bolug-san buyu : ügei
14 bügesü sira[133] öngge-tü ed

*7r

1   abuysan-ača yai boluysan
2   buyu ::[134] tegüni ǰoliy-a
3   yurban [   ] keseg sir-a

4   modon yulir-iyar kümün
5   kiǰi[135] [...] : lay-čas kiged
6   tarni-yin[136] usun-iyar bey-e-gini

---

118 For qabtayai.
119 Mong. 301, 4v:8: saralayulǰu.
120 Probably for ulayan. Mong. 301 has sibayun- i örbelge.
121 Mong. 301, 4v:10: qara.
122 bey-e-gini, "his body", reflects the colloquial language. On the accusative suffix -gi (for -yi) followed by ni (< inu), see Poppe, "Geserica", pp. 20–1.
123 Mong. 301, 4v:12: üde-yin čay.
124 Mong. 301, 4v:13–14: uruy kümün bolbasun-u idegen em-eče yai bolba.
125 bügesü is barely legible in the original.
126 Mong. 301, 4v:14–15: ese bügesü soqor kümün-eče ba.
127 Mong. 301, 4v:17 has tegün-ṯür.
128 Tib. gtor-ma.
129 Instead of kiǰü. On the suffix -ǰi, -či see Poppe, Grammar, § 372, p. 96.
130 The text is badly damaged. This word seems to have a final m. See bey-e-gini in *6r:10, *7r:6; Mong. 301, 4v:19–20 has bey-e ben.
131 Mong. 301, 4v19–20: tarni-yin usun-iyar bey-e-ben ugiyaǰu öröne ǰüg yary-a.
132 This is where the text in Mong. 301 (3r:21) begins.
133 sira is barely legible in the original.
134 Mong. 301, 3v:1–5: kümün-i yasun bariysan kümün dayariǰu iregsen-eče yai bolba. ese bügesü sira önggetü ed abuysan-ača yai bolba. ese bügesü kümün-i yasun dayariǰu iregsen kümün-dü ǰolyabuu.
135 kiǰi instead of kiǰü, showing the influence of the colloquial language. See Poppe, Grammar, § 372, p. 96.
136 -yin is still legible in the original.

7   *ugiyaǰu emün-e γarγ-a : ::*[137]
8   O *söni dülii-yin urida bayusang (?)*[138]
9   *raqui-yin čaγ-tur ebedbesü*
10 *qar-a čirai-tu*[139] *qoγoson*

*7v

1   *ünesün[-iyer] [n]aiman terigün kiǰi*[141]
2   *noqai-yin qubaqai toloγai*
3   *γulir-iyar kümün kiǰi ebed =*
4   *čin kümün-e kesiǰü (?) kiǰi*[142]
      γ[arγ]-a (?)::
5   *tarni-yin usun-iyar bey-e -gin[i]*

6   *ugiyaǰu ǰoliγ ǰam-tur γarγ-a ::*
7   *söni dülii-yin qoγina*
8   *[...]ba*[143] *raqui čaγ-tur*
9   *< > tuγur-a*
10 *< > [...]i -ača iregsen*[144]

11 *uyuta barigsan [...]*[140]
12 *bol[...] temür barigsan küm[ü]n*
13 *-eče γai boluγsan buy[u] ::*

*8r

1   *eme kümün-eče γai boluγsan*
2   *qara*[145] *öngge-tü yamayan barigsan*
3   *kümün-eče γai boluγsan bui :*[146]
4   *ese bügesü noqai daγaγsan*
5   *-ača γai bolǰi :*[147] *ünesün-iyer*

6   *γulir-iyar kümün kiǰi temür*
7   *kiǰi keriy-e ni ödön qadquǰu*[148]
8   *γarγ-a :: : ::*[149] *tegüs-be*
9   *sadu edgü*

The calendar dealing with the suitable or unsuitable days frequently indicates the days when people should or should not begin a nomadic journey: *negüdel ne[gü[küi... sayin bui* (*3:4–6); *negüdel ülü negükü* (*1:4), "It is good to set out on a nomadic journey. Do not set out on a nomadic journey". This demonstrates that a calendar like this served the needs of the Mongol nomads.[150]

---

137 Mong. 301, 3v:6–8: *tegün-e γurban modo γulir kümün kiǰü layčas kiged. tarni-yin usun-iyar beyeben ugiyaǰu emüne ǰüg γarγ-a.*
138 Mong. 301, 3v:9 has *bsang.*
139 Mong. 301, 3v:10 adds *kümün.*
140 Mong. 301, 3v:11: *ese bügesü.*
141 Mong. 301, 3v:12–13: *tegün-tür ünesün-iyer naiman terigün kiǰü.*
142 Mong. 301, 3v:13–15: *noqai-yin qubaqai toloγai-iyar γulir kiǰü. γulir-tur ebečin kümün-i keseg-i kiǰü.*
143 Mong. 301, 3v:17: *isgamba.*
144 Mong. 301, 3v:18–19: *tuγur-a boγoni qari-ača iregsen.*
145 *qara* is legible in the original.
146 Mong. 301, 3v:19–20: *qara öngge-tü ed abuγsan-ača γai bolba.*
147 The text has *γai bolǰi,* while line 3 reads *γai boluγsan bui.*
148 *qadquǰu* is still legible in the original.
149 Mong. 301, 4r:1–3: *tegün-e učarabasu γulir-iyar kümün kiǰü. temür keriy-e edön qadquǰu dorona ǰüg γarγ-a.*
150 In his article "Kalenderausdrücken" (p. 350), Kara mentions a calendar found by Rintchen in Xövsgöl, which, judging from the context, served the needs of the Mongol nomads.

We also find the expression *saday-a buu ög* (*2:8), "Do not give effigies".[151] In other texts however *yary-a* is used instead of *ög* (*saday-a yary-a*).[152]

The second text is used to make divinations according to the cycle of twelve days which are named after the twelve *nidāna* e.g.: *bolqui edür-tür qoor ada bolqu. törököi edür[-tür] jočid irekü* (*5r:2–4), "On the day of formation (*bhava*), there will be harm. On the day of birth (*jāti*), guests will come".

The text also shows that the twelve *nidāna* were employed to make divinations based on the observation of involuntary movements of parts of the body. For example: "If on the day of ignorance (*avidyā*) someone's eyes twitch, there will be danger to this person's father and mother" (*mungqay edür-tür nidün tatabasu ečige eke-tür ayul bolqu*, *5v:6–7).

To make divinations according to the movements of the body is a practice which has an old tradition in Asia.[153] A fragment of a text of astrology and divination from Olon Süme bears witness to this divinatory practice among the ancient Mongols of southern Mongolia.[154] We also have a great deal of evidence of the continuity of the divinatory practice discussed so far in Mongol areas.[155]

Finally, the third text describes a *joliy* ritual performed to counteract disease which is attributed to apparently harmless people such as a woman (*eke kümün*, *8r:1), someone who holds a black goat (*qara öngge-tü yamayan barigsan kümün*, *8r: 2–3), etc. The ritual instructions are given in these words: *ünesün-iyer yulir-iyar kümün kiji temür kiji keriy-e-ni ödön qadquju yary-a* (*8r:5–8), "Make a human figure with ashes and flour-paste, prepare a piece of iron, stick the feathers of a crow into it and expel these".

The text also uses terms pointing to a *joliy* ritual performed by a Buddhist practitioner. We have *tarni-yin usun* (*6r:9), "the *dhāraṇī* water", referring to water empowered with magic spells,[156] and *oydarm-a talbi* (*6v:4), "set up *tormas*". The *tormas* (*gtor-ma*)

---

151 According to Lessing (p. 655), *saday-a* means "paper doll used in shamanistic rites, human figure made of dough by a lama". Lessing lists the compound *joliy sadaya*, which is the same as *sadaya*; the *Dictionnaire ordos* (p. 550a) registers the compound *džolik sadaga = džolig*; on *saday-a* see Bawden, "The Supernatural Element", II, note 62, p. 100, see also pp. 100–1.

152 For example, Mong. 301 (17r) has *naiman sinede ese anabasu yai tayil saday-a yary-a*, "If the person did not recover on the 8th day of the month, counteract harm, expel an effigy".

153 An Uighur calendar from Turfan, which is based on Chinese calendars, deals with divinations based on the observations of involuntary movements of parts of the body. For this see Rachmati, "Türkische-Turfan Texte VII", No. 34, p. 331, and the remarks by Eberhard on p. 383; on this method of divinatory practice among the Tibetans, see Ekvall, *Religious Observances*, p. 272.

154 Heissig, *Handschriften-Reste*, OS IV/30, pp. 517–20.

155 See Namjildorji, *Ordos-un jang üile*, p. 435; Kürelbayatur and Urančimeg, *Qorčin-u jang ayali*, pp. 331–2; Sayrajab et al., *Mongyoljin jang tadqal*, pp. 507–8; see also the two following texts: *Bükü bey-e tat[a]qui üjekü bisig (bičig)*, "The book for investigating the involuntary movements of the whole body" = Heissig and Sagaster, *Mongolische Handschriften*, No. 88, pp. 63–4; *Eldeb kereg-tü qas qayurčay* = Heissig and Bawden, *Catalogue*, Mong. 234, p. 169; Sazykin, *Katalog: Bükü bey-e tataqu üjelge oršiba; Kümün-ü bükü bey-e tataqui-yi üjikü (üjekü) sudur bolai* (No. 1967, p. 346).

156 On the preparation of *rasāyana* in the Buddhist monasteries of Mongolia, see Pozdneyev, *Religion and Ritual*, pp. 443–7.

are closely linked with a *ǰoliy*-effigy since they form part of the ritual objects which are offered as a substitute for a person's life (soul).[157]

XBM 108

There is also a fragment of a folio of a text of divination and healing practices, which associates a day of the month with disease, which is ascribed to evil spirits or to actions performed by the patient. We can observe the occurrence of the term *üǰel*, which indicates a therapeutic ritual in this context.[158] The text shows the use of the compound suffix *-yaysan (qariyaysan)*, which also appears in XBM 107. It is also interesting to note that XBM 108 is the third text of astrology and divination from Xarbuxyn Balgas which is the same as that included in Mong. 301. The latter was brought from the Tümed, in southern Mongolia.[159] The coincidence of these texts points to a common body of Mongol traditions.

XBM 108 has 1 item of a *pothī* (1 fragment of a folio, 2 written sides), measuring ca. 14×5 cm, comprising 16–20 lines, without page number. The fragment is half-burnt, but the text is legible thanks to infra-red reflectography.[160]

recto

1	[ ] *kiǰü dorona yučin* [ ]	7	[...] *yarya* ::[162] [ ]
2	[ ] *anaqu yutayar ada en[e]* [ ]	8	*qariyaysan*[163] *kümün-i* **gerte buu**
3	[ ] *ükügsen ere kümün nut[uy]*[161]		*oro[yul]*[164]
4	[ ] *qoyar ebedkeyü te*[ ]	9	○ *qorin qoyar-a ebedbesü t*[ ]
5	[ ] *nigen ulayan dege[l]* [ ]	10	*gerün eǰen qoyar ebedkenem* [ ]
6	[ ] *bariǰu* [ ]	11	*metü boluyu* ::[165] *tegün yesün* [ ]

---

157 The *gtor-ma* are broken up by ritual weapons or by hand, thrown out, or scattered, and sometimes burned. See Ekvall, *Religious Observances*, pp. 164–5; the expression *baling ǰoliy* is found in the book by Altanyarudi et al., *Mongyolǰin-u šasin surtaqun*, p. 328.

158 Bawden discusses this term in "The Supernatural Element", I, pp. 77–8; in some *dhāraṇī*, the term *üǰel* often appears in combination with *ǰasal*. See *üǰel ǰasal* in the *Čayan sikürtei* (7v et passim), and *Činayči qariyuluyči mayui tarnis-un kürdün*, which also has *mayui üǰel* (31v), = Mong. 468.

159 See Heissig and Bawden, *Catalogue*, pp. 161–3.

160 Restored by Mrs. Nebel; old number 35/5.

161 Mong. 301, 16v:2.

162 The passage in Mong. 301, 16v:1–6 reads: *ükügsen em-e er-e. nutuy-tu ükügsen em-e kümün qoyar ebedkem. tegun-e arban qoyar ayaya darasu. nigen ulayan degel. tabun öngge-tü čayasu ildü bariǰu. dorona nom tarni ungsiǰu yary-a. qadquǰu yary-a.*

163 Note *qariyaysan*, i.e. the suffix *-ya* is an element in the compound suffix *-yaysan*.

164 Mong. 301, 16v:6–7: *qariǰu iregči kümün ayaya qoyar-i gerte buu oroyul.*

165 Mong. 301, 16v:9–11: *qorin qoyar-a +. tngri-yin yeke ongyod yaǰarun eǰen qoyar ebedkem yar köl ǰančiysan metü boluyu.*

12 *alqu yarγa :: anaqu*[166] *basa ad[a]* [   ]   15 *emüne qorin alqu yarγa ::*[168] [   ]
13 *tu eliy-e bui modon deger[e]* [   ]   16 *γutaγar ada ene bui*
14 *ulaγan čaγasun sömesön*[167] [   ]

verso

1   *üre niγun ükügsen qoγa[r]* [   ]   11 *[i]de[gen] iden [a]bumui*(?)[174] *üjel* [   ]
2   *γadana küiten dotora qalaγ[un]* [   ]   12 [   ] *γin idegen ö[röne]*
3   *toγola utasun yesün aγa[γan]* [   ]   13 [   ][175] *[qu]rdun a[naqu]*
4   *ayaγan ǰimis tabun önggetü* [   ][169]   14 [...]
5   *qonin-u utasun ebedčin küm[ün]* [   ]   15 *[aγ]ula-yin eǰen* [   ]
6   *kita[γ]an*[170] *bariǰu degegside tata[* [   ] 16 [   ]*mui idekü idegen* [   ]
7   *ǰiran alqui-a üǰügüre γal* [   ]   17 [   ] *[s]aγumui tabun sira* [   ]
8   *anaqu*[171] *ese masi berke bui buu*[172] [   ] 18 [   ] *alqu yarγa ::*[176] *basa a[da]*
9   *[e]bedbesü öröne-tü tergegürü[n]* [   ]   19 [   ] *[t]ergegür-ün eliy-e uduγ[an]*
10 *[e]bedbesü kündü [kö]nggen*[173]   20 [   ] *üküγsen em-e eliy-e* [   ]
       bolumui [   ]

XBM 109

Further evidence of the diffusion of texts of astrology and divination, dealing with disease provoked by evil influences and healing remedies is given by the 3 items of a text shown below.

---

166 Mong. 301, 16v:11–12: *tegün-e yisün ayaγ-a idegen emüne γarγ-a. arγul anaqu.*
167 The *Mongγol kitad toli* has the spelling *sömösö(n)*, p. 948.
168 Mong. 301, 16v:13–16: *basa ada ene bui. ulaγan niγur-tu eliy-e bui. modon degere saγumu. tegün-e tabun ulaγan čaγasu sömesön idegen kiǰü. dorona emüne döčin alqu γarγ-a.*
169 Mong. 301, 16v:18–17r:2: *oyir-a uruγ-un ükügsen ada qabasan ebedkem γadana küiten dotor qalaγun ebečin kümün-i nasu toγola utasu yisün ayaγ-a darasu jisün ayaγ-a ǰimis tabun öngge čaγasu ǰaγun naiman alqu γarγ-a.*
170 For *kituγan.*
171 Mong. 301, 17r:2–6: *qonin-iγar ebečin kümün-i ergigülǰü kituγan bariǰu tarni ugsiǰu öröne ǰaγun ǰiran alqu-yin üǰügüre γaldu tüle. yisün qonoγ-tu anaqu.*
172 These words are not found in Mong. 301.
173 Mong. 301, 17r:8 has *könggen.*
174 Mong. 301, 17r:10 has *yadamu,* wich makes sense.
175 Mong. 301, 17r:6–12: *qorin γurban-a +. öröne-tü tergegür-ün eǰen bui. kümün-i gerte odču ebedbe. kündü könggen bolumu bükü bey-e ebedčü qalaγun idegen iden yadamu. üjel inu tabun öngge torγ-a nigen ayaγ-a idegen öröne ǰaγun alqu γarγ-a.* As it is evident from this passage in Mong. 301, *üjel* also indicates the ritual objects.
176 Mong. 301, 17r:12–16: *qurdun anaqu basa ada ene bui. aγula-yin eǰen ongγod bui. ekin ebedkü idegen-e dura ügei degel deger-e saγumu tegün-e tabun sira čaγasu dorona qorin alqu γarγ-a.*

XBM 109 has 3 items of a *pothī* (6 written sides). The first item is a folio measuring ca. 13.5×5 cm, and consisting of 17–16 lines (r/v); the Mongolian page number is *yurban* (3). The second item is a fragment of a folio measuring 8×4cm, with 8–10 lines; the Mongolian page number is *tabun* (5). It is severely damaged on recto. The third item is a folio measuring 12.5×5.5 cm, with 14–13 lines (r/v); the Mongolian page number is

qoyitu

u m[i]q-a

ʾay[181] ide =

ba :

len

bedkü

lkü

us[182] bolqu :

ʾayun ǰegün

qonin-tur

ǰu ög =

ʾn arban

ʾigen

e edür

ʾi

old number 31/6. The sec-

Twelve Deeds, 60r, pp. 64,

deity).

sion by Sampilnorbu in his

182 *namursun yaras*, "ulcers". According to a Tibetan and Mongol belief, the spirit masters of earth and waters, if offended, inflict ulcers, abcess, sores etc. See XBM 47, 4r, in which the old term *güjügün*, "ulcer, abcess, sore", occurs.

183 The word *tusa* is written separately. On this orthographic feauture see Ligeti, "A propos de quelques texts mongols préclassiques", p. 274.

5r

1 *[...]g γaǰar-un eǰen-i (?)*   5 *[   ]*
2 *[...] bolai: ul[...]*   6 *[   ]*
3 *[   ] terigüte[n] [   ]*   7 *[   ]*
4 *[   ] ača (?) bol[   ]*   8 *[   ]*

5v

1 *ǰoliγ-luγ-a teg qo[   ]*   6 *tus-a bolqu : ○ [   ]*
2 *emüne ǰüg γary-a : nai[man]*   7 *sini arban tabu[n]*
3 *luus-un qadun [...] üil[   ]*   8 *qorin γurban [   ]*
4 *bandi toyin kümün [   ]*   9 *[   ] kiküi [   ]*
5 *nom ungsiγul tegü[   ]*   10 *[   ] dur [   ]*

7r

1 *○ γabuγsan-ača [   ]*   8 *ǰasaqu-a inu ekener-ün*
2 *teden-ü nigen-eče*   9 *dongli ba isganga*[184]
3 *[γa]i bolba: bey-e*   10 *namančilaqui subury-a*
4 *[...] [   ]gei qabanara =*   11 *ǰas-a*[185] *čimeg emüskeged*
5 *laγad (?) qalaγun ebedčin*   12 *nigen sar*[186] *üker öber*
6 *toloγai ebedkü*   13 *-ün degel γutul ačiγad*
7 *elige muskilqu*   14 *tegün-ü qoyin-a-ača*

7v

1 *öber-ün ǰil ali*   8 *-yin edür bui : bigar*[188]
2 *bolbasu tegün-i kiǰü*   9 *kiged tireng*[189] *gemgser (?)-ün*
3 *γary-a : tus-a bolumui ::*   10 *bandi-yin bombo kiged*
4 *○ naiman sini arban*   11 *baraγun emüne-eče*
5 *ǰirγuγan qorin dörben*   12 *boγoni beyetü olan*
6 *tede edür ödün*[187]   13 *γabudal-tu bandi (?)*
7 *üiledügči ökin tngri*

---

184   3v:1 reads *isgangga*.
185   The word *ǰasa* is also written separately.
186   For *šar*.
187   For *edün (ed-ün)*.
188   *bigar* should be Pe-har. On this protective deity see Nebesky-Wojkowitz, *Oracles and Demons*, pp. 94–133.
189   *tireng* for *teγireng*, reflecting the spoken language. The spelling *tireng* is also found in a shamanist invocation from Küriye Banner. See Heissig, "Schamanen und Geisterbeschwörer", pp. 24–5; the nine The'u-raṅ are deities of an evil nature, who belong to the retinue of Pe-har. For this see Nebesky-Wojkowitz, *Oracles and Demons*, pp. 282–3; on a *mdos* ritual to avert the harmful influence of the The'u-raṅ, see Eimer and Tsering, "T'e'u raṅ mdos", pp. 46–87.

The text says that the protective deities of a *bandi (ban-de)* and a *bombo (bon-po)* became angry (*bandi bombo kümün-i sakiγulsun aγurlaγsan buyu*, 3r:4–6). As a result,
misfortune and disease will occur.[190] Mongol folk texts of divination and *dhāraṇī* often
mention a *bandi,* "Buddhist monk" and a *bombo,* "follower of Bon" (in this context as
ritualists). Both are believed to provoke harm and disease, but also to be able to divert
evil with their magic rites.[191]

As in other texts dealing with this subject, this text also associates the harmful influence of humans with that of deities and demons, thus showing the high degree of
efficacy of Buddhist magic rituals.[192]

In this text the ritual instructions refer to the recitation of prayers such as *isgangga,*[193]
the "prayer of penitence" and the "100-syllable *mantra*" (*isgangga ungsi namančilaqui
ungsi ǰayun üǰüg ugsi,* 3v:1–3).[194]

The text also contains interesting terms. For example, *dongli* (3v:4),[195] and *ekener-ün
dongli* (7:8–9). The Mongol term *dongli* corresponds to the Tibetan *mdos,* "thread-
cross";[196] *mdos,* however, is also used as a general term for ritual devices of various
kinds.[197] It is thus possible that *dongli* is used as a general term for a ritual, while
ekener-ün dongli refers to a "female thread-cross" (Tib. *mo-mdos*)[198] in this text. As is

---

190   The Tibetans believe that the contact with a *ban-de* and a *bon-po* is a source of impurity, because their protective deities can send forth demons. See Tucci, *Le religioni,* p. 217.

191   See Bawden, "The Supernatural Element", I, pp. 74–75; on rituals performed to ward off the
misfortune provoked by a *ban-de* and a *bon-po,* see Nebesky-Wojkowitz, *Oracles and
Demons,* p. 391; on the black Bön, see Beyer, *The Cult of Tārā,* p. 353; see also *bandi bom-
bo-yin üǰel ǰasal* in *Činaγči qariγuluγči maγui tarnis-ün kürdün* (= Mong. 468, 31v).

192   On the significance of magic rituals performed by Tantric lamas, see Samuel, "Ge sar of
gLing", p. 54; for an account of rituals performed by a lama practitioner to avert the harm
caused by demons or evil spells uttered by people, see Altanγarudi et al. *Mongγolǰin-u šasin
surtaqun,* p. 529. As Lessing remarks, learned lamas adhere personally to more philosophical
theories, but at the same time they compromise with the needs of the populace ("Calling the
Soul", pp. 32–3).

193   The Tibetan equivalent of *isgangga* is *skaṅ-ba.* Das (*Tibetan-English Dictionary,* p. 82) lists
this word with the meaning of "a kind of expiatory sacrifice to make amends for a duty not
performed".

194   On the prayer of penitence to the 35 Buddhas *(namančilaqui),* see XBM 22 above; *ǰayun üǰüg*
translates the Tibetan *yi-ge brgya-pa',* which is recited by lamas after the prayer of penitence.
I am most grateful to Geshe Pema Tsering, Bonn, for this information; on the 100-syllable
mantra, see Savvas and Lodro Tulku, *Transformation,* p. 39.

195   On *dongli* see the discussion by Bawden in "The Supernatural Element", II, pp. 108–10, and
by the same author, "On the Practise of Sapulimancy", p. 137; see also Mostaert, *Manual of
Mongolian Astrology and Divination,* 41r; a *dongli* is also made to avert afflictions. A passage
in *Arban γurban čilaγu-tu-yin sudur* says: *yisün ǰüil γasalang-yi qariγuluγči dongli ki,* "Make
a *dongli* which counteracts the nine kinds of afflictions" (10v).

196   *Sumatiratna,* vol. I, p. 1092; see also Das, *Tibetan-English Dictionary,* pp. 676–7.

197   See Snellgrove, *The Nine Ways of Bon,* p. 300; see the terms *mdos,* "thread cross", *yas,*
"offerings" and *glud,* "substitute effigy", in Eimer and Tsering, "*Sun zlog:* Abwenden von
Störungen", p. 70.

198   On *mo mdos,* see Nebesky-Wojkowitz, *Oracles and Demons,* p. 373.

well-known a thread-cross is one of the most important magic devices used by the Tibetans in protective rituals.[199]

A notable feauture is the occurrence of *čay süm* (3v:4). It transcribes the Tibetan *cha
gsum*, "the ritual of three parts", i.e. offering to the wordly protectors of the ten directions, offering to the interfering spirits *gdon*, and offering to the interfering spirits
bges.[200]

The word *gsum* is pronounced *sum* in the Lhasa dialect, but is pronounced *gsum* in
the Amdo and Golok dialects. This should explain the Mongolian spelling *čay süm*.[201]

Moreover, we have *čangbu tibču* (3v:7), which occurs in other Mongol ritual texts.
The spelling *čangbu tebse* is found in a fragmentary text from Olon Süme dealing with a
substitute ceremony.[202]

The *Tibetan-English Dictionary* lists *chan-bu* meaning "the dough of barley-flour
squeezed or pressed within the hand and coming out between the fingers. It is given to
the ghosts", while *mtheb-kyu* is "a symbol resembling a finger which is offered with the
gtor-ma (offering made to the gods and demi-gods").[203] From other sources we learn that
mtheb-kyu represents the life of the person for whose benefit the ritual is performed, and
is offered with the *gtor-ma* as a substitute *(glud)*.[204]

---

199   See Hoffmann, *Quellen*, pp. 177–86; Nebesky-Wojkowitz, *Oracles and Demons*, pp. 369–71,
      381–3, 391; Beyer, *The Cult of Tārā*, pp. 318–354; Stein, "Trente-trois fiches", pp. 318–21.
200   The ritual is called the ritual of three parts because there are three groups of guests to whom
      offerings are made. The offerings include water, flowers, incense etc., praises and *tormas*. On
      cha gsum, see Savvas and Lodro Tulku, *Transformation*, pp. 153–9, and note 25, p. 191; see
      also *Zang han da cidian*, p. 777; the forms *čaysum*, *čagsum* appear in texts which Bawden
      quotes in "The Supernatural Element", II, note 89, p. 107.
201   de Roerich, *Le parler de l'Amdo*, p. 41.
202   Heissig, *Handschriften-Reste*, OS I/10r, pp. 410–11.
203   Das, pp. 408, 602.
204   Tucci, *Le religioni*, p. 221; on *chan-bu mtheb-kyu*, see Nebesky-Wojkowitz, who points out
      that these ritual objects are used in the *glud* ceremonies (*Oracles and Demons*, pp. 364–5). See
      also *Zang han da cidian*, p. 1217; Beyer, *The Cult of Tārā*, p. 324; Eimer and Tsering, "T'e'u
      ran mdos", note 9, pp. 69–70.

The Four Prayers of the *ǰayuradu (bar-do)*

XBM 110

The last manuscript included in this volume is one of the most important texts of the rich Xarbuxyn Balgas collection. It is a Mongolian translation from Tibetan of the four prayers of the *ǰayuradu (bar-do)*, "the intermediate state between death and rebirth", which are attributed to Padmasambhava. The end of the text reads: *orǰan-u mergen badma sambau-a baysi-da ǰokiyaysan sudur-i tegüs tuyulbai*,[1] "The sūtra composed by the wise Master Padmasambhava of Oḍḍiyāna has ended".

The four prayers form the original nucleus of the *Bar-do thos-grol*, while the prose parts are commentaries.[2] The prayers are located at the end of the *Bar-do thos-grol*,[3] but passages from them are also found incorporated in the text. The *Bar-do thos-grol* was translated into Mongolian as *Sonosuyad yekede tonilyayči neretü yeke kölgen sudur*, "The mahāyāna sūtra called The Great Liberation by Hearing".[4]

The text from Xarbuxyn Balgas provides evidence of the use of the prayers of the *ǰayuradu* in early 17th century northern Mongolia.[5] The prayers, however, were also known in southern Mongolia during the same period. One piece of evidence is two fragments of the prayers of the *ǰayuradu* from Olon Süme, which Heissig did not identify.[6] Thus the identification of the Olon Süme fragments in the light of the Xarbuxyn Balgas text, contributes to our knowledge of the history of the translation of the prayers of the *ǰayuradu*.[7]

I was lucky enough to have access to a complete manuscript of the prayers of the *ǰayuradu*, without a title, which can be dated from the first part of the 17th century. The

---

1 The Tibetan term *rdzogs-pa* corresponds to the Mongolian *tuyuluysan, tegüsügsen, büridügsen, urbayuluysan, dayusuysan* (*Sumatiratna*, II, p. 661).

2 Evans-Wentz, *The Tibetan Book of the Dead*, lxi.

3 *Bar-do'i thos-grol bžugs-so* (Kalsang, ed.) has the four prayers on pp. 110–117; on the English translation of these prayers see Evans-Wentz, *The Tibetan Book of the Dead*, pp. 197–208.

4 Heissig, *Blockdrucke*, pp. 33–4; Krueger edited *Sonosuyad yekede tonilyayči neretü sudur* in 1965. This version, however, does not include the four prayers. *Sonosuyad yekede tonilyayči* is found in various collections of Mongolian manuscripts and xylographs. See Heissig and Sagaster, *Mongolische Handschriften*, No. 362, p. 205; Heissig and Bawden, *Catalogue*, No. 466, p. 220; Ligeti, "La collection", Nos. 3592–3; Farquhar, "A Description", No. 14, p. 170.

5 Pozdneyev tells us that most lamas knew the *ǰayuradu-yin sudur* by heart, and read it to the dying person in Mongolian. See *Religion and Ritual*, p. 594

6 Heissig, *Handschriften-Reste*, pp. 446–9.

7 The Olon Süme fragments OS IV /109–110 are transcribed in notes 37, 38, 40, 42.

manuscript forms part of the Mongolian block-prints and manuscripts which were collected in southern Mongolia and Peking by Gösta Montell of the Sven Hedin expedition of 1927–1935. It is preserved in the National Museum of Ethnography in Stockholm.[8] The Stockholm text turned out to be especially valuable in the investigation of that from Xarbuxyn Balgas.

XBM 110 has 1 nearly complete booklet *(debter)* written in a beautiful hand. It is composed of 9 folios (17 written sides), measuring ca. 17 × 9 cm, and comprising different numbers of lines, without page numbers. Folio 1v is severely damaged and a section of the text is missing; 9v is also damaged and difficult to read. The other folios are stained and have numerous splits and holes, but the text is legible.[9]

1v

```
 1   namo [budday-a ::][10]
 2   namo darmay-a [::]
 3   namo sangga[y]a ::
 4   arban jüg-tür sayuysan [    ]
 5   bodisung-na[r]-un nigüles[küi-luγ-a] [tegügügsen][11]
 6   medeküi-luγ-a tegüsügsen : [    ]
 7   tegüsügsen : bilig-luγ-a tegüsügsen [:] [    ]
 8   [luγ]a tegüsügsen qamuγ amitan [    ]
 9   [bo]luysan nigül[e]sküi-yin erke[ber] [    ]
10   [    ] [ki]ged bolun soyorq-a : iledte [    ]
11   [    ] qubilyan-u ta[    ] amsan [    ]
12   [qamu]γ nigülesküi bi[    ]
13   [nigüles]küi ber jokiyaysan [üi]les ibegel-ün [    ]
14   sedki[s]i ügei [    ] yi sayitur [    ]
15   [    ] nigülesügtün bi ber ene [    ]
16   [čina]du kijayar-a yabu[ju] [    ][12]
```

---

 8 Aalto, "Catalogue", p. 69; for a brief description of the manusript H. 5827, which Prof. Aalto did not identify, see p. 98. As I mentioned in the introduction to this volume, Mr. H. Wahlquist most kindly put at my disposal a photocopy of this text.

 9 Restored by Mr. Bentchev; old number 9; the top corners of the folios had broken, and were found scattered among other fragments. Previously they were numbered 12 (folios 1, 2, 3, 4); 32/12 (folios 5, 6, 7); 26 (folios 8–9).

10 H. 5827 writes *buday-a;* this form also occurs in other Xarbuxyn Balgas texts.

11 H. 5827, 1v:6 *nigülesküi-luγ-a tegüsügsen.* See *medeküi-luγ-a tegüsügsen* in the next line.

12 H. 5827 has *yabuju bür-ün;* the Xarbuxyn Balgas text has *yabuju bürü[n]* in 2r:11. The complete passage in H. 5827 (1v:1–2r:8) reads: *namo buday-a. namo darmay-a. namo sanggay-a. arban jüg-üd-tür sayuysan qamuγ burqan bodisung-nar-un nigülesküi-luγ-a tegüsügsen. medeküi-luγ-a tegüsügsen. nidün-luγ-a tegüsügsen. bilig-luγ-a tegüsügsen. qamuγ amitan-i itegel boluysan. nigülesküi-yin erkeber ene oron-tur ögede bolun soyorq-a. ilete učaraysan ba sedkil-ün qubilyan-u takil-i amsan soyorq-a. qamuγ-i nigülesküi-ber qamuγ medeküi belge bilig-iyer kündülen nigülesküi-ber jokiyaysan üiles ibegel-ün küčün-ber sedkisi ügei auγ-a-bar sayitur qamuγ-i nigülesün. bi ber ene yirtinčü-yin činadu kijayar-a yabuju bür-ün.*

2r

1   *ene yirtenčü ber qoyin-a qo[č]orbai : yeke*
2   *ibegegči ber ügei : yeke nököčegči ber [ügei :]* [13]
3   *γasiγun ǰobalang-yi yeke aburayči ber ügei :*
4   *sitügen ber ügei [...] amin-i sönegegči :* [14]
5   *busu amitan-ṯur odču : [ye]ke qarangγui-ṯur*
6   *oroǰu : au* [15] *yeke yaǰar-tur unaǰu yeke [...]* [16]
7   *ükeger-tür oroǰu : ǰayayan-u erke-ṯür tü[l]ig =*
8   *deǰü :* [17] *teyimü eǰen ügei yeke yaǰar-tur [   ]*
9   *[   ] yabuǰu :* [18] *yeke dalai-yin dolkiyan-ṯur oqor =*
10 *[daǰ]u :* [19] *ǰayayan-u salkin-a toγtayaydaǰu :* [20] *čay ügei*
11 *[   ]un ǰüg-tür yabuǰu bürü[n] yeke dayisun-u*
12 *dotor-a oroǰu :* [21] *yeke adayin [ba]riγdaǰu :* [22] *erlig*
13 *qayan-u yarγačin-u ayul-ača ayuγad ǰayayan-u*
14 *sangsar-ača bas-a sangsar-tur tögöriǰü :* [23] *erlig*
15 *qayan-u yarγačin-u* **toli** *kiged* [24] *: qamtu ber törögsen*
16 *burqan čidkür qoyar čayan čilayun qara*

2v

1   *čilayun qoyar-iyar* [25] *belgedeǰü: erlig qayan-u yarγačin :*
2   *buyan kilinče-ḏü qoyar-i : bičig-tür tuγu =*
3   *laǰu üǰebesü :* [26] *niγuǰu buruγu kelelekü erke*
4   *küčün ügei : [n]ökör ügei : γaγčayar yabuǰu :*
5   *kereglekü čay bolbasu : edüge qam[uγ] yeke nigülesü =*
6   *[gči]: biber terigülen itegel ügei mandur ibegen*

---

13   H. 5827, 2r:8–10: *ene yirtenčü yabayrabai. yeke ibegegči ügei. nökör selte ber ügei.*
14   MLM *sönöge-*; H. 5827, 2r:13–2v:1: *ene nasun-u amin sönöbei.*
15   Instead of *ayu*; the γ between the two vowels is omitted; see *ayu* in XBM 66, 8v; H. 5827, 2v:3 reads *yeke ayuda.*
16   H. 5827, 2v:4 has *qarangγui.*
17   H. 5827, 2v:6: *küčülegdeǰü.*
18   H. 5827, 2v:6–7: *teyimü yeke kereg-tü yabuqu bolbasu.*
19   H. 5827, 2v:8–9 has *oqordaǰu.*
20   H. 5827, 2v:9–10: *dayustaǰu.*
21   H. 5827, 2v:10–13: *dürbel ügei aliba ǰüg-tür yabuǰu bür-ün. yeke ayul-un dotora oroǰu bür-ün.*
22   H. 5827, 2v:13: *ada-ṯur bariγdaǰu.*
23   *basa* is written separately; H. 5827, 3r:2–4: *ǰayayan-u orčilang-tur tögöriǰü. basa sansar-un yaǰar-tur baytaǰu.*
24   H. 5827, 3r:5 has *toli-ṯur.*
25   H. 5827, 3r:7: *čilayun-iyar.*
26   On Erlig qayan, the judge of the good and bad actions, see Poucha, "Das tibetische Toten-buch", pp. 146–8.

7   *[soy]orq-a :*[27] *abural ügei mandur aburan soyorq-a :*
8   *[ola]n*[28] *nököd ügei mandur olan nököd-tü bolyan*
9   *[s]oyorq-a: ǰayura-du yeke qara[ngyu]i-ṯur aburan*
10 *soyorq-a : ǰayayan-u yeke ulayan salkin-i*
11 *qa[riy]ulun soyorq-a :*[29] *erlig qayan-u yeke ayul*
12 *-nuyud-un ayul-ača aburan soyorq-a : ǰayu[ra]du*[30]
13 *yeke öndör qabčayai-ača getülgen soyorq-a : qam[   ]*[31]
14 *nigülesügči ülemǰi nigülesün soyorq-a : nigülesküi*
15 *ber kürgen soyorq-a : yurban mayui ǰayayan-ṯur*

3r

1   *buu ilegen soyorq-a : [   ]du*[32] *tanggariy [   ]*
2   *alyasal ügei nigülesküi [-yin] kücün-iyer [öd]ter*[33]
3   *büged iren soyorq-a :*[34] *[   ]*[35] *kiged bodisung*
4   *namai nigülesküi-yin ary-a-yin kücün ber egü[sün]*[36]
5   *soyorq-a: qamuy amitan-i mayui ǰayayan-u*
6   *er[ke]-ṯür buu ilegen soyorq-a : yurban erdenis*
7   *[   ]či (?) ǰayura-ṯu-yin yeke ayul-ača [i]begen soyorq-a :*[37]
8   *[a]buran suyurq-a: kemen bisi[r]el sedkil-iyer*
9   *qatayuda bisilyaydaqui qamuy öber busud-un*
10 *tula : yurban ḏa ügülegdeküi :: : ::*[38] *tedeger ǰayura =*
11 *ṯu amitan-i sonosuyad to[ni]lyaýči [qab]čayai-ača getülgegči :*
12 *ayulača aburayči irüger irü[gegdekü]i :*[39]
13 *yosotu burqan kiged : bodisung qamuy amitan-i*
14 *neken ülü talbiqui :*[40] *ene irüger-i orǰan badm-a*

---

27 H. 5827, 3r:12–3v:3: *nökör selte ügei. yaýčayar yabuqu kereg-tü čay bolbasu. edüge qamuy yeke nigülesügči. biber itegel ügegün-i mandur itegel bolun soyorq-a.*
28 H. 5827, 3v:4: *olan nököd-tü bolyan soyorq-a.*
29 H. 5827, 3v:5–7: *jabsar-un yeke qarangyui-ṯur aburaýči bolun soyorq-a. yeke ulayan salkin-i qariyul-un soyorq-a.*
30 H. 5827, 3v:9: *jabsarun.*
31 H. 5827, 3v:11: *qamuy-a.*
32 This word must be *uridu*; H. 5827, 4r:1 has *urida.*
33 H. 5827, 4r:2 has *ödter.*
34 H. 5827 (4r:1–3) shows some textual variants: *urida aman aldaysan-iyar nigülesküi-yin kücüber ödter soyorq-a.*
35 H. 5827, 4r:3 has *burqan.*
36 Line 3 has *iren soyorq-a*; H. 5827, 4r:5 has *yaryaýči* at this point.
37 H. 5827, 4r:7–9: *yurban erdenis kürtele yasiyun jobalang-yi ibegen aburan soyorq-a*; OS IV/ 109–110r, 1–4 reads: *ǰayayan-u erkeber buu il-gen soyorq-a. yurban erdeni-ṯür kürte[l]e yasiyun jobalang [ ] aburan soyorq-a* (Heissig, *Handschriften-Reste*, p. 448).
38 OS IV/109–110r, 5–8: *ene bisirel [se]dkil-iyer qatayu-da bisilyan qamuy öbere busud-un tula yurban ta [ügü]legdekü.*
39 H. 5827, 4v:2–4: *ayul-ača aburaqui irüger-i irügegdeküi.*

15 *sambau-a baysi-yin ǰokiyaysan buyu : dalai*
16 *[i]la[yu]ysan dagini ubadi[s]lan bičibe :: ene sansar-un*

3v

1 *orčilang qoyoson boluy-a inaru ülü tuyulqu*
2 *boltuyai :: siddi-dü garm-a ayulan-u dvib-tur*[41]
3 *sang niyuǰu talbiysan ene nom-i ǰalaǰu iregsen bui :*[42]
4 *qutuy orosiysan čoy-iyar*[43] *badarangyui-lagsan.*[44] *čambudvib*[45]
5 *-un čimeg boltuyai :: : :: oom a qung oom mani*
6 *badmi qung : qiri :*[46] *il[ayu]ysan amuyulang kiling-tü*
7 *burqan-tur mörgömü ::*[47] *ǰayura-tu-yin ǰiryuyan*
8 *ǰüil ündüsün üge : egüni yurban erdenis: yasiyun*
9 *-i manu sonos ::*[48] *biber ene ǰayura-tu-tu[r] [t]örögsen*
10 *-ü čay-tur : yambar üiledügsen [ǰ]egüdün metü nasun*
11 *-tur : amul ügei*[49] *alyasal-i tebčiǰü bür-ün :*
12 *so[no]s[q]ui sedkiküi bisilyaqui yurban-i*[50] *alyasal [ügei] :*
13 *nom-un mör-tür oroydaqui :: gegegen sedkil-ün [ ]*[51]
14 *üǰügülügči*[52] *yurban bey-e-yi iledte* **bolyan** *bisilyaydaq[u]i :*
15 *ene kümün-i bey-e-yi ile-de*[53] *oluysan čay-tu[r]*
16 *alyasangyui ene oron-tur sayuqun*[54] *-u yayun*[55] *yur[ban]*

---

40 The following lines in OS IV/109–110r contain scattered words: 8) *tedeger ǰayu[radu]* 9) *amitan-i sonosuy[ad]* 10) [ ] 11) *irüger* 12) *b[urqa]n kiged* 13) *amitan-i ül[ü]*.

41 No distinction is made between *i* and *v* in the word *dvib*. See also *čambudvib* in line 4.

42 H. 5827, 4v:7–5r:2: *ene irüger-i orǰan badma sambau-a baysi ǰokiyaysan buyu. dalai ilayuysan dagini ubadis-a bičibe. ene sansar-un orčilang qoyoson boluy-a inaru ülü tuyulqu boluyu. sisiten garm-a ayulan-u dib-tur sang niyuǰu talbiysan-u ene nom-i ǰalaǰu iregsen bui*; OS IV/109–110v (p. 449) reads: *ene irüger orǰan badma sambau-a baysi-yin ǰokiyay-san buyu. dalai ilayuysan dagina ubadisi bičibei. ene [san]sarun orčilang qoyoson boluy-a inar[u] ülü tuyulqu [boltuyai]. [ ] garma ayulan[-u] dvib [-tur] [niy]uǰu talbiysan-u.* (The rest of the text is missing, and only the word *amuyulang* is left in the last line).

43 H. 5827, 5r:3: *čoyčas-iyar*.

44 H. 5827, 5r:4: *badarangyuyilaysan*.

45 AT Čambudivip; Skr. Jambudvīpa (*Drevnetjurksij slovar'*, p. 138).

46 The word *qiri* is also written with *q* before *i* in H. 5827, 5r:6.

47 H. 5827, 5r:6–8: *amuyulang-iyar kilinglegsen ilayuysan burqan-tur mörgömü*.

48 H. 5827, 5r:8–10: *ǰiryuyan ǰayura-du-yin ündüsün üge egüni yurban erdenis sonos*.

49 Šaǰǰa (*Mongyol ügen-ü tayilburi toli*, p. 20) lists the word *amul*; H. 5827, 5r:12–13 has *uduriyulsun ügei*.

50 H. 5827, 5v:1–2: *yurban-tur*.

51 H. 5827, 5v:3: *möri*.

52 Instead of *üǰegülügči*; the text has both *üǰe-* and *üǰü-*.

53 Line 14 reads *iledte*.

54 Note the plural form of the *nomen futuri*.

55 H. 5827, 5v:5–8: *enegeken kümün-ü bey-e-yi oluysan-tür-i. alyasangyui ene oron-tur dura-bar sayuqun-u yayun*.

4r

1   *erdenis : enelküi manu sonos :*[56] *biber ǰegüdün-ü [   ]*
2   *ǰayuradu-ṯur töröküi čaγ-tur*[57] *mungqay-iyar [kü]mün*
3   *-ü yasun metü : kebteküi čaγ ügei tebčigdeküi : alγasal*
4   *ügei duradtaqui ber yo[s]otu ayui-yin činar-tur*
5   *or[o]γdaqui : ǰegüdün-i barimtalan qubilγan-i [orčiγu]l =*
6   *ǰu*[58] *gegen-e bisilγaydaqui : aduγusun metü ül[ü]*
7   *kebtegdeküi : untaqui- ṯüri*[59] *iledte büged*
8   *qoličal ügei uduriγulsun ab[un] [bisilγaydaq]ui*[60]
9   *γurban erdenis : sonos: enelküi manu :*[61] *biber möri*
10   *üǰegülügči ǰayuradu-ṯur töröküi čaγtur : alγasang =*
11   *γui ber qamuγ qudqulduγsad-i oγoγata tebčiǰü*
12   *bür-ün : alγasal ügei barimtalal [üge]i [eč]üs*[62] *qayačaysan-u*
13   *činar-tur oroγdaqui egüskedeküi [tuγu]lqui qo[γar]*
14   *-tur sitün kičiyen oluγdaqui :*[63] *mayui üiles-i tebčiǰü*
15   *bür-ün: nigen üǰügür-ḏü sedkil-i bisilγaydaqui : nisvanis*
16   *-un*[64] *qudqulduγsan-u erkedür ülü ilegegdeküi : γurba[n]*
17   *erdenis : sonos : enelküi manu : biber üküküi ene*

4v

1   *ǰayuradu-ṯur töröküi čaγtur yerüde tačiyang =*
2   *γui urin sedkil-i tebčigdeküi : ubadis-iyar geyigülküi*
3   *činar-tur alγasal*[65] *ügei oroγdaqui öber-ün sedkil-i töröl*
4   *ügei oγtarγui*[66] *činar-tur orgiγdaqui : čiγuluγsan*
5   *üiles čisun miqan bey-e-eče qayačaγulun üiledteküi :*

---

56   H. 5827, 5 v:8–9: *γurban erdenis sonos γasiγun-i minu sonos.* The Tibetan original has the excla-
     mation *kye-ma.*
57   H. 5827, 5 v:9–10:*bidaber ǰegüdün ǰayura egüni ǰegüdüleküi metü.*
58   H. 5827, 6 r:2:*orčiγulǰu.*
59   Instead of *-ṯuri, -tur-i*; H. 5827, 6 r:4 has *untaqui čaγ-tur .* On *-dur- i, -dür- i, / -tur- i, -tür- i*,
     see Weiers, *Untersuchungen*, pp. 79–87; see also Poppe, *Introduction*, § 155, p. 214; Cleaves,
     "The Sino-Mongolian Inscription of 1362", note 260, p. 131; see *töröysen-dür-i* in the *Erdeni-*
     tobči (Urga text, 76 r).
60   H. 5827, 6 r:6: *abun bisilγaydaqui.*
61   H. 5827, 6 r:7: *γasiγun-i minu.*
62   H. 5827, 6 r:11:*ečüs.*
63   H. 5827, 6 r:11–13: *aγar-tur oroγdaqui. egüskeküi tuγulqui qoγar-tur sitügen-e nigen-e*
     oroγdaqui.
64   H. 5827, 6 v:3: *nisvanis-a.*
65   For *alγasal.*
66   The word *oγtarγui* is written with diacritical points before the letter *γ* in first position.

6 *möngke busu-yi yili metü*[67] *kemen medegdeküi : yurban erdenis :*
7 *sonos : ene yasiyun-i manu : biber nom-un činar-un* **ene** *jayuradu*
8 *-tur töröküi čaytur : bügüde-eče silgüdün ayuqui-yin*[68]
9 *ayul-nuyud-i tebčijü : alin-tur töröbesü öber-ün*
10 *gegen sedkil-i <> ile uqan medeküi-tür oroydaqui :*
11 *jayur-a-tu sedkilün yoson-i mön ber medegdeküi : yeke*
12 *udqatu tüidtejü :*[69] *učiralduqui-a nigen čay irebesü :*
13 *öber-ün sedkil-i amuyulang kilinglegsed-ün čiyulyan-iyar ülü*
14 *ayuydaqui : yurban erdenis: sonos: yasiyun-i manu : biber*
15 *sangsar-un ene jayuradu-tur töröküi čay-tur : ken ni[gen] üjügür*
16 *-dü sedkil-iyer ungsibasu baribasu : [say]in [ölje]i*

5r

1 *-e*[70] *učiraysan-iyar : ulam degedüs-luy-a nayiralduju [ ]*
2 *qalya-tur*[71] *töröküi kiged : ayula unaysan metü [ ]d[ ]*[72]
3 *jirükeben ülü ulbadun :*[73] *ariyun sedkil-iyen nigen čaytur*
4 *kereglegdeküi nidün-ü quričal-i tebčijü bür-ün : ečige lam-a*
5 *burqan : eke dagini-yi bisilyaydaqui : ükül ireküi ülü*
6 *sanaqu: urtu oyutu tus-a*[74] *ügei : ene yirtenčü-yin*
7 *üile-yi bütügen üiledčü bür-ün :*[75] *edüge qoyoson*
8 *[ ]riqui üile-tür sedkil-i buu endegüre : maya[d] kereg =*
9 *leküi degedü nom bui :*[76] *edüge büged burqan nom-i*
10 *ülü üileddün :*[77] *yeke ačitu lam-a-yin aman-ača eyin*
11 *kemen nomlabai :: la[m]-a-yin ubadis-i sedkil-tür* **ese** *ayulba =*

---

67 The text reads *yili*, which must stands for *yilvi*; H. 5827, 7r:1 has *yelvi*. See *yilwi, yälwi* in von
    Gabain, *Grammatik*, p. 38; *möngke busu-yi yilvi metü* corresponds to Tibetan *mi-rtag*
    sgyu-ma, "impermanent and illusory" (*Bar-do thos-grol*, Kalsang ed., p. 114); *yilbi, yilvi*, "illu-
    sion, magie", (Kowalewki, p. 2346); see *möngke busu*, Skr. *anitya*; Tib. *mi- rtag- pa*, and *yilvi*,
    yilbi (māyā, sgyu-ma) in *Mahāvyutpatti*, Nos. 1191, 2816; *möngke busu yilvi-dür adali* is
    found in *Molon Toyin's Journey into Hell*, (Lőrincz p. 32).
68 See *silgüdüged ayuyad*, "Having trembled, having feared" in the *Hsiao-ching* = de Rachewiltz,
    "The Preclassical Mongolian Version", p. 29 and note 69, p. 61.
69 H. 5827, 7r:10–11: *yeke kereg-tü türidtejü.*
70 Following H. 5827, 7v:5.
71 For *qayalya.* H. 5827, 7v:7–8:*umai-yin qayaly-a-ača töröküi-türi.*
72 H. 5827, 7v:9: *sayadqaqui.*
73 For *ulbayidun.*
74 The word *tusa* is written separately.
75 H. 5827, 8r:1–4: *ükül irebesü bisilyan ülü čidan oyun tögöriyü. tusa ügei enegeken amin-u tula*
    üiles bütügejü bürün.
76 H. 5827, 8r:5–8: *qoyoson buruyu üiledür oroldubasu masi učaraqui-a. berke keregleküi niyur-i*
    taniyuluyči boyda nom buyu.
77 For *üiledün*; H. 5827, 8r:8–10:*edüge burqan-u nom-i ese üiledbei-e.*

12 *su : öber-iyen öber-ün kü aryadaysan buyu :*[78] *gün*
13 *amurlingyui kilinglegsed-ün sayin ǰarliy-i öber-iyen*
14 *getülgegči nom bui :*[79] *ǰiryuyan ǰayuradu-yi toliyayči*[80]
15 *ündüsün üge-yi tuyulbai :: tedeger ǰayuradu*
16 *qab[ča]yai-ača [get]ülgegči irüger bui :: : ::*

5v

1 *lam-a idam burqan daginis-un čiyulyan-tur mörgömü ::*
2 *ye[ke] yos[ ]*[81] *ber mör-i udurid-un soyorq-a :: bi[ber]*
3 *qa[...]i*[82] *orčilang-tur tögöri**küi***[83] *čaytur : sonosqui sedki =*
4 *[kü]i bis[i]lyaqui yurban-tur : alyasal ügei gerel geyigülküi*
5 *-yin* **mör-tür** *ǰarliy-un ündüs-ün-ü degedü qa[muy] lam-a-nar mör udu =*
6 *rid : degedü eke daginis-un [či]yulyan qoyin-ača qasi<n>: ǰayuradu*
7 *[a]yultu qabčayai-ača getülgen soyorq-a : üneger tuyu =*
8 *luysan burqan-u oron-tur kürbe : doysin urin-iyar orči =*
9 *lang-tur tögörigsen čaytur :*[84] *toli met[ü] [bel]ge [bili]g*
10 *-ün gerel-iyer geyigülküi-yin mör [-tür] [i]laǰu [ ]*
11 *sadau-a*[85] *burqan mör udurid : degedü eke dagini burqan-u*
12 *ni[dü]tü dagini qoyinača qasi : ǰayuradu ayultu qa[b]čayai*
13 *-ača getülgen soyorq-a: uneger tuyuluysan burqan or[o]n*
14 *-tur kürge ::*[86] *doysin omorqoqui-bar*[87] *orčilang-tur [tö]gö =*
15 *rigsen čaytur :*[88] *te[g]si [bel]ge bilig-ün gerel-iyer geyi =*
16 *gülküi-yin mör-tür [ila]ǰu tegüs-e radn-a sambau-a*
17 *burqan m[ö]r u[dur]id : degedü eke dagi[ni]*

---

78 *kü*, "exactly", is an emphasising particle. See Poppe, *Twelve Deeds*, p. 83, note 13; *aryada-* means "tromper" (Kowalewski, p. 152). The verb is found in this meaning in the *Secret History* (Haenisch, *Wörterbuch*, p. 9); H. 5827, 8r:13–8v:1 reads *öber-iyen [öber]-ün tonilqu ülü boluyu.*

79 H. 5827, 8v:2–3: *gün narin ene nom-i sedkigsen-ü tedüi öber-iyen tonilyayči buyu.*

80 For *tonilyayči*; H. 5827, 8v:5 has *tonilyayči.*

81 H. 5827, 8v:9: *yeke tayalal.*

82 This word is not clear; H. 5827, 8v:10 reads *qarsi.*

83 *tögöriküi* instead of *tögeriküi*; *tögeri-* appears in the next lines; See *töreksen, töröksen* in the *Secret History* (§ 1 et passim, § 281); H. 5827, 8v:11: *baytaysan-türi.*

84 H. 5827, 9r:8: *tögörigsen-tür-i.*

85 H. 5827, 9r:10–11: *geyigülügči-yin mör-tür. ilaǰu tegüs-e včir-a sadu-a.*

86 *Sonosuyad yekede tonilyayči* (Krueger ed.), 20r–20v: *ene doysin urin-iyar orčilang-dur tögeriküi čay-tur. toli metü belge bilig geyigülküi gerel-ün mör-tür ilaǰu tegüs nögčigsen včir sadu-a emün-e-eče udurid. degedü eke qutuy-tai namagi qoyin-a-ača qaši. ǰayur-a-du-yin ayul-tu qabčayai-ača getülgen soyorq-a. üneger tuyuluysan burqan-u oron-dur kürge.*

87 *omorqoqui* instead of *omorqaqui*, reflecting the pronunciation; H. 5827, 9v:4–5: *doysin ayidangyui-bar orčilang-tur tögörigsen-türi.*

88 *čaytur* is still legible in the original.

6r

1   *qoyinača qasi :*[89] *ǰayuradu ayultu qabčayai-ača getülgen*
2   *soyorq-a : üneger tuyuluysan burqan-u oron-tur*
3   *kürge : [doysi]n tači[yan]gyui-bar orčilang-tur tögerigsen*[90]
4   *čay-tur : öber-e öber-e uqaqui belge bilig-ün*
5   *gerel-iyer geyigülküi-yin mör-tür : ilaǰu tegüs-e*
6   *abida burqan mör udurid : degedü čayan degeltü*
7   *dagini qoyinača qasi :*[91] *ǰayuradu ayultu qabčayai-ača*
8   *getülgen soyorq-a: üneger tuyuluysan burqan-u oron*
9   *-tur kürge :: doysin bütegürgeküi (?)-ber*[92] *orčilang-tur*
10 *tögerigsen čaytur :*[93] *üile-yi bütügegči belge bilig-ün*
11 *gerel-iyer geyigülügči-yin mör-tür : ilaǰu degüs-e*[94]
12 *amogasidi burqan mör udurid : degedü tangyariy-du dara*
13 *eke qoyinača qasi :*[95] *ǰayuradu ayultu qabčayai-ača getülgen*
14 *soyorq-a : üneger tuyuluysan burqan-u oron-tur kürge ::*
15 *doysin [mun]gqay-iyar orčilang-tur tögerigsen čaytur :*[96]
16 *nom-un činar-un*[97] *belge bilig-ün gerel-iyer geyigülküi-[yi]n*
17 *mör-tür : ilaǰu tegüs-e viročan-a burqan mör*

6v

1   *udurid : egesig degedü [e]ke erke küčütü dagini qoyinača*
2   *qasi :*[98] *ǰayuradu ayultu qabčayai-ača getülgen soyorq-a :*
3   *üneger tuyuluysan burqan-u oron-tur kürge : doysin*
4   *tačiyangyui- yin abiyas ber quriyaysan-iyar orčilang-tur*
5   *tögerigsen čaytur : silgüdün ayuqui ayultu sedkil-i*

---

89 *Sonosuyad yekede tonilyayči*, 23r: *ene doyšin omoy-iyar orčilang-dur tögeriküi čay-tur. tegsi belge bilig geyigülküi gerel-ün mör-tür. ilaǰu tegüs radn-a sambau-a emüne-eče udirid. degedü eke budda lizani qoyin-a-ača qaši.*
90 See *tögörigsen* in the lines above.
91 *Sonosuyad yekede tonilyayči*, 26r: *ene doyšin tačiyangyui-bar orčilang-dur tögeriküi čay-tur. öbere öbere uqaqui belge bilig geyigülkü-yin mör-tür. ilaǰu tegüs nögčigsen degedü čayan debeltei eke qoyina-ača qaši.*
92 H. 5827, 10r:11: *qaram-iyar.*
93 H. 5827, 10r:12:*tögörigsen-tür-i.*
94 Line 5 has *tegüs-e.*
95 *Sonosuyad yekede tonilyayči*, 29r: *ene doyšin ayidangyui-bar orčilang-dur tögeriküi čay-tur. üile bütügegči belge bilig-ün geyügülküi gerel-ün mör-tür ilaǰu tegüs amogasidi burqan emün-e-eče udirid. degedü tangyariy-tu dar-a eke qoyin-a-ača qaši.*
96 H. 5827, 10v:8: *tögörigsen-türi.*
97 H. 5827, 10v:8: *nom-un egesig.*
98 H. 5827, 10v:12–13:*egesig küčütü qamuy kiling-den dagini; Sonosuyad yekede tonilyayči*, 17v–18r: *ene öber-ün doyšin mungqay-iyar orčilang-dur tögeriküi čay-tur. nom-un činar-un belge bilig-ün geyigülkü-yin gerel-ün mör-tür. ilaǰu tegüs virozan-a burqan emün-e-eče udirid. degedü eke krodisvari dagini qoyin a ača qaši.*

6 *geyigülküi gerel-ün mör-tür : ilaju tegüs-e amuyulang*
7 *kilin[g]ten-i čiyulyan mör udurid : eke küčütü qamuy*
8 *kiling-den dagini qoyinača qasi : jayuradu ayultu*
9 *qabčayai-ača getülgen soyorq-a : uneger tuyuluysan*
10 *burqan-u oron-tur kürge :: [doys]in qaram-iyar orči =*
11 *lang-tur tögerigsen čaytur : qa[m]tu ber törögsen čaytur :*
12 *belge bilig-ün gerel-iyer geyigülküi-yin mör-tür :*
13 *qamuy bayatud-un ijayur-i bariyčid mör udurid :*⁹⁹
14 *degedü eke daginis-un čiyulyan-iyar qoyinača qasi : jayuradu*
15 *ayultu qabčayai-ača getülgen soyorq-a :: üneger tuyuluysan*
16 *burqan-u oron-tur kürge :: : :: oytaryui-yin oron*
17 *-nuyud-ača dayisun buu edügülüged : qas öngge-tü*
18 *burqan-u yajar-i üjekü boltuyai :*¹⁰⁰ *usun-u*

7r

1 *oron-nuyud-ača [day]isun buu [edü]gülüged : čayan öngge-tü*
2 *burqan-u yajar-i üjekü boltuyai :*¹⁰¹ *yajar-un oron-nuyud*
3 *-ača dayisun buu edügülüged : sir-a öngge-tü burqan-u*
4 *yajar-a*¹⁰² *üjekü boltuyai :*¹⁰³ *yalun oron-nuyud-ača dayisun* **buu**
5 *edügülüged : ulayan öngge-tü burqan-u yajar-i üjekü*
6 *boltuyai :*¹⁰⁴ *salkin-u oron-nuyud-ača dayisun buu edügü =*
7 *lüged : noyayan*¹⁰⁵ *önggetü burqan-u yajar-i üjekü boltu =*
8 *yai :*¹⁰⁶ *dayun gerel öngge yurban-u oron-nuyud-ača*
9 *dayisun buu edügülüged : amuyulang kiling-den*
10 *sayitur ilayuysad-un oron-i üjekü boltuyai :*
11 *eldeb jüil solongyon-u*¹⁰⁷ *oron-nuyud-ača dayisun*
12 *buu edügülüged : eldeb jüil burqan-u yajar-i üjekü*
13 *boltuyai :: qamuy bügüde dayun-i öber-ün dayun metü*
14 *medekü boltuyai :: qamuy gerel bügüde-yi öber-ün öngge*
15 *gerel metü medekü boltuyai : qamuy* **öngge** *bügüde-yi öber-ün*
16 *öngge metü medekü boltuyai : jayuradu öber-ün*
17 *niyur-i öber-iyen taniqu boltuyai :: yurban bey-e-yin*
18 *mön činar bol[qu] boltuyai :: jayuradu*

---

99 H. 5827, 11v:4–5: *bayatud-un qamuy uqayan-i bariyči mör-i udurid.*
100 H. 5827, 11v:10–13: *oytaryui-yin oron-ača dayisun ülü edügülün qas öngge-tü burqan-u yajar-i üjügülün orosituyai;* the blue Buddha is Vairocana, placed in the centre (*Sonosuyad yekede tonilyayči,* 16v–17r).
101 The white Buddha is Vajrasattva, in the east (*Sonosuyad yekede tonilyayči,* 21r).
102 *yajar-a* instead of *yayar-i* in the preceding lines.
103 The yellow Buddha is Ratnasambhava, in the south (*Sonosuyad yekede tonilyayči,* 21r).
104 The red Buddha is Amitābha, in the west (*Sonosuyad yekede tonilyayči,* 24r).
105 *noyayan* instead of *noyoyan.*
106 The green Buddha is Amoghasiddi, in the north (*Sonosuyad yekede tonilyayči,* 26v–27r).
107 *solongyon,* instead of *solongya(n),* reflecting the spoken language; H. 5827, 12v:2 has *solongy-a.*

7v

1 *ayul-ača saki[   ]i*[108] *ene irüger buyu :: amuyulang kiling*
2 *-iyer ilayuysan burqan-t̲ur mörgömü :: yurban erdenis :*
3 *yasiyun -i manu sonos : ene yirtenčü-yin tus-a-t[u]-yi*
4 *ba[r]aydaysan čaytur :*[109] *ene yirtenčü-tür nut[a] ülü talbiqui*
5 *öber-iyen yayča-bar ǰayuradu-t̲ur o[dq]ui [te]düi :*[110]
6 *amuyulang kiling-iyer ilay[uysad] [nigüles]küi-yin*[111] *küčün*
7 *-iyer yary-a : mungqay qarangyui balamud-i arilyan [so]yorq =*
8 *a: amaray-un nököd-eče qayačaǰu yayčabar odqui*
9 *čaytur :*[112] *öber-ün sedkil qoyoson körög*[113] *bol-qui*
10 *čaytur : egüni: burqan-nuyud-un nigülesküi-yin küčün*
11 *-iyer yary-a :: silgüdün ayuquyin ǰayuradu ayul-nuyud-i*
12 *ülü üǰügülküi boltuyai :: belge bilig-iyer*
13 *geyigülküyin tabun gerel törögsen čaytu[r] : egün-eče*
14 *[ü]lü silgüdün ülü ayun öberün sedkil-ün niyur*
15 *öberiyen taniqu boltuyai :: amuyulang kilingtü-yin*
16 *öngge beyen törögsen-ü čaytur :*[114] *[e]gün-eče ülü ayun :*[115]
17 *sitügen : [ol]uyad :*[116] *ǰayuradu-yi taniqu boltuyai ::*
18 *mayui ǰaya[yan]-u erke-ber ya[s]iyun ǰobalang-yi*[117]

8r

1 *[üǰekü-y]in*[118] *čaytur : idam bur[qa]n yasiyun*
2 *ǰoba[lan]g-i arilyan soyorq-a : nom-un činar*
3 *ö[ber]- ün [d]ayun mingyan luu-yin dayun dayur =*
4 *[   ]-yin [   ] ::*[119] *yeke kölge-ü nom-un*
5 *dayun metü bolqu boltuyai :: itegel ügei ǰayayan-a*

---

108 This word must be *sakiyči;* H. 5827, 12v:13: *ibegegči.*
109 H. 5827, 13r:5: *baraydaysan-t̲ür-i.*
110 H. 5827, 13r:8: *odqui-yin tedüiken;* the Xarbuxyn Balgas text has *odqui* in line 8.
111 H. 5827, 13r:9–10 reads: *ilayuysad nigülesküi-yin küčün-iyer yary-a;* the Xarbuxyn Balgas text has *nigülesküi-yin küčün* in line 10.
112 H. 5827, 13r:13: *odqui-t̲üri.*
113 See the spelling *körög* in the *Mongyol kitad toli,* p. 711.
114 H. 5827, 14v10–11 reads: *amuyulang beyes-iyen kilinglegsed-ün-t̲üri ber ǰedkügči.* Note the genitive suffix in *-ün* before the dative locative *-t̲üri (-t̲ür-i),* followed by the particle *ber* in the form *kilinglegsed-ün-t̲üri ber.* According to Poppe, only the genitive in *-yin* or *-ai* can take a dative-locative suffix (*Grammar,* § 299, p. 78). Weiers gives an example of a genitive in *-un* taking the dative-locative suffix: *naqur-un-dur.* See *Untersuchungen,* p. 82.
115 *ayun* is legible in the original.
116 H. 5827, 14v:12 reads *sitügen-i oluyad.*
117 Instead of *ǰobalang-i.*
118 Line 8 reads *[ǰ]obalang-yi üǰekü čay-tur;* H. 5827, 14r:2: *üǰeküi-yin čay-tur.*
119 H. 5827, 14r:4–6: *nom-un dayun-i öber-ün činar-tur mingyan luu-yin dayun metü bolbasu.*

6 *dayal-duǰu*[120] *yabuqui bolbasu amuγulang [kil]inglen*
7 *ilaγu-ysan [na]mai-yi [i]begen soyorq-a :: abiyas*
8 *-un erk[e]-ber [ǰ]obalang-yi üǰeküi čay-tur*[121] *gerel*[122]
9 *-iyer geyigülügči amuγulang diyan-i üǰekü boltuγai[::]*
10 *sansar-un ǰayuradu-ača qu[bil]γu . töröküi čaytur :*
11 *yadayadu buruγu ud[uriduγ]či*[123] *simnus-un uduriγulsun*
12 *ülü üǰekü boltuγai ::*[124] *alin-i sedkibesü erkeber*
13 *kü[rkü]i-yin*[125] *tedüi ber maγui ǰayayan-a endegüreysen*
14 *ayuqui ayul-nuγud-i ülü edügülkü*
15 *boltuγai :: ariyatan gö[rögesü]n kürkireküi [day]un*
16 *[dayu]risqaqui čay-tur :*[126] *ǰirγuyan ü[sü]g-tü*
17 *[nom] -un dayun bolqu bo[l]tu[γai ::]*[127] *[č]asun [   ]*[128] *qurayin*
18 *qarangγui [-d]ur*[129] *[   ]*[130] *[bel]ge*[131]

8v

1 *bilig-iyer geyigül[ügč]i burqan-u nidün-iyer*
2 *üǰekü boltuγai :: adali iǰayur-du bari[l]duγsan*
3 *ǰay[ura]du amitan-nuγud : nidün irmeküi-yin*
4 *[ǰayu]ur-a*[132] *degedü oron-tur [bolqu] bol[tuγai ::]*
5 *nisvan[is]-un masi ölösküi umdayasqui* **čay**-tur[133] *ölösküi*
6 *umdayas[q]ui qalaγun küiten-i ǰobalang-yi*[134]
7 *ülü edügülkü boltuγ[ai] :: qoyit[u]*
8 *ǰayayan-a ečige eke egün-lüge*[135] *uči[r]ald[u]n üǰe[kü]-yin*
9 **čay**-dur : *amuγulang kilinglen ilaγuγsan . ečige*

---

120 The scribe of the text wrote the words *dayuldaǰu, ilaγuγsan* (line 7) separately because the folio (the birch bark) is uneven at this point.
121 H. 5827, 14r:12–13: *alin-tur tačiyaysan-iyar ǰayayan-u ǰobalang-yi üǰeküi čay-tur.*
122 The word *gerel* is legible in the original.
123 See *buruγu uduriduγči, buruγu tataγči* in Ishima and Fukuda eds., *Mahāvyutpatti*, No. 3162.
124 H. 5827, 14v:2–5: *sansar-un ǰayur-a lingqu-a-ača töröbesü. yadayadu buruγuduγči simnus-un uduriγulusun-i ülü edügülkü boltuγai.*
125 H. 5827, 14v:7: *kürküi-yin.*
126 H. 5827, 14v:10–12: *doγsin ariy-a-tan kürkireküi dayun-i sonosqui-tur.*
127 H. 5827, 14v:12–13: *ǰirγuyan üsüg-tü nom-un dayun bolqu boltuγai.*
128 There is a hole in the folio; as one would expect it, H. 5827, 15r:1has *kei.*
129 Judging from the orthography of the text, this was most probaby *-tur*; see *ǰayuradu-tu, üile-tür, oron-tur,* etc.
130 H. 5827, 15r:2: *učarabasu.*
131 Part of this word is legible in the original.
132 H. 5827, 15r:5: *ǰayura-du.*
133 H. 5827, 15r:9: *umdasqaqui-türi.*
134 The folio is uneven at this point, so the scribe wrote the suffix *-yi* (instead of the regular *-i*) a long way from the word.
135 The *ü* of *-lüge* is written with a superfluous *yod*; H. 5827, 15r:13: *egün-luγ-a.*

10 *burqan eke dagini-yin činar medü* [136] *üjekü boltuyai* :: [137]
11 *alin-tur töröbesü öber-tegen erke olǰu busud*
12 *[-t]ur* [138] *tusatu : laysas belges üliger-iyer čimegsen*
13 *[dege]dü bey-e-yi olq[u] bo[l]tuyai* :: *biber t[örölki]*
14 *-den-ü* [139] *degedü bey-e-yi oluyad sača : üjegsen*
15 *sonosuysan bügüde-yi [öd]ter büged tonilyaqu*
16 *boltuyai : qamuy may[ui] ǰayayan dayan ülü*
17 *dayuriyan* [140] *[a]liba buyan-nuyud-i üreigülün*
18 *dayan da[yu]-riya[qui] [boltuyai]* :: [141] *alin alin*
19 *[-t]ur* [142] *törö[besü] [   ] tede tede[ger-tür]* [143]

9r

1 *[   ] nuyud-tur idam burqan- luy[a] [   ]*
2 *[   ] boltuyai* :: [144] *töröged [sa]ča ödter*
3 *[büge]d ayalyus-i [...]leged [   ]ǰu:* [145] *töröl-i*
4 *medeged umartal [üge]i bey-e-yi olqu boltuyai* ::
5 *yeke ü[č]üken dumda eldeb ǰüil erdem-üd-i*
6 *sonosuysan [sed]kigsen* [146] *üjegsen tedüi ken-i medekü*
7 *boltuyai* :: *[a]lin-tur töröbesü tere ǰüg*
8 *-tür* [147] *qutuy orosiqu boltuyai* :: : ::
9 *qamuy ami[t]an amuyulang-luy-a tegülder*
10 *bolqu boltuyai* :: *amuyul[an]g kilinglen ilayuysan*
11 *činu bey-e yambar metü bügesü : nö[köd]* [148] *kiged :*
12 *beyen-ü nasun [ü]liger kiged : oron ba :* [149] *činü* [150] *degedü*
13 *sayin nere yayun-tur* [151] *adali bügesü : tegün-tür*
14 *adali : nasuda bi te[ri]gün törökü boltuyai* :: [152]
15 *kemen bisi[re]l-ün küčün-i egüden-eče öber busud*

---

136 The letter *t* in *metü* is written like a *d* before a consonant.
137 H. 5827, 15 v:4–5: *ödter büged üjekü boltuyai.*
138 Line 9, however, has *čay-dur.*
139 H. 5827, 15 v:10: *törölkiten.*
140 H. 5827, 16 r:1–2: *qamuy mayui ǰayayan-i ülü dayuriydaqui.*
141 H. 5827, 16 r:3–4: *dayan dayuriyaqui boltuyai.*
142 See *[a]lin tur* in 9r:7.
143 H. 5827, 16 r:4–5: *alin-tur töröbesü tedeger-tür.*
144 H. 5827, 16 r:6–7: *keb keǰiy-e idam burqan-luy-a učaralduqu boltuyai.*
145 H. 5827, 16 r:7–9: *töröged sača ödter bügüde ayalyus-i üjügülün yabuǰu.*
146 H. 5827, 16 r:13: *sedkigsen.*
147 H. 5827, 16 v:2: *tere yaǰar-tur.*
148 This word is barely legible; H. 5827, 16 v:7 has *nököd.*
149 H. 5827, 16 v:7–8: *beyen-ü keb üliger-ün oron ba.*
150 *činu* is legible in the original.
151 H. 5827, 16 v:9 has *im-e-tür.*
152 H. 5827, 16 v:8–11: *činu degedü sayin ner-e im-e-tür adali. tegün-tür adali. ürgülǰide bi*
     terigülen bolqu boltuyai.

16   -un tula yurban da ügülegdeküi : :: :
17   ǰayuradu-yi [ne]keǰü[153] [ü]lü talbiqu irüger kiged :
18   ǰiry[uya]n [ǰayura]du-yi tonilya[yči]

9v

1   [ündüsün] üge[154] sayin buyan-dan -luy-a učiraldu =[155]
2   [qu boltuyai ::][156] [   ]
3   [...] bajar guru badm-a[157]
4   [...] :: tendeče ǰayuradu-ača[158]
5   sonosuyad tonilyayči: kiged qabčayai-ača
6   getülgegči kiged ayul-ača ibegeküi irüger[159]
7   irügemüi qamuy <> burqan
8   bodisung-nar qoyinača kürgeküi-yin
9   irüger-i orǰan-u mergen badm-a
10   sambau-a baysi-da ǰokiyaysan sudur-i[160]
11   tegüs tuyulbai: sadu edgü :: : ::[161]

According to the Tibetan tradition, the *Bar-do thos-grol* is a *gter-ma*, "hidden treasure", referring to sacred books and objects which were hidden away in rocks, mountainsides, monasteries etc. and are revealed when the time is ripe. The person who brings to light a *gter-ma* is called *gter-ston* (Mong. *sang-i yaryayči*).[162] Various *gter-ma* are ascribed to Padmasambhava.[163] The *gter-ton* of the *Bar-do thos-grol* is Karma Gliṅ-pa, "the man of Karma Gliṅ".[164]

The *Bar-do thos-grol* has colophons which say: *o-rgyan-gyi mkhan-po padma 'byuṅ-gnas-kyis mdzad-de. mtsho-rgyal-gyis zin-ris-su bris-nas gter-du sbas. slar karma gliṅ-bas* (= *pas*) *sgam-po-dpal-gyi ri-bo-nas gdan-draṅs-ba'o* (= *pa'o*),[165] "The Master of Oḍḍiyāna Padmasambhava composed it. mTsho-rgyal[166] wrote down the original and concealed it as a treasure. Karma Gliṅ-pa took it out again"; *grub-thob karma gliṅ-pas*

---

153   H. 5827, 16v:12: *nekeǰü*.
154   *üge* is still legible in the original; H. 5827, 17r:2: *ene ündüsün üge*.
155   These words are still legible in the original.
156   H. 5827, 17r:3–4: *učiralduqu boltuyai*. This is where the text in H. 5827 ends.
157   *badm-a* is legible in the original.
158   *ǰayuradu-ača* is legible in the original.
159   This line is damaged, but legible in the original.
160   *sudur* is legible in the original.
161   There are two words which are written in a different hand.
162   *Sumatiratna*, I, p. 830.
163   See Christa Klaus, *Der aus dem Lotos Entstandene*, pp. 9–10.
164   On this person, see Evans-Wentz, *The Tibetan Book of the Dead*, pp. 73, 77; see also Tucci, *Il libro tibetano dei morti*, note 1, p. 10.
165   Kalsang ed., p. 113.
166   On mTsho-rgyal, see Fremantle and Chögyam Trungpa, *The Tibetan Book of the Dead*, xiii; see also Christa Klaus, *Der aus dem Lotos Entstandene*, p. 9, and picture No. 22.

sgom-po-gdar-gyi ri-bo-nas gdan-draṅs-pa'i gter-ma'o,[167] "It is a *gter-ma* brought by the Siddha Karma Gliṅ-pa from Mount sGom-po-gdar (Gompodar)".[168]

The text from Xarbuxyn Balgas has a colophon at the end of the prayer called *Ĵayuradu amitan-i sonosuyad tonilɣayči qabčayai-ača getülgegči ayulača aburayči irüger* (3r:10–12), "The prayer which liberates beings by hearing, saves from the narrow passage and protects from fear in the intermediate state". The colophon reads: *ene irüger-i orĵan badm-a sambau-a baysi-yin ĵokiyaysan buyu: dalai ilayuysan dagini ubadislan bičibei... siddi-dü garm-a ayulan-u dvib-tur sang niyuju talbiysan ene nom-i ĵalaĵu iregsen bui* (3r:14–3v:3), "The Master Padmasambhava of Oḍḍiyāna composed this prayer. Dalai Ilaγuγsan ḍākinī wrote it down as a teaching. The Siddha Karma brought this book, which was hidden as a treasure 'in the *dvib*' of the mountain".

The Tibetan colophon tells us that Siddha Karma Gliṅ-pa found the treasure on Mount Gompodar (or Gampodar), but there is no mention of the name of this mountain in the Mongol text. The latter reads *ayulan-u dvib-tur*. The term *dvib*, "island, country, continent",[169] translates the Tibetan *gliṅ*,[170] but *gliṅ* is a part of the name of the *gter-ston* Karma Gliṅ-pa, not a separate word. As a result, the Mongol translator erroneously interpreted the name of the famous *gter-ston* Karma Gliṅ-pa. As shown, the same error is found in both the Olon Süme fragment OS IV/109–110 and in the Stockholm manuscript H. 5827.[171] Hence this error must be traced back to the archetype of the Mongolian translation.

The prayers of the *ĵayuradu* from Xarbuxyn Balgas shed light on the history of Buddhist religious practices in early 17th century Mongolia. Furthermore, we have at our disposal an early Mongolian translation, which is also valuable from the linguistic viewpoint. For instance, the letters *i, y, yi, ĵ* and *v* are not distinguished (*amitan, yeke, yirtenčü, ĵayayan, dvib, čambudvib*, 2r:4; 2r:6; 2r:1; 2r:6; 3v:2, 3v:4); the letter *s* is written like an Uighur *z* at the end of a word (*erdenis, sonos*, 4r:1);[172] *d* is used instead of *t* at the beginning of a word (*degüs*, 6r:11); words such as *bas-a* (2r:14), *tus-a* (7v:3),[173] and the word *qiri* (3v:6) is written with the velar *q* before *i*.

The text shows the plural form of the future noun (*sayuqun*, 3v:16), and the frequent use of the future noun in *-qui/-küi* of the passive verb expressing the idea of necessity to act (*tebčigdeküi, bisilγdaqui*, 4r:3; 4r:6 et passim).[174] There is the occurrence of *boluy-a*

---

167 p. 109.

168 Other versions have *sgam-po-gdar* instead of *sgom-po-gdar*. See, for example, Tucci, *Il libro tibetano dei morti*, p. 10.

169 Kowalewski (p. 1778) has *tib, tiib, tvib*; Skr. *dvīpa*.

170 The Tibetan *gliṅ* means "island, isolated place, continent", see Das, pp. 257–258.

171 The Olon Süme fragment has *ayulan[-u] dvib[-tur]*; H.5827 reads *ayulan-u dib-tur*. See the passages quoted in note 42.

172 See von Gabain, *Grammatik*, pp. 26–27.

173 On this orthographic feature see Cerensodnom and Taube, *Turfansammlung*, p. 11.

174 See the remarks by de Rachewiltz in "The Preclassical Mongolian Version", note 37, p. 58; see also Poppe, *Grammar*, § 607, p. 169.

inaru in the following phrase: *ene sansar-un orčilang qoyoson boluy-a inaru ülü tuyulqu boltuyai* (3r:16–3v: 2) "May (this teaching) not end so long as this *saṃsāra* is not empty".[175]

175 The Tibetan text reads: '*khor-ba ma -stoṅs-kyi bar-du chos'di ma rdzogs-so* (Kalsang ed., p. 212); on -*yal-ge* followed by *inaru*, see Weiers, *Untersuchungen,* pp. 175–6; on *oluy-a inaru, inaysi* etc., see Cleaves, "*Bodisatw-a Čari-a Awatar-un tayilbur*", note 235, pp. 113, 114; see also *kürüge inaru* in the 3rd chapter of the *Bodhicaryāvatāra* (= de Rachewiltz, "The Third Chapter of Chos kyi 'od-zer's Translation", 21c, p. 1183); *yaruy-a edüi, oluy-a inaru* are found in the *Erdeni-yin tobči* (Urga text), 79v–80r.

Glossary[1]

abida burqan, XBM 42, *1v; XBM 47; *[burq]an*, XBM 50, 7v; XBM 110, 6r
abida ber burqan, XBM 49, 8r
abida burqan-u ulus, XBM 47, 4r; *[burq]an*, XBM 50, 7v
abida ber burqan-u ulus, XBM 49, 8r
abqui (nidāna), XBM 107, *3v (et passim)
ači ür-e, XBM 46, 2v
ači-tu ečige eke, XBM 2, 1v; XBM 3, *1r; XBM 5, 1r; XBM 7
ada, XBM 47, 3v; XBM 100, 2r; XBM 103, 4v; XBM 92, 2v; XBM 108r; XBM 110, 2r
ada todqar, XBM 47, 3v; XBM 100, 2r; XBM 103, 4v
adal-i barayan-i ab, XBM 73, 2v
adal mal, XBM 66, 8r, 10r
adas, XBM 65, 2v, 3v; XBM 109, 3r
adasun [čer]ig-üd-i terigün-i oytalǰu, XBM 65, 3v
adasi qariyulqui, XBM 65, 2v
aduyusun metü, XBM 110, 4r
aduyusun-u nasu, XBM 47, 4r
adayusun-u töröl oron, XBM 22, 3v
adayusun-u töröl-eče tonilqu, XBM 47, 2v; XBM 49, 4v
adistid, XBM 58, *1v; XBM 66, 6v; XBM 81, 3v
adistid-un eǰen, XBM 81, 3v
adistid-un takil, XBM 81, 3v
adqay ügei yeke sangun eǰen ariy-a avalogide isvari, XBM 29, 4r
aginista-yin eǰen šigemüni, XBM 66, 9r
ayul dayisun, XBM 73, 2v
ayulan-tu diya[n] sayubasu, XBM 106, 4v
ayulayin eǰen burqan, XBM 29, 3r; XBM 30, 3v; *ayula-yin eǰen burqa[n]*, XBM 37r
alaqui-tur orobasu, XBM 47, 3v
albin čidkör, XBM 86, *1v, XBM 88, 2r; *[alb]in čid[kör]* XBM 89, 3v; *[albi]n*,
   XBM 90, 3r
alyasal ügei, XBM 110, 3r
alin alin, XBM 110, 8v
altan včir-tu saran metü yabuyči burqan (500 Buddhas), XBM 28, 3r
altan mönggön kögeregen, XBM 30, 3v
altan mönggön kögergen, XBM 29, 3v; XBM 34, 3r

---

1 The glossary lists selected terms and expressions; it also includes names and epithets of deities.

altan mönggön kökörge, XBM 35, 7r; *[a]ltan*, XBM 33, 8v; *[m]önggön*, XBM 37v
altan möngeön kögergen, XBM 39, 8v
altan öngge-tü lingquu, XBM 46, 5r
altan nom, XBM 29, 4r; XBM 30, 5r; XBM 33, 4r; XBM 34, 4r; XBM 40, 9v
altan quyaytan, XBM 47, 1v
altan sečen qayan, XBM 79, 6r, 6v
altan toyona, XBM 66, 7v
altatu keyid, XBM 66, 2v
amaray-ud ba nököd, XBM 107, 5r
amaray-un nököd-eče qayačaju, XBM 110, 7v
amin sünesü, XBM 66, 10r
amin-i sönegegči, XBM 110, 2r
amin-u sakiyul[sun] kereg kilge, XBM 104, *2v
amin-u saki[yulsun] [kereg] kilge, XBM 105r-v
amitan-i kilinče, XBM 47, 3r
amitan-u kilinče, XBM 47, 3r; XBM 49, 6r
amitan-u tamu, XBM 22, 3v
amitan-u tusa-yin tula, XBM 6, 4v; XBM 9, 1r (et passim); XBM 11v; XBM 13, 6r;
    XBM 14r; XBM 16r (et passim); XBM 20r
amitan-u tusa-yin tulada, XBM 1, 2v
amogasidi burqan, XBM 110, 6r
amul ügei, XBM 110, 3v
amuyulang-un ary-a-tur učiraqu, XBM 107, *4v
amurliy[san] burqan (500 Buddhas), XBM 28, 4r
anda, XBM 106, 4r
angir sibayun, XBM 100, 2v; *anggir*, XBM 102r
aq-a degü, XBM 100, 3v
ara büle, XBM 82, *4v; *bule (büle)* XBM 83, 3v; XBM 84, 4r
aran boyol, XBM 83, 3v
arban yurban takil-un modon, XBM 81, 2r
arban jüg-ün burqan, XBM 66, 2v, 10r
arban jüg-ün burqan bodisug, XBM 82, *1r
arban jüg-ün bursang quvaray-ud, XBM 22, 3v
arban jüg-ün geser qayan, XBM 66, 12r
arban jüg-ün yurban čay-un qamuy tegünčilen iregsed, XBM 1, 1r; XBM 2, 1v;
    XBM 5, 1r; XBM 6, 1v; XBM 7; XBM 8, 2rXBM 9, 1r
arban jüg-ün yertinčü, XBM 22, 3r
arban naiman tamu, XBM 29, 3v; XBM 30, 4r; XBM 33, 3v
arban qar-a nigül, XBM 22, 5v
arban qoyar jil-ün qarsi, XBM 86, *1v
arča-yi[n] modon, XBM 81, *2v
ary-a-yin küčün, XBM 110, 3r
ariyun (35 Buddhas), XBM 22, 2r
ariyun gerel-iyer čenggen ülü medegči (35 Buddhas), XBM 22, 2v

ariyun gegen gerel-tü niyuča burqan (500 Buddhas), XBM 28, 2v
ariyun saysabad-un qubčad, XBM 54, 2v; XBM 57, *2v
ariyun takil, XBM 66, 2r (et passim); XBM 67, 1v; XBM 68, 2r, 2v; XBM 69, 2r, 2v;
   XBM 70v
ari[y-a] avaloyide suvar-a, XBM 51, 1v
ariy-a balo, XBM 58, 2r (et passim)
ary-a avalogi-de süvr-a, XBM 52, 1v
arsalan-u dayun, XBM 41, 1v
arslan dayubar ridi qubilyan-u köl (500 Buddhas) XBM 28, 2v
arslan dürüber altan včir-tu saran metü yabuyči burqan (500 Buddhas), XBM 28, 3r
asuri, XBM 47, 2v; XBM 49, 4v
atayatu dayisun, XBM 66, 8v
au (ayu) yeke yaǰar, XBM 110, 2r
auyan köbegün, XBM 97, 3v
avalogide šuvar-a, XBM 54, 1v
avalogi-de süvr-a, XBM 52, 1v
avaloyide suvar-a, XBM 51, 1v
ayay-qa tegimlig-nuyud, XBM 1, 1r, 2r
ayud tamu, XBM 46, 5r
ayul ügei, XBM 47, 4r
ayultu qabčayai, XBM 110, 5v, 6r, 6v

baǰar-bani, XBM 41, 3r
badm-a lingqu-a čečeg, XBM 48, 2v; XBM 49, 2v
badm-a lingqu-a sečeg, XBM 47, 2r
badm-a li[n]gqus, XBM 66, 9r
badm sambau-a XBM 29, 4r
badm-a sambau-a, XBM 81, 3v
badm-a sambau-a baysi, XBM 81, 3r; XBM 110, 3r, 9v
[bay]a sara, XBM 99, *4
bayatud-un ayimay (35 Buddhas), XBM 22, 1v
baydar sayari-tu, XBM 82, *4r; XBM 84, 4r; *sayaritu*, XBM 83, 3v
baysi, XBM 106, 4r
baysi sabi, XBM 66, 7r
baysi sibi (sabi), XBM 46, 2v
bayuqu quduy, XBM 81, 8r
bayuqu yoson, XBM 99, *2r
bayuqui nutuy, XBM 66, 12r
bayuri, XBM 66, 12r; *bayu[ri]*, XBM 99, *4
bal sikir, XBM 29, 5r
balamad amitan, XBM 58, 3r
baltu modon, XBM 82, *2v
bandi kümün, XBM 100, 1v
bandi bombo kümün-ü sakiyulsun, XBM 109, 3r

bandi toyin kümün, XBM 109, 4v

bandi-yin bombo, XBM 109, 7v

baraydasi ügei, XBM 82, *2v

barayun ǰüg γarγ-a, XBM 107, *6v

barayun ǰüg-ün küčün [auγ-a] yeke-tü burqan (500 Buddhas), XBM 28, 4v

baral ügei, XBM 66, 9r

bayasqulang čoγ-tu (35 Buddhas), XMB 22, 2r

belge, XBM 100, 2v (et passim); XBM 103, 4r (et passim)

belge bilig, XBM 4v; XBM 12r; XBM 16r; XBM 22, 4r, 4v; 56, 3v; XBM 66, 2v, 5r;
   XBM 69, 2r; XBM 73, 2r; XBM 110, 6v

belge bilig neretü qurča bolad ildün, XBM 73, 2r

belge-tü bayatur yeke nigülesügči, XBM 58, 3r

beri abubasu,, XBM 107, *2v

beri uγtuqu, XBM 107, *1v

berke qatayuǰil, XBM 42, 3r

berke üilš (üileš), XBM 28, 9v

bey-e-gini ugiyaǰu, XBM 107, *6r, *7r

bey-e tebčiküi, XBM 47, 2v; *bey-e-yi*, XBM 49, 5r

bey-e-tür ebečin, XBM 41, 7r

beyen-ü nasun, XBM 110, 9r

bičig-tü bičimüi, XBM 106, 4v

bičig-tür tuγulaǰu üǰebesü, XBM 110, 2v

bigar, XBM 109, 7v

bilig-ün činadu kiǰaγar-a kürügsen, XBM 28, 2r

bilig-ün kei, XBM 60, 3v

birid, XBM 49, 4v

birid-un γaǰar, XBM 22, 3v

bisirel sedkil, XBM 110, 3r

bisma[n] tngri, XBM 82, *1v, XBM 83, 2r

blam-a bolbasu, XBM 106, 4v

blam-a burqan nom-un činar, XBM 66, 6r–6v

bodalang ayulan, XBM 42, *2v; XBM 56, 3r (et passim)

boda bodalang ayulan, XBM 53, *2r

bodalang-un ayula, XBM 78, 1v

bodalan-i orgil, XBM 58, *1v

bodančay (bodančar), XBM 46, 2r

bodi modon, XBM 53, *2r

bodi qutuγ, XBM 11v; XBM 16r

bodi sedkil, XBM 6, 4r; XBM 15r; 16v; XBM 66, 2r; XBM 67, 1v

bodičid, XBM 6, 4r; XBM 9, 5r; XBM 11v; XBM 22, 6r; XBM 41, 5r, 7r; XBM 58, 2r

bodičid-un ǰirüken, XBM 41, 7r

bodi saduva ma ha a saduva, XBM 62, 1r

bodisug, XBM 29, 4r; XBM 30, 4v

bodisug-nar, XBM 25, *1v; XBM 40, 9r; XBM 82, *1v; XBM 83, 2r *bodisung*, XBM 34, 4r; XBM 47, 2v; XBM 49, 5r; XBM 81, 3v; XBM 90*1v

bodisung maqasung, XBM 87, 1v; XBM 90, *1v

boyda, XBM 65, 1v; XBM 42, *3r; XBM 43, 3v; XBM 65, 1v (et passim); XBM 66, 7r
    (et passim)

boyda dara, XBM 43, 3v

boyda dar-a eke, XBM 42, *3r

boyda yamandaga, XBM 65, 1v (et passim)

[boy]da-yin [j]arliy, XBM 65, 3v

boyol, XBM 82 *4v; XBM 83, 3v; XBM 84, 4r; XBM 106, 4r

boyoni beyetü, XBM 109, 7v

bolqui (nidāna), XBM 107, 4r (et passim)

bombo kümün, XBM 100, 2v; XBM 109, 3r

boro boljomor siba[yun], XBM 100, 2r

borqan bodančay (bodančar), XBM 46, 2r

bodhi saduva, XBM 28, 7r; XBM 88, 2r

bsang, XBM 66, 6r

bsang-un idegen, XBM 80, *1v

bu burqan, XBM 15r

bu buyan kesig, XBM 82, *4v

buy eliy-e daruqui, XBM 107, *3r

buyu kiged qonin-tur degel yutul ačiju ögbesü, XBM 109, 3v

buyulyan yeketü, XBM 82, *4r; *[buyu]lyan yeke-tü*, XBM 83, 3r; *bulya (buyulya)
    yeke[-tü]*, XBM 85, 4r

bujar idegen, XBM 109, 3r

bulya, XBM 47, 3r; XBM 49, 6v; XBM 97, 9r

burqan baysi, XBM 29, 4v, 5r

burqan burqan, XBM 13, 6r; XBM 29, 2r; XBM 30, 2r; XBM 35 3r

burqan čidkör qoyar, XBM 110, 2r

burqan nom lam-a, XBM 30, 2v; XBM 34, 2r

burqan tengri, XBM 29, 2r; XBM 30, 2r

burqan-u nidütü dagini, XBM 110, 5v

burqan-u qutuy, XBM 78, 1v

bursang quvaray-ud, XBM 5, 1v; XBM 22, 3v; XBM 23, 1v; XBM 25, *1v; XBM 41,
    7v; XBM 81, 3r, 8v

burtay idegen, XBM 46, 4r

buruyu kilinče, XBM 46, 4r

bu[r]uyu mayu yabudal-dan, XBM 65, 3v

buruyu törökü, XBM 22, 3v

buruyu üjel-i bariqu, XBM 22, 4r

buruyulasi ügei, XBM 82, *4v; XBM 83, 3v; *burulasi*, XBM 84, 4r

busu amitan-tur odču, XBM 110, 2r

busu yabudal, XBM 47, 4r

busud-da keregül temečel bolqu, XBM 107, *4v

busud-un kümün, XBM 73, 3r

buta büri burqan, XBM 81, 8r

buyan kesig, XBM 82, *1r (et passim); XBM 85, *3r, 3v; XBM 103, 5r

buyan kisig (kesig), XBM 83, 1v (et passim)

buyan kilinče-d̲ü, XBM 110, 2r

buyantu sayin üile üiledčü, XBM 97, 9v

bügüde-yi geyigül-ün jökiyagči čoγ-tü (jokiyaγči čoγ-tu) (35 Buddhas), XBM 22, 3r

büri büri, XBM 30, 3r

büü ög, XBM 99, *2r

čagirbad-un qaγan, XBM 100, 1v

čaγ süm, XBM 109, 3v

čaγ ügei, XBM 110, 2r

čaγan badm-a, XBM 58, 3r

čaγan čilaγun, XBM 110, 2r

čaγan čulu qulusun, XBM 81, *2v

čaγan darai-yi egeči, XBM 73, 1v

čaγan labai, XBM 81, *2r

čaγan gerel-tü degü, XBM 73, 1v

čaγan luus, XBM 73, 1v

čaγan naran-u gerel-tü duγulγan, XBM 73, 1v–2r

čaγan öngge-tü arban nigen niγur-tu naiman γar-tu, XBM 47, 2r

čaγan öngge-tü burqan, XBM 110, 7r

čaγarγu maγu dayisun-i simnus, XBM 66, 9v

čaγasi qariqu boltuγai, XBM 88, 2r (et passim)

čaγasi qariqu bold̲u-yai, XBM 88, 2v

čaγag-si qariqu boltuγai, XBM 90, *2r (et passim)

čalma orkimui, XBM 106, 5v

čalma-yi oγtalbasu, XBM 106, 4v

čambala, XBM 66, 2r (et passim)

čambudvib, XBM 110, 3v

čangbu tibču, XBM 109, 3v

časutan-u merged-ün oroiyin čimeg, XBM 41, 2; *[ča]sutan-u merged-ü[n] oroi-yin*
    čimeg, XBM 78, 2v

času-tu γajar, XBM 29, 4r; XBM 74, 1v

času-tu γajar-t[ur] mergen oroi[-yin] čimeg jongga-ba, XBM 29, 4r–4v

čečeg-ün čoγ-tu (35 Buddhas), XBM 22, 2v

čege[rle]jü y[a]bu, XBM 105r

čerig tataqui, XBM 107, *2r

čerig-ün terigün, XBM 66, 7r, 7v

čidayči küčütü, XBM 66, 11v

čider-iyer čiderlejü, XBM 47, 3v

čidder-iyer čidder-lejü (čider-iyer čider-lejü), XBM 49, 6v

čidkör kiged ada, XBM 92, 2v

čidkedün eliy-e, XBM 29, 3v

čidköd-ün eliy-e, XBM 35, 7v; XBM 39, 8v; *čidköd eliy-e*, XBM 34, 3v
čidöri saki, XBM 73, 3r
čigir-badun qayan, XBM 101, *1v
čiyuluysan üiles, XBM 110, 4v
čikin ungsibasu, XBM 107, *4r, *5r
čimeg emüskeged, XBM 109, 7r
činadusun čerig, XBM 66, 7v
činadus-un süri doroyitayuluyči, XBM 66, 8r
činaysi qariqu boltuyai, XBM 100, 4v (et passim); XBM 87, 1r (et passim); XBM 89, 3r
    (et passim)
čindamani erdeni, XBM 62, 1v; XBM 66, 6r
čindan-i modon, XBM 81, *2r
čing joriy sedkil, XBM 47, 3r; XBM 49, 5v
čirai öngge, XBM 66, 9v
čisun miqan bey-e, XBM 110, 4v
čisutu moren (mören), XBM 34, 3r
čisutu mören, XBM 29, 3r; XBM 30, 3v
čisu-tu mören, XBM 33, 8v; XBM 35, 7r; XBM 37v
čoy-ča, XBM 12r
čoy-čas, XBM 2, 1v
čoyčas, XBM 4r; XBM 5, 1r; XBM 8, 2r; XBM 47, 4r; XBM 49, 8v; XBM 92, 2r
čoy-i öggügči (35 Buddhas), XBM 22, 2r
čoy-tu ayulan, XBM 46, *2r; *[čoy]-tu* XBM 43, 2v
čoy-tu belge-tü masi oyoyata aldarsiysan (35 Buddhas), XBM 22, 2v
čoy-tu čindan (35 Buddhas), XBM 22, 2r
čoy-tu gerel-tü (35 Buddhas), XBM 22, 2v

daginis-un čiyulyan, XBM 5v
dayu dayusba, XBM 84, 4v
dayun gerel öngge, XBM 110, 6v
dalai ilayuysan dagini, XBM 110, 3v
dalai lama, XBM 78, 2r
dalai mören, XBM 97, 9v
dalai[-yin] [do]tora luu-yin ordo, XBM 30, 4r
dalai-yin dotora ki luu-yin ordo, XBM 34, 3v
dalai-yin dotoraki luu-yin oordo, XBM 29, 3v; XBM 35, 8r
dalai-yin jirüken, XBM 81, *2r
dalan doloyan etügen eke, XBM 82, *1v; *da[lan] dol[oyan] etügen eke*, XBM 81, 8r;
    [etügen]n XBM 83, 2r
dara, XBM 43, 3v; XBM 73, 1v
dara eke, XBM 110, 6r
dar-a eke, XBM 42, *3r
darasun uyuqui, XBM 107, *2v
daruqui üile, XBM 107, *1v

dayini daruysan, XBM 22, 1v

dayin-i daruysan, XBM 23, 1v; XBM 42, *1v

dayisun kümün, XBM 73, 3r

dayisun simnus, XBM 81, 8v

dayisun todqad-i ünesün tobaray bolya, XBM 73, 3v

dayisun-u adal-i barayan-i ab, XBM 73, 2v

dayisun-u yaǰar, XBM 106, 5r

dayisun-u küčün, XBM 73, 3r

dayisun-u mesei-i uyadqa, XBM 73, 3v

dayisun-u qoor ayul bolqu, XBM 107, *3v

degedü čayan degeltü dagini, XBM 110, 6r

degedü degedü, XBM 16v

degedü eke dagini, XBM 110, 5v

degedü nom, XBM 110, 5r

degedü nom-un qan qongsim bodi<i> sa[du]va, XBM 28, 9v

deger-e niskü sibayun, XBM 46, 3r

deger-e ügei degedü, XBM 22, 4v

deger-e tengri-ner-ün boyda, XBM 66, 7r

diyan-u idegen, XBM 57, *2v

doysin ada, XBM 90, *1r

doysin ada todqar-i qariyuluyči tarni, XBM 87, 1r

doysin qaram, XBM 110, 6v

doysin tačiyangyui, XBM 110, 6v

doloyan alqui-yin yary-a, XBM 107, *6r

doloyan ebüged, XBM 82, *2r; *[dolo]yan* XBM 83, 2r

doloyan erdeni, XBM 47, 1v

doloyan qonoy, XBM 29, 2v; XBM 30, 3r; XBM 34, 2v; *qo[noy]*, XBM 36, 7v

doloyan üy-e, XBM 29, 3r; XBM 37r; *dolo[yan]*, XBM 30, 3v

dongli, XBM 109, 3v, 7r

dorm[-a]-yin mandal, XBM 66, 12r

dorona qandun bayuba[su], XBM 97, 8r

dönürüb, XBM 73, 1v

dörben belčir-tü qaryui, XBM 109, 3v

dörben čaylasi ügei, XBM 8, 5r; XBM 19

dörben luusun qad, XBM 66, 10v

dörben ǰayun ebedčin, XBM 103, 4v

dörben ǰüil čaylasi ügei gerel, XBM 58, 2v

dörben költü, XBM 46, 3r

dörben qosiyun mal, XBM 66, 2v; XBM 69, 2r; XBM 70r

dörben qusiyu-tu aduyusun, XBM 82, *3v

[dör]ben qosiyun aduyusun, XBM 84, 4r

duyulyai saki, XBM 73, 2v

duradqui čoy-tu (35 Buddhas), XBM 22, 2v

duran-i qangyayči rasiyan-u usun, XBM 54, 2v

[du]rani qangɣayči rasiyan-u usun, XBM 57, *2v

dvib, XBM 110, 3v

ebderesi ügei, XBM 82, *2v; *[ügei]* XBM 85, *3v

ebečin kölčin, XBM 97, 9v

ebečin-eče amiduraqu, XBM 107, *4r

ebečin ügei, XBM 41, 7r

ebečidten-i emčilebesü, XBM 107, *1v

ebečiten taqul-dan, XBM 66, 4r

ebedčin-i arilɣayči otači burqan, XBM 41, 3v

ebedčin kümün, XBM 107, *7v

ebesün čečeg, XBM 100, 3r

ebesün usun degere ki burqan, XBM 30, 3r

ebösün modon-u ǰirüken, XBM 81, *2r

ebösün usun degereki büri burqan, XBM 29, 3r, *ebös[ün]*, XBM 33, 8r; *degere ki*,
　　XBM 34, 3r

ebösün usun-a degereki büri burqan, XBM 37r

ečige oytarɣ[ui], XBM 80, *2r; *[e]čige oytarɣui*, XBM 81, *2r

ebüge ečige, XBM 46, 2r

ebüge ečige eke burqan, XBM 29, 3r; *[e]büge*, XBM 30, 3v; XBM 37r

ečige eke, XBM 2, 1v; XBM 3, *1r; XBM 5, 1r; XBM 7; XBM 9, 1r; XBM 46, 2r;
　　XBM 81, 8v; XBM 97, 2r (et passim); XBM 107, *5v; XBM 110, 8v

ečige lam-a burqan, XBM 110, 5r

[e]čige oytarɣui-ača luus, XBM 81, *2r

ečige-yin töröl, XBM 109, 3r

ed idegen, XBM 107, *5v

ed tavar, XBM 107, *5r, *5v

edür söni ügei, XBM 62, 1v

eke burqan, XBM 29, 2v; XBM 30, 3r; XBM 33, 8r; XBM 34, 3r

eke delekei-eče ɣal, XBM 81, *2r

eke dagini, XBM 110, 5r, 5v

eke daginis, XBM 110, 5v

eke inu delekei bui, XBM 81, *2r

eke küčütü qamuɣ kiling-den dagini, XBM 110, 6v

ekener-ün dongli, XBM 109, 7r

eǰen qormusta tngri, XBM 65, 2r

eǰen ügei, XBM 110, 2r

elige-gi čöm oytaba, XBM 106, 4r

elingčüɣ qulingčuɣ (elinčüg qulinčuɣ), XBM 46, 2r

eliy-e nomoɣdq-ui, XBM 107, *2r

em nairaɣulqui, XBM 107, *2v

em-e eliy-e, XBM 108, v

em-e köbegün, XBM 66, 10r

eme kümün, XBM 107, *8r

eme kümün-eče ɣai boluɣsan, XBM 107, *8r

emegeli sakiyad qaǰayari saki, XBM 73, 3 r

emün-e yary-a, XBM 107, *7 r

emüne qandun bayubasu, XBM 97, 8 r

emüne-eče minu, XBM 66, 8 r

emüneside qandun bayubasu, XBM 99, *2 v

enelküi manu, XBM 110, 4 r (et passim)

eng urida, XBM 46, 1 v

[e]rdeni erdeni, XBM 41, 4 r

erdeni lingqu-a-tur sayitur sayuysan degedü oki ilayuysan čimeg-tü qayan (35
   Buddhas), XBM 22, 2 v

erdeni-sün altan delekei, XBM 52, 1 v

erdenis-ün altan delekei, XBM 53, *1 v; XBM 54, 1 v

erdeni-yi[n] qan bisma[n] tengri, XBM 82, *1 v

ere, XBM 97, 2 v (et passim)

ereyin degüner, XBM 97, 3 v

ergin toyoribasu XBM 47, 4 r; XBM 49, 8 v–9 r

erke küčün ügei, XBM 110, 2 v

eriküi üiles, XBM 107, *3 r

erketü manǰusiri, XBM 29, 4 r; XBM 41, 2 r

erketen-ü [man]ǰusiri, XBM 78, 2 v

erke-tür-iyen oroyuluysan, XBM 66, 10 v

erlig qayan, XBM 29, 3 r, 3 v; XBM 30, 4 r; XBM 33, 8 v; XBM 34, 3 r; *erl[ig],* XBM 37 v
   XBM 40, 9 r; *[erlig],* XBM 100, 3 r; 102 r; XBM 110, 2 r, 2 v

erlig qayan-u bi[čig], XBM 104, *2 r

erlig qayan-ü emüne, XBM 29, 3 r; XBM 34, 3 r; XBM 39, 8 r; *emün-e,* XBM 33, 8 v;
   XBM 37 v

erlig qayan-u tengsegül, XBM 102 r; *[erlig],* XBM 100, 3 r

erlig qayan-u yaryačin, XBM 110, 2 r, 2 v

erlig qayan-u yaryačin-u toli, XBM 110, 2 r

erlig qayan-u yeke ayul-nuyud, XBM 110, 2 v

erlig-üd[-ün] bičig, XBM 106, 5 r

erliy (erlig) qayan, XBM 38 v; XBM 39, 8 r

erl<l>iy qayan, XBM 35, 7 v

erte uridaki üile bolǰu, XBM 107, *4 r

esergüčel ügei, XBM 66, 4 r; XBM 68, 2 r

eserun qormusta, XBM 66, 9 r

esrun egesig, XBM 41, 1 v

etügen, XBM 46, 2 v; XBM 81, *7 v

etügen eke, XBM 66, 8 r; XBM 81, 8 r; XBM 82, *2 r; *[etüge]n eke,* XBM 83, 2 r

gabalad bariǰu, XBM 65, 3 r–3 v

gandaragud [ayulan], XBM 43, *2 v

gandarigudun ayulan, XBM 42, *2 r

gangg[a] mören, XBM 82, *2 v

garudi sibayun, XBM 100, 2v

gegegen sayiqan, XBM 66, 11v

gegen sedkil, XBM 110, 4v

geǰige oγtalun, XBM 100, 3r

gem-eče qaldaγsan, XBM 60, 4v

gem ügei, XBM 41, 7r

ger baraγan-ača qayačaqu, XBM 103, 4r; *[ba]raγan*, XBM 100, 4v

ger dotora yabuγči, XBM 47, 3r

ger tergen-ü do[t]or-a yabuγči, XBM 49, 6r

ger-ün eǰen, 107, *2r

gerel-tü yeke otači burqan (500 Buddhas), XBM 28, 3v

geser boyda, XBM 66, 9v (et passim)

geser qayan, XBM 66, 11v; XBM 73, 1v

ginǰi, XBM 49, 6v

graγ odon, XBM 73, 2r; XBM 91, 3v

graγ odon neretü qoor-tu sumun, XBM 73, 2r

güikü görögesün, XBM 46, 3r–3v

güǰügün uryuǰu, XBM 47, 4r, XBM 50, 7r

gürü norbu badm-a [sam]bau-a baγsi, XBM 81, 3r

γai boluγsan, XBM 107, *6v (et passim); XBM 109, 3r, 7r

γai ǰobalang, XBM 97, 8v

γai qarsi, XBM 88, 2r (et passim); XBM 89 3r; XBM 90, *3r (et passim)

γal erdeni-tü (35 Buddhas), XBM 22, 2r

γal erdeni-tü γarγaγči (35 Buddhas), XBM 22, 1v

γalun oron, XBM 110, 7r

γaǰar-un buyan kesig, XBM 82, *2r

γaǰarun buyan kesig, XBM 83, 2r

γaǰar-un eǰed, XBM 81, *7r

γaǰar-un eǰen, XBM 109, 3r

γaǰar-un oron, XBM 110, 7r

γaǰar usun, XBM 81, *7v, (et passim)

γarqui-yin oron, XBM 1, 1r; XBM 2, 1r; XBM 4r; XBM 5, 1r; XBM 8, 2v

γasalang ügei čoγ-tu (35 Buddhas), XBM 22, 2v

γasalaqu čaγ bolumui, XBM 106, 5v

γasiγun ǰobalang, XBM 110, 2r

γasiγun manu, XBM 110, 3v

γasiγun-i manu, XBM 110, 4v, 4r

[γ]olom-ta, XBM 99, *4

γoo-a sayin, XBM 107, *3v

γool-un eǰed, XBM 81, 8r

γool tasuraqu, XBM 100, 4r

γučin γurban qad tengri-ner, XBM 49, 9r

γučin γurban tengri-ner, XBM 47, 4r

γučin ǰirγuγan sakiγulsun, XBM 47, 1v

yu[lir]-iyar kümün kiǰi, XBM 107, *7r, *8r, *[kiǰi]*, *6v
yurban čay-yin (čay-un) burqan, XBM 66, 9v
yurban čay-yin geser boyda, XBM 66, 9v
yurban coy-ča, XBM 22, 5v
yurban da dalal, XBM 83, 1v
yurban delekei-yin ulus, XBM 41, 8r
yurban erdeni, XBM 41, 4r; XBM 47, 4r; XBM 66, 9v
yurban erdenis, XBM 110, 3r (et passim)
yurban erdeni-sün sitügen, XBM 47, 1v
yurban erdenis-ün sitügen, XBM 48, 2r; XBM 49, 2r
yurban gray, XBM 76, 2r
yurban mayui ǰayayan, XBM 110, 2v
yurban oroi-yin ebedčin arilyayči otači burqan, XBM 41, 3v
yurban oron-u sansar, XBM 92, 2r
yurban oros, XBM 42, *1v
yurban silüg, XBM 47, 1v
yurban silüg-üd, XBM 48, 2r
yurban üǰüg, XBM 60, 3r

ibegeküi irüger, XBM 110, 9v
ibsan, XBM 83, 1v
idam burqan, XBM 110, 8r
idam [q]ongsim bodisung, XBM 42, *2v
idegen umdayan, XBM 107, *5r, *5v
[i]la[yu]ysan dagini, XBM 110, 3r
ilaǰu degüs-e amogasidi burqan, XBM 110, 6r
ilaǰu tegüs baǰar-bani, XBM 41, 3r
ilaǰu tegüs-e abida burqan, XBM 110, 6r
ilaǰu tegüs-e radn-a sambau-a burqan, 110, 5v
ilaǰu tegüs-e viročan-a burqan, XBM 110, 6r
ilaǰü tegüs nögčigsen burqan-nuyud, XBM 22, 5r
ilaǰu tegüs nögčigsen sigemüni burqan, XBM 42, *2r
ilaǰu tegüs nögčigsen tegünčilen iregsen, XBM 22, 1v; XBM 23, 1v; XBM 25, *1v
ilegü [du]tayu, XBM 65, 2v
ilqayan [-u] ǰasay töröi köndeǰü, XBM 49, 6v
ilqayan-u ǰasay töröi-yi köndeǰü, XBM 47, 3v
ilqayan-u yirtinčü, XBM 47, 4r
imdo, XBM 83, 1v
imdos, XBM 82, *5r
irege üdügüi mingyan burqan (500 Buddhas), XBM 28, 4r
iregsen burqan, XBM 22, 4r
[i]rgen oryon, XBM 107, *4v
irügel-den, XBM 42, *1v
irüger, XBM 22, 4v; XBM 66, 4v; XBM 110, 3r, 8v, 9r

irüger irügemüi, XBM 110, 9v
irüger-ün ejen čigir-badun qayan, XBM 101, *1v
irüge[r]-ün qan čagibard-un qayan, XBM 100, 1v
isganga, XBM 109, 7r
isgangga ungsi, XBM 109, 3v,

ǰayučin kümün, XBM 97, 2r, 3r, 5v, 6v
ǰayun üǰüg ungsi, XBM 109, 3v
ǰayun galab-ud-un včir-tu sang burqan (500 Buddhas), XBM 28, 4r
ǰayuradu, XBM 110, 2v (et passim)
ǰayuradu ayultu qabčayai, XBM 110, 5v (et passim)
ǰayuradu yeke öndör qabčayai, XBM 110, 2v
ǰayuradu-tur töröküi, XBM 110, 4v
ǰayuradu-yi taniqu boltuyai, XBM 110, 7v
ǰalayu bey-e, XBM 63r
ǰalayu boyda yamandaga, XBM 65, 1r
ǰalayu čirayi, XBM 65, 1v
ǰalaman včir ǰida barin, XBM 65, 1v
ǰalyamai čoyolburi, XBM 53, *1v
ǰambala, XBM 67, 1v; XBM 68, 2r, 2v; XBM 69, 2r; XBM 70r-v
ǰamun ejed, XBM 81, 8r
ǰarliy dayun, XBM 76, 2r
[ǰ]arliy-iyar ülü yabu[yči], XBM 65, 3v
ǰarliy-un ündüs-ün, XBM 110, 5v
ǰasay törö, XBM 47, 3v; XBM 49, 6v
ǰasaqu-a inu, XBM 109, 7r
ǰayayan-u erke, XBM 110, 2r
ǰayayan-u qamuy tüidker, XBM 41, 6v
ǰayayan-u sansar, XBM 110, 2r
ǰayayan-u salkin, XBM 110, 2r
ǰayayan-u yeke ulayan salkin, XBM 110, 2v
ǰa[y]aya[t]u kölčin bayuǰu, XBM 105r
ǰebendü ülü dayariydaqu, XBM 47, 2v
ǰeben-dü ülü dayaydaqu, XBM 49, 4v
ǰegün ǰüg-ün yeke erdeni gerel-tü burqan (500 Buddhas), XBM 28, 4v
ǰil čayun yai qarsi, XBM 103, 4v
ǰiryuyan ǰayuradu, XBM 110, 5r, 9r
ǰiryuyan ǰüg-ün ǰiryuyan burqan (500 Buddhas), XBM 28, 4v
ǰiryuyan ǰüil amitan, XBM 58, 3r
ǰiryuyan költü, XBM 46, 3r
ǰiryuyan mayui töröl, XBM 47, 3r
ǰiryuyan orod (nidāna), XBM 107, 4v (et passim)
ǰiryuyan tarni, XBM 48, 3r
ǰiryuyan üǰüg, XBM 47, 2r, XBM 58, 3v

ǰirγuγan üsüg, XBM 110, 8r
ǰirmüsün bolbasu, XBM 47, 3v
ǰirüken aldaraqu, XBM 100, 4r
ǰob (ǰöb) toγola, XBM 98, *4
ǰobalang bolumu, XBM 106, 5v
ǰobalang-i aburayči, XBM 28, 9v
ǰobalang-tu dalai, XBM 29, 3r; *[dal]ai*, XBM 33, 8v; XBM 34, 3r; XBM 39, 8r
ǰoliγ, XBM 107, *7v; XBM 109, 5v
ǰoliγ-luγ-a, XBM 109, 5v
ǰoliγ ǰam-tur γarγ-a, XBM 107, *7v
ǰoliγ-a, XBM 107, *7r
ǰol-un tengri, XBM 66, 7r
ǰongga-ba, XBM 29, 4v
ǰonggaba-yin sasin, XBM 78, 2v
ǰongkaba, XBM 74, 1v (et passim)
ǰoriγtu ǰoriγtu, XBM 66, 11r
ǰovanggaba, XBM 76, 2v (et passim)
ǰovangkaba, XBM 75, 5r (et passim)
ǰöb ǰöb, XBM 66, 3v; XBM 68, 2r
ǰöngga-ba, XBM 41, 2r
ǰud turaqan, XBM 97, 10v
ǰüil ("chapter"), XBM 47, 4v; XBM 49, 9r

keger qalǰan morin kölge-tü, XBM 66, 11v
keger tala, XBM 66, 12r
kegür orosiγulqui, XBM 107, *2v
ke kes-ig, XBM 82, 2v
keb keǰiγ-e, XBM 106, 4v
kei boroγan, XBM 97, 10v
kei möndör, XBM 66, 7v
kei salkin, XBM 54, 2r XBM 66, 7v
keibüng kürtü, XBM 81, *7v
kelelčekü kele-besü, XBM 107, *5v
kelkü ulus, XBM 66, 11v
kereg kilge, XBM 104, *2v; *[kereg]*, XBM 105r
keregür temečel bolqu, XBM 107, *3v
keregür-ün ǰabsar, XBM 109, 3r
keriγ-e, XBM 107, *8r
keriγ-e ni ödön, XBM 107, *8r
kir ügei medegči erketü manǰusiri, XBM 41, 2r; XBM 78, 2v
kiir ügei bügüde-yi medegči erketü manǰusiri, XBM 29, 4r
kkir-eče qayačaγsan badm sambau-a baγsi, XBM 29, 4v
kkir ügegü, XBM 58, 2r
kkir ügei-tü (35 Buddhas), XBM 22, 2r

kiǰayalal ügei kündü ǰibqulang (35 Buddhas), XBM 22, 2v

kilyasun-u činegen ǰamun eǰed, XBM 81, 8r

kilinče üiles, XBM 46, 4r

kilinčesün üyiles, XBM 22, 2r

kilinčetü üiles, XBM 66, 5r

kinal-ḏan-un ǰasaγ, XBM 66, 5r

kinal-tu ǰasaγ, XBM 68, 2v

kirčegei mayu silmusi daruγsan, XBM 29, 4v

kitad utaisang ayulan, XBM 42, *2r

kitad-un utai sang ayulan, XBM 45r,

kitad kegüküd, XBM 83, 3v

kitad-un kegüked, XBM 82, *4v

köbčin yaǰar degereki burqan, XBM 29, 2v; *degere ki*, XBM 30, 3r

köbčin qamuγ moron (mörön, mören), XBM 29, 2v

köbčin qamuγ mör[en], XBM 30, 3r;

kög dayun, XBM 66, 12r

kögeler sara, XBM 97, 2v (et passim); XBM 99, *1r, *1v

köke ayur, XBM 29, 4v

köke oγtarγui, XBM 66, 8r

köke luu, XBM 66, 7v; XBM 100, 2v

kököge sibayun, XBM 100, 2r; XBM 102r

kökemdüge modon, XBM 82, *2v

kökemdüge nabčis, XBM 81, *2v

köl ebüdüg, XBM 66, 10r

köl ügei, XBM 46, 3r

kölčin, XBM 104, *1v; XBM 105r

kölčin bayuǰu, XBM 105r

kömčin yaǰar [de]gereki burqan, XBM 34, 2v

kömčin qamuγ mören, XBM 34, 2v

köndei qulusun, XBM 81, *2v

könggen singgen gilbelgen minaγa, XBM 73, 2v

könǰilei-yin činegen umai, XBM 82, *3v

könög-yi-yin činegen küi XBM 82, *3v

körisütü etügen eke, XBM 66, 8r

kötege sibayun, XBM 100, 2r

kötegö sibayun, XBM 102r

kötel-ün eǰed, XBM 81, 8r

küčir kelegsen, XBM 46, 4r

küisün čigeǰin, XBM 66, 10r

küǰisün ünüd, XBM 54, 2r

küǰis-ün ünüd, XBM 57, *1v

külüg boγda, XBM 66, 10v

kürgen, XBM 98; XBM 99, *4

kür-gen, XBM 99, *1v

kürteküi (nidāna), XBM 107, *3v (et passim)

lay-čas, XBM 107, *7r
laysas belges, XBM 110, 8v
lam-a bančen, XBM 78, 1v
lam-a idam, XBM 110, 5v
lingqu-a čečeg, XBM 47, 2r; XBM 48, 2v; XBM 49, 2v
lingqu-a sečeg, XBM 47, 1v
lingqu-a-sun qayan, XBM 81, 3r
lingqu-a-tača qubilyan, XBM 54, 2v
lingqu-a-yin gerel čenggen ile medegči (35 Buddhas), XBM 22, 2v
lingqu-a-yin erdeni masi darumta-tu (35 Buddhas), XBM 22, 3r
lingqu-a-yin nidü-tü, XBM 41, 6r
logisvari, XBM 61, 6r
luus-un erketü qayan (35 Buddhas), XBM 22, 1v
luu-yin oordo, XBM 29, 3v; XBM 35, 8r
luu-yin ordo, XBM 30, 4r; XBM 34, 3v
luusun qad, XBM 47, 3r; XBM 109, 4v
luusun qad yaǰar-un eǰen-i köndeǰü, XBM 47, 3v–4r

maytayal, XBM 60, 4v
mayui ayul-ača tonilači, XBM 89, 3v
mayui dayalta, XBM 89, 3v
mayui dayisun-tur qariqu boltuyai, XBM 100, 2v (et passim);*dayisundu*, XBM 103,
    4r, 4v
mayui ebedčin-tür odbasu, XBM 47, 3v
mayui ǰayayan, XBM 47, 4r; XBM 49, 8r XBM 62, 1r; XBM 110, 3r
mayui ǰayayan-u erke, XBM 110, 3r, 7v
mayui ǰayayan-u mör, XBM 49, 8r
mayui ǰayayan-a endegüreysen, XBM 110, 8r
mayui ǰegüdeni qariyuluyči, XBM 103, 5r
mayui ǰegüdülegsen, XBM 100, 1v (et passim)
mayui ǰobalang-ača tonilqu, XBM 47, 2v; XBM 48, 3v; XBM 49, 4r
mayui sedkil-ten irgen, XBM 47, 3v
mayui üiles-i tebčiǰü, XBM 110, 4r
ma ha a garuni ga arya avalovgide suvar-a , XBM 62, 1r
manayar erte, XBM 60, 4v
mangyus-un čalma, XBM 106, 4v
mangyus-un čerig, XBM 104, *3v; XBM 106, 5r
manǰusiri, XBM 29, 4v; XBM 41, 2v; *manǰus[ir]i*, XBM 42, *2v 43, *2v; XBM 65, 2r;
    XBM 74, 1v (et passim); XBM 75, 5v (et passim); XBM 76, 2v; *[man]ǰusiri*,
    XBM 78, 2v; XBM 104, *1v
[manǰusir]i bodis[un]g, XBM 65, 3r

manǰusiri-yin qubilyan-u bey-e-tü, XBM 74, 1v; XBM 75, 5v (et passim); XBM 76, 2v;
    XBM 77r

masi berke, XBM 108v

masi ǰiryalang-tu yirtinčü, XBM 47, 4r; XBM 49, 8r

masi sayin, XBM 99, *3

masi teyin büged daruyči čoy-tu (35 Buddhas), XBM 22, 2v

masi sayitur, XBM 66, 2v

mayidari, XBM 44, *2r; XBM 66, 12r

medeküi (nidāna), XBM 107, 4r (et passim)

menekei, XBM 47, 3r

mese-tür ükükü, XBM 107,* 2r

meseyigi saki, XBM 73, 2v

minaya, XBM 73, 2v

minekei, XBM 49, 6v

mingyan ada todqar, XBM 103, 4v

mingyan burqan (500 Buddhas)

mingyan yar-tu mingyan nidü-tü, XBM 47, 2r

mingyan luu, XBM 110, 8r

mingyan tabun ǰayun burqan (500 Buddhas), XBM 28, 4r

minu minu, XBM 73, 4r

mital ügei sedkil-tü, XBM 65, 2v

modon-u namči buri (büri), XBM 34, 3r

molor erdeni metü bey-e-tü geser qayan, XBM 66, 11v

m[on]čay jegügsen, XBM 65, 3v

mongyol ul[u]si eǰelegsen, XBM 66, 11r

morin qonin oroyulqui, XBM 107, *1v

morin urulduqu, XBM 73, 3r

mönggön duyulyatu, XBM 47, 1v; XBM 48, 2r

mönggön quyaytan, XBM 47, 1v

möngke tengri ečige, XBM 82, *1v

möngke busu, XBM 110, 4v

mör udurid, XBM 110, 5v, 6r, 6v

mören usun, XBM 97, 10r

mösön-i eǰ[e]d, XBM 81, 8r

mun [ü]gei, XBM 65, 3r

mungqay (nidāna), XBM 107, *4r (et passim)

mungqay qarangyui balamud, XBM 110, 7v

nayaǰuna, XBM 42, *2r

nayarǰun[a], XBM 43, *2v

nayur-un eǰed, XBM 81, 8r

naiman bodi saduva-nar, XBM 28, 9v

naiman takil, XBM 60, 4r

naiman terigün, XBM 107, *8r

naiman tümen ayaya, XBM 29, 1v; *ayaγ-a*, XBM 30, 1v

naiman tümen dörben mingyan nom-un čoyčas, XBM 41, 4v

namančilaqui ungsi, XBM 109, 3v, 7r

namursun yaras, XBM 109, 3r

narin qura, XBM 29, 2v; XBM 34, 2v *na[rin]* XBM 30, 3r

nasun qutuγ, XBM 46, 5v; XBM 75, 9r

nasun qutuγ boltuγai, XBM 46, 5v

nasun qutuγ nemekü boltuγai, XBM 75, 9r

[na]sun torqaru olǰei [q]utuγ orosiqu [bol]tuγai, XBM 71, 4r

nasu ürgülǰi, XBM 22, 1v

nayan dörben mingyan nom [-un] čoγ-čas, XBM 2, 1v

nayan d[örbe]n mingγ[an] nom-un čoγ-ča, XBM 12r

nayan dörben mingyan nom-un čoyčas, XBM 4r; XBM 5, 1r; *nom[-un] [č]oyčas*, XBM 8, 2r

nayan mingyan čidköd, XBM 100, 4v

nayan tümen dörben mingyan nom-un čoγč[as], XBM 1, 1r

negüdel ne[gü]küi, XBM 107, *2v

negüdel ülü negükü XBM 107, *1v (et passim)

[ne]gükü nu[t]uγ bayuqu [qu]duγ, XBM 81, 8r

negüküi-yin usu[n]-u qutuγ, XBM 66, 12r

nereber ügei, XBM 54, 2r (et passim); XBM 56, 3r (et passim); XBM 57, *1r (et passim)

ner-e orod, XBM 107, 4v (et passim)

ner-e öngge (nidāna), XBM 107, *3v (et passim)

nidüber üǰegči, XBM 41, 2r, 2v; XBM 62, 1r, XBM 78, 2v

nidüber üǰegči erketü, XBM 64

nidün irmeküi, XBM 110, 8v

nidün tataqui, XBM 107, *5v

nidün-ü ebečin, XBM 41, 6v–7r

nidün-ü quričal, XBM 110, 5r

nigen üǰügür-dü sedkil, XBM 110, 4r; 4v

nigülesküi-yin eǰen ariy-a avaloyide suvar-a, XBM 51, 1v

nigülesküi-yin eǰen ary-a avalogi-de süvr-a, XBM 52, 1v

nigülesküi-yin küčün, XBM 110, 7v

nigülesügčiyin sedkil, XBM 47, 3v

niγuča ǰarliγ, XBM 101, *1v

niγuča tarni, XBM 41, 3r

niγučasun eǰen včir-a-bani, XBM 42, *2v

niγ[uča]-yin e[ǰ]en manǰus[i]ri, XBM 65, 2r

niγun köbegün, XBM 100, 3v

nisvanis, XBM 110, 4r, 8v; *nisvsnis*, XBM 22, 5v

nisvanis-un qudqulduγsan, XBM 110, 4r

nisvanisun tabun orosi arilγayči, XBM 41, 3v

noyoyan kö[kemdüge] oγiui-yin aγulan, XBM 81, *2r

noγtoi-gi sakiyad čidöri saki, XBM 73, 3r

nom-i ǰalaǰu iregsen, XBM 110, 3v

nom-t̲ur [ü]lü kičiyegči, XBM 65, 3v

nom-un bey-e, XBM 41, 3r

nom-un činar, XBM 66, 6r–6v

nom-un daγun, XBM 110, 8r

nom-un qan qongsim bodi sa[du]va, XBM 28, 9v

nom-un sakiγulsun, XBM 5, 1v; s[a]kiγ[u]lsun, XBM 4v

nom-un sang burqan (500 Buddhas), XBM 28, 2v

noqai daγaγsan-ača γai bolǰi, XBM 107, *8r

noqai-yin qubaqai toloγai, XBM 107, *7v

noyan kümün, XBM 41, 8r

noyan qatun, XBM 101, *1v

noyaγtai kümün, XBM 49, 6r

noγayan öngge-tü burqan, XBM 110, 7r

nögčigsen doloγan burqan (500 Buddhas), XBM 28, 3v

nököd, XBM 84, 4r; XBM 107, 5r; XBM 110, 2v

nököd ügei, XBM 110, 2v

nökör següder, XBM 46, 2r

nökör ügei, XBM 110, 2v

nutuγ, XBM 66, 12r; XBM 99, *4; nu[t]uγ, XBM 81, 8r

odod-un quyaγ, XBM 66, 7v

odon neretü quyaγ, XBM 73, 2v

odon unan, XBM 100, 4r

oγiui-yin aγulan, XBM 82, *2r

oγoγata irüger, XBM 22, 4v

oγdarm-a talbi, XBM 107, *6v

oγtarγui kiǰaγar-a-luγa sača, XBM 2, 1v; XBM 41, 4r

oγtarγui metü ilγal ügei, XBM 41, 3r

oγtarγui-yin oron, XBM 110, 6v

olan γaǰar-a buu γabu, XBM 106, 5r

omoγ süri sitaraγuluγad qariγuluγči, XBM 66, 7r

on saraγin γai qarsi, XBM 103, 4v

onin-i činegen kötel-ün eǰed, XBM 81, 8r

orčilang nirvan, XBM 75, 1v

orčilang-un dalai-t̲ur tögörigsen, XBM 75, 6r

orčilang-tur orčiqui, XBM 22, 4r

orčilang-tur tögerigsen, XBM 110, 6r

orčilang-tur tögöriküi, tögörigsen, XBM 110, 5v (et passim)

orǰan badm-a sambau-a baγsi, XBM 110, 3v

orǰan-u mergen badm-a sambau-a baγsi, XBM 110, 9v

otočin-u qaγan burqan, XBM 42, *1v

öber-ün busud-un tula, XBM 110, 9r

öber-ün busud-un tusa, XBM 6, 4r
öber-ün ǰil ali bolbasu, XBM 109, 7v
öber-ün kümün, XBM 73, 2v
öber-ün sedkil qoyoson körög bol-qui, XBM 110, 7v
öber-ün sedkil-ün niyur, XBM 110, 7v
ödün üiledügči okin tngri, XBM 109, 7v
ödür söni, XBM 56, 3v
ödür kiged söni, XBM 54, 2r; XBM 57, *2r
öge[s]ün čisun čiburiqui, XBM 47, 4r
ögligeyin eǰen noyan qatun, XBM 101, *1v
öglige-yin eǰen qayan qatun, XBM 100, 1v
ökin, XBM 97, 2v, (et passim); XBM 98, *1 (et passim); XBM 100, 3r
ökin tengri, XBM 66, 9r; XBM 109, 7v
ölǰei qutuy, XBM 71, 4r; XBM 82, *4v; XBM 83, 3v; XBM 85, 4v; *qu[tuy]*, XBM 80,
    *1v;
ölǰei qutuy orosiqu boltuyai, XBM 71, 4r
ölǰei-tü qutuytu, XBM 47, 4v
ölǰei-tü qutuytu boltuyai, XBM 47, 4v
ölǰei ügei, XBM 107, 2r, 2v
ölöng qudqur sibayun, XBM 100, 2v
öngge bey-e, XBM 41, 3r
öngge beyen, XBM 110, 7v
önide ǰobaqu, XBM 107, *1v
ösiyeten dayisun, XBM 68, 2v
ösiyeten dayisud, XBM 66, 5v
ötelküi üküküi (nidāna), XBM 107, 4r
ötög qutuy ungsiǰu ungsiyutai, XBM 46, 1v

qab ǰayasu (ǰiyasu), XBM 47, 3r
qabčal ǰam, XBM 66, 8v
qabt-yai čilayun, XBM 107, *6r
qada büri [burqa]n, XBM 81, 8r
qadqulduyan teyin büged ilayuysan (35 Buddhas), XBM 22, 3r
qadum, XBM 98, *4
qadum ečige eke, XBM 97, 3v (et passim)
qayaly-a ǰasaqui, XBM 107, *3r
qayan kiged tüsimed, XBM 54, 2v; XBM 56, 3v; XBM 57, *2r
qayan qatun, XBM 81, 8v; XBM 100, 1v
qayaraqai sabatan, XBM 66, 4r
qaǰir sibayun, XBM 100, 2r
qakilig sibayun, XBM 100, 2r
qalayun ebedčin, XBM 109, 7r
qalturiqu köl, XBM 66, 8v
qamqay, XBM 81, *2v

qamtu törögsen, XBM 46, 2r

qamuy ada todqar, XBM 63v

qamuy amitan-i tusa-yin tul-a, XBM 15r

qamuy amitan-i tusayin tula, XBM 28, 2r

qamuy amitan-u tusa-yin tula, XBM 12v

qamuy bayatud, XBM 110, 6v

qamuy berke üilš (üiles)-eče tonilaqu, XBM 28, 9v

qamuy burqan-nuyud, XBM 28, 9r

qamuy ed-ün sang, XBM 67, 1v

qamuy kilinčesi namančilamui, XBM 22, 5v

qamuy kilincesi öber[e] öbere namančilamui, XBM 11v

qamuy mayui jayayan-tur odqui, XBM 47, 4r

qamuy mayui jegüdün jedker qariqu boltuyai, XBM 100, 1v

qamuy mayui jegüdün-i jedker-i arilyaqu boltuyai, XBM 101, *1v

qamuy modon-i nabči büri burqan, XBM 29, 3r; *büri büri,* XBM 30, 3r; *[b]üri,*
   XBM 33, 8r; XBM 37r; XBM 39, 8r

qamuy nom-ud-un qutuy, XBM 81, 8v

qamuy orod, XBM 22, 3r

qamuy qan yajar usun, XBM 81, *7v

qamuy ters buruyu sedkil-ten, XBM 66, 4r

qamuy torol (töröl) tutum-tur, XBM 41, 7r

qamuy tüidker, XBM 41, 6v

qamuy üiles, XBM 99, *3

qan kümün, XBM 100, 3v

qan oro sayuqui, XBM 107, *2r

qan yajar, XBM 81, *7v, et passim

qan sümbür tay, XBM 81, 6r

qančuni činegen yool-un ejed, XBM 81, 8r

qanilan yabuysan, XBM 46, 2r

qara čilayun, XBM 107, *6r; XBM 110, 2r–2v

qar-a jirüke-tü, XBM 66, 4r

qara öngge-tü bey-e, XBM 109, 3v

qara öngge-tü yamayan barigsan kümün-eče yai boluysan, XBM 107, *8r

qara negüresün, XBM 81, 3r

qara ragsa čidkör, XBM 100, 1v; *yaysa,* XBM 101, *1v

qara [ra]qui-yin čay-tur, XBM 107, *6r,

qara suqai mod[on], XBM 81, *2v

qarabtur qamqay, XBM 81, *2v

qarangyui-yi arilyayči, XBM 67, 1r

qarangyusi geyigülügči, XBM 41, 3v

qaryui, XBM 109, 3v

qarsi, XBM 86, 1v; XBM 87, 1r; XBM 90, *2r; XBM 95, 3r (et passim); XBM 92, 2v

qas öngge-tü burqan, XBM 110, 6v

qas qada, XBM 66, 8v

qatayu qurča bold, XBM 66, 10r

qatayuǰin [a]ryaysan, XBM 46, 2r

qatan bolad bolyaǰu XBM 73, 3v

qatuytai kümün, XBM 47, 3v

qočorlig tüyidkel ügei, XBM 41, 2v

qočorlig ügei, XBM 72r; *ü[gei]*, XBM 72r

qočorliy ügei, XBM 78, 1v

qoyolai uruyul tataqui, XBM 107, *4r

qoyoson kü ayar, XBM 46, 1v; XBM 48, 2v; XBM 49, 2v; XBM 66, 2r

qoyoson körög, XBM 110, 7v

qoyoson uyuta, XBM 107, *7r

qoličal ügei, XBM 66, 4v, XBM 68, 2r

qomsim bodisug-nar, XBM 60, 3r

qongsim bodi saduva, XBM 28, 9v

qongsim bodasug, bodisug, XBM 41, 8r, 8v

qongsim bodisung, XBM 47, 1v; *[q]ongsim*, XBM 42, *1v; XBM 49, 2r

qonsiim bodisung, XBM 48, 3r

qondan etügen, XBM 81, *7v

qorin nigen qonoy, XBM 41, 6v

qoor ada bolqu, XBM 107, *5r

qoor ada kiküi, XBM 47, 3v

qoor ayul, XBM 107, *3r

qoor kikü, XBM 104, *1v

qoor-a aldaraǰu, XBM 47, 3v

qoor-dan dayisun, XBM 66, 11v

qoor-tu dayisun, XBM 73, 2r

qoor-tu sedkil-den, XBM 66, 4r

qoor-tu sumun, XBM 73, 2r

qormusta, XBM 65, 2r; XBM 66, 9r

qormusta tngri, XBM 65, 2r

qota balyasun ülü bariqu, XBM 107, *2r

qoyar garudi, XBM 66, 8r

qoyar köl, XBM 47, 4r; XBM 49, 8v

qoyar költü, XBM 46, 3r

qoyar luu, XBM 66, 8r

qoyin-a qo[č]orbai, XBM 110, 2r

qoyinača qasi, XBM 110, 5v, 6r, 6v

qoyitu ǰayayan, XBM 110, 8v

qoyitu töröl, XBM 46, 5r

qubčan oldaqu, XBM 107, *4r

qubčasun eskeküi, XBM 107, *2v

qubi sara, XBM 97, 2v (et passim); XBM 99, *1r

qubilyan, XBM 66, 7r, 10r, 10v; XBM 74, 1v; XBM 75, 5v (et passim); XBM 76, 2v; XBM 77r; XBM 81, 3v

quda, XBM 106, 4r

qudal-tu, XBM 107, *2r, *3r

qudal ülü ügüleyü, XBM 28, 9r

qujir sara, XBM 97, 3r (et passim); XBM 99, *1v

qulayan, XBM 47, 3r

qulingčuɣ (qulinčuɣ), XBM 46, 2r

qumak[i]-yin eke burqan, XBM 30, 3r

qumaqi-yin eke burqan, XBM 34, 2v–3r

[quma]qiin eke burqan, XBM 37r

qumaqiyin eke burqan, XBM 29, 2v

qura oroɣuluɣči, XBM 109, 3v

quričaqui (nidāna), XBM 107, *3v

qurim ülü qurimlaqui, XBM 107, *2v

qurdun mori-iyan unuǰu, XBM 73, 2v

quričaqui ügei köbegün (35 Buddhas), XBM 22, 2v

qurča bolad, XBM 73, 2r

qurča bold, XBM 66, 10r

qurui (fire-*dalalɣa*), XBM 82, *1v (et passim); XBM 83, 1v (et passim); XBM 84, 4r

qutu[ɣ] olqu boluyu, XBM 90, *4v

qutuɣ orosiqu boltuɣai, XBM 81, 8v

qutuɣ-tu ayulas-un erketü qayan (35 Buddhas), XBM 22, 3r

qutuɣ-tu boyda dar-a eke, XBM 42, *3r

qutuɣ-tu dalai lama, XBM 78, 2r

qutuɣ-tu erdeni-tü burqan (500 Buddhas), XBM 28, 3v

qutuɣ-tu lingqu-a-yin nidün, XBM 41, 5v

qutuɣ-tu manǰus[ir]i, XBM 42, *2v

qutuɣ mör, XBM 47, 2v

qutuɣ-tu nagaǰuna, XBM 42, *2r; XBM 43, *2v

[qu]tuɣ-tu naɣarǰun[a], XBM 43, *2v

qutuɣ-tu qongsim bodi sadu, XBM 49, 9r

qutuɣ-tu qongsim bodisung, XBM 47, 4v;

qutuɣ-tu yeke nigülesküi, XBM 58, 2r

radn-a sambau-a burqan, XBM 110, 6r

raqu, XBM 107, *6v, *7r, *[ra]qu*, XBM 107, *6r

raqui-yin čaɣ-tu, XBM 107, *6v, *čaɣ-tur*, *7r

rasiyan, XBM 47, 3v; XBM 54, 2v; XBM 80, *2; XBM 81, *2r

rasiyan boluyu, XBM 47, 3v

rasiyan-u qura, XBM 80,*2; XBM 81, *2r

rasiyan-u usun, XBM 54, 2v

sača busu-luɣ-a sačaɣu, XBM 28, 2r

sadaɣ-a buu ög, XBM 107, 2r

sadu edgü, XBM 9, 6v; XBM 30, 5r; XBM 40, 9r; XBM 41, 5v XBM 46, 5v; XBM 47,
    4v; XBM 49, 9r; XBM 73, 4r; XBM 82, *5r; XBM 107, *8v; XBM 110, 9v

sadü öd̲gü, XBM 8

sadu sakituyai, XBM 22, 6r

sadud, XBM 107, *5v

sayad ügei, XBM 41, 9r

sayali jegümü, XBM 106, 5v

sayaral ügei sedkil-d̲ü, XBM 65, 2r

saysabad-un tergegür, XBM 47, 2v; XBM 49, 4r

saysabad-yi sakibasu, XBM 49, 8v

sayuysan yajar usun, XBM 81, 8r

salkin-u oron, XBM 110, 7r

samadi diyan, XBM 54, 2v

samayu mayu sedkil, XBM 66, 3r

samayu mayu simnus, XBM 65, 2v

sanaysan sedkigsen üiles, XBM 66, 6r

sang niyuju talbiysan, XBM 110, 3v

sang-gi-yin ejen, XBM 66, 9v

sangsar-un orčilang, XBM 110, 3v

sangsar-tu yabuqu amitan, XBM 65, 2r–2v

sangsar-tur tögörijü, XBM 110, 2r

sansar-un jayuradu, XBM 110, 8r

sar (šar) üker, XBM 109, 7r

sara (sira) jambala, XBM 67, 1v (et passim)

saran erdeni-tü (35 Buddhas), XBM 22, 2r

saran mandal, XBM 47, 2r; XBM 48, 2v; XBM 49, 2v

saran-u neretü bambai, XBM 73, 2r

sara-yin gerel erdeni-tü (35 Buddhas), XBM 22, 2r

sarayin yai, XBM 100, 4v

sasin nom-i ejelen sakiyči burqan (500 Buddhas), XBM 28, 3r

sayid tüsimed, XBM 100, 3v

sayin čoy-tu (35 Buddhas), XBM 22, 2r

sayin jarliy, XBM 110, 5r

sayin nere, XBM 110, 8v

sayitur nuta, XBM 66, 3r

[sn]aggsba kümün, XBM 100, 2r

šagi-a-muni, XBM 22, 1v

šagi-muni, XBM 41, 2v

šara sibayun, XBM 100, 2r

šari budari, XBM 75, 7r

sečen burqan, XBM 29, 5r

sedkil-i jögeleregüljü, XBM 47, 3r; XBM 49, 6v

sedkil-i-iyer nomoqan boluyu, XBM 49, 4v

sedkil-iyer inu nomoqan boluyu, XBM 47, 2v

sedkilün yoson, XBM 110, 4v

sedkisi ügei yeke sang nigülesküi nidüber üjegči, XBM 78, 2v

sereküi (nidāna), XBM 107, *3v

siddi-ḏü garma, XBM 110, 3v

siddi-tü törögsen geser, XBM 66, 11r

siditü, XBM 46, 4v

sidi ügei, XBM 46, 4v

sigemüni, XBM 42, *2r; XBM 66, 10r, 12r

sigemüni-yin sasin, XBM 66, 10r

sigiy-a-muni, XBM 25, *1v

sikür, XBM 54, 2r; XBM 56 3r; XBM 57, *1v

silege γarγaγsan, XBM 66, 11r

silgüdün ayuqui, XBM 110, 4v, 6v, 7v

silgüdün ayuquiyin ǰayuradu, XBM 110, 7v

siltaγantu qatun, XBM 97, 8v

silüg, XBM 47, 1v; XBM 49, 2r

simnus-un adasi qariγulqui, XBM 65, 2v

simnus-un čerig-üd-i un-i butaratal-a kiduγsan, XBM 65, 2v

simnus-un dayisun daruγs-an, XBM 65, 1v

simnus-un uduriγulsun, XBM 110, 8r

sinaγan-i [čine]gen mösön-i eǰed, XBM 81, 8r

sintaral üǰel ügei, XBM 66, 11r

sir-a čambala, XBM 66, 2r (et passim)

sir-a modon γulir-iyar kümün kiǰi, XBM 107, *7r

sir-a öngge-tü burqan, XBM 110, 7r

sira öngge-tü ed, XBM 107, *6v

sir-a toson, XBM 107, *6r

sir-a zambala, XBM 66, 3v

sirayiγo[l]-un qaγan, XBM 66, 11r

sira ulabir gerel-tü, XBM 73, 1v

sirgisi ügei, XBM 82, 2r

siroi kiged maqabud, XBM 54, 2r; XBM 57, *1v

siroi kiged maqa-bud, XBM 56, 3r

solongγa metü öbere öbere geyigülügči, XBM 41, 3r

solongγon-u oron, XBM 110, 7r

soq[or] kümün [abuγ]san-ača γai boluγsan, XBM 107, *6r-*6v

söni dülii-yin urida, XBM 107, *7v

subud erike, XBM 58, 2v

[su]baradisdi burqan (500 Buddhas), XBM 28, 3v

suburγ-a, XBM 22, 3v; XBM 109, 7r

suburγ-a ǰas-a, XBM 109, 7r

suraγ γarqu, XBM 107, *4r

sudur nom, XBM 47, 4v

suqai modon, XBM 81, *2v

suu čerig-ün geser qayan, XBM 73, 1v

südarasun-u eǰen qormusta tngri, XBM 65, 2r

sükavadi, XBM 42, *1v; XBM 47, 2v; XBM 49, 5r; XBM 52, 1v; XBM 53, *1v;
    XBM 54, 1v

sülder-tü küčütü, XBM 65, 2r

süm-bür ayulani bey-e-tü, XBM 29, 5r

sümbür ayula-yin giskigürleǰü yaruysan burqan (500 Buddhas), XBM 28, 3r

sümbür tay, XBM 81, 6r

sümbür-ün orgil, XBM 65, 2r

sünesün, XBM 82, *4r (et passim); XBM 83, 3v; XBM 84, 4r; XBM 96, 1v

sünesün yabuqui üǰekü, XBM 93v

sür sünesün, XBM 82, *4r (et passim); XBM 83, 3v; XBM 84, 4r

tabun belge bilig, XBM 59v

tabun bey-e-yin čoyčas, XBM 92, 2r

tabun čoyčas, XBM 47, 4r; XBM 49, 8v

tabun ǰabsar ügei, XBM 22, 5v

tabun titimtü, XBM 41, 2v; *titim-tü*, XBM 4v

tabun iǰayur, XBM 41, 3v

tabun<a> iǰayur-tu, XBM 59v

tabun ǰayun čečeg burqan (500 Buddhas), XBM 28, 4r

tabun čidkör kiged ada, XBM 92, 2v

tabun küčün tegüsügsen balyasun, XBM 42, *3r

tabun naiman takil, XBM 60, 4r

tabun-a naiman takil, XBM 60, 4r

tabun orosi arilyayči, XBM 41, 3v

tayalaydaqun čiyulqu, XBM 107, *5r

takil bsang, XBM 66, 6r

takil-un arban yurban modon, XBM 81*2v

takil-yi takibasu, XBM 71, 4r

tala yaǰar, XBM 79, 6v

tamturaqai-yi minu, XBM 82, *2v

tariy-a tariysan, XBM 79, 6v

tariyan, XBM 107, *5v

tarni, XBM 28, 2r, 2v,7r; XBM 41, 6r, 8r; XBM 47, 2r (et passim); XBM 48, 3r, 3v;
    XBM 49, 4r (et passim) XBM 50, 7v; XBM 60, 3v; XBM 90, 4v

tarni-yin usun, XBM 107, *6v, *7r, *7v

tarni-yin usun-iyar bey-e-gini ugiyaǰu, XBM 107, *7r, *-gin[i]*, XBM 107, *7v

tasuraqai-yi minu, XBM 82, *2v

tebčiǰü kesegeǰü, XBM 73, 3v

tegsi delekei yaǰad, XBM 54, 2r; XBM 56, 3r; XBM 57, *1v

tegünčilen iregsen, XBM 22, 1v (et passim); XBM 47, 4r; XBM 49, 9r

tegünčilen iregsed, XBM 1, 1r (et passim); XBM 41, 4r

temür barigsan küm[ü]n-eče yai boluysan, XBM 107, *7r

temür qadayasu, XBM 86, 1v

temür-ün ayulan, XBM 81, *2v

tenggel ügei, XBM 78, 1v

tenggeri yaǰar, XBM 35, 7v

tengri yaǰar, XBM 29, 2v–3r; XBM 30, 3; XBM 39, 8r; XBM 40, 9r

tengri-ner, XBM 66, 8v

tengri-yin noqai, XBM 103, 4r

tengri-yin tengri, XBM 66, 10v

tengsel ügegü, XBM 41, 4r

tengsel ügei, XBM 22, 4v; XBM 41, 4r

[t]ergegür-ün eliy-e, XBM 108v

terigülesi ügei töröl, XBM 22, 4r

ters irutan, XBM 66, 10v

ters ulus-dayan ürgügdekü, XBM 107, *4v

tetürü orčilang, XBM 58, 3r

teyin büged daruyči (35 Buddhas), XBM 22, 3r

tireng, XBM 109, 7v

tngri-ner, XBM 81, 3v; XBM 107, *1v, *2r

tngri-ner-ün qan, XBM 81, 3v

tngri-yin noqai, XBM 100, 4v

todqar-nuyud, XBM 41, 3r

toya ügei, XBM 29, 2v

toyo ügei, XBM 30, 2v; XBM 34, 2v

toyoriyu sibayun, XBM 100, 2r

toyos sibayun, XBM 103, 4r

toliyin činegen nayur-un eǰed, XBM 81, 8r

toloyai-yin eǰed, XBM 81, 8r

toniltuyai törötügei, XBM 46, 4v, 5r

tory-a debüsčü, XBM 106, 4r

toti sibayun, XBM 100, 2r

[tö]bed-ün čidköd, XBM 100, 1v

törögsen ečige eke, XBM 46, 2r

törögülügsen köbegün, XBM 46, 2v

törökü boltuyai, XBM 42, 42, *1v (et passim); XBM 43, *2v (et passim); XBM 44, *1;
     XBM 45; XBM 54, 2v; XBM 56, 3r (et passim); XBM 57, *1r

törökü boluyu, XBM 47, 4r; XBM 49, 9r

töröküi (nidāna), XBM 107, *4r

tunumal čayan gerel, XBM 66, 6v

tus-a, XBM 109, 3v, 7v; XBM 110, 5r, 7v

tus-a bolumui, XBM 109, 7v

tus-a ügei, XBM 110, 5r

tusa-i bütügegči, XBM 66, 11v

tüdel ügei, XBM 66, 6r

tüg tümen, XBM 29, 4r; XBM 30, 5r; XBM 34, 4r; XBM 65, 3v; XBM 82, *2r;
  XBM 83, 3v
tüg tümen adasun čerig-üd, XBM 65, 3v
tüg tümen költi odod, XBM 82, *2r; XBM 83, 2r
tügemel neretü ayulayin ejen burqan (500 Buddhas), XBM 28, 3v
tümen odon neretü quyay, XBM 73, 2r
türgen čakilyan neretü qurdun morin, XBM 73, 2v
türidkel ügei, XBM 81, 8v
tüyidkel ügei, XBM 41, 1v

ubadis, XBM 110, 4v
ubsang, XBM 66, 12r; XBM 81, *2r
ubsang-un ečige [oyta]ryui, XBM 81, *2r
učir ("time"), XBM 41, 6v
uyuli sibayun, XBM 100, 2r
ulabir gerel-tü jarudasu, XBM 73, 1v
ulayan öngge-tü burqan, XBM 110, 7r
ulayan öngge-tü ed, XBM 107, *6v
umai, XBM 82, *3v
umar-a-ţu jüg-ün ariyun gerel-tü burqan (500 Budhas), XBM 28, 5r
ungyaril-du čayan qamqay, XBM 81, *2v
un-i (uni) butaratal-a, XBM 65, 2v
untaqui-ţüri, XBM 110, 4r
uralaqui üiles, XBM 107, *2v
uralaqui üile-si kičiyeysen, XBM 66, 9r
urbal ügei, XBM 66, 2r; XBM 67, 1r
urida ükükü XBM 107, *1v
urtu nasutu tengri, XBM 22, 3v
urtu oyutu tus-a ügei, XBM 110, 5r
uruy, XBM 100, 3v
usun čečeg, XBM 107, *6v
usun tngri (35 Buddhas), XBM 22, 2r
usun tngri-yin tngri (35 Buddhas), XBM 22, 2r
usun-ţu yabuqu amitan, XBM 107, *6r
usun-u oron, XBM 110, 6v–7r
utaisang ayulan, XBM 42, *2r-*2v
utai sang ayulan, XBM 43, 3r; XBM 45
üčüken köbegün, XBM 97, 8v
üčüken üile, XBM 107, *5v
üčüken yabayaqu, XBM 107, *4r
üdesi manayar, XBM 92, 2v
üge bulyalduqu, XBM 73, 3r
üge sonostaqu, XBM 107, *4v
ügen dayun, XBM 107, *3r

ügegü dutaɣu, XBM 66, 3v

ükükü belge, XBM 100, 2v (et passim); XBM 102v; XBM 103, 2v (et passim)

ükügsen lagsan, XBM 107, *4v

ükül učiraqu, XBM 93v

üile kereg, XBM 107, *1v

üiles učirabasu, XBM 47, 3r

üiledküi (nidāna), XBM 107, *4v

üliger, XBM 22, 4r; XBM 110, 9r

ülü bolqu, XBM 91, 3v (et passim); XBM 92, 2v

ülü bütükü, XBM 47, 3r; XBM 49, 5v, 6r

ülü kičiyegči, XBM 65, 3v

ülü negügdekü, XBM 107, *2v

ülü qalda[ɣu], XBM 47, 3v

ülü qaluɣu, XBM 47, 3r; XBM 49, 6v

[ü]lü silgüdün ülü aɣun, XBM 110, 7v

üǰegseger tüsa (tusa)-tu (35 Buddhas), XBM 22, 2r

üǰel (ritual), XBM 108v

ündüsün üge, XBM 110, 5r

üneger tusa kürgegsen, XBM 29, 4v

ünen ünen, XBM 29, 4v

ünesün, XBM 73, 3v; XBM 66, 10r; XBM 107, *8r

ünesün[-iyer] naiman terigün kiǰi, XBM *7v

ünesün tobaraɣ bolɣa, XBM 73, 3v

ünesün butaratala kiduɣči, XBM 66, 10r

ür čaɣiqui, XBM 60, 4v

üre niɣun, XBM 108v

ütegerümtegei maɣu daɣisun-i silmus, XBM 66, 9r

ütele busu üile, XBM 66, 9v

üy-e üy-e, XBM 66, 9r

üɣer usun, XBM 97, 9r

vaiduri erdeni gerel-tü, XBM 41, 3v

vayiduri erdeni oron, XBM 42, *1v

vasudari ökin tngri, XBM 109 3r

včirabani, XBM 43, 3v

včir-a dara, XBM 81, 3v; *včira dara* XBM 82, *1r

včir ǰirüken sayitur daruɣsan (35 Buddhas), XBM 22, 1v

včir-tu kölgen, XBM 84, 4v

včir-du küy-e, XBM 82, *5r

včir-tu sedkil, XBM 60, 4r

viročana burqan, XBM 60, 3v; XBM 110, 6r

yabuqui saɣuqui, XBM 62, 1v

yala bolqu, XBM 107, *2v

yalačin kümün, XBM 107, *4v

yayaramtayai dayun, XBM 65, 1v

yamandaga burqan, XBM 65, 1v (et passim)

yeke adayin [ba]riydaǰu, XBM 110, 2r

yeke buly-a qadqulduyan, XBM 97, 9r

yeke dayisun buly-a, XBM 97, 11r

yeke dayisun-u dotor-a oroǰu, XBM 110, 2r

yeke erdeni-tü burqan (500 Buddhas), XBM 28, 5v

yeke yamsiy, XBM 100, 4v

yeke kölge, XBM 47, 4v, XBM 110, 8r

yeke kölge-ü nom, XBM 110, 8r

yeke köl-gen, XBM 22, 5v

yeke küčü-den, XBM 42, *2v; *küčüten*, XBM 43, 3v

yeke öndör qabčayai, XBM 110, 2v

yeke nigülesügči, XBM 47, 3r (et passim); XBM 49, 8r; XBM 58, 3r; XBM 61, 6r;
    XBM 62, 1r

yeke udqatu tüidteǰü, XBM 110, 4v

yeke uqayan-u tarni, XBM 28, 2r

yeke sara, XBM 98, *4

yeke tergegür, XBM 41, 8r

yeke tüimer, XBM 100, 4v; XBM 103, 4r

yeke ü[č]üken dumda, XBM 110, 9r

yeke-yin yeke degedü tngri-ner-ün qan, XBM 81, 3v

yerü idegen, XBM 57, *2v

yesün küsel, XBM 72v

yesün siǰimi tasu[l]umui, XBM 61, 6r

yirtenčü degere, XBM 97, 10v

yirtinčü-yi orkiǰu XBM 106, 4v

yirtinčü-yin qubčad, XBM 54, 2v; XBM 57, *2v

yirtinčü-yin üile, XBM 110, 5r

yoro-a buu üǰegül, XBM 107, *3v

yoron-u üile irekü, XBM 107, *4r

zambala, XBM 66, 3v

Bibliography

Mongolian Texts

Altan erike by Nata, edited and commented on by Čoyiǰi, Kökeqota 1989

Altan gereliyin xurangyui (4 texts), Institute of Language and Literature of the Mongolian Academy of Sciences, Ulaanbaatar, Nos. 143, 144, 145, 535.

Altan kürdün mingyan kegesütü by Dharma, edited and commented on by Čoyiǰi, Kökeqota 1987

Altan quyay-tu kemekü neretü yeke kölgen sudur, Heissig, "The Mongol Manuscripts and Xylographs", No. 27, p. 174.

Altan quyay-tu-yin sudur, manuscript belonging to the author (Ulaanbaatar).

Altan tobči by Blo-bzaṅ bstan-'dzin= *Erten-ü qad-un ündüsülegsen törö yoson-u ǰokiyal-i tobčilan quriyaysan altan tobči kemekü orosibai, Ėrtnij xaadyn ündėslėsėn tör yosny zoxiolyg tovčlon xuraasan altan tovč xėmėėx oršvoj, The Golden Summary Which Relates Briefly the Deed of Civil Governing Established by Ancient Emperors*, ed. Š. Bira Ulaanbaatar 1990.

Arban yurban čilayu-tu-yin sudur, manuscript belonging to Prof. Walther Heissig.

Arban yurban sang orosiba, manuscript belonging to the author (Ulaanbaatar).

Arban ǰüg-ün eǰen geser qayan-u tuyuǰi orosiba, 2 vols., Kökeqota 1955–1956.

Ariyun oron-du getülküi sudur, Ulaanbaatar Central State Library, No. 294.2 A–816.

Arban xoyor ǰiliyin ǰiran nigen tömür yadasu-tu doqšin ada todxor arilyaqči tarni, Institute of Language and Literature of the Mongolian Academy of Sciences, Ulaanbaatar, No. 171.

Ariyun sang orosiba, Heissig, *Mongolische Handschriften*, No. 88, Ms. Asch 124, pp. 63–4.

Ariyun sang orosiba, Heissig, "The Mongol Manuscripts and Xylographs", No. 24a, pp. 173–4.

Ariyun ubsang, Heissig, *Mongolische Handschriften*, No. 420, Ms. or. fol. 1590–2, pp. 238–9.

Ary-a avalogide šuvari-yin arban nigen niyur-tu kemegdekü, Zungdui, 205v–209v.

Ariy-a balo-yin maytayal, Ulaanbaatar Central State Library, No. 294.2 A–819.

Asarayči neretü-yin teüke by J̌amba, edited and commented on by Bayan-a and Süke, Beijing 1984.

Badma yatang sudur (Pad-ma bka'-yi thaṅ-yig), Heissig, *Mongolische Handschriften*, No. 489, Libr. Mong. 48, p. 264.

Bodhi sadva-yin unal namančilaxui orošiboi, Heissig, *Mongolische Handschriften*, No. 415, Ms. or. fol. 594–3, pp. 236–237.

Bolor erike. Mongolian Chronicle by Rasipungsuy, eds. Antoine Mostaert and Francis Woodman Cleaves, 5 vols., Cambridge, Mass. 1959.

Bolor toli by J̌imbadorǰi, edited and commented on by Liu Jinsuo, Beijing 1984.

Čayan dalalya kemekü sudur orošiboi, copy of the manuscript belonging to the author (Ulaangom Museum, Uvs Ajmag).

Čayan lingqu-a neretü degedü nom yeke kölgen sudur (Saddharma-puṇḍarīka-nāma-mahāyāna-sūtra), Ganǰur, vol. 66, No. 868, pp. 2–466.

Čayan lingqu-a erikes by Demčoyiǰamso, edited and commented on by He. Čoyimbal and S. Dorǰi, Beijing 1996.

Cay-a-yin geser. Gay-a version of Kesar Saga, ed. Rintchen, Ulaanbaatar 1960.

Činayči qariyuluyči mayui tarnis-un kürdün kemekü, Heissig and Bawden, *Catalogue*, Mong. 468, pp. 230–1.

Činggis eǰen boyda-yin sakiyulsun čayan sülde-yin sang takily-a kiged sarqud čai sayalin-u ǰüil-üd ǰang yoson tegüs orosiba, photographic reproduction of the manuscript belonging to the author (Alabur, Üüsin Banner).

Čiqula kereglegči tegüs udq-a šastir, Heissig, *Geschichtsschreibung*, I, pp. 28–83.

Čoytu čindan, *Zungdui*, pp. 434 v–437 v.

Čoytu čindan-u yučin tabun burqad-un emün-e gem unal namančilaqu yoson orošiba, Heissig, *Mongolische Handschriften*, No. 410, Libr. Mong. 18, p. 235.

Čoytu čindan sudur, Heissig, *Blockdrucke*, No. 6, pp. 11–12

Čoy-tu čindan-a orosiba, Heissig, *Mongolische Handschriften*, No. 409, Ms. Asch 125, pp. 234–5.

Čoytu qara yeke ökin tngri činggegči ušnisa neretü tarni, Heissig and Bawden, *Catalogue*, Mong. 468.

Čoytu vačir kimusutai neretü tarni, Heissig and Bawden, *Catalogue*, Mong. 468.

Collection of prayers to Geser qayan, manuscript belonging to the author (without a title page; incipit: *ǰegün nidüben aniysan. ǰegün yar-iyar adquysan*, 2r, Ulaanbaatar).

Eldeb kereg-tü qas qayurčay nere-tü bičig orosiba, Heissig and Bawden, *Catalogue*, Mong. 234, pp. 166–70.

Ene sara ǰimbhala-yin takil in *Tngri-yin qara noqai-yin sudur*, Heissig, *Mongolische Handschriften*, No. 89, Ms. Asch 128-A, p. 65.

Erdeni ǰoo-yin ba öndör gegen-ü namtar orosibai, Ulaanbaatar Central State Library, No. 517–3 E–734.

Erdeni-yin tobči, ed. Erich Haenisch, *Eine Urga-Handschrift des mongolischen Geschichtswerkes von Sečen Sayang (alias Sanang Sečen)*, Berlin 1955.

Erdeni tunumal neretü sudur orosiba, edited and commented on by J̌ürongy-a, Beijing 1984.

Erdeni-yin erike kemekü teüke bolai by Galdan, ed. Ča. Nasunbalǰur, Ulaanbaatar 1960.

Erten-ü mongyol tögen-e-yin bičig, edited and commented on by Duvan Gombojab, Ulayanqada 1992.

Erten-ü mongyol-un qad-un ündüsün-ü yeke sir-a tuyuǰi orosiba, edited and commented on by Ölǰeyitü and Ba. Bayan-a, Beijing 1983.

Ganǰur = *Mongolian Kanǰur*, ed. Lokesh Chandra, 108 vols., New Delhi 1976.

Gegen toli = *Qutuytu gegen toli kemekü sudur orosiba*, Ligeti, "La collection", No. 3598, p. 173.

Geser-ün ubsang neretü sudur, Heissig, *Mongolische Handschriften*, No. 75, Libr. Mong. 130, p. 54.

Fayar usun-i sang, photocopy of the manuscript belonging to the author (Mr. P. Süxbat's private collection, Ulaanbaatar).

Fal-un eke kölgen sudur; Fal-un sudur orosibai, manuscripts belonging to the author (Ulaanbaatar).

Fal-un takiqu-yin ǰang üile bayasqulang-un yarqu-yin oron kemekü orosiba, photocopy of the manuscript belonging to the author (Mr. Süxbat's private collection, Ulaanbaatar).

Fangy-a-yin urusqal by Gombojab, edited and commented on by Čoyiǰi, Kökeqota 1980.

H.5827 (The four prayers of the *jayuradu*, without a title), Aalto "A Catalogue of the Hedin Collection", p. 69.

Incense offering to Yamāntaka (without a title) in *Sammlung von Hymnen und Anrufungen*, Heissig, *Handschriften*, No. 466, Ms. or. quart. 771–5, pp. 253–4.

Itegel orošiboi, Institute of Languages and Literature of the Mongolian Academy of Sciences, Ulaanbaatar, No. 352.

Itegel yabuyulqu-iyan yoson kemegdekü, Heissig and Bawden, *Catalogue*, Mong. 449, pp. 220–1.

Itegel yabuyulqu maytayal, Heissig and Bawden, *Catalogue*, Mong. 392, pp. 220–1.

Itegel yabuyulqu neretü orosiba, Heissig, *Mongolische Handschriften*, No. 441, Libr. Mong. 134, p. 245.

Itegel yabuyulqu-yin surtayal-un tobči quriyangyui, Ulaanbaatar Central State Library, No. 294–2 U–913.

Jayun eki-tü-yin sudur-a, photocopy of the manuscript belonging to the author (Mr. Süxbat's private collection, Ulaanbaatar).

Jegüden-ü qariyulqu nom ene bui, Heissig, *Mongolische Handschriften,* No. 111, Ms. Asch 129, pp. 74–5.

Jegüden-i tayilburi neretü sudur, Ulaanbaatar Central State Library, No. 294.2 J–995.

Jiryuyan jayuradu, Heissig, "The Mongol Manuscripts and Xylographs", No. 39, p. 179.

Kümün-tü mangyus-un birid kölčin qoor kiküi üjekü bičig, Heissig and Bawden, *Catalogue,* Mong. 301, pp. 161–3.

Louvain No. 35 (without a title), Heissig, "The Mongol Manuscript and Xylographs", p. 178.

Mahākāruṇika-nāma-āryāvalokiteśvara-dhāraṇī, Heissig, *Mongolische Handschriften,* No. 202, Ms. or. oct. 422–6, p. 125.

Mañjuśirī jñān-a saduva-yin ner-e-yi üneger ügülegči, Zungdui, 3v–21v

Mani gambu-yin terigün bölög, nögöge bölög orosiba, Heissig, *Mongolische Handschriften,* No. 334, Libr. Mong. 47, p. 192.

Mergen gegen Lobsangdambijalsan-u 'bum jarliy kemegdekü orosiba, edited and commented on by Ralluu and Jiryatai, Beijing 1986.

Mong. 301 (without a title page), Heissig and Bawden, *Catalogue,* pp. 161–3.

Mongyol-un niyuča tobčiyan (The Secret History of the Mongols) = Igor de Rachewiltz, *Index to the Secret History of the Mongols,* Bloomington 1972.

Noyoyan dhar-a eke orosiba, xylography belonging to the author (Ulaanbaatar).

Öljei qutuy-tu tarni, Heissig and Bawden, *Catalogue,* Mong. 468.

Payba lama-yin tuyuji, edited and commented on by Čoyiji, Kökeqota 1991.

Qad-un ündüsün quriyangyui altan tobči, edited and commented on by Liu Jinsuo, Kökeqota 1989.

Qalq-a-yin mongyol-un yajar-a burqan-u šasin delgeregsen-ü daray-a boyda činggis-un iǰayur-tu qalq-a-yin tüsiyetü qan gombodorji-yin-du angq-a öndör gegen-ten qubilaysan-u namtar terigüten-i tarqayalan bičibei, manuscript belonging to the author (Ulaanbaatar).

Qas erdeni-yin qayurčay kemegdekü toy-a bičig orosiba, Heissig, *Mongolische Handschriften,* No. 101, Libr. Mong. 121, p. 70.

Qongsim bodisung-un aldarsiysan dügüregsen neretü sudur, Heissig, *Mongolische Handschriften,* No. 453, Ms. Asch 130, p. 249.

Qutuy-tu degedü altan gerel-tü erketü sudur-nuyud-un qayan neretü yeke kölgen sudur (Ārya-suvarṇa-prabhāsottama-sūtrenda-rāja nāma mahāyāna-sūtra), Ganjur, vol. 13, No. 177, pp. 393–692.

Qutuy-tu degedü altan gerel-tü erketü sudur-nuyud-un qayan yeke kölgen sudur orosi-ba, Heissig and Bawden, *Catalogue,* Mong. 395, pp. 204–6.

Qutuy-tu burqan baysi-yin jokiyaysan yal-un burqan-yi takiqu sudur-nuyud orosiba, Heissig and Bawden, *Catalogue,* Mong. 401, pp. 123–4.

Qutuy-tu lingqu-a-yin nidün neretü tarni, Ganjur, vol. 14, pp. 286–7; vol. 23, pp. 237–8.

Qutuy-du mariči nertü tarni, Heissig and Bawden, *Catalogue,* Mong. 468, pp. 8r–9v.

Qutuy-tu qayurčay-un jokiyal kemegdekü yeke kölgen sudur (Ārya-kāraṇḍa-vyūha-nāma-mahāyāna-sūtra), Ganjur, vol. 66, No. 871, pp. 512–633.

Qutuy-tu tegünčilen iregsen-ü oroi-ača yaruysan čayan sikür-dei busud-da ülü ilaydaqu yeke-de qariyuluyči degedü bütügsen nertü tarni, Heissig and Bawden, *Catalogue,* Mong. 468.

Quva yi yi iui, Hua yi yi yu, edited and commented on by Ü. Manduqu, Qayilar 1998.

Sayin galab-ud-un mingyan burqan ner-e, Heissig, *Mongolische Handschriften,* No. 486, Ms. or. 732, p. 262.

Sayin ügetü erdeni-yin sang neretü šastir by Saǰa Bandida Güngyaǰalsan, translated by Tarniči Toyin Sonomgar-a, edited and commented on by J̌ayunasutu and Sečenčoytu, in coll. with Rinčingava, Kökeqota 1989.

Sira ǰambala-yin ubsang, photographic reproduction of the manuscript belonging to the author (Mr. Damdinsüren's private collection, Dašinčilen Sum, Bulgan Ajmag).

Sonosuyad yekede tonilyayči neretü yeke kölgen sudur, ed. John R. Krueger, Bloomington 1965.

Sukavadi-yin oron-u namtar orosiba by Čaqar Gebsi Blam-a Blo-bzaṅ tshul-khrims, manuscript belonging to the author (Ulaanbaatar).

Ündüsün-i sang, Heissig, *Mongolische Handschriften,* No. 421, Ms. Asch 122, p. 239.

Ya ma ndaga-yin dbang sudur orosiba, Heissig, *Mongolische Handschriften,* No. 366, Libr. Mong. 101, p. 208.

Yamandaga sudur orosiba, Heissig, *Mongolische Handschriften,* No. 374, Libr. Mong. 57, pp. 210–11.

Yeke külgüni altan gereliyin xurangyui, Heissig, *Mongolische Handschriften,* No. 446, Ms. or. quart. 770–2, pp. 246–7.

Zungdui = Qutuy-tu tarnis-un quriyangyui zungdui kemegdekü yeke kölgen sudur orosiba, Peking 1727.

Other Literature

Aalto, Pentti, "Notes on the *Altan gerel*", *Studia Orientalia,* 14, 1950, pp. 3–26.

—, "A Catalogue of the Hedin Collection of Mongolian Literature", *Statens Etnografiska Museum Stockholm,* 1953, pp. 69–108 (reprinted from *Reports From the Scientific Expedition to the North-Western Provinces of China Under the Leadership of Dr. Sven Hedin. The Sino-Swedish Expedition.* Publication 38).

—, "*Ayay-qa tegimlig*", *Studia Altaica,* 5, 1957, pp. 17–22.

Altanyarudi, Buu De, Manduqu, Toytanbayar, Tungyalay, *Mongyolǰin-u šasin surtaqun,* Qayilar 1995.

Altan-orgil, *Köke qota-yin süm-e keyid,* Kökeqota 1982.

Arjasürėn, Č. and X. Njambuu, *Mongol jos zanšlyn ix tajlbar tol',* vol. I, Ulaanbaatar, 1992.

Bang, Willi and Annemarie von Gabain, "Türkische Turfan-Texte", in *Sprachwissenschaftliche Ergebnisse der deutschen Turfan-Forschung. Text-Editionen und Interpretationen* von Albert A. von Le Coq, Friedrich W. K. Müller, Willi Bang, Annemarie von Gabain, Gabdul R. Rachmati, Wilhelm Thomsen. Gesammelte Berliner Akademie-Schriften 1908–1938, mit einer Einleitung von Georg Hazai, Leipzig 1972, vol. 2, pp. 241–68.

Banzarov, Dorji, "The Black Faith or Shamanism Among the Mongols", translated from the Russian by Jan Nattier and John R. Krueger, *Mongolian Studies. Journal of the Mongolian Society,* 7, 1981–2, pp. 53–91.

Bar-do'i thos-grol bźugs-so/The Tibetan Book of the Dead. By the Great Acharya Shri Sing-ha, ed. E. Kalsang, Varanasi 1969

Bawden, C. R., *The Mongol Chronicle Altan tobči,* AF 5, Wiesbaden 1955

—, "Vitality and Death in the Mongolian Epic" in W. Heissig ed., *Fragen der mongolischen Heldendichtung,* Teil 3, AF 91, Wiesbaden 1987, pp. 7–32.

Bawden, Charles R., "The Supernatural Element in Sickness and Death According to Mongol Tradition", I, II, in *Confronting the Supernatural: Mongolian Traditional Ways and Means. Collected Papers,* ed. Bawden, Wiesbaden 1994, pp. 41–110.

—, "Two Mongol Texts Concerning Obo-Worship" in *Confronting the Supernatural,* pp. 1–19.

—, "Calling the Soul: A Mongolian Litany" in *Confronting the Supernatural,* pp. 204–26.

Bergmann, Benjamin, *Nomadische Streifereien unter den Kalmücken in den Jahren 1802 und 1803,* Riga 1804.

Beyer, Stephan, *The Cult of Tārā. Magic and Ritual in Tibet,* Berkeley/Los Angeles 1973.

Bira, Sh., "The Worship of the *Suvarṇaprabhāsottama-sūtra* in Mongolia", *Bulletin. The IAMS News Information on Mongol Studies,* No. 2 (14), No.1 (15), 1994–1995, pp. 3–14.

Bischoff, F. A., "The First Chapter of the Legend of Padmasambhava. A Translation", in Rudolf Kaschewsky, Klaus Sagaster, Michael Weiers eds., *Serta Tibeto-Mongolica. Festschrift für Walther Heissig zum 60. Geburtstag am 5.12. 1973,* Wiesbaden 1973.

Bod-rgya tshig-mdzod chen-mo, Zang han da cidian, ed. Zhang Yisun, 3 vols., Beijing 1985.

Bosson, James E., *A Treasury of Aphoristic Jewels: The Subhāṣitaratnanidhi of Sa skya Paṇḍita in Tibetan and Mongolian,* Bloomington 1969.

Buddyn šašin, sojolyn tajlbar tol', compiled by Š. Čojmaa, L. Tėrbiš, D. Bürnėė, L. Čuluunbaatar, Mongolian State University *(Mongol ulsyn ix surguul'),* Ulaanbaatar 1999.

Bulay, *Mongɣolčud-un ɣal takily-a-yin sudur orosibai,* Kökeqota 1995.

Čeringsodnam, D. *Mongɣol uran ǰokiyal (XIII–XX ǰaɣun-u eki),* Beijing 1989.

Čeringsodnam, D., *Mongɣol-un niɣuča tobčiyan-u orčiɣuly-a tayilburi,* Beijing 1993.

Cerensodnom, Dalantai and Manfred Taube, *Die Mongolica der Berliner Turfansammlung,* Berliner Turfantexte XVI, Berlin 1993.

Cėrėnsodnom, D., *Mongolyn burxany šašny uran zoxiol,* Ulaanbaatar 1997.

Cėvėl, Ya., *Mongol xėlnij tovč tajlbar tol',* Ulaanbaatar 1966.

Chabros, Krystyna, *Beckoning Fortune. A Study of the Mongol dalalɣa,* AF 117, Wiesbaden 1992.

Chavannes, Edouard, "Le cycle turc des douze animaux", *T'oung Pao,* 7, 1906, pp. 51–122.

Chen Manchao, *The Origin of the Chinese Deities,* Beijing 1995.

Chiodo, Elisabetta, "The Book of the Offerings to the Holy Činggis Qaɣan. A Mongolian Ritual Text", *Zentralasiatische Studien,* part I, 22 (1989–1991), pp. 190–220; part II, 23 (1992–1993), pp. 84–144.

—, "History and Legend: The Nine Paladins of Činggis (Yisün Örlüg) According to the Great Prayer *(Yeke öčig)*", *Ural-Altaische Jahrbücher (UAJb),* N.F., 13, 1994, pp. 175–225.

— and Klaus Sagaster, "The Mongolian and Tibetan Manuscripts from Xarbuxyn Balgas: A Preliminary Description", *Zentralasiatische Studien,* 25, 1995, pp. 28–42.

—, "The Worship of the White Standard *(čaɣan tuɣ sülde)* in Üüsin Banner", *Mongolica. An International Annual of Mongol Studies.* A special issue containing the papers of the Sixth International Congress of Mongolists (August 11–15 1992, Ulaanbaatar), Vol. 6 (27), 1995, pp. 618–26.

—, "The J̌arud Mongol Ritual Calling the Soul with the Breast *(köke-ber sünesü daɣudaqu)*", *Zentralasiatische Studien,* 26, 1996, pp. 153–71.

— and Klaus Sagaster, *Saɣang Sečen: Erdeni-yin tobči. A Manuscript from Kentei Ayimaɣ,* edited and commented on by Elisabetta Chiodo, with a study of the Tibetan glosses by Klaus Sagaster, AF 132, Wiesbaden 1996.

—, "A Mongolian Hymn to Qongsim Bodisung on birch bark from Xarbuxyn Balgas (Bulgan Ajmag)", *UAJb,* N.F. 15, 1997 /1998, pp. 223–49.

—, "The Black Standard *(qara sülde)* of Činggis qaɣan in Baruun Xüree", *UAJb,* N. F. 15, 1997/1998, pp. 250–4.

—, "Yamantāka and the *Sülde* of Činggis", *Tractata Tibetica and Mongolica. Festschrift für Klaus Sagaster* (in press).

Čimeddorǰi, "Ligdan qaɣan nögčigsen-ü daɣaraki aru qalq-a-yin mah-a samadi sečen qan", *Öbör mongɣol-un yeke surɣaɣuli erdem sinǰilgen-ü sedkül,* 2, 1998, pp. 16–25.

Clark, Walter Eugene, *Two Lamaistic Pantheons,* New York 1965 (reprinted).

Clarke, Geo. W., (translated by) "The Yü-Li or Precious Records", *Journal of the China Branch of the Royal Asiatic Society*, 23, 1898, pp. 30–400.

Cleaves, Francis Woodman., "The Sino-Mongolian Inscription of 1362 in Memory of Prince Hindu", *Harvard Journal of Asiatic Studies (HJAS)*, 12, 1949, pp. 1–133.

—, "The Sino-Mongolian Inscription of 1335 in Memory of Chan Yin Ying-jui", *HJAS*, 12, 1950, pp. 1–131.

—, "The Sino-Mongolian Inscription of 1346", *HJAS*, 15, 1952, pp. 1–123.

—, "The Mongolian Documents in the Musée de Téhéran", *HJAS*, 16, 1953, pp. 1–107.

—, "*Daruya* and *Derege*", *HJAS*, 16, 1953, pp. 237–59.

—, "The *Bodistw-a Čari-a Awatar-un tayilbur* of 1312 by Čosgi Odsir", *HJAS*, 17, 1954, pp. 1–129.

—, "An Early Mongol Contract from Qara Qoto", *HJAS*, 18, 1955, pp. 1–49.

—, "The *lingǰi* of Aruγ of 1340", *HJAS*, 25, 1964/65, pp. 31–79.

Coloo, Ž., *BNMAU dax' mongol xėlnij nutgijn ajalguuny tol' bičig*, II: *Ojrd ajalguu*, Ulaanbaatar 1988.

Conze, Edward, *Vajracchedikā Prajñāpāramitā. Edited and Translated with Introduction and Glossary*, Roma 1957.

—, *Buddhist Thought in India*, Ann Arbor 1973 (third printing).

Čoyiji, "Tutuγar dalai-blam-a-luγ-a aγulǰaqu-yin uridaki altan qaγan ba töbed-ün burqan-u šasin", *Menggu xue xinwen*, 3, 1996, pp. 10–26.

Damdinsürüng, Č., *Mongγol-un uran ǰokiyal-un degeǰi ǰayun bilig*, 4 vols. Kökeqota, 1982.

Damdinsürüng, Č. and D. Čengdü, *Mongγol-un uran ǰokiyal-un toyimu*, 2 vols., Kökeqota 1982.

Dandekar, R. N., "Yama in the Veda", in D. R. Bhandarkar, K. A. Nilakanta Sastri, B. M. Barua, B. K. Ghosh, P. K. Gode eds., *B. C. Law Volume*, part I, Calcutta 1945.

Das, Sarat Chandra, *Tibetan-English Dictionary*, compact edition, Kyoto 1969 (reprinted from the original edition, Calcutta 1902).

Dobo and Ba. Bayan-a, *Uyiγurǰin mongγol üsüg-ün durasqaltu bičig-üd*, Beijing 1983.

Doerfer, Gerhard, *Türkische und mongolische Elemente im Neupersischen*, Vol. 1: *Mongolische Elemente im Neupersischen*, Wiesbaden 1963; Vol. 2: *Türkische Elemente im Neupersischen*, Wiesbaden 1965; Vol 3: *Türkische Elemente im Neupersischen*, Wiesbaden 1967.

Dorongγ-a and Na. Asaraltu, *Paǰai geser-ün tuγuǰi*, 2 vols, Beijing 1989.

Douglas, Nik, *Tibetan Tantric Charms and Amulets*, New York 1970 (with 232 plates).

Drevnetjurkskij slovar', Leningrad 1969.

Dumas, Dominique, *Aspekte und Wandlungen der Verehrung des Herdfeuers bei den Mongolen*, doctoral dissertation, University of Bonn 1987.

Duyvendak, J. J. L., "A Chinese Divina Commedia", *T'oung Pao*, 41, 1952, pp. 255–316.

Eimer, Helmut and Pema Tsering, "*T'e'u raṅ mdos ma*", in Rudolf Kaschewsky, Klaus Sagaster, Michael Weiers eds., *Serta Tibeto-Mongolica. Festschrift für Walther Heissig zum 60. Geburtstag am 5. 12. 1973*, Wiesbaden 1973, pp. 47–96.

—, "*Sun zlog*. Abwenden von Störungen", in Klaus Sagaster and Michael Weiers eds., *Documenta Barbarorum. Festschrift für Walther Heissig zum 70. Geburtstag*, Veröffentlichungen der Societas Uralo-Altaica, Band 18, Wiesbaden 1983, pp. 55–80.

Ekvall, Robert B., "Significance of Thirteen as a Symbolic Number in Tibetan and Mongolian Cultures", *Journal of the American Oriental Society*, 79, 1959, pp. 188–92.

—, *Religious Observances in Tibet. Patterns and Function*, Chicago/London 1964

Erdemtü, Mingγad, "Mongγol uran ǰokiyal-du tusqaγdaγsan ǰegüdü ǰöng", *Öbör Mongγol-un baγsi yeke surγaγuli-yin erdem sinǰilegen-ü sedkül*, 2, 1996, pp. 64–77.

Erkimbayar, "Mongγol baγatur-un tuuli-daki ǰegüdü-yi sinǰileкü ni", *Öbör mongγol-un yeke surγaγuli*, 1, 1995, pp. 114–18.

Essen, Gerd-Wolfgang and Tsering Tashi Thingo, *Die Götter des Himalaya. Buddhistische Kunst Tibets. Die Sammlung Gerd-Wolfgang Essen*. Tafelband, mit einem Geleitwort von S.H. dem Dalai Lama und einer Einführung von Roger Goepper, Photographie von Hans Meyer-Veden, München 1989.

Evans-Wentz, W. Y., *The Tibetan Book of the Death*, London/Oxford/NewYork 1968 (reprinted).

Even, Marie-Dominique, *Chants de chamanes mongols, Études mongoles et sibériennes*, 19–20, 1988–1989.

Farquhar, D. M., "A Description of the Mongolian Manuscripts and Xylographs in Washington", *Central Asian Journal*, 1, 1955, pp. 175–91.

Franke, H., *Mittelmongolische Kalenderfragmente aus Turfan*. Sitzungsberichte der Bayerischen Akademie der Wissenschaften, Philosophisch-Historische Klasse, München 1964.

Fremantle, Francesca and Chögyam Trungpa, *The Tibetan Book of the Dead. The Great Liberation Through Hearing in the Bardo by Guru Rinpoche according to Karma Lingpa*. A new translation from the Tibetan with commentary, Berkeley and London 1975.

Gabain, Annemarie von, *Alttürkische Grammatik*, 3rd edition, Wiesbaden 1974.

Gockel, Eberhard, *Kuan-shi-yin*, Bonn 1992.

Goodrich, Anne Swann, *Chinese Hell: The Peking Temple of the Eighteen Hells and Chinese Conception of Hell*, St. Augustin 1981.

Grupper, Samuel N., review of *Die Weiße Geschichte. Eine mongolische Quelle zur Lehre von den Beiden Ordnungen Religion und Staat in Tibet und der Mongolei* by Klaus Sagaster, *Mongolian Studies. Journal of the Mongolia Society*, 7, 1981–2, pp. 127–33.

gZuṅ-'dus: Byin-brlabs dṅos-grub bkra-śis char-'bebs-pa'i / bstan-'gro'i phan-bde'i dga'-tshal rgyas-pa'i phyir / ṅo-mtshar 'dzam-gliṅ sa-steṅ dkon-pa'i mchog / gzuṅs-mdo brgya daṅ drug-bcu rtsa-bdun bźugs-so (Kangxi period 1662–1722, without an exact date).

Γongγor, Da., *Qalq-a tobčiyan*, 2 vols., Beijing 1992.

Haenisch, Erich, *Sinomongolische Glossare*, I, *Das Hua-i-ih-yü*, Abhandlungen der Deutschen Akademie der Wissenschaften zu Berlin. Klasse für Sprachen, Literatur und Kunst, Berlin 1957.

—, *Wörterbuch zu Mangḫol un niuca tobca'an (Yüan-ch'ao pi-shi)*, Wiesbaden 1962.

Harva, Uno, *Die religiösen Vorstellungen der altaischen Völker*, Porvoo/Helsinki 1938.

Heissig, Walther, *Der Pekinger lamaistischen Blockdrucke in mongolischer Spache. Materialen zur mongolischen Literaturgeschichte*, AF 2, Wiesbaden 1954.

—, "Zur geistigen Leistung der neubekehrten Mongolen des späten 16. und frühen 17. Jahrhunderts", *Ural-Altaische Jahrbücher*, 26, 1954, pp. 101–16.

—, "The Mongol Manuscripts and Xylographs of the Belgian Scheut Mission", *Central Asiatic Journal*, 3, 1957, pp. 161–89.

—, *Die Familien- und Kirchengeschichtsschreibung der Mongolen*, I, *16.–18. Jahrhundert*, AF 5, Wiesbaden 1959.

—, in coll. with Klaus Sagaster, *Mongolische Handschriften, Blockdrucke, Landkarten*, Wiesbaden 1961.

—, "Eine kleine mongolische Klosterbibliothek aus Tsakhar", *Jahrbuch des Bernischen Historischen Museums in Bern*, 41/41, 1961/1962, pp. 557–90.

—, "Ein mongolisches Handbuch für die Herstellung von Schutzamuletten", *Tribus*, 11, November 1962, pp. 69–83.

—, *Beiträge zur Übersetzungsgeschichte des mongolischen buddhistischen Kanons*, Abhandlungen der Akademie der Wissenschaften in Göttingen, Philologisch-historische Klasse, 3. Folge, 50, Göttingen 1962.

—, *Mongolische volkreligiöse und folkloristische Texte aus europäische Bibliotheken mit einer Einleitung und Glossar herausgegeben*, Wiesbaden 1966.

—, *Die mongolische Steininschrift und Manuskriptfragmente aus Olon süme in der Inneren Mongolei*, Abhandlungen der Akademie der Wissenschaften in Göttingen, Philologisch-historische Klasse, 3. Folge, 63, Göttingen 1966.

—, *Die Religionen der Mongolei*, in Giuseppe Tucci and Walther Heissig, *Die Religionen Tibets und der Mongolei*, Stuttgart 1970, pp. 293–428.

— and C. R. Bawden, *Catalogue of Mongol Books, Manuscripts and Xylographs*, Copenhagen 1971.

—, *Geschichte der mongolischen Literatur*, 2 vols., Wiesbaden 1972.

—, *Die mongolischen Handschriften-Reste aus Olon süme Innere Mongolei (16.–17. Jhdt.)*, AF 46, Wiesbaden 1976.

—, "Zwei mutmaßlich mongolische Yüan-Übersetzungen und ihr Nachdruck von 1431", *Zentralasiatische Studien (ZAS)*, 10, 1976, pp. 8–115.

—, "Geser Khan-Rauchopfer als Datierungshilfen des mongolischen Geser Khan Epos", *ZAS*, 12, 1978, pp. 89–135.

—, *Geser-Studien. Untersuchungen zu den Erzählstoffen in den "neuen" Kapiteln des mongolischen Geser-Zyklus*, Abhandlungen der Rheinisch-Westfälischen Akademie der Wissenschaften, Band 69, Opladen 1983.

—, "Schamanen und Geisterbeschwörer im Küriye-Banner", in Walther Heissig and Hans-Joachim Klimkeit eds., *Schamanen und Geisterbeschwörer in der Östlichen Mongolei. Gesammelte Aufsätze*, vol. 24, Wiesbaden 1992, pp. 1–48.

—, "Invocation of a Female Shaman", in *Schamanen und Geisterbeschwörer*, pp. 51–60.

—, "A Mongolian Source to Lamaist Suppression of Shamanism", in *Schamanen und Geisterbeschwörer*, pp. 91–135.

—, "Banishing of Illness into Effigies in Mongolia", in *Schamanen und Geisterbeschwörer*, pp. 157–67.

—, "From Verse Epic to Prosimetrum in Recent Mongolian Oral Literature", in Joseph Harris and Karl Reichl eds., *Prosimetrum. Crosscultural Perspective on Narrative in Prose and Verse*, Cambridge 1997.

Higuchi, Koichi, "Mongolian Versions of the *Saddharmapuṇḍarīka* from the Linguistic and Philological Viewpoint", *Zentralasiatische Studien*, 26, 1996, pp. 7–21.

Hoffmann, Helmut, *Quellen zur Geschichte der tibetischen Bon-Religion*. Akademie der Wissenschaften und der Literatur, Wiesbaden 1950.

Huth, Georg, *Die Inschriften von Tsaghan Baišiṅ. Tibetisch-mongolischer Text mit einer Übersetzung sowie sprachlichen und historischen Erläuterungen*, Leipzig 1894.

Imaeda, Yoshiro, "Note préliminaire sur la formule *oṃ maṇi padme hūṃ* parmi les manuscrits tibétains de Touen-houang", in M. Soymié ed., *Contributions aux études sur Touen-houang*, Gèneve-Paris 1979, pp. 71–6.

Jagchid, Sechin, "Buddhism in Mongolia After the Collapse of the Yüan Dynasty", *The Mongolian Society Bulletin*, 10, No. 1, Spring 1971, pp. 11–47. Reprinted in Sechen Jagchid, *Essays in Mongolian Studies*, Provo, Utah 1988, pp. 121–6.

Kara, G., "L'inscription mongole d'Aruγ, prince de Yun-nan (1340)", *Acta Orientalia Academiae Scientiarum Hungaricae (AOH)*, 17, 1964, 145–73.

—, "Old Mongolian Verses Without Alliteration", in *Annales Universitatis Scientiarum Budapestinensis de Rolando Eötvös Nominatae*, Budapest 1972, pp. 161–8.

— D., *Knigi mongol'skix kočevnikov (sem' vekov mongol'skoj pis'mennosti)*, Moskva 1972.

—, "Une version mongole du *Maṇi bka'-'bum*", *AOH*, 27, 1973, pp. 19–41.

— and Peter Zieme, *Fragmente tantristischer Werke in uigurischer Übersetzung*, Berlin 1976.

—, "L'ancien ouigour dans le lexique mongol", *Journal Asiatique*, 169, 1981, pp. 317–23.

—, "Zu den mittelmongolischen Kalenderausdrücken", *Altorientalische Forschungen*, 11, 1984, pp. 247–352.

Kaschewsky, Rudolf, *Das Leben des lamaistischen Heiligen Tsongkhapa Blo-bzaṅ-grags-pa (1357–1419). Dargestellt und erläutert anhand seiner Vita 'Quellort allen Glückes'*, AF 32, Wiesbaden 1971.

Klaus, Christa, *Der aus dem Lotos Entstandene. Ein Beitrag zur Ikonographie und Ikonologie des Padmasambhava nach dem Rin chen gter mdzod*, AF 85, Wiesbaden 1982.

Kotwicz, Wladyslaw, *Formules initiales des documents mongols aux XIIIe et XIVe ss.*, Rocznik Orientalistyczny, 10 (131–157), 1934, pp. 131–57.

Kowalewski, Joseph, Étienne, *Dictionnaire mongol-russe français*, 3 vols., Kasan 1844, 1846, 1849.

Kullmann, Rita and D. Tserenpil, *Mongol xèlzüj, Mongolian Grammar,* Hongkong 1996.

Kürelbayatur and Urančimeg, *Qorčin-u ǰang ayali,* Qayilar 1988.

Laufer, Berthold, "Bird Divination Among the Tibetans (notes on document Pelliot No. 3530, with a study of Tibetan Phonology of ninth century)", *T'oung Pao*, 5, 1914, pp. 1–110.

Lessing, Ferdinand D., *Yung-ho-kung. An Iconography of the Lamaist Cathedral in Peking. With Notes on Lamaist Mythology and Cult,* Sino-Swedish Expedition: Publication 18, Stockholm 1942.

—, "Calling the Soul: A Lamaist Ritual", in Lou Tsu-k'uang ed., *Ritual and Symbol. Collected Essays on Lamaism and Chinese Symbolism by Ferdinand D. Lessing,* Taipei 1951, pp. 31–43.

—, "The Topographical Identification of Peking with Yamāntaka", in Lou Tsu-k'uang ed., *Ritual and Symbol,* pp. 89–90.

—, (general editor), compiled by Mattai Haltod, John Gombojab Hangin, Serge Kassatkin and Ferdinand D. Lessing, *Mongolian-English Dictionary,* Bloomington, Indiana 1995 (third reprinting with minor type-correction).

Ligeti, Louis, "La collection mongole Schilling von Canstadt à la Bibliotèque de l'Institut", *T'oung Pao*, 27, 1930, pp. 119–78.

—, *Catalogue du Kanǰur mongol imprimé,* Budapest 1942–44.

—, "Deux tablettes de T'ai-tsong des Ts'ing", *Acta Orientalia Academiae Scientiarum Hungaricae (AOH),* 8, 1958, pp. 201–39.

—, "Un vocabulaire mongol d'Istanboul", *AOH,* 14, 1962, pp. 3–99.

—, "Les fragments du *Subhāṣitaratnanidhi* mongol en écriture 'phags-pa. Mongol préclassique et moyen mongol", *AOH,* 17, 1964, pp. 239–92.

—, "A propos de quelques textes préclassiques", *AOH,* 23, 1970, pp. 251–84.

—, *Monuments préclassiques, 1, XIIIe et XIVe siècles,* Monumenta Linguae Mongolicae Collecta II, Budapest 1972.

—, "Le sacrifice offert aux ancêtres dans l'*Histoire secrète*", *AOH,* 27, 1973, pp. 145–61.

Lobsangčoyidan, *Mongɣol-un ǰang ayali-yin üilebüri,* Kökeqota 1981.

Lőrincz, László, *Molon Toyin's Journey into Hell. Altan Gerel's Translation,* 2 vols. (vol. 1: introduction and transcription; vol. 2: facsimile), Monumenta Linguae Mongolicae Collecta VIII, Budapest 1982.

Mcdonald, Ariane W., "Une lecture des Pelliot tibétain 1286, 1287, 1038, 1047 et 1290", in Mcdonald ed., *Études tibétaines dédiées à la mémoire de Marcelle Lalou,* Paris 1971, pp. 190–321.

— and Yoshiro Imaeda, *Choix de documents tibétaines conservés à la Bibliothèque Nationale complété par quelques manuscrits de l'India Office et du British Museum,* I, préface de R. A. Stein, introduction par Marie-Rose Séguy, Paris 1978.

Mahāvyutpatti = Jumiko Ishihama and Yoichi Fukuda eds., *A New Critical Edition of the Mahāvyutpatti. Sanskrit-Tibetan-Mongolian Dictionary of Buddhist Terminology,* Materials for Tibetan-Mongolian Dictionaries, vol.1, The Tokyo Bunko, (Tokyo) 1989.

Majdar, D., *Mongolyn arxitektur ba xot bajguulalt,* Ulaanbaatar 1972.

Maṇi bka'-'bum glegs-bam daṅ-po thugs-rje chen-po saṅs-rgyal stoṅ-rtsa'i lo-rgyus chae-mo bźugs, Dha-sa/Dharamsala: Bod-gźuṅ śes-rig par-khaṅ/Tibetan Cultural Printing Press 1984.

Mėnd-Oojoo, Gombožavyn, *Bilgijn mėlmij nėėgč*, Ulaanbaatar 1997.

Mongγol kitad toli, Meng han cidian, compiled by the Research Institute of Mongolian Language of the Inner Mongolia University *(Öbör mongγol-un yeke surγaγuli-yin mongγol kele bičig sudulqu tasuγ)*, Kökeqota 1977.

Mongγol üges-ün iǰaγur-un toli, compiled by Sečenčoγtu and Rinčingava, Kökeqota 1988.

Monier-Williams, Monier, *Sanskrit-English Dictionary*, Delhi 1970 (reprint).

Moses, Larry William, *The Political Role of Mongol Buddhism*, Bloomington, Indiana 1977.

Mostaert, Antoine, "Les Erkut, descendants des chrétiens médiévaux, chez les Mongols Ordos" = *Ordosica* in Bulletin No. 9 of the Catholic University of Peking, 1934, pp. 1–20.

—, *Dictionnaire ordos*, 3 vols., Peking 1941–1944.

—, "Sur quelques passages de l'*Histoire secrète des Mongols*", *Harvard Journal of Asiatic Studies*, 13, 1950, pp. 285–361.

—, "Sur le cult de Sayang sečen et de son bisaïeul Qutuγtai sečen chez les Ordos", *HJAS*, 20, 1957, pp. 534–66.

—, "Introduction" = *Erdeni-yin tobči. A Mongolian Chronicle by Saγang Sečen*, part I, with a critical introduction by Reverend Antoine Mostaert and editor's foreword by Francis W. Cleaves, Cambridge, Mass. 1957, pp. 1–77.

—, "A propos d'une prière au feu", in Nicholas Poppe ed., *American Studies in Altaic Linguistics*, 13, Bloomington/The Hague 1962, pp. 191–223.

— and Francis W. Cleaves, *Les Lettres de 1289 et 1305 des ilkhan Arγun et Öljeitü à Philippe le Bel*, Cambridge, Mass. 1962.

—, *Manual of Mongolian Astrology and Divination*, with an editor's foreword by Francis Woodman Cleaves, Cambridge, Mass. 1969.

— and Igor de Rachewiltz, *Le matériel mongol du Houa i i iu de Houng-ou (1389)*, part II, commentaries, Bruxelles 1995.

Muniev, B. D., *Kalmycko-russkij slovar'*, Moskva 1977.

Munkuyev, N. Ts., "Two Mongolian Printed Fragments From Khara-Khoto" in Louis Ligeti ed., *Mongolian Studies*, Budapest 1970, pp. 341–57.

Murayama, S., "Zwei mongolische Manuskripte aus Ost-Turkestan", *Central Asiatic Journal*, 4, 1958/59, pp. 279–88.

Namǰildorǰi, *Ordos-un ǰang üile-yin tobči*, Qayilar 1992.

Naranbatu, Ü., J̌alsan, Pe. Rasinim-a, Oyunbatu, *Mongγol buddha-yin soyol*, Kökeqota 1997.

Navaan, D., *Övgön Dėndėvijn durdatgal*, Ulaanbaatar 1995.

Nebesky-Wojkowitz, René de, *Oracles and Demons of Tibet. The Cult of the Iconography of the Tibetan Protective Deities*, Graz/Austria 1975 (reprint).

Nima, "Böge mörgöl-ün tuqai kedün asaγudal" in *Γabiy-a ǰidkül durasqal. Dedicated to Doctor Professor Walther Heissig's 80th Birthday*, Qayilar 1993, pp. 266–87.

Olschak, Blanche Christine in coll. with Thupten Wangyal, *Mystik und Kult Alttibets*, Bern/Stuttgart 1972.

Ordos-un tayily-a takily-a irügel maytaγal, Kökeqota 1991.

Osamu, Inoue, "Harubohin Barugasu shutsudo no mongoru-go. Chibetto-go juhi shahonjoron", translation of "The Mongolian and Tibetan Manuscripts on Birch Bark from Xarbuxyn Balgas: A Preliminary Description" by Elisabetta Chiodo and Klaus Sagaster, *Nihon mongoru-gakkai kiyō, Bulletin of the Japan Association for Mongol Studies*, 27, 1966, pp. 105–22.

Pallas, P. S., *Sammlungen historischer Nachrichten über die Mongolischen Völkerschaften*, 2 vols., St. Petersburg 1776/1801.

Öljei, Ma. Sa., *Mongγol töbed 'geser'-ün qarilčaγ-a*, Beijing 1991.

'*Phags-pa Phuṅ-po gsum-pa źes-bya-ba theg-pa chen-po'i mdo = gZuṅ-'dus*, pp. 272v:5, 274v:7.

'*Phags-pa Pad-ma'i spyan źes-bya-ba'i gzuṅs, bKa'-'gyur* = Ui et al. eds., Vol. 11, No. 491, p. 98/4/ 7–8.

Pelliot, Paul, *Les Mongols et la Papauté*, chapitre II; I: Le nestorien Siméon Rabban-Ata; II: Ascelin, extrait de la *Revue de L'Orient chrétien*, 3ᵉ série, T. IV (XXIV), Nos. 3 et 4, 1924, pp. 225–335, (here pp. 29–139), Paris 1924.

—, "Notes sur le 'Turkestan' de M. W. Barthold", *T'oung Pao*, 27, 1930, pp. 12–56.

Pėrlėė, Xödöögijn, *Mongol ard ulsyn ėrt dundad üeijn xot suuriny tovčoon*, Ulaanbaatar 1964.

—, "*Xalxyn šinė oldson caaz-ėrxėmžijn dursgalt bičig*", *Monumenta Historica*, Tomus 6, Fasc. 1, 1974, pp. 5–139.

—, "*XVII zuuny ėxėn möčlögijn mongol jaruu najrgijn üjsėnd bičsėn xojor züjl*", *Studia Mongolica*, Tomus 3 (11), Fasc. 1–25, 1976, pp. 127–51.

—, "*Kidančuudyn modon ongodyn tuxaj*", *Studia Mongolica*, Tomus 3 (11), Fasc. 1–25, 1976, pp. 154–5.

Petech, Luciano, "Tibet", *Handbuch der Orientalistik*, Erste Abteilung Der Nahe und der Mittlere Osten, Fünfter Band Altaistik, Fünfter Abschnitt Geschichte Mittelasiens, ed. B. Spuler, Leiden/Köln 1966, pp. 311–71.

Pjotrowskij, Michail ed., *Die schwarze Stadt an der Seidenstrasse. Buddhistische Kunst aus Khara Khoto (10.–13. Jahrhundert)*, Museum für Indische Kunst, Staatliche Museen zu Berlin, Preußischer Kulturbesitz 16. April bis 3.Juli 1994, Mailand 1993.

Poppe, N., "Zum Feuerkultus bei den Mongolen", *Asia Major*, 2, 1925, pp. 130–45.

Poppe, N., "Geserica. Untersuchung der sprachlichen Eigentümlichkeiten der mongolischen Version der Geserkhan", *Asia Major*, 3, 1926, pp. 1–32.

Poppe, N. N., "Opisanie mongol'skix šamanskix rukopisej Instituta vostokovedenija", *Zapiski Instituta vostokovedenija Akademii nauk SSSR*, Vol. I, Leningrad 1932, pp. 151–200.

—, *Mongol'skij slovar' Mukaddimat al-Adab*, Moskva/Leningrad 1938.

—, "Zolotoordynskaja rukopis' na bereste", *Sovetskoe vostokovedenie*, 2, 1941, pp. 81–136.

Poppe, N. "The Groups **uya* and **üge* in Mongol Languages", *Studia Orientalia*, 14, 1950, pp. 3–15.

Poppe, Nikolaus, *Khalka-mongolische Grammatik, mit Bibliographie, Sprachproben und Glossar*, Wiesbaden 1951.

Poppe, Nicholas, *Grammar of Written Mongolian*, Wiesbaden 1974 (third printing).

—, *Introduction to Mongolian Comparative Studies*, Helsinki 1955.

—, "Eine mongolisches Fassung der Alexandersage", *Zeitschrift der Deutschen Morgenländischen Gesellschaft*, 107, 1957, pp. 105–29.

—, "On Some Mongolian Manuscript Fragments in the Library of the India Office", *Central Asiatic Journal (CAJ)*, 5, 1959/60, pp. 81–96.

—, "Ein mongolisches Gedicht aus den Turfan-Funden", *CAJ*, 5, 1959/60, pp. 257–94.

—, "Antworten auf Professor Fr. Wellers Fragen", *CAJ*, 7, 1962, pp. 42–59.

—, *The Twelve Deeds of Buddha. A Mongolian Version of the Lalitavistara*, Mongolian Text, Notes, and English Translation, AF 23, Wiesbaden 1967.

—, *The Diamond Sutra. Three Mongolian Versions of the Vajracchedikā Prajñāpāramitā, Texts, Translations, Notes, and Glossaries*, AF 35, Wiesbaden 1971.

Poucha, Pavel, "Das tibetische Totenbuch im Rahmen der eschatologischen Literatur. (Ein Beitrag zu seiner Erklärung)", *Archiv Orientální. Journal of the Czechoslovak Oriental Institute*, Prague, 20, 1–2, 1952, pp. 136–62.

Pozdneyev, Aleksei M., *Religion and Ritual in Society: Lamaist Buddhism in Late 19th-Century Mongolia,* translated from the Russian by Alo Raun and Linda Raun, ed. John R. Krueger, Bloomington, Indiana 1978.

Qaserdeni, Danzan, Bürinbatu, Γarudi, J̌alsan, N. Batuǰiriγal, Engkebayatur, *Arǰai ayui-yin uyiγurǰin mongγol bičigesü-yin sudulul,* Shengyang 1997.

Qorin nigetü tayilburi toli, compiled by the Research Institute of Language, Literature and History of Inner Mongolia *(Öbör mongγol-un mongγol kele udq-a ǰokiyal teüke sudulqu yaǰar),* Zhangjiakou 1979.

Qurča, N., "Yekes lamanar činggis-un tayily-a-yi šasin-daγan abču gesen ni", *Öbör mongγol-un neyigem-ün sinǰilekü uqaγan,* 4, 1997, pp. 31–43.

Qurčabaγatur, Solongγod L., *Qadagin arban γurban atay-a tngri-yin tayily-a,* Qayilar 1987.

Rachewiltz, Igor de, "The Preclassical Mongolian Version of the Hsiao-ching", *Zentralasiatische Studien,* 16, 1982, pp. 7–109.

—, "The Third Chapter of Chos-kyi 'od-zers' Translation of the *Bodhicaryāvatāra*: A Tentative Reconstruction", in G. Gnoli and L. Lanciotti eds., *Orientalia Iosephi Tucci Memoriae Dicata,* Roma 1988.

Rachmati, G. R., "Türkische Turfan-Texte VII", mit sinologischen Anmerkungen von Dr. W. Eberhard, *Opuscula III,* 2, Leipzig 1972, pp. 290–411.

Ramstedt, G. J., *Kalmückisches Wörterbuch,* Helsinki 1935.

Rasisereng, Ge. ed., *Blo-gsal rin-chen me-loṅ, Oyun-i dotorayuluγči erdeni toli, Minghui baojing,* Kökeqota 1998.

Ratchnevsky, Paul, "Über den mongolischen Kult am Hofe der Grosskhane in China", in Louis Ligeti ed., *Mongolian Studies,* Budapest 1970, pp. 417–43.

Regamey, Constantin, "Motifs vichnouites et śivaïtes dans le *Kāraṇḍavyūha*", in *Études tibétaines dédiées à la mémoire de Marcelle Lalou,* Paris 1971, pp. 411–32.

Rigzin, Tsepak, *Tibetan-English Dictionary of Buddhist Terminology* (revised and enlarged edition), New Delhi 1993.

Rintchen, B., "En marge du culte de Guesser khan en Mongolie", *Journal de la Société Finno-Ougrienne,* 60, 1958, pp. 3–50.

—, *Les matériaux pour l'étude du chamanisme mongol. I. Sources littéraires,* AF 3, Wiesbaden 1959.

Rintchen, Y., "Manuscrits Mongols de la collection du professor J. Kowalewki à Vilnius", *Central Asiatic Journal,* 19, 1975, pp. 105–17.

Rintschen, "Zum Kult Tschinggis-Khans bei den Mongolen", in *Opuscula Ethnologica Memoriae Ludovici Bíró Sacra.* Budapest 1959, pp. 9–22.

Roerich, Georges de, *Le parler de l'Amdo. Étude d'un dialecte archaïque du Tibet,* Serie Orientale Roma, 18, Roma 1958.

Roerich, George N., *The Blue Annals,* part I and II (bound in one), Delhi 1979, 1988 (reprinted).

Róna-Tas, A., "The Mongolian Version of the *Thar-pa čhen-po* in Budapest", in Louis Ligeti ed., *Mongolian Studies,* Budapest 1970, pp. 445–93.

—, "Dream, Magic Power and Divination in the Altaic World", *Acta Orientalia Academiae Scientiarum Hungaricae,* 25, 1972, pp. 227–36.

Sagaster, Klaus, "Ein Dokument des Tschinggis-Khan-Kults in der Khalkha-Mongolei", in Walther Heissig ed., *Collectanea Mongolica. Festschrift für Professor Dr. Rintchen zum 60. Geburtstag,* Wiesbaden 1966, AF 17, pp. 193–234.

—, *Die Weiße Geschichte (Čaγan teüke). Eine mongolische Quelle zur Lehre von den Beiden Ordnungen Religion und Staat in Tibet und der Mongolei. Herausgegeben, übersetzt und kommentiert,* AF 41, Wiesbaden 1976.

—, "Bemerkungen zur Dreizehn im mongolischen Epos" in *Beiträge zur Turkologie und Zentral-asienkunde. Annemarie von Gabain zum 80. Geburtstag am 4. Juli 1981 dargebracht von Kollegen, Freunden und Schülern*, Wiesbaden 1981, pp. 141–55.

Saγrajab, Wu Jinbao, *Mongγoljin ǰang tadqal*, Qayilar 1993.

Sampilnorbu, S., *Mongγol-un ǰang aγali-yin toyimu*, Ulaγanqada 1990.

—, *Mongγol ündüsüten-ü idegen umdaγan-u soyol*, Shenyang 1997.

Samuel, Geoffrey, "Ge sar of gLing: Shamanic Power and Popular Religion" in Geoffrey Samuel, Hamish Gregor, Elisabeth Stutchbury eds., *Tantra and Popular Religion in Tibet*, ata-Piṭaka Series. Indo-Asian Literatures, vol. 376, New Delhi 1994.

Saran and Nima, "Qar-a buq-a-yin balγasu-ača oldaγsan mongγol töbed üisün bičig-ün tuqai angqan sinǰilge", translation of "The Mongolian and Tibetan Manuscripts on Birch Bark from Xarbuxyn Balgas: A Preliminary Description" by Elisabetta Chiodo and Klaus Sagaster, *Ündüsüten-ü bülgümdel/Ethnic Unity* 82, April 1996, pp. 44–9.

Sárközi, Alice, "A Mongolian Hunting Ritual", *Acta Orientalia Academiae Scientiarum Hungaricae (AOH)*, 25, 1972, pp. 191–208.

—, "Toyin Guiši's Mongol *Vajracchedikā*", *AOH*, 27, 1973, pp. 43–102.

—, "A Mongolian Picture-Book of Molon Toyin's Descent into Hell", *AOH*, 30, 1976, pp. 273–307.

—, "A Thanka from Mongolia", in Louis Ligeti ed., *Proceedings of the Csóma de Kőrös Memorial Symposium Held at Matrafüred, Hungary, 24–30 September 1978*, Budapest 1978, pp. 393–401.

—, "A Text of Popular Religious Belief: Cutting Of the Lasso", *AOH*, 39, 1985, pp. 39–44.

—, *Political Prophecies in Mongolia in the 17–20th Centuries*, AF 116, Wiesbaden 1992.

—, ed., *A Buddhist Terminological Dictionary. The Mongolian Mahāvyutpatti*, in coll. with János Szerb, AF 130, Wiesbaden 1995.

Savvas, Carol and Lodro Tulku, *Transformation into the Exalted State. Spiritual Exercises of the Tibetan Tantric Tradition*, Rikon/Zurich 1983.

Sayinǰirγal and Šaraldai, *Altan ordon-u tayilγ-a*, Beijing 1983.

Sazykin, A. G., "Die mongolische Erzählung über Güsü-Lama", *Zentralasiatische Studien*, 16, 1982, pp. 111–40.

—, "Mongol and Oirat Versions of the Description of Naranu Gerel's Descent to the Buddhist Hell", *Acta Orientalia Academiae Scientiarum Hungaricae*, 42, 1988, pp. 281–306.

—, *Katalog mongol'skix rukopisej i ksilografov Instituta vostokovedenija Akademii nauk SSSR*, vol. I, Moskva 1988.

—, "The Oirat (Kalmyk) Version of the Story of Güsü-Lama", *Manuscripta Orientalia*, 3, (2), June 1997, pp. 33–8.

Šaγja, *Mongγol ügen-ü tayilburi toli*, Beijing 1994.

Scheftelowitz, J. von, "Die Zeit als Schicksalsgottheit in der Indischen und Iranischen Religion (Kāla und Zruvan)", *Beiträge zur Indischen Sprachwissenschaft und Religionsgeschichte*, 4, 1929, pp. 1–58.

Schulemann, Günther, *Die Botschaft des Buddha vom Lotos des guten Gesetzes*, Freiburg im Breisgau, 1937.

Schwieger, Peter, *Ein tibetisches Wunschgebet um Wiedergeburt in der Sukhāvatī*, St. Augustin 1978.

Sečenmöngke and Gerelčečeg, *Oyirad mongγol-un irügel maγtaγal*, Kökeqota 1993.

Sérinde: Terre de Buddha. Dix siècles d'art sur la Route de la Soie. Galeries nationales du Grand Palais, Paris 24 octobre 1995–19 février 1996.

Serruys, Henri, "*Pei-lou Fong-sou. Les coutumes des esclaves septentrionaux de Siao Ta-Heng suivi des tables généalogiques*", traduit par Henri Serruys C.I.C.M., *Monumenta Serica*, 10, 1945, (reprinted New York/London 1970), pp. 117–208.

—, "Early Lamaism in Mongolia", *Oriens Extremus*, 10, 1963, pp. 181–216.

—, "A Mongol Prayer to the Spirit of Činggis-Qan's Flag", in Louis Ligeti ed., *Mongolian Studies*, Budapest 1970, pp. 527–35.

—, "A Mongol Lamaist Prayer: *Ündüsün bsang*, Incense Offering of Origin", *Monumenta Serica*, 28, 1971, pp. 321–418.

—, *Kumiss Ceremonies and Horse Races. Three Mongolian Texts*, AF 37, Wiesbaden 1972.

Siklós, Bulcsu, *The Vajrabhairava Tantras*, Tring, U.K. 1996.

Sørensen, Per K., *Tibetan Buddhist Historiography. The Mirror Illuminating the Royal Genealogies. An Annotated Translation of the XIVth Century Tibetan Chronicle: rGyal-rabs gsal-ba'i me-long*, AF 128, Wiesbaden 1994.

Skrynnikova, T. D., "Sülde: The Basic Idea of the Chinggis-khan Cult", *Acta Orientalia Academiae Scientiarum Hungaricae*, 46, 1992/93, pp. 51–9.

Snellgrove, David L., *The Nine Ways of Bon*, Boulder, Colorado 1980 (reprinted).

Stein, Rolf A., "Trente-trois fiches de divination tibétaines", *Harvard Journal of Asian Studies*, 4, 1939, pp. 297–371 (with 8 plates).

—, *Recherches sur l'épopée et le barde au Tibet*, Paris 1959.

—, *Tibetan Civilization*, translated by J. E. Stapleton Driver, with original drawings by Lobsang Tendzin, London 1972.

Strickmann Michel, *Mantras et mandarins. Le bouddhisme tantrique en Chine*, Paris 1996.

Sumatiratna: Bod-hor-kyi brda-yig miṅ-tshig don-gsum gsal-bar byed-pa'i-mun-sel-sgron-me, Corpus Scriptorum Mongolorum, 2 vols., Ulaanbaatar 1959.

Tachikawa, Musashi, Masahide Mori, Shinobu Yamaguchi, *Five Hundred Buddhist Deities*, National Museum of Ethnology, Osaka 1995.

Taube, Manfred, "Mongolische Birkenrinden-Fragmente in Taschkent", *Ural-Altaische Jahrbücher*, N.F., 11, 1992, pp. 152–5.

Toyka-Fuong, Ursula, *Die Kultplastiken der Sammlung Werner Schulemann im Museum für Ostasiatische Kunst, Köln (Ikonographie und Symbolik des Tibetischen Buddhismus*, vol. B, ed. Klaus Sagaster), AF 78, Wiesbaden 1983.

Tsultem, N., *Mongyol ǰiruy. Development of the Mongolian National Style Painting 'Mongol zurag' in Brief*, Ulaanbaatar 1986.

Tucci, Giuseppe, *Il libro tibetano dei morti. Il libro della salvazione dall'esistenza intermedia*, Milano 1949.

—, *Tibetan Painted Scrolls*, Roma 1949.

—, "Il tempio di Bsam Yas", in *Les symbolisme cosmique des monuments religieux. Actes de la conférence internationale qui a eu lieu sous les auspices de l'IsMeo, à Rome avril-mai 1955, avec la collaboration du Musée Guimet*. Conférences par R. Bloch, J. Daniélou, M. Eliade, M. Griaule, C. Hentze, H. Puech, G. Tucci. *Serie Orientale*, 14, Roma 1957, pp. 118–23.

—, *Le religioni del Tibet*, Roma 1970.

Ui, H., M. Suzuki, Y. Kanakura, T. Tada, *A Complete Catalogue of the Tibetan Buddhist Canons (Bkaḥ-ḥgyur and Bstan-ḥgyur)*, with Catalogue-Index, Sendai 1934 (reprinted 1973).

Vangjil, Borǰigidai Ba., *Köke ǰula. Mongyol ulamǰilaltu amidural-un toli*, Qayilar 1990.

Veit, Veronika, "Das Testament des Sečen Qan Šoloi (1577–1652)", in Klaus Sagaster and Michael Weiers eds., *Documenta Barbarorum, Festschrift für Walther Heissig zum 70. Geburtstag*, Veröffentlichungen der Societas Uralo-Altaica, Band 18, Wiesbaden 1983, pp. 405–11.

—, *Die Vier Qane von Qalqa*, 2 vols., AF 111, Wiesbaden 1990.

Vladimircov, B.Ya., "Nadpisi na skalax xalchaskogo Coktu-tajdži", *Izvestija Akademii nauk SSSR (Bulletin de l'Académie des Sciences de l'URSS)*, 1926, pp. 1253–80 (2 plates).

Vladimirtsov, B., *Le régime social des Mongols. Le féodalisme nomade*, Paris 1948.

Vreeland, Harold, *Mongol Community and Kinship Structure*, New Haven 1953.

Waddel, L. A., "The Dhāraṇī Cult in Buddhism, its Origin, Deified Literature and Images", *Ostasiatische Zeitschrift*, 1912, pp. 155–95.

—, *The Buddhism of Tibet or Lamaism*, Cambridge 1958.

Wayman, Alex, *The Buddhist Tantras. Light on Indo-Tibetan Esoterism*, Delhi 1990 (reprinted).

Weiers, Michael, *Untersuchungen zu einer historischen Grammatik des präklassischen Schriftmongolisch*, AF 28, Wiesbaden 1969.

—, "Bemerkungen zu einigen sprachlichen Eigenheiten des Südostmongolischen im 17. Jahrhundert", in Walther Heissig and Klaus Sagaster eds., *Gedanke und Wirkung. Festschrift zum 90. Geburtstag von Nikolaus Poppe*, AF 108, Wiesbaden 1989, pp. 366–72.

Wu-t'i Ch'ing-wên-chien, Translated and Explained, eds. Jitsuzo Tamura, Shunju Imanishi, Hisashi Sato, 2 vols., Kyoto 1966.

Ya Hanzhang, *Bančin erdeni-yin namtar*, (translated from the Chinese), Beijing 1990.

—, *Dalai lama-yin namtar*, (translated from the Chinese), Beijing 1992.

Yang Haiyin, "*Kinsho*" *kenkyū he no josetsu. An Introduction to Altan Bičig*, Senri Ethnological Reports, 7, National Museum of Ethnology, Osaka 1998.

Žamcarano, C. Ž., *The Mongol Chronicles of the Seventeenth Century*, translated by Rudolf Loewenthal, AF 3, Wiesbaden 1955.

Zieme, Peter, *Religion und Gesellschaft im uigurischen Königreich von Qočo. Kolophone und Stifter des alttürkischen buddhistischen Schrifttums aus Zentralasien*, Opladen 1992.

—, *Altun yaruq sudur, Vorworte und das erste Buch*, Berliner Turfan-Texte XVIII, Turnhout 1996.

Zimmer, Heinrich, *Miti e simboli dell'India*, Milano 1993 (translation of *Myths and Symbols in Indian Art and Civilization*, Princeton 1946).

Zhang Wenban, *Meidai zhao*, Kökeqota 1984.

Facsimiles

XBM 1,
1 r

XBM 1,
1 v

XBM 1,
2 r

XBM 1,
2 v

XBM 2,
1 v

XBM 3,
*1 r

XBM 3,
*1 v

XBM 4,
recto

XBM 4,
verso

XBM 4,
6r

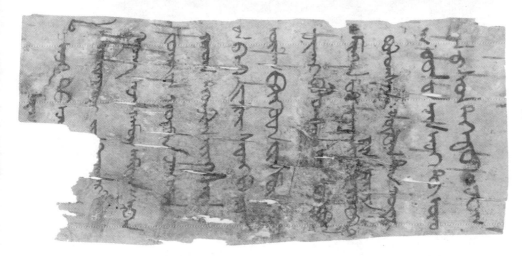

XBM 5,
1r

XBM 5,
1 v

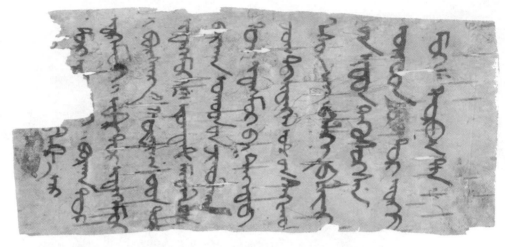

XBM 6,
1 v

XBM 6,
4 r

XBM 6,
4 v

XBM 7

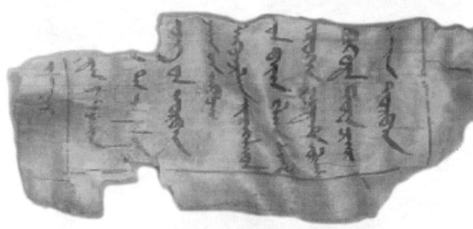

XBM 8,
2r

XBM 8,
2v

XBM 8,
5 r

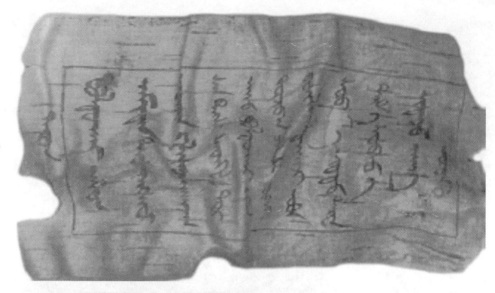

XBM 9,
1 v

XBM 9,
5 r

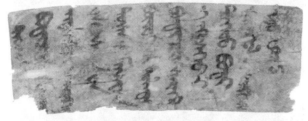

XBM 9,
5 v

XBM 9,
6 r

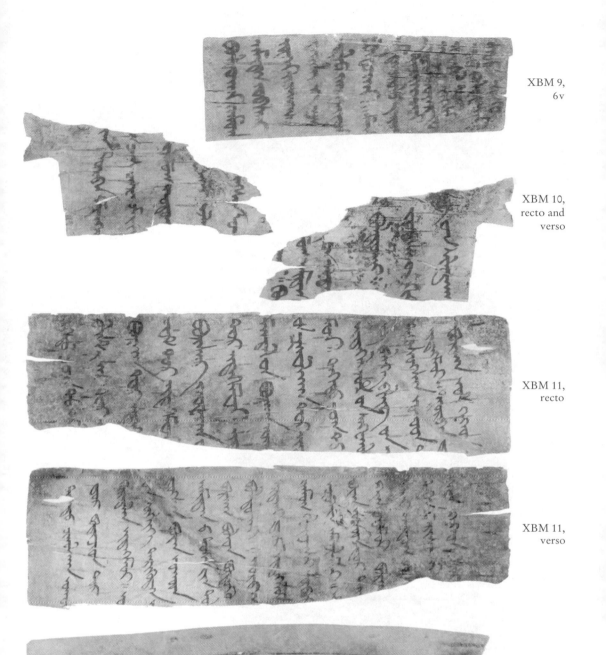

XBM 9,
6v

XBM 10,
recto and
verso

XBM 11,
recto

XBM 11,
verso

XBM 12,
recto

XBM 12, verso

XBM 13, 6r

XBM 13, 6v

XBM 13, 7r

XBM 13,
7v

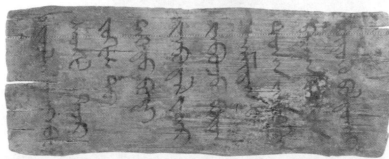

XBM 14,
recto

XBM 14,
verso

XBM 15,
recto

XBM 15,
verso

XBM 16,
recto

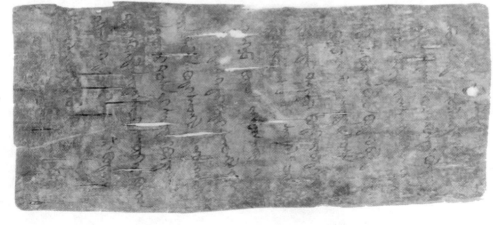

XBM 16,
verso

XBM 17,
recto and
verso

XBM 18,
4r

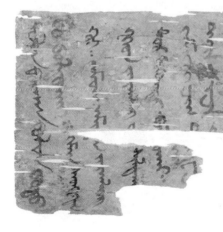

XBM 18,
4v

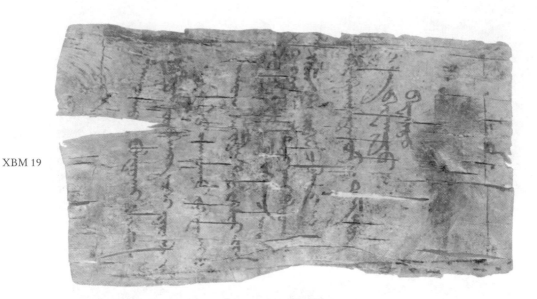

XBM 19

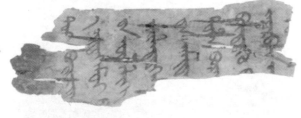

XBM 20,
recto

XBM 20,
verso

XBM 21,
5r

XBM 22,
1 v

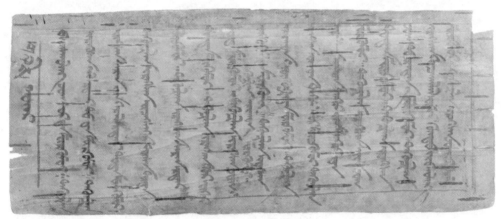

XBM 22,
2 r

XBM 22,
2 v

XBM 22,
4 v

XBM 22,
5 r

XBM 22,
5 v

XBM 22,
6 r

XBM 23,
1 v

XBM 24,
3 r

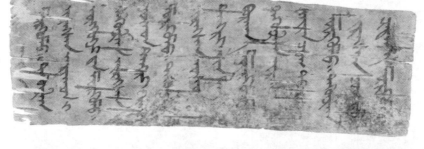

XBM 24,
3 v

XBM 25,
1 v

XBM 26,
11 r
and 11 v

XBM 27,
9 r

XBM 27,
9 v

XBM 28,
2 r

XBM 28,
2 v

XBM 28,
3 r

XBM 28,
3 v

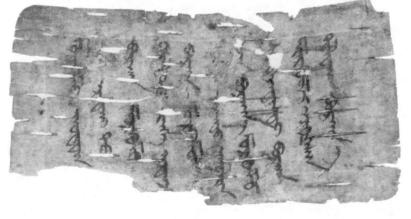

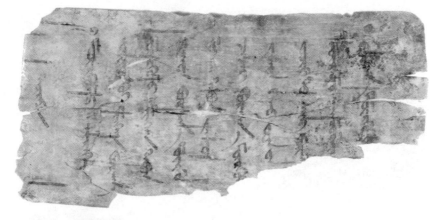

XBM 28,
4 r

XBM 28,
4 v

XBM 28,
5 r

XBM 28,
5 v

XBM 28,
7 r

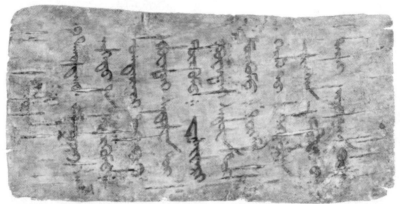

XBM 28,
7 v

XBM 28,
9r

XBM 28,
9v

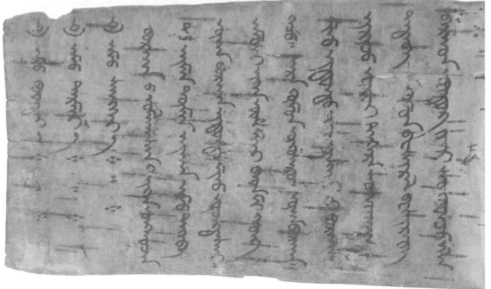

XBM 29,
1v

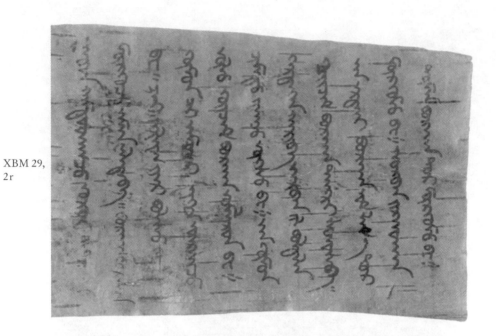

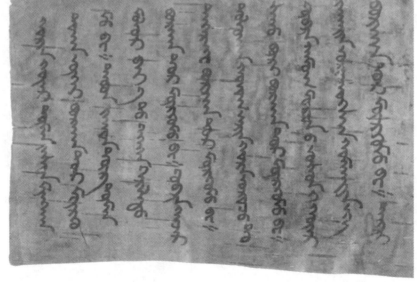

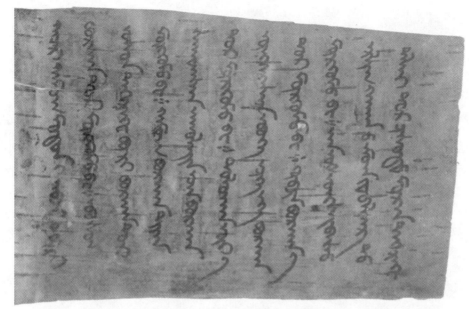

XBM 29,
3r

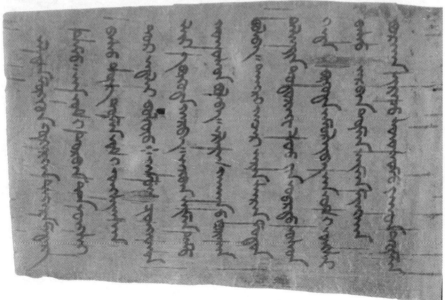

XBM 29,
3v

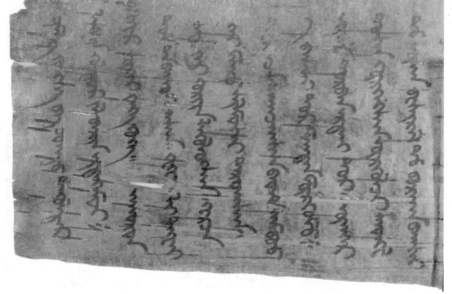

XBM 29,
5 r

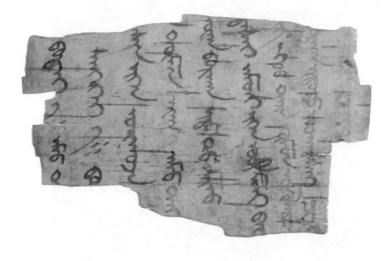

XBM 30,
1 v

XBM 30,
3 r

XBM 30,
3 v

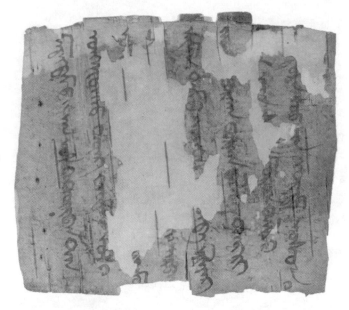

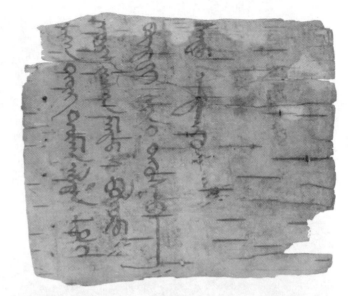

XBM 30,
5 r

XBM 31,
1 v

XBM 32,
2 r

XBM 34,
2 r

XBM 34,
2 v

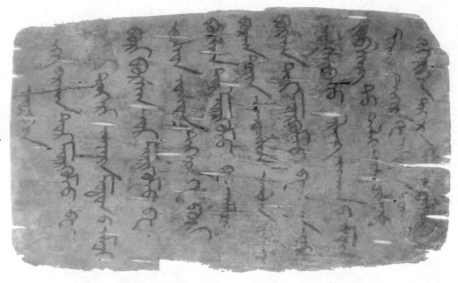

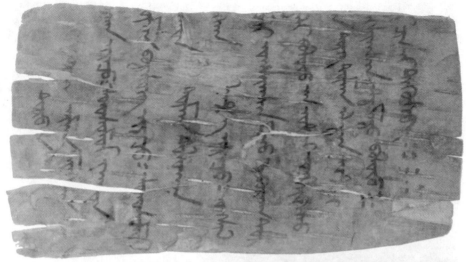

XBM 34,
4r

XBM 35,
2r

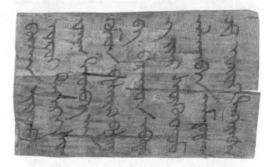

XBM 35,
2v

XBM 35,
3r

XBM 35,
7r and 7v

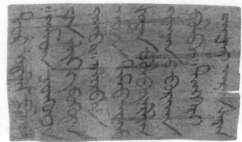

XBM 35,
8r

XBM 36,
7r

XBM 36,
7v

XBM 37
recto

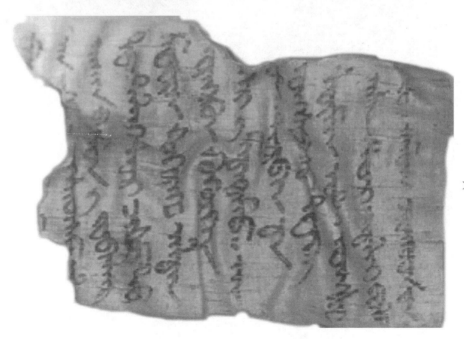

XBM 37
verso

XBM 38,
recto

XBM 38,
verso

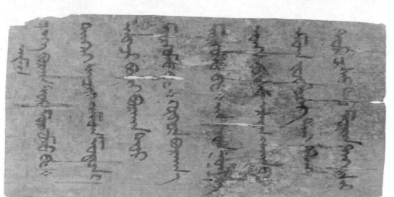

XBM 39,
8r

XBM 39,
8v

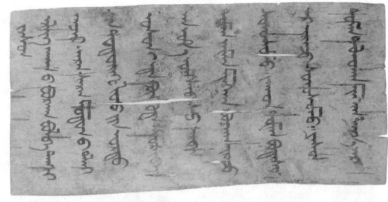

XBM 40,
9r

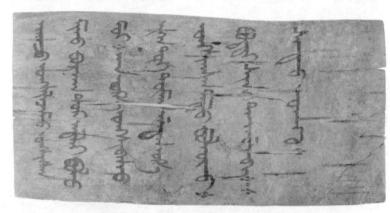

XBM 40,
9v

XBM 41,
1v

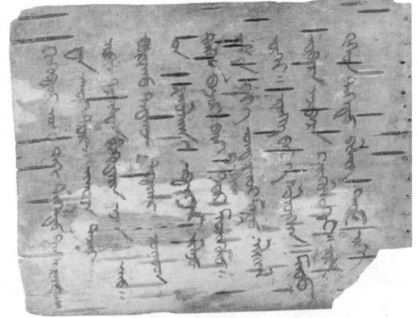

XBM 41,
3r

XBM 41,
3v

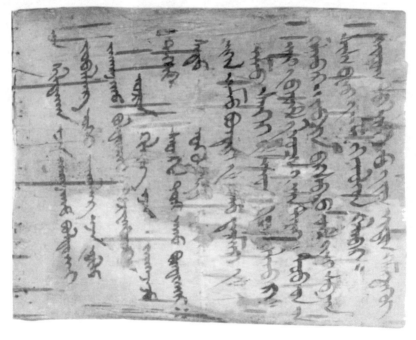

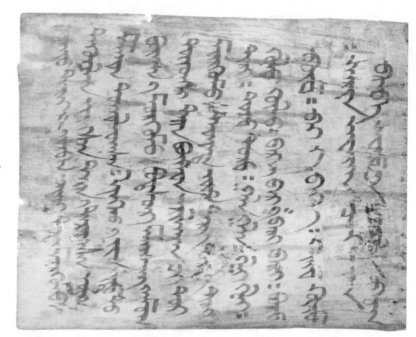

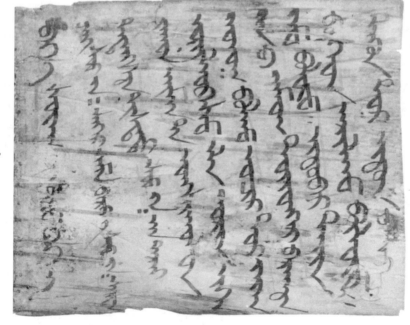

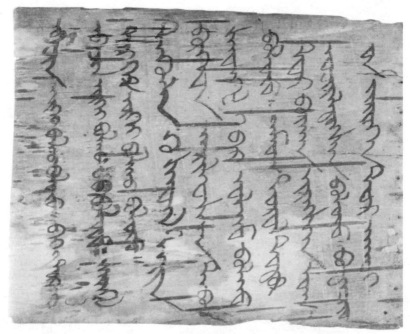

XBM 41,
7r

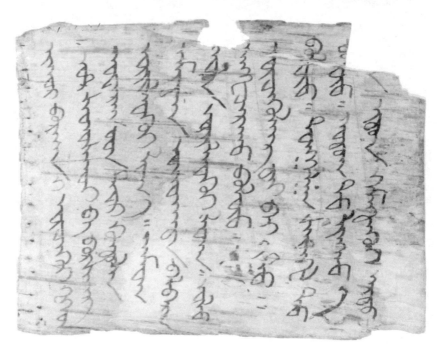

XBM 41,
7v

XBM 41,
8r

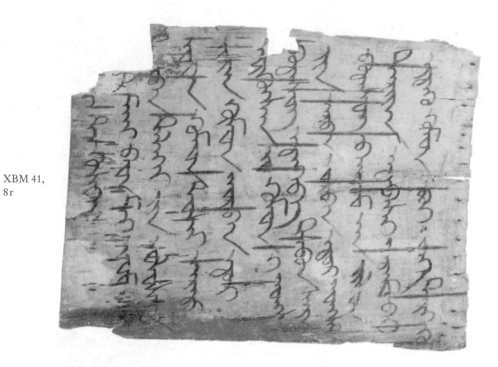

XBM 41,
8v

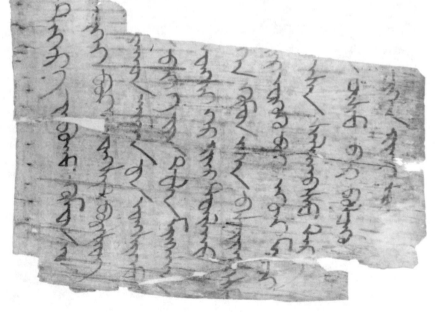

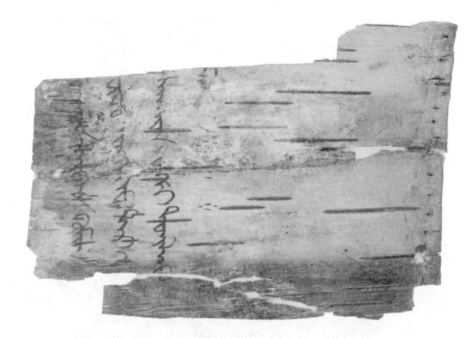

XBM 41,
9r

XBM 42,
*1v

XBM 42,
*2r

XBM 42, *2v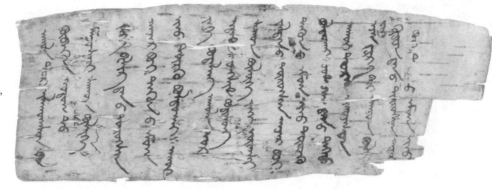

XBM 42, *3r

XBM 43, *2v

XBM 43, 3r

XBM 43,
3 v;
XBM 44,
*1

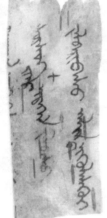

XBM 44,
*2 r
and *2 v

XBM 45

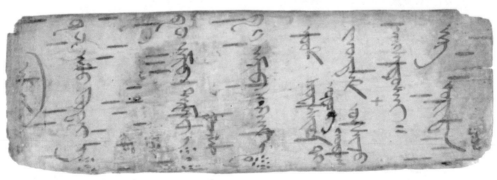

XBM 46,
1 v

XBM 46,
2r

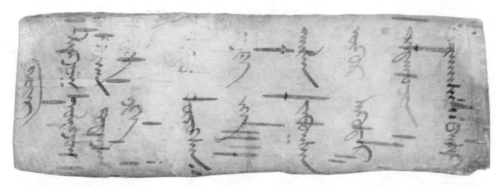

XBM 46,
2v

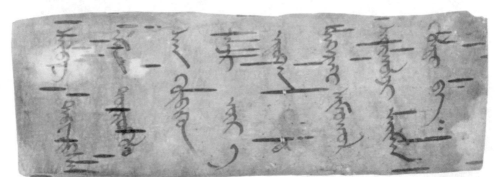

XBM 46,
3r

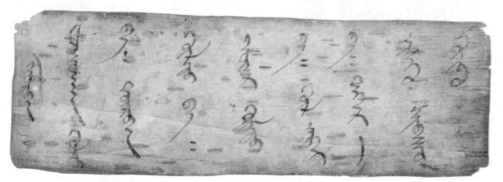

XBM 46,
3v

XBM 46,
4r

XBM 46,
4v

XBM 46,
5r

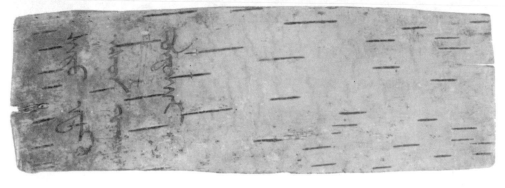

XBM 46,
5v

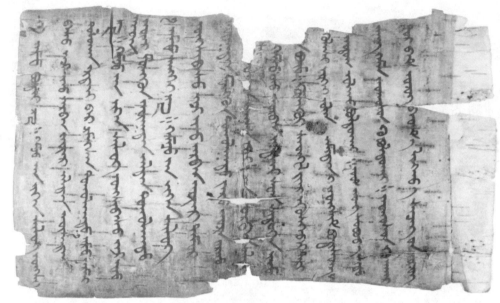

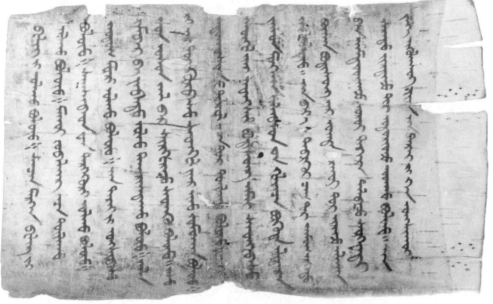

XBM 47,
2 v

XBM 47,
3 r

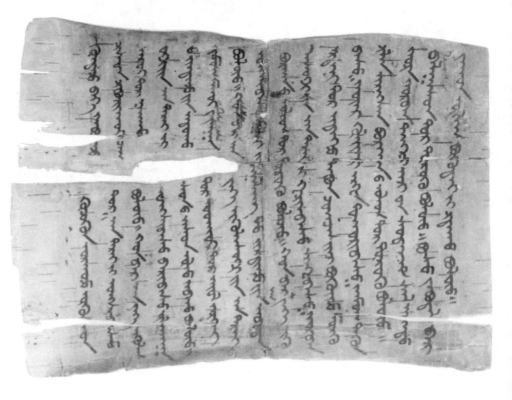

XBM 47,
4v

XBM 48,
2r

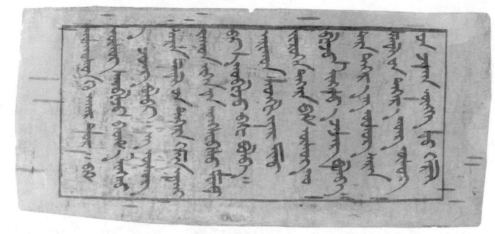

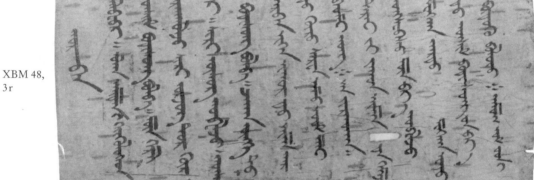

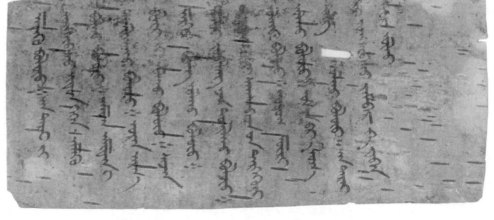

XBM 49,
2r

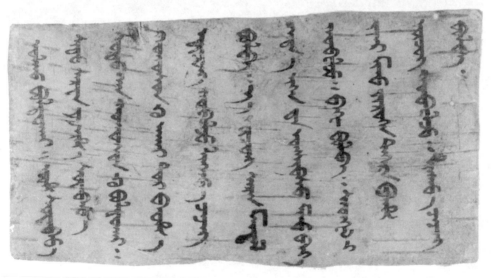

XBM 49,
2v

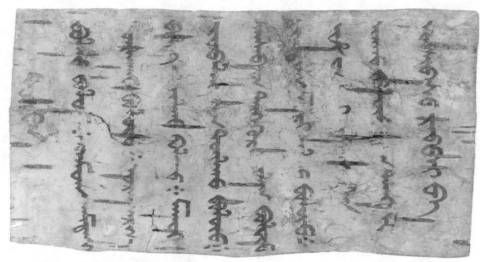

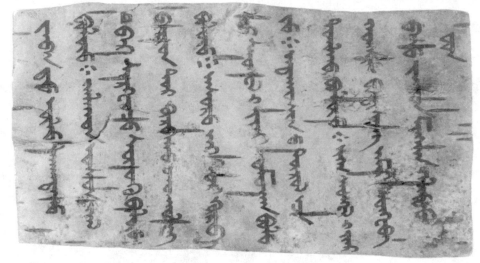

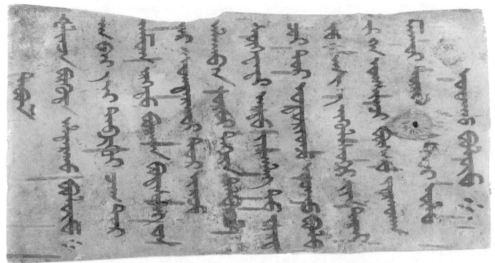

XBM 49,
5 r

XBM 49,
5 v

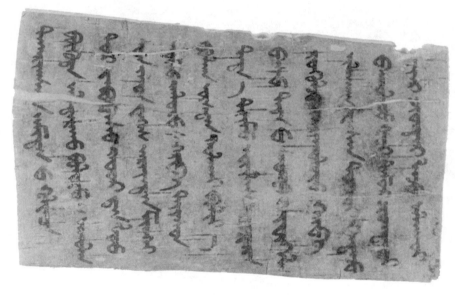

XBM 49,
8r

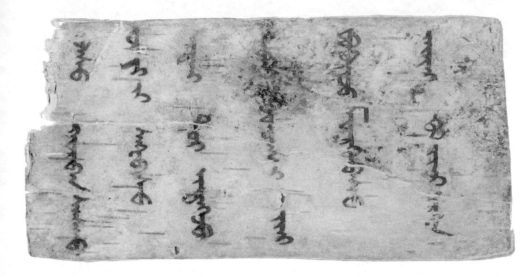

XBM 49,
8v

XBM 49,
9r

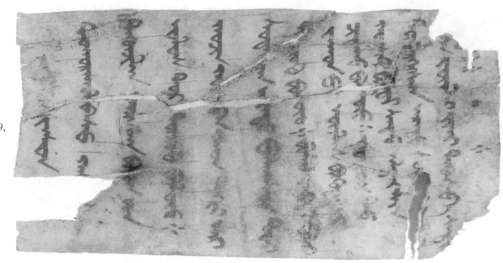

XBM 50,
7r

XBM 50,
7v

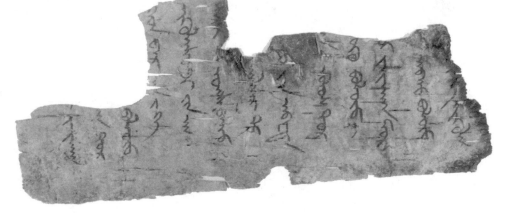

XBM 51,
1 v

XBM 52,
1 v

XBM 53,
*1 v

XBM 53,
*2r

XBM 53,
*2v

XBM 54,
1v

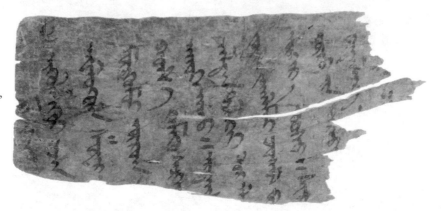

XBM 54,
2r

XBM 54,
2v

XBM 55

XBM 56,
3r

XBM 56,
3v

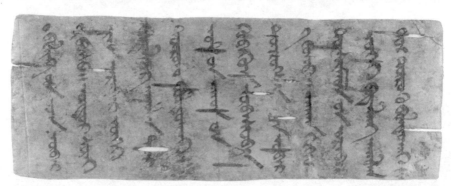

XBM 56,
5r

XBM 56,
5v

XBM 57,
*1r

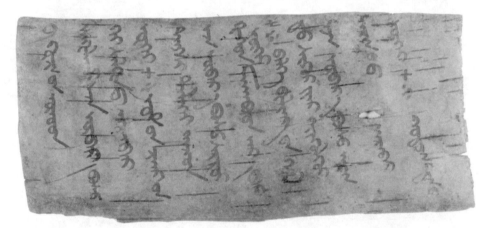

XBM 57,
*1v

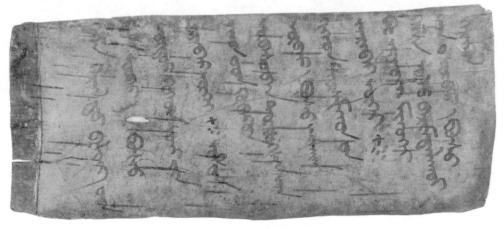

XBM 57,
*2r

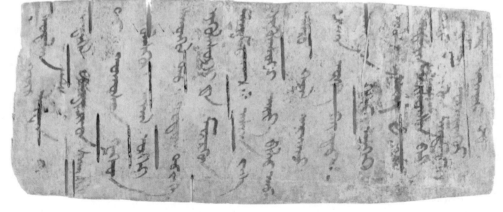

XBM 58,
2v

XBM 58,
3r

XBM 58,
3v

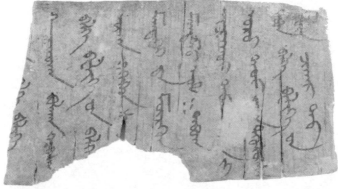

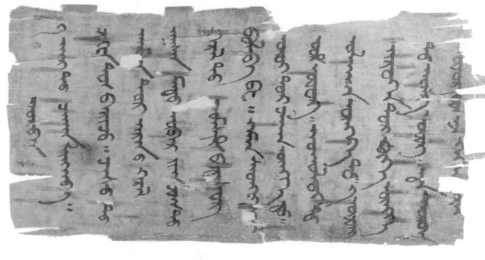

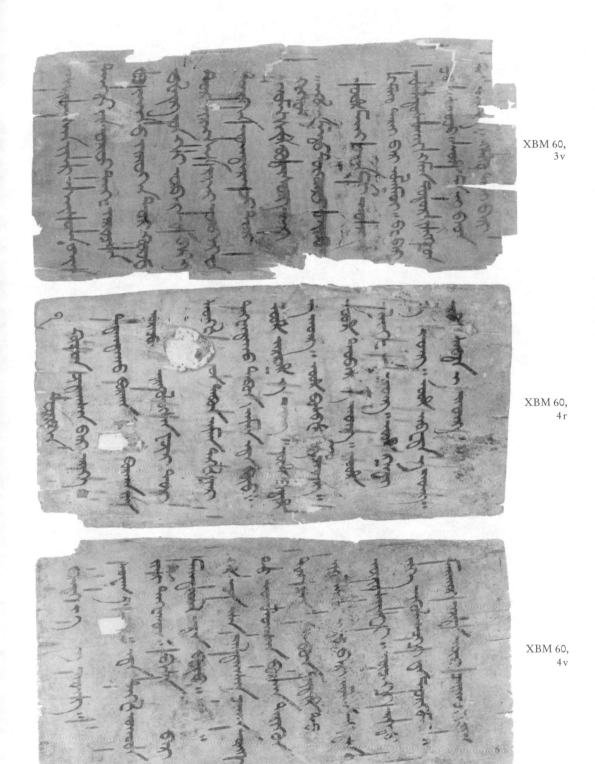

XBM 61,
6r

XBM 62,
1 r

XBM 62,
1 v

XBM 63,
recto

XBM 63,
verso

XBM 64

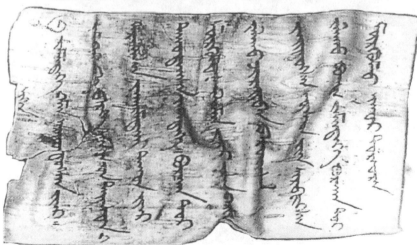

XBM 65,
1 v

XBM 65,
2r

XBM 65,
2v

XBM 65,
3r

XBM 65,
3 v

XBM 66,
1 v

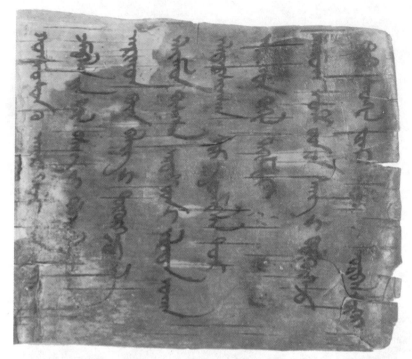

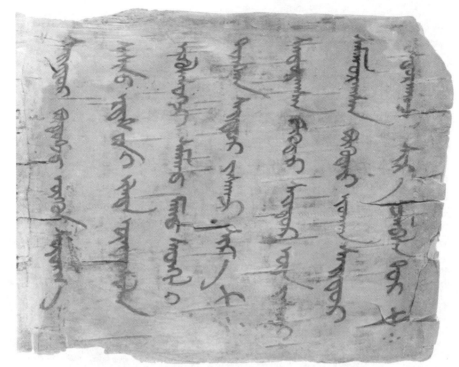

XBM 66,
3 r

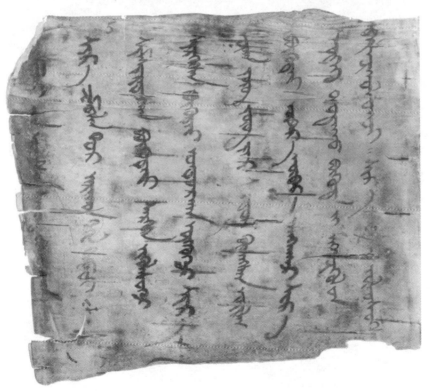

XBM 66,
3 v

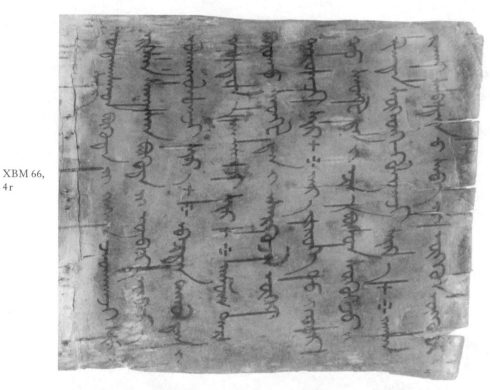

XBM 66,
5r

XBM 66,
5v

XBM 66,
7r

XBM 66,
7v

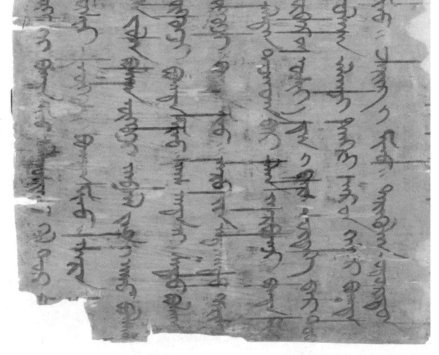

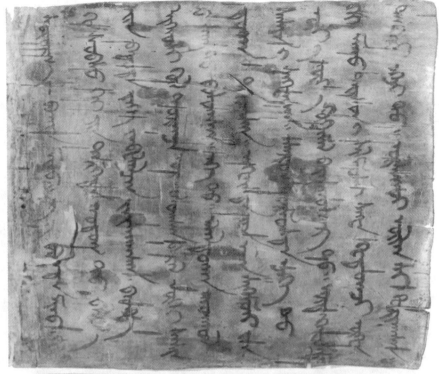

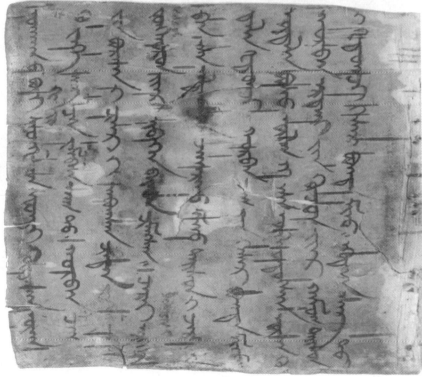

XBM 66,
10r

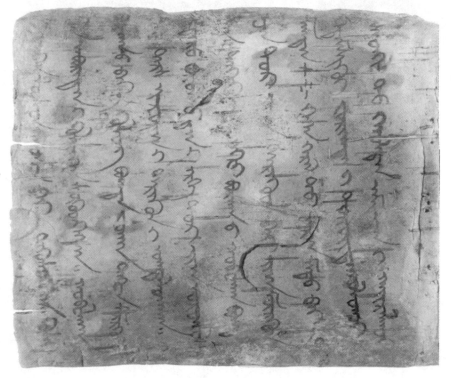

XBM 66,
10v

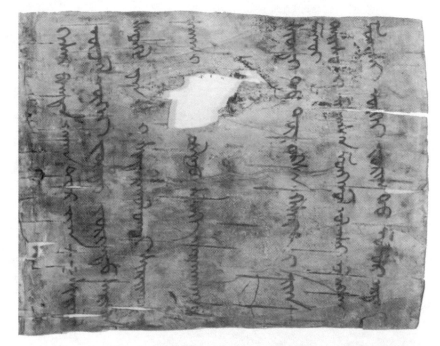

XBM 66,
11 r

XBM 66,
11 v

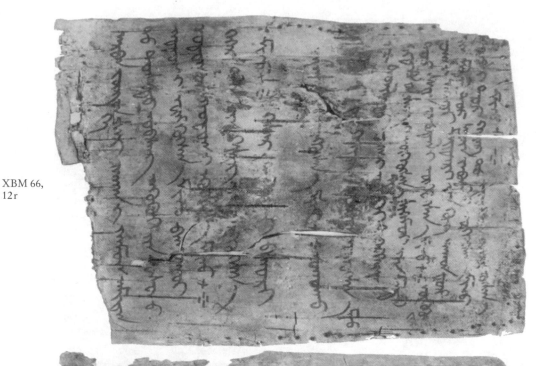

XBM 68,
2v

XBM 69,
2r

XBM 69,
2v

XBM 70,
recto

XBM 70,
verso

XBM 71,
4 r

XBM 72,
recto

XBM 72,
verso

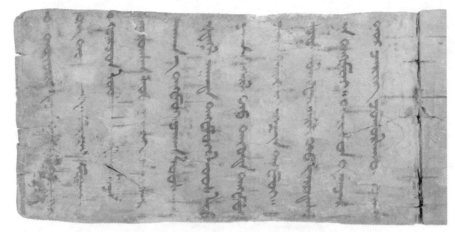

XBM 73,
1 v

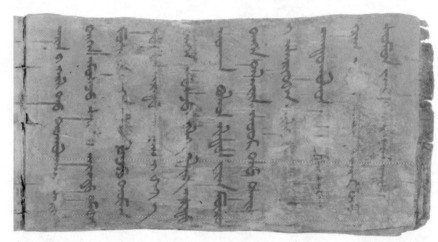

XBM 73,
2 r

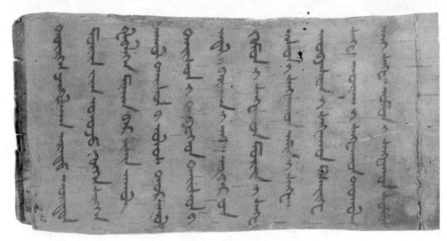

XBM 73,
2 v

XBM 73,
3r

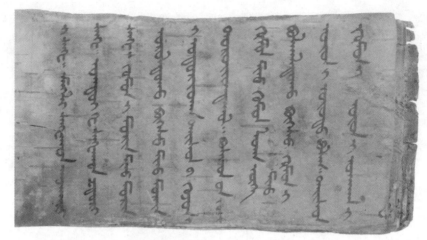

XBM 73,
3v

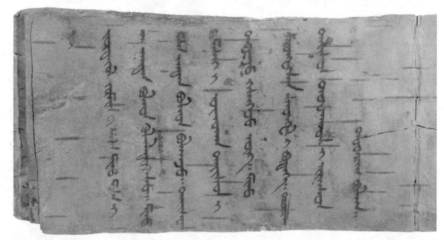

XBM 73,
4r

XBM 73,
4 v

XBM 73,
5 r

XBM 74,
1 v

XBM 75,
6 v

XBM 75,
7 r

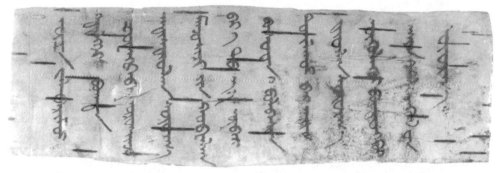

XBM 75,
7 v

XBM 75,
9 r

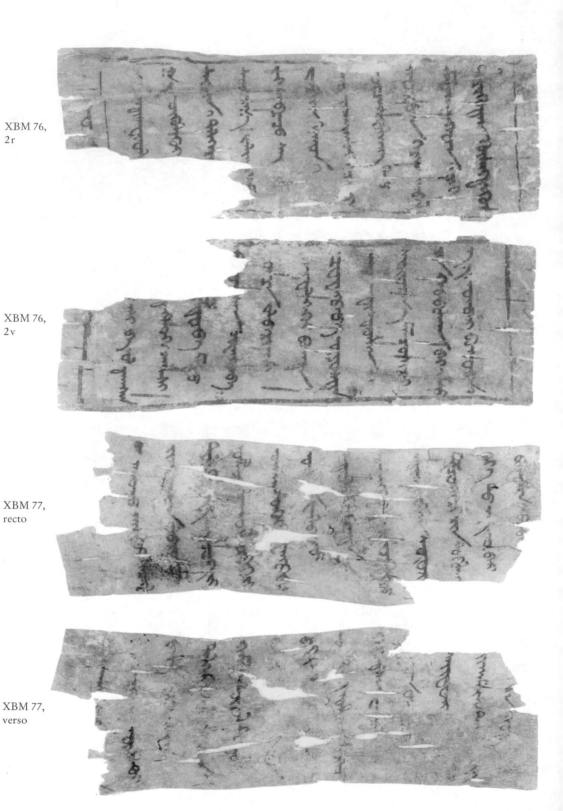

XBM 76,
2r

XBM 76,
2v

XBM 77,
recto

XBM 77,
verso

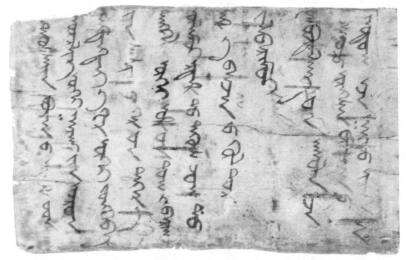

XBM 78,
1v

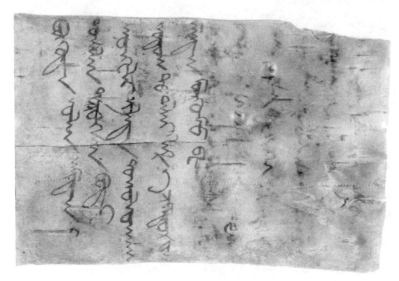

XBM 78,
2r

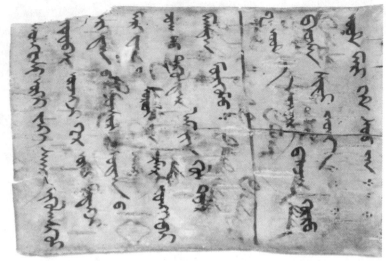

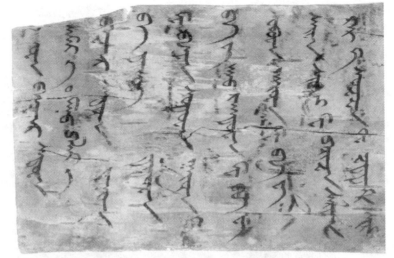

XBM 78,
3 v

XBM 78,
4 r

XBM 80,
*1 v

XBM 80,
*2 r

XBM 81,
3v

XBM 81,
6r
and 6v

XBM 81,
*7r

XBM 81,
*7v

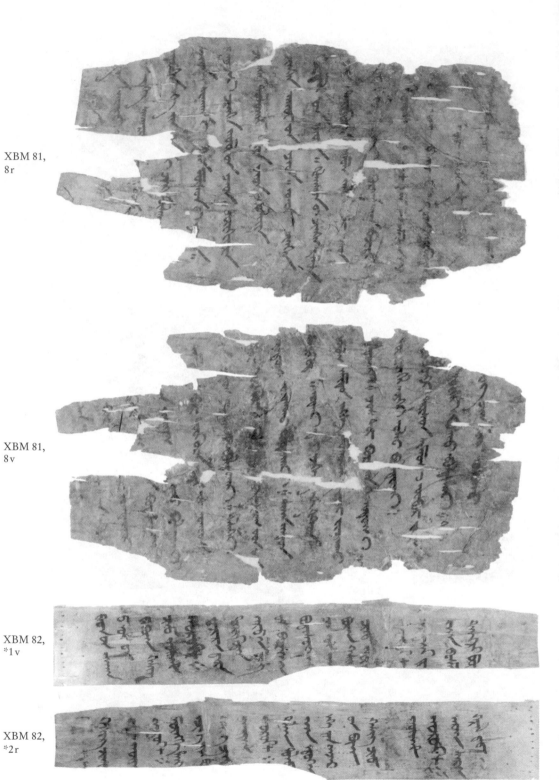

XBM 81,
8r

XBM 81,
8v

XBM 82,
*1v

XBM 82,
*2r

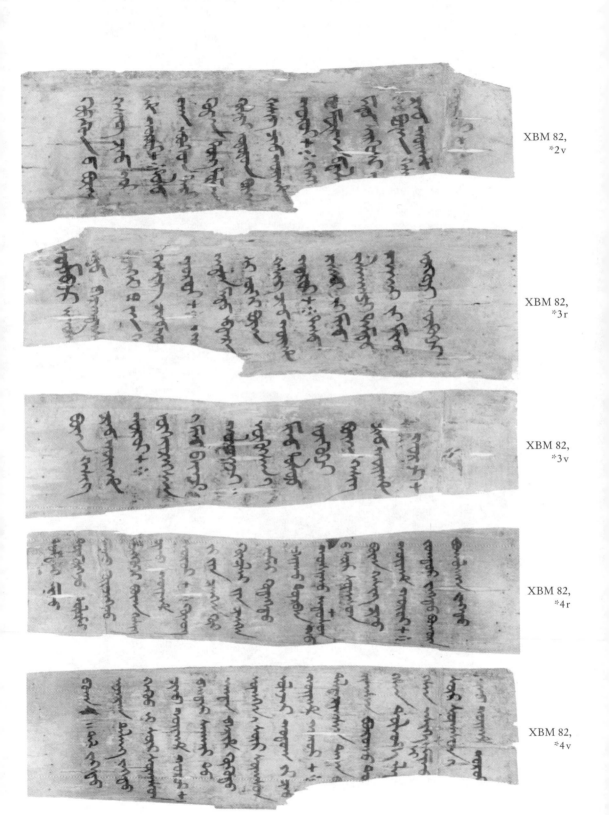

XBM 82,
*2v

XBM 82,
*3r

XBM 82,
*3v

XBM 82,
*4r

XBM 82,
*4v

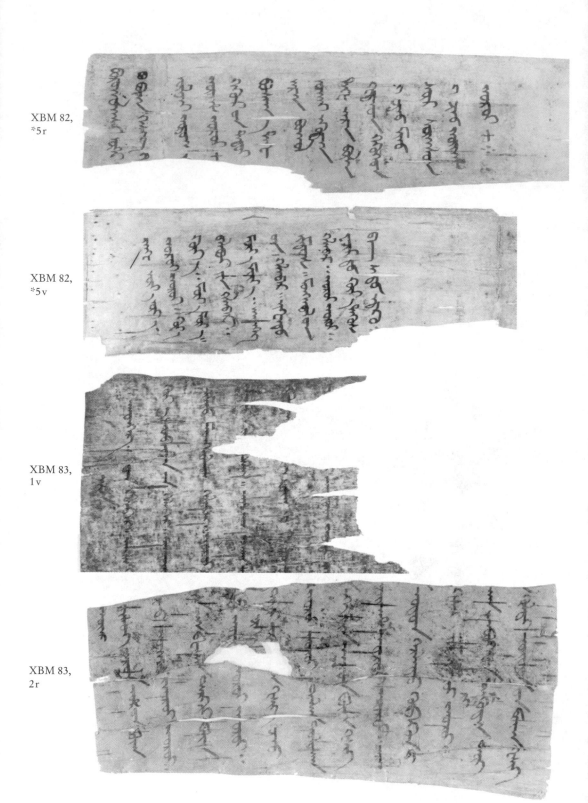

XBM 82,
*5r

XBM 82,
*5v

XBM 83,
1v

XBM 83,
2r

XBM 83,
2 v

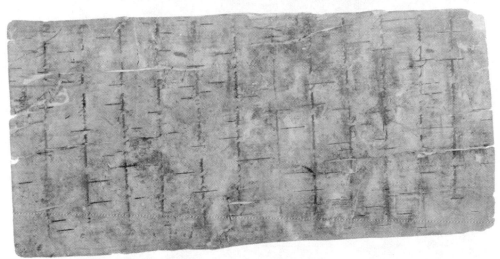

XBM 83,
3 r

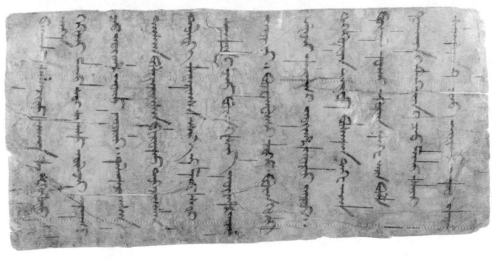

XBM 83,
3 v

XBM 84,
4r

XBM 84,
4v

XBM 85,
1 and *3r

XBM 85,
*3v

XBM 85,
4r

XBM 85,
4v

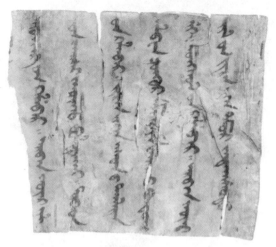

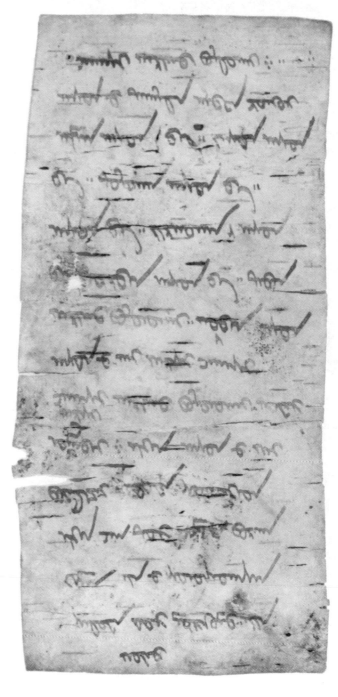

XBM 88,
2r

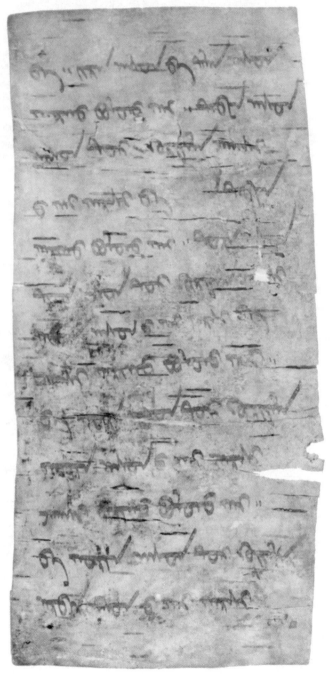

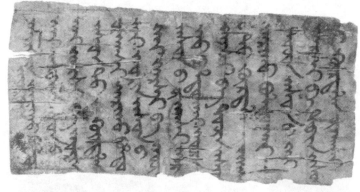

XBM 89,
3 r

XBM 89,
3 v

XBM 90,
*1 v

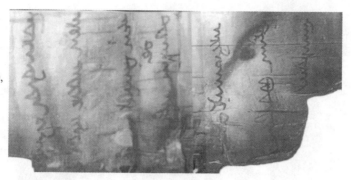

XBM 90,
*2r

XBM 90,
*2v

XBM 90,
*3r

XBM 90,
*3v

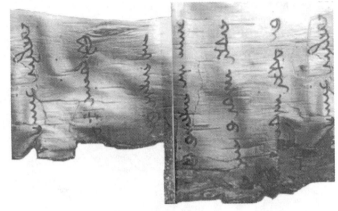

XBM 90,
*4r

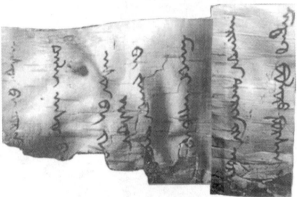

XBM 90,
*4v

XBM 90,
*5r

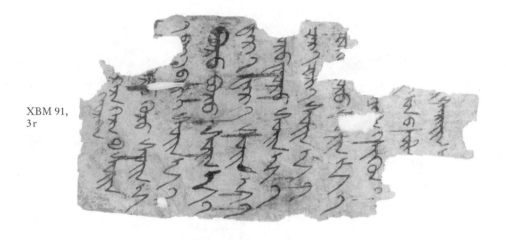

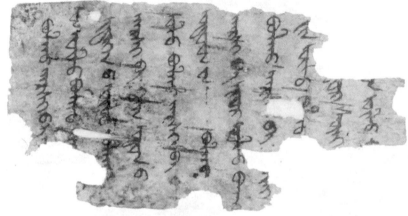

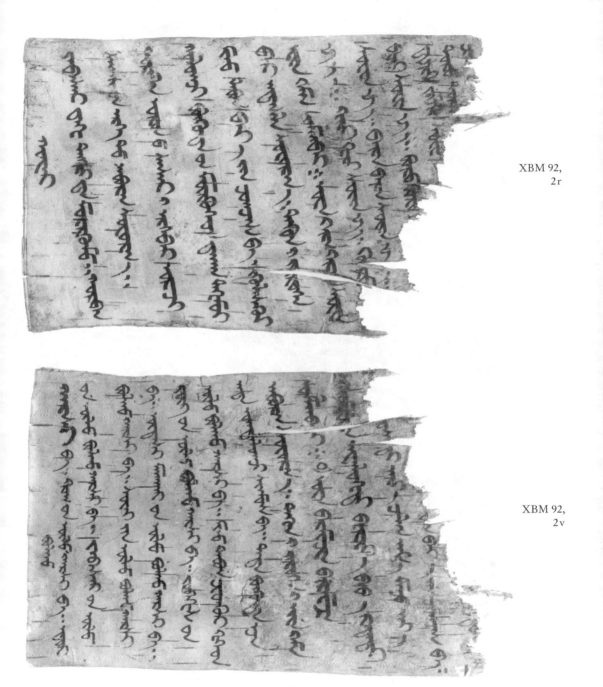

XBM 92,
2r

XBM 92,
2v

XBM 93,
recto

XBM 93,
verso

XBM 94,
3 r

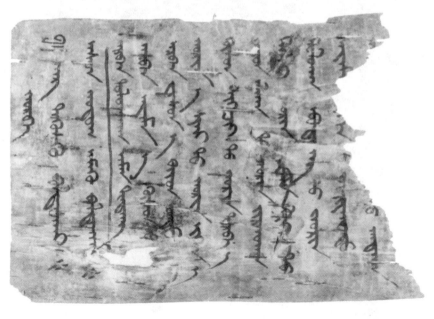

XBM 95,
4 r

XBM 95,
4 v

XBM 96,
1 v

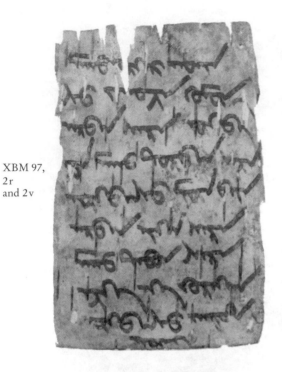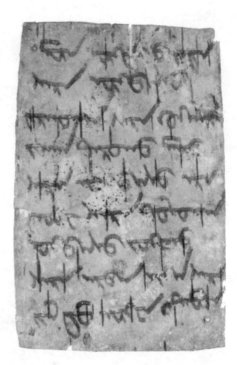

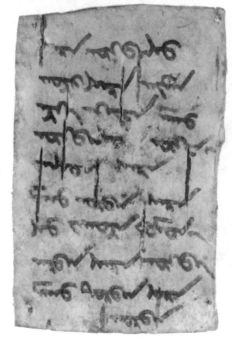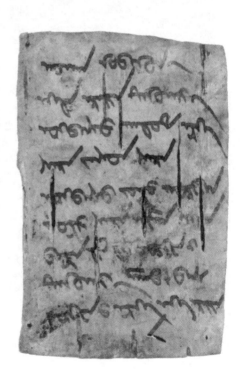

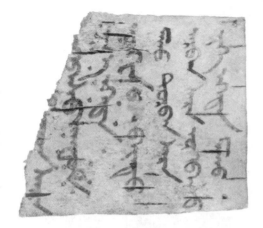

XBM 97,
*4r
and *4v

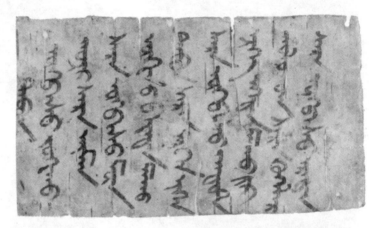

XBM 97,
5r

XBM 97,
5v

XBM 97,
6r
and 6v

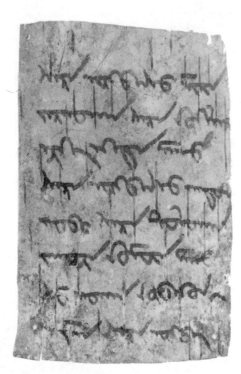

XBM 97,
8r
and 8v

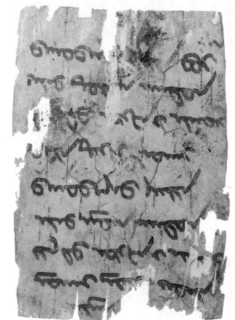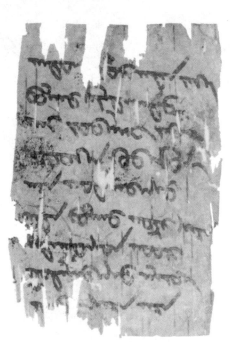

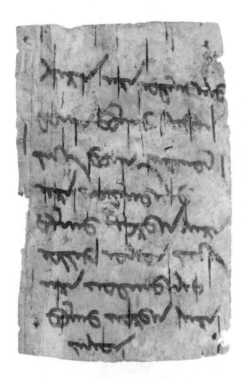
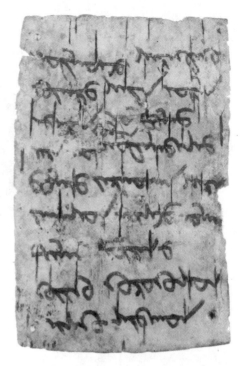

XBM 97,
9r
and 9v

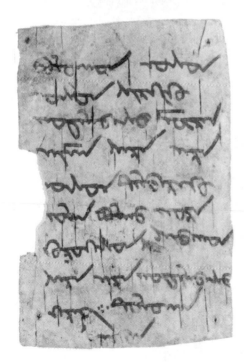
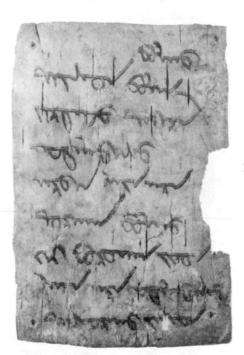

XBM 97,
10r
and 10v

XBM 97,
11r

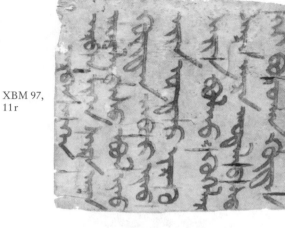

XBM 98

XBM 99,
*1r

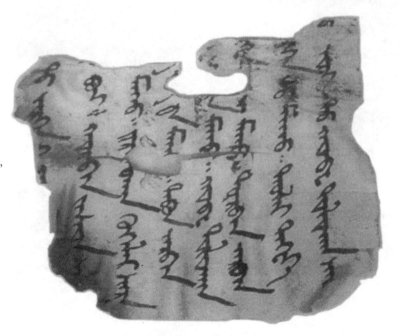

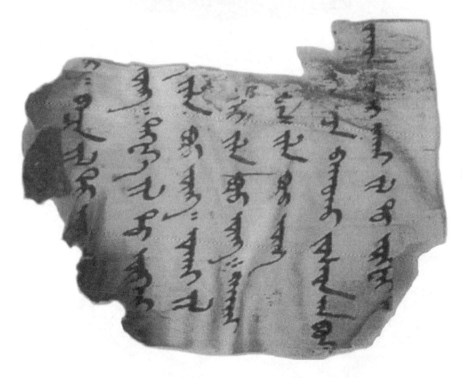

XBM 99,
*2v

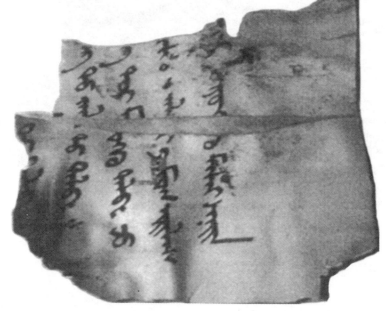

XBM 99,
*3

XBM 99,
*4

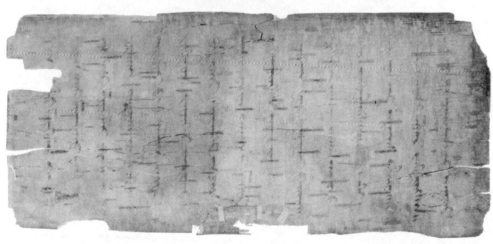

XBM 100,
1 v

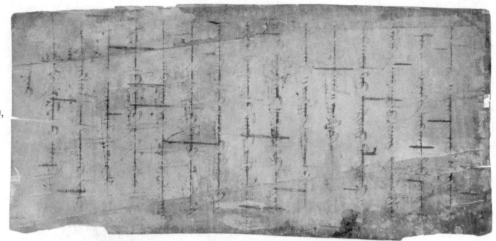

XBM 100,
2r

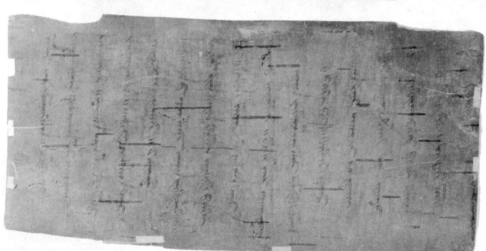

XBM 100,
2v

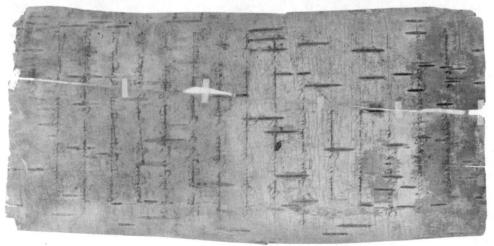

XBM 100,
3r

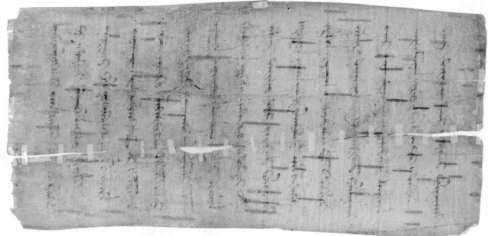

XBM 100,
3v

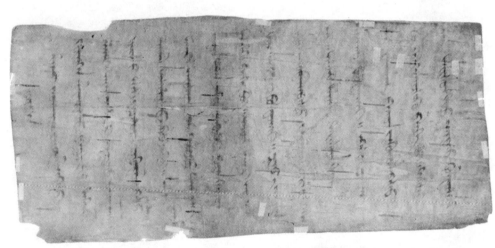

XBM 100,
4r

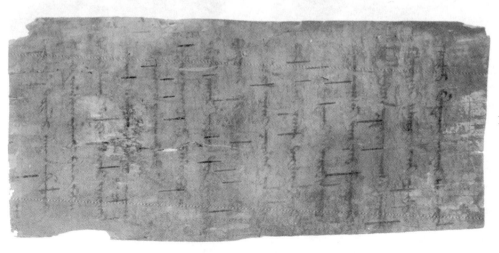

XBM 100,
4v

XBM 100,
5 r

XBM 101,
*1 v

XBM 102,
recto
and verso

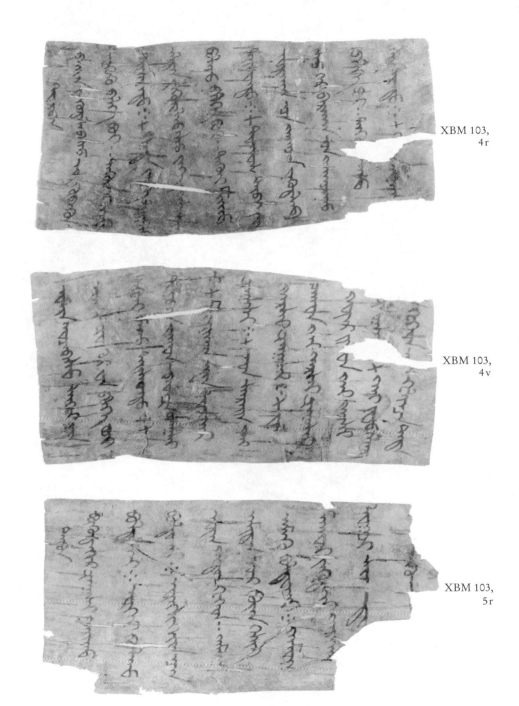

XBM 103,
4r

XBM 103,
4v

XBM 103,
5r

XBM 104,
*1 v

XBM 104,
*2 r
and *2 v

 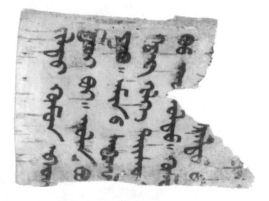

XBM 104,
*3 r

XBM 104,
*3 v

XBM 105,
recto

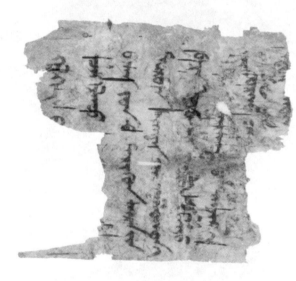

XBM 105,
verso

XBM 106,
4r

XBM 106,
4v

XBM 106,
5r

XBM 106,
5v

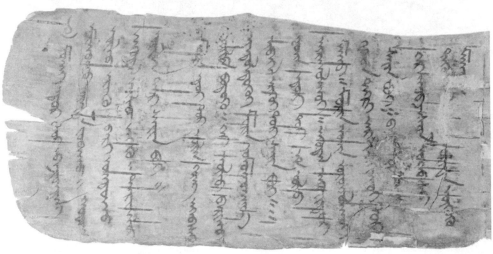

XBM 107,
*1v

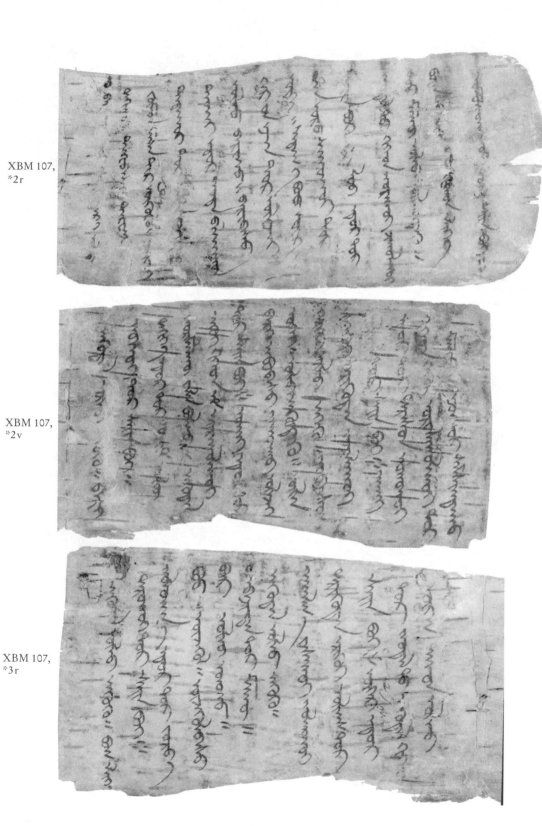

XBM 107,
*2r

XBM 107,
*2v

XBM 107,
*3r

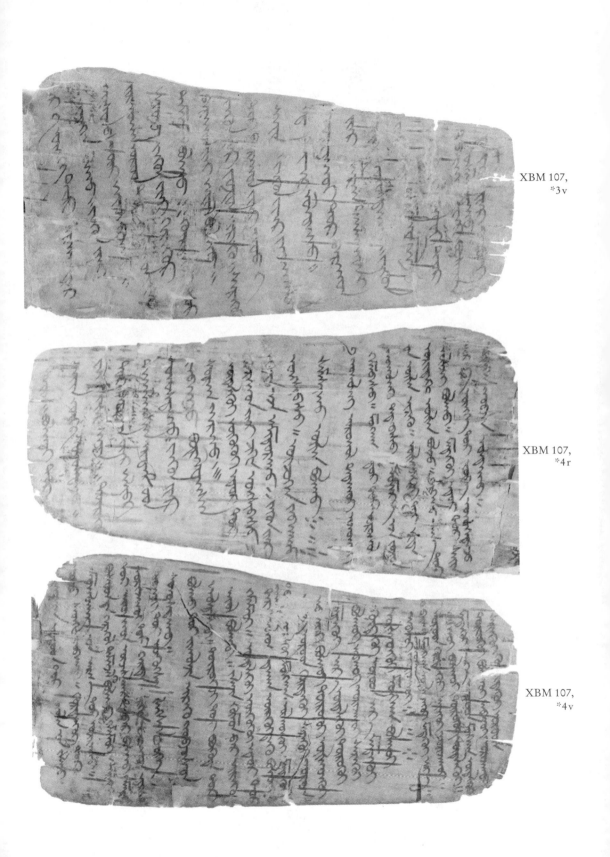

XBM 107,
*3v

XBM 107,
*4r

XBM 107,
*4v

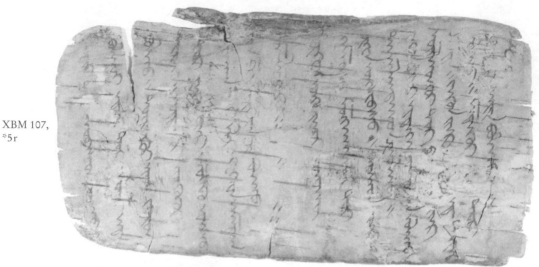

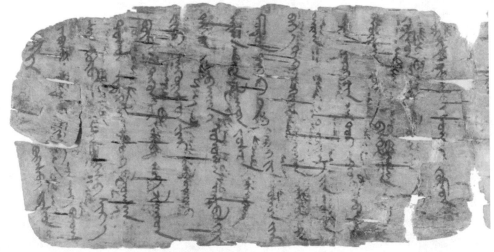

XBM 107,
*6 r

XBM 107,
*6 v

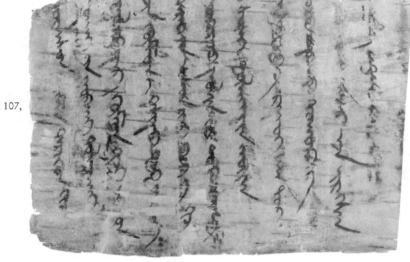

XBM 107,
*8r

XBM 108,
recto

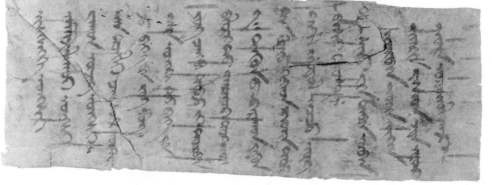

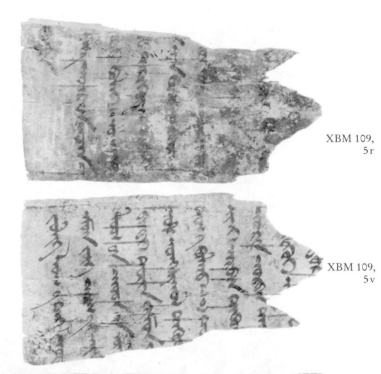

XBM 109,
5r

XBM 109,
5v

XBM 109,
7r

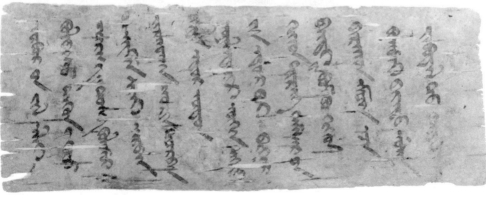

XBM 109,
7v

XBM 110,
1v

XBM 110,
2r

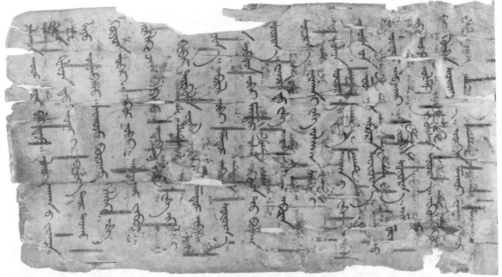

XBM 110,
2v

XBM 110,
3r

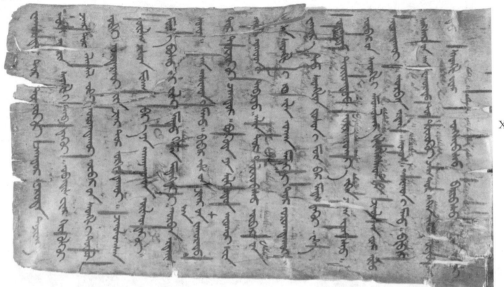

XBM 110,
4v

XBM 110,
5r

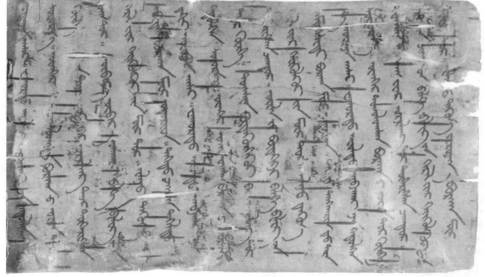

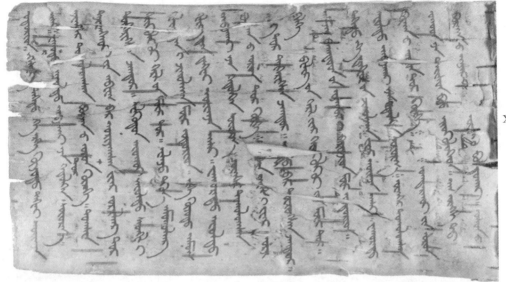

XBM 110, 6v

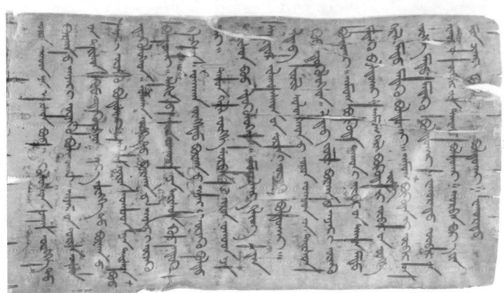

XBM 110, 7r

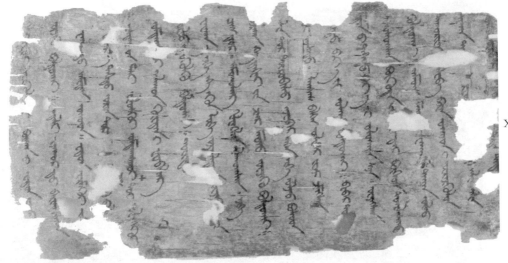

XBM 110,
8 v

XBM 110,
9 r

XBM 110,
9 v